HENRY

# RURAL ENGLAND

## BEING AN ACCOUNT OF
## AGRICULTURAL AND SOCIAL RESEARCHES
## CARRIED OUT IN THE YEARS 1901 & 1902

### VOLUME I

Elibron Classics
www.elibron.com

# RURAL ENGLAND

## VOL. I.

# WORKS BY H. RIDER HAGGARD.

## PARLIAMENTARY BLUE-BOOK.

REPORT TO H.M.'S GOVERNMENT ON THE SALVATION ARMY COLONIES IN THE UNITED STATES, WITH SCHEME OF NATIONAL LAND SETTLEMENT. [Cd. 2562.]

## POLITICAL HISTORY.

CETEWAYO AND HIS WHITE NEIGHBOURS.

## WORKS ON SOCIOLOGY, AGRICULTURE AND COUNTRY LIFE.

| | |
|---|---|
| RURAL ENGLAND (2 *vols.*). | A FARMER'S YEAR. |
| THE POOR AND THE LAND. | A GARDENER'S YEAR. |

## BOOK OF TRAVEL.

A WINTER PILGRIMAGE.

## NOVELS.

| | |
|---|---|
| DAWN. | BEATRICE. |
| THE WITCH'S HEAD. | JOAN HASTE. |
| JESS. | DOCTOR THERNE. |
| COLONEL QUARITCH, V.C. | STELLA FREGELIUS. |

THE WAY OF THE SPIRIT.

## ROMANCES.

| | |
|---|---|
| KING SOLOMON'S MINES. | MONTEZUMA'S DAUGHTER. |
| SHE. | THE PEOPLE OF THE MIST. |
| ALLAN QUATERMAIN. | HEART OF THE WORLD. |
| MAIWA'S REVENGE. | SWALLOW. |
| MR. MEESON'S WILL. | BLACK HEART AND WHITE |
| ALLAN'S WIFE. | HEART. |
| CLEOPATRA. | LYSBETH. |
| ERIC BRIGHTEYES. | PEARL MAIDEN. |
| NADA THE LILY. | THE BRETHREN. |

AYESHA : The Return of She.

(*In collaboration with Andrew Lang.*)
THE WORLD'S DESIRE.

# RURAL ENGLAND

## BEING AN ACCOUNT OF
## AGRICULTURAL AND SOCIAL RESEARCHES CARRIED
## OUT IN THE YEARS 1901 & 1902

BY

## H. RIDER HAGGARD

'I will make a man more precious than fine gold; even a man than the golden wedge of Ophir.'—ISAIAH

'The highways were unoccupied . . . the inhabitants of the villages ceased.'—JUDGES

## IN TWO VOLUMES—VOL. I.

**WITH 46 ILLUSTRATIONS FROM PHOTOGRAPHS**

*NEW EDITION*

## LONGMANS, GREEN, AND CO.
### 89 PATERNOSTER ROW, LONDON
### NEW YORK AND BOMBAY
### 1906

I DEDICATE THIS WORK

TO

ARTHUR H. D. COCHRANE

THE COMPANION OF THESE JOURNEYINGS AS OF MANY
PREVIOUS ADVENTURES

AND TO ALL THROUGHOUT ENGLAND

WHO HAVE ASSISTED ME IN MY UNDERTAKING

# PREFACE

## TO NEW EDITION

I DO not know that I can begin a Preface to this new and cheaper edition of 'Rural England' better than by thanking the Press and my readers for the extremely kind reception which that lengthy and laborious work has met with at their hands. Of this I will only say that it was almost without exception favourable, and indeed far surpassed my modest expectations. May it prove an augury of the continued use and vitality of the book in time to come.

I wish I could add that I was able to point to any tangible fruits of its publication. This, however, I cannot do. Personally, I have made every effort to bring the reforms urged in its pages to the benevolent notice of those in authority. At some private cost I have inflicted upon them copies of these expensive volumes and been favoured in return with polite notes of thanks. I have interviewed certain of them who wished to receive me. I have neglected other work in order to travel up and down the country addressing every kind of meeting and explaining my views ; in short, of would-be agricultural reformers, I may say almost that I have 'laboured more abundantly than they all.'

Now after four years are gone by I must with humiliation report that nothing of consequence has happened. 'Perhaps,' I wrote upon the last page of this book, 'it is too much to hope that my humble and unaided efforts will influence those who have power so to do, to stir in these grave matters before time takes away their opportunity. At least I have done my best, and doubtless things will go as they are fated.' Well, time has taken away their opportunity and things have gone as they were fated, that is, for years at least the Unionist Party has been almost destroyed. During the decade or so that they were in power nothing would induce that Party to do anything for the land or those connected with it, except to pass the Agricultural Ratings Act, which has recently been renewed as a makeshift for a short period of time, and appoint a Departmental Committee to consider the question of Small-holdings.  I believe that I am right in saying, indeed, that in the course of the last period of the deceased Parliament, a few hours were all that a Government with a great majority could find to spare for questions dealing directly or indirectly with agriculture.  No Bill bearing a rural complexion—and several were introduced—was even given a chance of passing.  Whole sessions could be devoted to such matters as an Education Act which, whatever its virtues, has caused much bitter controversy, and, as was to be expected, largely increased the rates, also to a Licensing Act of the merits or demerits of which I will say nothing, and so forth, but to the great subjects of Agriculture, the Land and that rural population which is still the backbone of the Empire, not a minute.  These were taboo.

It is permissible to wonder why.  Perhaps because there are, or are supposed to be, no votes in the thing.  Perhaps because the idea is engrained in so many members of our hereditary governing classes in both branches of the Legislature, that the land of Britain is first and foremost a retreat for sportsmen and a tabernacle for the givers of fashionable house-parties.  Perhaps because £120,000,000 or so of the national cash having been devoted to a scheme for the purchase of Irish estates, whereof some £12,000,000 is, I

believe, a gift without security or hope of repayment, nothing
was left to be expended in or advanced to the rest of the
United Kingdom. Perhaps because the whole business was
too troublesome to be faced by an Administration that did
not wish to be burdened with the solution of intricate
problems.

At any rate nothing was done, nothing was even attempted; that great opportunity has gone by for ever.

It will be admitted that such a record of progress, or
rather of the utter lack of it, is not very encouraging to a
private person who has devoted years of his life and the best
labour of his brain, every hour that can be spared of both of
them from the actual task of earning his living indeed, to the
furtherance of what are acknowledged to be national needs by
the most reflective and able minds in all the political parties.
At times I confess that I have been tempted to abandon the
crusade in despair. Yet I have gone on with it to the utmost of my powers, utilising such small opportunities as
came my way for its furtherance. At least I have had
this reward—the ideas I advocate are spreading. In the
absence of more exciting subjects, the papers write about
them a good deal from time to time; politicians and
pamphleteers also make use of them occasionally, with or
without acknowledgment. This is something; for it shows
that the seed sown by myself and others, or certain grains
of it, are beginning to germinate.

Meanwhile, what is to be said of the present state of
the agriculture of Great Britain? But little, I think, except that since the publication of 'Rural England' it appears on the whole to have still further disimproved, though
whether this is actually so or not, I cannot of course say
with certainty without a renewed and elaborate investigation
of its existing conditions. At any rate in the counties with
which I am best acquainted, I can see no advance. Further,

the whole matter has been complicated and some confusion caused by the reappearance of the fiscal problems which are now before the Country.

In view of their far-reaching issues, I must ask leave to write briefly of these problems, especially as my own opinions in connection with them have been more than once much misrepresented.

Personally, my private belief for what it is worth, and I am quite ready to admit that it may be wrong, is, and always has been, that in face of the attitude taken by the rest of the world towards this matter and of our urgent need for increased revenue, some modest but general measure of Protection such as did not suffice to raise the price of food to any appreciable extent, would greatly benefit the inhabitants of this kingdom. Under the circumstances of our case no argument that I have seen, and, to the best of my ability, I have studied them all, has converted me to the other and more popular view. I have, however, again and again said in these pages that in my judgment, this remedy, so far as Agriculture and the Land are concerned, is purely one of academic interest, seeing that I was certain that the people, the vast majority of whom live in towns, would never tolerate any tax upon food-stuffs unless and until some crushing disaster falls upon the Nation. That this is so I will prove by one or two quotations. Thus, as may be seen in my Introduction, p. 18, I say: 'For too long, landowners and farmers together, we have schooled our minds to believe that there is but one salvation, protective duties on imported food-stuffs which are unattainable, and even if attained, might work ills not now foreseen. Let us cease, then, to pursue this marsh-light— this phantom—of Protection and combine to secure moderate but effective measures of reform, against which it cannot be urged that they would raise the cost of a people's daily bread.'

Again in a speech which I made to the Institute of Journalists at Fountains Abbey in Yorkshire reported on pp. 310-12, vol. ii., I remarked :—

'Mr. Foljambe, alluding to my work, said—if he were reported aright—that the keynote of it was Protection. Now I myself have not pleaded that cause in my articles, though I have at different times quoted the arguments of people who do ; and I take this opportunity publicly to wash my hands of Protection. Whatever arguments there may be in favour of it, and they are many, we, as men of the world, have to face facts. Believe me, Protection can only be introduced into this country after some disaster too serious for us to contemplate. To talk about Protection as a remedy for the evils by which we are surrounded is merely to dash our heads against a wall. We must look for other palliatives.'

I might multiply such extracts, but these two are perhaps sufficient.[1] Not very long after the appearance of 'Rural England,' Mr. Chamberlain sprang his fiscal Policy upon the Country, and sundry people who believed that it would be straightway adopted with enthusiasm, told me, with no uncertain voice, that the position I had taken up was a great mistake ; that I had, in common parlance, 'put my money upon the wrong horse.' The late Prime Minister, Mr. Balfour, also introduced to public notice a modified scheme of his own which eliminated the element of taxation of foodstuffs. In considering the state of affairs thus created, I saw at once, and was, I think, the first to see, or at any rate to point out, that Mr. Balfour's scheme would complete the ruin of the land and agriculture of the United Kingdom. The first public opportunity that I could find of explaining these conclusions was at the Annual Dinner of the Framlingham Farmers' Club, which was held in October, 1903. Now again

---

[1] See also Vol. ii., pp. 537-539.

I fear that I must quote from an almost verbatim press report of my remarks upon that occasion. I said :—

It would be idle to pretend otherwise than that there is one great question which now overhangs us all, to the exclusion of almost every other, and that is the question of the various fiscal policies which have been placed before the Country. I don't want to sail under any false colours, and therefore I say at once that I have always been a Fair-trader of a moderate sort. I hope that those who think otherwise will pardon my infirmity, though I may say that of late I have found myself in quite distinguished company. (Laughter.) However, I propose to consider this matter for a few minutes, if you will allow me, not from any party point of view—for I wish that the word 'party' might vanish altogether where agriculture and its interests are concerned (hear, hear), but from the point of view of agriculture. I may preface what I have to say by observing that although by conviction a Fair-trader, yet in my book, to which allusion has been made ('Rural England'), I stated perfectly clearly that I did not myself believe that the people of this country would consent to the imposition of taxes upon food. . . . Mr. Balfour wishes to establish retaliatory duties—that is to say, to provide that we should tax the goods of those countries by which our goods are taxed. He says, however, that there is to be no tax upon food-stuffs, and therefore no preferential arrangement with the Colonies. As far as I can gather from his speeches, Mr. Balfour says this, not because he does not approve of such taxes, but because he does not think that they will be acceptable to the electorate. His position is in fact a very ancient one. What he says in practice is 'all things may be lawful to me but all things are not expedient'. (Laughter.) . . . But the point to which I wish to call your particular attention is this : Let us suppose that Mr. Balfour's scheme succeeds ; let us suppose that leaving out all taxation on food-stuffs, and all ideas of preferential treatment of the Colonies, he succeeds in establishing retaliatory duties. What would that mean ? First one trade and then another would ask to be protected in this way. . . . But I also think, and this is a point that no one else has touched on so far as I am aware, that it would end in something very like ruin to agriculture. (Hear, hear, and a voice : Why ?) It is easy to see why. You would have everything in this country protected except your produce ; you would have to compete against the whole world with your corn and your meat and whatever else you had to sell, and yet on the other hand you would have to pay a tax upon everything coming from foreign countries that you had to buy. I can put the argument to you in a nutshell. You want to sell a quarter of wheat, say, and in so doing you have to compete with other wheat growers all over the world, particularly in America. Very well, but if you want to buy an

American plough or reaper, you must pay a tax in addition to the prime cost of the article. Follow that out through all its details and you must see, I maintain, that such a scheme as that will end in nothing more nor less than the destruction of your industry. . . . All these things, in my humble judgment, would result from the introduction of these partial fiscal reforms, under which everything would be taxed except the produce of our industry ; therefore, I say to you, let it be Chamberlain or nothing. (Applause.) I am not prepared to say that it should not be nothing, but let it be the whole scheme, or no scheme. (Renewed applause.) A half-scheme of the sort proposed would be your ruin, and I only wish that my humble voice of warning upon this point could reach every man, woman and child connected with agriculture in these islands—that I could put before them this view, which somehow seems to have escaped attention, but which I believe to be perfectly sound. . . . I very much doubt, you know, whether the walls of the Free Trade Jericho are going to fall down at the first blast of Mr. Chamberlain's trumpet, however shrill and clear it may be. I think you will be wise not to count upon Protection in any form, but to rely upon your own energy, upon your own hands and your own heads. Urge on minor reforms. Seek to have the burdens which crush us, such as that of unjust taxation, lessened ; seek to have the cost of the transfer of land lessened ; seek to have the cost of the carriage of agricultural produce lessened. (Hear, hear.) There is another thing I would venture to say, which is not always a popular thing to say to large farmers, though I know there are many who agree with me : Seek to promote unity among the various classes connected with the land, by interesting the labourers in the land—to keep the population on the soil by giving them a stake in the soil.

After the delivery of this Framlingham speech I was unexpectedly asked to move a Resolution at the Central Chamber of Agriculture in favour of the 'proposals submitted by Mr. Chamberlain.' Once more I venture to quote very shortly from the official report in the Journal of the Proceedings :—

'He (Mr. Rider Haggard) said that he had been honoured within the last few minutes with a request to move this Resolution. He confessed that personally he should have preferred a somewhat different Resolution, as the one which he was now submitting seemed to him to bind the Council, and through the Council its affiliated bodies, a little too closely to the chariot-wheels of Mr. Chamberlain. He thought that, so far as he understood the proposals put before the Country by Mr. Chamberlain, they were not made by him with any special reference to agriculture. Agriculture, if it came into the question at all, would only come in by a side wind; and therefore, when, as in this Resolution, they spoke of "proposals submitted by Mr. Chamberlain," it might be supposed they thought that those proposals were made in the interest of the agriculture of the country. This, however, was not the case.'

The debate which ensued upon this Resolution was very keen, several prominent persons taking part in it, so keen indeed that it was adjourned for future consideration. In winding it up, as I had the right of reply, I said by way of emphasising the arguments which I had already adduced at Framlingham and in the Chamber, that in my opinion there was 'no site for a half-way house upon the steep road which runs from Free Trade to Protection,' a remark that I have often seen subsequently quoted. In the end the Resolution was carried in a crowded Chamber with only seven dissentients.

I must apologise for writing so much about my own views, but after all it is my views that are in question, and I do not think that I can make them clear better than by quoting the actual words I uttered in the past. Did I content myself with a summary or interpretation of them, as I should have preferred to do, it might be thought that I had dressed them up to fit in with existing circumstances. As it is, it will be seen that so far I have proved perfectly accurate in my political prognostications. For this, however, I take no credit at all, since in the future I may prove to be perfectly wrong. Thus the great forces of Labour may turn round and insist upon duties on imports as some people think likely, although even then they will probably, either at once or afterwards, make an exception in the case of food-stuffs. Ireland may do the same before or after it wins Home Rule. The cause of Protection may in the end triumph all along the line. For the present, however, the mooting of it, assisted it is true by other matters, has resulted in the crushing of the Unionist Party.

For my part I do not see, and never was able to see, how this recent political overthrow could have been avoided, at any rate in our rural districts where the majority of the voters are generally indifferent to questions connected with the Empire or Home Rule, and being very poor not unnaturally consider politics chiefly from the point of view of their own pockets. The raising of this great issue of Protection *versus* Free Trade made it inevitable.

However these things may be, and I am not arguing upon the rights or wrongs of them, I adhere entirely to the views I have expressed in 'Rural England' and the above extracts. Agriculture, or rather the agricultural interest, did not engineer this demand for Protection, which was made on behalf of the towns, quite independently of it and its advantage. If it is wise, in my humble opinion, it will leave the whole matter severely alone, and content itself with pressing forward just and reasonable reforms. If, however, Mr. Balfour's or some subsequent but similar scheme of retaliatory duties upon foreign imports other than food-stuffs ever becomes a serious issue, then I hold that Agriculture should fight it by all means in its power. This I know at least, that every vote I have and every vote that I could influence would be given against candidates pledged to such a scheme, which, whatever prosperity it might or might not bring to the cities, must, unless my reason is utterly at fault, complete the ruin of the rural industries. In short, taking everything into consideration, I repeat that I incline to the belief that so far as the land of the United Kingdom and its welfare are concerned, it would be better that this question of the reintroducing of Protective duties, which at the highest must be very trivial, should be omitted from the programme.

The Land and those connected with it have enough enemies as it is without raising a new army, every man of them bent upon their destruction, by the sowing of these dragons' teeth of proposed duties upon imported meat and corn. How bitter those enemies are may be seen in any newspaper. Already some of them clamour (I quote from 'The Times' of January 19, 1906, which publishes extracts from a book called 'Britain for the British' by Robert Blatchford, editor of 'The Clarion') for 'Removal of Taxation from articles used by the workers, such as tea and tobacco, and increase of taxation upon large incomes and upon *land.*'

Another way by which it is now commonly proposed to strike at the person who owns real estate, is to give to District and Parish Councils the right to take any portion of his property that pleases them for the purposes of Small-holdings, and to rate him for the erection thereon of cottages and buildings which can pay no interest. As the danger of the introduction of some such measure seems really imminent, although I do not desire to enter at length into political questions, I wish to say a few words on this matter. Any student of the methods of these minor elective bodies will be aware that in sundry cases such authority might be cruelly used, often enough from other motives than the desire to procure Small-holdings ; for instance, from petty malice or envy or the wish to tyrannise, injure and annoy. Pieces of land could be picked out here and there in such a fashion that the whole property must be rendered practically valueless ; the best and most accessible soil could be taken, and that which was worst or most inconvenient to reach left upon the owner's hands, and so forth, by the mandate of some conclave ruled over or inspired, perhaps, by the local agitator.

The same thing might happen, but upon a larger scale, if tenants are to be given an absolute power of buying their farms without the consent of the owner and with the aid of money advanced by the State. Here and there a farm would be purchased in the middle of a property whereof the rest was thus ruined for residential purposes, and probably in the end bought up, perhaps at rubbish prices, by the District Councils or other purchasers.

The truth is, of course, that if any land-purchase Act is found to be necessary, and nothing of the sort ought to be introduced until efforts to obtain sufficient and suitable areas by voluntary agreement have entirely failed, the last people who should have to do with its administration are the smaller local authorities, or the army of petty officials who live out of the rates. Such powers should be left to the County Councils, or better still, in the hands of the Government of the day, acting only through one of the great central departments of the State; for example, the Board of Agriculture. Moreover, in my judgment they ought not to apply to properties of less than a certain size, and in each instance all the surrounding circumstances should be taken into consideration. Further, if an estate is meddled with at all, the owner should have the option of electing to sell every acre of it at a fair and independent valuation, so that he might go away to some other place or country where he can possess his own in peace, as the holders of Stocks and Shares are allowed to do. The man who buys land and pays hard cash for it, does so under a tacit agreement with the State that he shall not be ruined by its breaking up or seizure, or even interfered with in his unoffending possession of it, any more than he would have been interfered with, of course beyond the payment of his lawful taxes, in the possession of the money that he expended for its purchase.

It is no answer to say that the State, or Companies acting under its authority, can already take some of his land for the purposes of rifle ranges or of railroads, for if they do so the State, or the said Companies, must fully compensate him for disturbance. If these conditions are to be altered, then due notice must be given of the new arrangements under which real property is henceforth to be possessed, and the existing arrangements put an end to upon equitable terms. Otherwise it seems to me that the State will be guilty of conduct which no British law-court would tolerate as between man and man since it is in direct contravention of the principles of equity.

I am aware that the object of these proposals, when they are made with an honest purpose, which is not always the case, is to subdivide the land; to bring it into more hands; in my opinion a most desirable consummation. If such a subdivision is held to be imperative, however, could it not be better and more surely effected by abolishing the law of primogeniture and, thus, at any rate in the case of intestacy, making real property divisible among the children, male and female, or other heirs at death, as it is in every case in the Channel Islands and I understand in France? I am not prepared to express any final opinion upon this matter, or even to say that such a fundamental alteration in our system would be wise. Still, although the process might be slow, it would certainly result at last in a much freer circulation of the land, and while tending to closer settlement, avoid the great injustice of forced purchase at an arbitrary price.

In the Channel Islands, I may add, as can be seen from these pages, this plan, even in its extreme form of forcible division at death, seems to work very well and to advance the welfare of the community. At least it is clear that our feudal system, or what remains of it, has broken down; its day is gone, and the time has come when the whole matter should be reconsidered from the point of view of the future welfare of the nation. Also from another point of view, that of equity, why should an eldest son, or next heir, take all the heritage, if it chances to be real estate?

As readers of this book and other writings of mine will be aware, no one is more convinced than I am of the absolute necessity, if our Country is to continue in its present place, of the reconstruction of the lost yeoman class, who rear a stamp of children very different to those that are bred in the great towns. The only question is—How can this best be done under our present conditions? At the moment I know not what to answer. As I have said in this work, save under exceptionally favourable circumstances and on suitable soil, I am still inclined to doubt the general success of artificially created Small-holdings in the United Kingdom, and to think that small-holders should be encouraged to arise naturally and by degrees through the slow devolution of landed property, or by its purchase under fair and well-considered regulations, with funds advanced by the State. But to tell the truth without further and extensive research I am in no position to give a definite judgment upon so intricate a matter, complicated as it is by the difficulty of earning a living profit out of the heavily burdened and unhelped land of Britain.

In the Report which as a Commissioner I made to the Imperial Government some months ago,[1] I offered to investigate this question of home land-settlements, and after the completion of such investigations to submit my conclusions for what they might be worth. That offer was neither definitely accepted nor definitely declined before the Government to which it was made disappeared. It is therefore probable that this research will never be carried through by me, especially, amongst other reasons, as my views

[1] Report on the Salvation Army Colonies in the United States and at Hadleigh, England, with Scheme of National Land Settlement, republished under the title of *The Poor and the Land* (Longmans).

on these matters may be thought too out-of-date for the times.

Meanwhile, I am glad to see that Mr. Herring has placed a large sum of money at the disposal of the Salvation Army to be used at home upon lines very similar to those that I suggested in my Report (which is still being considered by a Departmental Committee), as expedient and quite feasible in the case of Colonial land-settlements. From this experiment there should be much to learn, but years will go by before we, or those of us who survive, are in a position to digest and apply its results, and ere then it seems probable that some decided step must be taken in one direction or another. At any rate it is clear that unless very grave national evils are to ensue, by this means or by that the land of Britain ought to be made more productive and more easily available to the people of Britain, the question being how these ends can best be attained with equity to the present holders and to the general advantage.

In the interim, I again venture to urge upon the new Government the introduction of those moderate and practicable reforms which I have suggested in these pages, and especially in the last chapter which is named 'Conclusions.' I would urge also that all questions connected with the Land, its population and its prosperity, should not continue to be met with a mere *non possumus*, or thrust aside with a shrug of the shoulder, as has been the case for many years, but in view of their intense importance to the welfare of the nation, and indirectly of the whole Empire, that they should be made the subject of earnest and consistent thought, enterprise and experiment. Thus, to begin with, amongst other Continental countries, a new and exhaustive report might be obtained upon the underlying causes of the agricultural prosperity of Denmark, a territory having poorer soil and a worse climate than our own, expressly with a view to ascertaining whether the methods and institutions which have produced that wonderful prosperity could not be introduced into the United Kingdom under the auspices and with the active encouragement of the State.

Lastly, I would urge that the owners of land should cease to be over-taxed, unjustly rated and continually threatened, as is now the case. Rather ought they to receive assistance in the promotion of reforms since the object of true statesmanship should be to multiply holders of land, not to render that position impossible to all save the very rich. Even if they are naturally for the most part conservative in their tendencies surely that is no good reason for wishing to complete their ruin. The party to which many of them belong is practically annihilated and perhaps will not return to power for years, with the result that they are left naked to their enemies. The net rent which they receive after the payment of legal dues, sundry outgoings and repairs, is exceedingly small. The city dwellers and the labourers whom they employ and remunerate out of their scanty profits, if any come to them from the land, can and do enormously out-vote them, and are therefore in a position to secure the passing of oppressive laws. Yet it should be remembered that the only fruit of the further impoverishment of the landowner would be that fewer of these rural workers could be supported, while the rest, deprived of occupation, must go to swell the masses in the towns.

If by way of answer to this argument the Socialist or the Labour leader should point to a certain sprinkling of quite modern landlords of whose notorious proceedings this perhaps is not the place to speak, I reply that a whole class should not be made to suffer for the vulgarity and ostentatious folly of the few. If great wealth is held to be undesirable—and the point is one which I will not argue—it can be made to pay toll by means of a graduated income-tax ; if excessive game-preserving is proved to be a public evil, then the owners of those large estates which are entirely given up to sport, could, and probably would be willing to contribute something more to the Exchequer than is extracted from land where it is pursued upon a modest scale, or not at all.

This is certain, the Liberal Government of 1906 has a great opportunity before it if it is really anxious to do good in these directions, and will turn a deaf ear to vast and nebulous schemes of 'land nationalisation,' of 'abolition of rent,' 'absolute security of tenure,' 'dual ownership,' 'taxing out' and so forth, which in my belief can only end in the wasting of huge sums of money, injustice, confusion and disaster.

Many are the things which it might do.   It might establish Credit Banks and foster Co-operative Societies.   It might introduce a juster incidence of the rates, especially as regards education and the upkeep of the roads, and equalise their weight as between real and personal property.   It might —if such a thing be possible—arrange that the burden of tithe should always bear some proportion to the net profits, as in the first place it must surely have been meant to do.   It might abolish copyhold upon equitable terms and cheapen the cost of land transfer.   It might largely develop the existing parcel-post system, so as to facilitate the transport of agricultural produce, including milk.   It might check fraud, strictly enforce the laws against adulteration of food products, and prevent the artificial blending of water with butter.   It might investigate the question of water carriage and arrange for the reopening of our silted-up canals, some of which, in order to avoid competition, have, I believe, been bought and purposely destroyed by the great railway companies.   This, I am thankful to say, indeed, it has already announced its intention of attempting.   It might advance money for the building of cottages, the purchase of farms when both parties are willing to deal, and after due inquiry, for the increase of Small-holdings by whatever means are found to be wise and feasible, for instance, by devoting the Crown and Glebe lands to that purpose.[1] It might make a national business of afforestation, which can seldom be undertaken by short-lived individual landowners.

In short it might formulate and develop a settled agricultural policy, a thing that no modern British Government as yet has ever thought of, and thus try to bring back to, or to re-create some part of their lost population in the rural districts of the United Kingdom, which as I and many others believe, is one of the most urgent needs of our age. But who can say whether or no it will deal with these things in a spirit of enterprise, wisdom and moderation? The task is arduous and if we argue from the experience of the past with its story of perpetual neglect, the prospect is not promising.

On one matter, however, all who are interested in these problems may congratulate themselves, namely, that of the appointment of Lord Carrington as President of the Board of Agriculture. Lord Carrington, as is well known, is an earnest and practical advocate of closer settlement. Also he is a landlord who understands the needs and difficulties of the land, though I imagine that owing to the character of

[1] Since this Preface was written it has been announced in the King's Speech that the 'social and economic conditions of the rural districts in Great Britain require careful consideration'. It is stated further that 'inquiries are proceeding by means of which a large number of the population may be attracted to and retained on the soil'. I presume that the reference is to the investigations of the Departmental Committee on Small-holdings whereof I have written and before which I have recently given evidence. At any rate the news is good, so far as it goes, although at present not very definite. A published correspondence also seems to indicate that Mr. Balfour's fiscal views are now more or less in line with those of Mr. Chamberlain. It does not follow, however, that they will stay there, or that new and quite different developments may not occur in this connection. Indeed, I remain of opinion that Agriculture would be wise not to pin its faith to hopes of Protection for the reasons given above and throughout this book.—H. R. H.

their soil, his estates have not been so severely smitten as is commonly the case in the clay, corn-growing districts. We may hope, therefore, that if he remains in his office, which few of its holders seem to do for long, he will try to effect permanent and useful reforms and will succeed in impressing the necessity for them upon the powerful Government of which he is a member.

I am glad to be able to say that since its publication, among all the persons interviewed or alluded to in this very extensive work, to the best of my memory but one has found any fault with the accuracy of its statements, a gentleman of Cambridgeshire, who wrote to 'The Times' to complain of 'minor inaccuracies and blemishes' . . . 'so far as I can judge from the few pages with which the author honours me.' What the inaccuracies and blemishes may be I cannot say, as, although I answered his letter, he did not and has not since made any attempt to quote them. I think, however, that they must be very 'minor,' for on comparing the 'few pages' with the notes of this gentleman's evidence taken down in his presence from his own lips and the documents which he produced, I find that in every respect they appear to be quite identical. I should add that the General Manager of the Great Eastern Railway also called my attention to the fact that in two places their rates of carriage were wrongly stated. For this, however, I am not responsible, as in each case I merely recorded on their personal authority figures given to me by my informants.

With these results I consider that I have every reason to be satisfied in the case of a book of this magnitude, in which the views of scores, or hundreds of informants are quoted under their own names. In effect it is a greater testimony to its general correctness than I could have reasonably anticipated.

On one point, however, I wish to correct myself. In my

' Conclusions ' I spoke doubtfully of the Garden City project. Since these were written, however, I have had a good deal to do with this movement and become convinced of its great possibilities. To say that its success is assured is too much, but success is certainly in sight. That it may be fully attained all who are acquainted with the objects of the scheme will earnestly desire.

Glancing through its pages to-day it is borne in upon me how soon a work of this character begins to partake of the nature of past history. It is true that the state of affairs with which it deals has not materially changed, but in the course of the four years that have elapsed since it was published, to my knowledge a considerable number of those who are interviewed or quoted here have passed away, and doubtless there are many others of whose departure I have not heard. Thus Mr. Arkwright of Hampton Court, Herefordshire; Mr. George Beck of Ormesby, Norfolk; Miss Boucherett of Willingham, Lincolnshire; the Right Hon. A. F. Jeffreys; Mr. Richard Green of the Wittern, Herefordshire; Mr. Thomas Grierson, agent to the Flixton estate, Suffolk; Mr. W. H. Hall of Six-mile Bottom, Cambridgeshire; my old friend, Mr. Clare Sewell Read of Norfolk, whose death was a loss indeed; Mr. Edward Turnour of Stoke Rochford, Lincolnshire, and Sir Henry Wiggin of Alvechurch, Worcestershire, are all gone from among us. So quickly do things change in this world where only the land that bore us remains comparatively immutable.

I very much regret that the price at which this new issue of ' Rural England ' is published has rendered it impossible to include therein the agricultural maps that are to be found in the former edition, as the reproduction of them would be too costly.

H. RIDER HAGGARD.

Ditchingham,
*25th January*, 1906.

# INTRODUCTION

FOR a long while past I have been anxious to undertake a very heavy task, that of the investigation of the conditions of the rural England of our day. Towards the end of the eighteenth and the commencement of the nineteenth centuries my great predecessor, Arthur Young, wrote many volumes on this subject which must always remain our chief source of information as to the agriculture of England during that period. William Marshall also treated of it between 1787 and 1800 in his 'General Survey of the rural Economy of England.' Later, in 1830, William Cobbett published his 'Rural Rides,' which are full of useful information, but, perhaps, somewhat too highly tinged with the hue of the writer's own political opinions. Lastly, fifty years ago, Sir James Caird, under the title of 'English Agriculture,' collected into a volume the valuable and interesting letters which he wrote upon this matter as Commissioner for 'The Times,' since which date, so far as I am aware, no one has attempted to carry out similar researches on any considerable scale.

During the last half-century, however, our agriculture, and indeed everything connected with the land, landowners, and husbandmen of England, have undergone great changes; it seemed to me, therefore, that there was some need for a new work treating of these questions. Such a work I purposed to write, and at length, through the enterprise of the 'Daily Express' newspaper, discovered an opportunity of carrying out my design. The articles that form the foundation of these volumes, expanded now to full three or four times their original bulk by the addition of matter for which it would have been impossible for a journal to find space, appeared in the columns of that paper in 1901, and were the result of a journey of about eight months' duration through the greater part of England, accomplished by myself in that year.  Since its conclusion I have continued my inquiries in Norfolk, Suffolk, and other counties, and largely supplemented the store of facts and deductions that I was able to collect during its progress.  The results are now offered to the reader in these volumes.

When a man straightens his back after building the chief corner-stone into the labour of a life that has not been idle, he is apt, perhaps, as its weight leaves his hands, to congratulate himself unduly.  But reflection will tell him how much more massive that stone might have been if he could have found the strength to quarry and to lift it, and of how far finer a material, and less marred with flaws, had he known where best it should be searched for, and in what way most shapely hewn.  For instance, let me admit at once that my work is incomplete.  I have, I think, examined into the state of twenty-seven counties, exclusive of the Channel Islands, whereof none of those who went before me seem to have treated.  But other counties remain unexplored, and beyond them lie Scotland, Wales, and Ireland.  Whether I shall ever find time and strength to continue my investigations in these places is to be doubted, so meanwhile I must content myself with the reflection that I have perhaps covered almost as much of England as any of my predecessors—the entire task proved too vast for every one of us.

Arthur Young, I believe—although of this fact I am not certain—described in all about the same number, namely, twenty-six counties; William Marshall fewer, but in great detail; Sir James Caird more, but in less detail.  He says that he 'traversed thirty-two of the forty counties of England.' Should, then, the finishing of this quest be left to a hand or hands unknown, perhaps unborn, I will venture to give him or them, out of the store of my own experience, a few hints as to the qualifications needful to the perfect investigator of agricultural matters and the English land, to which eminence, needless to say, I lay no claim.

Physically such a person must be very strong, since the work is the hardest that I have ever undertaken. Not only are the necessary correspondence and arrangements in themselves troublesome, but when these are completed, he must travel week after week and month after month, by rail, with horses, in motor-cars, on bicycles, and on foot, in order to fulfil his hundreds of engagements. He must never fall ill, or, if he does, must go on as I did, until he is well again, or collapses utterly, which I am thankful to say I did not. Every night he must be prepared, at the end of the toil of a long day, to plunge into unknown society, to make acquaintance with many new faces and listen to many fresh views or arguments, without showing signs of an exhaustion which his hosts or their guests might, not unnaturally, attribute to a lack of interest and proper gratitude. Never for one instant must he allow his attention to flag, his powers of observation to become dull, or his sight and hearing to miss anything that is of importance to his cause.

His mind should be that of a trained lawyer, able to weigh and sift evidence, discriminating between the true and the false, the weighty and the trivial. His intelligence must be of that patient and prosaic order that scorns no detail, however oft repeated, knowing that in each there is some difference from all that went before, if only it can be grasped. Vexations, disappointments, even occasional impertinences and rebuffs, should not disturb him ; with a smile he must try again elsewhere. Also he must have money at his command, since such long journeyings are costly. He must learn to write accurate articles and notes under any circumstances and at any time, and, what is still more important, how to read the latter afterwards. To heat, cold, and bodily weariness he must be indifferent. Lastly, not to prolong the list, he should really know something about agriculture, and must have given adequate study to those great questions of which he proposes to treat.

Of these qualifications and others left unrecorded, I can with humility lay some claim to one—an acquaintance with my subject. I was born in a farmhouse, among high-hedged pastures near to the silence of a great wood, and I suppose the first sounds that my ears heard were the lowing of kine and the bleating of sheep. Perhaps, if there be any truth in such theories, it is to this fact that I owe my rural bent.

Since then all my life has been more or less connected with the soil, at home and oversea; and before ever I thought of writing on it I was, mayhap unconsciously, engaged in observing in many lands the ways of Nature and of those who dwell in her constant fellowship. Thus, amongst other places, I have travelled in and tried to learn what I was able of the physical peculiarities, climate, and husbandry of Holland, Norway, France, and Italy in Europe, of Cyprus and Syria in the Mediterranean, of Egypt and the Southern Territories and States in Africa, of Mexico in Central America, and of Iceland in the Northern seas. I have owned and own land, have in Natal worked with my own hands on the land, have hired and hire land, and for the last thirteen years or so have been myself a practical farmer of a considerable acreage of land in England, as once I was abroad. This, then, is the main equipment which emboldened me to make the great attempt that is now at length concluded.

When I began it one of the questions that perplexed me was the exact fashion in which I ought to treat my subject.

Now of fashions, as ' of writing tribal lays,' there may be many: for instances, the somewhat violent way of Cobbett ; the descriptive way illustrated with copious examples of Arthur Young, perhaps the best for a leisurely age ; the compressed way of Sir James Caird, which alone is possible where much matter must be crowded into a minimum of space, and so forth.

All of these, however, appeared to me to be open to the objection that they are too liable to be coloured to the tint of the author's own mind. Every man has his predilections and opinions, and if his work is worth anything, they will reappear therein. But it seems to me desirable that these should be kept out of records of facts, whatever prominence he chooses to give, or cannot help giving to them in the deductions which he draws from those facts. It was for this reason that, notwithstanding the great extra labour involved, I determined to adopt a new system—that of the interview. By this means I am enabled to preserve, together with something of their personalities, the individual experience and opinions of many witnesses which, if I had been content to melt them down in the crucible of my own intelligence, might have acquired, perhaps, qualities derived from myself rather than from my informants.

Therefore, separating his evidence from my comments, I have recorded the substance of what each man said to me as he said or wrote it, always from notes taken in his presence, or from written documents with which he has furnished me, and, except in cases where I have been asked to omit it, under his own name.

Although here and there misinterpretation may have occurred, such testimony is in the main incontestable. It does at least furnish an actual record of what a certain number of people intimately connected with English land and agriculture, thought and said on these matters in the years 1901 and 1902. Of course the method, like every other, has its draw-

backs. Thus it may seem to involve a certain amount of
repetition. This, however, as any careful student will note,
is more apparent than actual. Each county, and all its
districts, have peculiarities of their own. Also the husbandman always wears his rue with a difference. Even as no
two leaves are alike, although to the casual eye they appear
so similar, so there exist variations between every one of a
thousand tales of agricultural woe.

These variations, however, can in the end be classified,
therefore it is useless to pursue them beyond a certain point.
Thus I am persuaded that if the views of each landowner,
tenant farmer, agent, clergyman, doctor, small-holder, labourer, optimist, pessimist and moderate man, which I have
recorded, were multiplied by a hundred of those of the
same class in the same districts, the results would be in
fact identical. Such as I have set down are a fair 'sample
from bulk' taken very much at hazard, as the merchant
takes corn which he wishes to buy. The evidence that I
have collected, therefore, may be accepted, I believe, without
doubt or cavil as typical of the state and opinions of the
counties and classes of which it treats.

I may add that it was not always quite easy to collect,
especially, though not exclusively, in the case of farmers of
the less educated sort, some of whom are by nature very suspicious. Such men often find it difficult to understand that
a person could undertake a wearisome mission of the kind
without an ulterior object tending to his own advantage
or to their disadvantage. One gentleman of this stamp, who
chanced to be in a very large way of business, was, I remember, quite unable to explain my real aims to his private
satisfaction. At last his curiosity led him to consult me
on the point, when I discovered he had evolved the theory
that the true end for which I was engaged in travelling
the length and breadth of England was a thirst, not for

rural information, but for—*free drinks!* The instance, in its utter absurdity, is illustrative of the mental calibre which finds it impossible to conceive that a man will devote himself to anything, solely to forward the accomplishment of a large and public object.

Indeed such an idea, I am sorry to say, is often foreign to farmers as a whole; whence perhaps their rooted dislike and mistrust of co-operation. They look too much to their intimate and private interests, and allow their views to be hedged in too closely by the conditions of their immediate neighbourhood. Therefore they will not combine for the good of their class, though combination is to their own good also, or be convinced even that circumstances vary in different parts of this great land and that they have anything to learn from them.

As I write, two examples occur to me. One man, after reading certain of my articles, sent me a letter to the effect that he had observed I described agriculture in England as depressed. Now, he said in substance, if you will come to see my farm I will show you that you are quite mistaken. To that man the affairs of his little farm were the husbandry of England. The second example comes from nearer home. In the midst of my journeyings I returned here for a night and sent for my own worthy steward to ask how things were progressing on the farms. When our business conversation was finished I inquired of him if he had read the articles I was writing. He replied he had seen 'some of them.' I suggested that he might do well to continue his studies and so improve his mind by finding out what farmers were doing in other places. He answered with decision: 'I don't want to know what folk are doing in *other* places; I want to know what they are doing *here*.'

After this I did not feel equal to pursuing the argument, but I reflected that the spirit shown by the remark was far too common among British husbandmen, and is indeed one of the causes of their failure to cope with these difficult times. They will not learn and they will not combine, and until they do so they must be content to bear the sorrows and scorns that are heaped upon them.

Personally, although it is hard to know in what direction to look for light, even in face of so much that is discouraging, I do not take a hopeless view of the future of British agriculture, at any rate in so far as the cultivator as distinct from the owner of land is concerned. The wheel of fortune may go round with some quick and unexpected turn, as in this world it is always going round. Also our land is as good as ever it was, and has the advantage of all the enormous improvements made upon it at great cost in the prosperous past. But we must change our methods and above all we *must* co-operate, for the case of the agricultural interests is an instance of the old story of the single stick that can, and of the faggot that cannot be broken.

As I have pointed out, this work does not deal with every district in England, or indeed with every division in those districts whereof it treats. That circumstance seems sometimes to have given great offence to gentlemen resident in the omitted places, who have expressed themselves strongly upon the subject in their local newspapers. I appeal to such critics to remember that it is not possible for a busy man to give up more than a certain proportion of his life to the execution of a task which, for obvious reasons, is one that in the main must be its own reward. Further, the whole of Mudie's would not contain the works that might be written about English agriculture, were it to be treated with the detail that some correspondents appear to desire. As it is, these volumes are long enough; a fact which has prevented me from dealing with certain subjects whereof I wished to speak, such as the history of English land tenure and the gradual extinction of the peasant proprietor.

Whilst alluding to this subject of criticism, I venture to express the hope also that I may be judged by what I have actually said or written, and not, as too often has been my lot, by what I am supposed to have said or written. To take a single example. It is nothing short of alarming to a man who holds such quack and predatory remedies in strong dislike, to read in journals which circulate throughout the world, that Mr. Rider Haggard by 'his advocacy of the enforced cultivation of derelict land . . . has given the Radicals a new electoral programme.' Or again, that the taxation of waste land ' derives fresh strength from the advocacy of Mr. Rider Haggard, who seems to have imbibed certain advanced ideas from long residence in Radical Norfolk.' Strange as it may seem, these exceedingly erroneous interpretations of my views were evidently founded upon the following passage taken from a speech which I made before the Central Chamber of Agriculture in November 1901 :—

' Within forty miles of where he was now standing he had seen some thousands of acres of land absolutely derelict, and he had seen many more thousands of acres practically derelict. It was a sad thing to look at this land and to know that if it were furnished with suitable communications and put beneath the spade, it could be made to produce a great amount of food, though it might not pay under corn now-a-days. Surely it would be desirable to adopt some method to bring together the men who wanted to till those acres and the acres that wanted to be tilled.'

My reason for mentioning this matter here, since contradictions rarely overtake such statements, is that for aught I know these somewhat serious allegations against my agricultural character may still be repeated and believed by news-

papers and their readers.  Therefore I wish to deny them
once and for all.  Indeed, had I been capable of advocating
the monstrous injustice of penalising men because they
could find nobody to cultivate their land, and were unable
to afford to do so themselves, I should be quite unfit to pose
as an impartial investigator of the grave problems connected
with the present state of agriculture in England.

The illustrations in these volumes are from photographs
taken, nearly all of them, upon my travels.  They are in-
serted, not to add to the attractiveness of the book, for which
purpose hand-camera pictures are scarcely suited, but to its
value, by the representation of certain things, such as cattle,
small-holders' or other typical houses, specimen landscapes,
remarkable trees, &c. as I saw them.

The maps, for which I am so largely indebted to the
labours of my friend Mr. Cochrane, and to the care of
Messrs. G. Philip & Son in reproducing them, have been
compiled upon a new principle from information which we
collected during and since our journeyings.  The idea occurred to me that it would be most useful, and furnish an
easy mode of reference, if a certain amount of local agricultural lore could be conveyed to the inquirer upon the
face of each map; a method that, so far as I am aware, has
as yet scarcely been attempted.  It must be remembered,
however, that the sum of facts which can be included is
necessarily limited by the small surface area of the maps
themselves.  Doubtless also, although every care has been
taken to ensure accuracy, some errors may be found by
persons intimately acquainted with particular districts.  For
these I apologise beforehand.

Indeed the same remark applies to all this book.  Here
or there a name may have been misspelt, a place or a field
misdescribed, or even, when several gentlemen were talking together—though I think that this has happened very

rarely, if at all—words spoken by one may have been attributed to another. Also now and again a figure or a sentence hurriedly scrawled in a note-book, perhaps in the rain or the dark, may have been misread. If so, for all of these things I am truly sorry, as I am for any shortcomings in my descriptions of particular spots. I observe that one gentleman made a speech that was reported in the newspapers, complaining that, although all I said was true and accurate enough, I had given him no fresh information about the system of agriculture practised in a locality where he had farmed for forty years. How could this be expected of me who had bided there but a single day? Yet it is possible that to readers in other parts of England I may have been successful in conveying new information concerning that neighbourhood.

I trust, then, and indeed believe, that in these volumes will be found a fair summary of the state of rural affairs in those counties of which they treat. At least I can conscientiously declare that no fatigue or effort has been spared to ensure this result. I may add that the work involved in dealing in many places and among many people with these problems and inquiries has proved by no means light. In short, my labours have been not unlike to those of a Royal Commission, faced single-handed and without the ample resources, assistance, and lordly leisure of such august bodies. If, however, the effort has been the most arduous and exhausting of my life, it proved also the most interesting, although at times that interest was of a somewhat painful character.

Before I lay down my pen, even at the risk of seeming insistent, I take this opportunity of calling attention to my scheme for the establishment of an Agricultural Post under Government control, upon which I have dwelt in more detail in the concluding chapter of these volumes. The longer that I consider this project, the more am I convinced of its perfect feasibility. Further, I make bold to assert that if it should be adopted in conjunction with the other remedies that I have proposed, it would go some way towards changing the present gloomy aspect of agricultural affairs in Great Britain and Ireland to one of moderate and increasing prosperity. Without cheap transport small-holders cannot flourish except under the most favourable conditions of soil and markets, and without small-holders co-operation does not flourish—at any rate in England. An Agricultural Post, in my opinion, therefore would multiply small-holders, and induce what our land so sorely needs—co-operation. I am certain, moreover, that such a Post must exercise an appreciable influence in checking the migration from the country into the cities.

For too long, landowners and farmers together, we have schooled our minds to believe that there is but one salvation, protective duties on imported food-stuffs which are unattainable, and even if attained, might work ills not now foreseen. Let us cease, then, to pursue this marsh-light—this phantom—of Protection and combine to secure moderate but effective measures of reform, against which it cannot be urged that they would raise the cost of a people's daily bread.

I appeal to the Government, and especially to the President of the Board of Agriculture, to give fair consideration and trial to this idea; to formulate further a settled rural policy on some such lines as those that I have ventured to suggest, and to pursue it with energy and despatch. I appeal also to the Press to help the matter forward. Still more strongly do I appeal to the members of Parliament representing country districts, to league themselves together quite irrespective of party considerations, and to insist that a portion of the public time should be devoted to the amendment of evils which all who think must admit to be most real and urgent.

With this petition I end the last of many pages by returning my heartfelt thanks to those of every class throughout England—and their name is legion—who have so kindly assisted me with information—written or verbal—hospitality, and in other ways. Most of them I cannot hope to meet again, but their goodness I never shall forget.

DITCHINGHAM,
*November*, 1902.

---

## NOTE

The approximate total areas of Counties given in the text are for the most part taken from Longmans' Gazetteer.

# CONTENTS

OF

## THE FIRST VOLUME

|  | PAGE |
|---|---|
| PREFACE TO NEW EDITION | vii |
| INTRODUCTION | xxvii |
| WILTSHIRE | 1 |
| HAMPSHIRE | 51 |
| GUERNSEY | 68 |
| JERSEY | 84 |
| SUSSEX | 104 |
| KENT | 137 |
| DEVONSHIRE | 175 |
| CORNWALL | 218 |
| SOMERSET | 225 |
| DORSETSHIRE | 257 |
| HEREFORDSHIRE | 287 |
| WORCESTERSHIRE | 323 |
| GLOUCESTERSHIRE | 389 |
| WARWICKSHIRE | 404 |
| SHROPSHIRE | 422 |
| ESSEX | 486 |
| HERTFORDSHIRE AND MIDDLESEX | 509 |

# ILLUSTRATIONS

TO

# THE FIRST VOLUME

WILTSHIRE:

    STONEHENGE, SHOWING THE FALLEN MONOLITH.
      (*Since re-erected*) . . . . . . . *facing page* 17

    MR. DIBBEN'S HAMPSHIRE-DOWN TEGS . . .   ,,    17

    IMPORTED SCOTCH SHEEP, NEAR SWINDON . . .   ,,    32

    A SMALL-HOLDER AND HIS COWS, DAUNTSEY VALE   ,,    32

GUERNSEY AND JERSEY:

    TYPICAL GUERNSEY COW . . . . . .   ,,    84

    A FARMHOUSE, GUERNSEY . . . . . .   ,,    93

    COMBINED JERSEY POTATO CULTIVATOR AND CLOD
      CUTTER, WITH SEED POTATOES IN BOXES . .   ,,    93

SUSSEX:

    GROUP OF YOUNG CATTLE ON MR. EAMES'S FARM .   ,,    113

    FOWLS IN FATTING COOPS . . . . .   ,,    128

    CHICKEN CRAMMING . . . . . . .   ,,    128

KENT:

    KENTISH CHERRY TREE, SAID TO BE THE LARGEST
      IN ENGLAND . . . . . . .   ,,    149

    SPECIMEN APPLE TREE AND NUT BUSHES ON MR.
      LENEY'S FARM, SHOWING KENT METHOD OF
      PRUNING . . . . . . . .   ,,    156

DEVONSHIRE:

    Cottage at Broad Clyst   .   .   .   .   *facing page* 209

    Sir Thomas Dyke Acland's Devon Bull.  .  .    ,,   209

SOMERSET:

    Cottages near Williton   .  .  .  .  .   ,,   224

    Dorset Horn Sheep .  .  .  .  .  .  .   ,,   241

    Bird-scaring ! .  .  .  .  .  .  .  .   ,,   241

DORSETSHIRE:

    Mr. Tory's Sheep   .  .  .  .  .  .  .   ,,   256

HEREFORDSHIRE:

    Hereford Cow, the Property of Mr. Stephen

        Robinson .  .  .  .  .  .  .  .   ,,   321

WORCESTERSHIRE:

    An Evesham Orchard   .  .  .  .  .  .   ,,   336

    Wickhamford Manor   .  .  .  .  .  .   ,,   353

    Four-year-old Damson Tree, grown on Cold

        Clay  .  .  .  .  .  .  .  .   ,,   368

    Training Hop-bine (East Kent System) on Mr.

        Savory's Farm .  .  .  .  .  .   ,,   368

    The Earl of Coventry   .  .  .  .  .   ,,   373

    Young Hereford Bull .  .  .  .  .  .   ,,   373

    A Teme Valley Orchard .  .  .  .  .   ,,   380

    Sheep-shearing by Machinery   .  .  .   ,,   380

GLOUCESTERSHIRE:

    The Hyde Farm   .  .  .  .  .  .   ,,   389

    View of Stroud from the Cotswold Hills.   .   ,,   396

WARWICKSHIRE:

    Mr. Cooper's Lifting Stack-roof  .  .  .   ,,   433

    Lord Camperdown's Oxford-down Ram  .  .   ,,   433

ESSEX:

IN DEDHAM VALE, NORTH ESSEX . . . *facing page* 448

HOMESTEAD, DENGIE FLATS . . . . . . ,, 448

'PUGGLING' STRAWBERRIES, TIPTREE FRUIT FARM . ,, 453

THE HONBLE. E. G. STRUTT'S DAIRY COWS . . ,, 460

DENGIE FLATS, LOOKING SEAWARDS . . . . ,, 469

A MOATED GRANGE, THE ROOTHINGS . . . . ,, 476

A ROOTHINGS COTTAGE . . . . . . ,, 476

THE PARLOUR AND KITCHEN OF TWENTY ESSEX
LABOURERS . . . . . . . . ,, 497

HERTFORDSHIRE:

MR. PROUT'S WHEAT, BLOUNT'S FARM . . . ,, 512

LORD SALISBURY'S COTTAGES, NEAR HATFIELD . . ,, 529

A HERTFORDSHIRE FARMHOUSE . . . . ,, 529

A DAIRY COW, KNEBWORTH ESTATE . . . . ,, 544

NEW HAY-SWEEP ON A HERTFORDSHIRE FARM . ,, 549

MOLE-DRAINING DERELICT LAND . . . . . ,, 556

MOLE-DRAINING PLOUGH . . . . . . ,, 556

# RURAL ENGLAND

## WILTSHIRE

In this work I propose to confine myself, so far as may be convenient, to an account of my own experiences in those parts of rural England which I visited during the years 1901 and 1902. To expand its scope almost indefinitely would be a mere matter of time and labour. But each county has already books of reference devoted to it, which can be consulted by those who desire detailed information upon any particular point; and to such compilations it is not my object to add. As well might one man try to write a rural encyclopædia, which would, after all, prove somewhat weary reading.

It seems to me that if any value can be attached to these labours in our own days, or in those to come, it will be more or less personal—of a nature connected with him who undertook them. Their interest must lie, at any rate to a material extent, not only in the facts recorded, but in the things which he saw, as he saw them in his time; in the opinions that he formed according to his lights and opportunities, and in the views of the men whom he met and with whom he corresponded. These, when pieced together, will, it is hoped, add a not uninteresting chapter to the story of our generation. Doubtless that chapter may be full of faults: many omissions it must have, together with some errors of view, and deductions that are perhaps mistaken. One thing only I can promise— it shall be honest. To the best of my ability, I strive to record the truth as the truth appeared to me, and to give an equal weight to every voice and argument.

Indeed, the subject also is worthy of earnest consideration and of treatment by abilities far higher than my own. In this twentieth-century England we seem to have grown away from the land; we have flocked into cities, and are occupied with the things of cities ; we have set our hearts on trade, and look to its profits for our luxury. But the land is still the true mother of our race, which, were it not for that same land, would soon dwindle into littleness. Although it no longer produces the bulk of the food they eat, from it our towns draw their strength, for with its healthy men and women their pale blood is replenished. Though to-day they be so poor, yet the might of England is in her villages, those villages so many of whose homes are crumbling, and whose arable fields go back daily to the wasteful and unproductive grass out of which our forefathers reclaimed them. Thus our national neglect of husbandry, and of the welfare of the soil and those who till it, has decreed that it shall be.

For my part—although I know all the arguments in its favour—I think such a decision short-sighted and ill-advised, but perhaps it is I who lack wisdom and am blind. At the least, thus matters stand at present, and it is useless to rail at them—rather must we try to adapt ourselves to circumstances which we cannot control. In our country, if anywhere, the command of the people appears a judgment of Heaven. If it pleases them that our agriculture should be crippled by unbridled foreign competition, and our hamlets emptied, chiefly through the desire for a wage which a broken industry cannot pay, right or wrong so it is ordained and so it must befall. My present business is not to find fault with things as they are, but to describe them, and, if I can discover any, to suggest remedies to those who have power to direct the course of the country. Perhaps thus I may be of service, however slight, to a cause that seems to have few advocates, and, before it is too late, may succeed in bringing home to the minds of some of authority in Parliament and the Press, the need of combating those admitted and far-reaching evils which are involved in the decay of agriculture and in the desertion of the English land by its inhabitants.

In the very early spring of 1901, or before it, I began my investigations in the south-western inland shire of Wiltshire, one of the largest in the country, since it measures about 880,000 acres, of which some two-thirds are chalk downs or uplands.

Looking through the windows of his railway carriage, the traveller from London to the old cathedral city of Salisbury sees, stretching on either side of him, the great Hampshire fields of light and very chalky land, through which winds the placid stream of the Test, famous for its trout. Presently he passes into Wiltshire, where, at that winter season of the year—for as yet no sign of spring was visible to the eye—the grey plough-lands stretch themselves out to an indefinite horizon. It is a country of long views and vast unhedged expanses, broken here and there by villages nestling in sheltered vales, about whose churchyard elms the storm-tossed rooks swing and circle. Around the ancient city of Salisbury this character is maintained and even accentuated. My first day's investigations led me out to Stonehenge, some nine miles away, by the road which, for the most part, follows the banks of the Avon, running past the mighty earthwork known as Old Sarum, where, until Salisbury dispossessed it, once the city stood. But long before its first house was built, the dim and forgotten forefathers of our race, by what patient and continual toil no man will ever know, reared these colossal earthworks which have so long outlived them, and will outlive all the following civilisations.

Close by, embowered in trees, stands a house, now in process of demolition or repair, where, as our driver informed us—I do not guarantee the statement—once lived William Pitt. Beyond this the scenery is beautiful, especially in contrast to the desolate surrounding plain. Yonder, to our right, stands a grey old hall backed by a wood-crowned hill, with purple-budded trees broken here and there by masses of sombre yet shining fir. In front of it winds the Avon, its gentle stream embanked by marshy bottoms, lined everywhere with water from the brimming dykes, which now gleams and now turns black, as the storm-clouds come and go and the squalls hiss through the red growths of the pollard willows. On either side are the Wiltshire Downs rolling away endlessly like the veld of Southern Africa.

Presently we halted at the gate of a brand-new, villa-like residence, planted round with small and struggling firs. As we had been told that the farmer whom we were to visit was ' quite of the old school,' the appearance of his dwelling, which reminded me of that of a retired tradesman, was disconcerting. For this, however, as we discovered presently, there was a reason. The door was opened by an elderly woman, of very comely appearance and pleasant manners, who led us into the sitting-room, where we found her husband, a hale, shrewd-faced old gentleman. After compliments—as they say in the East—he asked me what I wanted to know. I replied, everything that he could tell me with reference to farming in his part of Wiltshire. Indeed, as it proved, our host could tell us a good deal. Wrapping himself against the icy wind—for the weather was bitter—he led us, pausing now and again to rest and talk, up some six or seven hundred yards of steep slope behind the house, until we came to the crest of a great earth-swell, whence the landscape lay outstretched beneath us for miles and miles. To the left the square-towered church of Upper Woodford nestled amid trees in the hollow, and about it stood the houses of the village. In the vale far below was a lambing pen, where, even from that distance, we could distinguish the ewes moving over the scattered yellow straw. Beyond that, again, on the opposite rise, were buildings used as carters' houses and a training stable for racehorses ; and beyond these at various points, masses of thick wood. Over all this wide expanse the gale roared and whistled, and great shadows chased each other as the storm-clouds raced across the sun.

Here is the history of this farm, not large as they are reckoned in that county, although it covers 700 acres, and may be taken as a fair specimen of those in the neighbourhood. In 1812 it was sold for £27,000. This happened when corn was so high in price that the farmers of that day ploughed up the downlands to put them under wheat, a crop to which they are little suited, being very thin-soiled, although for a few years it paid them well enough. Afterwards, when it ceased to be remunerative to work these downs, of which the first fertility was now exhausted, their owners would have been very glad to restore the close natural turf that sheep find so sweet and fattening. But this they could not do. Once destroyed, the down grasses cannot be replaced, at any rate for generations. Land which has been broken thus is called 'bake.'

Time went on, and again the farm came into the market, on this occasion in 1892. Now it sold for £7,000, a drop of £20,000 on the glorious total of eighty years before. When our host hired it twenty-seven years ago he paid £600 a year in rent, and £196 a year tithe. In 1901 he paid £250 a year rent, and the landlord pays the tithe. So far as I can see, therefore, after he has discharged all the other customary outgoings, with repairs and sundries, that gentleman must be fortunate if this property puts £100 a year into his pocket. Even on a purchase price of £7,000, plus the cost of the new house which he has built for the tenant, this return does not seem encouraging to such as contemplate investment in Wiltshire acres.

'But,' added the old farmer, 'those times was better for I than these is. I made more money when I paid £800 a year than now when I pay £250.' Surely an eloquent admission. Yet, if I understood him aright, being hardheaded, saving, and experienced, he still makes some money. It is the landlord who makes none. Also in the past, having farmed through all the fat years, he made a good deal—enough to enable him to start a considerable family on farms of their own, where, with the help of dealing, they are doing

well. Doubtless, too, he had something put by against a
rainy day. I asked him what he considered the worst feature
of the present times. 'Labour, sir, labour!' he answered
with emphasis, striking his stick into the ground. 'The
labour is worse than all the rest. There is none to be had.
The trouble is that we cannot pay the men enough to keep
them on the land.'

Just then a young man passed driving a water-cart of
home manufacture. Two ancient wheels, a large barrel, and
a couple of fir poles for shafts—these were its rude but
sufficient elements, an indication of its owner's frugal mind.
Water, by the way, is the great difficulty on this and many
similar farms. It must often be carted to the stock, and
such carting up steep hillsides costs both money and time.

' You have a lad there,' I said, pointing to the youth walking by the wheeler—for this job two horses are necessary.

' Ay!' he answered; 'he is the last left to I, and he will
be off soon.' The wage of this young fellow, by the way,
was 10s. 6d. a week.

Taken altogether, I should describe the farming of this
land as rough, at least we should call it rough in Norfolk.
On the other hand, it must be cheap. Thus, no drainage is
needed, and there are no fences to trim or holls, that is,
ditches, to clear. Sainfoin—that most useful crop upon a
chalk soil, as Arthur Young pointed out 130 years ago—is
largely grown. Our informant sold a quantity of this seed
recently at 44s. a quarter, which, as he remarked, 'paid better
than wheat.' Sheep, however, of the Hampshire Down
breed were his mainstay. Also, there was a herd of cows,
but these, under a system which was quite new to my
experience, were hired out to a dairyman in the vale below
at £10 a head per annum. All that the dairyman can make
over the £10 is his profit. Beyond the necessary labour of
attendance and milking when the cows are in yield, he
has no further responsibility. The farmer finds their food
throughout the year, and when they go dry takes charge
of them until they come again to milk. His advan-

tages seem to be that he is sure of a fixed return from his animals, which, with their offspring, remain his property. The advantage of the dairyman, on the other hand, is that he has no anxiety as to the provision of the cows necessary to his trade, and no need for capital wherewith to buy them. In short, his position is very much that of the individual who jobs his horses at an agreed rate per month.

On our way back to the vale we came to a pen containing 150 ' tegs,' that is, hoggets or sheep not yet of an age to bear lambs, which were being fed upon a crop of mixed swedes and turnips. I noticed that, as was to be expected after this severe winter, a good number of these roots, perhaps a quarter, were rotten. By way of inquiry I poked my stick through one of them. 'Ay,' answered the farmer, ' they should have been pitted' (that is, earthed up) 'and fed to the "tegs" from the heaps, but I could not get the labour to do it, so they just had to take their chance.' Another eloquent admission. These 'tegs,' by the way, their owner valued at 40s. to 50s. as they run out. Just beyond the pen a man was engaged in collecting flints from the stone-strewn soil. On inquiry it appeared that he was the servant of the road authorities, who pay 1s. 4d. a load for the stone, for the collection and carting of which the farmer is at no expense. As flints are plentiful, this seems money easily earned.

I cannot leave this farm without mentioning the ancient house which stands in the fertile bottom, surrounded by noble Spanish chestnuts and approached through an avenue of great elms, beneath which just then the turf was white with snowdrops and golden with the bloom of aconites. It is a peaceful-looking place nestling there among the rich water-meadows upon the banks of Avon, and its appearance seems to proclaim that it has a history. So it has, indeed, for here, when Heale House belonged to the Hyde family, Charles II. lay hid for fourteen days after the battle of Worcester. Thus at least says tradition, speaking through the mouth of our host, who for more than twenty years lived in this house, until he found a home in his present villa-like farmstead. Another story tells that some lady of that far-off day—Mrs. Hyde, I believe—under cover of a coursing party, smuggled the future king to Southampton, whence he escaped to France.

Beyond Woodford the road runs through lovely country to the little town of Amesbury, about five miles away. Here, with some qualms of conscience—since it has nothing to do with farming, and on this unsentimental journey, at any rate, I had resolved sternly to repress the archæological instincts of my nature—we made a digression to enable us to visit the stately monument of Stonehenge.

I wonder whether the traveller has often seen this solemn ruin, if so it may be called, under circumstances much more impressive. To begin with, we were quite alone in the place—always, I think, an advantage in such pilgrimages to the shrines of departed gods. Then, as it chanced, there overtook us one of the most furious squalls of wind and sleet that ever I remember to have experienced in any country. Out of the bosom of an inky cloud leapt the sudden gale and rain. On drove the storm, roaring across the vast veld till we were glad to cower under the shelter of an 'upright,' and, from this insufficient hiding-place, watch it sweep over and past us. Like wind-borne smoke it streamed by in dense clouds lined with horizontal streaks of hail which at times seemed to be rising up from the earth, to break into white showers upon the desolate monoliths. The sound of the tempest wailed and echoed through the trilithons with a music wild and indescribable, while a blackness as of night fell upon the face of earth. The solitary tumuli standing on the surrounding plain were wreathed round and blotted out beneath the storm-palls, the distant clumps of trees grew shadowy and vanished, the horizon seemed to draw near. Then suddenly the gloom above lightened, until once more, by slow degrees, the grey arch of heaven became visible. The wind still raged on, but the rain had passed.

We made a careful examination of the great monolith,

which with its cross-piece or impost—I think that is the right term—fell on the last night of the nineteenth century, humbled at length by the remorseless hand of Time. Indeed, as we huddled under its lee it occurred to me to hope that this savage hurricane might not prove the doom of its still standing twin, and, incidentally, of the human mites beneath. Looking at the pillar which had fallen, I observed that the turf at its base was only lifted up to a height of about two feet. This puzzled me, as I had imagined that, like dolmens which I have seen in Brittany and elsewhere, these stones were set deep into the earth by the ancients who reared them. Afterwards I discovered my mistake. Here the chalk lies but a little way beneath the surface, and the primitive races knew that this is the very best of all foundations. In it they made a little hollow, and in the hollow placed the base of the monolith. How, I wonder? Perhaps, like the old Egyptians, by the help of mounds of earth built up beneath. I examined also the fallen cross-piece, now, I believe, restored to its ancient place, which was broken in two. During all these unnumbered centuries the weather does not seem to have discoloured the stone to a depth greater than that of a fraction of an inch. Within, the material glistened like fine quartz, in which appeared small black pebbles. Here, with apologies for touching on the subject, I bid farewell to Stonehenge.

In this neighbourhood all the land is very light in character, with a chalk subsoil. Sheep graze in numbers on the downs, but such proportion of the richer soil as is under the plough produces good crops of barley and oats. Wheat is also grown to some extent. The cottages are, many of them, very picturesque, being relieved with white stones worked into the walls that are crowned with heavy thatch, above which rise the red chimneys.

It was on the day after my journey to Stonehenge that I made a very interesting—perhaps my most interesting—expedition from Salisbury, to visit the Don Quixote of the Hampshire Downs, Major Poore, of Old Lodge, near Winterslow. I name him thus, which I trust will not displease him, since the title is meant as one of compliment, because Major Poore is the first gentleman whom I have met whose originality of mind and perseverance have enabled him to carry a certain very desperate enterprise to a successful issue. In other words, in the teeth of a thousand protestations of its impossibility, he has succeeded—on a small scale, it is true—in re-establishing on somewhat unpromising land, without the loss of a penny piece to himself, a thriving settlement of little freeholders. Like the famous knight of La Mancha, he has tilted at this formidable windmill, but with results very different from those which befell his prototype. It is the windmill that has gone down. How he conceived the idea and why he conceived it I will not discuss, since to do so would involve explanations that must be somewhat long and intricate. A brief summary of the facts will be sufficient for the purposes of this work.

By the advice of a village council, a kind of twentieth-century 'Court of the Tything' which he established at Winterslow, on the borders of Hampshire—a hamlet situated upon the crest of a wide, wind-swept plain dotted with juniper bushes, and in the immediate neighbourhood of great woods, which it overlooks—Major Poore purchased for £1,500 a holding known as Cooper's Farm. About eighty acres of this farm, however, were resold in one lot at an improved price, thus minimising the risk of his experiment with the remainder. The balance of the land was mapped out into lots, varying in size from a quarter of an acre to sixteen acres, to suit the pockets and prospects of intending purchasers. Of these—for all the plots were taken up—a small proportion paid in full at the rate of £15 per acre. Others, whose circumstances would not admit of so simple a discharge, entered into agreements under which they bound themselves to pay down a fraction of the capital sum and the balance of principal and interest within a period of fifteen years, these payments to be made half-yearly and in advance.

The experiment began in 1892, and its results in 1901 were roughly as follows: Of the freeholders who elected to pay by instalments—to be more correct they are lease-holders for 2,000 years—or their representatives, none had defaulted or fallen into arrear, although one, I think, had sold his plot for cash at an advance of 50 per cent. over cost price. The surplus of assets over liability in the hands of the managers of the venture was about £650, increased to nearly £800 in the account ending July 31, 1901, which, as it must prove interesting and instructive to all students of small holdings, I reproduce in full (pp. 12-14).

When I visited Winterslow over thirty houses had been erected on their plots by the owners of the settlement, and to assist them in the erection of these houses they had among them found it possible to borrow, upon security which satisfied friendly societies and other lending institutions, a sum of about £6,000.

Now I ask the reader to accompany me from Major Poore's house—the scene, by the way, of a remarkable whirlwind, such as we call a Rogers-blast in the Eastern Counties, which a few years ago swept away his outbuildings in three seconds of time—to Winterslow itself, over the Wiltshire border, a matter of half an hour's drive. Here we were most kindly received by Mr. John King, a large farmer in the village, whose forefathers had tilled the same fields for some generations. Mr. King, strange as it may seem—for farmers rarely welcome new ideas—has been Major Poore's right-hand man from the inception of this enterprise, and is himself a holder of two acres of the settlement land. He led us to the borders of the old village, and with a sweep of the hand pointed to a score or so of neat residences. 'Those are the houses of the settlement,' Mr. King said. I looked at them, and was astonished. I had expected to find very humble cottages, but in the majority of instances, at any rate, these dwellings were much more. Some of them are constructed of red brick; others of the chalk, lime, and straw concrete which is common in the

NINTH ANNUAL

## LANDHOLDERS' COURT,

*Statement of Receipts and Expenditure*

REVENUE

| PAYMENTS | | £ s. d. | £ s. d. | £ s. d. | £ s. d. |
|---|---|---|---|---|---|
| March 16, 1901. | Cheque Book 2s. 6d., Stamps 2d. . . | 0 2 8 | | | |
| „ 25, 1901. | Tea . . . . . . . . | 1 19 5 | | | |
| „ „ | Postage . . . . . . . | 0 5 0 | | | |
| „ „ | School Subscription . . . | 1 1 0 | | | |
| „ „ | Rent of Oddfellows' Hall . . . | 0 6 0 | | | |
| | | | 3 14 1 | | |
| May 22, 1901. | Registration Stamp . . . . | 0 5 0 | | | |
| July 14, 1901. | Bennett, Printing . . . . . | 1 8 8 | | | |
| | | | 1 13 8 | | |
| | | | | 5 7 9 | |
| March 25, 1901. | Secretary's Salary . . . . . | | 5 0 0 | | |
| „ „ | Auditors' Fee . . . . . . | | 1 1 0 | | |
| | | | | 6 1 0 | |
| | | | | | 11 8 9 |
| Sept. 20, 1900. | Tithe, Rev. J. C. Noel . . . . | 8 10 10 | | | |
| March 26, 1901. | „ . . . . | 8 10 10 | | | |
| | | | 17 1 8 | | |
| Oct. 18, 1900. | Tithe, Rev. W. Dowding . . . | 2 4 9 | | | |
| April 17, 1901. | „ . . . | 2 4 7 | | | |
| | | | 4 9 4 | | |
| | | | | 21 11 0 | |
| Dec. 7, 1900. | Rate . . . . . . . . | 2 8 10 | | | |
| June 29, 1901. | „ . . . . . . . . | 1 16 8 | | | |
| | | | | 4 5 6 | |
| | | | | | 25 16 6 |
| June 29, 1901. | Loan to Mr. Alexander Hardy . . | | | | 50 0 0 |
| | | | | | 87 5 3 |
| | Balance at Bank { On Deposit . . | | | 300 0 0 | |
| | { Current Account . | | | 111 1 1 | |
| | | | | | 411 1 1 |
| | | | | | £498 6 4 |

STATEMENT OF ACCOUNTS

# WINTERSLOW

*for the Year ending July* 31, 1901

ACCOUNT, 1900-1901

| | RECEIPTS | £ | s. | d. | £ | s. | d. | £ | s. | d | £ | s. | d. |
|---|---|---|---|---|---|---|---|---|---|---|---|---|---|
| Balance from July 31, 1900 . . . . . . | | | | | | | | | | | 170 | 2 | 7 |
| Half-year ending September 29, 1900— | | | | | | | | | | | | | |
| Division 1 . . . . . . . | | 15 | 5 | 10 | | | | | | | | | |
| 2a . . . . . . . | | 7 | 8 | 0 | | | | | | | | | |
| 2b . . . . . . . | | 17 | 0 | 0 | | | | | | | | | |
| 3 and 4 . . . . . . | | 11 | 3 | 0 | | | | | | | | | |
| 5 . . . . . . . | | 2 | 8 | 9 | | | | | | | | | |
| | | | | | 53 | 5 | 7 | | | | | | |
| Half-year ending March 25, 1901— | | | | | | | | | | | | | |
| Division 1 . . . . . . . | | 13 | 7 | 0 | | | | | | | | | |
| 2a . . . . . . . | | 7 | 18 | 0 | | | | | | | | | |
| 2b . . . . . . . | | 17 | 0 | 0 | | | | | | | | | |
| 3 and 4 . . . . . . | | 10 | 3 | 0 | | | | | | | | | |
| 5 . . . . . . . | | 2 | 8 | 9 | | | | | | | | | |
| | | | | | 50 | 16 | 9 | | | | | | |
| | | | | | | | | 104 | 2 | 4 | | | |
| PAID OFF CAPITAL ACCOUNT. LAND— | | | | | | | | | | | | | |
| Dec. 11, 1900. J. W. Loviboud, in full, 11a, Plot 4 | | 5 | 0 | 6 | | | | | | | | | |
| " " W. Baugh, to make £3 table, 9a, Plot 4 . . . . | | 0 | 19 | 7½ | | | | | | | | | |
| | | | | | 6 | 0 | 1½ | | | | | | |
| April 16, 1901. T. Hale, paid off No. 2, Plot 4 . | | 9 | 12 | 0 | | | | | | | | | |
| " " Hy. Annetts, paid off Nos. 3, 4, 5, Plot 1 . . . . | | 20 | 3 | 0 | | | | | | | | | |
| " " Herbert Annetts, paid off No. 19, Plot 2a . . . . | | 19 | 15 | 7 | | | | | | | | | |
| June 4, 1901. Silas Stone, paid off No. 3, Plot 4 . | | 8 | 19 | 2 | | | | | | | | | |
| | | | | | 58 | 9 | 9 | | | | | | |
| | | | | | | | | 64 | 9 | 10½ | | | |
| MORTGAGES PAID OFF— | | | | | | | | | | | | | |
| Oct. 18, 1900. Eli Collins, paid off from £150 . | | 35 | 0 | 0 | | | | | | | | | |
| April 9, 1901. Eli Collins, " " £115 . | | 15 | 0 | 0 | | | | | | | | | |
| | | | | | 50 | 0 | 0 | | | | | | |
| April 16, 1901. Henry Annetts, to complete payment on £20 . . . | | 14 | 10 | 0 | | | | | | | | | |
| " " Henry Annetts, to complete payment on £10 . . . | | 8 | 0 | 0 | | | | | | | | | |
| | | | | | 22 | 10 | 0 | | | | | | |
| " " T. Hale, to complete payment on £10 | | | | | 8 | 10 | 0 | | | | | | |
| " 30 " John Shears, " " £30 | | | | | 21 | 0 | 0 | | | | | | |
| | | | | | | | | 102 | 0 | 0 | | | |
| MORTGAGE ACCOUNT— | | | | | | | | | | | | | |
| Sept. 29, 1900. Principal paid off . . . . | | 9 | 12 | 6 | | | | | | | | | |
| March 25, 1901. " " . . . | | 7 | 14 | 6 | | | | | | | | | |
| | | | | | 17 | 7 | 0 | | | | | | |
| Sept. 29 1900. Interest paid . . . . | | 7 | 10 | 8½ | | | | | | | | | |
| March 25, 1901. " " . . . | | 6 | 14 | 1 | | | | | | | | | |
| | | | | | 14 | 4 | 9½ | | | | | | |
| | | | | | | | | 31 | 11 | 9½ | | | |
| Sept. 29, 1900. Tithe . . . . . | | 11 | 5 | 0 | | | | | | | | | |
| March 25, 1901. " . . . . . | | 11 | 5 | 0 | | | | | | | | | |
| | | | | | 22 | 10 | 0 | | | | | | |
| " " Rate . . . . . | | | | | 3 | 4 | 9 | | | | | | |
| | | | | | | | | 25 | 14 | 9 | | | |
| Stamp . . . . . | | | | | | | | 0 | 5 | 0 | | | |
| | | | | | | | | | | | 328 | 3 | 9 |
| | | | | | | | | | | | £498 | 6 | 4 |

## SHARE ACCOUNT

NOMINAL CAPITAL—2,400 Shares at 5s. each.

|  |  | £ | s. | d. |
|---|---|---|---|---|
| 240 ,, | paid up | 60 | 0 | 0 |

## SURPLUS FUND AND MORTGAGE ACCOUNT

| Division | Name | Repayment Loan began | Original Amount £ s. d. | Paid-off £ s. d. | Value after March 25, 1901 £ s. d. | £ s. d. |
|---|---|---|---|---|---|---|
| 1 | Andrew Sheppard | March 25, 1898 | 100 0 0 | 17 10 0 | 82 10 0 | |
| | | May 27, 1899 | 20 0 0 | 1 10 0 | 18 10 0 | |
| 2b | Hy. Shears | March 25, 1900 | 120 0 0 | 19 0 0 | 101 0 0 | |
| „ | Eli Collins | ,, 25, 1900 | 25 0 0 | 1 5 0 | 23 15 0 | |
| 4 | Alex. Hardy | June 29, 1901 | 150 0 0 | 50 0 0 | 100 0 0 | |
| 5 | John Coleman | March 25, 1900 | 50 0 0 | | 50 0 0 | |
| „ | John Shears | Sept. 29, 1898 | 100 0 0 | 5 0 0 | 95 0 0 | |
| | | | 10 0 0 | 1 5 0 | 8 15 0 | |
| | Stephen Williams | Temporary Loan at 3% | | | | 378 10 0 |
| | | | | | | 10 0 0 |
| | | Total Mortgage Account | | | | 388 10 0 |
| | | Balance at Bank | | | | 411 1 1 |
| | | | | | | 799 11 1 |

Audited and found correct, Nov. 21, 1901.

HENRY T. WITT.

district, set upon brick pinnings, and roofed with slate or corrugated iron, with proper water troughings, large underground cemented cisterns to collect the rain, and all necessary outbuildings.

The houses vary in size. The best of them must contain six rooms, while others are on a more humble scale, but all seem thoroughly well built and comfortable—such habitations as men put up with their own money to dwell in for the remainder of their days and to leave to their children after them. We entered the first, and were introduced to the wife of its owner, a woodman, who during parts of the year works at hurdle-making and tree-felling in the neighbourhood. On a table in the sitting-room lay many rolls of cloth. These were the produce of the Winterslow spinning and weaving industry, founded and, as I gathered, to some extent subsidised by Mrs. Poore, the wife of Major Poore. The cloth, which is manufactured from the wool of Hampshire Down sheep, is an excellent and closely woven homespun that, as is shown by the certificates hung upon the wall, has gained much commendation at the Albert Hall exhibitions and elsewhere. Up to the date of my visit, however, this venture could not be said to pay, chiefly for the reason that customers will not purchase home-carded woollen goods, and at Winterslow no perfected carding machine was available. Therefore the raw material had to be sent to Scotland to be carded at an expense greater than it could bear. The price of it is 5s. a yard of 30 inches in width. This is not exorbitant, but homespun at that figure must face competition. Thus, as it chanced, my companion on this visit was wearing clothes made of a most admirable and lasting cloth which he purchased in Connemara. It cost him 2s. 6d. a yard of 36 inches in width, that is, 50 per cent. less than the Winterslow product.

The husband of the manageress of this weaving industry was the owner of an acre plot, and his house, I understood, cost about £150 to build, some of it borrowed money. This acre, which is a strip twenty-two yards in width, was divided into a little flower garden in front of the house, planted with well-trained and pruned espalier apples, thirty yards of kitchen garden set with winter vegetables, thirty yards of springing rye, and a hundred yards of mixed white turnips and swedes. The balance was fallow. Near by lay a second typical plot of five-and-a-half acres, of which one-and-a-half were rented from another owner. The house was good and very neat, built of chalk concrete and plastered over. Its master worked on a farm during part of the year, and the wife took in washing. They had a well-planted garden, and, with the exception of a small portion reserved for roots, the land was laid down to sainfoin. There was a pigsty with an iron roof and a cow-house—in the pig-sty two sows, in the cow-house two cows and a calf. Also there was a pen with about a dozen fowls, and on the land was an unbroken 'hale' of beet : here, I think, it is called a 'pit.' The establishment looked and was, I believe, most thriving.

Next we came to a four-acre plot, with the usual good house. This was laid down in sainfoin after barley, the sainfoin being cross-drilled to secure a thinner and more equal distribution of the seed. The owner, a baker, worked his land by help of the horse which he used on his rounds. It was, by the way, customary to hire horses when they were needed to plough the plots.

I might quote many other examples, but perhaps the above will suffice. The conclusions to which they lead the observer are sufficiently astonishing. Whenever, in my search for a remedy against rural depopulation, I have in past years ventured to suggest that something might be done by small holdings and the sense of ownership, many well-informed voices have promptly cried out that I was a theoretical enthusiast, since under few conceivable circumstances could such holdings be made to pay. Yet I found this Winterslow settlement established upon poor land, with an insufficient water supply and a severe winter climate, where small holdings *do* pay, and their owners have built upon

STONEHENGE, SHOWING THE FALLEN MONOLITH
(*Since re-erected*)

*Page 8*

MR. DIBBEN'S HAMPSHIRE-DOWN TEGS

*Page 25*

them comfortable homes, in which they take as much pride and pleasure as does the rich man in his mansion.

As I hope to show presently, the common cry in Wiltshire and Hampshire seems to be that, like those of other counties, the villages are in course of depletion. It is alleged, on the contrary, that here in Winterslow the population will show a considerable increase when the new census returns are announced. This is one of the very suggestive results of the system of small holdings, which after all is not wonderful when it is remembered that whereas on the 195 acres of the original Cooper's Farm only three labourers earned a livelihood, some fifty or sixty men with their families now live on, and more or less live out of, that portion of it which is the subject of Major Poore's experiment. Again, the villagers seemed well contented. I heard of no grumbling, and was told that even the members of the landholders' court, by which the settlement is managed, do not quarrel among themselves. Moreover, the general tone and intelligence of the inhabitants appear to have been raised.

One of the complaints of country dwellers is that our system of education is not adapted to rural needs. I visited the school at Winterslow, and what did I find? On the blackboard that had been in use that day were chalk drawings illustrative of the effects of shallow and deep culture upon root action, and of those of good and bad tilth upon the growth of plants. The schoolmaster, Mr. Witt, went to a shelf and took from it a roof-tile, sprinkled with soil and set in a pan of water, whereon some of his pupils had been testing the germination of the beans, which were to be set in their school gardens. Thus they learn to love and understand the land. What is the reason of it all? I cannot say, unless some explanation may be found in the fact that for a century or more there have existed at Winterslow a number of freeholders who in the beginning established themselves on some waste land. None other occurs to me, as I have not heard that the inhabitants of this place are congenitally superior to their neighbours. Moreover, I may mention that Major Poore has tried very much the same experiment at Bishopstone, some ten or twelve miles away, but on a larger scale and in bigger lots. Here the holders, finding the payment of instalments irksome, actually approached Major Poore and offered to take over the land with all responsibilities. To this he consented, with the result, as I understood, that the freeholders were doing well.

And now one question : If the system succeeds at Winterslow, why should it not succeed elsewhere? Major Poore, who had no faith in county councils, suggested that individual owners should follow his example in their respective districts. But few of them possess his enterprise and energy, even if they have the capital and the time to devote to a somewhat intricate business. Also many landlords, for various reasons, are deeply averse to the principle of small holdings. In the face of the admitted evils of rural depopulation, and the obliteration of the yeoman class, is it not worth the while of Parliament to look into the matter?

This Winterslow settlement, by the way, furnishes an amusing instance of the evil—and expensive—results of giving way to superstition. Everywhere in England there seems to exist a somewhat general belief in the magical powers of ' dowsers ' or water-finders—that is, of men who allege themselves to be able to discover hidden springs by means of a hazel twig, which goes through mysterious bendings and convulsions at the spot where the water lies hidden in the earth. Of the results of the divination of one of these inspired persons I have told a rather amusing story in my book ' A Farmer's Year,' and here at Winterslow they were exemplified again. Water being scarce on the settlement, a dowser was employed to reveal the spot where a well should be sunk, which would provide it with a general and perpetual supply. At a likely looking place near the bottom of a hollow the twig jumped in the orthodox fashion. For some reason, however, the work was not begun before this magnetic expert died, and when the time came to undertake it nobody was quite certain of the precise place which he had pointed out. So another 'dowser' was retained, whose powers led him to the same spot, where the infallible evidence of the twisting rod enabled him to assure his employers that at a depth of 100 ft. a splendid supply of water would be struck. Filled with faith by this double revelation, they set to work and dug. As no water was found at the 100 ft. level, however, they went down another 100 ft.; indeed, the issue being still unsatisfactory, greatly daring, they sank yet a third hundred.

The results as I saw them were an enormous heap of white chalk, a 300-ft. shaft with a little water at the bottom of it, such as accumulates in what are there called 'weeping wells,' and a bill for about £150! At Winterslow the subject of that experiment is somewhat delicate ground to tread on. I ventured to suggest that by way of a change it might now be wise to take the opinion of a competent water engineer. To hazel twigs and those who hold them they seem to have given a fair trial.

At the back of this Winterslow settlement once ran a Roman road, leading, I believe, from Old Sarum to Winchester. One of the freeholders had recently cut into it, revealing its foundation. This is constructed of flints closely cemented together; how I cannot say. When I was there this man had taken out some twenty loads of them, and so fast do they cling, that he found it a great labour to break them up. Evidently the old Romans understood the science of road-making as well as, or better than, we do to-day.

On one bitter morning—for the sou'-westerly gale had now veered to the north-east—we set out from Salisbury to visit Mr. Dibben, of Bishopstone, a very noted breeder of Hampshire-Down sheep, with the single exception of Mr. Flower, perhaps, indeed, the most noted in the county.

After recent and painful experience of the dreadful tracks of mud and stone, which in certain parts of Suffolk are called roads, the smooth and beautifully made highways of Wiltshire were very pleasant to the traveller. Our path

led us through five or six miles of country much less wild
and lonely in its general aspect than that which lies around
Stonehenge.    Indeed, in spots the appearance of the fertile
bottom to our left, through which wanders the river Ebele,
with its rich pastures and low-towered Gothic churches
of Stratford Tony and Bishopstone, its pollard willows and
poplars, reminded me of certain scenery in Holland.

Mr. Dibben's farm covers 1,100 acres.    Like most of
these holdings, which in some remote age seem to have been
divided out upon a fixed plan, it runs from the valley to the
crest of the opposing ridge, a strip of land measuring about
half a mile in breadth and over two miles in length.    Thus
each farm is made to contain a stream frontage, a proportion of water meadows and of deep soiled arable land
running gradually up to the thin-skinned 'bake,' or downs
which have been put under the plough.    This farm, with
others, belongs to Lord Pembroke, a good landlord, who,
even in these bad times, is in a position to meet the needs
of the land and of his tenants.    As a result, we found
Mr. Dibben's buildings in capital order, spacious, well constructed, and fitted with most of the modern conveniences.

Very different was the case upon another large farm
which we visited, not far from Salisbury, whose owner,
it was reported, had been crippled, if not crushed, by the
fall in the value of property.    There the cow-houses were
narrow sheds which in Norfolk would be indicted as insanitary : the walls, made of chalk concrete, were cracked
and crumbling owing to the decay of the thatch wherewith
in Wiltshire it is the fashion to protect them, and the roof
of one large building was only prevented from collapsing
bodily upon the valuable horses which it sheltered, by a rude
prop that would fall the first time a waggon backed against
it.    I asked the tenant how he managed to put up with such
buildings, to which he answered that as the landlord had
no money to repair them, at a probable cost of several
thousand pounds, either he must do so or leave the farm.
He added that there were many worse.

Another very frequent complaint was of the lack of cottage accommodation. Mr. Blake, a well-known and much-respected farmer, land agent, and county councillor in the Amesbury district, told me that in many places there were practically no houses in which young folk could settle down and marry, while of such as existed those which fell into disrepair were often not rebuilt because such dwellings are not remunerative to their owners. Sometimes also the cottages lay two miles away from the homestead, and now-a-days men and women refuse to live isolated upon the Downs. As a remedy Mr. Blake suggested that money should be advanced to landowners at a nominal rate of interest, repayable over long terms of years by means of a sinking fund, to enable them to provide suitable cottage accommodation. But, as I pointed out to him, to expect the State to come to the rescue of the land or any class that has to do with it, is somewhat Utopian.

On Lord Pembroke's estate all this was different. There, as we were told by two of the best-known auctioneers and land agents in Salisbury, cottages are good and plentiful, and are either occupied free or let to labourers at a shilling a week, for the most part with gardens attached. Thus, on Mr. Dibben's farm there were, I understood, no fewer than twenty-two such cottages. If things are different on other estates their owners must not be blamed, since without money they cannot build cottages, which give little or no return on the capital invested. Great landlords, such as Lords Aylesbury, Pembroke, and Radnor, the Marquess of Bath, Sir C. Furness, who bought Mr. Hooley's property, Mr. Walter Long, &c., most of whom, perhaps, have sources of income other than the land, can afford to do what the small owner, and more especially the mortgaged owner, who has nothing to look to except his acres, cannot afford. Indeed, I heard in every direction that in Wiltshire and Hampshire such men are practically ruined. 'The small landowner is being squeezed out of existence.' . . . 'The landowners are very badly hit, except those who are arti-

ficially supported.' Such are two sample opinions uttered
by people who, above all others, ought to know the facts in
these counties, and who themselves are not owners of land.

How can it be otherwise? Here are a few instances of
the present rent values of Wiltshire land taken from cases
which came under my own observation. I must state,
however, that in each case I have altered the totals proportionately in order to avoid the identification of the actual
farms, which might displease their tenants.

A farm which up to 1870 used to pay a rent of £2,100
a year in 1901 was let for £825, tithe free. A farm of 1,500
acres, in excellent order, with good buildings, &c., that let for
£1 an acre had fallen to 13s. an acre, out of which the
landlord paid 5s. an acre tithe, all main repairs, and half
the minor repairs. A farm of 1,600 acres, which used to
let for £1,600, had been reduced to £400, tithe free. Three
other typical farms in 1901 brought in respectively 6s. 8d.
per acre, 8s. an acre, and 5s. an acre, all tithe free. These
figures speak for themselves, so I need not enlarge upon
them.

But if the rent question is ruining the landlord, almost
equally destructive to the farmer is that of labour. ' The
labour difficulty is the blackest cloud of the lot,' said Mr.
Blake. ' Unless something unforeseen occurs farming must
come to an end for lack of labour,' said Mr. Rawlence, of
the well-known firm of Waters and Rawlence. He added
that on the day of our interview a farmer who milked thirty
cows had told him that his cowman was leaving, and, as he
could get no one else, he could see nothing for it but to try
to do the milking himself. I suggested that the difficulty
might be met to some extent by laying down more land to
grass. He answered that the land was not suitable for
laying down. Boys, also, my informants declared, were
scarcely obtainable ; even shopkeepers found it difficult to
hire them. Especially does the Wiltshire labourer object
to Sunday work. We were told of a farmer with a large
herd of cows who was obliged to bring his three sons home

every Saturday from their school in a distant town in order that they might milk on Sunday. This aversion to Sunday labour does not, I heard, arise from religious prejudices, since the labourers of this district are declared to be very indifferent upon that point. They regard the Sabbath as a day of recreation, and no more. The clergy also were reported to be unpopular as a body; 'but,' added my informant, 'so they would be if they were angels.'

The quality of the labour was described as poor —far worse, indeed, than it used to be. Many of the men, allowing for the time walking to and fro and for meals, were not actually at work for more than eight hours a day; while the pace was set by the slowest hand. Knowing that they could not be replaced they did not fear dismissal. In the neighbourhood of Stonehenge things were particularly bad, since the great Bulford Camp, that was being laid out by the War Office, which has purchased about 45,000 acres of the plain for military purposes, was said to draw away 100 men a week, who earned high wages on the works.

'Young men,' said Mr. Squarey, jun., 'are now seldom to be seen upon the land, while hedgers, ditchers, and thatchers are all over fifty years of age. The race is dying out.' Again his father, Mr. Squarey, senior, a gentleman of great experience, whom unfortunately I missed, as he was absent from Salisbury, writes to Mr. E. G. Strutt, who has kindly sent me on the letter :

'Mr. Rider Haggard does not put the case a bit too strong, and certainly the labourers will not stay on the land for any wages which a farmer can afford. But "gloria ruris" has not lost all its power, and I have faith that if opportunities were offered akin to those of the fourteenth, fifteenth, and sixteenth centuries, men would be found to reconsider their town tendencies, and would go back to their villages.'

'If this state of affairs goes on,' said Mr. Blake of the labour question, 'it may make farming impossible.' Various reasons were given for this wholesale migration by these and other gentlemen, among them the lowness of the wage, and that our system of education, which is unsuited to the needs of the land, breeds dislike of rural life. At the least such are the facts in the neighbourhood of Salisbury; the reader must interpret them for himself.

In these melancholy circumstances it is pleasant to be able to record that Mr. Dibben himself suffered from no labour difficulty. I ventured to suggest personal popularity as a factor in this happy result, and although the most modest of men, he could not altogether deny that impeachment. Doubtless, also, the excellent supply of cottages on his farm accounted for much. His shepherds seemed to me men of a good stamp, rough, but open-mannered and honest-faced; indeed, I was favourably impressed with those specimens of the Wiltshire labourer with whom I came in contact. The wages paid on this farm ranged from 11s. to 16s. per week, to which must be added harvest and other extra moneys, amounting in all, perhaps, to an average sum of 3s. a week throughout the year.

Mr. Dibben grew wheat, oats, and barley—more oats than in former days. All the growers to whom I spoke in this district, declared that the Wiltshire barley is not so good as it used to be; that it is 'feathery,' by which seems to be meant that it comes unevenly into ear, some of the heads standing up and others drooping down, with the result that the sample ripens in patches. Many attribute this to the summer frosts, which are now so frequent; but Mr. Blake believed it to be owing to the robbing of the soil of its natural element of silica, as a result of the close modern mowing of the reaping machine, which removes almost every inch of stubble. The straw, he said, contains this silica, but loses it when thrown into the yards to be trodden to manure. He overcame the difficulty by thickly strewing the land with fresh clean straw once in every four years, which he distributed evenly upon a mown clover or other seed layer. During the winter the worms draw it into the soil, which it serves to keep moist and open. In the following year the layer is fed, then broken up for roots to be succeeded by wheat. Mr. Blake said that his experience proved that no manure is so valuable on these lands as an occasional coating of this clean straw. He added, what all agriculturists know, that those who sell their straw are, more than any others, those who fail as farmers.

To return to Mr. Dibben, although of necessity an arable farmer—since food must be provided for his flock —sheep were his stand-by. Of these he kept 800 breeding ewes, with 300 tegs or hoggets, to which in the season must be added a fall of over 1,000 lambs. In the year of 1901 the lambs, which under the rules of the Hampshire Down Association must not be dropped before January 1, had been rather disappointing in numbers, since the wet and stormy weather chilled the ewes and caused over 100 of them to cast their offspring. Of each year's fall about 250 are let out as stock rams, 100 of the best bringing in the good average price of £10 10s., and the remaining 150 averaging about £5 5s. Of the rest a picked proportion of the females are kept as tegs, to be used for breeding another year, and the remnant are sold off for what they will fetch.

As we trudged up the rain-soaked roads to the first lambing-pen we passed a pit newly dug and puddled with clay to make it hold water. Here Mr. Dibben showed us a beautiful specimen of the ancient British ring-money, which was found among the soil thrown from this pit, looking as bright to-day as it did when the old down-dweller dropped it thousands of years ago.

The lambs in the fold, all picked males, were a beautiful lot, bold-headed, thick-built, and very even. They were folded on rape and swedes mixed, with lamb hurdles set in the fold that allow the lambs to creep through to the next enclosure, so that they may get the 'forward bite,' but keep the ewes suffering the sorrows of Tantalus on the further side. Also they had hay in feeding crates, with cake and other delicacies, since no expense was spared in getting these creatures up for market. Mr. Dibben's sheep, by the way, never suffered from foot-rot, which on this land, he said, was only caused by neglect. Leaving the lambs we walked on a mile or so to the teg pens, which were set on the crest of the rise overlooking the valley of the Fovant, low-lying land broken by wood-clad peaks; a lovely and peaceful scene, more especially in the rare rays of sunshine which shot athwart its spaces. These tegs, which were worth £3 3s. a head as they ran out, were folded with hurdles of wattle to break the wind—none others are used in this country—on as much swedes as could be covered by an oblong of sixteen hurdles by thirteen, the ground being changed every twenty-four hours. Also they were given all the unchopped oat straw that they could eat and one sack of mixed cake and corn among the 300 of them per diem.

The rotation followed by Mr. Dibben seemed to be wheat, barley; then two root crops in succession, and wheat or oats again. Of wheat he grew from 120 to 140 acres. His oats, Black Tartar and Abundance, gave an average yield of 8 quarters per acre, and his barley, Webb's Chevalier and Archer's Stiff Straw, about 6 quarters per acre. Most of this barley fetched 34s. a quarter at the previous thrashing, the worst bringing in 27s. 6d. The season of 1900 was not good for this grain here owing, he thought, to a summer frost which struck it before it came into ear, and to some extent to the subsequent scorching weather. Below the Downs line nearly all the land is good, much of it being a sound loam well worth the very moderate rent it fetches, the exact amount of which I do not, however, feel at liberty to state.

On our way up to the Down I saw an interesting pasture. For a number of years it was in sainfoin. Then grasses came and choked the sainfoin, but Mr. Dibben did not plough it up, as is the common custom. For several seasons he sheeped it heavily, with the result that the twitch and other bad grasses were killed out, only the good remaining. Now it is a very serviceable meadow. Here I may state that my experience is that, even if land is never laid down with good seeds in the proper fashion, almost any class of it, except light sands or gravel, can in time be brought to produce fair grass with the aid of sheep and dressings of farm manure, basic slag, or even road scrapings. Certainly the above instance goes to prove that this is so, and I have seen others quite as striking.

Mr. Dibben grew swedes for his ewes and rape and kail for the lambs. The latter crop he did not hoe out much, since if this is done the stems become too thick for feed, and obstruct the subsequent tillage of the ground. The swedes he never, or rarely, pitted, taking the risk of damage from the weather. I think that he used to use steam tackle, but had abandoned it in favour of horses on account of the great expense of the up-keep of machinery. I might say more about this typical and interesting farm, had I the space. One adjoining it, of similar character, sold, by the way, not long before my visit, for the miserable sum of £6 an acre. So, wishing him and his beautiful flock all good fortune for many years to come, I bid farewell to Mr. Dibben.

On our way home that night we saw a sky and landscape of exceptional loveliness—one which I shall always remember. Behind us the enormous copper-coloured ball of the half-vanished sun burned upon the horizon. In front the sky was spread with a pall of cloud of intensest black framed in the giant arch of a perfect and resplendent rainbow. Before us lay a wide stretch of fresh-ploughed land, rose-purple in the conflicting lights and shadows, while in mid air, betwixt sun and storm, a countless flock of wind-blown plover wheeled and tumbled, their under-wings shining like silver discs in the rays of the sunset.

My investigations of Salisbury Plain and its neighbourhood came to an end with the day that I spent on Mr. Dibben's farm. In closing my remarks upon the district, I wish to express my thanks to Mr. Nightingale, the manager of the South-West Farmers' Association, a useful co-operative society, for his kindness in helping me to obtain the information which was necessary to my work.

The agricultural conditions of North Wiltshire, of which the little town of Wootton Bassett may be called the centre, vary considerably from those of South Wiltshire. Here the land is nearly all good pasture, fit for dairying purposes, whence it results that the hand of agricultural depression has fallen much more lightly upon the northern than upon the southern half of the county. The arable lands, it is true, have sunk 50 to 60 per cent. in their rental value, but then there is not much arable, and the grass lands have only dwindled 15 to 20 per cent. Here, as in most places, the trouble was one of labour. 'We are masters now. I would sooner go to penal servitude than work for a farmer,' was the remark made to one of my informants by a labourer of about thirty-five, when explaining his reasons for leaving the land. It seems to be typical of the general feeling among his class in this part of England, although wages run from 14s. to 15s. a week, and the farmers are, for the most part, considerate to their men.

The greater part of North Wiltshire is in the hands of about half a dozen owners of huge estates. Putting aside those who, like Lord Lansdowne, hold by ancient succession, these domains seem to have been formed during the past half-century by the buying out of the yeomen and small holders. So long as they would consent to stand no more between the wind and the nobility of the rich man who desired to found a family in a fashionable neighbourhood, these small owners were paid almost any price they liked to ask—as much, I am told, as forty years' purchase on the top rentals of the last century. Indeed, notwithstanding the agricultural depression which exists here, this process is still going on. A large land agent of my acquaintance informed me that he had in his office half a dozen applications for such estates from men who had made large sums of money. What they say is: I have a million or half a million, and I am prepared to spend 25 per cent. of it upon a suitable landed property with the usual amenities. I care nothing whether it pays me or does not pay me, since for my income I look to my remaining fortune. All I want is sport, the right sort of society, and a place that will be pleasant to live at during the hunting and shooting seasons.

Such men, of course, are a blessing to a country or the reverse, according to the view which the student of land-questions may take of the matter. My own opinion is that they are very much the reverse, believing, as I do, that vast estates acquired and held merely for the purposes of pomp and pleasure, and not that the land or its population may be advantaged, are an actual source of evil. Better by far that the soil should still be in the hands of the bought-out yeomen. Nevertheless such proprietors have their advantages. Thus, their cottages are good, while their fine houses and park lands undoubtedly add to the picturesque charm of the country-side. Yet in North Wiltshire all these things do not keep the labourer on the land.

Among the many gentlemen whom I met in this district perhaps the most able and interesting is Mr. Herbert Smith, agent for Lord Lansdowne and Lord Crewe, and author of a well-known and valuable work, ' The Principles of Landed Estate Management.' He told me that the labour position was bad ; that ' we cannot get half enough labour, and what we do get is very inferior.' Yet on these estates of 14,000 acres there is an ample supply of excellent cottages at a low rent—1s. to 2s. a week, I believe. Also, there are reading-rooms and libraries, and the largest system of allotments in England, amounting in all to about 600 acres, though, with reference to them, he added : ' Alas ! many of these, which formerly were well cultivated, are now going out of cultivation for lack of tenants.' Further, a system of sale of small plots of land to labouring men had been tried and failed in the village of Foxham. He thought, however, that this might be because the experiment was not properly managed by the land company who purchased the farm from Lord Lansdowne.

Mr. Smith said, further, that some farmers were giving up
dairying, owing to want of milkers, and taking to grazing
instead—a much less profitable business—adding that when
the older labouring men were gone he could not say what
would happen.   Upon this point he saw no hope unless industrial depression set in, and the towns became congested.
Even then he believed that most of those who had migrated
thither would go upon the rates rather than return to the
land.   As it was, he said, the labour deteriorated day by day,
and became continually scarcer.   The men no longer put
their hearts into their work ; they had grown to look upon
their employer as their enemy.   Young fellows were not to
be had, although in individual instances early marriages would
sometimes keep them upon selected estates.   If the worst
came to the worst, he supposed that the only thing to do
would be to cut up the land into small holdings which could
be worked by farmers and their sons.   Indeed he thought it
a mistake to rely too much upon the old class of farmer.

Mr. Smith mentioned various hill farms wherewith he
had to do, which, after meeting the expense of tithe and
repairs, did not even bring in interest upon outlay.   These
farms are rather stiff corn-lands which have gone down to
grass and been fenced with wire for sheep.   The pasture,
however, is of a very inferior nature, being full of moss,
although it cost £1 an acre to seed, and £80 a mile to fence.
In short, on the highlands the arable is practically worthless, and even in the vale but of doubtful value ; the industry,
such as it is, depending upon the good pastures for the sake
of which the farms are taken.   For such lands there were
plenty of applicants, many of whom had been agricultural
labourers.   These will take farms of from 80 to 100 acres,
doing the milking and other work by the help of their
families.   Thus, having no labour-bill, they still make
money.   Indeed, Mr. Smith said that some of them
were very successful, instancing one man who had been
a labourer and was now worth £3,000.   He was a very
industrious person who eked out his farming profits

by dealing, with the result that his sons were taking holdings of their own. Mr. Smith believed that if small freeholds could be created in quantity, it would bring back a considerable degree of prosperity to the land, but the difficulty was how to create them. Once they existed in large numbers in this district, but as I have said they are now nearly all of them swept into the net of the great landowners.

As regarded remedies, his only suggestions were farming large blocks of pasture with the aid of a few very highly paid men, which might to some extent meet the difficulty in that immediate neighbourhood ; or, possibly, some system of small freeholds, to establish which the landlords would have to be backed by the State. Beyond these, he said, there seemed to be nothing that would retain the rural population, unless it were some total change in our land system such as has not yet been formulated.

Through the kindness of Mr. Herbert Smith, who is the chairman of the company, we had the advantage of going over the Wiltshire bacon and butter factory at Chippenham, which, I suppose, turns out some of the best bacon in the world. This factory was established about eleven years ago, and deals with a total of from five to six hundred pigs a week. During these eleven years ten factories have started in different places in England, of which I believe only three remain, the Chippenham establishment being one of them. I asked the reason of the non-success of the others, and was informed that the explanation lay in the fact that Wiltshire bacon had deservedly won a name, which gave it an advantage over that manufactured elsewhere. No other bacon, indeed, can stand up against the foreign competition. As the householder will be aware, he must pay about one shilling retail for a pound of prime Wiltshire, whereas he can buy American down to sixpence and eightpence, and good Danish for, I think, about tenpence.

The subject is a delicate one, and I did not like to inquire into it too closely ; but I gathered that even these Wiltshire

factories are feeling the competition very keenly. At least
it is certain that their profits are not what they were, since
the public will buy in the cheapest market, although they
know nothing of how the animals they eat may have been
fattened—an important point where such foul feeders as
pigs are concerned—or of what processes they may have
undergone in the curing—by the aid of borax, for instance—before they appear on the domestic breakfast table.
Most of all, however, do these factories complain of the
frequent frauds whereof they are the victims. Great quantities of hams and bacon which are sold as 'Best Wilts'
were never on English land until they passed through it in
a railway train. Do what they will, the manufacturers of
the real article cannot altogether cope with this dishonesty.

One thing is certain, that looked at in an agricultural
light it will be a thousand pities if these factories are
squeezed out of existence, seeing that they cause the production of a vast number of pigs, to the great benefit of the
farmer, and especially of the small farmer. Indeed, the Chippenham factory cannot always get enough pigs, although to
foster their growth they have added a butter department to
the works, so that the separated milk, which is so necessary
to the feeding of swine, can be sold to the neighbouring
farmer at the low price of, I think, a penny a gallon.

This factory is beautifully arranged and managed upon
the most modern and approved principles, but to the
squeamish I cannot pretend that it was altogether a pleasant
place to visit. First we were taken to the pens, where we
saw a great quantity of hogs, mostly crossed Tamworths
and Yorkshire-Middles, with some Berkshires which had
been bought in at the weight of five-score pounds, to be
fattened on barley meal and milk to the desired average of
nine-score, or 180 lb. The factory does not undertake this
fatting from choice, I should explain, but because it must,
since in no other way could it get sufficient pigs to keep
the establishment fully employed, at any rate at that time.
The manure from these animals, by the way, is wasted, as

IMPORTED SCOTCH SHEEP, NEAR SWINDON

A SMALL-HOLDER AND HIS COWS, DAUNTSEY VALE  *Page 44*

the farmers will not go to the trouble of carting it even at the price of 2s. a waggon-load. The barley fed to the swine is all foreign, ground at the factory, and is given to them unscalded, mixed with the skim-milk. The pigs are bought in at about 50s., and after eight to twelve weeks' fatting reach a value of about 75s.

Next we went to the slaughter pens whence—when their time comes—the wretched animals are caught up by some devilish machinery and, hanging head downwards, travel along oiled bars to meet their doom in the pit—an awful place which I will not describe. Bereft of life, they still travel on at the rate of sixty an hour, till they fall into an iron framework that runs on rails into the mouth of a veritable inferno of a furnace, where they remain for half a minute while every scrap of hair is burned off their bodies. Out they come again brown and naked—this scorching, I should say, is a peculiarity of Wiltshire bacon, and takes the place of the ordinary scalding—to slide along the endless iron bar to another department, where they are cleaned. Then the bar brings them, their decapitated heads perched between their hams, to the weighing machine, where they are weighed, so that each owner may receive his price. After this and the branding with the trade mark 'Royal Wilts' they go to the vast cooling chamber, which is chilled by the ammonia process with chloride of calcium brine at a temperature of from 40 to 45 degrees. Now, reduced to sides, they are salted and treated by the injection of brine with a special force-pump. Here they remain three weeks being cured, after which they migrate to the smoke-chamber, where they hang for three days over a smouldering heap of elm sawdust. Then at length they are ready for sale, and within another fortnight or month have all been converted into rashers of bacon.

The by-products are lard, sausages of various size, colour and degree, chaps, trotters, graves, and black puddings; but I have no space to describe the manufacture of these delicacies. Everything is made use of except the brains—

even the stomachs, which are sold for pepsine. Nobody will buy pigs' brains, as the manager informed me sadly.

A speciality of this factory is the curing of the famous Bradenham hams, which we saw in process. Each ham lay in an earthen vessel of its own, but the details of that cherished art we did not see or hear, as it is a trade secret of the first water, purchased for no mean sum. How uneasy must lie the head weighted with the awful responsibility of the secret of curing Bradenham hams! Supposing that in sleep the lips became unlocked! Its discoverer, by the way, was a butler in the time of Queen Elizabeth, and until bought by the present proprietors, the receipt was handed down from father to son in a single family.

After a long and intimate association with so much departed and departing pig it was, I confess, pleasant to exchange the odours and sights of death, unavoidable in spite of every possible sanitary arrangement and cleanliness, for the cool, sweet butter factory. Here several thousand pounds of butter are manufactured every week from about 7,000 or 8,000 gallons of milk, bought at the season of my visit at an average price of $5\frac{1}{4}d.$ a gallon. The processes employed in this great dairy are absolutely perfect, every drop of milk being Pasteurised before it is separated and churned. Cheese is also made here, but this manufacture had been reduced because of the unprofitable price of the finished article. The capital of the factory, I forgot to state, is £100,000. It was a wonderful place to visit, and I hope that it may long prosper in spite of foreign competition and of the damage that it suffers from those imitations of its products which are sometimes fraudulently palmed off upon the public.

Swindon, as all the world knows, is the site of the works of the Great Western Railway, and to its populous streets draws no small proportion of the available labour of North Wiltshire. In this district I visited a good many farmers and some landowners or their representatives, among them Mr. Story Maskelyne, of Basset Down, chairman of the Agricultural Committee of the Wiltshire County Council. Among much interesting information Mr. Maskelyne told me that he put the average rental value of the pasture land in the valleys at 40s. an acre, the lower Down lands at 12s., and the higher arables at 7s. The prosperity or otherwise of the local farmer depends greatly, he thought, on the man himself. He did not seem to believe in small holdings, and had tried, without success, to induce farmers to co-operate. This effort having failed, being enterprising and public-spirited, he proposed to erect a small central dairy in the benefits of which his neighbours may share if they choose. I trust that it will succeed, since there is not the slightest doubt that co-operation among farmers is urgently needed in Wiltshire as in other counties. Mr. Maskelyne was of opinion that the exodus of the rural population is not merely a matter of cottages— although some of these in the district are far from good— but rather of the pleasures of the town, which draw men to it, even if in truth they do not better their lot by the change.

I walked over Mr. Maskelyne's farm, which, as might be expected, was well and intelligently managed with the help of his Scotch bailiff, Mr. Kelly. Particularly noticeable and worthy of imitation was his system of feeding calves with separated milk, in which is mixed crude cod-liver oil to replace the cream. The milk is warmed to the natural temperature, for without this precaution the oil refuses to mix, and the dose given is at first very small, increasing by degrees to one ounce of oil to the gallon of milk, administered twice daily. Upon this unattractive mixture, as I can testify by personal inspection, the calves do splendidly, while the saving of cost in comparison to that of the various calf foods is said to be very great. On this same farm we saw a stack of forty tons of clover hay—a striking object lesson of what can be done on 12s. an acre 'lower Down' land by good farming. This hay, which Mr. Kelly described as one of the heaviest crops that ever he saw, was saved from a thirteen-acre field at a single cut. The land when under roots was fed off by 170 sheep, to which were given, in addition, three-quarters of a pound of cake per diem, and when the seeds were growing was dressed with three-quarters of a hundredweight of nitrate of soda to the acre.

The next farm we visited was that of Mr. Ferris, of Upper Salthrop, who held 400 acres, half arable, half pasture, and complained much of the lack of labour. Mr. Ferris had a flock of Dorset-horn sheep, and told me what, oddly enough, I never learned when in their country, that they will produce two crops of lambs a year if well kept, one about March and one about October, of which a large proportion will be twins.

A very interesting farmer of the smaller sort was Mr. Jimmy Newman, of this neighbourhood, who farmed 200 acres, of which sixty were high-lying arable, under the Charterhouse Trustees, at a rent of 33s. an acre. The pasture land, he said, is as good 'as ever a crow fled over,' but of the arable he had a very different tale to tell. This, he declared, was not worth 1s. 6d. an acre, adding that the whole sixty acres only brought him in £30 in 1900. It has no fences, no water, no buildings, and, according to him, swallows up any amount of manure that can be put upon it. 'I've drawn muck up there for twenty-five years, and I'll draw no more,' he concluded with energy.

He said that when he took the holding twenty-six years before he used to make a little money, but that latterly all that he could do was to add somewhat to the value of his stock. The whole farm was worked by himself, his son, a carter, and one cowman, as he could find no other hand. To the cowman he gave 16s. a week, a cottage, and a quart of beer a day, as the labourers here refuse to drink cider. In addition this cowman's wife received 6s. a week for milking and 1s. a day when she worked in the fields. The carter also had an extra shilling every time he went to market. Mr. Newman tried to compound the beer allowance for an additional 1s. 6d. a week, but to this the men would not consent. His comments on the labour question amounted to a positive wail. He said that he and his son—a fine and pre-possessing young man—were obliged to work from five in the morning to seven at night to keep 'the books square,' and added that in 1900 he had not made a halfpenny profit, and did not expect to better things in 1901. I asked him why, under these melancholy circumstances, he continued to farm. He replied that he made a living, and had nothing else to turn to ; but that if he were in his son's place he would not stay a day, 'father or no father.' How-ever, they did their best to help each other, but his advice to the son was to be off the moment the breath was out of his—the father's—body.

Mr. Newman, who is a sportsman, had an artificial earth upon his farm, out of which, by way of varying our agricultural investigations, we set to work to bolt a fox. A little terrier dog was fetched and induced to enter the earth, while we stood round expectant. 'He's at home,' said his owner excitedly, lifting his head from the ground. 'I can hear him scrapping at him.' Scarcely had he spoken the words when, like a pigeon from a trap, out shot a great mangy fox followed by the yapping terrier. ' O Lord ! ' said Mr. Jimmy Newman as he watched the diseased animal vanish over the crest of the rise, 'if only I had a gun, he shouldn't have gone far.' I parted from Mr. Newman with regret, for his is an engaging personality, hoping that, after all, things were not so bad as he imagined. On this farm water was very short, as, indeed, is the case with all lands that lie on the Oxford clay.

I devoted one day of my time in this district to visiting the splendid property of Lady Meux, which covers, I believe, some 25,000 acres in the neighbourhood of Wootton Bassett and elsewhere. Mr. Baines, the agent, who received his agricultural education in Yorkshire, most kindly furnished me with a large number of figures, covering a period of about twenty years, illustrative of the average rental values of the various estates which comprise the property. Of these I propose to quote a few in due course.

Mr. Baines said that owing to its proximity to Swindon, house property in this neighbourhood was valuable, since mechanics and others who work there like to take the cottages, of which there are some five hundred on the estate, that cannot therefore be considered as purely agricultural. The fact that water has been laid on at great expense by the proprietor is an added attraction. Here, as elsewhere, it is common for labourers to agitate to obtain the direct hire of their cottages from the owners, which in most cases means a yearly or half-yearly tenancy, instead of through the farmer, which means a possibility of ejection at a week's or a month's notice to quit. In the first event the man is more or less in a position to defy his employer, who cannot dismiss him, as without a cottage he could not in all probability obtain anyone to replace him; in the second the employer has a great hold over his man, who in most cases does not wish to lose his home. Mr. Baines quoted an instance in which the would-be hirer put the matter very baldly. He asked whether the cottage was to be let to him direct, not through the tenant of the land upon which it stood, 'because then,' he said, 'if I go away and leave the milking he might turn me out.' In other words, he wished to be able to leave his master's cows unmilked if he liked without suffering the natural penalty of dismissal.

I have found this question of the direct or indirect tenure of cottages a burning matter in most parts of England, and read much fine writing on the subject. A free labourer, it is argued, ought not to be dependent on the whim of his employer for his home, and so forth. But let us consider how the thing works, which perhaps can best be done by quoting an actual example. On a farm that I hold in the parish of Ditchingham is only one cottage occupied by the horse-keeper and stockman, which is therefore absolutely necessary to the place. A while ago the horseman in charge left his horse harnessed to a machine in the harvest field and departed early in the afternoon to a public-house, whence he returned at midnight. Later in the day the animal in his care was found dragging the rake about at random, to the great risk of itself, the instrument, and anyone whom it happened to meet. Notwithstanding its gravity the offence was overlooked. A few days before I write I chanced to pass a public-house in the neighbouring town of Bungay, and to see standing unattended in front of it two of my horses attached to a loaded tumbril. I entered the house and found this same man drinking beer at the bar. As the case was flagrant—seeing that the horses might easily have run away and done damage to life and property to the value of hundreds of pounds, for which, of course, I should have been liable under the law—I gave orders that their driver should be dismissed. His answer was, ' I don't care ; I can easily get another place, and you can't turn me out of the house.'

As it happened, on investigation the man was found to be in error, for the cottage had been granted to him gratis as an addition to his weekly wages, and its continued occupation was therefore dependent upon the duration of his service. Had it been otherwise my position would have been hard, since then for many months, although I needed the house for another servant, I should have been obliged to retain as a tenant a man who had been dismissed for repeated gross and dangerous neglect of duty. This is a fair example stated from the farmer's point of view, although it is possible that in the case of capricious or unjust employers, hardship may sometimes ensue to the tenant-at-will whose tenancy must terminate with his employment. Speaking generally, however, it would be madness on the part of the farmer to subject himself to the necessity of giving a year's—which in practice often means nearly two years'—or even six months' notice to the occupier of a cottage that is necessary to the carrying on of the farm when he can be rid of the man's actual services in eight days. For an exposition of the other side of the case I refer the reader to the views of a correspondent published at the end of this chapter.

To return. Since the year 1886, on this particular Meux estate, which has a good many advantages, the grass lands do not seem to have suffered a depreciation of more than about 10 per cent., but on the arables it is, of course, considerably heavier. There are on this property no fewer than 1,212 allotments, but for the most part they seem to be of small size. I should add that in the Dauntsey Vale the soil overlies Oxford clay, and from Wootton Bassett to Calne, coral rag and coarse sandstone.

Now I give some figures, beginning with

### The Dauntsey Property

|  | Acres | Rent £ |
|---|---|---|
| One of the worst farms . . | 130 | 130 |
| ,, ,, ,, . . | 180 | 200 |
| Better farm . . . . | 214 | 300 |
| ,, ,, . . . . | 160 | 240 |
| ,, ,, . . . . | 150 | 220 |
| ,, ,, . . . . | 132 | 220 |

### Christian Malford Property

|  | Acres | Rent £ |
|---|---|---|
| Cheap farm . . . . | 190 | 260 |
| Larger farms . . . . | 377 | 600 |
| ,, ,, . . . . | 200 | 350 |
| ,, ,, . . . . | 200 | 360 |
| Bad ,, . . . . | 150 | 130 |

### Downs Property

|  | Acres | Rent in 1884 | Rent in 1901 |
|---|---|---|---|
| Farm of . . | 550 | £620 | £430 |

(This farm comprises 245 acres arable, 75 Down and 220 pasture.)

### Overton Property

| | Acres | Rent in 1882 | Rent in 1901 |
|---|---|---|---|
| Temple Farm . | 390 | £250 | £120 |

(This farm, which has no road and no water, comprises 190 acres arable, 67 pasture, and 130 Down. Forty more acres were laid down in grass in 1901.)

| | Acres | Rent in 1882 | Rent in 1901 |
|---|---|---|---|
| Wick Farm . | 740 | £300 | £220 |

(This farm is all Down, and very much out of the way.)

| | Acres | Rent in 1883 | Rent in 1901 |
|---|---|---|---|
| Clatford Farm . | 900 | £620 | £500 |

(This farm comprises 560 arable, 130 pasture, and 200 Down. It has upon it seventeen cottages, and is situated one and a half miles from Marlborough.)

### North Overton Property

| | Acres | Rent in 1882 | Rent in 1901 |
|---|---|---|---|
| Farm . . | 960 | £800 | £490 |

(This farm comprises 530 acres arable, 360 Down, and the balance pasture. There are upon it thirteen cottages.)

### Avebury Property

| | Acres | Rent in 1882 | Rent in 1901 |
|---|---|---|---|
| Farm . . | 840 | £600 | £440 |

(This farm comprises 560 acres arable, 80 pasture, 200 Down.)

These comparative rentals will suffice to give a good general idea of the approximate letting value of land in this part of Wiltshire at the present time.

There is still practised an ancient and mysterious ceremony connected with the lands of this estate by virtue of which some of them are freed from the payment of tithe.

The story, so far as I could follow it, is that a long-departed abbot, whose monastery owned the land, remitted the tithe thereon for the sole consideration of the annual performance of certain rites. Should the said rites be neglected, then the land concerned must once more bear its burden of tithe. Like Herodotus when he deals with the mysteries of the religion of old Egypt, those that have to do with this ceremony declare that 'it is not lawful to speak' thereof, so I did not press my inquiries. It is, however, called 'Wordale,' and appears to involve the taking of solemn oaths by the owner or agent of the estate and the tenants for the time being of the land affected, together with a religious celebration at which these persons only are present, followed by a dinner and the cutting of a notch upon a hazel wand.

This wand, which resembles a lath, we saw. It has 170 notches cut upon it during the last 170 years, and is, I presume, the successor of some earlier wand. However this may be, the old one is full of notches, and a new lath has now come into use. Of course, the interest of this quaint performance lies in the fact that in the present year of grace rights of property can still be affected by the fulfilment or otherwise of so obsolete a secret custom. Those concerned, however, seemed to believe—I know not with what justice—that were it neglected even for a single year the burden of tithe would once more fall upon the land. The tale goes, moreover, that in past generations the ecclesiastics who would have benefited by the receipt of that tithe, resorted to many quaint artifices to prevent the holding of the annual court, but always without success. So much for the custom of Wordale.

The first farm that I visited upon this property was Midge Hall, the holding of Mr. White, who is said to be, as I can well believe, one of the best and most enterprising farmers in the neighbourhood. He complained greatly of the labour, saying that were it not for two sons who worked with him at home, he would have been obliged to sell his cattle, and that, try as he might, the shortage prevented him from keeping his farm in tip-top order. All he could do was 'to get on without getting behind.' Young fellows, he declared, would not take to the land; indeed, he had given some twenty of them characters to enable them to find places in the towns. He still kept, however, some good old men who had been with him for years, but was obliged to work like a slave himself. The wages he paid were, roughly, 14s. a week, plus beer to the value of 2s. a week, plus a house worth 2s. a week, with gratis garden and allotment, plus, I think, an extra 2s. a week during the summer months, and 4d. an hour for overtime. Mr. White believed that if more good houses were erected, surrounded by fair-sized plots of land, they would tend to keep men in the country. As it was, all his cottages were occupied. The question, in his opinion, was not one of wages. He considered that the land in that locality could not be properly farmed on a less capital than £10 the acre. His farm covered 600 acres, of which only 100 were arable, and his wages bill in the year 1900 amounted to between £400 and £500.

He used from seventy to eighty tons of cake per annum, and in addition manured very highly with blood manure, which he considered better than phosphates. It cost £6 a ton, and was applied in the proportion of 4 cwt. to the acre. Also he applied farmyard muck—'pot manure' it is called in these parts, I gather, because of the heaps in which it is laid upon the fields. Mr. White kept six working horses, besides colts. His cattle were of the Shorthorn breed; and of dairy stock, young and old, he had 170 on the place, in addition to a considerable flock of Hampshire-Down sheep.

The character of his farming is shown by the fact that twice he has taken the first prize that is given to the tenant of the best farm on the estate. I am glad to be able to add that, in spite of the bad times, Mr. White still makes his business pay—to some extent, he stated, owing to the kind way in which he had been met by his landlord.

I now pass on to some instances of smaller men, which, in a sense, are perhaps even more instructive than that of Mr. White. Thus there was Mr. Potter, who farmed sixty-eight acres in 'Dauntsey Vale,' of which only four were arable. By sheer energy and hard work this gentleman had raised himself to his present position from very small beginnings, which shows that these qualities still bring their reward in Wiltshire—even to a farmer. When I saw him he milked twenty cows, sending their produce to London, or, if milk was low in price, making it into butter. He employed two men, one of them very old, and a boy if he was obtainable. He had great trouble with his labour, and said that it was impossible to keep a young man. He had one for a few weeks, but on the Saturday before our visit this youth vanished without notice or explanation, and appeared no more. In order to feed his large stock of cows Mr. Potter bought a hundred tons of mangold a year at the average price of 8s. 6d. per ton, which, he said, cost less than growing them, even if he had the land. His one complaint was of the difficulty of obtaining labour, otherwise, I am glad to say, he was prospering.

Another specimen small-holder was Mr. Stokes, who farmed sixty acres and had fourteen cows. He was so busily engaged with his milking that he carried on conversation with his head half buried in the ribs of a cow, explaining that as he could not get help he must do the work himself. He told us a melancholy tale of what he had suffered at the hands of his men. The last one, he said, would go away for two or three days at a time, and leave him to shift for himself. He even played this trick in haysel, showing an utter indifference to the fate of the hay. Mr. Stokes had no sons to help him. 'I could do with a son or two,' he said reflectively, withdrawing his head from the ribs of the cow. Then down it went again, and our interview came to an end.

Mr. Freegard, who had been a tenant on the estate for fifty-one years, holding the same farm that his grandfather held before him, told us the same story as to the lack of labour. They all went away, he said. He suggested that the matter might perhaps be met by cutting up the land into small lots, only then, he added, he did not see who was to pay for the necessary buildings.

On our homeward way we passed the Lynham Hills, whence this part of the Meux estate is supplied with the water which it is so difficult to find in the Oxford clay. That the work was costly is proved by the fact that, in addition to the making of the reservoirs, it involved the labour of laying no less than ten miles of 3-in. pipes, which run to the villages and various cottages and farms in the Dauntsey Vale.

One expedition that we made was from the village of Wroughton, where the subsoil is mostly clay, to Avebury, a drive of eight or nine miles. The road runs along the base of the upper Downs, and the prospect is everywhere very wide and open. Here the Downs are semicircular, trending to the west, the chalky cultivated lands, which looked as though they would grow good barley, lying at the foot of them only, for all the upper parts are devoted to sheep. On our way we passed one of the White Horses cut out of the chalk upon the hillside, which are a famous feature of this county. This particular specimen, however, is, I believe, of modern origin.

Although I made this journey late in April, the weather was that of March, and the plough-lands were looking white for the first time that spring as they dried out beneath the breath of the hard easterly gale. Indeed, on this sticky, chalk soil the sowing of the spring corn had everywhere fallen into arrear. We passed various small villages of which the cottages struck me as poor. In most cases they were built of chalk. As we drew near to Avebury I noted that many of the houses were furnished with fine stone gate posts and lintels, which, we were told, had at some time or other been cut from the monoliths that make the place remarkable.

The most striking thing about the ancient Druidical—if they are Druidical—remains at Avebury is the huge dry fosse with which they are in part surrounded. In comparison with those of Stonehenge the remaining monoliths are of small account, though when their inner and outer circles stood in lonely grandeur on the plain they must have been impressive enough. The mighty tumulus of Silbury Hill, however, heaped up to the height of 130 feet, it is said by the labour of primitive men, is a majestic object, though if it were only a natural hill it would not strike us as wonderful, the circumstance of its human origin being that which appeals to the imagination.

Here we visited an ancient and beautiful manor house, once a monastery, but now tenanted by the Misses Kemm, who farmed 900 acres, most of it arable, upon the Meux estate, a somewhat heavy task, it struck me, for two ladies in these difficult times. They complained much of the want of labour, saying that they could not even get a man to tend the garden. Indeed, everywhere in Wiltshire it is the same story, and that this trouble is spreading from the purely agricultural classes, the following anecdote will show. In one of the houses in which I stayed my host had a head-gardener, a Scotchman, who when he first arrived worked wonderfully well. After a while, however, his employer observed him watering the garden during a drought while the afternoon sun was still full on it. He pointed out to him that this was a very bad thing to do, as the water should be applied at the close of the day. The gardener answered that he agreed; but as the other men about had protested against his working after six o'clock, even at his gardening duties, he had to water before that hour, whether it suited the plants or not.

I will conclude my remarks upon Wiltshire with a few quotations of opinions, amongst them those of a farmer of about 600 acres in the neighbourhood of Chippenham, which

I select as being, in my view, fairly representative of those of his class. He puts his grievance against the sporting landlord which is so common in this and some other counties, very clearly.

It seems that before taking his present holding he had previously occupied a large corn and sheep farm which— here I will quote his own words—'was bought by one of those people who have made money in trade, solely for the sporting. I feel rather strongly about that. Mine was a very useful farm. I could make it pay well at a moderate rent so long as I had it, shooting and all. But when he bought it and got me to give up the shooting I would not have it rent free. Indeed, it would have been dear at no rent. So gave it up. He is farming it himself, as of course he could not find a man with capital who would take it under such conditions (must not touch even rabbits, or would get notice). He is likely to lose £1,000 a year on it, besides his rent, and after a few years it will probably lapse from cultivation. I think this is wrong. A man can do what he likes with his own to a certain extent, but ought not to be able to do so to the injury of the country at large. There are several instances in that neighbourhood of the same kind. The landlord takes the farm over, farms it for a time, finds it useless to cultivate with a great stock of game. One or the other is sacrificed. If he is not a rich man, most likely the game; but if he is drawing a large income from other sources he lets the land go out of cultivation, at least for a field out from all coverts, and does very little to the remainder.'

The same gentleman writes, 'I could milk a quantity of cows, but only milk about a score. The labour difficulty and dislike of Sunday work is very much against the milk.' Labour, he thinks, is very scarce, although the wages, including harvest money and extras, average about 18s. a week. In his opinion the young men migrate to the towns, not so much on account of the present system of education, as from a dislike to Sunday work and a desire for the excitement of a city life. The labourers, he considers, are well off; the landlords, who depend solely upon the rents, very badly off indeed; and the tenants of the old school gradually losing their all, although some who adapt themselves to the times, and possess brains and capital, are doing fairly well. He can see no signs of a general revival in agriculture, and believes that a continuation of the exodus will probably mean that all land capable of being laid down will go to grass, while arable will be cropped in a very rough fashion without the aid of hoeing or other hand labour.

By way of contrast to the foregoing opinions I now instance those of a correspondent in Mid-Wilts, who takes a different view of things. From internal evidence I should imagine that he is an educated, labouring man. He says :

My view is when you extend the scope of your inquiries you will discover that after all farmers are not in such a bad way. In a few isolated cases, as in other businesses, no doubt there has been loss, but on the other hand—and I speak with a knowledge of a wide district—the most striking commercial fact of my lifelong observation is the prosperity of farmers. I wish you would look into this yourself. I ask if it is not a fact that men by the score who started with three acres and a cow less than twenty or thirty years ago are now well-to-do people and drive to market as swells. They have done well—are doing well. Upon this point I defy contradiction. I could give names, and support my contention with undeniable evidence.

You, when you consult another class will learn the true explanation of the labour question. The slavish system of tied cottages is the great factor. The farmers used this as a whip, and drove away the best of the labourers, and now the people themselves use the system against its own defenders. Security of tenancy will mean, as anyone can see, security of labour. If a man were responsible for his garden and cottage for twelve months, he would not run away from his place a day or two after the first tiff with his employer. The uncertainty, the unrest, the dissatisfaction—take these things into your account and ask what they have done. It is the ' Can any good thing come out of the country ? ' which is driving the people to the town. Other causes I know. The Egyptian bondage presses so hard upon the English in the people, hence the exodus. It is a wretched system. I know it, and I know too what the people think of it. Bad cottages too many, but that is not it. Too few cottages perhaps, but that difficulty is being painfully overcome automatically. Hereabouts we have cottages empty, not a few.

A remedy? Split up the land into not more than fifty-acre lots. This will give such an impetus to the industry as would save it from this continual parade of poverty, this fretting and grumbling of which we get so much. To begin with the Crown lands throughout the country. This surely is within the power of any Government of moderate strength. You may depend upon it men are not going to be tied in cottages and be ruled by the iron hand of employers. Create hope in the people and provide for its realisation. Oh! the hopelessness of village life. No wonder people flee from it as from the haunted castle of Giant Despair.

I need scarcely assure the reader that without waiting for my correspondent's advice, I *have* looked into all these matters myself, with results that from time to time I shall strive to chronicle in the pages of this work. Much looking into, indeed, has convinced me how many-sided are the great problems connected with the present condition of land and rural interests in England. It is this conviction that leads me to welcome and to introduce for the consideration of others, all shades of opinion, even if to my judgment they seem extreme. For instance, earlier in this chapter I have touched upon the matter of cottages on a farm held independently of the tenant of that farm, and pointed out the grave inconveniences which may ensue from such a tenure.

In the foregoing extracts the reader has an opportunity of studying the other side of the case, put forward in a very earnest and able manner by a man who evidently thinks for himself, if in a somewhat one-sided fashion. In forming his conclusions, however, that reader should, I think, bear one point in mind. Few farmers now-a-days wish to get rid of a good servant in any unjust or arbitrary fashion. Nor need deserving men lack the opportunity of other employment. The labourer is no longer a slave. My correspondent's proposed remedy of cutting up the land into fifty-acre lots is heroic, but, as I fear, scarcely practicable, even if it is really desirable. Doubtless, however, Government might make experiments in this direction if it chose, but will it choose? My belief is that nothing short of a revolution will induce those in authority to take any steps that would radically alter the conditions and tenure of English land, and indeed the necessity must be grave and well demonstrated which would justify them in so doing. Violent revolutions are apt to produce more evils than they are designed to cure.

## HAMPSHIRE

ALTHOUGH I did not visit Hampshire till quite the end of
the year 1901—that is, with the exception of a single brief
expedition—as it lies contiguous to Wiltshire I propose to
supplement my remarks upon that county by a description
of one or two typical Hampshire farms and a summary of the
views of a few residents in the district.   The southern mari-
time county of Hampshire, which includes the Isle of Wight,
has (excluding the Isle) a greatest length from north to
south of about forty-six miles, and a greatest width from
east to west of about forty-one miles.   Its area (including
the Isle of Wight) is about 1,037,000 acres.   The chalk hill
ranges called the North and South Downs, where many
sheep are grazed, follow a north-westerly course across the
county.   This shire has suffered a good deal from the prevailing agricultural depression.

   The first farm that I have selected to describe is that of
Norman Court, Upper Clatford, a village on the Anton, not
far from Andover, over which I was shown by Mr. F. C.
Ellen, the well-known estate agent and valuer, who is
managing it on behalf of the owner.   The country here is
very wide and open, and upon the borders of the stream
beautiful to look at, with its green and fertile meadows
dotted and lined by willows.   The soil is mixed on chalk—
most of it light loam.   On the whole the farm, which covers
540 acres, is a good one, although until recently the land
had been much neglected and the buildings are very poor,
the walls being mud-plastered and thatched, as in Wiltshire,
to keep the wet from their crowns.   As the land is in hand
of course there is no fixed rent, but including the water-

meadows its letting-value, exclusive of the sporting, would be about 15s. the acre. The selling value of such land in Hampshire, if well situated near to a town with facilities and sporting rights, seems to be about £30 the acre. The buildings to which I have alluded were wood-clad, thatched, and in very bad order. The bailiff told me that there was on them no less than an acre of thatch which required to be kept up, and what that means every landlord will know. Indeed, before long they will have to be pulled down and rebuilt, though probably, as Mr. Ellen seemed to think, it would pay the owner better to divide the farm, lying as it does near to Andover, into holdings of 100 acres and put up upon these smaller sets of premises. Upon this farm, as on the majority in that neighbourhood, sheep of the Hampshire Down breed are the mainstay. Here they keep 400 ewes, which produced in 1901 a fall of 450 lambs. In July 240 of these lambs were sold at 33s. a head; 120 of the best were kept for stock, while the cull lambs were to be sold during November at Andover Fair, being estimated then to produce about 38s. a head. These selected ewe tegs I saw folded upon rape, nor during all my travels can I recall meeting with a better-countenanced little company. Indeed the shepherd told me that in his long experience he could remember no finer or more even lot.

This man, George Piper by name, was a person worthy of remark. Then over seventy years of age, for sixty of them he had been a shepherd, forty years of that time being spent in the employ of a single master. Sunk as he was in eld, it was easy for anyone accustomed to watch his class, to see that in very many cases the services of two men of the present generation would be of less value than those of this shepherd, who knew his sheep and was known of them. There he stood in the cold wind upon the bleak Down crest watching the fold much as a dog does, and now and again passing the hurdles to do some little service to his flock, every one of which he could distinguish from the other.

This, too, on a Sunday, the day on which it is so difficult to keep the modern stockman to work, however necessary.

The view from the sheepfold was very fine. On the south, wide, open country running to the dim line of the old Danish encampment of Danebury Ring. On the south-west, the dense mass of Wherwell Woods still tinged with their autumn foliage, where, according to local tradition, Queen Elfrida stabbed her stepson Eadward about the year 980. This, however, must be a mistake, since Eadward is said to have been done to death at Corfe Castle in Dorsetshire; but it is undoubted that her son Ethelred granted lands to a monastery at Wherwell for the good of his mother Elfrida's soul, which it is not uncharitable to suppose stood in some need of this pious and filial attention. There at any rate to this day stands the priory, or the house built upon its ancient site. To the west, open country stretching to Salisbury Plain ten miles away, and but a little space above the fold, the old Roman road, now a sheep track, which linked Andover with Winchester.

The cereals grown upon this farm are barley, wheat, and oats. Of barley in 1901 there were forty acres, but the land, which had only been in hand two years, being still in poor heart and the season dry, the yield averaged but three quarters to the acre, which sold for 30s. a quarter. Of wheat there were seventy acres, giving a good all-round crop of about four quarters to the acre. Of oats sixty-five acres, that produced only three quarters to the acre owing to the ravages of wire-worm. The land upon which these oats were grown was worthless grass broken up. Of such pastures there are many in Hampshire. Owing to the low price of corn they have been laid down in grass, although the thin, stony soil is quite unsuitable to that crop, which in most cases never comes to any value. Of sainfoin there were forty acres, producing from a ton and a half to two tons of hay per acre. Here I may remark that sainfoin is the salvation of this district and out of it many a man pays his rent. It was, I find, grown so early as Arthur Young's day, for speaking of such land he says :

> The white chalky soil is, in general, of a cold wet spewy nature and will not bear ploughing in winter unless the weather is very dry or frosty. . . . It is a cold hungry soil of little profit except with very peculiar management and answers best if tolerably dry laid down to sainfoine.

Of sainfoin and its uses in Hampshire I was told the following story, which is authentic. Not many years ago a 400-acre farm in the neighbourhood was sold to a shrewd man at about £10 the acre. The purchaser, who knew that it was fresh to that crop, laid it all down to sainfoin. In a few cuts he recouped himself for the entire price of the land, which, after felling every stick of timber, he resold at about the same figure as he had originally given for the holding. Such a method of farming does not fit in well with the old local saying that ' nothing should go off a Hampshire farm that cannot walk,' still its cleverness may be admired.

In addition to the above crops there were grown in 1901 ten acres of peas for feed which produced four quarters to the acre and a field of mixed clover and rye-grass. The pastures were skimmed over, producing in that dry season only about five hundredweight of hay per acre, and then fed. The horse strength on the farm was eleven, excellent animals of the Shire stamp, very stoutly made, and mostly roan in colour. The labour bill came to about £1 the acre, which is rather above the local average.

In walking over this farm the first field I visited was upland pasture-land which had been laid down six years. It was not in very grand condition, but then, as I have said, much of the Hampshire land is put into grass, however unsuitable it may be to that purpose. This is done to save labour on unremunerative arables when they are already beggared out, with the result that from nothing nothing comes. Speaking generally, if near the rivers the land lays down fairly, but not well; above them, although the rainfall is of an average quantity, it generally lays down very badly indeed.

Field No. 2, separated, I think, from the first by rough wire fencing, was a new-laid pasture that had been recently broken up. In the spring of 1901 it was under vetches, and in the summer was drilled for turnips, which, however, were taken off by the fly in the drought. When I saw it, it was sown with winter barley, to be folded with sheep in the following spring, after which it will come again for turnips. The pasture which had been broken up is, I was informed, absolutely valueless.

Field No. 3 was sown with rye—much punished by wire-worm—after oats. This rye will be fed off with sheep. Then will come swedes, then turnips, then wheat. The bailiff reckoned that it would cost £5 an acre in tillages to get a wheat crop.

Field No. 4, which is all part of the same stretch of high land, was under late turnips, that had grown more at the top than at the bottom. These were to be fed off with sheep about the middle of the following January, when the ewes lamb.

Fields 5 and 6 were water meadows, worth 50s. an acre rent. These meadows are fed with sheep in April and May, after which the water is let over them. In July they are hayed, and when the grass is off, fed with cattle till the end of November. After this the dykes are drawn or 'fyed' at a cost of 5s. the acre, and the meadows laid under water until March 25, when they again come into use. On field No. 6 even in November twenty head of stock steers were feeding. These were bought in at two years old at £8 a head. When they left the meadows they were to be yard-fed with cake and straw, as in the barren year of 1901 there was no hay to spare for them. They were to come out again in the following May, and after running the summer to be sold as stores for fatting in September at the probable price of about £12 a head. These figures will scarcely leave much profit, seeing how long the animals remain in hand, but of course the real benefit to the farm is to be looked for in the manure that they make.

Field No. 7, twenty-three acres of winter oats, following wheat on a broken-up new-laid pasture. These oats looked well, and were to be kept for crop, not fed.

Field No. 8, sown with vetches to be fed off with sheep in the following June and then to come for swedes.

Field No. 9, winter barley for sheep feed, following rye, and to be followed by vetches. In this county winter barley is one of the commonest provenders for sheep, but locally it is not considered to be of use for malting purposes.

Field No. 10, root which had been fed off by sheep, the second of two root crops on the same land that was now to be ploughed for wheat.

No cows were kept upon this farm.

In considering the above details and the returns given by the various crops, the reader must remember that this land had only been two years under its present management, and was taken over in very indifferent order. Doubtless the results will soon be much improved, both in quality and quantity. Still in these days it is a hard struggle to make a profit out of such soils, especially in seasons of drought when feed and hay are short. Indeed, many such Hampshire farms are now chiefly valuable for the shooting and fishing rights that attach to them. Mr. Ellen told me, however, he believed that in future the better class of tenants will insist upon being given the shooting, either for their own use or to let. Good tenants are going fast in Hampshire and often enough can only be kept by this concession. To some extent their place is being taken by men who come from Devonshire, but I was informed that the majority of these immigrants do not stay. Employing little labour, they are beaten by the land and prices, and, finding that they cannot make a living, depart to pastures new.

Mr. Ellen, who like his father before him has been a large Hampshire land agent all his life, was so kind as to give me his views upon the general agricultural position in that county. Of these the following is the summary. He said that farms let more readily than they did three or four years ago, but many farmers were tempted by reduced rentals to take more land than their capital justified. A quarter of a century ago it was reckoned that a farm ought to produce three rents, one for the landlord, one for labour, and one for profit. Thus, say that the rent of the farm was £700, the labour would be about £700, and the profit about £700. Now the labour-bill remains practically the same, while the rent has been reduced from 40 to 50 per cent., and the profit also has been much lessened. In those old days leases were often bought at a premium, but now there are few leases, and the banks are very unwilling to advance money upon any farming security. In these times a number of tenants are barely rubbing along. Some of them do not make enough of a business of their farming, do not take it as seriously as they ought ; but those who have sufficient capital, ability, perseverance, and decent land, still prosper as such men would in any other profession, that is, if they do not expect too much.

Nearly all Hampshire farms continue to let at a price, but the difficulty is to find responsible tenants with sufficient capital, especially for the larger farms which fetch less per acre than those of smaller size. Nowadays it is common for tenants to come in with less than £5 per acre capital, whereas formerly £10 per acre used to be considered necessary. The results of this change upon farming methods and production can be imagined. Rents now run from 21s. an acre to 5s. the acre, tithe free, the sporting rights being generally reserved.

In the Vernham and Combe neighbourhoods there are thousands of acres of derelict land that practically fetches no rent at all, being given up to rabbits. It is stony soil, but Mr. Ellen can remember when it was farmed on the four-course system and produced good crops. Now so much less food is grown in the county, and so many more rabbits, of which Australian competition is lowering the value.

Of all the problems that agriculture has to face in Hampshire, Mr. Ellen thought that of labour the most serious. It is now very difficult to procure young men, who do not like stopping in the country districts. They go to work at the Tedworth Barracks on Salisbury Plain and to the towns. Moreover, the exodus is progressive, so that only the old fellows are left. These are the best, but very independent. He thought that when they dropped out it was difficult to say what would happen, or how they could be replaced. Even now, if it were not for the self-binders, it would be hard to get in the harvest. Thus, on a farm of 400 acres which he knew, situated about two miles from a town, the tenant was left quite without labour in haytime, and was obliged to get up the hay with the help of a casual hand and rick it as best he could. This, however, was an extreme instance. Mr. Ellen said that it is now essential that tenants should be provided with numerous and good cottages, otherwise they would find themselves unable to procure labour. On many estates the houses are bad and the landlords in no position to build, as such investments bring in practically no interest on outlay. For instance, a pair of good cottages cost about £400, and in a rural district produce only 1s. 6d. a-piece a week in rental. Further, the tenant in taking a farm generally stipulates that he must have a certain number of cottages included in his rent, and he cannot afford to pay additional money for new dwellings, even if the landlord could afford to build them, which in many instances is not the case.

As regarded wages, day-labourers in Hampshire earned 13s. a week, harvest work with other extras bringing their wages up to about 16s. a week—that is, when they are in regular employ. Many farmers, however, cannot afford to keep on the men throughout the year, and such people find it very difficult to get labour at the time they want it most. Carters' wages are 15s. a week, with £4 Michaelmas money,

£2 beer money, 3$d$. an acre reaping, 1½$d$. an acre drilling, and 1½$d$. an acre cutting hay, bringing the total up to from 19$s$. to 20$s$. a week. Shepherds receive 14$s$. a week, with £4 Michaelmas money, 1$d$. for every lamb, and 1$s$. for every lamb over a lamb to a ewe. It is customary to hire carters and shepherds by the year.

Tenants now press for more open covenants—that is, for greater liberty in the system of farming. Also the sale of hay and straw has become very general, with the result that less stock is kept and the land not cultivated so well as it used to be. It is on this account that few tenants derive any benefit from the Agricultural Holdings Act; for if a claim is made under it, it is generally found that the landlord is in a position to make a counter-claim, that reduces or swallows up the tenant-right demand made under the Act. A large tenant-right claim also often increases the difficulty of letting a farm, as it is a very hard matter to find applicants with sufficient capital to meet it, and an easy incoming facilitates the letting of a holding that is in poor condition.

Mr. Ellen was of opinion that too much is habitually expected in return from capital invested in farming. Thus, say that £4,000 is invested and 8 per cent. realised; £320 is not sufficient income to keep up a house of the rental value of, as is often the case, £60, with horses, carriages, &c., which are essential to persons residing and making their living in the country.

He added that those of the smaller farmers who succeed are generally men who do a certain amount of dealing. This, indeed, has been my experience throughout England, though how there can be so many dealers and who they deal with remains to me a mystery. I have heard it said that farmers ought to deal more, but it is impossible that everybody should live by making a profit out of his neighbour, in other words, as a middleman. Some there must be who provide that profit, otherwise no dealers could flourish; the race would die out like the Jews who tried to do business in

Aberdeen.   In short, to be a successful dealer means that
you must be sharper than the majority of your fellows
and, fortunately perhaps, all farmers are not preternaturally
sharp.

The great difficulty in the way of establishing more
small-holdings is, Mr. Ellen thought, the houses and
buildings which they necessitate.   It was, however, an undoubted fact that the smaller the holding the easier it is to
let.   The average size of Hampshire farms is now about
400 acres.   They used to be larger.

In the districts of Vernham and Combe, where, as has
been said, so much land is practically out of cultivation, to
such an extent, indeed, that in many instances it would cost
the value of the farm to clean it, the villages that used to
be prosperous are greatly depopulated.   In these out-of-the-
way places it is difficult to persuade labourers to live.   In
conclusion Mr. Ellen said that few sons now succeed their
fathers in farms, and that the capital employed is less than
it used to be.

Another farm which I inspected in Hampshire was the
Enham home-farm of 450 acres, which has been worked for
the last three years by my friend, Dr. Lyne Stivens, under the
management of a bailiff, Mr. Edward Butler.   This farm
includes forty acres of park, twenty-five acres of sundry grass,
and forty-three acres of new-laid pasture, which was almost
worthless and ought, Mr. Butler thought, to be ploughed up.
Indeed, almost all the pasture land in this neighbourhood is of
poor quality.   Three hundred and twenty ewes are lambed
upon this farm, producing 325 lambs in 1901, and 354 lambs
in 1900; a very good fall.   Here a lamb for a ewe is reckoned
a satisfactory increase.   Of these lambs 100 were sold out in
July at 29s. 6d., and eighty more at the end of that month
for 34s.   The rest were sold on October 10, 100 making
38s. 6d., and twenty-five 33s. 6d.   The balance were consumed in the house or died.   The wool of the flock was
disposed of at 7½d. a pound—a poor figure enough.

This district is not good for barley, and only seventeen

acres were grown upon the farm in 1901. Of wheat there were about sixty acres, producing a little over four quarters to the acre. This crop had suffered a good deal from rabbits. No cattle are fatted on the farm, but about a dozen yearlings are bought in at an average price of £6 10s., kept for a year, and sold out for stores or as down-calvers at from £10 to £12 a head. Of sainfoin about fifty acres are grown. The land suits this crop well, and it produced over two tons to the acre. There are six cows, of which the produce is sold to the house, but sheep are the mainstay ; indeed, Mr. Butler said it would be impossible to get on without them, as in addition to the value of their produce they manure the land. The year of 1901 had been very bad ; thus there were on this farm four haystacks less than it produced in the previous season. With the exception of swedes, however, the roots were all good, kail which was to be fed off with lambs in the following April, being very good. Upon this farm the lambs are timed to be dropped about January 4, some ten days earlier than is usual in the neighbourhood. Mr. Butler thinks that they do best thus ; at any rate he has always had more luck with the early lambs.

The wages-bill on the farm comes to £640 a year, or about 27s. 6d. per acre. The receipts are eked out by a certain amount of stone hauling done for the road authorities ; also timber is carted for the estate, the charge made for carting, including that which is done for the house, being 6s. a day.

Mr. Butler has been employed in managing land in Wiltshire and Hampshire since 1882—that is, all his working life—and is therefore well qualified to give an opinion upon agricultural matters in these counties. He thought that if a man is a competent farmer and has plenty of capital he can still get on at his trade. By this he meant that he can pay his rent and make a fair living, the interest on capital invested being counted towards the living. Few can do better than this, although there is more to be made out of some farms than from others. A great number of Hampshire farmers, however, are, he believed, in considerable distress. Notwithstanding this there is still a good application for farms, especially for those of small size; but men frequently enter upon the business with too little capital. The local rent he put at about 15s. the acre for ordinary land in good heart. Of cottages, he said, there is a great scarcity, and most of those that exist are not very good. Very few new ones were being built.

Speaking generally, he considered that the condition of the land was going back throughout the county, owing to the indifferent character of modern farming. As regarded labour, he declared that the old men still stay on, but young ones were practically unattainable. Thus, wanting an under-carter he advertised for three weeks, and as a result received but a single application. This man he engaged, ' but,' he added feelingly, ' I wish I had never seen him.' This carter's wage was 11s. a week, with £4 harvest-money at Michaelmas, and 1s. a day extra beer money when employed upon any kind of harvest work that keeps men to seven o'clock. Also he received 6d. a day beer money when drawing corn from the thrashing-machine, and 6d. a week lodging money throughout the year. The young men, Mr. Butler said, all go into the building trade, or to the Government work at Tedworth Camp, where they receive high wages. What would happen when the old men die he could not say. ' Heaven only knows ! ' He thought that perhaps the people would come back to the land; but wherever they have gone to, they were not learning farm work, and would be of little use if they did. As regards the financial results upon this farm, as yet nothing had been paid out beyond an allowance for rent and the amount of his own salary. There was, however, a cash balance in the bank. Of the future he could not think well, being unable to see from what quarter improvement was to come. What outlook was there, he asked, when he had to sell beautiful wheat at 29s. 6d. a quarter ? Labour was perhaps the worst of all their difficulties, and about it the outcry amongst Hampshire farmers was great and general. Although wages were 2s. a week higher than they had been three years ago, the men no longer seemed satisfied; they were always grumbling.

Upon this point, indeed, the evidence is ample. Thus, Mr. C. R. Knollys writes to me from the Grange Estate Office, Alresford : ' It is not only the scarcity of agricultural labour, but the appalling inferiority of the men that one gets nowadays. Their sole object seems to be to get through the day somehow and bustle off to the public-house as soon as possible.'

Mr. Henry Way, of Pyle, Chayle, Isle of Wight, which is technically a part of the county of Hampshire, says : ' There is an ever-increasing trouble as to labour.'

Mr. Jeffreys, M.P., the well-known agricultural authority, writes to me : ' Carter boys are very difficult to obtain, and both men and boys dislike a breeding flock or a dairy because of the constant work, including Sundays.' He points out that the difficulty of the Hampshire farmers in getting labour during the last three years, has been accentuated by the building of various railways in the county; also by the embodiment of the Hampshire Militia and the despatch of the Yeomanry to South Africa. He adds that if it had not been for these circumstances, he thinks they would have been fairly well supplied with labour on the farm. My own experience is, however, that in almost every district, not only of Hampshire but of many other counties, some such local reason is advanced as a cause of the lack of labour. Either it is a railway, or a sewer, or harbour works, or an embankment, or a spurt in the building trade. Everywhere there is something, but I take the fact to be that everywhere the present generation of Englishmen desire to escape from the land to some more congenial and remunerative employment.

Mr. F. M. Jervoise, of Herriard Park, near Basingstoke, a large landowner, said that ordinary farm labourers are scarce, but more plentiful than they were a year before. In his opinion farmers must spend more and more upon machinery, labour-saving appliances, steam cultivation, and implements upon which men can ride instead of walking. In short, the farm work must be carried on by a few permanent hands and whatever casual labour can be procured in busy seasons. He thought that a small proportion of the young men stay on the land, but that many go into the police or the army, while some take service as porters on the railways, some as bricklayers' labourers, and others as mechanics. The great facilities for moving about induce many to leave the village. Education, in his opinion, had also without doubt much to do with it, as its result was to inspire boys with a repugnance for work on the land, or even to learn the more remunerative labour of thatching and hurdle-making. Mr. Jervoise had no great faith in the idea that a change in the system of education would make a difference in this matter. Teaching gardening and botany might, he thought, produce more gardeners, but not more agricultural labourers.

He believed that tenant farmers who understand and stick to their trade are still making a fairly remunerative business of farming, but that landlords who are dependent on rent were very hard hit, as so much of their remaining income goes out in repairs and new buildings. In his district, on the contrary, the labourers appear contented, and with cottages at a shilling a week and constant work are, he said, better off than their fellows in towns, where the rents were high. Unless the prices of produce improved, he could see no chance of revival in Hampshire agriculture, and certainly not of a return to its old prosperous condition.

In curious contrast to those expressed by Mr. Jervoise as to the advantages of teaching gardening, &c. in rural schools, are the views of Mr. F. J. Ames, the headmaster of the Board school at Crondale, in Hampshire, which has a population of about 1,300, and an average school attendance of about 235. Mr. Ames, who had held his position for more than forty years, and is certainly therefore entitled to speak with authority, stated that in his district allotments have been tried and have failed, for the reason that allotments are large gardens, and are generally taken by men with large families who have a small garden or none at all. Such men work them to eke out their wages and to provide vegetables of the grosser sorts, such as potatoes, cabbages, and turnips, together with corn, for sale. They are, on the other hand, seldom taken from a love of gardening; and on very few of them is any attempt made to grow fruit, since no one will plant trees without security of tenure. Cottage gardening, as it is sometimes taught in country schools, is, in his opinion, of little avail, as such small patches can generally be as well attended to in the suburbs of towns, where the gardens are often reproductions of the model school cottage garden.

He thought that what is necessary is to give the villagers a stake in the land. If they cannot have, and do not require, 'three acres and a cow,' such a stake may be created by inducing them to take an interest in the cultivation of fruit-trees, roses, &c., which cannot readily be removed with their owner to a suburban garden. He suggested that in place of or in addition to cottage gardening as it is taught in some villages the children in the day-schools, and the young men in the evening classes, might be instructed in budding and grafting. Between those who graft and that which is grafted there grows up a fellowship not easy to sever. He was certain, indeed, that if the owners of village property would but plant fruit trees in every cottage garden, many might be kept on the land who at present migrate to the towns. By way of example, Mr. Ames stated that he has two Quarantine apple trees the fruit of which he sold to a dealer at the price of 3s. a bushel. They produced thirty bushels, for which he received £4 10s. 'If I were a labourer,' said Mr. Ames, 'and had been offered a better place with a rise of 2s. a week, should I have moved? No, thank you; only two of my trees nearly paid me that.' Indeed, he knew an instance where a man labouring on a fruit farm had 'worked' some trees in his cottage garden. Having left his situation he was offered a better place at a distance from his village, but he replied : ' I shall not leave my fruit trees.' It was his experience that a child or young person generally becomes much attached to any tree that he has grafted.

He believed that many young men (thanks to School Penny and Post Office savings banks) are anxious to become owners of a cottage and garden. Unfortunately, however strange it may seem, this desire can, he said, be more easily gratified in the suburb of a large town than in a country village, where the land is generally in the hands of a few persons, who do not care to sell, or of public bodies such as the Church and the Ecclesiastical Commissioners. He thought that if this matter of the provision of garden plots were taken up by those in authority, a great deal of good might be done, and many of the rural population who at present leave it would be retained upon the land. Further, he said, villagers require recreation like other people, and although games and fêtes may suffice for the summer, none is provided for the long winter evenings. Being gregarious, therefore, they assemble in the taverns where publicans cannot allow them to remain unless they continually call for drinks. This evil, Mr. Ames believed, might be obviated by providing non-political and unsectarian village clubs, where men could resort and enjoy innocent recreation, with, if they desired them, newspapers, books, and ale or other drinkables. Many clubs and institutes, he declared, are strangled by the ' goody-goody ' manner in which they are conducted, no smoking or intoxicants being allowed upon the premises. If such advantages and innocent pleasures are not provided, can we wonder, asked Mr. Ames, that people migrate to the towns or their suburbs ?

For my part I think that Mr. Ames' views are very sound and sensible, although by no means capable of universal application. I have, however, observed, especially in the Eastern Counties, that cottagers often neglect the fruit trees which they find in their gardens, although in many instances this may arise from ignorance. Not one labouring man in ten seems to understand that an apple tree—to take an example—requires to be lime-washed to kill the moss and insects, to be occasionally manured at the root to promote fertility, or to have the surplus wood removed, especially in the centre, so that the sun and air can get to the hearts of the trees. Certainly, as Mr. Ames suggests, they should be instructed in these matters, and good would result from the cultivation of such wholesome and natural tastes.

## GUERNSEY

THE island of Guernsey, whither I travelled from Wiltshire, has an area of only about 15,560 acres, of which I believe some 10,000 are cultivated.

In planning this journey of agricultural research my intention was to commence it in the Channel Islands. In fact, however, a return of furious winter weather made this almost impossible until the seas should moderate, especially as these islands suffer from the drawback that, with the exception of a few months in the summer, boats run thither only through the night. As it chanced, this accidental delay was fortunate, since I can imagine no better preparation for a study of Guernsey than that of the unfrequented rolling Downs of Wiltshire. It is the finest example of the advantages of education by contrast that I know. The student comes from a country where land sells for £6 an acre to one where it fetches as much as £500 an acre (for agricultural purposes, be it understood); from a country where land lets at from 5s. to 15s. per acre to one where it lets at from £4 (for the rougher furze-bearing soil) to £9 per acre; from a country where the average holding covers a thousand acres to one where it covers but a single acre.

There are other contrasts equally strange. In the one place vast expanses are in the hands of great landlords, and to them, for the most part, but ruinous possessions; in the other the soil is held in tiny patches by a multitude of smallholders. In the one place the population is extraordinarily sparse I drove there for a whole day and scarcely met a dozen people on the road—in the other I believe it to be the densest in Europe. In Wiltshire, Hampshire, and the adjacent counties the labouring inhabitants are pouring from the soil; the cottages are, at least in very many cases, wretched and insufficient in number, and few working men can hope to rise to independence, much less to wealth. In Guernsey, on the other hand, the population own the soil and cling to it; most of the houses are excellent; indeed, there is no such thing as a hovel to be seen, except, perhaps, in certain parts of St. Peter's Port and St. Sampson; and instances are common in which men who begin life with no other endowment than health and strength end it in the possession of fortunes of from £5,000 to £10,000—earned, every farthing of it, not by trade or speculation, but out of those small-holdings which we are so often assured cannot possibly be made to pay.

Of course there are reasons for all this. Guernsey, for instance, has considerable advantages of climate, although whether these greatly surpass those of the south coast of England may be doubted. Her soil also is very fair, though not so good as is often imagined, and her people are extraordinarily hard-working, thrifty, and intelligent. Moreover, taxation is ridiculously light, while criminals and paupers are strangely few. But I think the true cause of her triumph and of that of her sister islands is to be found in the character of their people, which character for generations has been profoundly influenced by the magic power of ownership. Here every man works for himself, and not for the benefit of others, or at least intends so to work in the near future. Therefore he has ambition, and ambition in due course leads him to attainment. *O si sic omnes !* Were Britain as is this little isle of Guernsey, what true and immovable prosperity would be hers !

Yet there is scarcely one of our cherished shibboleths that Guernsey does not dare to violate. Its cattle are protected from admixture of blood and disease by the absolute prohibition of the landing of imported animals, and until quite recently, at any rate, it boasted no system of compulsory education. Yet its inhabitants seem singularly

intelligent. Primogeniture entails no rights beyond one to
the principal house, and about twenty perches of land. All
property must be left to be divided among the children in
varying proportions, while from the moment of marriage a
wife has an indefeasible right to the revenue of one-third of
her husband's estate, and at his death to one-third of his
personal possessions absolutely. Again, the Channel Islands
submit to and flourish under a system of military con-
scription, the very mention of which would strike horror
here in England. All males, of whatever condition, must
serve in the ranks of the Militia, and between the ages of
sixteen and sixty-five remain liable to be called out in case
of emergency.

The cost of the land being so enormous, and its rent
value so high, the farmers are forced to wring from it all
that the intensest cultivation can produce. They have two
main sources of revenue—their glass-houses and their cattle,
of the famous Guernsey breed. In the year 1900, from a
summary kindly furnished to me by the Guernsey Board of
Agriculture, the cereal total seems to have amounted to
924 acres only out of the 10,000 under cultivation. Much
of the hay and straw necessary for the cows has to be imported, while corn is little grown in the island.

It is scarcely too much to say that parts of Guernsey are
nearly roofed in with glass; indeed on one occasion, coming
to a rise and looking over into a valley, for some moments I
imagined that the shimmering surface beneath me was that
of water. And still day by day more goes up—everywhere
the eye falls upon gaunt, pink-hued skeletons which in a
month or two will be finished greenhouses full of tomato
plants. Indeed, there are few farms left in Guernsey: glass
culture is killing farming, and large stretches of the island
resemble a scattered township rather than a countryside.
As to whether so much glass will continue to pay is a
debated question. Many experienced islanders think that
the thing is being overdone. Moreover, there is another
point that should be noticed. In a few years the soil

covered in by the houses, deprived as it must be of the natural atmospheric conditions and moisture, and heavily cropped as it is from month to month, becomes exhausted, notwithstanding the frequent applications of every possible manure and restorative. Then it is necessary to remove it and to bring in new soil, which, however, often does not answer in Guernsey, partly, as I believe, because fibrous turf or virgin loam is now hard to come by in that much cultivated island. Once the soil is thoroughly exhausted, it breeds various insects and bacteria, and the crops become affected by wire-worm, ' finger-and-toe,' with other blights and maladies.

There are in Guernsey to-day men, some of whom began with nothing, who own acres of these glass-houses. Thus Mr. Ozanne, of Lily Vale, whom we visited, and who most kindly showed us over his holding, farms seventy-five vergées, that is, thirty English acres, of which seven and a half vergées, or three acres, are covered with glass. On this area he had in all eighty head of cattle and employed fifteen hands. It is difficult to imagine the face of an Englishman were he asked to keep eighty head of cattle on thirty acres of land.

Here I may state that most of the hired labour both in Guernsey and in Jersey is French, the peasants of Normandy and Brittany finding it possible to earn about twice as much in the Channel Islands as their toil would bring to them at home. Sometimes these men are lodged and fed by the farmers, in which case their cash wage is less, and sometimes, at any rate in Jersey, they live in hired cottages.

First, we inspected Mr. Ozanne's cows, a truly beautiful lot of animals, some of which have taken the highest possible honours at the London Dairy and other shows. For one of these cows he had been offered £75, but declined to part with it for less than £100. Then we went on to the heifers, of which he had recently sold thirteen at prices ranging from £15 to £18, and lastly looked at a few bull calves that he was keeping. Most of these male calves, however, are sold at three days old to the butcher, who pays 5 fr. a head for them.

Leaving the cattle we went to the glass-houses, huge span-shaped structures, many of them measuring over 200 ft. in length, and from 30 ft. to 40 ft. broad. Outside their doors were piled great heaps of anthracite, of which Mr. Ozanne uses about 300 tons a year. This coal is one of the great expenses of the Guernsey grower, since in addition to its price, which during the season of 1901 was as high as 32s. a ton, there is a harbour charge of 2s. 6d. a ton wharfage to be met.

House No. 1 contained arums and orchids overshadowed by the arching rods of vines, just then beautiful with their first green leaves, and thousands of tiny bunches coming into flower. Of the arums, whereof Mr. Ozanne grows some 10,000 and sells as many as 150 dozen blooms in a single week, there were in this house alone many hundred plants, all of them throwing up their glittering white cups above the rich green of the shining leaves. At that time—the month was March—these arums fetched from 1s. 4d. to 1s. 6d. a dozen, whereas a fortnight earlier their price was from 3s. to 4s. They are grown in strong loam with occasional doses of liquid cow-manure. Immediately after Easter, when their flowers are much in request for church decoration, they will be turned out of the houses and laid down upon their sides in the open, in which condition they are kept quite dry until July, when they are re-potted and started into life again. As for the orchids, a class of plant of which I know a little, the less said of them the better. Evidently their needs and culture are not understood in Guernsey, and it is a pity that money should have been wasted upon their purchase.

House No. 2 contained vines more recently started and arums like the first. No. 3 was devoted to Malmaison carnations, which looked very healthy, and, like the arums, were cleaned by daily syringings of water and nothing else. These, too, are rested—under glass of course—by being kept dry from November to March. House No. 4 was small and contained more orchids and the day's plucking of daffodils, mostly of the Princeps, Tenby, and Golden Spur varieties. These daffodils are plucked in the bud and bunched by Mr. Ozanne's children. They stand in water under glass until they are packed for market, where at the time of my visit to the island they sold for about 4s. the gross of 3½ lbs. in weight minus freight and commission, the freight amounting to 0¾d. per pound.

In house No. 5 were Eucharis lilies, which bloom three times a year and are sharply rested in summer ; also vines in flower, which are kept clean with periodical dressings of sulphur and soft soap. Grapes, by the way, do not pay as well as they did ; still, at 3s. a pound in May down to 1s. in October, Mr. Ozanne seemed to find no cause for complaint as to prices. Many growers have, however, given them up in favour of more remunerative crops.

In house No. 6 were a great number of peach trees in pots, for the most part maidens. These stand abroad during the summer. This house also was planted with a new vine called 'Matersfield Court,' of which great things were expected. House No. 7 was devoted to arums and forced daffodils grown in a corner. House No. 8, a very large one, contained about 5,000 tomatoes in pots, and coming into flower. These tomatoes are trained up strings depending from the roof. They stand until June, when the house is replanted with other tomatoes, grown this time in the ground. House No. 9 was filled with potatoes, which would be dug in April, and house No. 10 was also given up to potatoes more highly forced, which would be ready for lifting in a fortnight. Such are the contents of a sample Guernsey glass farm.

After we had gone through the houses I asked Mr. Ozanne how he managed to support so many cattle on such a tiny acreage. He replied that he feeds them on bought hay, cakes, and mangold, some of which are purchased.

In summer he grazes them on his meadow land, each animal being tethered to an iron peg driven into the ground.

'You all seem very rich in Guernsey,' I said.

'No, sir,' he answered, 'we are not rich, but we are thriving.' This remark appears to me to describe very exactly the condition of these prosperous and fortunate folk. It must be remembered also that this prosperity comes from the land alone, and that land not of the best. Moreover, the glass did not bring it, for it existed long before there was a greenhouse in the island; and if the glass should fail through competition or from other causes, such as the working out of the soil, which some experienced islanders think possible, it will, I am convinced, still continue. Guernsey, it is true, has no manufactures to fall back upon; indeed, the export of her excellent granite seems to be her only source of extraneous wealth. The real cause of her well-being, however, must be sought, not in any particular products which she puts out at a given period—for these may and will vary with market requirements—but rather in the enterprise and energy of her inhabitants, the small yeomen proprietors of the island, and in those land-laws which prevent the aggregation of her acres into large estates.

Of course these islanders have their faults like all men, although I am not one of those who count their assumption of independence and of equality with others of higher rank and standing as a fault. In truth I think it in many ways worthy of admiration. Their sin seems to be that of the king who coveted Naboth's vineyard. Here such vineyards lie at the foot of every man's field, and often he seems to covet them. The result is many bitter feuds and much malice and suspicion, for, as the old French saying runs, 'Qui a terre a guerre.'

Through the kindness of our host, Lord De Saumarez, who is perhaps the largest individual property-holder in the island, with which his family has been connected for many generations, and of others, we were enabled to inspect sundry farms and gardens during our stay in Guernsey.

One of the most interesting of these is that belonging to the well-known grower, Mr. Parsons, who has no less than four and a half acres under glass. The general appearance of this establishment was wonderfully tidy and prosperous.

House No. 1 contained fig trees, not in pots, but planted, and tomatoes of the varieties called Stirling Castle and Sarnia. This tomato—Sarnia—was raised by Mr. Parsons himself. It is excellent, as I can testify, having last summer in my own garden grown some plants of it which he gave me. Four or five seasons of successive plantings with tomatoes, Mr. Parsons informed us, exhausts the soil in a greenhouse, which after this time must be changed.

House No. 2, which measured 230 ft. by 38 ft., contained vast quantities of lilies, and was set with Black Hambrough vines, which it seems pay well when the grapes fetch 1s. 6d. a pound. To lessen labour in this and other houses their owners have arranged a system of Décauville trams, which run earth in, and run out the plants in pots when they are done with.

House No. 3 was filled with beans of the variety known as Guernsey Runner, that grows up to twenty feet in height. These beans, which were already being picked for market, early though it was in the year, are grown in pots in order to spare the soil in the houses, which would presently be required to bear a crop of tomatoes. This question is one of the most important in connection with Guernsey glass culture, and a not uncommon form of sharp practice is for owners of houses to work out the soil they cover and then sell them to unsuspecting English companies, who find that it must be replaced at great expense. Even then, as Mr. Corrie, a well-known resident, informed me, the remedy is not effectual, since the new soil, when carted into the houses, seems to become baked and is 'killed' by the heat. Many experts, therefore, consider digging out to be almost useless, and that the only alternative when the earth has been exhausted, especially by crops of peas and potatoes, is to grow produce in pots. For this pot-work the big growers buy and pile up great heaps of turf, which is largely consumed in the culture of chrysanthemums, among other products. Suitable turf, however, is now beginning to grow scarce in Guernsey.

Enormous sums have been laid out on glass-house work in the island, a form of investment that, in the opinion of some residents, is being considerably overdone. Thus it is not uncommon for carpenters to build greenhouses as a speculation, either on their own land or on land that is mortgaged to them under the peculiar Guernsey system, of which I shall have something to say. Then, if a tenant of the glass-house fails, the speculator obtains possession of them as well as of the land. Sometimes also these houses are jerry-built with dry-rot timber.

I forget the exact cost of a properly constructed and completed house, but it is incredibly low—I believe under £1 per foot run. Every expedient, also, is adopted to combine economy with efficiency. Thus in Mr. Parsons' houses the glass comes down to the ground, and instead of resting on a wall each principal is carried by sunk pillars, which system is said to be a great saving. He also stated that the principal complaints of the Guernsey growers were first, the cost of anthracite, which in 1901, as Mr. Ozanne told us, was 32s. the ton wholesale. Now I presume that it is cheaper, notwithstanding the new coal tax, which I have heard—although of this I am not sure—Channel Island consumers are expected to pay. Their second great grievance is the cost of sea and land carriage to the English markets. They say that there is no competition, and that, therefore, they are forced to pay any charge which the railway and steamship company chooses to inflict upon them. Doubtless this is the case ; but, as I ventured to point out, the problem could be more or less met if the islands agreed together to run their own cargo boats. There seems, however, to be among those concerned, a lack of that unanimity of opinion which is necessary to the success of such a scheme. Also it must be remembered that the Channel Islands trade, as has been proved by frequent disasters—some of them very terrible—is full of risks, which may perhaps justify the owners of ships in charging a high rate of sea carriage.

There are not many farms in Guernsey as we understand the word; but I went over one of forty acres, there quite a considerable holding, on which were actually only two glass-houses. Some of it was unproductive, high-lying furze land, which, poor as it is, would sell any day for £100 an acre—that is, for ten times as much as sound corn land in Suffolk. Only about a fourth of the farm was under the plough, the rest being grass, with a field of lucerne. Cows were the mainstay of the place, and it was pretty to see these docile animals, each of them pegged to her little patch of pasture, since the inhabitants of Guernsey are far too thrifty to allow their cattle to roam at will, treading and fouling much that they do not eat.

The view from the uplands of this farm, as from other spots that I visited in the island, was beautiful, stretching as it did over marsh lands, unmarred by the glittering roofs of greenhouses, to the blue and quiet sea with its fringe of rugged, formidable rocks. Here also, or near to it, stood the one ruined building that I saw in Guernsey, a broken-down, sail-less windmill. It seems that now-a-days but little corn is ground in the island, where, as I have said, practically it has ceased to be cultivated, therefore mills are superfluous. Everywhere I noted the same air of prosperity—in the neat stone cottages, in the charming villas nestling in nooks that overlook the sea, and in the busy streets and quays of St. Peter's Port, the latter crowded with crates of vegetables and fragrant flowers. It is, indeed, pleasant to see a place where, as in Madeira, every yard of ground is made to produce as much as possible; still the general effect is somewhat cramping to the mind, which at times turns with relief to the broad prospect of the surrounding sea. Only in the beautiful park of our host, Lord de Saumarez, with its bending bamboos, its camellia bushes, red and white with waxen flowers, and its stretches of emerald grass dotted with fawn-hued stock, could I ever feel quite alone with Nature. For the rest much of the island has begun to resemble the suburbs of a prosperous town.

From Mr. John Le Messurier, a local lawyer of great experience and repute, I obtained much valuable information as regards the conditions prevalent in Guernsey, and some of its more peculiar customs. He said that the prosperity of the island was increasing rather than diminishing, but he thought that the over-building of glass-houses would sooner or later result in great loss, as the amount of money borrowed upon them was enormous. He gave me many instances, quoting the names of those concerned, of men who had begun with nothing and died, or retired, with considerable fortunes, made, all of them, out of the products of the soil, and this in a place where land seems to rent for £8 the acre, and to sell at from £100 to £500 the acre. Thus one man began as a spade labourer and ended possessed of property valued at £6,000. Another—a woman—made a fortune out of flowers. Another from nothing rose to the enjoyment of £400 a year, and so forth. To industrious beginners the local banks are very liberal in the way of advancing money, often taking the known character of the applicant as their sole security, and I gathered from Mr. Le Messurier that they rarely find their confidence misplaced.

Of the transport question he spoke strongly, saying that since their amalgamation the southern English railways, on which the prosperity of Guernsey really depends, had pressed the island hard, as there was no longer any competition. As regarded the possibility of establishing a rival line of steamers, it would cost £100,000, and so far had gone no further than talk; moreover, in that event it was suggested that the railway company might refuse to carry the produce when it reached the English shore. Also, after an expensive harbour had been built for their convenience, the company had obliged the States—that is, the Guernsey legislative body—to reduce the wharfage charges. It was, however, a proof of the prosperity of the island that in 1901 the harbour debt of £300,000 incurred in 1853 had, with the exception of £20,000, been all paid off. Still the taxation was rising, and in time would be heavier.

The point, however, on which Mr. Le Messurier's information struck me as perhaps most interesting and valuable, was that of the peculiar land tenure of Guernsey with its complications of ' quarters ' and ' *rentes*.' This, for the subject is one upon which the uninstructed person is likely to err, I will give as nearly as possible in the words in which he summed them up. He explained that the local tenure of property can be held either subject to the payment of annual *rentes* or as freehold in perpetuity. Thus a purchase of land may be completed by the immediate payment of the agreed price in cash, or by the payment of a part of the sum, and the conversion of the remainder into corn *rentes*, to be annually liquidated on October 10 in each year. Lastly, the whole of the purchase price may be converted into these *rentes*. In the two latter alternatives— that is, where a part or the whole of the stipulated amount is to be discharged in annual *rentes*—the purchaser becomes to all intents and purposes as fully the proprietor of the estate as he does in the first case, where the entire sum is paid down in cash. In short, so long as the agreed *rentes* are paid, he and his heirs can never be disturbed, but hold the land as freehold for ever. These *rentes* are guaranteed to the vendor on the security of the land sold, and the collateral security of all other properties owned by the purchaser at the time of sale. *Rentes* being transferable also, and such security being always in demand, money can be raised by the sale of them as easily as it could be upon the land itself before they were created. In short, they can be passed from hand to hand, as is often done in the case of tithe-rent charges in England. Thus it comes about that without the necessity of cultivating, or even of remaining in occupation of the soil, the vendor continues to enjoy the income of his estate secured upon that estate itself, of which he can resume possession in case of non-payment. The purchaser, on the other hand, upon the due payment of the agreed *rentes*, becomes the real and perpetual owner of the fee-simple, and thus acquires an interest in the soil far greater and more effectual than that of farmers under any other system of tenure. Mr. Le Messurier pointed out that experience has proved that under this tenure, which might be thought onerous, is, in fact, generated a spirit of industry and economy that results in competence, and even wealth, won from estates which in other countries would often hardly be thought capable of affording a bare sustenance to their occupants.

This power of acquiring land in perpetuity without the actual payment of purchase money is, he said, proved to be of great benefit to the inhabitants of Guernsey. It is, however, obvious that the custom could never have existed without a well-guaranteed and unquestioned security vesting in the vendor of the land. Mr. Le Messurier exemplified the working of the system by the following example : Suppose A. F. to possess land in Guernsey valued at £1,000, which he desires to sell, or, as we say, 'to give to *rentes*,' A. F. would either convey his estate to a purchaser wholly in ' quarters,' receiving no cash, or, as is a more usual fashion, he would receive part of the agreed sum in cash and convert the remainder into annual quarters, payable yearly on October 10, either in wheat or in its equivalent of fixed quarters at the rate of £1 per quarter. The annual value of wheat *rentes* is fixed yearly by the Court at the Easter Chief Pleas in accordance with the average price of wheat between October 1 and April 1. A Guernsey quarter is equivalent to £20 currency. Generally these quarters, when charged upon property, are redeemable by certain instalments at a price varying at from £20 to £24 each, according to the agreement made at the time of sale.

In case this explanation should leave any lingering doubts upon the mind of the reader as to the exact nature of ' quarters,' ' *rentes*,' and the system of land purchase in

Guernsey, since it is really as curious and important as it is intricate, I will give a second explanation of the matter. This I quote from Gardner's 'Guide to Guernsey,' a very admirable little pamphlet, now, I believe, out of print, published in 1885 by the proprietor of a local hotel. Mr. Gardner defines 'quarters' by saying, 'All property for purposes of taxation is technically supposed to be converted into wheat *rentes* at a rate of £25 per quarter, or four quarters to the £100 of capital.' Later on he adds :—

Intimately connected with the land tenure of the island is a system of creating *wheat-rentes* upon real estate. These may be regarded as a kind of permanent mortgage, and as this relation of landlord and tenant is peculiar to the Channel Islands, it may perhaps be most clearly explained to strangers by an example : Suppose that A possesses land valued at, say, £1,200 which he desires to sell, as we should say in England, or *to give to rent* (*bailler à rentes*), as the phrase runs in Guernsey, the following would be the process :—

The vendor A would either convey his estate to B, the purchaser, wholly in quarters, without receiving any cash, or—as is the more usual mode—he would receive, say, one fourth of the price in cash, and convert the remainder into quarters. One Guernsey quarter—in this relationship to landed property—is equivalent to £20 local currency. According to the first arrangement, B would have to pay annually to A £60, being the interest on £1,200, the assumed cost of the estate, at the rate of 5 per cent. per annum ; in the second case he would have to pay annually £45, being the interest on the forty-five quarters created. The reason why it is usual to pay about one fourth of the purchase money in cash is, that such payment may be some guarantee to A that B will faithfully work the estate, and pay the *rentes* regularly. Should the *rentes*, however, fall into arrear, then A, by a process called *saisie*, may totally eject B from the property, and in that case the £300 paid by B when the contract was passed, would be lost to him for ever. In this manner, then, is the vendor or landlord secured in the receipt of the equivalent for which he has parted with the estate. As soon as the contract is executed, however, the property really belongs to B, who can fell timber, convert meadow into arable, or arable into meadow, and perform any and every act that a tenant in fee-simple can do in

England, while the estate thus acquired also descends to the lawful heirs of the purchaser, or can be willed by him if he die without issue. The fundamental difference between this system and the ordinary mortgage is that the vendor can never come upon the purchaser for the capital represented by the quarters, as an English mortgagee can for the money lent. The quarters may, however, be made redeemable by mutual consent ; and under certain conditions, and within the town barriers, they are now compulsorily redeemable by the holder of the property, who can buy up the *rentes* from the original vendor, and so free the estate. But the vendor has no reciprocal power of compulsion against the holder of the property. Again, some *rentes* are not permanently settled at £1 per quarter, but fluctuate with the price of wheat. If corn is high, then the farmer can afford a high *rente* ; if it is low, he is thus relieved from paying more than his crop warrants. Within the past century these variable *rentes* have fluctuated from as high as £2 down to 12s. 6d. per quarter. *Rentes* can also be freely sold and transferred, and are much sought after as investments when secured on substantial properties.

Lucid as is the above exposition of the somewhat involved and difficult matters with which it deals, it will be observed that it gives no clear account of the origin and growth of this system of ' quarters.' Nor indeed was I able to obtain such an account from any expert whom I consulted in the island. When did a quarter first become a quarter, and why ? I asked with an iteration that may have been thought troublesome, to be on various occasions answered at length. Whether it is owing to my own stupidity, or whether the origin of the system is so nebulous that it cannot be defined in words, I know not, but to this moment I confess its details have remained unmastered by me. I gather, however, that rent must have originally been paid in wheat ; that the amount of the payment varied with the quantity and quality of the crop ; and that when money was substituted for produce as a medium for the discharge of this debt, the term ' quarter ' was still retained, the value being arbitrarily fixed at £25 for purposes of taxation, and £20 where landed property is concerned, on which the interest at 5 per cent. is of course £1.

Now, trusting that I have fallen into no pit of error, I will leave the subject of *vergées, rentes,* and *quarters,* remarking only that upon the last of these no dictionaries or encyclopædias that are within my reach deign to throw the smallest light. Perhaps the writers of these also found that 'quarters' are hard to comprehend.

In the old days Guernsey was one of the great havens of refuge for the persecuted Huguenots, who flocked thither in large numbers, especially after the massacre of St. Bartholomew. Probably it is to this beneficent infusion of Huguenot blood that its inhabitants owe much of their enterprise, energy, and other good qualities. Certainly they derive from it the sturdy Protestantism which is so marked a feature in their character. One of the quaintest of the experiences of the visitor to the island is to attend some ancient church, such as that of St. Sampson, and listen to the English service read word for word in French.

## JERSEY

THE island of Jersey is much larger than that of Guernsey, its area amounting to about 28,700 acres, of which some 25,000 are under cultivation. Its soil also is better, while the climate is practically the same; that is to say, one of the most favourable in our latitudes for the purposes of agricultural production. The country varies very much. Thus on the east it is wooded and the soil is richest; on the west it is light and sometimes sandy. On the north it rises steeply from the sea; on the south the slope is gradual. Narrow valleys intersect it, leading to stretches of low-lying land that are among the earliest and best in the island. As in Guernsey, the holdings are small, averaging, according to Colonel Le Cornu, perhaps the greatest agricultural author-ity in Jersey, from fifteen to twenty acres. Many, however, are under ten, and but very few above fifty acres. The same gentleman states in a paper on the Jersey dairy industry, read by him in 1901 before the local Agricultural Society, that on an average farm of twenty acres, (reckoning $2\frac{1}{4}$ vergées to the acre, as against $2\frac{1}{2}$ in Guernsey), which is not given up to grass or fruit, the holding would be divided much as follows :—

|                      |   |   |   |   | Vergées |
|----------------------|---|---|---|---|---------|
| Hay and pasture      | . | . | . | . | 20      |
| Potatoes and roots   | . | . | . | . | 15      |
| Corn                 | . | . | . | . | 10      |

This specimen farm would be stocked with two horses, twelve cows and heifers, and about six pigs.

The agricultural returns of the island for 1900 showed

TYPICAL GUERNSEY COW

that it was divided among 2,797 occupiers of land, and that the proportions of the various crops and live stock were as shown by the following table :—

|  | Vergées |
|---|---|
| Corn crops . . . . . . | 5,184¾ |
| Potatoes and roots . . . . . | 17,020 |
| Vetches, tares, and lucerne . . . | 290¼ |
| Bare fallow land, from which no crop was taken . . . . . . | 418¼ |
| Clover and rye grass : |  |
|    For hay . . . . . . | 7,866 |
|    Not for hay . . . . . | 4,527¼ |
| Permanent grass (exclusive of furze and heathland) : |  |
|    For hay . . . . . . | 3,257¼ |
|    Not for hay . . . . . | 5,787 |
| Small fruit . . . . . . | 252¼ |
| Orchards . . . . . . . | 1,837¼ |
| Market gardens . . . . . | 182¾ |
| Nursery gardens . . . . . | 47¾ |

### Live Stock

| Horses for agricultural purposes . . | 2,186 |
|---|---|
|    ,,    ,,    unbroken | 157 |
| Cows and heifers of all ages in milk or in calf . . . . . . . | 6,762 |
| Cattle other than those in milk or in calf, two years old and above . . . | 732 |
| Cattle under two years of age (including calves) . . . . . . . | 4,397 |

As Guernsey lives and prospers upon fruits, daffodils, and arums, so Jersey grows rich upon the potato. All of us are familiar with the well-shaped, round, white-fleshed new potato of the London restaurants, a very tasteless esculent, quite different, indeed, from that which we raise in our own gardens. On the point of flavour, however, the market is careless. Among the great public of consumers the sole requisites seem to be that the potato shall be good to look at and obtainable in advance of its natural season ; whether or not it is good to eat matters very little. So to satisfy that public the Jersey growers invented the 'Royal Fluke,' which is early, prolific, and handsome. That their customers are pleased is proved by the fact that they paid to the said growers in the year 1900 a sum of £445,872 in exchange for 54,012 tons of 'Royal Jersey Fluke' potatoes, produced from the 25,000 acres which are under cultivation in the island, or such proportion of them as are given up to this crop.

There appears to be no information to show the exact date of the introduction of the potato into Jersey, but this seems to have been somewhere about the year 1775, at which date the parsnip was largely grown. In 1811 experiments began to be made with the view of proving the possibility of producing two crops of potatoes on the same land during a single year. From that time forward the culture of this root increased continually until it has reached its present huge proportions. Some authorities, however, are of opinion that, in face of the growing competition in France, Cornwall, and elsewhere, the Jersey potato has seen its best days ; that it is 'as high up the ladder as it can go.'

By way of exemplifying the importance of the trade, I reprint here the statistics of the Jersey potato crop for 1900, together with a comparative statement of the number of tons exported and their value from the year 1883. The reader will observe how the value per ton—that between April 30 and May 12 amounted to £31 4s.—between July 16 and 21 sank to £3 0s. 8d.

Statistics of the Jersey Potato Crop—Season 1900,

*giving the number of packages and weight exported, also the average price per week at the States' Weighbridge (St. Helier), viz. :—*

| Weeks | Date of Shipments | No. of Packages | Tons | Average weekly price per ton | | | Weekly Totals | | |
|---|---|---|---|---|---|---|---|---|---|
| | | | | £ | s. | d. | £ | s. | d. |
| 1 | April 30 to May 12 | 7,449 | 185 | 31 | 4 | 0 | 5,772 | 0 | 0 |
| 2 | May 14 ,, ,, 19 | 26,499 | 885 | 19 | 10 | 0 | 17,257 | 10 | 0 |
| 3 | ,, 23 ,, ,, 26 | 50,899 | 1,700 | 16 | 5 | 0 | 27,625 | 0 | 0 |
| 4 | ,, 28 ,, June 2 | 98,838 | 4,942 | 10 | 18 | 10 | 54,073 | 14 | 4 |
| 5 | June 4 ,, ,, 9 | 184,077 | 10,226 | 8 | 0 | 4 | 81,978 | 8 | 8 |
| 6 | ,, 11 ,, ,, 16 | 201,786 | 11,210 | 7 | 3 | 0 | 80,151 | 10 | 0 |
| 7 | ,, 18 ,, ,, 23 | 194,046 | 11,414 | 7 | 7 | 4 | 84,083 | 2 | 8 |
| 8 | ,, 25 ,, ,, 30 | 154,845 | 9,109 | 7 | 11 | 8 | 69,076 | 11 | 8 |
| 9 | July 2 ,, July 7 | 61,771 | 3,633 | 6 | 3 | 6 | 22,433 | 15 | 6 |
| 10 | ,, 9 ,, ,, 14 | 11,686 | 688 | 4 | 17 | 8 | 3,359 | 14 | 8 |
| 11 | ,, 16 ,, ,, 21 | 347 | 20 | 3 | 0 | 8 | 60 | 13 | 4 |
| | Totals . . | 992,243 | 54,012 | — | | | 445,872 | 0 | 10 |

*Comparative Statement.*

| Years | Tons | Value | | |
|---|---|---|---|---|
| | | £ | s. | d. |
| 1883 | 36,468 | 262,472 | 3 | 4 |
| 1884 | 53,655 | 375,841 | 18 | 0 |
| 1885 | 48,524 | 319,464 | 3 | 4 |
| 1886 | 64,820 | 309,155 | 6 | 11 |
| 1887 | 50,073 | 423,888 | 18 | 10 |
| 1888 | 60,988 | 242,109 | 11 | 8 |
| 1889 | 52,700 | 264,153 | 15 | 0 |
| 1890 | 54,109 | 293,681 | 9 | 2 |
| 1891 | 66,810 | 487,642 | 1 | 8 |
| 1892 | 66,332 | 376,535 | 15 | 10 |
| 1893 | 57,762 | 327,366 | 13 | 4 |
| 1894 | 60,605 | 462,895 | 10 | 5 |
| 1895 | 54,290 | 359,989 | 4 | 6 |
| 1896 | 64,583 | 435,192 | 0 | 6 |
| 1897 | 53,555 | 402,274 | 9 | 10 |
| 1898 | 56,227 | 338,269 | 0 | 0 |
| 1899 | 65,040 | 330,421 | 0 | 0 |
| 1900 | 54,012 | 445,872 | 0 | 10 |

Jersey, however, has a second string to her agricultural bow—her cow. Most people who know anything of country life, are familiar with this beautiful, deer-like animal with its gazelle eyes, its fawn-hued skin, and its slender legs, the fancy cattle of the rich man and the model farm. Agriculturists know also that—as their large, level udders, set well forward and back, denote—these cows are splendid milkers ; indeed, when in full flush a good one will give as much as five gallons a day. For this reason, and because of its extreme richness, a proportion of Jerseys is often kept with herds of Shorthorns in order that their milk may raise the general standard of quality. But they have no other use. Once myself I kept a few Jerseys, only to abandon them because they proved impossible to fat ; nor indeed did they do well in our severe Norfolk climate.

As Captain Le Brocq, an enterprising and advanced agriculturist in the island, of whose views I shall speak more at length later in this chapter, said to me, 'the Jersey is a one-purpose cow—a machine to manufacture milk.' As he pointed out also, although it is true that the very pick of the cows will still fetch £80 or £100 for exportation, the average price for the inferior animals is but £12 or £14. Again, the male calves are quite useless, the custom being to knock them on the head and to throw them to the manure heap. One large farmer explained to me that the milk of the cow is worth 15s. a week, whereas after being kept on her for a month, drinking up most of the milk, the calf only fetches from 10s. to 12s. So the poor little creatures have to go, except, of course, a fortunate few which are saved for bulls.

On the day following our arrival on the island, I accepted the kind invitation of Mr. Perrée, the secretary of the Agricultural Society, to inspect a butter competition which was being carried out under his superintendence in a large, cool building. To watch the various operations of separating the milk and churning the cream till it was converted into the golden-coloured Jersey butter, which, by the way, is often absent from the breakfast tables of the hotels, was a very interesting experience. It appears, however, that these competitions are no longer so popular as they used to be.

Thus at the same time in the previous year there were thirty candidates for the prizes, whereas on the occasion of our visit in 1901 there were but nine. Mr. Perrée attributed this falling off to the engrossment of the islanders in the cultivation of the potato, which has resulted in the comparative neglect of the Jersey cattle industry. The best cow of the nine by the way—a four-year-old animal—produced 2 lb. 11 oz. of excellent butter from milk given by her during the twenty-four hours of trial.

After the tests, accompanied by Mr. Perrée, we visited the farm of one of the largest cowkeepers and early potato-growers in the island. Mr. Durrell—for that was our host's name—is also, I may mention, one of the few in Jersey who have taken up vegetable and flower growing under glass. On leaving St. Helier the horses—a pair are always used in Jersey—have to face a steep climb up to the valley-seamed tableland which occupies the centre of the island, the road running past several fine and picturesque residences set upon commanding points. As we went Mr. Perrée and some gentlemen whom we met in his company upon this and other occasions, including Colonel Le Cornu, gave me much interesting information. They said that the rent of Jersey land if good was about £12 the acre per annum, that is, more than the fee-simple value of tens of thousands of acres in England. If the landlords cannot obtain this sum from tenants, they will often take the farms in hand and work them themselves.

Potatoes upon the earliest lands will sometimes bring in a return of £90 or over, an acre, though they may not realise more than £30 under special conditions. Competition is the great danger ahead. Thus the labour supply is for the most part drawn from Brittany; and when the Bretons have thoroughly mastered the Jersey methods of growing, they return to their own country and put them into practice in the neighbourhood of St. Malo. When it chances, however, that the mainland is visited by spring frosts which the island escapes, Jersey makes a great profit, and in the same way those of the local growers who do not happen to be afflicted by this scourge succeed much better than their fellows, for here the fall of frost is often so patchy that it will smite one field and spare another fifty yards away.

What really gives the island its prosperity, however, is the fact that it can as a rule put its produce on the English market a fortnight earlier than any competing district. Still the potato remains a speculative crop, and the cost of its cultivation enormous, owing largely to the heavy expense of artificial manures. Indeed, the total outlay is said to amount to as much as £31 per acre. Captain Le Brocq, it will be seen, puts it at from £40 to £50 the acre. For these reasons the industry is not quite so popular as it was, with the result, as I was informed, that some leases at Christmas, 1900, were renewed at a 20 per cent. reduction of rent. In short, the great prosperity of Jersey has to a certain extent received a check. Especially, as I was told, is this the case in the matter of the cattle trade, the English market being no longer what it was. As all the best blood is now represented across the Channel, owners of Jersey herds there are able to replenish them from other English herds, of which the animals fulfil the strict requirements of the English Jersey Cattle Society. Thus it comes about that the demand for choice bulls and heifers has fallen off considerably, although of course a number of the finest beasts are still exported.

Perhaps the best evidence upon this point, however, which to some extent contradicts, or at any rate qualifies, the information that was given to me in the island, is to be found in the Royal Jersey Agricultural Society's Report for 1900, which says :—

The cattle export trade has on the whole been satisfactory. A fair demand prevailed during the spring and summer, though towards the autumn it somewhat abated, and was not equal to the corresponding season in former years. . . . The continent of Europe, including Russia and Belgium, have purchased a few small lots of cattle, whilst an experimental shipment has been made to Brazil, the outcome of which will be watched with interest. Since the last report was issued 182 head have been exported to the United States of America, and judging by the result of Mr. T. S. Cooper's sale of stock imported in 1899, and sold by auction in May of this year, there is a good demand in that country for first-class cattle, but animals of average merit will not pay their expenses of exportation. It is necessary to repeat what has been said in your Committee's reports of the two preceding years, namely, that there is a continued demand, at remunerative prices, from England for animals fit to win at the large shows.

To sum up the matter, it would seem that the best Jersey cows still pay well to export, but of course the best of anything are rare. For the moderate animals—that is, those that are produced in the greatest number—the market is no longer remunerative.

Mr. Durrell is the owner of the (for Jersey) enormous area of 200 vergées of land, or eighty-nine English acres, according to the Jersey measure of $2\frac{1}{4}$ vergées to the acre. On this he kept sixty milch cows, besides young stock, and employed twenty men, all Bretons—for none but French labour is available—at a wage of from 15s. to 18s. per week, with extra moneys for the potato lifting, which answers to our harvest.

At the farmhouse we were told that its master was engaged in planting potatoes. Walking up a steep lane, we came to a field of about four acres. The scene was busy, about a dozen men being employed in the various operations connected with planting its friable, chocolate-coloured soil. If the potato is to flourish as it should, it requires a great deal of attention. First, I must repeat that there are two different classes of potato land, the early and the less early, the former being much more valuable than the latter. Indeed, some of these lands, such as those of L'Etac, which I hope to describe, fetch as much as £16 or £17 an acre rent. This earliness or the contrary is determined by the liability of the land to frost, though why some fields should escape this scourge and others suffer from its attack is, as I have said, difficult to explain.

The aspect and altitude have to do with it without doubt, but the question of subsoil must also be considered, farms which lie upon warm red gravel proving more immune than others with a colder bottom. Further, lands over which the air moves continually from the sea, preventing the fall of the frost, are safer than others where it remains stagnant. Shelter from the east is also desirable, not, as the reader might think, because of its protection from cold winds, but for the reason that it prevents the sun from shining upon the tender plants before the frost particles have melted in the soft air of morning. Should these be violently dispersed by the direct action of heat, the curious result is that the young sprouts of the tuber, which would otherwise escape unharmed, turn black and perish.

To show the extraordinary difference in value between the earliest and the later land, I may emphasise the facts, which will be found detailed in the table printed on page 87, that potatoes sold before May 12, 1900, fetched £31 a ton ; those between May 12 and May 19, £19 a ton ; between May 23 and May 26, £16 a ton ; between May 28 and June 2, nearly £11 a ton ; between June 4 and June 9, £8 a ton ; and so on down to the wretched figure of £3 a ton between July 16 and July 21. Owing to the backwardness of the spring the season of 1901 was, however, from ten days to a fortnight later than that of 1900, the weather at the date of our visit on March 13 and subsequent days being intensely cold and sunless.

Mr. Durrell's land, although not of the earliest, is early, and therefore very valuable.

The expense of potato cultivation is, as I have pointed out, enormous. According to Mr. Durrell—for it is instructive to note the varying estimates of individual growers—allowing for and inclusive of a rent of only £4 a vergée, or £9 the acre, it amounts to about £16 4s. per vergée, or £36 9s. the acre. This is not wonderful when we remember that it

A FARMHOUSE, GUERNSEY

COMBINED JERSEY POTATO CULTIVATOR AND CLOD CUTTER,
WITH SEED POTATOES IN BOXES          *Page 93*

is not unusual to dress these lands with from twenty to
thirty tons of farmyard manure per acre, *plus* half a ton
of crushed bones, *plus* a ton of 'guano,' costing from £7 to
£8. Further, the land must receive various scarifyings and
ploughings, one of them known as *la grande charrue*—to
effect which some six horses are necessary—to a depth of no
less than 14 in. The result is a tilth as fine as that of a
garden-bed, and free from even the most inconspicuous weed.
There is another result—that nowadays the potatoes never
suffer from disease, though some suggest that this is because
they are out of the ground before the disease appears.
Further, they can be planted in the same soil for a number
of years, of which the limit has not been reached, without
any deterioration in the quantity or quality of the crop,
living as they do in practice upon the yearly replenishment
of manures, rather than upon the soil itself.

This was the method of planting as I saw it. First
little trenches are drawn on the fine surface of the soil to a
depth of about 2½ in., and at a distance from each other of
from 15 in. to 18 in. Along these trenches go men scattering
with the hand from buckets which they carry, the grey
guano that contains among other ingredients about 8 per
cent. of sulphate of ammonia, 20 to 23 per cent. of soluble
phosphates, and 2 to 5 per cent. of potash. I should have
mentioned, however, that before the furrows are drawn the
land receives a final treatment from a cultivating machine of
peculiar ingenuity, which is worked by three horses. This
instrument is, as to its fore part, a cultivator with the usual
hook-shaped teeth that tear the soil to a depth of about six
inches; and, as to its hind part, a ridged iron roll of very
curious construction which cuts and grinds every little clod
to powder.

When the manure has been sown the potatoes are set
by any hands who may be available down to those of little
children. These seed tubers, by the way, are started in
boxes, fitted with handles for convenience of carrying, which
are placed on the rafters in the byres that the warmth from

the cows below may foster the growth of the germinating shoots, which must be neither too long nor too short at the date of planting. If too long they are apt to break; if too short the harvest is retarded. Large potatoes, which are halved before setting, are started thus about September; small ones, which are not cut, at Christmas. After the seed has been set with carefulness and regularity, the green shoots pointing upwards, a blunt-edged one-horse plough, with a specially designed share, is passed along the row in such fashion that it buries the tubers to the appointed depth beneath a coating of fine soil. Afterwards the field is raked by hand, which completes the process of seeding. As soon as the potatoes have been lifted in the month of June mangold is sown and yields a heavy crop which is pulled in October. On some very early lands, indeed, three crops are taken—two of potatoes, following each other, and one of roots—but this is unusual.

Having finished our inspection of the planting, we visited the cow-stables, which were large, good, and, like most of the outbuildings of the island, solidly built in stone. Here in an endless succession were tied up the beautiful Jersey cows and, when they were not in use, the eleven horses employed upon the farm. These cows were fed upon bran, hay, carrots, and parsnips. The straw Mr. Durrell buys—it comes from France in bales—but in most seasons he grows all the hay he requires. As he has only eighteen vergées of meadow land, at first this seemed to me almost incredible, considering the number of stock which must be fed. The mystery is more or less explained, however, by the fact that good land in Jersey produces five tons of hay to the acre at a single cut; indeed, so thick does the grass grow that it cannot be mown by any English-made machine. From the cowsheds we went on to the glass-houses, that need not be particularly described, as their fashion and contents are similar to those in Guernsey, of which I have already spoken. These houses, heating pipes included, cost 25s. a foot run, their width being 18 ft. When it is necessary to change the soil in them they are dug out to a depth of 2½ ft. The fuel used is anthracite and coke mixed.

Bidding farewell to this interesting and prosperous farm, we paid a visit to Mr. Perrée's cows, some of them famous prize-winners, and valued at £100 a piece or even more. They were pegged in a row on a grass field, and beautiful to look at, but to the eye of an English stock-keeper very small and light-boned. In considering these cattle a suspicion will force itself upon the mind that they are too much inbred; indeed, as the island is small and no fresh blood may be imported, in-breeding cannot be avoided.

To take some examples of the herd. For cow No. 1 £100 had been refused. Cow No. 2, which was remarkable for the perfect shape of its bag, took the local championship prize. No. 3, a small heifer, was the only living grand-daughter of a very famous bull. She cost £100. And so forth.

On Mr. Perrée's farm I saw a patch of the famous and imposing Jersey cabbage that grows to a height of six feet or more. Of the stems of these cabbages walking-sticks are made, while their leaves are culled to feed the pigs. Here also was a layer sown after wheat in the spring of 1899. In the summer of that year it yielded two tons per vergée, or four tons and a half of hay per acre. The cutting, a task which two gangs of men abandoned, cost 15s. per acre. This layer receives about fourteen tons of farmyard manure the acre per annum, and was expected to stand for three or four years. Mr. Perrée fed his cows with cotton cake, but most Jersey men prefer bran for this purpose.

The next farm I visited was that of Mr. R. Peppin, a highly educated gentleman who, if I remember right, in company with his brother, had taken to this pastoral occupation for the benefit of his health. We found him setting potatoes, to which he applies 12 cwt. of guano per vergée, as against the 18 cwt. used by Mr. Durrell. On this holding, which I think measured thirty vergées, or about thirteen acres, were kept six cows, seven heifers, and two horses. Here we saw a little meadow lying along the banks of a rivulet, which is irrigated by allowing water from the stream, in which have been steeped quantities of cow-manure, to overflow it, with the result that an enormous crop of grass is obtained. Mr. Peppin reckoned his harvest of potatoes at an average of ten and a half tons to the acre, but sometimes, I believe, as much as twenty tons are obtained. After the potatoes are off he grows a crop of mangolds on the same ground, which keep the cattle through the winter. From his layers he obtains, first year, two cuts of hay, after which they are grazed; second year, one cut of hay and the grazing; third year, the grazing only. He ploughs to a depth of fourteen inches with a strength of six or eight horses. Here we were told that the French labourer is gradually ousting the Jersey labourer, as the Frenchman is more thrifty, harder working, and closer living. Moreover, he will work for a master, while the Jersey man, as a rule, will only work for himself.

Another very interesting holding was that of Mr. P. Bree, of La Rocque, who farmed thirty acres, of which twenty vergées were under potatoes, ten vergées in wheat, and the remainder under meadow hay, parsnips, and mangolds. Of stock he kept from sixteen to twenty cows, from fifty to sixty pigs, and three horses. Needless to say his farming is of a most intense order. Straw and cake are bought; hay is a scarce commodity, although the grass land devoted to it produces five tons to the acre, but the heavy crops of roots secured are sufficient for the needs of the farm. On these thirty acres were employed eight men; that is, roughly, a man to ten vergées of land, which on places that are cultivated like a garden, is no more than is required. Indeed, some of it is garden, two vergées being devoted to gooseberries of a new variety, and an apple orchard. Also there was about half an acre of daffodils, chiefly of the lovely Princeps kind, and pears were grown—Doyenne de Comice and the famous Jersey Chaumontel. Tomatoes were also cultivated upon this farm. The price realised for the second or outside crop of this fruit by Jersey growers seemed to be about 2*d*. the pound.

Here, while looking at the cows, it was explained to me that the horns of Jersey cattle are trained to shape by means of bands tied across the forehead, which are kept on for a month or six weeks while the animals are young. On this farm we saw the Jersey system of draining low-lying land, which is very simple and effective. First a trench is dug to a depth of three feet, then it is filled in with stones, and the drain is complete.

On one day of our stay in the island Colonel Le Cornu was so kind as to take me on a very interesting expedition to visit various farms, including one in the famous early district of L'Etac. The scenery as we drove over hill and vale to reach our host's house was singularly charming. Every inch of ground seems to be cultivated, sometimes, as in Madeira, by means of terraces built on the steep hillsides. Another instance of the thrifty character of the Jersey husbandman is to be observed in the curious method of growing trees along the sides of the roads or the divisions of fields. These are so severely pruned that only a tuft of foliage is allowed to remain at the top. The effect is not beautiful, but the custom has a twofold reason : to prevent shade falling on the land, which lessens its produce, and to obtain the boughs for fuel.

In sheltered nooks here and there we saw pleasant-looking country-houses. These houses, by the way—and the remark applies to all districts of the island—are not so well filled or so valuable as once they were. Formerly both Guernsey and Jersey were favourite places of residence for English families who wished to economise. Now the islands are no longer very cheap to live in, except in the matter of spirits and tobacco. Meat, on the contrary, is dear, while butter in Guernsey costs 2*s*. the pound. Also domestic servants other than Frenchwomen are practically unattainable. Moreover, the dreadful shipping catastrophes of recent years, to say nothing of the inconveniences of the

midnight passage, have frightened the public to such an
extent that, as I was informed, the hotels have been seriously
affected in their business.  One gentleman said to me that
strangers have come to believe that if they are tired of life
the best thing they can do is to take a trip to the Channel
Islands, while residents find it difficult to persuade their
friends to visit them.  All these causes combined keep
people away, with the result that at the present time the
islands are even more self-contained and conservative than
they were in past generations.

As we drove Colonel Le Cornu pointed out some land that
had been sold about a year before by auction.  It only contained forty-eight vergées, or 21⅓ acres, yet with the house
on it it fetched £5,760—for agricultural purposes, be it
remembered !  He told us also that the reason why swedes
are not grown is that they would get ' finger-and-toe ' on old
potato ground ; therefore mangolds, which do not suffer in
this way, are invariably planted.

On our road to L'Etac we passed the holdings of Messrs.
Duval Brothers, one of whom farmed fifty vergées and the
other, at whose place we stopped, sixty vergées, or about
twenty-five acres.  On this patch of ground, in addition to the
crops it bears, he kept no fewer than thirty cows and heifers,
in which—if I remember right—he carried on an export trade
with America.  Here we saw in practice the system of which
I have spoken, whereby the warmth of the cow-stables is used
to start the seed potato into activity, the tubers being placed
in trays that are set on racks above the animals.  This is
another instance of the ingenious economy of the Jerseyman.
Mr. Duval informed us that during the following week he
was going to ' cut the seaweed,' an ocean harvest which
furnishes a valuable manure for the land.  As the system
of cultivation practised here and on some other farms was
similar to that on those which I have already described, it
is not necessary that I should set out its details.

Driving across the black marsh and commonage of
St. Ouen we came to the district of L'Etac, named from the

rock which is one of the most curious and noticeable on the coast of Jersey. The land of L'Etac, which sixty years ago was the poorest in the island, is now the most valuable, owing to the extraordinary earliness of its potato yield. From soil such as we saw on the farm of Mr. Hacquoil which we visited, three crops can be taken in a single season, one of potatoes, one of barley—which is reaped in June —and one of roots. The subsoil, that lies about 3 ft. from the surface, is red gravel or decomposed granite, which is very favourable to the growth of potatoes. The situation may be described as a flat plain running down to the sea, swept with the mellow ocean air and bounded to the north and east by high granite hills. It is the existence of these hills that makes it so early, since if frost falls upon the land at the foot of them it melts before the sun strikes the sheltered fields. On lands that lack this advantage the hot rays of morning striking the frost-covered foliage burn and kill the plant. Thus it comes about that such lands will fetch a rent of £17 10s. per acre, and increase yearly in value. For instance, a field of about three and a half acres was pointed out to me which thirty years ago was worth £590. The year previous to my visit this same field sold for £1,500.

Potatoes on the medium early ground such as that of Mr. Durrell were, it will be remembered, in process of planting. Here on Mr. Hacquoil's farm they had been in for over a month, and were already showing above the ground. The spring in 1901, however, was very late in Jersey as in England and elsewhere. Thus in L'Etac the appearance of the potatoes had been delayed ten days beyond the usual date. On this farm, which comprises thirty vergées—we should call it a market-garden in England— we saw some Breton women at work. One of them was topping and tailing beet, and another engaged in breaking granite with a hammer. To the visitor from England, where for the most part women will no longer perform even the lightest agricultural task, this sight was strange.

Mr. Hacquoil had some splendid cows of the famous

Mona blood. One of these, an animal with a big frame and a wonderful bag, was producing five gallons of milk a day, and when in flush gave up to six gallons.

After leaving L'Etac we visited the beautiful manor of St. Ouen, which is owned by Colonel Malet de Carteret. This is indeed a lovely spot, surrounded by deep ravines of grass and wood through which runs water. The castle, which was undergoing repair, is of very ancient date, having been built by Renault de Carteret in the twelfth century. It is moated and approached through a massive gateway, and possesses a splendid hall from which a grand oak staircase leads to the tower and rooms above. This residence, with its surrounding grounds, was the most impressive place that I saw in Jersey.

At St. Peter's, where Colonel Le Cornu lives, I visited the school. It is under Government control and inspection, and receives pecuniary assistance from the State. In Jersey, however, education is not, I gather, entirely free as in England, since it seems that each child pays threepence to fivepence a week according to the school standard to which it belongs. I was told that there is no difficulty in collecting these fees. The children appear to be remarkably intelligent, and some of their original drawings that hung framed upon the wall were well worthy of notice.

We ended the day by inspecting Colonel Le Cornu's cattle that stood in beautifully arranged buildings, and were of the usual excellent quality. Here I examined the milking vessels which are used in Jersey. In England, as the reader knows, milking is done into an open pail, with the result that much dust and other refuse often enter it which it would be desirable to exclude. Not so in this more advanced island. Here the vessels are round and have covers. Moreover, straining cloths are fixed across the mouths to prevent the entry of any foreign substance and to break the force of the milk as it is stripped into the vessel. Near these buildings stands a curious dovecote dating from the feudal times, and not far away a single field was pointed out to me with an easterly aspect which, however much the neighbouring lands may be afflicted, is for some mysterious reason never smitten with frost. The selling value of land in the neighbourhood of St. Peter seemed to be about £225 the acre.

I will close my remarks on Jersey with a short summary of the views expressed to me by Captain Philip Le Brocq, a well-known agriculturist, whose opinions seemed on some points to vary from those that are common in the island. Thus, as I have already stated, he was no whole-souled admirer of the Jersey cattle, and did not appear to think that the trade in them will always continue profitable. The average price of 1,200 exported during 1900 was, he said, not £15, from which must be deducted the transport costs of from £2 to £3 a head. Most of the balance left in the island, which I understood produces about 5,000 calves a year, were, he said, useless for meat, although a good many were slaughtered for export to Guernsey. In England, he added, they have already bulls and cows of the best blood, and can hire land for as many shillings the acre as the islanders pay pounds. 'How, then, can we compete with them?' Captain Le Brocq would like to see the present laws against the importation of cattle abolished. He thought it would be a good thing to bring them in for fatting purposes, instancing the fact that if he could feed bullocks on cake it would save him more than £200 a year in artificial manure.

As it was, the Jersey calves will not fat, and the last 1,500 or so that had been slaughtered did not realise an average of 15s. a head. The island bulls were, he declared, inbred and small. The 'Americans have ruined us' by picking up and 'booming' certain strains, with the result that to satisfy the demand, the Jersey stockowners breed into that strain until they lose the best characteristics of the race. The land, he considered, was decreasing in value, although it still commanded such enormous rents and there was plenty of money in the island. He seemed to think that the legislature would be the better for some new blood, as those in power, many of whom had never been out of the island, would tolerate nothing new.

Jersey he called the 'Isle of White Slavery,' since during the potato season men worked from 3 A.M. to 10 P.M. I gather, however, that he referred to farmers slaving on their own account, since he said also that where there is money to be earned capitalists with from £1,400 to £1,600 a year are to be seen toiling in their shirt-sleeves. The cost of the French labour he put at from 12s. to 14s. a week, adding that what a Frenchman will do for £1 the Englishman, by which I suppose he meant the Jerseyman, will not do for 25s. or 30s. He said that the heavy crops of hay which are obtained exhaust the soil, and to get five tons the acre you must put much of that value into the land in manure. As regarded the flower trade, he considered it a fashion, but that the early blooms will always pay. For the rest Lincolnshire could compete with Jersey in flowers.

Himself he grew a great quantity of potatoes, many of them for seed, which he sold as high as £14 a ton. He also grew for market on the early land, the seed being produced upon his late land. The advantages of the early land were, he said, (1) the higher price; (2) the absence of disease which does not develop so soon; (3) the certainty of a good second crop and perhaps a third crop to follow. The cost of producing an acre of potatoes he put at from £40 to £50, and the return at £100, while the manure required per acre was a ton of guano, half a ton of bones, and thirty tons of farmyard muck. He considered also that Cheshire was pressing Jersey hard in the potato trade. Still he thought that there was more to be feared from English competition with flowers and grapes, which reached market in a better state and at a lower cost than those grown in Guernsey and Jersey. His general conclusion was that the early lands— say half the total acreage—would hold their price, but that the later lands must fall very heavily, and that ' these islands have seen their best days.'

Many Jersey men, and others who have studied the local conditions, among whom I may number myself, will think Captain Le Brocq's views too pessimistic. Certainly in England we should be happy if we only found ourselves called upon to face such somewhat shadowy signs of agricultural decay. Still they represent one shade of local opinion, even if it be the darkest, and are therefore well worthy of record.

I can only state in conclusion that for my part here, as in Guernsey, I was amazed at the prosperity of the place. That so small an area of land can produce so much wealth is nothing short of astonishing. It is true, as I have shown, that the inquirer hears some grumblings and fears for the future ; but when on the top of them he sees a little patch of twenty-three and one-third acres of land, such as I have instanced, and is informed that quite recently it sold at auction for £5,760, to be used, not for building sites, but for the cultivation of potatoes, he is perhaps justified in drawing his own conclusions. Even on the supposition that these values have touched high-water mark, and that the tide of agricultural wealth may be expected to recede to some extent, the industrious husbandmen of Jersey are, he feels, in no danger of immediate ruin.

Doubtless they are greatly favoured by climate, soil, and other circumstances. Still, it is safe to conclude that the facts that they own the land they till, and work upon it with the intelligence and energy which in every clime men will devote to their immediate and peculiar interests, are the mainsprings of their success.

## SUSSEX

THE beautiful sea-bounded shire of Sussex, which measures seventy-six miles in length by twenty-seven in breadth, and contains about 933,200 acres, belongs chiefly to the chalk foundation, that is in the south of the county. Here run the Downs for a length of fifty miles, with a breadth of seven miles and an altitude of about 500 feet. To the east are lowlands and marshes, and to the north lies the great area of the Wealden. Its agricultural products are various. Hops in the east, wood on the highlands, market gardens in the Worthing district, sheep on the South Downs (from which the famous breed is named), cattle in the lowlands, and wheat on the Wealden clay—such are the general characteristics of the county.

The agricultural districts of West Sussex, whither I travelled from the Channel Islands, lying as they do round the cathedral town of Chichester, are by nature divided into two sections. The southernmost of these—a belt of land varying from four to about seven miles in breadth, which stretches from the sea coast towards the South Downs—is very fertile, containing, it is said, some of the best wheat-growing soil in England. The northern portion, on the contrary, where the hill farms lie, consists of poor, sticky, chalk land, for the most part surrounded by beechwoods, and only capable, according to the melancholy accounts of those who farm it, of producing but little grass and less corn.

Although my expectations of these hill farms were not great, on the lowlands I hoped to find prosperity, for surely if farming can flourish in any part of England it should flourish here. The climate is good and sunny, the soil is bounteous, the markets are plentiful and close. Brighton, Portsmouth, and London all lie within two hours' rail of Chichester, nor are any of the districts distant from a station.

To a certain extent I was not disappointed. Undoubtedly, in some cases where the capital is ample, intelligence and enterprise are great, the land in good heart, not over-rented, and devoted chiefly to producing milk, butter, and sheep, there is prosperity. No one, for instance, who walks over a farm like that of Mr. Pitts, with its splendid herds of pure-bred Guernseys and Jerseys—much bigger boned here than they are on their native islands—its steam butter-factory, turning out 700 lb. of butter a week, and its flocks of carefully managed poultry, can fail to feel prosperity even through the north-east wind that in the cold spring season of my visit howled across those naked fields.

Yet Mr. Pitts himself did not seem enthusiastic or confident as to the position of the industry, since he remarked of the farmers of the district that they were all hard hit. Upon his farm of 500 acres I spent an interesting afternoon. In the main he is a dairy farmer, and most of the produce of his ninety cows, pure and cross-bred Guernseys mixed, which he valued at from £17 to £20 apiece, goes, I believe, to London. Besides the cows there were about fifty head of young stock, but he stated that the meat of these Channel Islands cattle runs to yellow fat, which the butchers do not like. It fetches no more than from 3s. to 4s. the stone. At a week old the calves, which are fed on Thorley's food and separated milk, sell for about £1 apiece. The cows, that give an average yield of two gallons of milk a day, receive no cake. Their rations consist of oat straw and hay chaff steamed in a special apparatus for half an hour as a pre-ventive of indigestion ; mangolds, beanmeal, oatmeal, and bran. The labourers upon this farm received 14s. a week, with double wages at harvest time, and the cowmen 17s. a week. Personally, Mr. Pitts said, living as they did upon the borders of Chichester, they were in luck about labour. But upon this subject complaints were general. Skilled men could not be got, and nearly all the young fellows went away to the towns at the age of fifteen or sixteen, so that only boys and old men were left. The Sunday milking was a great grievance; in towns there was no Sunday work. He declared that if it went on, it would be impossible to find the men to milk. Still, on the whole, they were in better case than some other districts. Farmers, he thought, who chose to work could still make a living at the prevailing rents of from 25s. to 30s. an acre, although wages had risen so much and the margin of profit was very fine.

In addition to his cows Mr. Pitts also kept Southdown sheep, in these parts practically the only breed. We saw 160 of his tegs feeding upon yellow-globe turnips grown after vetches, but I believe there were more elsewhere. His pigs were of the Berkshire and Sussex breeds, the Sussex sows being very long and fine in quality. Poultry were a feature upon this farm, Langshan and Minorca for laying, Dorking and Game for the table. They are hatched out by means of Hearson's Incubators, each of them fitted to hold a hundred eggs.

The subsoil of the land, of which two-fifths are pasture, is gravel, and the strength employed on the farm fifteen men, two boys, three milkers, and twelve horses. Barley was grown, but during the previous three years had been a poor crop, nor had the oats done very well. The buildings upon this holding were good, airy, and spacious, and for other than structural repairs the rule is that the landlord finds the material and the tenant the labour. In the laying down of pasture the same custom prevails, the landlord paying for the seed which the tenant sows. I noticed that a goat was kept among the cows and asked the reason. The answer was that it was to prevent them from slipping their calves, and that it seemed to have this effect. Surely this must be a superstition, but if so it is one that I have found to be very widely spread.

Living as he does on the very outskirts of Chichester, and having so many other advantages, Mr. Pitts' holding,

however, can perhaps scarcely be called representative
of the common run in West Sussex. The reader will, I
think, be able to form a sounder opinion of the local conditions from the example and experience of more typical
farmers.

I will begin with Mr. Eames, who is well known in this
neighbourhood as a good and intelligent agriculturist.

The traveller from Chichester to Bepton, twelve miles
away, where the Linch Farm lies, passes through a wide
open country, dotted here and there with farmsteads and
hamlets, set snugly in sheltered vales between the slopes of
the South Down. In this Bepton neighbourhood the soil
is chalk marl of a stiff character, and the subsoil flinty chalk,
while the chief crops are the common cereals. On the
north side of the hills, as he goes, he sees the little town of
Midhurst, a mere blot in the distance, its pine forests on the
day of our visit, only just discernible through a haze of
sleet and vapour. Passing through Cocking, where the soil
is chalky and the subsoil for the most part clay and rock, a
ride of about two miles over steep and muddy roads brings
him to the Linch Farm, a somewhat lonely place, near to a
church with a low ivy-clad tower.

Mr. Eames' land is of the variety called 'upper green
sand,' or 'Malm,' so named, I suppose, from the bluish
rock which underlies it within about a foot or so of the
surface. This soil is fertile and well suited to the cultivation
of the hop plant, of which Mr. Eames grew about forty
acres. He farmed in all some 700 acres, whereof 200 are
coverts and waste, leaving 500 available for cultivation. On
this total his wages bill amounted to £1,400 a year, or 40s. an
acre gross. Before starting on our walk round the farm, I
had the advantage of hearing his views on this subject of labour
and on the local condition of agriculture generally. He said
that in his district all the young men were leaving the land,
giving as an instance the fact that during the previous
week he had lost two unmarried carters, who departed from
their native fields to become warders in a lunatic asylum—

a strange taste truly! As to boys, sometimes he could get them for a year or two, after which they went away.

He was of the opinion that if farmers could afford to pay 50 per cent. more wages they might keep the men upon the land; but to do this, he declared, would swallow up every halfpenny of possible profit. 'I should have to go into the workhouse, and the men would have the farm.' Of cottages there are a good supply at rents of 1s. to 1s. 6d. per week. He himself had then an excellent cottage which had stood empty for a year. The average wages of a labourer, including harvest money, &c., were at the very lowest 16s. The women also could earn a great deal at hop-training in May and June—up to £5 or £6 for a woman and two or three children—and about as much for hop-picking in September. Many of them, however, refused to work. Employers were left with all the old men. When these died out, unless the conditions altered, it seemed as though the farming industry in his part must come to an end. As regarded the farmers, he thought that those with enterprise and capital were making a living, especially if they kept plenty of stock. The rents in that district averaged about 15s. an acre. The tithe appears to have been redeemed.

Armed with this and other information we set out in a snowstorm to inspect the farm, on which, owing to the severity of the weather, no corn had yet been sown. First we visited the cow stables. Mr. Eames kept about 100 cows, but made no butter, as all the milk went to London. They were fine cross-bred animals of the Shorthorn type, and their milk averaged 16 per cent. of cream. When they became unprofitable as cows he could sell them fat at a price of from £14 to £15. As he had only 160 acres of arable, the rest of his farm being pasture and hops, lack of straw was one of his difficulties. This he overcame to some extent by buying; also he chopped up the stiff brown hop bine into 6-inch lengths by means of an oil-engine, and used it as litter. Hard as they are, these dry stalks have great power of absorption, and, as he said, although I have heard a different opinion, make a good manure. In addition to his cows, upon which he principally relied for profit, he had a small flock of sheep. The ewes, however, did very badly in 1901, with the result that he lost 20 per cent. of the lambs and 6 per cent. of the ewes.

Beyond the fold lay some of the hop gardens, then mere forests of bare poles. By looking at the ground, however, one might see, set at distances 6 feet or 9 feet apart, according to the system of planting, brown masses of fibrous roots, each of them large as a child's head, on which purple-tipped shoots were already starting into life. These shoots an aged man was engaged in cutting off with a knife, since if they are allowed to grow too early, the hops will not do so well. A friend has pointed out to me, by the way, that in Belgium a very delicious dish is made of these hop shoots, which are boiled and served with melted butter sprinkled with chopped parsley. In our more wasteful country I believe they are always thrown away.

Hops are a very expensive crop to grow, costing, Mr. Eames said, if properly cultivated, about £60 an acre per annum, although some farmers, he added, do not spend more than £20 or £30 the acre. To begin with, the land must be quite clean and the ploughing deep. Then it should receive twenty tons of farmyard manure with from £2 to £5 worth of artificial per acre, which manuring must be renewed in each subsequent year. The plants, that are grown from cuttings and do not come into full bearing for three years, cost from £5 to £10 per acre. More or less are used according to the system favoured by the planter, some setting as many as 2,000, and some as few as 800 per acre. Mr. Eames planted 800 'hills' on one plan and 1,200 on another, his squares measuring respectively 6 by 9 feet and 6 by 6 feet. Once set, he considered that here the plants last from ten to twenty years. The poles, if pickled with creosote, should stand as long as the plants. With the wire they cost about £30 an acre— that is, when arranged upon the modern system. As regarded profit, Mr. Eames estimated it at £10 an acre on the average.

In bad years, of course, there is none at all, but in very good ones, on the contrary, it may run up to as much as £40 the acre. Mr. Eames explained to me that to plant hops the permission of the landlord must be obtained, since if a tenant sets them without it he can make no claim for compensation on leaving. No extra rent, however, is charged for the hop lands.

The view looking southward from Mr. Eames's meadows was one of singular charm, even when seen through the snow showers of this bitter day. In the foreground were the green pastures backed by the brown hop lands thickly studded with thin tall poles. Beyond these appeared a line of a deeper shade of green, that of the swedes upon which the sheep were penned, and beyond, again, above the dip where stands the house, the bold swelling ridges of the South Downs flanked here and there with clumps of yew and beech growing in thin shallow kloofs.

On our way back to Chichester from Mr. Eames's farm we visited the ancient town of Midhurst, which has a population of about 1,700, and until 1832 returned two members to Parliament. Now it is disfranchised. Near to it stands one of the loveliest ruins I ever saw, that of Cowdray House. To-day it is but a shell, but its Tudor façade still remains to charm the eye of the traveller. It was the home of the Montgomerys, of whom, we were told, eight generations lived here. The last unlucky owner of that name, said our cicerone, was drowned in Switzerland, and at the same time his ancient home, by a strange coincidence, was destroyed by fire. About sixty years ago the property was bought by an Earl of Egmont, whose representative, the present earl, still lives, I believe, at Cowdray Park. The old house, however, was never rebuilt, possibly because it stands low and very near to water. Still, it seems sad that a place so beautiful should be allowed to crumble into utter ruin.

Another farmer whom we visited was Mr. Gorringe, who held some 280 acres near Chichester. His rent stood at £1 the acre, with the proviso that if he stopped on the farm—

which he did not intend to do—for more than four years it was to rise by £25. Previous to his occupation this farm had only two tenants in sixty years, the first of whom paid a rent of £800 a year for it with thirty acres of pasture, which do not now belong, thrown in ; and the second, I think I am right in saying, £500 a year. Most of the soil is somewhat 'shravey,' which is the local term for stony, and very apt to scald in summer. 'Unless,' said our host, 'we have a shower every week, the crops dwindle on this land. Last year they were 50 per cent. below average.'

Mr. Gorringe belonged to the class of gentlemen-farmers; which fact I do not state to his agricultural disparagement, who am myself of that same tribe, since I have seldom met with a tiller of the soil who showed a more practical acquaintance with his land, or greater ingenuity in making the best of it under somewhat adverse circumstances. It is painful to have to add that as the net result of his four years' farming he had lost £500, which melancholy fact he attributed to drought and low prices. Also he was of opinion that the rent of the land was at least £50 more than it should bear. As regarded labour, personally he had not felt the pinch, but all his men were old with the exception of one carter. This *rara avis* came to his work late in the morning, but his employer dared not speak to him on the subject, 'lest he should take umbrage and cease to come at all.' Upon this holding of 280 acres Mr. Gorringe employed— at a total cost of £12 the fortnight—two cowmen, two carters, one shepherd, and two odd men. The wages, he said, had risen a shilling a week since the previous year. Water seemed to be somewhat short here, as he stated that during the first year of his tenancy the wells gave out in March. He had, however, a good pond out of which he had fyed 5 feet of mud.

Here I saw twenty-six acres of wheat which had been sown in a peculiar way with a drill fixed on to the cultivator. This system, Mr. Gorringe said, saved expense, and answered well. Of spring corn he had forty acres. The yield of his cows, which gave an average of about two gallons of milk a day, he put at a value of £18 per cow per annum gross. Of ewes he kept ninety-nine, which had produced him 111 lambs, four of them proving barren. Amongst other crops he grew kale, for some of which he had been offered during the previous year £15 the acre, as that vegetable was in demand for table purposes. He made use upon this land of an admirable and very light American plough, called the 'Oliver,' which turns a furrow 16 inches in width and, as he thought, pulverises the soil much more thoroughly than do our English ploughs. He had also a double-furrow plough of the same make, which could work to a depth of 11 inches. With six horses and two men he said that this implement is capable of ploughing five acres in a day, whereas it would need five ploughs of the local make, with ten horses and five men, to till the same amount of ground in the same time.

Mr. Gorringe appeared to look forward without unmixed regret to the date when he and his farm would part company.

One of the most interesting of many interviews that I had in this district was with Mr. Stride, a well-known Chichester auctioneer, who is also a large farmer both of his own and hired land, and very evidently a gentleman who thinks for himself. In answer to my question as to the condition of the landed interest in the county, he replied that in his opinion it was 'rotten.' He said that the new style of owner who, having accumulated money in some commercial pursuit, buys a large estate makes no legitimate use of the land. His, as a rule, is merely a sporting interest, and the rent being a matter of indifference to him, he seeks to grow, not produce but partridges. The small owners who lived on the land were for the most part broken and gone, unless they chanced to possess other resources.

The tenants, he declared, were quite a different race from those of forty years ago, and many of them paid their way by the sale of hay and straw, which meant that the land was being worked out. The end of it would be, he thought, the splitting up of the large estates—in his opinion a desirable

GROUP OF YOUNG CATTLE ON MR. EAMES'S FARM

consummation—and the laying down of the fields to grass. As regarded labour, all the young men were draining from the land ; no one who was fit for anything else stopped on it now-a-days. This must result in the going down to grass of the good land and the use of the poor for purposes of sport alone. The only chance of keeping people on the soil was, he thought, by means of ownership. If individual labouring-men could get twenty or thirty acres of their own and live upon them, it would, in his opinion, be an excellent thing for the country.

As it was there was no labour. He himself had a man of sixty employed in doing boy's work as a herd. He believed that half of the hill farms were in hand, and a great number of tenants had been ruined. These men were not made bankrupt, so that no one heard of their end. They compounded with their creditors and vanished, and very frequently died soon afterwards of chagrin and the change of life. He instanced a man in a good holding, with whose case he was acquainted, who had farmed all his days. Not long before he had died suddenly, when it was found that he owed £6,000 and that his estate was not worth more than £1,200. Now that we have to deal with foreign competition the land, he said, would no longer support three classes—that is, the owner, the tenant, and the labourer. Gradually a change was coming about; the old landed aristocracy were breaking up. 'If,' added Mr. Stride in conclusion, 'I advertise a farm of 300 acres I get no applications; but if I advertise a little lot of thirty acres, with house and buildings, I have many applicants.'

This gentleman's view of the hill farms was confirmed by those of another agriculturist from that district, who, however, desired that his name should not be mentioned. He said that they are 'worthless : what you make on the bottom land you lose on the top.' The condition of the labour market in his district he described as 'shocking.' He himself wanted three men, whom he was unable to get. He ended his expressions of opinion by declaring that he

could see no light, and that the prices, both of wheat and of
labour, were 'something awful.' An old gentleman who
contracted for the purchase of underwood also said that
labour was very scarce, almost impossible to get, indeed;
and there were others who told me the same tale. 'You
never see a young man hoeing turnips,' declared one of them.

Chichester market is held once a fortnight—upon Wednesday. I attended it, and, although the day was particularly
wretched, with pouring rain and a gale of north-east wind,
I can well believe that its repute as the best in England,
Norwich alone excepted, is no exaggeration of the facts.
The company was large, and there was a great deal of stock
on sale, some of which fetched good prices. Thus two
pens of lambs belonging to Mr. Pitts, whose farm I have
described, which had been dropped before Christmas,
were knocked down at 43s. and 43s. 6d. apiece for butchering purposes. Such lambs, however, cost a good deal
in care and cake before they come to the hammer. In
a field adjoining the market a patent American hayloader,
called the 'Ohio,' was exemplifying its merits by picking
up wet straw strewn thickly about the grass, and deposit-
ing it upon the waggon to which it was affixed. It is
claimed for this ingenious machine that it can handle a
ton of hay in ten minutes. But although American implements may do their work almost as effectively as the
men whom they replace, none of them can restore its lost
legions to our English land. We need more men, not
more machines.

From Chichester I went on to investigate the conditions of East Sussex and in particular that of its great
industry, the production of the 'Surrey fowl.' Journeying
thence to Uckfield, the traveller passes through some of the
most beautiful country in England. To the right is a rich
alluvial plain stretching to the sea. To his left lie wide lands
rising gently upwards to the beech woods of the South
Downs, whose southern slopes are dotted with the stately
houses of the great landlords, such as Goodwood, Eartham,

Slindon, Dale Park, and the Duke of Norfolk's seat, tower-crested Arundel. Indeed, this is a country of lovely views. Take that, for instance, which is to be seen from the topmost turret of Lewes Castle. Looking inland a vast and fertile plain stretches northwards further than the eye can follow. To the south it catches a gleam of the far-off sea seen through a dip in the Downs, beyond which lies New-haven. To the east are more downs scarred with white chalk pits, around the edge of one of which crawl a team of coal-black oxen at their work of ploughing, for here oxen are still in use. To the west lie yet other down lands crowned by a windmill, beyond which the battle of Lewes is said to have been fought; then to complete the scene, looking map-like as viewed from that great height, the red-tiled roofs of the ancient city, the straight line of a railway, and the silver stream of the Ouse wandering gently through the valley.

Beautiful as is this prospect, it is equalled, if not sur-passed, by that to be seen from the churchyard of All Saints', in the parish of Waldron, whereof the hill-encircled amphi-theatre is so vast that the rector, Mr. Humble-Crofts, told me that on the night of the Diamond Jubilee he counted dotted about it no fewer than fifty beacon fires. There to the east are the Sussex Downs; to the south-east, just to the right of Eastbourne, Beachy Head; to the south, Birling Gap and Cuckmare Haven, far, far away the landmark of Chanctonbury Ring; and to the west the dim line of the Hampshire hills. Such is the frame, but the picture can scarcely be described, lovely-hued as it was even beneath the shadows of a wild March sky sweeping over mile upon mile of some of the fairest champaign country in the world.

The land in the neighbourhood of Uckfield cannot be called first-class, indeed much of it is indifferent, consisting for the most part of a hungry, sandy loam, which when wet becomes paste-like both in appearance and to the touch. The pastures are particularly poor even under liberal treat-ment, this soil being little suited to the production of grass.

Perhaps this is the reason why there are so many woods in
these parts of Sussex.  I imagine that if the Uckfield and
Heathfield districts of the county were dependent on agriculture alone, their depression would be deep.  Fortunately for
them, however, this is not the case, since here has been
practised from time immemorial the art and craft of chicken-
cramming, which is reported to put into the pockets of its
votaries a gross sum of about £150,000 per annum, or even
more.  Doubtless, at least in many instances, this industry
would have supplanted all others were it not for the fact,
which the keepers of poultry farms pure and simple find it
so hard to learn, that fowls will not pay, whether as egg or
flesh producers, unless they are worked in conjunction with
other farming.

Fowls need pastures to run on—and, I may add, the pastures need and are greatly improved by them—woods to feed
and shelter in, and stubbles to scratch at, otherwise very soon
they become diseased, and the soil where they are penned,
poisoned.  So it comes about that all the fatters, or ' higglers,'
as they are called, have farms, varying in size from 100 to
300 acres, upon which they grow general produce.  But for
profit they look not to their farms but to their fowls.

This is the process of chicken-fattening as I saw it in
practice on various holdings.  The names of the owners of
these establishments I do not, however, specify, as one of
them begged me especially not to do so, giving as a reason
the fear that he would be  troubled with letters in
consequence asking him ' how much a chicken would eat.'
The industry, indeed, is somewhat of a ' close borough,'
where publicity is not sought, at any rate by its smaller
practitioners, perhaps because they fear that knowledge
may induce more competition, of which, in their opinion,
there is already enough.  As a general rule the ' higgler '
does not by any means rear all the fowls he fats.  Frequently, indeed, this is a separate business, every cottage and
small farm turning out so many per annum, which, when
ripe for the coop, are bought up eagerly by the higgler,

whose cart travels that particular district, at prices that in the Eastern Counties we should consider good for fatted fowls. At the time of our visit the rearers were receiving about three shillings a piece from the fatters. I understand that sometimes the price rises as high as four shillings, but during the summer months, on the other hand, it may sink as low as two. Irish fowls, which are imported in enormous numbers in 'tops' or crates realise less. When I was in the district they were being bought at 2s. 3d. a head.

The breed kept is in the main 'barndoor,' or, in other words, the indigenous race that probably has crowed upon the Sussex Downs since the times of the ancient Britons. This class of fowl has been proved to be the hardiest and the best suited to cramming, but occasionally a dash of Dorking, Brahma, or Game blood is thrown in by way of change. On arriving at the fatting place the chickens are thrust into pens, fifteen to a pen. These pens are made very roughly of round bars of willow or other suitable wood, set about 2 in. apart, and divided into three sections, each of which accommodates five fowls. They are perched upon poles to a height of 3 ft. from the ground, and, beyond occasional disinfecting and limewash, need no cleaning, since the droppings fall through the open bars to the earth beneath, whence they are from time to time collected to be used as dressing for the pastures.

The process of fatting takes about a month. For the first fortnight the pens are stood in the open air in a double line, leaving room for a man to walk between, and protected by hedges of underwood fixed upon a pole framework, with boards or thatch laid over them. In front are fastened the narrow feeding troughs at such an angle that the fowls can reach them easily. Here I must explain that for this first fortnight the chickens feed themselves, food in ample quantity being supplied to them twice a day. After this, when they take disgust and will not eat, art comes to the aid of nature, as shall be described in its place. While as yet satiety is far from them, it is indeed a sight to see them eat. At one end of the long line appears a man with a bucket and a wooden spoon. Instantly hundreds of heads are thrust through the bars of the pens ; hundreds of long necks crane and bend themselves towards him, while the air is rent with jealous crows and clamour.

The man gets to work. With the spoon he ladles out portions of grey and greasy stuff composed of mutton tallow, oatmeal, and skim milk, and skilfully disposes it at equal distances along the trough. Then comes a sound as of woodpeckers tapping upon a thousand trees, till presently every particle is gone, and with a curious noise of satisfaction, not unlike the purring of cats, the birds draw in their heads to spend the ensuing hours in digestion that grows gradually to appetite renewed.

When the best of mutton tallow will no longer tempt them, the fowls are removed to other pens, this time under the shelter of a roof, and here make acquaintance with a new delight. At the appointed hours of seven and four-thirty a man wheels up a stand supporting a tin hopper, to which are affixed a pump worked by foot and an apparatus not unlike a garden syringe, ending in a stiff indiarubber tube of about half an inch in diameter. This tube the operator greases with some of the compound. Then, opening the pen, he seizes a shrieking chicken by the leg and drags it out. Another instant and it is tucked beneath his left arm. Then, with a swift movement, he opens the beak, and bending forward impales that fowl upon the stiff indiarubber tube, of which about eight inches—by the gods, no less !— vanish down its throat.

We have all of us heard of the aspect of a dying duck in a thunderstorm, by tradition supposed to be supremely tragic, but I make bold to declare that it cannot equal, cannot even approach, that of the rooster penetrated for the first time by a feeding machine, with the sweet uses of which he is as yet unacquainted. His feathers bristle, his bright, expressive eye turns upward as though in appeal to Heaven, grows pale, and disappears, his limbs quiver with the agony of this new emotion. The foot of the crammer gives a quick stroke, and as it swells, the fingers of his right hand gently play upon the victim's crop. In an instant it is full. Without search or labour on its own part that bird has absorbed a good half-pint of satisfying nutriment. The ordeal is over, and, snatched from the tube, it is restored to its coop, where it sits silent and replete, reminding the observer of an after-dinner alderman according to the comic papers. Fourteen crowded days go by, after which, although our fowl still takes its food because it must, this does it no good. Ceasing to lay on the yellow fat so prized by the epicure, it begins to retrograde, or would begin were its owner so foolish as to allow it so to do. As a fact, however, at the exact high-water mark of flesh production its neck is scientifically stretched.

It cannot be pretended that this process of artificial feeding—an expert hand, by the way, is able, as I understand, to cram twenty dozen in an hour—affords an agreeable sight. Indeed, the observer is haunted by a fear lest the operator should make a mistake and feed the same fowl twice over, with results too awful to contemplate. But as to its efficiency there is no doubt. Long before the invention of the present machine chickens were crammed by hand with a specially constructed paste rolled into pellets, a system as slow as it must have been laborious. Now all that is needed is to thrust the creature on to the indiarubber spike and touch the pedal. The machine does the rest to the satisfaction of crammer, fowl, and purchaser. Its career ended, that is, so far as it is consciously concerned, the fowl is at once plucked and 'stubbed,' while it is still warm, indeed. This plucking is done by men at 6*d.* a dozen, and the stubbing, or the removal of the undeveloped feathers, by women, at 7*d.* a dozen, the head being left untouched.

Thus finished, the fowls are placed, undrawn, in a rectangular trough, where they lie side by side in such a fashion that their hinder parts, pressing against the back of the trough, acquire in cooling a certain squareness of shape which the trade approves. Next a little flour is sprinkled over them, after which a narrow board is laid upon their breasts and weighted by means of fragments of iron placed upon cross pieces which project so as to give them leverage, with the result that all angularities of breast disappear, to be replaced by a pleasing plumpness. Thus they remain for some hours, till the collector calls, when they are skilfully packed in boxes with open barred lids, each layer being separated from that above by paper or straw. Twenty-five of them, averaging perhaps 5 lb. apiece in weight, go to a box. Then, an invoice having been neatly tucked under the wing of one of the top birds, they pass from the hands that have nurtured and tended them into those of the salesman and the public; in other words, to Leadenhall and Central Markets, where, for some inscrutable reason, they are sold as ' Surrey fowls.' For his trouble in delivering them to the railway the collector receives a penny a head, out of which he must pay carriage, the difference between this penny and the actual freight being his profit, while the middleman at Leadenhall Market takes 5 per cent. of the price realised.

At the time of my visit this price, according to what I was told and from an invoice which I saw, was 5s. a bird. In the height of the London season it rises to 6s., and occasionally to 7s., whereas in October and November, when game is in, it falls to 3s. or 3s. 6d. Of course, these are wholesale prices; what the public pays I do not know. When I mentioned them, however, to certain housewives of my acquaintance, they were incredulous, declaring that they had never paid so much as 10s. or 12s. a couple for chickens in their lives. Yet a great number of people must give that, or even a higher figure, since middlemen are not in the habit of losing money on their goods. Probably these Surrey fowls, whether they hail from that county or from Sussex, are consumed by the very rich in London and other great cities, to whom the price is a matter of indifference.

Different higglers rear them in various quantities, according to fancy or the capacity of their lands. Thus, one farmer whom we visited turns out about 16,000 a year, and another from 50,000 to 60,000. Some of them make use of incubators for hatching and some do not, though the general opinion seems to be in favour of using the incubator, but not the foster mother. So soon as they come out of the egg these incubator chickens are taken and placed at night under hens which have just hatched off, whose broods, however, are generally small in the winter season. Eggs are not produced for sale in these districts, since from them, as one farmer said, ' the money does not come fast enough.' Indeed, they reckon that it costs a halfpenny to breed an egg. What the exact profit is on a fat fowl I cannot say, as upon this point all concerned are reticent. I imagine, however, that, allowing 1s. as the cost of the cramming, it must average at least 8d. a bird. Some experts put it at a lower figure, and some at considerably more, but of this matter the higglers alone know the truth.

Having treated of the specialty of chicken farming, I now pass on to the consideration of some general matters connected with Sussex agriculture, and especially to those which have to do with its supply of labour. It must never be forgotten that, however important are other problems that bear upon the prosperity of the land, that of the labour conditions is perhaps the most vital of them all. Without labour farming must cease, or at least become what a paralytic is to a healthy man. Moreover, lack of labour means that the best of its population is leaving the land, and the desertion of the land by its population, if allowed to continue over wide areas, will in the end mean the decay of England, or at the least its change into another England sprinkled with unwholesome and bloated cities set in the midst of wastes of thinly-peopled, unfruitful territory.

My informants on these matters at Lewes were Messrs.

Powell & Co., the well-known firm of land agents and surveyors. They said that with regard to the general position of the rural industry in Sussex in their opinion it was as good as it had been for the last few years, but that the price of corn was very much against the hill farmers. Hops, at the figure obtainable in 1900, had proved a help to many of the Weald farmers, while the chicken industry was of considerable importance in their district, and on the increase. The business of fruit growing also had received favourable consideration in recent years, and if they possessed—as they ought to possess—better railway facilities, they believed that it might go ahead.

The landlords in the district, no doubt, had been, and were, much affected by the great drop in their rents. There was no doubt also that these gentlemen now have to pay considerably more than in the past towards the upkeep of buildings on their properties, since it was impossible to persuade tenants to continue to bear the same proportion of this burden as they did in former days. The outlook as regarded labour they thought very bad. What the upshot of this question would be they could not tell. In some places, to a certain extent, the difficulty was being met by the erection and improvement of cottages, but they doubted whether this change for the better would be sufficient to allay the trouble. It was a question for the future whether it would become possible to import labour from other parts. However this might be, the fact could not be overlooked that in the year 1901 dairy farmers found the greatest difficulty in securing men to do their milking, and that those whom they could obtain were of a very inferior class as compared with the hands of the old school.

With reference to the education question they should say that the present system was far from sound, and that much more was attempted than was really required, certainly where the rural districts were concerned. It would be better if the children were thoroughly instructed in reading, writing, and arithmetic, and all the etceteras left alone. In their neighbourhood, speaking generally, the rents of farms were low, although they hoped that these had touched bottom. At the prevailing prices lands were letting without much difficulty. The size of the farms in that district varied according to their position from 1,500 to 50 acres. The hill farms were large, but in the Weald they ran down to quite small holdings.

Another very interesting informant was Mr. Jones, of Halland, where he has had many years' experience as a land agent. He pointed out that in the past century the tendency of the Poor Law was to prevent the migration of the labourer. Indeed, no man with a large family was permitted to enter another parish, and to supplement the small wages of such people, and save them from starvation, outdoor relief was granted universally to folk who had their quivers full.

The labourer in those days, however, was a fine specimen of humanity, and well skilled in all agricultural work. On some farms such men were still to be found, but they are no longer common. This method of supplementing wages caused the poor-rate to be very high. Thus, to go back nearly 120 years, in 1789 in East Hoathly it came to 3s. 6d. in the pound for the half-year ! Before 1832 nearly all the labourers were paupers. Mr. Jones said that he was told some thirty years ago by a Mr. Martin, who at that time was churchwarden for the parish of Hellingly, which now has a population of about 1,500, that in the winter season as many as seventy men and boys applied daily for work.

Then it was common for parish officers to resort to every kind of device to save the community from being imposed upon by these people. Thus in one parish a persistent applicant—a kind of Poor-law Sisyphus—was forced to dig holes by the highway and when they were dug to fill them in again. The ridiculous nature of this occupation, however, did not suffice to keep him off the rates. Here I may say that the race of this digger is not extinct, for in my own time I have known one of them whose feats may be found chronicled in my work 'A Farmer's Year' (page 431).

In another case an old Sussex carpenter seeking for parish relief was ordered to peck in the ruts on the roads. Shortly afterwards the astonished overseers found him sitting in the middle of the highway hammering at it with a mallet and chisel. When remonstrated with he replied that the tools he was using were the only ones to which he was accustomed.

In those days three or four strong young men, who had charge of the stock, were boarded in each farmhouse. They worked hard and fared harder, since the usual morning and evening meal consisted of bread and milk, and they rarely tasted meat other than fat pork. This diet may with advantage be compared with that common under similar circumstances to-day in Yorkshire, of which I shall speak later in this book. Mr. Jones stated, however, that most of the best labourers who are now left, talk affectionately of the times when they were in ' sarvice.'

About sixty years ago numbers of the more enterprising farming hands, growing very dissatisfied with their scanty pay and wretched condition, emigrated to the colonies. There, he said, they have retaliated upon their late employers by flooding our markets with their produce and keeping down the prices of English meat and corn. These men generally did well, and many of them have sent back sufficient money to remove all their relatives to their new homes. As education spread and national wealth increased, the labourer no longer felt tied to the soil and afraid to leave his parish. High wages induced him to enter the towns, where long apprenticeship had gone out of fashion. Thus it happened that the farm hand easily converted himself into a bricklayer's assistant, a porter, or a van or 'bus driver.

At the beginning of the last century, Mr. Jones added, there was a more cordial feeling between master and man and more direct association than exist at present. Then they met daily on familiar ground and amusements were provided which were common to all classes. The festival of Harvesthome, May-day celebration, the local fair, and the village cricket match afforded convivial enjoyment to rector, squire, and master as well as to the labourer. In this respect times were now changed, and the worker's daily round is rarely diversified by such entertainments. Even the itinerant circus has ceased to visit the village. This change, in Mr. Jones's opinion, is one of the great causes why not five per cent. of the boys, who year by year leave the national schools, remain upon the land, which infinitesimal residuum is of a far lower mental calibre than that of the great majority who go. The present race of stalwart labourer, he declared, is fast dying out without any prospect of its replacement. This state of affairs, he thought, amounted to a serious national problem, but it was one which the nation refused to face.

By way of remedy he suggested that efforts should be made to better the conditions of village life, and to bring employer and employed into closer fellowship. He thought also that dwelling houses in many districts might be improved, and that as in Sussex men can easily earn £1 a week at piecework, they ought to be given allotments to cultivate in their spare time upon which they could keep a cow and rear a few hundred chickens. Indeed, Mr. Jones, more hopeful than some, seemed to think that if the labourer can earn enough to satisfy himself, he may be content to stop upon the land. This, however, partakes of the nature of a pious opinion which is not held by many other authorities. In fact, the suggestions that he made as to the advisability of planting oak timber, which does so well in the Wealden woods, on a large scale show that in his own mind Mr. Jones admits it to be nothing more.

By way of a pendant to the foregoing opinions, I will quote those which have been given to me by a Sussex clergyman, whose name I do not print because I am not sure whether or no he would wish me so to do. It will be seen that he takes a very hopeful view of the condition and prospects of the labouring class in his county. He said that he wished to put before me a few facts concerning the labourer as he knew him. I give them in his own words.

We often hear it said, ' Pity the farm labourer. He toils and has no pleasure.' Now toil to a healthy man is pleasure. I heard a labourer's widow tell one of her children so only the other day. The farm labourer has more pleasure than those who pity him think. His work is hard, but easy to him. Most of them hereabout ask for overtime employment all the summer through, and when cultivating their own gardens after their regular daily work is done, they use the spade like children at play digging sand upon the shore. They rear the best of vegetables in plenty for themselves, and some they sell. They send such specimens to Shows that those who keep a gardener often wish they could get as good. And if freedom from anxious care has anything to do with happiness, then they are happy enough. They are never anxious about the future for themselves or their children. They never beg. They have enough. They dress well and eat well. Most of them are in some sick and benefit club. If not, when they are ill they have the parish doctor; when very ill they are sent to the infirmary; when very, very ill they are sent to a London hospital. That is the rule. Rather often £100 a year goes into one cottage as wages. Rent, 2s. 6d. week, is the most. No rates, no school fees, no anything to pay outside their own immediate needs. The young men give £7 perhaps for a bicycle on which they ride about. The children are well clad, clean, and attractive as those of any other class. They are trained at school to habits of punctuality, obedience, order, and good manners, and thus fitted for living useful lives. No girls make better servants. One girl from this village a short time ago had £5 given her by her master (head of a public school) for good conduct over and above her wages. The boys leave school equally well prepared; but, alas ! are too often dragged down by bad company, becoming lawless and blasphemous, when parents give up the reins, as they frequently do now. At school they are patterns of obedience, and have the keenest sense of shame under rebuke. At home parents give way to them a very great deal more than parents of the upper and middle classes. Whenever the lads keep steady the parson is always ready to give then a good ' send-off' if a chance comes, and if inquiry is made it will be found that our railway servants and police are largely supplied from this source. The country fellow can now read, write, and cipher sufficiently. The way is open to him for self-improvement and intellectual pleasure. There is the village library free; the village reading-room free; County Council technical classes practically free—well, at about one thirtieth the cost. (Carpentry, dressmaking, cookery, health, gardening, and drawing classes have all been held here, the first and second of these with marked success.) History, geography, biography are not sealed to the country lad, any more than to the son of a lord. Good papers and monthly periodicals are made as accessible to him as if he lived in a town. All that opens and ennobles the mind, and lifts it above the dirt, is his—if he likes. He has, in some ways, more opportunities for self-improvement than the town fellow, because he has less distractions. And when an offer comes, as come it does to every man, the country fellow has as good a chance as the town fellow. Read the lives of distinguished men and notice where they hail from. The country, sir, as often as the town. There is in most villages a savings bank or provident club. Here, with a population of under 250, the deposits were above £60 last year, returned with £3 12s. interest at Christmas. As to the education given in the country schools, there is no reason why it should be thought inferior to town schools. Here the buildings, apparatus, course, teachers, and reports will bear comparison with those of any town school. Sword and rifle drill were taught to the boys long before the South African war led 'educationists' to suggest their utility in the school curriculum, and when four thousand school children were gathered at the Jubilee of 1897, those of this country school were the only ones receiving special commendation for marching and discipline from the chief organiser, a military man.

Now let us see what are the 'pleasures' the townspeople think would fill up the measure of the peasant's bliss. Is it town 'pleasure'? Well, when our young fellows take to town 'pleasures' we know where it ends. When I see one going off to the town in the dusk of the eve pretty regularly I find he has no health. His labours of the day conduce to health, strong health. His 'pleasures' of the eve do not. His mother tells me he is never well. He is in no club, his 'pleasure' takes his money. He worships no God, he worships himself and his 'pleasures.' So great is his desire for town 'pleasures' that he migrates at length into the town, and the first thing you hear is that he flourishes. His country friends tell you this. They have been to see him, and to be introduced probably to his 'pleasures.' But the next thing you hear is that he is not flourishing; he is in a hospital and in a very bad way. This is not a fancy picture—it is fact. The country fellow is more likely to suffer from town pleasures than the town fellow, for the same reason that the Red Indian suffers more from intoxicants than the white man. He is carried away by them. They are good for none—they are death to him.

Another representative witness is Mr. J. Moreton Lord, of Goatley Grange, Northiam, in the Rye division of Sussex, where he has had many years' experience as a farmer, and I believe as a landowner also. He said that rents in his district have in many instances fallen more than a half since 1875, and that the rental value of average lands might be put at from 12s. 6d. to 15s. the acre. Farms of from fifty to 100 acres were almost certain to let readily, but the larger holdings hung heavy on hand. In most cases the rents were more or less readily paid. Labour was becoming exceedingly scarce, owing, he believed, to a new railway that was being made in the locality, to activity in the building trade, and perhaps to the effect of education upon the younger men. The average wages for ordinary day labourers were 2s. 6d. per diem, rising to 3s. 6d. in summer during the different harvest operations. But teamsters and cowmen, who worked longer hours and on Sundays, received more. Of cottages there was about a sufficient supply, and those which had been built during the last twenty years were good and roomy. The rents varied from 1s. 9d. up to 4s. a week. Nearly all the young men were leaving the land for other and easier occupations. What he meant was that their education teaches them that they need not exercise their muscles in heavy farming operations at what they consider low wages, when they can and do obtain easier and less tiring work in the towns or elsewhere. Even if they obtain no higher wage in such places, they can enjoy there a 'kind of wild life' after work hours, for which they are very eager. 'Early to bed and early to rise' was certainly not their motto.

CHICKEN CRAMMING

FOWLS IN FATTING COOPS

The tenant farmer in his district was, he considered, almost invariably a very energetic man. Unless his ' speculative crop,' hops, did well his lot, however, was extremely hard. In that event for a month or two he was flourishing, after which he must settle down to hard and steady work for the rest of the year in the hope of making both ends meet. Of the position of the landowner Mr. Lord added that he could hardly speak with confidence. The labourer, however, was the best off of the three. This could be seen by comparing his wages and the cost of living twenty-five years ago with those of 1901. Indeed, he believed that this class was nearly twice as prosperous now as it had been at that date.

He could see no prospect of a revival of agriculture. The land which used to be under corn had to a large extent tumbled down into good-for-nothing pastures. In that district it was the hop crop alone that kept the larger sort of farming on its feet. In the cultivation of hops horses were necessary, and as these required corn and straw some of the best corn lands were still under the plough in his neighbourhood. Personally he was hopeful as to the future, that is, so far as his minor farm-produce was concerned. Thus fowls from twelve to fourteen weeks old were fetching 4s. 6d. a bird in Leadenhall Market; honey in nominal pounds 9s. the dozen ; fat tegs sixteen months old 45s. each ; and tomatoes from 4d. to 6d. the pound, which were fair prices. Apple and pear trees also, grown as pyramids like cabbages, produced fine fruit which sold at from 5s. to 8s. the bushel. All these small things, said Mr. Lord, go towards making a nice little living for the man who works both with his hands and his brain, but not for the man who walks about telling others what to do and doing nothing himself. If labourers became unobtainable the hop lands would gradually go down to pasture, bringing that industry to an end. The only remedy that he could suggest was a duty upon imported hops. This would cause a revival of the industry, and give remunerative employment to thousands upon thousands of men, women, and children. I fear, however, that Mr. Lord must sigh in vain for such assistance. To convert the beer drinkers of England to protectionist views would prove no easy task.

Mr. B. Wells, of The Fruit Nurseries, Crawley, near Horsham, whose orchards—in which he had planted some 30,000 young apple trees—unfortunately I was not able to visit, favoured me with some views which seemed to bear out the opinion of Mr. Lord on the advantages of fruit culture. He said he thought that fruit growing, if rightly carried out, would induce both labourers and their employers to go back to the land; first, because people want the fruit; secondly, because to all appearance it must be profitable to produce it for many a year to come; and thirdly, because should it become so plentiful that it would pay little on the open market, it makes a splendid beverage which might be sent almost all over the world at a remunerative price. 'Three acres and a cow' in his opinion offered but a poor inducement to the labouring man in comparison with that afforded by fruit growing coupled with fixity of tenure.

The Rev. Mr. Nicholls, who for twenty-five years farmed between three and four hundred acres in West Sussex, some of which is now occupied by his son, declared that there the depopulation, and especially the exodus of the best labourers, has become more and more acute. This he attributed to the direct action of Free Trade, which makes it impossible for farmers to pay higher wages, with the result that the children of the labourers forsake the country and flock into the towns, and that owners have seen their capital dwindle by one-half. He said that he was not blind to the boon which unrestricted foreign imports had proved to certain classes, nor was he sorry that the experiment had been fully tried. He thought, however, that if in the face of the divergent policy of the other great nations, we still persisted in treating Free Trade as a fetish, we were doomed to lose our country village life, and with it the only healthy recruiting ground for all our industries.

Sir William Grantham, the well-known judge, very kindly wrote me a letter, which by misfortune I only received after I had left the county, offering to show me over his property at Barcombe. Here, he said, he had succeeded in keeping a good many farmers' sons and labourers on the land by subdividing holdings and improving cottage farmhouses. He instanced one farm of 400 acres which used to be held by a single tenant. Now it is divided among twenty-four tenants occupying from 2 or 3 up to 125 acres. In addition to improving cottages he builds some new ones every year, which I understand are taken the moment they are ready to be let.

Doubtless these are excellent methods which, where landlords can put them into practice, are likely to do much to retain population in the country. But how many owners are there who, greatly as they may desire it, can afford to subdivide farms into little holdings and erect upon them numbers of cottage-steadings with their necessary outhouses? Landlords who would do this must have other resources beyond the acres which used to suffice for their support, but now—in many an instance—must be supported by them.

Mr. Justice Grantham, it is evident, is a severe critic of farmers and their ways. At least, when trying a case during the Norfolk Assizes of January 1902, in which a dealer was found guilty of stealing fleeces belonging to a local farmer, he said, according to a newspaper report, that

the case showed how foolish farmers were; how they robbed themselves and did not use that intelligence which God had given them, to make their business a success. They went on selling things for less than their full value, and then they grumbled and abused the Government because farming did not prosper. It was their own fault in a lot of cases.

A member of the jury said most of the jury were farmers, and they thought that farmers generally did not deserve the severe criticism passed upon them by his Lordship.

His Lordship replied that he was glad he had hurt somebody's feelings. (Laughter.) As a rule, perhaps, farmers did not do what he had suggested, but a good many of them did.

With all respect I venture to suggest that, however much it may have been deserved in this individual instance, the above censure of our class is too sweeping. It is not difficult for men of very high intelligence to find fault with the methods and habits of the average tenant farmer, especially if, like Sir William Grantham, they chance to be personally experienced in matters connected with the land and its management. Indeed, everybody— experienced or not—seems to have a stone in his pocket ready to throw at the head of the agriculturist and a stick wherewith to beat his back. Yet what are the facts? Although owing to loss of capital and other causes, now-a-days it is not so in all cases, are there any farmers in the world who as a body do better, or so well, by their land and get more out of it than those of these islands? They have their faults it is true, such as an undue conservatism and a liability—as in the present example—to be outwitted by commercial sharpers, whom, as the prosecutor said, they are so foolish as to take for honest men. But belief in the probity of a neighbour, although it may be inadvisable, is scarcely a fault of which anyone need feel ashamed. I imagine, however, that his Lordship did not quite intend that his words should be taken *au pied de la lettre*; that he spoke more in humour than in anger. Still in these days of misfortune farmers have much to bear. Naturally, therefore, like the Norfolk jury they are inclined to be sensitive when criticism which they deem unjust is added to their load.

To return to the subject of Sussex labour. Another gentleman, a landowner and farmer, told us that the average wage of his men was about 17s. 6d. a week and a house. He said: 'I have one man who knows how to hedge, ditch, and dry hops; no one else can, and no one else cares to learn. Even he, although he is the stockman, cannot milk. One of my gardeners can milk; otherwise only the cowman. For the boy's own benefit I directed that the cowboy should be taught to milk, at the same time telling him that he would not have to do it while with me. He promptly gave notice to leave rather than learn.' This informant told us also that it was the same with most of them now-a-days; that, as a class, they are very pig-headed, and apt to interpret any attempt to teach them into a desire on the part of the teacher to get something out of them.

Mr. Humble-Crofts, the Rector of Waldron, a clergyman of much experience, informed me that none of the young people are staying on the land. He said also that more cottages are required in his district. The old folk cling to what there are, so that young couples have little room to live. Captain Cochrane, our host in that neighbourhood, who practically manages the excellent East Hoathly Schools, said that small attempt is made to give agricultural education to the students. The master of the school, however, in a letter to the press, which unfortunately I have lost, demurred to this statement, saying, if I remember right, that he held certain classes devoted to instruction on such subjects. However this may be, so far as I could gather, this branch is much neglected in all the schools of that neighbourhood, whether Board or Voluntary. How can it be otherwise, indeed, when so many of the teachers are townsfolk, and quite ignorant of rural matters?

A chicken-fatter whose farm we went over, declared that if extra hands were wanted they were not to be had, and that he could not say what would happen when the old men dropped out. He considered the matter serious, and one with which the Government ought to deal. He reckoned the wages he paid at from 18s. to £1, and the average letting value of land at about 15s. the acre.

I will conclude my remarks upon Sussex labour by quoting an interesting suggestion which has been made to

me by Mr. W. D. Scull, of The Pines, Crowborough Beacon,
in that county, who is anxious that Italians should be
introduced into England to take the place of the farm hands
who are migrating to the towns. He said, ' Since our
happy land's wise rulers have decreed that we are to be a
dumping ground for Europe, and since we have Malatesta
and other such human wolves in our bosom, may we not
just as well accommodate others of the same nation who
have at least the qualities of industry, sobriety, and thrift?
Our towns are already becoming ghettos, receptacles for
what is too bad for the ghettos of the Continent. Whatever
the especial beauties of the Jew may be, even his most
ardent adorers have never called him an agriculturist. Now
the Italians are as good agriculturists as any in the world.
Surely it is not unreasonable to feel that since our England
has become a home for the bad Italians, it may just as well
become a home for the good ones. If we have the men of
the Mafia, we may as well have the men of the mattock.'

I have said that the suggestion is interesting; I fear I
must add that it is also impracticable, although I have
heard that in one of the English counties—perhaps I shall
come across the reference later—some Italians are employed
upon a fruit farm. Speaking generally, I am convinced that,
however little the English labourer may wish to cultivate
the land himself, he would earnestly object, even with
violence, to its being cultivated by Italians at about one
half the wage which he considers a meet reward for his
own services when he is pleased to render them. In this
matter the colonies and their alien-exclusion bills furnish a
sufficient object lesson. Still I may add that I know one
lady who imports Italian women servants with the most
satisfactory results, and another who does the same with
Scandinavians.

During my visit to this part of East Sussex I was shown
over the 400-acre holding—of which a third was grass—
of a farmer of the old school, one of the few who have not

bowed the knee to the Baal of chicken-fatting. The place did not look particularly prosperous, although the poor sandy soil commands but 10s. an acre rent; indeed, as its occupants informed me with evident sincerity, they only 'just managed to live.' I was the more astonished, therefore, when, in answer to my question, I was informed that they had plenty of labour. Further research explained the mystery. There were five sons on the farm, who worked for their father, and some of these were the parents of growing lads. That is why labour was plentiful. The crops on this holding included hops and corn, eaten very bare by rabbits. Also there were sheep and cows. From the seven and half acres of hops the average returns seem to have been from fourteen to fifteen cwt. per acre, rising to twenty-five cwt. in very good years. The owners said, however, that this was 'an unreliable crop.' The cost of its cultivation they put at £30 the acre.

Once a great mansion stood upon this place, and local tradition, going back a hundred years or more, tells how its lords used to drive down from London in their four-horsed coaches with a retinue of servants and French cooks. Now all that remains of that splendid establishment are the fine stone stables used as a barn, a massive outer wall that encloses the hop garden, and certain depressions in a meadow, formerly part of the park, which once were stew-ponds for the breeding of coarse fish. It is a melancholy example of prosperity passed away, and considering it the visitor cannot refrain from wondering what its former occupants, who dwelt in pomp amongst its pleasure grounds and spacious halls, would think of these broken ruins and half-starved pastures.

My general conclusion on this district is that were it not for the fowl industry, and for the fact that many rich men from London occupy large houses, which absorb much produce at a good price, it would go very hardly both with tenants and with landlords. As it is, the latter are much crippled, while, save in exceptional instances, the farmers make no more than a bare living. Those who are left of the labourers, however, are more prosperous than their class has ever been before. In the midst of the decay of Sussex agriculture they thrive. Yet year by year their numbers dwindle.

## KENT

THE beautiful and fertile county of Kent, which I visited on leaving Sussex, has an area of about 975,000 acres. Its soils are very various: chalk downs, which furnish pasturage for thousands of sheep; rich alluvial lands in the Weald between the North and South Downs; gravel and clay, are all represented within its borders. There are few agricultural products which it does not grow, some of them better perhaps than any other shire in England. Thus of hops I believe that there are quite 30,000 acres, about half the total English area devoted to this important crop. They come chiefly from the Weald of Kent, East Kent, and Mid-Kent, and especially from the valley of the Medway. Also the common cereals are largely cultivated, and the county is the great home of the fruit industry. With Kentish filberts and cob-nuts we are all familiar, and these are supplemented by apples, cherries, pears, plums, and small fruit. Market-garden stuff comes from the neighbourhood of Deptford and other places, with spinach and watercress from the Gravesend district, and canary and radish seed from the Isle of Thanet. The woods are very large and yield much timber, and in addition, in Romney Marsh and on the banks of the Medway, Thames, Swale, and Stour, are more than 80,000 acres of fat marsh-land devoted for the most part to the grazing of sheep and cattle.

The traveller from Sussex to Kent sees in the neighbourhood of Winchelsea, running down to the Channel, flats, a mile or more in breadth, of rich marshes, already in the early spring dotted over with sheep. To his right appears a hoary castle about which the sea-gulls wheel, and to his left, or northwards, here and there little valleys of arable land lined with pollard willows. Then comes Rye with its fertile fields and woods, and the picturesque town crowned by an ancient church. To the north the highlands are wide and open to the eye; to the south the river runs sluggishly through stretches of green marsh. Now appears another wide expanse running down to Dungeness, dotted with poplars and more pollard willows. Here some of the fields seem rushy and underdrained, although the brimming dykes are kept clean and open. By Appledore the land begins to rise and the seaward marshes to increase in width. In the neighbourhood of Ham Street orchards appear, the whitened stems of the fruit trees in ordered lines, and their carefully tended soil contrasting pleasantly with the great flats beneath. Here and there also are hop-lands well placed for sun and light and sheltered by great woods. Evidently in this district, however, all the soil is not good, since many of the oaks look somewhat hide-bound and stunted. On the spacious, undulating meadows, bordered by hedgerow timber, are seen many sheep feeding unconcernedly in the awful weather, quite heedless of the bitter blasts and driving storms of sleet and snow.

From Canterbury my first visit was to the charming village of Wingham, some seven miles away, to which we drove through wide, well-farmed land that must be very beautiful in summer when the green hop-bine hides the naked poles and wires. These, at the time I saw them, were, however, irritating to the eye. Indeed, it would not be too much to say that they spoiled the aspect of the country, since, although so different from those of summer, if left unmarred, the winter landscape has beauties of its own.

Mr. Maxted, whom we went on to visit at the Well Farm, cultivated about 400 acres in the village, part of it hired land and some his own property. Of this area 100 acres were under hops, and about 20 under fruit, the rest being grass and arable, farmed in the usual fashion. First we walked with him over the Wingham Well Farm, which he took in poor condition about three years before my visit, and was engaged in bringing into order. Near to the homestead, a very ancient house, he had planted a hop garden upon one of the improved systems—that known as the East Kent—at a cost of about £30 the acre. Its third season was just completed, and he expected it to come into full bearing in the summer of 1901, the year of my visit. In the old days hops were grown up single poles, which lasted a few years only ; but now things are done in a much more scientific manner, the uprights being of choice chestnut or larch soaked in creosote, which will preserve them for the best part of a generation. To these is fastened a network of galvanised wire, strained tight by special instruments, and from it strings are tied to pegs fixed in the ground or to the lowest wires, in such fashion that the clinging bine may travel up them easily. Spraying machines can pass between the rows, and the admission of light and air encourages the production of the largest possible crop.

The soil, a hazel loam on brick earth, which in turn rests upon the chalk, is, when well dug, dressed and tended, perhaps the best known for hop culture, unless, indeed, the 'Kentish rag' soil of West Kent may be excepted. Hops will stand upon it for almost any length of time without change of plant, although some growers prefer to reset every twenty or thirty years. Mr. Maxted showed us a garden still in good bearing where the plants are known not to have been renewed for the last two centuries, and another garden, which he himself cultivated with great success, where they have been undisturbed for ninety years. In order to protect the fruiting bines from devastation by the high winds, which are so much dreaded by the hop farmer, quick-growing poplars are planted round the exposed parts of the fields. In the instance of the new garden which I am describing, these saplings, set during its first season, were already growing strongly, and after another ten or fifteen years will be trees of considerable size. They are planted quite close together and pruned in so as to form a kind of living wall. Hops are also protected by the hanging of close-woven nets on the outermost wires of plantations. When they are not wanted for this purpose, that is, during the winter and spring seasons, these nets are sometimes used by the more provident farmers as a shelter for their lambing sheep. Near to this hop garden Mr. Maxted had planted a quantity of strawberries for market purposes. He used nothing but ' Paxtons.' 'Royal Sovereigns' he had tried and discarded, declaring that, although they may be a little earlier, they have not the flavour or the travelling qualities of the ' Paxton.'

Leaving the hops and strawberries we went on to the sheep, which were Kents of pedigree breed. This particular lot were what are called 'hogs' in Kent, answering to the ' tegs ' of Wiltshire and the 'hoggets' of the Eastern Counties. In this part of England it is common to shear the lambs during the summer of their birth, so these tegs, though only a year old, had been clipped. The points of the Kent sheep are that it should have fine, long ears and a very wide back and chest. It makes excellent mutton, and although its wool fetches twopence a pound less than that of the Downs, it produces six and a half pounds of it on an average, compared to about three and a half pounds yielded by the Southdown. Mr. Maxted told me that in his farming experience he had seen wool selling at 2s. 6d. a lb., and down as low as 6d. a lb., while as for hops, he had known them at £30 a cwt. and at 29s. a cwt. The then prevailing price of about £5 10s. he considered too low. Indeed, he thought them an uncertain crop, and that the man who cleared £10 an acre was fortunate. ' Hop-growing,' he added, ' is just like a rubber of whist. I have lost £1,000 a year at it, and I have made £1,000 a year.'

As we walked over his land, inspecting the fat stock, the peas already well up above the soil, and the primitive Kent plough—which the experience of generations, however, has proved to be the best suited to this land—Mr. Maxted spoke of farmers and their prospects in the district. It was no very cheerful tale he had to tell. Many, he said, to his own knowledge, had gone through the ' Court ' of late years, and many more had compounded with their creditors and vanished. Work as they would, month by month they continued to lose money, till at length the long-delayed day of reckoning came, and their place knew them no more. Mr. Maxted told me also that he put the average rents in his district at £1 or £1 1s. an acre, tithe free. Resident landlords were scarce, and he added that this class had been very hard hit by the times, especially the small men who have nothing but their acres to depend on. In his opinion, ordinary farming gives no profit nowadays. Indeed, he thought that it was ' all loss,' and that those who would make anything must look to fruit and hops. As for labour, in 1900 they could not get a man ; but in the year 1901 they had plenty in his neighbourhood.

I asked the reason of this change. He explained that labourers were drifting down from the ' backbone of Kent,' leaving the poor lands of the Dover Hills, which were going to grass, and migrating into the rich valleys, where they stay awhile on their road to the towns. Only the old men remained permanently on the land ; the younger ones departed. I inquired what he thought would be the upshot of this state of affairs. He answered that apparently it must mean the depopulation of the rural districts and the laying down of all but the best lands to grass, larch, and woods. He complained that there was no agricultural education ; that nothing was taught in the schools which would tend to tie the rising generation to the soil. Also he said that the district is short of cottages, which perhaps hurries the departure of young folk. He thought, however, that if farmers could pay them as much as they could earn in towns many men would be glad to stay ; at any rate, in the better and more convenient neighbourhoods. Still, as will be seen when I come to talk of West Kent, there are facts which do not appear altogether to confirm this view.

After luncheon we drove to Mr. Maxted's fruit farms, stopping on the way to inspect a very ingenious ' oast,' or hop-drying kiln, built upon a new design of his own, which, unfortunately, it would take too long to describe. Some of these lands are his property. He valued ten acres of sandy loam, beautifully planted with young standards, small fruit, and strawberries, at from £30 to £50 an acre. The same land in 1870 would easily have fetched £100 an acre, which shows a depreciation of 60 per cent. since that date. By way of illustration, he quoted the example of a farm that lay close at hand, which used to be worth £90 an acre, but was sold recently at £30 an acre. Reckoning 1,700 trees and small fruits to the acre, he laid the cost of planting at £20, or half the fee simple value of the land, whereas for hops, he said, ' You must buy the land twice over to get a crop.' No wonder, he added, that it is better to own than to hire.

In this garden the trees were planted at distances of eighteen feet from each other, and the bushes set between them, gooseberry and currant alternately—six feet apart. Between the bushes again ran strawberries. On the grass orchards, however, the standard trees were set thirty feet apart. Mr. Maxted considered Cox's Orange Pippin the best apple for their district, and for cookers, Wellington, and, I think he added, Stone Loddington. Of plums he preferred Rivers, the Czar, and Black Diamonds ; of gooseberries, Crown Bobs ; while in selling value black currants surpass all others. He considered Waterloo, Napoleon, and Common Black the best cherries. Cherry and plum orchards, by the way, which take a long time to mature, still command a high price—say £200 an acre for plums, and £250 an acre for cherries of twenty years old and over. From four acres of such fruits a hard-working man should be able to get a good living, even at present prices.

Later in the afternoon we visited a young cherry orchard, which when under hops in 1883 cost Mr. Maxted, I think,

£80 an acre.   Six years ago he planted cherries among the
hops that were subsequently grubbed up, the land, which is
very rich and strong, being laid down to grass around the trees.
These grass orchards, I should state, are not hayed, but fed
heavily with sheep, whose manure nurtures the shallow
running roots of the trees.   The presence of geese and pigs
is also desirable for the same reason, but no cattle should
ever be admitted into an orchard.   When I saw these
particular young cherries I estimated their age at fifteen
years, so splendid was their growth, whereas in fact it
was only six.   This is accounted for by the circumstance
that, for thirteen years in succession, the deep hop ground
on which they stand had received heavy coatings of farm
manure, to say nothing of dressings of 'meat guano.'   All
growers, however, do not believe in allowing young trees
to make such rapid progress.   Some of them declare,
indeed, that when they have sucked the land of its rich
elements, seeking their accustomed nutriment in the after
years and finding none, they suffer very sorely and fall a
prey to disease.   Disease, I should state, is the terror of
the fruit grower, since, do what he will, American blight is
killing many of the apple trees, while bacteria of various
degree are playing havoc with the cherries.

Thus on the occasion of our visit Mr. Maxted was much
disturbed to find that a blight, which he believed to be new,
was busy in his young plantations.   Its symptoms are an
exudation of gum upon the trunk and boughs of the cherry
trees, and beneath, wood turned to a white tinder by the
working of the scourge as it saps the life-blood of the tree.
Also there are others, too numerous to describe, which
caused one farmer to declare to me that unless they could
be checked, cherry growing in Kent would become a thing
of the past.   Perhaps he was too pessimistic in this view,
but, as every observer of nature will have noted, it is
remarkable how high culture is almost invariably followed
by the Nemesis of pest.   In this connection it struck me as
possible that the extensive slaughter of small birds by

shooting during the fruit season may have something to do
with the increase of insect plagues.   Certainly birds seem to
be growing scarce in this district, although farmers declare
that there are plenty of them when the cherries are ripe.   At
any rate, during a whole long day, although I kept my eyes
and ears open, I saw and heard but two or three thrushes
and blackbirds, whereas in Norfolk, at the same season, they
may be counted by scores.   This must be because so many
are shot during their breeding time.

Most of the soil in this parish of Wingham is rich loam,
full of round, water-washed pebbles.   Mr. Maxted called it
‘ sea-drift.’   Underneath lies clay, and below the clay, chalk.
In favourable conditions, I understood, the roots of the hop
plant will penetrate the earth to a depth of twenty or thirty
feet, forcing themselves into the crannies of the rock beneath.
It would seem that there are hop farmers *and* hop farmers.
Thus some old-fashioned men still refuse to syringe their
plants with the special washes that keep them clean and
healthy.   The results of an instance of the sort, of which I
heard in this parish, were that the farmer who ‘ washed ’
his hops obtained a return of 7 cwt. the acre, whereas his
neighbour over the road, who would not wash them, only
secured 1½ cwt.

In Kent there is some complaint of the lack of fixity of
tenure for the tenants of fruit and hop farms.   Doubtless
this has worked hardship in the past to men who took their
land before the recent protecting Agricultural Holdings
and Market Gardeners’ Compensation Acts became law, and
planted without arriving at an agreement with the owner.
I was told of a man in East Kent who had planted a cherry
orchard upon his farm, which was then estimated at a
value of £60 the acre.   In due course he took his son
into partnership, and the two of them carried on the
business for twenty years, when the father died.   By this
time the growth of the cherry trees had raised the land
to a value of £300 the acre, as against its unimproved
value of £60.   Seeing this, the landlord gave the son notice

to quit. As he could not take his cherry trees with him, finally this tenant compromised by agreeing to pay an extravagantly high rent for the improvements, which he himself had made without the expenditure of a farthing of the owner's money. For a while he carried on, but the rent crushed him. He was ruined, and shortly afterwards died of chagrin. This, at least, was the story, which I believe to be authentic.

Another farmer, whom I myself saw in a different part of Kent, told me that, although he was rented much higher than his neighbours, it was impossible for him to leave his holding, on which were hop lands that had cost him about £5,000 to plant and bring to their present condition. It would seem that, under an agreement which he had been obliged to sign as the alternative of sacrificing what he had already invested in these hops, foolishly enough without any written security from the owners of the soil in the event of his quitting the farm, he was only to receive the value of twenty-five acres of poling and wiring as it stood, and the breakdown price of the remainder. Nothing at all was to be allowed to him on account of the hop plants, or for the unexhausted manure which he had put into the land. This, if he went, would, he declared, mean a clear loss to him of £3,000. Therefore he must stay on and pay such rent as the landlord, knowing the difficulties of his position, chose to exact.

Yet another farmer told me practically the same story of his own case. He took his holding years ago, when things were very prosperous, and apparently made so bad an arrangement with his landlord, as to any improvements he might carry out in the way of fruit and hop planting, that in practice the compensation due to him in the event of his leaving amounted to nothing at all. Yet he had committed the folly of investing thousands in hop-plants, poles, and trees, which he must leave behind him.

It will be understood, of course, that I give these histories for what they are worth; but personally I am convinced that the last two of them, at any rate, are true enough. Nor do I wish to imply that any considerable proportion of the Kentish landlords treat their tenants thus. Still it is my duty to point out every aspect of the agricultural case in those counties which I have visited; therefore when I come across such examples I must chronicle them. Generally, in fact, the tale runs differently; in most counties it is the landlord who has to complain of the conduct of the tenant. That it should be otherwise in some few instances in Kent, may be attributed to the universal truth that in every walk of life men are to be found, ready to take advantage of their neighbours in any way that the strict letter of the law allows. Also sometimes those complained against are trustees or executors, who must do the best for their beneficiaries or themselves be held liable for neglect. People in this position cannot be generous : they must take all that the law gives them. As it stands now, however, I believe that the tenant is amply protected, and that it will be his own fault if in the future he has to complain of any hardship in these respects.

Some of the orchards in Wingham and its neighbourhood are very valuable. Thus I saw one of four acres of, I think, plums and small fruit, said to be worth about £1,000, off which I was told a man earned a good living. Another, fifteen acres of cherries, with a nice house on it, had recently been bought in at the price of £5,200. It must be remembered, however, that it takes twenty years for a cherry orchard to come into bearing. The prices of fruit obtainable in 1900, the season before my visit, which is supposed to have produced the biggest crop that had been gathered during the last fifty years, were approximately: cherries, from 10s. to 14s. the sieve of, I think, eight gallons; pears, from 5s. to 7s. the bushel; apples, from 4s. to 6s. the bushel; gooseberries, from 2s. 6d. a bushel upwards, according to demand; and raspberries, from £26 to £32 per ton. Sometimes small-holdings do well here. Thus I saw one belonging to a young married man who had been a gentleman's servant and understood gardening. He began by hiring three acres, and saved enough to buy seven additional acres at £20 the acre, most of which he was cultivating as a fruit farm. This man, I was told, worked twice as hard as any hired labourer, but he made a good living. I should add that he was on his three-acre holding for ten years before he found himself in a position to purchase extra land.

Here in Wingham also—it was upon one of the farms that Mr. Maxted hires—I saw what he believes to be the biggest cherry in England. It is a noble tree.

There are few more charming places in the neighbourhood of Canterbury—that is, to those who love such things—than the hundred-acre nursery of Messrs. Mount, the well-known rose-growers. Never have I seen apples and pears better managed than they are here, or hops either. Even at that dead season of the year to those who know what a tree should be, the Cox's Orange pyramids of from three to five years' growth were a perfect sight, and, to come to another class of plant, so were the forced roses in the houses, some of which were already being cut for market.

The Messrs. Mount, by the way, are strong believers in the Paradise stock for apples and the quince for pears. Also they hold that the pyramid is by far the best form of tree—of course, on cultivated land—as it produces finer and more plentiful fruits, which can be gathered without the help of ladders, and is not so liable to be knocked about by gales. They think also that the end of March or even the beginning of April, when the roots are getting to work, is the best time for moving most shrubs. This surprised me, who have always been a believer in November planting. Of labour, their establishment being situated on the outskirts of the city—the land here rents for £8 the acre—they have sufficient, at a price. 'Only,' said young Mr. Mount, ' where we had five applicants for a vacancy we now get one.'

In Canterbury, as elsewhere, I sought an interview with some of the leading auctioneers and land agents. As a result I had a very interesting conversation with Mr. Wacher, of the firm of Messrs. Cooper and Wacher, who for many years has had to do with the management of estates in the district. He estimated the average fall since 1875 in the rental value of land at 33 per cent., and in the fee simple value at 50 per cent., instancing farms which within the present generation his firm had sold and resold at the above loss. Another holding of 191 acres, with which his family had been connected for many generations, was valued in 1870 at £14,000. In 1899 it sold for £4,000. The land, which was in good order, comprised arable and marshes, but was not suitable to the growth of hops. He said that practically there was no market for land, so that not much changed owners. With residential places things were little better; thus one had been knocked down not long before for about the cost of the house that stood upon the property.

As regarded the landlords, he was of opinion that they were 'like the eels which are said to grow accustomed to being skinned.' They had resigned themselves to their misfortunes. The feeling between them and the tenants was good, as the latter know that rents have fallen to a minimum. Mr. Wacher said that unless they had special advantages the farmers as a class were very poor; indeed, almost starving on the unprofitable lands. All those with whom he was acquainted on inferior soils owed money. In fact, poor land —that is, for the most part, corn-growing land—meant a poor tenant. Fruit and hops require a large capital, and even if he does not succeed, at least the man with capital lasts longer. The person without such resources is often knocked out in two years of hop-growing, for it is certain that if good farming scarcely pays, bad will not.

On the whole, farmers of fruit, hops, and stock were moderately prosperous. He thought that the best of them might perhaps make rent, interest on capital, and a living, but that none did more. Owing to three good harvests, things, Mr. Wacher said, have been looking a little brighter

KENTISH CHERRY TREE, SAID TO BE THE LARGEST IN ENGLAND

*Page 147*

of late, but with the best wheat at 29s. a quarter, he expected difficulties at the following Michaelmas. In short he added, 'We live on hope in this district.' Labour he believed to be very scarce everywhere, and although there were some good men to be had near the towns, their number was few. On his own farm he relied upon machinery without the assistance of which they could not pull through. Amongst other instances of this shortage he mentioned the case of a buyer of underwood who, when he asked him recently why he had not purchased more, replied that he would have done so but that he could get no one to cut the stuff. I inquired of him what he thought would be the end of this matter. He replied that the question was very serious, and one which nobody could answer. The education, in his opinion, is of the wrong sort, no agricultural teaching being given in the schools. At the same time he recognised the enormous difficulty of reconstructing the system.

Cottages, Mr. Wacher said, were wanted in some districts, but at the same time did not pay to build. As an example, he quoted two in the erection of which he had been interested. With water laid on, &c., they cost £550, and, after allowing for repairs and rates, bring in a little over £10 rent, or about two per cent. This he did not think a sufficient return. Farmers have, he thought, deteriorated, and as a class are no longer what they used to be. Many of them, indeed, belonged to the order of land 'skinners,' and when it comes to going out, thoroughly understood how to make up a big 'tillage bill.'

Labourers earned good wages, and the best of them £1 a week, or perhaps more; and, if they chose, the wives and children could bring in a great deal of money by hop training and picking. As a set, however, he had found them very improvident, and that an increase of wages meant, as a rule, more pints of beer. 'There is nothing cheery to look forward to,' said Mr. Wacher in conclusion; and after listening to his interesting account of agricultural matters in the Canterbury district, I inclined to agree with him.

Between Hythe and Rye, on the coast of Kent, lies a wide
district, measuring roughly ten miles from east to west and
thirteen from north to south, of some of the richest alluvial
soil in England. This is called Romney Marsh, and doubtless in a remote age was reclaimed, or reclaimed itself, from
the sea. A certain portion of this area, indeed, was drained,
or made otherwise fit for agricultural purposes, about forty
years ago. It is known as 'fresh land' to the present day,
and, as I was told, without the aid of any manure produces
enormous crops of grass and as much as six or eight quarters
to the acre of wheat. The 'stale lands,' on the other hand,
which are supposed to have been under the plough for
at least two centuries, are sometimes dressed, though not
often. I presume, however, that sheep are fed over all
these flats impartially, and that the soil is thus refreshed.
Up to 1875 the lands of Romney Marsh were some of
the most valuable in the country, and sold readily for £100
an acre. Those were the days of the 'Romney Kings,' men
who accumulated large fortunes out of sheep and corn, and
who were famous for their hospitality and high living. Now,
I am informed, with one or two exceptions, they have all
vanished away, most of them through the doors of the Bankruptcy Court. Of the prodigality and quaint characteristics
of some of these men strange stories are still told.

The Rev. Mr. H. Harbord was so good as to give us
particulars of a small property of fifty-one and a half acres
that he owned in this district. I quote them, as they are
typical and instructive. In 1840 this land was bought for
£4,000  In 1869 his family were offered for it £5,000, that
is, a fraction less than £100 an acre. I gathered that in
1901 he would have been a happy man if he could have
sold for £2,000 ; but, alas ! there was no bid forthcoming.
In the eighties the rental was £180 a year, the tenant, I
think, paying the ' Scots,' or sea-defence rate, which in 1900
amounted to 7s. an acre. In 1901 it was in hand, and he
could not let it at any reasonable rent. This fifty-one acres
will carry in winter 120 ewes, and, in addition, through the

summer 130 lambs and seventy-five tegs, to which in wet seasons must be added ten or twelve bullocks that eat the grasses which the sheep refuse.

On one of the bitterest days of the bitter spring of 1901 we set out from Wye on a thirty-mile drive to Romney Marsh, through it, and back again by another road. It was a terrible journey, of which the memory will long dwell with me. I recollect so cold were we, that at the end of six hours of it we could scarcely crawl from the cart. Mr. Amos, our host, who kindly escorted us, farmed about 420 acres—240 at Wye, of which ninety were hop lands, and 180 on the Marsh—and paid away no less than £2,500 in wages, of which £1,000 went in the hop-picking. Himself a hard-working and skilful man, he was of opinion that in his district farmers who have capital and who attend to their business, can just live—and no more. He said that there were practically no resident landlords, and that the only rural education given in the schools consisted of a few pictures of agricultural implements hung upon the walls. The depreciation of land values he put at 50 per cent., and the average rent at £1 the acre. He himself paid £2 ; but then, as he said with some bitterness, ' I have been here for years and improved my farm.'

Between the fertile fields of Wye and the Marsh lies a great stretch of undulating country. Its features are woods interspersed with arable and pasture lands, which grow gradually poorer and more sodden-looking towards the crest of the ridge, and are enclosed by somewhat ragged hedges. One farm we passed had sold not long before for £20 an acre. This land, that is of average quality, will grow ' fuggles,' or common hops, but not the finer sorts, which are very particular as to soil. At length we came to the edge of the high country, and saw the great grey Marsh stretched out beneath us far as the eye could reach, its expanses broken only here by a church tower and there by some solitary farm building or cottage that in past generations, when there were no roads, had been the home of smugglers,

Driving on through the flat dyke-bordered fields and pastures, some of them badly farmed enough, as the couch-grass and rushes showed, we came at length to Mr. Amos's holding and his steward's house, which are situated in the parish of Orgarswick. To be more correct, this is the parish which, population on the Marsh being somewhat thin, contains no other dwelling. Just in front of the little house is a patch of grass, rather greener than the surrounding fields, in which can be traced the outline of foundations. They were those of the village church when there was a village, and doubtless beneath this green plot of grass lie the bones of its ancient inhabitants. A little enclosure of land across the road is still glebe, now the property of some neighbouring parish. It would be hard to find a more desolate place, at any rate in the snows of winter or the hurricanes of spring, than this portion of the great Marsh. We walked round the holding, that is all pasture, and inspected Mr. Amos's pedigree Romney sheep, which were just then beginning to lamb behind queer V-shaped shelters made of three straw-lined hurdles. Several of the lambs had succumbed to the weather; indeed, we found one poor little thing lying dead with its eyes picked out by rooks, which are always on the watch for such delicacies.

Our inspection finished—at that time of year there was not much to look at—we started off again, and, circling through a portion of the Marsh down to the wall which protects it from the sea, turned homewards by the western road. About half-way we climbed a backbone of very poor land, remarkable for its hungry soil and bare brown pastures, which looked as if they would scarcely feed a rabbit. Presently, driving along the frost-bound road downwards towards the vale, we reached a richer country. One farm we passed had forty acres of hops, which seemed well tended and were protected by poplar fences, some fruit orchards, and a milk walk, carrying, I think, eighty cows. Its master, we were informed, had failed a while before for

£10,000, and at that time was said to be working the farm for the creditors at a wage of £2 per week.

Mr. Amos told me that he considered larch to be the best material for hop poles, though chestnut and spruce are also good. The new plan of creosoting these poles is ingenious. When quite dry they are placed in a chamber from which the air is exhausted. Then tar is let into the vacuum and at once penetrates every fibre of the wood. When properly prepared, these poles, or wire-props, will last from thirty to forty years.

The average rents upon the marshlands, which, when wool and corn were valuable, used to command so much money, and yet leave so fine a profit to their farmers, are now from £1 to 25s., out of which the landlord must pay tithe, taxes, and 'Scots,' except a proportion of 2s. of the last, which is payable by the tenant. This land when under pasture is all the better for being fed quite bare, and if treated thus with horses, the result is gradually to destroy the rush growths to which it is so liable. The soil is very rich and will produce as much as six—and sometimes eight —quarters of wheat to the acre ; but it ought to be ploughed early, as if left till later it becomes very sticky and hard to manage. To judge from some fields I saw, also, unless properly farmed it is liable to couch-grass. 'Emmet' or ant-hills are also very frequent and unsightly. If these are not cut away and scattered every three years they grow large and spoil the land.

The system of drainage on these marshes is somewhat elaborate, each field being surrounded with dykes that connect ultimately with the main sewer which, I think, runs to the sea past the beautiful church of All Saints at Lydd. Mr. Amos told me that many farmers spend £15 an acre on manure for their hops, and that the syringing of ninety acres cost him £250 a year. This is done from five to eight times in the season with a mixture of dissolved soap, quassia chips, and a little tobacco. Amongst many others, I heard one view on this visit which I trust does not apply to the vast majority of cases in Kent, namely, that 'it is an absolute disadvantage to be a good farmer because then the rent is put up.'

Before I left Canterbury I visited, or rather revisited, St. Augustine's, now once more, as in the earliest days, a missionary college. When I was here on a previous occasion to lay the foundation-stone of a new building, I was told that a piece of almost waste land then cumbered with sheds and, I think, pigsties, which adjoined the college grounds, was coming into the market. Long ago this place was the site first of a heathen temple and afterwards that of the noble fane of St. Pancras. Naturally, therefore, the authorities of the college were most anxious to find the money wherewith to purchase a spot, of old so hallowed, since the opportunity once let slip might never return again. On this occasion I was delighted to learn that owing to the unselfish action of several guarantors, this sum, about £3,000 I think, had been provided, and, after centuries of alienation, that the land again belonged to St. Augustine's.

Already the shanties, modern masonry, and débris had been cleared away and a few excavations made in what was the chancel of the ancient church and elsewhere with interesting archæological results. Thus the original square tiles of the flooring and the bases of the old walls were brought to light and proved to be of Roman origin. In the south chapel also, which is believed to have been built in the time of Ethelbert, the foundation of the Augustine altar was uncovered, and the plan of the Roman building, with its Anglo-Saxon imitations and mediæval additions, more or less made clear. Amid carved stones and pieces of coloured glass, bones too were found that doubtless had been those of princes, spiritual or temporal. These are relics which even the most unimaginative could not contemplate without emotion, although the mortal remains of St. Augustine himself, which it is thought may have been hidden away here, have not yet been discovered.

Millionaires are many : will not one of them come

forward and give £100,000 to restore the ruins of St. Pancras to their ancient glory? The money might be worse spent; in few ways, indeed, could it be better spent. Moreover, here there is good precedent for such liberality. Had it not been for the late Mr. A. J. Beresford-Hope, who in 1843 purchased the Abbey grounds and ruins, which, with the assistance of Mr. Edward Coleridge, afterwards, to a great extent, he restored upon the old lines, it is probable that now the former would have been cut up into building lots, and most of the latter swept away. Indeed, when he bought them, the beautiful gateway was a brewery, the state bed-chamber over it held the cooling vat, the 'Guesten' hall was a place for public dances—not always of the most refined description—and the kitchen a pot-house. The Great hall, the Chapel, and the Infirmary had vanished, the dormitories were ruins, the great tower had fallen down, and one of the walls of the Abbey Church served as a fives-court. All this is altered now, and I think that Mr. Beresford-Hope could have no finer monument to his memory than these buildings which he caused to re-arise, and dedicated anew to their sacred purpose of educating teachers for the heathen.

I called upon the Rev. Mr. Watkin Wynn Williams, the librarian, at his chambers over the Gateway. It was strange to drink tea in that mediæval apartment, practically unchanged, I believe, from its ancient state, which before the Dissolution had been occupied by so many honoured guests of the old abbots, and after it, served as a bedchamber to Queen Elizabeth; to Charles I., who here spent the first days of his honeymoon with the Princess Henrietta Maria; and to Charles II., who slept in it on his triumphal progress to London at the time of the Restoration.

From Canterbury, the centre of East Kent, we travelled to Maidstone, which may, I suppose, be considered the capital of West Kent, in many ways the most favoured district in England. Here I had the advantage of seeing Mr. Bracher, the secretary of the Maidstone Farmers' Club, and of going over the splendid fruit and hop farm of Mr. Herbert Leney, of Court Lodge, West Farleigh, a well-known and respected gentleman and county councillor of that division. Mr. Bracher could give no glowing report of the state of the agricultural industry. Many of the farmers, he said, were hard pressed, and hung on almost in a condition of insolvency, hoping for a change for the better. The banks, that had suffered much through the depression caused by the fall in the value of corn and of wool, which in the Romney Marsh district had declined from 2s. to about 6d. the pound, had, moreover, grown timid of advancing money even upon hops. In places where fruit is grown on the finest soil, such as the neighbourhoods of East Sutton, Langley, and Leeds, which might be called the pick of Kent, the land, he informed me, still held its own, and commanded a rent of from 40s. to 50s. the acre, but in the hill districts it brought in only about 10s. the acre, or even less. Such land fetched little when sold, sometimes not £20 the acre. The supply of labour, Mr. Bracher said, was bad, and the population in the rural parishes decreased steadily. He added that in most of the schools no agricultural education was given.

Our road from Maidstone to East Farleigh, a small village some three miles distant, situated on the south bank of the Medway, where the soil is rich loam with a rag-stone and chalk subsoil, ran through very beautiful country. Following the line of the wide vale where flows the broad stream of the Medway, we passed first by highly cultivated orchards and hop gardens. Then came rich fresh-looking pastures stretching to the ancient bridge by which we passed the river to reach Mr. Leney's house, that lies among trees upon its further side.

Mr. Leney's holding is, I believe, one of the finest in the country-side. In all it covers about 300 acres, of which some 10 per cent. are arable and pasture, leaving 100 acres or more under hops and about 100 acres of fruit land. This is a very large area for such crops, as will be readily

SPECIMEN APPLE TREE AND NUT BUSHES ON MR. LENEY'S FARM, SHOWING KENT METHOD OF PRUNING

understood when I state that on it his labour-bill comes to a total of between £4,000 and £5,000 per annum, of which sum £2,000 goes in the hop-picking alone. Although it was still the dead season of the year, when the bare trees and bushes are unadorned with leaves, until I saw this place I never understood to what perfection the culture of fruit and hops can be brought. The latter, by the way, were, if I recollect right, mostly trained upon the umbrella plan of wiring. There are, however, various other systems, amongst which the Worcester is one of the best known. This wiring is very expensive; also the price of the poles seemed to be double what it was five years before. Another favourite system is the 'Butcher,' so named after a famous grower, now, I believe, deceased. This has three strings to a hop hill, and leads the bine very evenly to the permanent wires above. Of these hills there were, I understood, some 1,100 to the acre. Indeed everything to do with the cultivation of hops is expensive, the labour, the manures, and even the lime, which here had to be carted a long way and cost Mr. Leney 12s. a yard, or, allowing for a dressing of seven loads, 70s. an acre.

Of fruit he grew many varieties, among apples, Lord Suffield, Lord Derby, and Worcester Pearmain being the favourites. These used to fetch 10s. the bushel, but at that time brought in from 5s. to 6s. only. His pyramid apples, planted five years, showed extraordinary growth, and those ten years of age were really wonderful. All of them were very carefully pruned so as to allow the maximum of light and air to reach the individual fruits. The nuts also were not grown in the tangled bushes to which we are accustomed in the Eastern Counties, but on a single stem like trees. From this stem, at a distance of a foot or two above the ground, issue three or four stout branches of which the shoots are cut back very hard, leaving the centre of the tree quite open. Treated thus they produce enormous crops, even when set upon very stony soil. In one orchard which we visited, a man was engaged in whitewashing the apple and

nut trees that grew here together.   First the bark is roughly
scraped, after which the following mixture is applied :—

| | | | | |
|---|---|---|---|---|
| Paraffin | . | . | . | 1 quart. |
| Salt  . | . | . | . | 1 pound. |
| Soft soap . | . | . | . | 1 pound. |
| Lime | . | . | . | 1 bucket. |
| Water | . | . | . | 30 to 40 gallons. |

When well mixed in a tub and applied thickly to the
trunk and branches of a tree, this compound, I was told, is
a great protective against moss and insect pests.

We also saw a cherry orchard which we were informed
would let for £10 the acre.   Mr. Leney, by the way, was
beginning to plant cherries as pyramids, which of course
would come into bearing much more quickly than do the
standard trees.   Under-fruit, such as currants and gooseberries, he said, no longer paid.   Therefore in some of his
orchards he had laid down grass beneath the standard trees,
upon which he grazed pedigree sheep.

Cottages, of which he had only eight upon his farm,
were let at 2s. 6d. a week, somewhat dearer than is general
in most counties.   To men, however, who can earn from
30s. to 35s. the week at hop drying while it lasts, and
9d. a 'packet' for hop pressing, with 1s. a day beer money,
the extra 6d. or 1s. for rent should not prove onerous.
Mr. Leney told me that there were a few small-holders—
twenty to thirty acre men—in that neighbourhood.   Out of
such patches of ground, when under fruit, they used to be
able to get a livelihood, but now, he said, they were obliged
to live like labourers ; indeed some of them virtually starved.
To this short account of Mr. Leney's fine farm I should add
that he kept a few prize-bred shorthorn cattle.   A bull and
heifer which he showed us were grand animals.

Of the condition of the labour market Mr. Leney spoke
with great emphasis.   He stated that, taking the year through,
many of the men with their wives and small children can

earn an average of £2 a week, and that, although the wages
are so high, still the young men go. He considered that the
labourer earned 30 per cent. more now than was the case ten
years before, for which he did 30 per cent. less work than
he used to do. In his opinion in the present state of affairs
the labourer was doing the best; the landlord, who could
still get from £2 to 50s. per acre for planted farms, the next
best; and the tenant the worst. If men were to be kept
on the soil, he thought that they would have to be paid at
the rate of mechanics in towns, and that the agricultural
industry would not bear the burden; also that good cottages
must be provided, of which there was a scarcity in that
neighbourhood.

Here is a summary of his views on the position and
prospects of the hop farmer in Kent. He said that it was the
most speculative of all trades, 'that the Stock Exchange is
a fool to it.' According to him, once the tenant was in on
a long lease—for here many of them still held under agreements of the old stringent sort—the money goes out and
must go out. He cannot stop, since—the Agricultural
Holdings Act not being retrospective—under the terms of
the lease, if he goes or defaults, the landlord benefits by his
tenant's capital invested on the holding in the shape of trees,
hop plants, wiring, and cultivation. So he continues to increase the value of the farm, sinking deeper and deeper,
and hoping that 'times will mend.' They do not, but still
he hopes and spends, and still circumstances combine to
keep down prices. At last, but too frequently, the day
comes when the load of debt overwhelms him, and the
landlord and the in-coming tenant reap the benefit of his
life's work. Meanwhile the state of speculative unrest in
which he lives often has an evil and unhinging effect upon
his mind. He becomes prematurely worn out and old. The
prices the Kent hop farmer realises for his produce seem
attractive enough to those who do not know the facts, but,
said Mr. Leney, there is no need for the grower of corn and
stock, who wrings a bare living from the soil, to envy him.

Before leaving the subject of this farm, I must state how sorry I was to read recently in the papers, that in the destructive hail-storm that devastated this district of Kent in September, 1902, Mr. Leney suffered loss to the extent of £8,000. I can only hope that the extent of the damage done to his hops and fruit has been exaggerated.

One of the most interesting general views of agricultural conditions in Kent which I have received, is from Sir Edwyn S. Dawes, K.C.M.G., who owns a large property near Faversham. Of course, as he himself points out, it must be remembered that with Sir Edwyn, husbandry, and indeed land-owning, is a means of recreation rather than of livelihood. He is what is called in that useful work of reference 'Who's Who' a 'scientific farmer,' and when ordinary working husbandmen are frequently unable to do so, it is difficult for 'scientific farmers,' by which generally, may be understood gentlemen who improve their properties regardless of expense, to make the occupation pay. At the same time it is foolish to underrate the value of opinions derived from such sources, seeing that they are for the most part those of highly intelligent men who, having succeeded brilliantly in other walks of life, have really brought their intellects to bear upon the problems connected with the land. Were they content to do only as their neighbours do, it is probable that they would surpass those neighbours in the results attained. As it is, possessing ample capital to spend, they do more than their neighbours, leaving the profit of their improvements to be reaped by those who come after them. Thus Sir Edwyn Dawes said :—

'I have about 2,000 acres of my own, which I farm highly and cheat myself into the belief that my improvements add to the value of the property. My farm accounts year by year show a substantial balance on the wrong side, but as I keep on planting fruit largely, those who come after me will reap the benefit. Meanwhile, it is to me the pleasantest of recreations, giving me health and pleasure far beyond yachting and horses.'

The result is that he has succeeded not only in keeping the agricultural labourers on his estate in full employment, but also in increasing their numbers.

Sir Edwyn said he did not think that rents had fallen much in his immediate district since 1875. Large farms, however, were difficult to let, and he was told that a landlord in his neighbourhood had several on his hands. Small farms with land suitable for hops and fruit, were sought after, and would let at from 30s. up to as high as £5 the acre. The fee-simple value of large farms had certainly fallen since 1875, but small-holdings adapted to fruit had advanced in price. In the autumn of 1900 a little farm of 14¾ acres with a nice cottage on it was bought in at £5,100. On the whole, he thought that in his district farms let readily, and that rents were fairly well paid. There were but few resident landlords. During the three last generations their number had greatly diminished.

Of labourers there was a good supply, who received 2s. 6d. per diem in winter and 3s. in summer. They could, however, earn more than this at piece work in the hop gardens and fruit plantations. For twenty years he himself had employed fully a hundred agricultural labourers at an average wage for able-bodied men of from 20s. to 22s. a week. Cottages were fairly numerous, and rented at from 2s. to 3s. a week, according to position and size. His own cottages, of which he possessed about seventy, had six rooms. A good many of the most intelligent young men found places in the police and on the railway; also several went to the brick-fields, but a fair proportion stayed upon the land. They married young, and if they could get a cottage it helped to keep them. Latterly in his neighbourhood they had suffered a good deal through the drain of the boys into the Navy, so much so indeed that 'mates' to go with the waggoners and look after the horses were hard to find. Education, in his opinion, had not much to do with their leaving the land, except indirectly by fitting them to fill railway and police appointments.

On the whole, he thought that landlord, tenant farmer, and labourer in his district had not much of which to complain. They grumbled at high railway rates, increasing taxes, and low prices for produce, but when he looked around him he saw hard-working, intelligent men doing very well ; those who came to grief being generally idle, unsteady, or thriftless. He could see no signs of any improvement in the general state of agriculture. The very low prices of grain, cattle, sheep, wool, &c., left but an infinitesimal margin of profit even for those who farmed the best. Hops and fruit kept the farmers going in his neighbourhood, but even this class of produce was hard pushed by the competition of foreign importations. This view, I may remark, is in somewhat strong contrast to that expressed by Sir Edwyn in the preceding paragraph.

The desertion of the country districts was undoubtedly, in his opinion, an unmitigated evil, but one for which it was not easy to suggest a remedy. Higher prices for farm-produce could only be secured by protection, which it seemed hopeless to expect. He thought that he foresaw a falling off in our manufactures, and probably a reduction of wages as a result of foreign competition. When this happened there would be less inducement for labourers to leave the land. This, however, was mere conjecture. Cheaper railway rates and a lessening of taxes on the land seemed to him the only reliefs for which we could contend at present. For the rest we must look to the energy and intelligence of those who have to wring a living out of the soil.

The Rev. J. A. Boodle, of Boughton Vicarage, Faversham, a connection of my own, said of this district also, ' our farmers, although not making the *large* fortunes they used to make, are all well-to-do, and the cultivation of hops (of which there are 600 acres in the parish) gives so much work to men, women, and children, that the labouring class is very thriving.'

The above views are, I think, the most hopeful that I heard in Kent. Still, it must be remembered that a gentleman in the position of Sir Edwyn Dawes, would naturally look at these questions through rosier spectacles than those which are worn by the ordinary much-harassed tenant farmer, or by the impecunious and too often mortgaged landlord.

To turn to another subject, I received an interesting communication from Miss Mary L. Russell, of St. John's, Sutton-at-Hone, Kent, dealing with the housing and general condition of the hop-pickers, who in the autumn of the year flock in thousands from the great towns to this county. I will quote the substance of her letter.

Miss Russell began her statement by assuring me that it was founded upon personal observations made while visiting the children of these people, and was in no wise exaggerated. She said that the habitations provided for hop-pickers are of tin, fitted with doors and iron ventilators, but without flooring or windows. One covered-in brick oven for cooking in wet weather and two or three sanitary huts are found, but there are no coppers or places for washing clothes. On some farms there is a tank to which water is brought in a cart, but at other places it must be fetched by the pickers, who sleep upon straw which is given to them, though rarely changed. The huts stand in the full sun, without any shelter from trees. They have no wells. The adult pickers can scarcely any of them read, the young men being as ignorant as the old, but the younger children can most of them read a very little, although this is not so in some cases.

The majority, both of men and women, have no thought except for the public-house and drink, and the girls are very wild. Owing to the insufficient arrangements made for personal cleanliness, the condition of the children, who are infested with insects, is extremely bad. Some of them suffer from ophthalmia, caused by dirt, and one little fellow of five, whom she knew, was covered with sores. As the doctor cannot carry on his business in such places, when children are taken ill they must be brought to him, even if their ailment is bronchitis. The condition of a woman whose child was born in one of these huts was, she said, too awful to describe to me.

Miss Russell thought that by way of remedy the Education Department should send travelling teachers to places where large numbers of children live in huts. Such children should not be allowed to pass all their time in the fruit fields, but ought to receive three hours' instruction at the beginning of the day before they were tired out. She believed that much might be done if the dwelling huts were made more suitable to their purpose, and that this could only be brought about by insisting on the local authorities building decent and sanitary tin houses and charging interest to the farmers for their use. Such houses could be moved from place to place as they were required. Miss Russell added that she knew it might be argued that, bad as these conditions were, still they are better than those of the dens in a London slum. She maintained, however, that in these country places there is a chance of improving the habits, morals, and education of a portion of our future labouring class, and that it is our duty not to allow such an opportunity to slip.

Doubtless all that Miss Russell says is true, and at any rate in a large proportion of the places which they frequent, the sanitary and moral surroundings of the hop-pickers are deplorable. But this question remains, Who is to better them? The majority of hop farmers make no more than a living; some, indeed, make less. If they were to be forced to provide respectable accommodation for the scores or hundreds of hands whom they employ for about a month of the year with their families, the workhouses of Kent would soon be overflowing. To insist upon such a thing would, I believe, in practice bring the hop industry to an end, for large tin buildings with wells, outhouses, &c., are costly. Miss Russell suggests that the work should be undertaken by the local authorities, by which I suppose she means the County or District Councils. But these bodies have to look to the rates for funds, and in Kent, as elsewhere, rates are already high enough. We may be sure that the interest which she thinks ought to be charged to the farmers, even if they did not refuse to pay it, would by no means be adequate to the capital expenditure, especially as the depreciation of movable tin buildings which must be frequently renewed, and, by the way, would be required almost everywhere at the same time, would be very heavy.

There remains the State, but the State already staggers under its load of obligations, local and imperial, like Christian beneath his sins in the Slough of Despair. How much more can its broad back carry? For my part I can see but two remedies. One—the heroic method—would be to forbid the employment of hop-pickers unless their accommodation was such as a sanitary Board would approve, which, I suppose, in most cases would mean an end of hop and fruit growing, since without ample labour at the proper season, these crops are useless. The other—a more humble expedient—is to let things go on as they are, and trust to the efforts and purses of philanthropists to better them. After all, it must be remembered that around these crowded insanitary hovels breathes the sweet, fresh air, and above them stretches the blue sky of English summer. In the festering slums of London such blessings are absent, and hop and fruit picking is the annual holiday of tens of thousands of their denizens—to them, indeed, what the autumn visit to sea or country-side is to other classes of town dwellers.

The question remains whether, with all these disadvantages which Miss Russell so movingly describes, the balance of good is not therefore still in favour of the yearly exodus to the evil-smelling shanties of the gardens of Kent, with its accompaniment of healthful labour in a pure atmosphere sweetened by the sights and sounds of Nature undefiled. After all, at the season of the year when their services are required the days are few on which the pickers or their children need pass more than eight hours out of the twenty-four beneath the shelter of a roof.

I put forward this side of the case because, where the cure of evils seems difficult, if not hopeless, it is as well to bear in mind their compensations.

I ventured the opinion just now that rates are already high enough in Kent. Certainly it is shared by the gentleman whose views I now proceed to quote, a Kentish landowner, who does not, however, desire that his name or address should be published. He dwelt on the tithe question and ' the present iniquitous manner in which rates are levied,' saying that he spoke as a landlord, and by way of example instanced his own case.

He owns a considerable extent of poor land in the hill district of Kent, and ever since he came into the property many years ago, which was then mostly in hand, said that he had been endeavouring to find tenants for his farms, but without success. Land, he stated, rarely pays if it is unlet, and in attempting to farm it year by year he had lost money. The principle of ' rateable value ' was supposed to be based upon what the land will let at, taking one year with another, and he contended, believing the argument to be sound and just, that if a man cannot let his land at all, and is able to prove to the satisfaction of the rating or other authorities that farming it means a steady loss of money, it has *no* rateable value. In such a case there ought, in his view, to be a right of obtaining a repayment of the rates on production of accounts, similar to that which exists in the matter of income tax. He thought, further, that the deficiency which the exercise of such a right would cause in the rates should, at least in some measure, be made good out of Imperial revenue. As it was, if an owner appealed to the assessment Committee, in all probability the answer he received would be to the effect that his land cannot be reduced to prairie value, and that a similar farm to that concerning which the appeal was laid was let at so much an acre. Yet very possibly the actual holding instanced as an argument against him, might in fact, be let to one of the appellant's own tenants, who, in practice, paid little or none of the nominal rent, but was allowed to remain in possession, because if he were sent away no one could be found to take his place, and capital must be forthcoming to farm the land.

As regarded tithe, he contended that it was put upon the land at a time when such land was a paying investment, and he could not see why, when that land brought its owner nothing but actual loss, he should have to find money elsewhere to satisfy the tithe. In his case it amounted to this, that the only persons who had ever received a penny out of a great deal of his property, or rather out of money which was supposed to have been derived from that property, were the rating authorities and the tithe owners. Not only had he taken nothing, he had been obliged to find a great portion of the sums necessary to satisfy rates, tithe, and other charges upon his land out of extraneous resources which he happened to possess. Had he not possessed them he would by now have become a bankrupt for no other fault or reason than that chance had made him a landowner.

Into the accuracy of my informant's definition of the origin of tithe I cannot enter at length, as the scope of this work scarcely comprises such a subject. I may say, however, that I believe that tithe in England was not originally charged upon land, or on things that could not exist except for the land, alone. There were also personal tithes which might be collected from moneys earned in business or other occupations, and were so collected until the time of Edward VI. and, I imagine, subsequently. In the early centuries, copying, probably, the example of the Jewish law, the payment of tithe was enjoined by the authorities of the Church and recognised by the Saxon and Danish kings of England, it is to be presumed, without reference to whether or not land was or was not in those days ' a paying investment.' Still he must be right to this extent. If there were no profit to be wrung from the land and its products, the most pious-minded owners could scarcely have paid tithe, which, I gather, was then collected in kind, as I think was common until the passing of the Tithe Commutation Act of

1836. Had it not paid, directly or indirectly, to cultivate the land, there would have been no produce, and from nothing it is impossible to subtract a tenth, nor could the tithe owner, lay or spiritual, distrain upon nothing. At present, without doubt the charge in many cases works great injustice, and, although it is regulated by the price of cereals, frequently absorbs a sum out of all proportion to that which the land produces.

Here is an instance taken, not from Kent, but from Norfolk :—I myself have a farm which from a rent of £230 a year dropped to £50 a year. Out of this £50 I had to pay from £26 to £28 in tithe. When the farm produced £230 the tithe, I believe, was about £30—more even then, it will be observed, than the Scriptural tenth, which, by the way, ought surely to be calculated upon net income. At the present moment this farm is let for £75 the year, and the tithe comes to £24. That is to say, after allowing for the cost of repairs, remissions, taxes, rates, agent's expenses, &c., the tithe practically absorbs all profit that is derived from the land. Such a result as this is not right and can never have been intended. Still it is a hard case, for which it seems difficult to devise a remedy. Nor indeed is any attempt being made, or likely to be made, in this direction.

As regards rates also, in such examples as that of my informant, the case is exceedingly hard. It is, as he said, most unjust that a man who receives nothing should have to pay rates upon what he does not receive, because his more fortunate neighbour receives, or is supposed to receive, something. This gentleman thinks that under these circumstances the rates ought to be paid by the Imperial Exchequer. But does he really imagine that the Treasury would ever undertake such a burden, any more than the local authorities would undertake to pay for the housing of 'hoppers,' as was suggested by Miss Russell ? Their answer would be brutal but plain :—

'If your land cannot pay its way, or you are not prepared to pay for it, then abandon your land, or sell it for what it will fetch.' In truth, the fact must be faced that there is always this resource. Even a tenant for life can now sell for whatever he is able to obtain upon the market, the mansion-house and its appurtenances alone excepted, to part with which he must have the consent of the Court of Chancery. If he could only obtain 10s. an acre I presume that he might sell for that amount as men do in South Africa and other distant countries. Then at least he would be clear of his annual loss. Yet nobody does sell for 10s. the acre. We prefer to meet our obligations of tithe, rate, &c. as best we can, and to cling to our property hoping for better times, or a change of fortune. Yet until we adopt this heroic course, it is useless to call upon the Imperial Exchequer to come to our aid. We cannot both carry the burden and ask that it should be borne by somebody else. If a holder's shares in any enterprise become valueless, he does not beseech the Treasury to pay him dividends, or to find money to meet the unpaid calls thereon. He writes off those shares at a loss, and his estate is liable for the uncollected charges if any.

The case is not wholly analogous, still there is something in the parallel ; for instance, these shares might conceivably, especially in an unlimited company, be liable to something answering to a rent-charge, payable whether they were profitable or not, and fixed upon them in times when they had been profitable. To be brief, my point is, that however hard the case may be in the instance of land, it gives the sufferer no claim to relief from the State. It is a misfortune that comes from Heaven, and he must bear with it, or, by cutting himself wholly adrift from the cause, be free of it. Of course, if it proved absolutely impossible for him either to sell or to give away the property that brought about his woes, his position would not only be painful but absurd. But in England, at any rate, I believe that this case has yet to arise. When it becomes general the State may intervene ; but until that happens of such help there is little hope.

Lord Northbourne—whose estate I was unfortunately unable to visit, as I had already left the county when I received his kind invitation to do so—has been so good as to give me some interesting information upon the past history and present prospects of Kentish agriculture. He said that in the middle ages the greater part of the land in East Kent was cultivated by the monks. It might then be described as divided into three different areas : the open down-country, which is by far the largest; the district of Romney Marsh, covering about 40,000 acres; and the heavy alluvial land at present used for market gardens. Now things are changed. After the Reformation, and again after the Civil Wars, the Church lands were much broken up. In this county the population had never been very large, and here less record remains of the effects of these convulsions than in many other places. There existed no great landowners or territorial potentates, so gradually the Kentish yeoman came into being, and with him the small squires of moderate fortune. These were by no means an unintellectual class, and lived a simple but comfortable life on incomes varying perhaps from £500 to £1,000 a year. For a while they struggled on, but he could say that in his own lifetime he had seen the disappearance of the whole of them. They had been absolutely engulfed. Rather later, or almost *pari passu* with them, the tenant farmers came into existence. Thirty years ago there were many of these men who risked £5,000, or £10,000, or even £20,000, in the cultivation of hired land. Of this class here and there a few still remained, but of the rest some had been ruined and some had gone away. Now such men were not forthcoming, and the land is very largely in the hands of its owners.

Lord Northbourne said that he lived about thirteen miles from Canterbury, and between his property and Canterbury there was scarcely an estate which was not farmed by the proprietor. But a few weeks previously a neighbour of his had sold 1,300 acres for £12,000, that is, for about £9 the acre. His own estate was bought by his father in 1847, and would, he thought, compare favourably with most residential properties, although it was in rather a dilapidated condition when he succeeded to it about ten years ago, the social changes of the last thirty years not having been faced and considered. Personally he found that the worries and anxieties were considerable, and the actual financial results from year to year small ; but although the returns might be poor, as yet he did not find agriculture a losing game.

In his district it was of no use growing corn, but directly the farmer got away from corn then his troubles began. Personally he relied entirely upon the very best stock, and he intended to continue much upon his present lines. He added that he was certain of very little, but with regard to land no one can run off with it, nor can it be destroyed by fire. It must always have *some* value, and its intelligent cultivation was quite the highest and best occupation to which anyone could aspire, involving as it did endless per-severance, courage, patience, faith, industry, and pursuit of knowledge. He was quite sure also that no legislation could ever bring about changes in social conditions like the touch of a magician's wand, and that no two properties, no two fields even, should receive similar treatment. Probability was the guide of life, and we must take measure of our methods in accordance with our means and opportunities. He had no special panacea to offer, and no special confi-dence that the course that he pursued was a wise one ; but according to his imperfect lights he did what seemed prob-ably the best, leaving Time to be the final arbiter in the matter. There were not many good practical farmers, and if he could be justly deemed of their number, he would be amply satisfied.

Upon these ably expressed views I have but one criti-cism to offer. Lord Northbourne says he is certain that no legislation can ever bring about great changes in social con-ditions. I presume he means in matters connected with the land. But did not the passing of Free Trade bring about such a change ? And would not a reversion to Protection—

should such a thing ever happen—bring about another equally far-reaching ?

Another interesting informant in Kent was the wife of a poor gentleman who had been in business as a hop and fruit farmer for thirty-two years, but recently had found himself obliged to file a petition in the Bankruptcy Court, and was then engaged in carrying on the farm for the benefit of his creditors. Into this tale of trouble it is not necessary to enter, and I only mention it as showing that there are parts of the county where things are less prosperous than in the Faversham district, in which Sir Edwyn Dawes and the Rev. Mr. Boodle reside. I believe that the farmer to whose case I allude—and I have seen testimony concerning him other than that of his wife—certainly could not be called 'idle, unsteady, or thriftless.' On the contrary, he is reported to have been a thorough master of his business, whose ruin was due to misfortune and the pressure of the times.

It will be gathered from what I have written that hop growing is the chief agricultural industry of Kent, more important even than that of fruit culture. Although its profits are sometimes large, this crop, as I have shown, is very costly to produce, and owing to its liability to disease, to injury by wind or weather, of which the season of 1902 has furnished so sad and striking an example, and the uncertainty of the price which it will fetch, it is also, I suppose, the most speculative in England. Further, it has to contend with another trouble.

Like almost every business and profession, the hop trade suffers from the burden of the middleman—in this case he is called the factor—whose occupation it is to negotiate between the producer of hops and the buyer of hops. I think that I spoke to few farmers, land agents, or solicitors in Kent who did not complain bitterly of these factors. For obvious reasons, it is impossible to give names, but here are one or two specimen opinions. Said one gentleman : ' It is monstrous, but the " ring " makes the grower take its price. We have tried to combine, but it is useless ; they are too strong. The small man borrows from the factor, who then has the crop completely in his power.' Another gentleman told me that they—that is, the growers— were not allowed to be present when the factor sold their produce to the merchant; so that they never knew what took place, and that the merchants refused to deal with them direct. A third, a solicitor, alleged, and showed documents connected with resulting bankruptcy proceedings to prove what he said, that some of the factors make a habit of attending the markets before the hop picking, and of offering advances to any farmers whom they may find short of cash, as he instanced by a certain very pitiful case. From that moment the borrower is in the power of the lender, and must put up, he declared, with any neglect or maltreatment which the latter chooses to heap upon him. The end of this state of affairs may be imagined.

Still it is right to add that hop factors, or certain of them, strongly disagree with this version of the matter. Thus, when my articles, which are incorporated in this book, were appearing in the *Daily Express*, one of these gentlemen, Mr. John Gulland, of the London firm of Selmes, Jackson, and Gulland, wrote to me saying, ' I cannot but think that you are under some misapprehension as to the respective position of the hop factor and hop grower. As one of a hard-working and, I trust, honest body of men, would you permit me to say a word or two from the hop factor's point of view ? Practically it has been found impossible to sell the hop crop without a "middleman," and the hop factor's business being essentially a commission one, his interests are identical with those of the hop grower whom he represents. Far from working to get prices down, it is always to his own interest to keep prices as high as possible.'

I print this denial gladly, since, as Mr. Gulland suggests, certainly I do not wish any words of mine to be ' misleading,' and it is possible, as he suggests further, that I do not ' quite understand ' the points at issue. My only comment is that the complaints of the growers, or some of them, are as I have set them out above. Between their case and that of the hop factors my readers must judge. They, I am sure, believed what they said, as Mr. Gulland believes what he says. But it strikes me as possible that as there are solicitors *and* solicitors, so there are hop factors—*and* hop factors.

As I have stated, another rather common cause of complaint, at least among those Kent farmers who went into their holdings under the old form of lease, or who had some 'verbal understanding' with a respected owner, perhaps long since departed to the Shades, is that they have no adequate security for their improvements, which on their death or giving up of the farm will go to the landlord practically without compensation. It must be remembered, however, that in these questions there is a landlord's as well as a tenant's side to be considered.

In conclusion, I am sorry to have to state that I ended my visit to Kent considerably disappointed and discouraged. To sum up. The condition of the poor lands and those who worked them appeared to be very bad, if not desperate. As regarded the rich hop and fruit growing districts, I believe much of their seeming prosperity to be hollow, and that but a small proportion of the farmers who depend upon their farming and not upon other means, are really making money in this uncertain business. Worst of all, however, because it threw its shadow over all, was the question of labour. No wage that employers can pay seems to be sufficient to induce the young men of Kent to stop upon the land, and when the old ones die—what then? So at least it was in 1901. Such, at any rate, are my opinions briefly stated, but formed after some consideration and research. I only trust that they may be wrong.

# DEVONSHIRE

THE south-western county of Devonshire, to which I travelled from Kent, has an area of about 1,667,000 acres, and is the third largest in England. It is a hilly and very well-watered county, remarkable for beautiful scenery, and, except upon the moors, for its mild, moist climate. A great deal of the moorland is still uncultivated, but the rest of the county is famous for its rich arable soils, and especially for its pasture land. With the exception of hops, almost every crop grows there. Apples are also cultivated, although for the most part in a somewhat careless fashion, and much cider is made. The red Devon cattle, of which there are several strains, have many excellent qualities. The majority of the population are of the old English stock, intermixed here and there with the Cornish blood. Such, in few words, are the main characteristics of the shire.

Even beneath the stormy skies of a wet, unseasonable April, perhaps no English county that I have seen is quite so lovely as this land of Devon. Nowhere else are the pastures so verdant, or, at any rate in South Devonshire where I began my investigations, the fresh-turned ploughs of so beautiful a red. The enclosures are small also, giving the idea that here the land is valuable—a desired possession—and surrounded, each of them, by sheltering banks of earth and stone, on which grow tall straggling hedges. Through these undulating fields run brooks of rapid water; indeed, in that time of rain water was everywhere—in the deep, narrow lanes, standing superfluous on the fallows, and in each hollow of the pastures.

Sometimes the gentle landswells are crowned by tree-clothed heights, beneath which lie slopes of gorse. Below these, perhaps, are orchards, very ill-cared for, it must be admitted, to the eye which has just studied those of Kent, but none the less picturesque because of the irregular, leaning trunks of the apples and matted boughs smothered in lichen. Between the orchards probably appears a farmstead, stone-built, and, in exposed positions, covered with a roof of slates cemented over; and round it some unpretentious buildings, at the gate of which, knee-deep in mud and water, stand the cows, waiting to be milked. In colour they are red as the soil that bred them. I wonder, by the way, if this similarity of hue is accidental or the effect of environment working through countless generations. Below the buildings again stretch the pastures – quite half the land seems to be pasture—dotted over with the Devon long-wool ewes and lambs, that contrive to frisk and look happy in spite of the tearing winds and bursts of rain.

A general characteristic of the county seems to be small farms—indeed, really large holdings are rare, while many do not comprise more than from twenty to fifty acres. Often these farms have been rented by the same families for three or four generations; thus among those that I visited this proved to be so in several instances. In the Eastern Counties to-day, by way of contrast, it is not easy to find a sitting tenant—that is the term in Devonshire—whose father and grandfather wore their lives out on the same fields before him. The circumstance shows a curious love of the soil, but, alas! the hand of fate is prevailing against this hereditary instinct. Nearly every farmer I spoke with in Devon told me that he did not mean to bring up his son to follow the land. When I congratulated one of them on the appearance of his boy, his answer was, ' I will take good care he shall not be a farmer,' and many others said likewise.

As a first instance of Devonshire farms I propose to describe one that I visited at no great distance from the ancient and interesting city of Exeter, whence I began my investigations. The farmer, a man of intelligence and, I should say, exhaustless energy, held about 250 acres at the high rent of £550 a year—his land being very good and of the order known as 'accommodation.' It used to stand at £120 more in the best times, but even in 1901, when rates and other outgoings were added, averaged nearly £3 an acre.

The tenant, whose father and, I think, grandfather held the same farm, considered that £2 would be a fair rent, but at the same time acknowledged, the land being so good and so conveniently situated for markets, that if he were to give it up, there would be many applicants at the present price. He instanced a farm that was to let close by, to see which, he said, people were streaming all day long. When I asked how this came about in such times, he replied that many of them were folk who had given up their holdings in the poorer districts and poured down here thinking that it was 'honey land.' 'They don't stay long for the most part,' he added. 'Two or three years, and off they go.' He was of opinion that, good as are the neighbourhood and markets, the farmers about him were not prosperous—that plenty of them, indeed, were losing money.

He himself, I gathered, made his rent and a living, and in addition added to the value of his stock. But he worked as few men would work, killing his own pigs and sheep, doctoring his own bullocks, milking his own cows, toiling in short from dawn to dark. Most of his earnings also came more from dealing than from legitimate farming. Thus between the previous October and the April of my visit, 200 bullocks had passed through his yards, coming in thin, but not so thin that they would not answer at once to high feeding, and going out fat. If he averaged 10s. profit a head on these animals he was pleased, for, considering the risks of sickness and the bad 'doers,' this trade is hazardous. In addition he had a good flock of sheep, and by the help of manure dragged everything out of the land that it would grow.

Labour was his greatest difficulty. All the boys went, he

said. He had but one lad left, who wanted a man's wage. The rest were old men, very good hands. 'When they go,' he added, 'I hope that I shall go too.' The wages were nominally 14s., but, with all the extras and privileges, such as ten pounds of beef at Christmas, straw, cider, potato ground, and 3s. a day in harvest, they amounted to nearly £1 a week. Still Sunday labour was almost unobtainable ; indeed, I gathered that, with the help of some aged servants who had been with him and his father for over thirty years, he had to do it himself. On this point he considered the outlook hopeless. 'We get the leavings,' he said, 'and you must not say a word ; you must bridle your tongue, or they are off.'

Wheat, he thought, was quite an unremunerative crop, although he sowed broadcast because it was quicker—2½ bushels of seed to the acre, from which his average return was 4½ quarters per acre. From barley he looked for a return of 6 quarters to the acre. As wheat had only the value of 'pig's food,' he was ceasing to grow it in favour of oats and barley. On this farm all the land was heavily manured, and a great deal of cake used. The tenant grew catch-crops wherever possible, and in addition bought straw and mangolds to help him to feed the five or six hundred cattle that he turned over in the course of the year. Also he dealt in horses whenever he found a chance, although he had been obliged to give up his hunting, of which he was fond. He said that he had proved that there was no profit to be made out of general farming, so he had to look to cattle and dealing for a livelihood, his principle being never to keep anything, but to turn it into cash so soon as he saw a profit, however small. Thus he did not breed from his cows, but fattened them as they milked, selling them out for beef at £16 or £17 when they went dry. As he bought in at from £10 to £13, by this method—after deducting the price of their food —he made £3 or £4 on each animal, in addition to the milk it yielded.

Generally, the cows stayed with him from six to twelve

months, according to their value as milkers. They were fed with chaff, hay, mangold, and oat straw pulped and mixed, an allowance of cotton cake being spread upon the top of the ration. His cows were milked by contract, the dairyman living rent free as part of the bargain. The fatting bullocks were fed with barley and maize meal, our host being of opinion that maize, of which he bought about 200 quarters a year, 'lifts a bullock' better than any other food. Half the land on this farm was pasture, and its tenant said he was prepared to lay down most of the rest, as it went well to grass.

Of mangold he grew 14 acres, in addition to the 200 tons that he bought, gathering about 40 tons to the acre. We saw some of these mangolds stored in a 'cave,' or earthed-up heap, which answers to our Eastern Counties 'hale,' but is made much wider. Of hay he had secured a good crop in the previous year: it averaged a ton and a half to the acre, and the sample was very clean and bright. The land on this farm, over which I walked, seemed excellent. Field was divided from field by 'banks' of stone, that, although they are costly to keep up, have the merit of giving good shelter to stock. Indeed, our host said that he would not care to be without them. Some of the pasture was particularly good, and one field that was pointed out to us was declared to be the earliest bit of grass in Devonshire. A flock of a hundred ewes, which had produced 120 lambs, was kept upon the farm. During the previous week fifty tegs had been sold off it at 45s. a head.

This gentleman informed us that the cottages in the neighbourhood were bad, insufficient, and the cause of general complaint. Most of them had only two rooms upstairs and one below, and were places in which respectable people ought not to be asked to live. Summing up, he said he hardly knew a farmer who was holding his own, and that although he was better off than many, he wished he could get a good berth as a steward, and have the spending of somebody else's money. 'I've got four boys. I only hope

they won't be farmers.   It's a dog's life, sir !   It's a dog's
life ! '

Another sample farm which I will describe is that
belonging to Mr. Tucker, who lives beyond the quaint little
town of Totnes, at Hazard, some twenty or five-and-twenty
miles from Exeter.   This farm, which is beautifully situated
upon a hilly slope, had been held by Mr. Tucker all his life,
as his father and grandfather held it before him ; but here it
was the same story, his son was being brought up to some
other trade.   Of its area of 300 acres, about two-thirds were
pastures.   Some of these he had laid down himself, and with
great success, as he made a special study of this branch of
agriculture.   It must be remembered, however, that the conversion into good grass of this kind of land, watered by the
plenteous rains of Devonshire, is one thing, and that of cold,
parched clays or sandy downs quite another.   Here Nature
fights for the sower ; there, against him.

In one of his fields situated on a steep hill-side, Mr.
Tucker was engaged in planting Magnum Bonum and
Imperator potatoes, manuring the red and friable soil with
8 cwts. per acre of phosphate and kainit.   In another were
running some of his herd of South Devon cows—South
Hams I think they are also called—which are of the same
red colour as the other cattle of the county, but, it seemed
to me, larger and longer on the leg.   This breed, by the way,
has of recent years been raised to the dignity of a herd-book
of its own.   Some of the selected yearling bulls sell for as
much as £40.

One of the most interesting features of Mr. Tucker's
beautifully cultivated farm was furnished by a vast and
picturesque limestone quarry, the haunt of thousands of
jackdaws.   This quarry has been worked for unknown generations, not for building purposes, but that its stone may be
converted into lime, which makes mortar of great strength
and excellence.   The rock, that pays a royalty of 4d. a load
to the landlord, is, so much of it as is not used for roadmaking
purposes, converted into lime in funnel-shaped pits twenty

feet or more deep, which we saw. When it is desired to start burning, brushwood is laid at the bottom of the pit, then alternate layers of coal and rock, each about nine inches in 'thickness. After the stone has been properly burned, the lime is withdrawn by gravitation at a lower level, the pit being kept constantly replenished with more coal and stone laid in atop. There are three of these kilns on the farm, but now-a-days only one is used. Lime used to be in great demand for dressing land, to which 6 hogsheads, or 84 cwts., costing about 24s., were applied per acre once in seven years, to lighten the soil and nourish the grasses. Now, however, when farming is not so thorough, this form of manure is largely dispensed with in the neighbourhood, artificial being used in its place. As a result finger-and-toe is rampant among the root crops.

It was pleasant to learn from Mr. Tucker that in his part of Devon, where the land is mostly in the hands of small owners of under a thousand acres, the yeoman class is by no means extinct, and that many of these occupy their own farms. Also there is a good sprinkling of tenant farmers, now working from fifty to a hundred acres, who began as labourers and have risen by the sheer hard work which throughout the county I found to be a characteristic of most Devon farmers. Of the quantity and quality of labour Mr. Tucker complained like everybody else, saying that the young men were leaving to a deplorable extent. The cottages he described as poor and small, for the most part without sufficient rooms, and the old ones as very bad indeed. He thought that more good cottages would help to keep the labourers on the land, but at the same time pointed out that, as they would only command a weekly rent of from 1s. to 2s., they could not be built to return an interest. He could see no issue to this labour problem.

As regarded the general question, he was of opinion that in his part of the county farmers who were fairly rented, ought to have held their own during the previous three years. He was certain, however, that they could have done no more than pay rent and live, and feared that many had not succeeded even to this extent ; indeed, he himself knew several who had 'faded away.' The average rent he put at 25*s.* an acre, though in some cases on poor lands this had been much reduced. Thus he instanced a farm which used to let at £400 a year, but then brought in only £160.

He complained that in many cases landlords would not meet the farmer soon enough. Thus the sitting tenant, who perhaps had held a farm for years, was impoverished and obliged to go, the incoming man getting the benefit of concessions which had been denied to his predecessor. On the whole he could only say that the outlook was not promising, because of the low prices and the threatening aspect of the labour question, but more on account of the latter than of the former. Indeed, with the best beef at £3 a cwt. and mutton at 8*d.* to 8½*d.* a lb., there was no particular cause of complaint. With wool, however, the question was different, as in 'the yoke' it was only fetching about 4½*d.* a lb.—a price at which it is quite unremunerative. Mr. Tucker seemed to consider that one of the few possible remedies for the present state of affairs, both as regards agricultural interests and rural population, is the multiplying of small-holdings by every possible means. This he believed would benefit the nation at large. 'We want the land in many more hands,' he said, adding that by means of dairy produce, pigs, poultry, and hard work, small-holdings could be made to pay.

In travelling south-west from Exeter to Plymouth, the first indication that we were running out of the fertile valley lands into the poorer district of Dartmoor Forest, was the appearance of stretches of hungry, paste-like clay, blotched on the fallows with patches of yellow sand. Many of the pastures, too, looked poverty-stricken and clogged with moss, being broken here and there with bushes or thickets of gorse, while in places the shaly rock cropped to the surface. Bolder and bolder grew the country, till after leaving Oke-hampton the tor-crowned moor became visible in all its rugged beauty, while through the desolate valley foamed the swift-streamed Tavy. Although the month was April, on the distant hills lay many a deep drift of snow, and the pitiless, beating rain caused even the hardy moorland-ponies to take shelter under the lee of the clumps of wild hollies. It was a dreary but imposing landscape.

From Plymouth to Yelverton the road winds through valleys and around the sides of hills, gradually ascending as it goes. On either hand forests, for the most part of oak and larch, clothe the hill-slopes and creep down the vales to the edge of mountain streams. The meadows are scarcely more than paddocks, 'pightles' we should call them in Norfolk, enclosed with high bush-clad banks that give shelter to the Devon cattle and the lambing sheep. Here and there are rich patches of arable, formed doubtless by washings from the hills, but the bulk of the soil is of a moorland character. Indeed, the landscape comprises curious contrasts. Here the valleys smile with fatness; yonder the hillsides are stark with poverty. It is typical of Devonshire, a county in which the richest and the poorest land may be found lying almost side by side.

Beyond Yelverton stretches the great expanse of Dartmoor. On the yesterday, as we travelled past it to Plymouth, it was swept by torrents of rain; on the morrow it would be once more deep in snow, but this day a roaring easterly gale tore across its spaces, and the sun shone upon purple stretches of dead heather, thickets of green gorse tipped with gold, and wide brakes of rusty bracken. Here and there yawned granite quarries, unworked apparently at that season; yonder flashed the great reservoir which supplies Plymouth with its water, while everywhere, far as the eye could reach, dotted about the plain like game upon the veld of Southern Africa, appeared scattered, rough-coated ponies, white-fleeced mountain sheep, and red herds of cattle. Even in the sunshine it was a sombre, impressive scene.

The great landlords on Dartmoor are the Duchy of Cornwall and Sir Massey Lopes. The farmers, who are called 'Moormen,' work an average of about seventy acres of good arable and pasture on the borders of the moor at a rent of from 10s. to 14s. per acre. They seem generally to hold under a peculiar lease for seven, fourteen, or twenty-one years, which is granted to a father and his son jointly, whereby it is supposed that the rising generation will be retained upon the farms. These Moormen are said to love their birthplace, and, although I have heard different opinions on the subject, on the whole they still appear to be fairly prosperous. Among their privileges is a right to run as much stock upon the moor as they can feed in winter at their homesteads. They work hard and live largely on bacon and ham, supplemented by fresh meat twice a week, with plenty of poultry and as many rabbits as they care to catch. Most of their money they make by breeding, grazing some of the stock, and selling the rest as 'stores.' Besides these farms there are stretches of enclosed land called 'newtakes,' which are not so valuable as they used to be, but still bring in a rental of from £30 to £100, according to their size. The letting value of pure moorland, by the way, appears to be from 4d. to 6d. an acre. These new-takes are used for the summer grazing of cattle and sheep from South Devon, which go out from them in good con-dition in the autumn months.

I was informed by old inhabitants of the moor that ten thousand cattle could easily be run during the season, whereas not more than two thousand are sent up between May and October. The Moormen, it is said, are glad to graze and tend a beast for these months at the moderate price of 7s. 6d.; but, as it is, much of the keep is wasted. During the summer the grass grows plentifully on Dartmoor, which remains green when the lowlands are burnt up, and is so nutritious that it will turn out sheep fit for the butcher without the aid of artificial foods. The Dartmoor sheep are a small, long-woolled breed, with distinct characteristics. They are very hardy, and are driven from the moor in the autumn to be sold to the lowland butchers. Here, as elsewhere, the great complaint of such of the farmers as were unable to work their holdings with the aid of their own families, was of a lack of labour. Thus we were informed by Mr. Rowe, of the Duchy Hotel, who, like his forefathers, had farmed on Dartmoor for many years, that the competition of the quarries forced him to pay labourers no less than 4s. a day. Also, the young men drew away to the great towns.

Mr. Rowe said that he was well acquainted with the squalor and poverty of Plymouth, and certain that the man who earned 15s. a week and had his cottage, garden, pigs, and fowls upon the Moor, was infinitely better off than his fellow who had migrated to the slums of that city, although the latter took a ' bigger shilling.' Still, they went. Thus the policeman or the London porter who is a native of Dartmoor or of some neighbouring village, returns home on his holiday wearing rings and an Albert chain, to fill the ears of listeners with fine stories, which so stir their imaginations that they are never content until they have also set out to seek their fortunes in the towns. Some of the blame of this he laid on the lack of cottages, which, were they in better supply, would, in his opinion, help to keep the people on the land.

To the agriculturist the most interesting sight upon Dartmoor is the great Prison Farm of about 2,000 acres. This establishment is worked by convict labour, under the direction of an able and experienced Scotch bailiff, Mr. Gourlay, and four assistants. Prison discipline and management are no part of my subject, which is already sufficiently large. Perhaps, however, I may be allowed to say how excellent seems to me a system which, while it turns the labour of those convicted of crime to a remunerative purpose, at the same time affords them healthy out-of-door employment, and enables them to acquire knowledge and skill, which will always put it in their power to earn an honest living in the future.

By the courtesy of Mr. Russell, the governor, we were

able to make a thorough inspection of this farm, of which at least 1,000 acres have actually been reclaimed from the moorland. This is the process of reclamation as I saw it. A stretch of moorland is enclosed with a wall built of stones collected from the area to be treated. Then the field within it is trenched—a very heavy labour, since it is sometimes necessary to go down 5 ft. and break the ' pan,' a kind of concrete of clay and granite, that lies beneath. If this were not done the surface moisture, unable to escape, would waterlog the ground. When it has been trenched and the cast-out stones removed on stretchers, it is drained by means of deep rubble drains, wintered and levelled. After this it is treated with five tons of white lime per acre, and, I think, with all the manure that can be spared. The first crop is roots, after which grasses are sown down with oats. These grasses come up luxuriantly, and produce heavy crops, but will not stand for more than about twelve years, when the natural mosses and flags conquer them. I saw some fields which had thus run their course, and, the soil having gone down tight, the bailiff informed me that it would be necessary to break them up afresh, re-treat and sow them. It will be obvious to the reader that so costly and laborious a system could not be followed with advantage under conditions other than those which prevail upon a prison farm.

As we drove from place to place, half frozen in the bitter gale, we saw gangs of convicts at their toil, some of them unearthing a splendid crop of swedes out of the pits where they had been buried from the weather, others quarrying and dressing granite, others drawing hand-carts at a pace almost as slow as that favoured by the new generation of agricultural labourers, and yet others, milking and tending the kine and horses. It was strange to watch these involuntary husbandmen, shepherded by their armed guards ; but I think it right to add that on the whole their work seemed to me to be well and intelligently done.

One of the principal supports of this farm is the breeding

of ponies, of which we saw many very useful-looking animals that sell unbroken at the annual sale at from eighteen to twenty-seven guineas. Great care is taken in their breeding, Arab and Welsh blood being blended with the original moor stock to whatever extent experience proves will not interfere with their native hardiness. The sire then in use was a strong, serviceable animal, and the average height of his progeny seemed to be about thirteen hands three inches. Also cart-horses are bred—animals of a very good class. Of sheep, at the time of our visit, there were, in addition to wethers, about 250 ewes and 200 lambs, of which Mr. Gourlay remarked, with justifiable pride, that, notwithstanding the fearful weather they had experienced, he had not lost a single one. Part of his good fortune, however, must be attributed to the fact that he was able to house them in the splendid range of piggeries, just then rather bare of swine owing to an outbreak of fever that necessitated the slaughter of 132 of them. These realised £260 by sale and compensation; still the loss to the farm was very heavy. The other stock, in addition to twelve working horses and the fifty ponies, comprised 103 bullocks and twenty-eight excellent cows. Oats were the only white crop grown, and these are not thrashed, but chaffed, and fed to stock with the straw, after the South African fashion.

Mr. Gourlay informed me that he found this practice the most profitable, as at so great an elevation the cast of grain is not good. The best grass land is dressed every four years or so with the refuse and manure from the gaol, spread upon it in the proportion of twenty tons to the acre. The soil, which may be described generally as peat upon clay, answers marvellously to this treatment. Indeed, a crop of two tons of hay an acre is not uncommon. He said that he rarely took the sheep and cattle off the pastures until May 1, and then was disappointed if he did not mow a ton an acre. Mr. Gourlay added that on a certain twenty-acre meadow twenty-seven bullocks could not keep

the grass down in summer, and that when they had
gone, it was still possible to let it stand and to take a cut
of hay.

In short, the Dartmoor Prison Farm is a very good
instance of the triumph of the ingenuity and perseverance
of man over difficulties of soil, situation, and climate. To
my mind it reflects great credit upon all concerned in its
up-keep and management. Still it must be remembered
that here the authorities have not to face the common difficulties of labour and capital which confront the ordinary
farmer. Also their buildings are massive, commodious, and
well appointed, and must be even more so now if the new
stable then in contemplation is completed. This farm, by
the way, is not the property of the Directors of County
Prisons, but is held under rent from the Duchy of Cornwall.

One of the best known and most skilful agriculturists in
the neighbourhood of Plymouth is Mr. Vosper, of Merri-
field, who held a thousand acres and employed from fifty to
sixty men. His farm, indeed, was perhaps the most highly
cultivated of any that I had so far inspected in the course of
my journey, which is not strange seeing that it absorbed
capital at the rate of £20 the acre, and that £3,000 a year
was spent in feeding-stuffs alone. Mr. Vosper's great
difficulty was labour, of which he said that he found it
hard to 'put his view strong enough.' He declared that
in his district he scarcely knew a young fellow who
was staying on the land, as directly they were useful,
young men went off to the railway or to other employment.
Especially did they object to milking on Sunday; indeed,
that task was only accomplished by coaxing old men and
young boys, and paying them highly to do the work. He
mentioned the instance of a lad to whom he was paying
14s. a week, with a promise of from 6d. to 1s. extra on
Sundays, if he would take to milking, who, rather than do
so, gave him notice on the spot. Perhaps from his own
point of view that boy was wise, since, though still living
with his parents on the farm, he was then earning 18s. a

week as a mason's assistant ; thus encouraging others to go and do likewise.

Mr. Vosper had done everything possible to keep the people on the land, by encouraging classes for technical education, giving prizes for good work, &c. His complaint was, however, that the young men would not learn, and even those who did learn and secured the prizes, went away. The wages were good, averaging 16s. a week, with cottage, manure, milk, and sundries, which brought them up, perhaps, to the value of £1. Indeed, some of them took £1, and even as much as 22s., in cash ; while the old men, to whom he used to pay 12s. a week in their prime, now drew 17s. It is in the cities that we hear the cry of 'too old at forty,' not upon the land ; but this the young people who migrate thither do not stop to remember.

As regarded cottage accommodation, Mr. Vosper said that it had increased, and that such landowners as Lord Morley, were building or remodelling many dwellings. Indeed, he added that they were driven to it, and must do so, 'whether they could afford it or not.' Yet he said also that cottages would not keep the people on the land ; that wages would not keep them ; that nothing of which he knew would keep them ; that he was at his wits' end ; and that unless some change took place 'the next five years would leave us without men.' Indeed, he added, there was a general feeling that dairy work might have to be abandoned.

With reference to the position of farming outside the question of labour in this beautiful and fertile district of the South Hammers, which stretches along the coast as far as Torquay and measures about twenty miles in depth, Mr. Vosper said that he could not call it prosperous. The rents, which have been reduced from 25 to 30 per cent. during late years, were paid, and there was still some competition for small, desirable farms, although the new class of tenants were for the most part not so satisfactory as the old. But, in spite of the good land and the good markets, farmers, in his opinion, must be content to 'rub along.'

They were, he thought, just living, and no more. The rent varied very much according to the quality of the soil, but on the whole was rather high. He estimated that from 25s. to 35s. per acre would be a fair average for the best mixed lands of, say, half pasture and half arable, and from 15s. to 25s. for the poor ordinary lands, according to quality. Of course, however, the finest marsh pastures were much dearer, fetching up to £3 an acre, or even more. The moorland farmers, he considered, did well with store cattle, which were very dear in proportion to the price of beef, but the fall in the value of grease-wool, that had then sunk to 4½d. per pound, had hit them very hard.

Mr. Vosper's farm is beautifully situated. As we drove we saw the Laira Water lying beyond the park lands, and further off the city of Plymouth, shadowed by its canopy of smoke. Then, to the left, were the wooded heights of Mount Edgcumbe, rising from the sea, while presently, just beneath us, appeared the thriving village of Plympton, the birthplace of Sir Joshua Reynolds, backed by a distant view of Dartmoor, now once more shrouded in its snows. The soil seemed to be a rich loam lying upon shale, and I noticed that where the shale strata were flat, it was deeper and of a better quality than where they had been forced into a vertical position by the convulsions of Nature. One of the first fields we stopped at contained five and a half acres of early cabbage for table eating, a truly splendid crop, of which Mr. Vosper hoped to make £40, or even £50, an acre. The sorts were Wheeler's Imperial and Early Dwarf, sown in August and set out in October, about 32,000 of them to the acre, and heavily manured with gas lime, nitrates, and farmyard compost.

A little further on we had the advantage of an object lesson in the treatment of pastures. Almost side by side lay two meadows, one quite bare and brown, the other, even in this backward spring, luxuriant with rich-hued grass—No. 2 farmed by our host, and No. 1 by somebody else. The secret of the difference was that Mr.

Vosper had dressed his field with a thick coating of slaughter-house and fish manure—which, by the way, the thousands of clamouring gulls seemed to appreciate—whereas the neighbour had left his to Nature. The mangold in the sheds told the same tale. They had received fifty tons per acre of fish and farm manure, with the result that the land yielded the enormous crop of seventy tons an acre of the biggest mangold that I ever saw, although some of them were rather coarse. These mangold were not pulped, but fed whole to the cattle in the sheds.

Mr. Vosper kept about 250 horned stock—'bullocks' is the generic term in Devonshire—of which from 160 to 180 were cows in profit. His milk realised 10$d$. per gallon all the year round in Plymouth, where it was retailed at the average price of 1$s$. 4$d$. a gallon. In other words the middleman took about 35 per cent. of the value of the article for his trouble. Besides the cattle, there were, including lambs, some 800 sheep upon the farm, of which 300 were ewes. In one of the dairies we saw the interesting process of the manufacture of the famed Devonshire cream. First the milk is stood from 12 to 24 hours, according to the season of the year, to allow the cream to rise. Then the pans are lifted and placed in iron boilers of special construction filled with water heated by a furnace. Here the milk is scalded till it reaches a temperature of from 160° to 170°. It is then immediately removed from the boilers and, when cool, skimmed. The result is Devonshire cream, which is sold for 1$s$. 4$d$. a pound, the skim being retailed at 5$d$. a gallon. I asked many people in the county whether it would not be possible to apply this simple process in other places. They answered, 'Yes, but the product would not be Devonshire cream.' I suppose, therefore, that this luscious article of diet depends for its perfection partly on the cattle of the county, and still more upon the quality of the local grasses which form their food. This view, I find however, is not always endorsed by experience. Thus Mr. Frederick Thomas writes to me from Stambourne, Halstead, Essex:—

I have been reading your articles with great interest. In your reference to Mr. Vosper's farm, you describe the process of making Devonshire cream, and, from information received, the impression seems to be left on your mind that the same process applied in other counties would not produce the same results. In your own words, the 'perfection' 'depends partly on the cattle of the country, and still more on the quality of the grasses which form their food.' I came into Essex from Cornwall about four and half years ago, and had always made cream by the process common to the two most westerly counties. I still adhere to the Devonshire method, and it may perhaps interest you to know that I find the cream in all respects as good as that produced in Cornwall.

I also have a nephew settled in Suffolk, about seven miles from here : he was saying to me before we saw your article, that the cream produced on his farm was equal both in quantity and quality to that he formerly made in Cornwall on meadow land for which he paid *quite* 50s. *per acre.*

A good example of quite another type of farm is one which I visited between Honiton and Exeter. Here the holder worked some 400 acres, to which he was adding another 300, as he thought that it would be more economical to farm on a large scale than on a small one. Out of these 400 acres a tenant who held them in the sixties and seventies was said to have made a fortune of £40,000, while one of his successors, who had to face the following lean years, they reduced to ruin. This is an instructive illustration of the recent history of English agriculture. The present holder, being a man of enterprise, had started a shop in the neighbouring town, to which he sent the produce of his dairy. This, he hoped, would answer well in time, but when we met it cost him nearly £200 a year in out-of-pocket expenses, which, he remarked, 'takes a lot of getting back.'

On his farm he employed nine men and, the proportion of grass being very considerable, but six horses. Also there were twenty-five acres of orchard, from which in the past he had made cider. This practice, however, he proposed to discontinue, except for domestic purposes, chiefly on account of the labour trouble. In 1900 he had sent fifteen tons of apples to be sold, but all that the salesman handed over to him was 17*s*. 6*d*. a ton, out of which magnificent return he must pay the cost of gathering and other expenses. On the other hand, he stated that once, under specially favourable circumstances, he had netted £250 from this twenty-five acres of orchard. On this farm we walked over the best bit of barley that we had yet seen. It was got in during February, before the heavy rain of 1901, and did not seem to have damped. On that land, however, barley is an uncertain crop. Thus, the previous year a field which was expected to yield fifty bushels to the acre only thrashed out thirty. This difference between promise and fulfilment was due to the sudden drought striking into the shaly land, and causing the kernels to wither.

The rent paid on this farm amounted to something over 28*s*. an acre—twenty years ago it was 43*s*.—but even at this reduced price I did not gather that it was easy to wring a profit from the land. Indeed, its tenant had been obliged to find more capital for his shop and other ventures.

' And if you had been unable to do so, where would you have been ? ' I asked.

' Up the spout ! ' he replied in terse if colloquial idiom.

As it is, however, that retreat will doubtless be avoided ; indeed, he thought that out of the whole 700 acres and the shop he ought, with care, to make £1 a day, in addition to his rent. Considering that this result, if attained, involved the investment of, as I understood, not far short of £15 an acre capital, or £10,500, plus the care and labour of the investor, it does not seem as good as might be hoped. Indeed, some will wonder whether the owner of the money would not do better to invest it in the War Loan or Consols at present prices, and save himself from the risk and anxiety of sinking it in the land, whence it, or some of it, may never reappear. Perhaps, however, our host took too ' conservative ' a view of the situation, and his profit will be larger than he thought. Let us hope so.

This gentleman showed us, hanging in his hall, a very interesting relic of the past. It was a pair of deer's horns of unusual size. Upon one of these horns was engraved 'I. R.,' with a crown between the letters and beneath:

NOBL KING JAMES DID KILL THIS BUCK IN
THE FOREST OF WHICHWOOD

## WILLIAM ESINGTUNE

ANNO DOMINI
1610

On the other side was cut a harp, a lion, and a *fleur-de-lys*, and beneath:

GOD PROSPER HIM THEM DOWN TO PLUCK THAT SEEK
TRUE CHRISTIAN BLOOD

WAS THERE WHEN IT WAS DON. 1610.

This William Esingtune was, I understand, an ancestor of our host's wife. It would be interesting if any antiquary could unravel the meaning of the second inscription. For my part I had forgotten that his late Majesty James I. was famous as a Nimrod.

Among the land agents and managers of estates with whom I had the advantage of exchanging views in Devonshire were Mr. Stevens, agent to Sir Thomas Dyke Acland; Messrs. Hussey, father and son, the well-known Exeter auctioneers; and Messrs. Body, father and son, valuers and land agents, of Plymouth.

Mr. Body came from Cornwall about sixty-six years ago, and told me that things had changed much since that date. Especially was this so in the matter of labour. Then good men could be had for 9s. a week and cider; now, he said, they cost 18s. a week and grumbled at their wage. In short, labour was scarce and the difficulty of obtaining it increased daily. It was a case of more money for less work. It seemed to him that the country people wanted to huddle together and to be paid more upon the land than they could earn even in the towns. Selling values had decreased to an extent of quite six years' purchase on the reduced rents. These rents he put at an average of about 25s. the acre for the district, but accommodation land near the city fetched a much higher sum. During the last thirty years, as Mr. Body informed me, much of the land had been laid to grass. In South Devon it went down well, but on the carboniferous soils in the north of the shire, badly. A number of farmers were leaving Devonshire and migrating to the Eastern Counties, where they took almost derelict land, draining, cleaning, and getting it into order. He thought that most of them did well, and certainly would not come back. These Devon men, he added, were very hard workers, much more so than those in Eastern England.

A solicitor, in large practice, whom I saw in Plymouth, told me also that the value of land in the district had fallen very much, instancing a small estate of about 180 acres with a large house, not more than a dozen miles from the city, which had been sold recently for £7,500. Formerly this property, which was one of the best in the neighbourhood, had been mortgaged for £12,000, nearly double its present sale value. He said that the real state of affairs among farmers came to light when their wills were proved. Then it was not uncommon to find that men who were supposed to be rich were in fact worth little or nothing. He thought, however, that tenants who had runs on the moors attached to their holdings were still doing well.

Mr. Stevens lives at Broadclyst, where Sir Thomas Dyke Acland has his seat. Mr. Richards, a resident landowner, was so good as to show us round this village—a beautiful, prosperous-looking place with a population of about 2,000. The cottages, which I believe all belong to Sir Thomas, are well constructed and commodious, having been for the most part rebuilt in recent years after a destructive fire, and there is a plentiful supply of good allotments. Moreover, the village has other advantages. Thus the grass on seventy acres of rich water meadow is annually put

up to auction in small lots for the benefit of the inhabitants, who pay a good price for it, and stack their cut on
common ground. Again, the Red Lion, the principal if not
the only public-house in the place, belongs to the People's
Refreshment House Association, now, I believe, known
as the Public House Trust, with which Earl Grey is
prominently connected, an admirable institution that, for
my part, I hope will take root throughout the length and
breadth of the land. It is, however, possible that the
People's Refreshment House Association is not identical
with the Public House Trust. But whether this is so or
not, their objects seem to be the same. This excellent
society pays the manager a fixed wage and a commission
upon all non-alcoholic drinks and on food disposed of to
customers. The result is that, unlike the landlord of a
'tied house,' he has no inducement to press the sale of
drink, as, after deducting the 5 per cent. payable to the
shareholders in the company, the object of his employers
is philanthropy, not profit. Still, in the year 1900, at Broadclyst, a gain of £65 was made, which, I was informed, had
been handed over to be spent for the general advantage of
the community.

The school is good, but, as I was told, gives no special
agricultural education; in fact, when I visited it, the
scholars were employed in making drawings from cones
and cubes. Also there is a row of excellent cottages with
gardens, especially devoted to the use of the widows of
labourers who die upon the estate. For these they pay
the small rental of 1s. 6d. a week. Although I admit that
this sketch of it seems rather Arcadian, such is Broadclyst;
but the reader must remember that all Devonshire villages
are not so fortunately placed or so well cared for.

On our second visit to Broadclyst I had a long and
interesting interview with Mr. Stevens, whose many years
of experience make his opinions very valuable. Rent, he
said, had fallen 20 per cent. on good and 30 per cent. on
poor lands, the arable farms being chiefly affected. The

best farm with which he had to do was let at a little under £2 the acre. The selling value of freeholds had dropped on an average from thirty years' purchase on the old high rentals to about twenty-two on the reduced rent. He thought that the farmers were to some extent holding their own, by which he meant that they were paying their rent and making a living, but earning no interest on the capital employed. Many of them, however, were not doing so much as this. As regarded the agricultural outlook, for grain he could see no prospect; but of the price of meat there was little cause to complain, as owing to the increased cost of freight on imported stuff it had risen, at any rate for a while.

On the estates which he managed they had sufficient labour of a sort, but in this respect the farmers had great trouble. The young men were going away, but not very rapidly, from that parish. They looked upon farm work as 'dirty,' and he said that if they asked for more money the choice lay between giving it or losing them. The labour question had greatly increased in intensity during the past eighteen months; even youths of seventeen treated the 'master' as nobody, and would become abusive if rebuked. The cost of labour, he considered, was now 30 per cent. higher than it used to be, and the quantity and quality of the work 30 per cent. less. Labourers had many advantages in addition to their wage, but still they did not consider that they were well paid. The cottages only returned an interest of 1 per cent., while of allotments there were 250 in the village, although many of them were not occupied. The labouring class, Mr. Stevens remarked, did not seem to care for vegetables. He added that it was common in riding about the estate to find the men smoking and talking instead of doing their work; indeed, he had recently been obliged to tell some of them that they were 'simply robbing their employer.'

I asked what he believed would be the end of this state of affairs. Mr. Stevens replied, he supposed that the burden must, for the most part, fall upon the landlord, whose rent would dwindle still further. He thought, however, that there were grounds for hoping that men would tire of the towns and return to the land. I suggested that even if they did they would know little or nothing of agricultural work. He answered that most of them did not ' know much now.' He laid a great deal of the blame for present agricultural troubles, from the issues of which he could see no escape, upon our system of education, that unfitted the children for a country life. He thought the only hope of the farmer lay in more grass and less corn, but as a subsidiary remedy suggested co-operation.

By this I suppose that he meant the establishment of local co-operative agricultural associations to enable the farmer to buy cheaper, and by means of combination to sell at a better price. These, I may mention here, are the objects of the Agricultural Organisation Society (Limited), to which everyone interested in the welfare of the land and land-dwellers should wish good fortune. This I do very heartily, especially as it hopes to establish credit banks to enable deserving labourers to take holdings upon their own account.

Almost equal in interest to those of Mr. Stevens were the views of Mr. Hussey, senior, the Exeter auctioneer, who spoke with the weight of a business experience extending over fifty years. Like Mr. Stevens, he had no good word for our system of education. Rents, he contended, were still too high, though that is a statement which landlords would dispute. Tenants—in his opinion, for the most part, a much less reliable class than they used to be—were, in many cases, on the verge of bankruptcy. They would, he thought, give up if they saw any other way of making a living, but struggled on in the trust that times might improve. This hope, according to him, was the secret of the competition which still existed for farms. Like Mr. Micawber, they thought that something might turn up, or that luck would be better on the new holding. As regarded the labour question, Mr. Hussey expressed himself to be of opinion that when the old generation of agricultural hands died off, farms in the districts with which he was acquainted would often have to be abandoned, or cut up into lots small enough to be managed by one man and his family. I may remark on this point that in such an event the question of the provision of the necessary buildings must be faced. Who is to find the money to pay for them? In most instances it is clear that the landlord could not do so.

Mr. Hussey, jun., was of opinion that the general agricultural position, in spite of the fall in rental and selling values, was decidedly better in Devonshire than in the north and east of England. The proportion of pasture being so much larger, less labour was required, and the fall in the price of corn was not so crushing. The land, he said, was much encumbered, and as there were no merchant princes among their landlords, those of them who depended upon it for a living income were hard hit. His views on the subject of labour were very much the same as those of the other gentlemen of whom I have written; therefore I need not quote them at any length. His conclusion, however, was that we shall be driven to the importation of foreign work-men, or must do the best we can by the aid of machinery. He held that the exodus from the land was more a question of education than of wages; that lads now desired to work with their heads rather than to work with their hands. He considered that small owners were increasing a little, and that among this class of men there was a wish to hold land; thus a farm of fifty or sixty acres, with house and buildings, was easy either to let or sell.

He thought that a system of small ownership would be beneficial, but that as things are the population was decreasing in the villages, and especially in the outlying districts. The farmers who throve best were those who had many sons, and labourers did not go so fast from places where the cottages were good and comfortable. These, he said, were not high-class as a whole, though better than they had been ten years before. His general conclusion was that if the land must go to ruin everything will follow the same road.

The fall in rentals between 1875 and 1885 he put at about 30 per cent. on the better lands. Since 1890, however, they had risen a little. On the poor, outlying properties they had come down 40 per cent. The good lands fetched from 20s. up to 50s. an acre for the pick of them. The wages ran from 12s. to 17s. a week plus a cottage free or at a nominal rent of 1s. plus cider, a quarter of an acre of land, and sometimes manure thrown in. Large holdings were, he said, difficult to sell if situated far from a town or station, but when near to these could be disposed of readily enough. Farmers generally were much pinched owing to the drop in the prices of corn and wool and the increase of that of labour. In many cases where they used to spend a thousand pounds, they did not now spend £200. They were a hard-working and close-living class, and generally acted as their own shepherds and stockmen.

From among many that were given to me by word of mouth or in writing, I now select some further views of the agricultural situation in Devonshire which, by reason of the experience or position of my informants, strike me as being of value.

Mr. Edgar Dudley, F.S.I., of Plymouth, land agent and surveyor to H.M. War Department, said that he had fifteen years' experience of the West of England. In his opinion agricultural depression in Devonshire was nothing like so acute as in most other parts of the country. The present average rental value of land he put at 20s. the acre. Farms were always in good demand, and the rents were regularly paid. Labour was becoming scarce, but the question was not of such paramount importance as in many places, on account of the small size of the holdings and of the fact that nearly all the farmers and their families worked with their own hands. Of cottages there was a fair supply.

Most of them had three or four rooms, and as a rule their condition was satisfactory. Among the young men there was a tendency to migrate to the towns, although not to the same extent as in some other districts. The cause of this migration was the better wage and the brighter life that were obtainable in cities. He did not think that in Devonshire the question of education bore much upon the matter. Although his energies were not always well directed, the tenant-farmer was usually a hard-working man. As farmers go he was fairly contented, and, owing to the large proportion of land that was under grass and the small total of his labour bill, could live in reasonable comfort.

Most of the landlords were more or less resident, but many of them were considerably involved and in the hands of lawyers. He did not consider that solicitors were good managers of estates, but remarked that upon this matter he might be 'open to the charge of partiality.' The labourers, who, as a rule, had satisfactory cottages and gardens, were fairly comfortable and without any great cause of complaint. In the Plymouth neighbourhood there was, he thought, a distinctly more hopeful tone, though upon what it was based he could not say. The labour problem was certainly most serious. He believed that, as in America, more labour-saving machinery would have to be used in the future, and that, as was the case with other industrial problems, the wit of man would, at any rate to some extent, solve the difficulty on lines that were not at present apparent. The only means that he could suggest to keep people on the land was to pay them higher wages. This, however, seemed to be out of the question.

I will now quote the interesting and experienced opinions of a large farmer, Mr. Sparrow Wroth, of Aveton Gifford, South Devon. He began by regretting that he had not been able to write to me sooner, but by the time that he had finished attending to the cattle, of which he kept about a hundred, and the sheep, that numbered three hundred, 'it was always ten o'clock at night.' It fell to the master's share, he said, after doing a day's work with his hands on the farm, to look to the beasts in the evening, since without his personal superintendence 'nothing seemed to go right.' Mr. Wroth said that of late years rents had fallen from 20 to 50 per cent. in his neighbourhood, and in some cases even more. The average rental he put at £1 the acre, and near towns at from 25s. to 30s. the acre. He thought that rents were still too high. There were a good many resident landlords in South Devonshire, although in his district none who owned large estates. He said that they were all very hard hit by the bad times, as the expenses of repairs were heavy and the burdens on land excessive. He feared that they found it difficult to make both ends meet out of rents from their landed property.

Farms were letting fairly well and the rents were paid. It seemed to him, however, that the class of tenant was not what it used to be. The new men did most of the work with the help of their own families, and in many cases did not farm the land as it ought to be farmed. Often their families had to work 'harder than slaves,' and through their being kept at home to help in busy times were not so well educated as the children of the labourers. Many of them were poor also; 'but,' remarked Mr. Wroth, 'I suppose those are rich whose requirements are few.' Labour was very scarce and inferior, only a few of the old hands being left that understood general farm work. The youths, he declared, were most impudent, indolent, and useless. Many of the young men went into the Navy and the rest to the towns, only about 1 per cent. staying on the land. Education, he thought, had much to do with this, as the children were taught at school that farming means hard work and poor pay, and long before they left it, announced that they did not intend to stay upon the land. The educational system might certainly be improved. Mr. Wroth was of opinion that the scholars 'are taught too much about dodos'—an amusing and comprehensive criticism that, rightly understood, is not without truth.

He paid his men 15s. a week, with 2s. a day and 1s. a day extra for corn and hay harvest respectively. Also he gave cottages and sufficient potato ground to grow fifteen bags of 140 lb. a bag, free, with other advantages, such as a certain amount of gratis firing and the haulage of coals. Still neither he nor his neighbours were able to get sufficient labour, and on Sundays had to do almost all the work themselves. Of cottages there were enough for present requirements, most of them with two or three downstairs rooms and two or three bedrooms. They were not, however, of modern construction, and many had been pulled down. Thus in his parish of Bigbury sixty had disappeared since his father commenced business half a century before. In this village the new census showed that since 1891 the population had fallen from 365 to 271 souls.

As regarded the relative positions of tenant-farmers, landlords, and labourers, he said that anyone who farmed in his part of Devonshire had to do all the hardest and dirtiest work himself. Thus he with his own hands had just sown a hundred acres of corn and root land to nitrate of soda and salt, a total of four tons of each material, because none of his labourers cared to undertake the job. Nor was his experience singular, as his neighbours were in the same case. They had to live sparingly, to work very long hours, and often to labour from dawn till dusk. Landlords had anything but a good time, owing to the excessive expenses on the land. The labourers, however, were the best off of the three, as their living was very cheap, they were most independent, and had few responsibilities to trouble them. His parents and many of his friends often said that the small farmers would be better off as day labourers.

He could see no sign whatever of British agriculture attaining to a better position than it occupied at present. How could farming improve with good quality 'long wool' hardly saleable at 4d. a pound, wheat at 7s. a bag of 125 lbs., barley at 6s. 6d. the 112 lbs., corn and every other saleable product very low in price? The efforts of the Americans to place their products on the English market were obvious, and as yet these enormous undertakings were but in their infancy. Why, he asked, had the old yeomen, whose families should have taken their places in due course, vanished away? Because they had been driven from the land, never to return, by taxation of their property, and by labour so heavy that it could not be borne. Everything the farmer bought went up in price, and everything he sold sank lower and lower and cost more to produce. Further, fresh expenses were continually thrown upon the rates and upon the land, quite irrespective of whether these could carry them or not. He affirmed that it was this continual sucking of the farmer's life-blood which had brought things to such a pass that a great deal of the land was going to waste. But a nation that wastes, in his opinion, must sooner or later pay the penalty.

He supposed that the end of it would be that the best of the land would go back into small holdings, but that would not make things better than they were at present. His parents could remember when nearly the whole of their parish, and indeed all that neighbourhood, was farmed in small holdings, but when these people died few of them left enough behind them to pay their funeral expenses. This was in what was called the good time. How, then, if the farms were re-divided, could any little tenants make them pay now? He believed that none of them would even win a livelihood, at any rate in the more isolated places. About fifteen years ago a good many acres in that parish were let at £5 the acre for the cultivation of early potatoes; now that land was producing nothing more than brambles, bracken, and rabbits. The competition of the early French potatoes had killed the business.

Farmers had many kind advisers. Some of these counselled them to grow fruit and make jam, but the facilities given to the foreigner by steam and cold-storage would prevent him from trying such a venture in Devonshire. Others told them to lay the land down to pasture; but their forefathers, whom he thought were not fools, used to say, 'It breaks a man to make a pasture.' From experience he knew that it was a very costly process, as, except upon favoured soils, nature is slow in bringing permanent grasses to perfection.

Mr. Wroth concluded his eloquent and earnest, if somewhat pessimistic, sketch of things agricultural as they are in South Devon, which he states is in no way overdrawn, by saying that he supposed it would all work out right in the end, and he only hoped they might find that this was so. By the way, he has been driven to import Irish labour, and is pleased with the result of his experiment.

My next evidence comes from East Devonshire. Mr. H. N. Pope, licensed valuer, estate and insurance agent, who lives in the neighbourhood of Honiton, said that except in the case of those farms that have very little arable, and special advantages in the way of watered meadows, &c., rents in his district had fallen quite a third since 1875. The fee-simple value, however, had not fallen more than five or six years' purchase. Unless they were desirable, the farms did not let readily ; indeed for poor high holdings on the hills it was very difficult to find tenants. Rents were paid fairly well, but not as they were thirty or forty years ago, when to be in arrear was thought disgraceful.

Labour had become scarce since the outbreak of the war, but had it not been for that event his opinion was that it would have been easier to get than during many years past. The average money wage was 12s. or 13s. a week, but all his men on a farm which he rented, cost him 15s. or 16s. a week. The extras they received were good cottages and gardens rent free, two quarts of cider per diem, Sundays included, 1s. a day in haymaking and harvest in lieu of food which used to be provided, and land enough ready worked and manured, to grow what potatoes they required for themselves and their families. His treatment of the labourers, however, was by no means exceptional, and he considered that his men were better off than porters and such people in the large towns earning 25s. a week. As he had lived for ten years in Manchester he knew something of the value of money in cities.

Good cottages were scarce, most of those in that neighbourhood had two rooms below and two above stairs. The young men went away to the towns. With this result education had everything to do, but he thought this matter would right itself. It was because they, or rather their parents, knew so little that they went. The scant education which young people received in our elementary schools, was of no use at all to them if they stayed upon the land; it only made them uneasy and discontented. The authorities were trying to alter this state of affairs, but before their efforts could bear fruit another generation of teachers must grow up. He instanced a Devonshire parish where a young woman of twenty-two was in charge of the school. What, he asked, was the use of telling this young lady to take the children out into the fields and give them object lessons, when she did not know a dock from a thistle, and perhaps not barley from oats, or wheat from beans? Most of the present race of teachers, in his opinion, ought to be cleared away and replaced by people of a different stamp.

Of the three classes connected with Devonshire land the labourer was, he considered, the best off, next came the landlord, and last of all the farmer. Only the up-to-date farmers were doing, or likely to do, any good. Many of the old-fashioned men had gone to the wall, and he feared that more were doomed. He could see very little sign of a brighter future for agriculture, although, except in the case of wool and corn, prices were high enough. The only hope seemed to lie in putting more capital into the land, using artificial manures and cake food with minuter knowledge, and thus making every acre of land produce half as much again as it does at the present time. Much of the land with which he was acquainted, and indeed throughout England, was not half farmed.

The wages question would right itself if the profits from

farming increased, as one reason why men had gone to the
towns was that they found it impossible to support themselves and their families in the country. He had never
experienced any difficulty in getting all the hands he wanted ;
what exercised him and his neighbours was to find money
enough to pay them out of farm profits. It was easy to keep
good cottages tenanted. A better class of cottage in every
respect would, he thought, do more than anything else to
bring labour back to the land. In thousands of existing
dwellings women refused to live, and as these were only
hovels really he could not blame them.

One of my most interesting and thoughtful informants
from the north of Devonshire was the Rev. J. Worthington,
of Northlew Rectory, Beaworthy, who, as he told me, had
reached the age of threescore and ten. For twenty-seven
years he had been a guardian and district councillor, and
during all his long life had taken a deep interest in questions
connected with the land. He said that farms in his neighbourhood consisted of a certain amount of more or less
cultivated and enclosed lands with some moor attached, their
tenants in many cases having the right of turning bullocks,
ponies, and geese on to the moor in numbers proportionate
to the size of their holdings. In his opinion, one of the
necessities of the situation was to find out what is the
'living wage' needful to the agricultural labourer, which
should at least be enough to enable him to provide a sufficient
home for his family. He must be taught that for his part
his first duty should be to supply a home in which the
decencies and proprieties of life can be observed. To secure
this, where boys and girls are growing up, there should
never be less than three bedrooms in the house, for which he
should pay a fair rent sufficient to remunerate the landlord
for his capital outlay. The ' cheap cottage' had been, and
was, one of the curses of the rural population.

Education given in a village school ought, he believed, to
differ from that given in town schools. As a rule there was
nothing taught in villages which would impress on a child

the fact that agriculture, horticulture, orchard and fruit culture are full of interest and delight, and both require and are worthy of the best work of their heads and hands. The country boy goes out from school knowing nothing of the soil on which he lives, and nothing of what a crop puts into or takes out of land. Probably he cannot measure his father's field or haystack—perhaps cannot tell one tree from another or the comparative value of their timber, what birds, or beasts, or insects are good or bad for crops, what meal makes bone and what makes fat ; what manures are valuable or how they should be applied, or even how to shape and manage a muck heap. All he has learnt are the three R's and a little geography and grammar, armed with which information he departs to a shop in the town, or to serve as a porter or a policeman. As it was, all the intelligent boys and girls went away, and those who were left took no pride in their work ; a fact to which the building and thatching of the hay and corn stacks bore witness.

Mr. Worthington was much in favour of the increase of small-holdings, to be placed within the reach of honest and industrious labourers. He believed that the establishment of such holdings would work to the interest of the larger farmers, since he did not advocate the cutting up of the whole country into three-acre lots. He was acquainted with districts in Warwickshire where small-holdings were numerous, and had found that their tenants were the best and most obliging labourers, who were glad to spend their spare time in the service of a farmer. Working well for themselves, they get into the habit of working well for their employers also. He knew parishes where the only men who could be trusted to do a really fair day's work for those who hired them were the small-holders.

He thought that the farmers in his locality kept their heads well above water. Their rents were low, their wants were few, and they did almost all their own work. Besides making the butter, &c., their wives 'meated' the calves, pigs, and poultry ; but the sons and daughters were

SIR THOMAS DYKE ACLAND'S DEVON BULL.

*Page 195*

COTTAGE AT BROAD CLYST

*Page 196*

deserting them. If this went on, he asked, what will be done in the end thereof? Mr. Worthington said, further, that of late years the rents in that neighbourhood had fallen 15 per cent., and that the average rental was about 10s. the acre. The selling value of poor land had in many cases sunk 50 per cent.; indeed, much of it had gone out of cultivation; but good lands near towns or villages had kept its value. There were many small proprietors who were resident, and the rents were paid. Labour was scarce, the wages running from 12s. to 15s. a week, with extra money at harvest. Cottages were scarce and in bad condition; very few of them had more than two bedrooms. The young men and women were migrating to the towns, and had lost interest in all country work, which they regarded as 'dirt and drudgery.' He thought that unsuitable education had much to do with this state of affairs, and that the system should be adapted to the country and its needs. The tenant was fairly well off, but worked hard; the landlords were not wealthy and the condition of the few labourers who remained was much improved. The stamp of all sorts of stock was much better than it had been, but the methods employed in local agriculture were wasteful and ignorant. Personally he was hopeful as to the future, but believed the effect of the desertion of the land by the labouring classes on the farming industry, and the country at large, would be 'disastrous all round.' The only remedies he could suggest were really suitable education, good cottages, and small-holdings brought within the reach of industrious men.

Another view of the position of affairs in Devonshire came to me from a large landowner in the county whose name, however, I do not give, as he marked his communication *Private*. He said that rents had fallen on some of the larger farms, but not enough to meet the present prices. Too often the agents let the best men go because they want reductions, and then put up the estate to tender and pick out hard-working men with large families. These, if report be true, were often financed until they could pull themselves round by work and industry.  In many cases, however, the children of such men will not stop upon the land, as they say that if they want to start for themselves their parents can give them neither help nor money.  Still this was not so in all cases ; thus he knew a farm of that stamp where all the family, varying in age from forty to eighteen, still lived and worked together.  As they had no labour-bill that family saved money.  There were no cake bills to pay, but they had just sold sixteen oxen at over £16 a head, and three young cart-horses for £140.  Here I may remark that my informant did not state how they fed their cattle without cake.  I presume that these oxen were sold out, not as finished beasts, but as well-grown 'stores' in good condition.  However this may be, all small farmers do not thrive so well, since with some of them, as he said epigrammatically, ' Saturday night kills the show.'  Here in this part of Norfolk we pay our labour on Friday night ; at least that is my own habit, but doubtless the custom varies.

The average rental of the best lands with a fair mixture of grass and tillage he put at 25s., and of second-class lands at 17s. 6d. the acre.  The fee-simple values had not fallen much on first-class estates which were well situated.  On others without these advantages they had shrunk to a certain extent, but much Devonshire land could be bought to pay five per cent.—as he remarked, as good an investment as anyone would want.  The second-class land had declined about thirty per cent. in value.  Most of the landlords were resident, and their farms were all let to tenants who generally paid the rents well.  In some districts there was just enough labour, but in others it was very scarce.  Wages averaged about 13s. a week, with cottage, garden, and potato land free, and forty shillings harvest money.  Cottages were plentiful, and for the most part fairly good, with excellent gardens.  They have a kitchen and back kitchen, larder, and always two or three bedrooms.  Still some useful cottages had been pulled down, and their occupants driven into the towns.

Some young men remained with good farmers, but wherever it was possible they left. The country gave no encouragement to them either in the matter of wages or the circumstances of life. He believed that education turns English working-class folk into upstarts, and makes them think that if only they are educated they need not labour. Better pay might help to remedy this failing, but present prices did not point that way. The condition of the tenant farmer was very uncomfortable, and too often his wife was but a white slave. Where it was possible most of the landlords were letting their large houses and living in smaller ones, although in his district they were not so hardly hit as in many others. On the contrary the labourers were distinctly better off than they had been in the past. There was no sign of a revival in agriculture, and he could not see any hope in that direction, as it was killed by the free imports, which would continue to increase. The result would be that in the future only the best lands would be cultivated, those that are poor going back to rabbit warrens and fox-coverts to the damage of the country at large.

The remedies he suggested were that taxes should be taken off the land, bounties given, and agriculture encouraged in all practical ways. Thus Government might buy their remounts direct from the farmers, standing good stallions, and pedigree bulls, at low fees in the different districts. They might help the factory system in the matters of butter and bacon, and send the army cart-mares to be sold in the large home-breeding centres, reserving the right to buy back their produce at some fixed price which would be remunerative to the farmer. They might lend money at cheap rates to farmers, landowners, and also to labourers to enable them to buy their cottages. They might arrange that the public analyst should visit farms and put his services at the disposal of the owners, and that agricultural colleges and stations should be established and worked as in America.

Doubtless it will strike the reader, as it does the writer of this work, that Government might do these and other things, but that before it undertakes a tithe of them the attitude of those in authority towards agriculture must be greatly changed. I say here what I shall probably have cause to say again before this book is finished, that it must always be remembered that English Governments look upon the land and its interests in a totally different light from that in which it is regarded by those of most other civilised nations. Here they cannot be brought to recognise that the matter is one of any real importance. Intoxicated with our recent, but now it would seem, waning success as a trading nation, and for the most part owing their place and power to the votes of traders and dwellers in the cities, to them the great questions of the prosperity of agriculture and of that which is dependent on it, the holding of the rural population to the fields and villages where their forefathers have dwelt for centuries, are things of small account. They will not face the fundamental facts that it is well that we should grow all the food we can within the limits of our own shores, and that of this we could grow a much larger quantity than we do to-day ; that men are more than money and deteriorate when crowded into towns, and that without a continually renewed supply of men and women, healthy in mind and body, the greatness of the nation must dwindle. Other countries are wiser ; they see and do their best to guard against the danger. Here, if we see it, we shrug our shoulders, say that any party or Cabinet that attempted remedies would lose popularity in the cities, and leave things to take their chance.

Another gentleman, himself a solicitor, writing to me from North Devon, said that his father was the tenant of a farm of 400 acres rented at £350, of which about a hundred acres were rough land not worth more than 4s. the acre. Of this farm, of which the family seem to have been tenants for generations—over two hundred years indeed—the rent used to be considerably higher, but had been reduced with the times. In that district, my informant said, there was a great scarcity of labour, most of the able-bodied men and youths having gone away to the large towns and the collieries of Wales. Owing to this labour question tenants were constantly giving up their farms. The greater part of the land is pasture, and the farmers sell very little corn, which is chiefly grown for home consumption, the rent being made out of the stock.

Two of his brothers assisted his father in the business, out of which they just managed to earn sufficient to pay the rent. He stated that, like himself, they were strong and in good health, men of six feet high or over. One of them had just returned from the war, where he had been serving with the Devon Yeomanry. Now the three of them had come to the conclusion that it was useless for them to continue to attempt to earn a living in England. They had determined therefore to emigrate, and the real object of the letter which gave this incidental information, was to ask me to advise them as to what country they should choose for their new home. I regret to say that I receive many such epistles, but when everything is said, it is not altogether a matter for regret. These fine young men, and hundreds like them, depart from our shores indeed, but they go to help to build up the new Englands beyond the seas, countries that have not yet adopted free trade, and where there is therefore a better chance of success for those who hope to spend their lives and earn their living on the land.

Mr. John Stone gave me some interesting information on the condition of the Devonshire labouring man as it used to be in and before the year 1845—a time which he remembered well. Then the peasant's wage was 7s. a week. One he knew who had 8s., but he worked for the squire and was a kind of foreman. He said that it was difficult for people of this generation to understand how such a man could exist, with bread costing from 10d. to 1s. a loaf. But exist he did, living principally upon potatoes, which before the disease broke out only fetched from 1s. 6d. to 2s. a bag of 120 lbs. Moreover he had a good suit of clothes in which to go to church on Sundays. In those days farmers used to work hard. He could recollect men of that stamp with their five or six strapping sons, every one of whom could reap and mow, plough and sow. The wives and daughters worked also, milking the cows, making the butter and cheese, brewing the beer, pressing the cider, and baking the bread ; indeed a farmer's wife of that generation would have been ashamed to buy a loaf of bread.

He said that he thought one of the great causes of the downfall of the class was the 'drinking habit,' which then was far worse than it is to-day. Such people were wanted now—minus their love of liquor ; but he thought the only way to get them was by means of smaller holdings and freeholds. The labourer, too, should have a freehold cottage with sufficient ground on which to keep a cow, and be able to pay for it as building societies enabled a member to pay for a house. It was, he said, astonishing what a man would do when he had something which was his own, and not the squire's. Then instead of running away from the land, he would manage his own little holding and work for the larger farmer in his spare time.

When Mr. Stone was a boy he was at school at Hatch Beauchamp, a village in Somerset. The schoolmaster was the secretary of seven or eight clubs or friendly societies, of which the members were for the most part labourers. He used to accompany him to take the monthly or quarterly subscriptions, and to the annual dinner provided in an orchard at the back of the village inn. To many of the poor fellows who had hardly tasted butcher's meat all the year this was a great occasion. First they marched to church headed by their band of music, calling at farmhouses on the way to be regaled with cider, brought out in milking pails, from which it was dipped with mugs, with the result that by the time they got to church some of them were hardly fit to attend service. These clubs were provident institutions, by means of which their members were kept off the parish, receiving in case of illness 7s. a week 'bed-pay,' or 3s. 6d. a week ' walking pay.'

Some sixty years have gone by since the days of which Mr. Stone spoke, and whoever they may have harmed in their passage, certainly they have bettered the lot of the labouring man. In those days, however, the fortunes of the Devonshire farmer seem to have been very good, and he was able to say, as I found inscribed on a mug of this period which I bought in Exeter :

> Let the Wealthy & Great,
> Roll in Splendor & State,
> I envy them not I declare it ;
> I eat my own Lamb,
> My Chickens & Ham,
> I shear my own Fleece & I wear it.
> I have Lawns, I have Bow'rs,
> I have Fruits, I have Flow'rs,
> The Lark is my morning alarmer ;
>   So jolly Boys now,
> Here's, God speed the Plough,
> Long Life and success to
>    the Farmer.

I might adduce more evidence as to the agricultural conditions of Devonshire. Thus among much other information Mr. T. Goss, of Iddesleigh, where he farmed, said that labour grew scarcer every year. Young men went away to towns where they received higher wages, had more company, and saw more life. 'Education may have something to do with this. I think that children who do not take well to learning should not be bound to stay the full time at school, as it tends to make them dissatisfied and lazy.'

Again, Mr. William J. Harris, of Halwill Manor, Beaworthy, told me that in his parish alone in that part of the county, the population had increased. In 1871 it was 243, in 1901, 434. This increase, he said, may be attributed entirely to the number of small-holdings, which, I believe, he has done much to foster. This is interesting testimony to the value of a system whereof many deny the advantages. I much wish that I could have found occasion to visit Beaworthy, as Mr. Harris kindly asked me to do.

Here I must cease my quotations. I have tried to select views representative of all classes and districts of the county, and from these I must leave the reader to form his own judgment of its general conditions and agricultural outlook. Perhaps, however, to the mass of evidence adduced above I may add an opinion or two of my own on Devonshire and its rural inhabitants. A very large part of the county is as fertile as it is beautiful, and it seemed to me that, except in the case of the apple orchards, which are often neglected, those who till its soil put it to the best possible use. In other words, the land is made to bear all that it can under the existing circumstances of comparatively large holdings. Nine Devonshire farmers out of ten, as Mr. Hussey, jun., and others said, are very hard-working. They stick to business, and seem to love their labour as they love the land that bore them. Here it is, I think, that we find the secret of the competition for farms even when farming is not too profitable. On the whole, also, they do fairly well, for their rich grass lands save them, enabling them to earn a rent and a living, if no more.

In the vast majority of cases this is the limit of their prosperity, for few, I imagine, are putting money by as farmers used to do. In Devonshire, or elsewhere in the South of England, lack of labour is the great trouble, but even in this particular the county is not so hard hit as are many others. On grass lands the labour-bill is light, and at the worst the farmer can give up his cows, take to sheep and store cattle, and lay down most of the arable, sure that in that moist atmosphere and on so kindly a soil it will in time make a good return as pasture. Many Devonshire and Cornish men, tempted by the low rents prevailing in the Eastern Counties, have migrated thither during the last fifteen years, where, by the help of energy, hard work, and new ideas, they are, I understand, doing fairly well. But their success, whatever it may be, is not, as I was informed, sufficient to tempt others to follow their example, since the migration seems practically to have ceased. On these matters, however, I may have something to say when I come to deal with that part of England.

The cry of all classes connected with the land in Devonshire is for some form of Protection, at any rate against imported manufactured articles, such as flour, barley meal, and other feeding stuffs. I scarcely spoke to a farmer or land agent in the county who did not urge the justice and necessity of such a change, although the labourers who see their wages increase by leaps and bounds, and benefit by the cheap foreign food, may have different views upon the subject. Whatever are its merits or demerits as a fiscal policy, a matter on which I do not pretend to enter here, it may be argued however that Protection, even if attainable, would not prove a panacea for all these ills—at any rate in Devonshire and counties that are similarly situated. Rents might rise, and farms be more eagerly competed for than they are at present. But would the root of the question be touched? Can there be any real or abiding agricultural prosperity without a sufficient rural population that is content to stay and labour on the land? Would Protection and the slight increase of wage which it might bring to the worker suffice to keep him there?

For my part, I am not quite sure, since I incline to agree with many of my informants, that in Devonshire this matter of the rural exodus is more one of the effects of education and of shrinking from hard manual work than of wages. On the other hand, Protection, should it ever be introduced, must tend to foster that very desirable person, the smallholder, who works his fields with his own labour and that of his family.

## CORNWALL

Although on this journey I did not, I think, actually cross
the borders of Cornwall, it will perhaps be useful if I quote
as briefly as possible, a selection of the evidence that I
gathered as to the agricultural conditions prevailing in
that county, which I have visited on previous occasions.  In
Cornwall the land was formerly in a very great number of
hands.  Thus, according to the 'Owners of Land Return'
for 1873, it appears that out of 13,866 proprietors, 8,717
owned less than a single acre, and the average size of the
estates was 54 acres.  What it is now I cannot say, but it will
be noted that Mr. Dingle, whose views I quote below, states
that very many of these little ownerships have been sold,
information that is confirmed from other sources.  Out of a
total cultivated area of, I think, 606,524 acres in 1901, 121,166
acres in Cornwall were under corn crops, 46,531 under green
crops, 188,026 under rotation—clover, sainfoin, and grasses—
and no fewer than 245,090 under permanent pasture.

Cornwall, the most westerly of the English counties, in
which are included the Islands of Scilly, covers an area of
about 868,000 acres, is very narrow, and has an extreme
length of nearly 80 miles.  The land, although it is falling in
value, seems in some places to be still by comparison highly
rented, for which reason, among others, a great number of
Cornishmen have migrated to shires where it can be hired
very cheaply.  One of these emigrants whom I met in Hertfordshire, informed me that the Cornish farmers were not
doing well, and that farming there 'means white slavery,' and
I have heard much the same story from others.  Between
1851 and 1871 the population appears to have increased

2 per cent., but whereas in 1861 it was 369,390, in 1891 it had fallen to 322,571. The results of the last census I have not yet seen.

I now give the opinions and experience of Mr. John W. Dingle, whose remarks strike me as especially interesting.

Mr. Dingle has farmed all his life at North Darley near Callington, in the north-east of Cornwall, and described himself as a survivor of the old yeoman class. He inherited a small estate, of which no record exists to show that it had ever been bought or sold. For four hundred years, or perhaps longer, it has descended from father to son through the male line, until it reached his hands—a curious circumstance in this changeful world. Cornwall, he pointed out, was in former days largely a county of small proprietors who farmed their own estates. Now for the most part these have passed away, and he believed that the days of the few yeoman farmers who remained, were numbered. He could point to whole parishes which used to be farmed by the owners of the soil. Now these properties have been sold, and are occupied by tenants whose education, mode of living, and social position are very different from those of their former owners. During his own remembrance the ownership of the land had completely changed; a result brought about, he considered, by the Free Trade policy inaugurated by Sir Robert Peel.

In reply to my queries, Mr. Dingle said that during the last quarter of a century, rents in his district had fallen about 15 per cent., and the fee-simple value of the land about 20 per cent. In 1901 the average rental value might be put at 18s. the acre. This rent was fairly well paid, but the competition for farms was less than it used to be. Labour was very scarce, the old men only being left upon the land. This was one of the farmer's greatest difficulties, which, bad as it was, seemed likely to become worse. The young men migrated into the towns, where there is more excitement which they call 'life.' Education, by keeping boys at school until they reach thirteen years of age, together with the reading of newspapers, has a tendency to make them discontented with the country. The corrective of reading-rooms had been tried in his district, but with little effect, and lectures they declined to attend.

The wages of a labouring man, including a cottage and garden, potato plot, harvest money, &c., came to an average value of 18s. or 19s. a week. Owing to the stoppage of the local mining industry and the exodus of those employed in it, cottages were plentiful in that neighbourhood. In his parish of Linkinhorne between 1891 and 1901 the population had decreased from 2,012 to 1,341. Most of the cottages contained four rooms and they were kept in fair condition.

Those tenant farmers who had considerable capital and employed labour, were not even holding their own, and there was a general complaint that the industry is unremunerative. Also the pedigree herds of cattle had been given up. The small farmers who, with the help of their families, do all the work on the land, were more successful, but they work harder and for longer hours than the labourers. The small land-owners who used to farm their own properties were nearly extinct, and the middle-class landowners, who have to provide jointures and portions for younger children charged upon their estates, were badly off. The large men, however, who possess other means or unencumbered estates, and are able to retrench a little and still live, were in a better position. The state of the labourer, who received much higher wages and could buy all commodities cheap, was far more pro-sperous than in the past.

He could see no signs of a revival of agricultural prosperity in Cornwall. The English farmer might perhaps compete with any one foreign country, but under our system of Free Trade he must compete with the whole world. Every year some foreign land, or lands, had a supply of foodstuffs greater than they required, of which the surplus was sent to the English market to be sold for what it would fetch. Against this competition British products had no chance. The effect of the desertion of the land by the labourer would, he thought, be the increasing dependence of this country on imported produce for its food supply, followed perhaps, when it was too late to remedy it, by the sudden awakening of our people to their peril. Our system of party government and the power of the dominant democratic element, in his opinion, prevented the possibility of a change for the better, at any rate for the present.

The views of Mr. Edward Mucklow, J.P., of Whitstone, also in North Cornwall, where he is lord of the manor and, I think, the largest landed proprietor, were on the whole more hopeful. He put the fall of rents and of the selling value of land, which was principally owned by persons residing in the district, at from 10 to 12 per cent. and from 12 to 15 per cent. respectively, and the average rent on average soil at about 12s. 6d. the acre. Small farms of from 70 to 150 acres, he said, let readily, and their rents were well paid. There was greater difficulty in the case of large farms. Of labour there was a moderate supply, but it grew more scarce. The young men were going fast to the towns, where the wages were higher and the hours of work were not so long. Education had made them more fit to fill situations in cities, nor did he see how the system could be altered. The average wage of the labourer was 15s. a week. Cottages were scarce, and the state of the older ones very bad. The general condition of the tenant farmer was socially better than it had been twenty or twenty-five years ago, and financially he was holding his own.

This view, it will be remarked, is in somewhat strong contrast to that expressed by Mr. Dingle.

The landlord, whose income depended solely upon rents received out of his property, was badly off, but the land in that district was for the most part owned by persons having other sources of income. The condition of the labouring man was never better. There was a good demand for his services, wages were high, food and clothing cheap. Personally he was hopeful as to the future of agriculture, although at present he could not point to any signs of a

revival in that business.    He thought that the effects upon
the farming industry of the desertion of the land by the
labouring classes, must be that more arable would be laid
down to grass, or go out of cultivation, and that the country
at large would be more dependent upon foreign supplies.
This, he added, was 'not a nice position to contemplate in
case of war with a neighbouring Power.'    The remedies he
suggested were : more and better cottages with good gardens,
and, when required, a plot of ground whereon to keep a
cow.    These, he thought, with fair wages, would induce the
young men to marry and settle down in the country.
Technical education in all branches of farm labour should
also be provided and rewarded with prizes.    This would
make work on the farm more interesting, with the result
that it would be better done.

Mr. T. Rickard, a wholesale grocer in the country
town of Wadebridge, was so good as to confer with six
leading agriculturists in his district, and to furnish me with
their joint opinions upon the various points which I submitted to them.    They said that since 1875 rents had fallen
quite 33 per cent., and selling values eight years' purchase
on the rentals, that is, from thirty years to twenty-two years.
The average rent they put at 15s. the acre ; at this price farms
let fairly well.    There were few resident landlords in the
district, and labour was scarce.    Wages ran from 15s. to 20s.
a week, men receiving extra pay at harvest time.    The
number and condition of the cottages varied.    In some parts
of the neighbourhood they were plentiful and in good condition, in other parts scarce and out of repair.    The young men
migrated to the towns to a very great extent for the reason,
my informants thought, that they found more amusement
and company there than in the rural districts.    The general
condition of the tenant farmer was not good, and the landlords were feeling the depression as much as the farmers.
The labourers, on the other hand, had never been so well
off.    They could see no signs of an improvement in the
agricultural situation, nor could they say they were at all

hopeful as to the future. As to what the ultimate result of the desertion of the land by the labouring classes would be, they could not express any opinion, but machinery was helping to replace them.

Mr. Rickard added that he thought that if landlords and other resident gentry would take an interest in the farm labourer, and if cricket clubs in the summer and social indoor clubs in winter could be started, it would, to a large extent, help to keep the young men in the country districts.

Mr. H. H. Vivian of Tregavethan, where I believe he owns all the land and has farmed since 1886, put the fall in rents and in selling values at from 20 to 25 per cent. The rental was from 15s. to 20s. the acre, at which price the farms let well. Labour was scarce and dear, the wage being 15s. a week with free cottage and extras, amounting in all to about 18s. a week. Cottages were plentiful and four-roomed, many of them being built of 'cob' and thatched. A number of the young men went abroad, for the most part to South Africa, being led thither by the prospect of higher wages and a love of change. The general condition of the tenant farmer and the labourer was good, but of the landlord less so. He could see no sign of any agricultural revival, and was not hopeful as to the future. He thought that the results of the exodus from the country-side would be that a good deal of poor land must go out of cultivation.

A study of the above samples of local opinion seems to point to the conclusion that the condition of the agricultural interests in Cornwall does not materially differ from that in the neighbouring county of Devonshire, especially in the matter of the migration of the agricultural inhabitants, who everywhere seem to be leaving the land. Of course, however, there are occasional exceptions. Thus Messrs. W. & F. Craze, auctioneers and fruit brokers of Penzance, told me that they had planted fifty acres with fruit trees and flowers, and by this means were 'doing our part in keeping people on the land.'

I may add that in various parts of England I conversed with farmers who had emigrated from Cornwall, and that all of them gave me a poor report of the farming outlook there, and seemed to be glad that they had left the county.

COTTAGES NEAR WILLITON

## SOMERSET

THE hilly, well-watered county of Somerset, whither I travelled from Devonshire, has an area of about 1,043,400 acres, of which some two-thirds are under pasture. In the main it may be described as a land of sheep and cattle, although of course large areas are under cereals, fruit and other crops. The moors also are famous for their red deer and hardy breed of ponies.

Travelling from Taunton to Williton I noted that the red soil of Devonshire is still to be seen in Somerset. The country, however, opens out more widely, the enclosures become larger, and the horizon is shut in with wood-clothed, down-like lands. There are many ditches, more fences, and fewer 'banks,' and here these seem to be lower than in Devonshire. In the neighbourhood of the fertile parish of Bishop's Lydeard the soil is quite red again, so that the sheep on the fallows are stained the same hue, and the turgid water in the overflowing brooks runs red also. Here the views are very wide, and the eye, looking across bare pastures and through leafless trees—for although the month was April the earth showed no signs of spring—rests on the heights of Exmoor far away, draped with dark and threatening storm-clouds. At Stogumber bare hills appeared upon our right, and to the left a fertile valley backed by swelling lands of rich hue and promise. Here all the bottoms were flooded and sodden, while the lanes about a thatched village of which the appearance suggested decay and neglect, ran like rivers.

Hitherto the views presented to the readers of this book have in the main of necessity been those of the landowner, the land agent, and the farmer. As all who are acquainted with him know, the labourer is very shy; also he is suspicious. In any case it is difficult to persuade him to talk, or to be sure, when he does talk, that he is saying what is really in his mind. Ask him why his class is leaving the country for the town, and in nine cases out of ten, if he gives any answer at all, it will be to the effect that it is because they get a 'bigger shilling' there, or because 'the missus finds it dull.' In short, the tradition, and in some cases the memory, of the evil days when his people were little better than serfs, existing on a starvation wage in hovels, many of them scarcely fit to shelter swine, are with him still.

Things have gone round since then, and the power is in his hands. Armed with his vote he is the real master of the situation, but in his heart he is still timid, and still looks upon the farmer with fear, if not with hatred. The efforts made for his amusement and the amelioration of his state do not in the least soften this mental attitude—at any rate that is so in very many instances. He puts them down to a desire on the part of his employers to conciliate him and to retain his services, not because his company is wanted, but because he is necessary. So—drawn by their glitter, like moths to a flame—shaking the dust of his native village off his feet, he departs for the great cities, where there is always a demand for youth and strength to feed the ceaseless mills of competition, in due course, perhaps, to be pressed aside and trodden down beneath the eager feet of the new-comers who follow on his path.

I propose, therefore, to begin my remarks upon the county of Somerset by giving prominence to the views of Dr. Killick, a man who for years has made a study of the labouring classes there. This gentleman is, moreover, in true sympathy with their trials and grievances, with which his profession brings him into daily contact, and is therefore well qualified to speak for them. In short—as it is wise to study every side of a matter—I wish to present for the consideration of my readers, certain aspects of our rural problems as they appear to the labourer in the West of England.

Dr. Killick, who struck me as an exceptionally able and clear-headed man, is the medical officer of health for the parish and district of Williton, with a population of about 5,000, and for half of the Union with a population of 10,000 more. On the great education question he said his experience was that truly educated people love the country, and wish to live where they can enjoy the sights and sounds and watch the operations of nature. The education which is given in the Board schools, however, is, he believed, just sufficient to make the labouring classes dislike these things and long for the glare and company of the towns. Also as a doctor he had found that the law which obliges the attendance of children at school, whither they must trudge through any weather, however wet and foul, is responsible for much sickness, and in some cases for the permanent ruin of their constitutions. It was this inconvenience or danger in many instances that made the village mother pine for clean streets, where the children could walk dry-shod to the schools, and never rest until she reached them.

The cottages he described as, on the whole, bad, many of them being very inconveniently situated in damp hollows, which, although they afford shelter, cause the walls and floors to reek. Also year by year they were becoming older and less healthy. Here I called Dr. Killick's attention to a village we had visited on the afternoon of our interview. Never in England have I seen any other hamlet in such a state of decay; therefore I hope and believe that the case is quite exceptional. In this Arcadian retreat the walls were falling down, the thatch was rotting on the roofs, the windows and doors were loose and unpainted. In short, the settlement, which, from its position and natural advantages, ought to have been both healthy and beautiful, was a scene of unwholesome desolation. Yet people lived in those ruinous homes, and children are bred there, for I saw them standing about the sodden gardens.

Dr. Killick replied: Yes, he knew it well, and that it had been responsible for much misery. The health of the district he described as bad generally among the labouring classes, indigestion being the most common of the local ailments. For this he considered that the constant drinking of inferior and ill-prepared tea and the use of so much sugar, which decays the teeth, were largely responsible. In the old days when the labouring folk had been content to drink skim milk, their health was better. He stated further that there were no trained nurses in the district.

I asked him why this should be so, seeing that in such a place as the village of Ditchingham, in Norfolk, and others which I could name, where land is of less value and the farmers are so much poorer, a trained nurse had been established. He shrugged his shoulders and replied that no one knew the need of such skilled assistance more than he did, and the unnecessary suffering that was caused by its absence. He had tried to establish nurses, but had met with no support. So they did without them, depending in emergencies, such as lying-in cases, on the help of the ordinary 'village women,' whose knowledge was worse than none at all.

Reverting to the question of unwholesome houses, I asked why he did not call upon the authorities to condemn them. He pointed out that this was a lengthy and troublesome business, as first there was a district Council, and after it the Bench of magistrates to be convinced. The worst of it was, however, that even if a house were ordered to be pulled down no new one was built, so its inhabitants had to find a home elsewhere. Dr. Killick held that to mitigate this evil public authorities should have power to build cottages. He added that the labourers as a class earnestly desired to rent dwellings which did not belong to their employers, of whom they wished to be independent so far as their homes were concerned. Turning to another matter, he was of opinion that, except in a few instances, the clergy were not popular, and that the trust and belief in an overruling and personal Providence was dying out of the hearts of the rising generation of villagers. Among their fathers this had been strong and constant, a living factor in their lives.

It was this trust, with the patience which it bred, that in the past had enabled them to bear their trials and privations with so little murmuring. Now, he thought, things were different, and the young people, unfettered, for the most part, by religious considerations, were determined to lead the easiest and pleasantest life which lay within their reach. I asked him whether he considered that as a class agricultural labourers were honest, having in my mind the many tales of scamped work to which I had listened of late. He answered that, speaking generally, the old folk were honest, but the young ones were not—at least they took a different view of their duties and responsibilities. As regarded wages, he believed them to be barely sufficient to enable a man to feed and bring up his family in a decent fashion. That was one of the reasons why the smartest lads had left the land. Those who stayed were sometimes ' a bit silly,' and in other cases too fond of drink.

This alleged insufficiency of wages gives point to a story which was told me by a farmer in the district. He said that he found a man who was employed to build up a bank, doing his work very badly, and told him that he should put ' more back into it.' The son of toil promptly answered, ' I ain't a-going to put no more back into it for the money that you gives me.'

As for remedies, Dr. Killick could only suggest two : the establishment of good relations between the labourer and the farmer, and the subdivision of the land. He believed that the working of big farms would become impossible, and that the ultimate burden of those changes which seemed to be inevitable must fall upon the shoulders of the land-owner.

While we were at Williton I visited a farm about a dozen miles away, of which the tenant, having assigned his stock and crops to his creditors, was being sold up by public auction. It was situated not far from the town of Minehead

—a rising watering-place that owes much of its prosperity to the stag-hunting on the heights of Exmoor close at hand, which brings numbers of rich people from London and elsewhere to share the sport. Some farmers, by the way, declare that there are too many of these red deer, which do great damage to the crops, and that the compensation paid is not really adequate, as it allows nothing for the ultimate manurial value of the roots and straw which they destroy. It would be a thousand pities if these stately creatures, some of which we saw on the hillsides, were allowed to vanish from one of their last haunts ; still, in deer, as in other things, there must be moderation.

The farm where the auction was to be is approached by a long lane leading up a beautiful valley that has on either hand rich pasture, diversified by clumps of covert which harbour the deer, and here and there with ploughed fields of fertile red earth, so steep that we wondered how a harrow or a drill could be dragged up them. The labourers, by the way, as we were told, show an increasing disinclination to take service on these precipitous farms, which involve a weary deal of hill climbing. Besides rough land and woods, this holding comprised some 400 acres of arable and pasture, and brought in, I understood, a rent of £530. At this, or even a higher price, however, no difficulty in reletting it was anticipated. Indeed, although it had not been advertised, the agent, Mr. Andrew, of the firm of Messrs. Hawkes & Andrew, informed us that he had already received some forty applications ; a fact which spoke well for the prosperity of Somersetshire farmers.

Walking by the edge of a valley, where we saw the white tents of woodmen engaged in cutting pole willows into clogs for sale in the North of England, we came to the scene of the auction. Here were gathered a large company of farmers from the surrounding districts. They were fine, independent-looking men, with loud, jovial voices and keen-lined faces, most of them full of enterprise and vigour, some of it due, perhaps, to the practice of the sport of deer-hunting, of which they are so fond. The stock put up, both fleece and horn, was of an indifferent quality, and prices ruled low, but all present seemed to look upon the occasion as a holiday, and a good deal of laughter and bantering of the usual sort passed each time the hammer fell. Ewes with two lambs fetched from 38s. to 51s., and the best of the cows, in milk or in calf, from £12 to £15 ; a result that must have been somewhat discouraging to the creditors.

For my part, after standing for three or four hours in six inches of mud, fanned by a biting wind, and employing the time in conversations of more or less interest with a bewildering succession of agriculturists, I felt depression creeping over me like the rising valley mist. Notwith-standing the beauty of the scenery and the fact, which soon came home to my mind, that farming was on the whole more prosperous in this part of Somerset than in any other district that I had yet visited, my thoughts would revert to the poor, broken man hidden away in the grey old Tudor house close by, while the auctioneer made jokes and the multitude of his brethren divided up his goods, specu-lating the while as to which of them would step into his home. Indeed, I was not sorry when at length it was time to tramp back through the pouring rain to catch the train for Williton.

There is no doubt that, on the whole, agriculture still prospers in Somerset—that is to say, those who follow it make their rent and a living, and, if they be exceptionally able and hard-working, pay off borrowed capital or put by money. This is more than could be said, so far as my judg-ment and experience went, of almost any other district that I had then visited, the Channel Islands alone excepted. As a consequence, the competition for farms was eager, while rents had not on the whole fallen more than 20 per cent. since the good times, and showed no tendency to further shrinkage. In some cases, indeed, it is still possible to relet at an advance, partly because the hard-working Devonshire farmers arrive in considerable numbers and enter into competition for the smaller holdings. The soil is splendid, a rich loam varying from red to black in hue. Of course, I speak of that of the lowlands. The hillsides, which have been denuded by æons of washing, are poor, and the moorlands seem what moorlands are all the country through.

I do not think that I ever saw more luxuriant or finer pasture lands than some of those round Williton; indeed, notwithstanding the cold of the weather, the deep green grass was coming through them with a rush, suggesting to the eye of experience how rich would be the sward in six weeks' time. In short, in the better parts of Somersetshire the farmer has every advantage that England can afford. His rainfall is ample, his breadth of pasture wide, his arables are deep and cool, his breeds of sheep and cattle good. Save on the large and well-tended estates, however, the farm buildings struck me as indifferent, and in some cases as bad. This, it must be remembered, is always apt to be the case where there is considerable competition for farms, since, if the landlord can let readily without renovations or repairs, it is scarcely strange that he should keep money in his pocket which he is not asked to spend.

The cottages, also, taken as a whole, did not appear to me to be so good as they are in many other counties. Although in Somerset, as elsewhere, as I shall show when I come to specific instances, the outcry over the scarcity of labour was very general, my conclusion is that in this respect, the hill farms excepted, the county has not suffered to anything like the same extent as most others that I have seen. The causes of this difference seem somewhat obscure, especially as Bristol and the Welsh coal mines are close at hand, and the wages, which average about 12s. a week, with cottage and some extras, are lower than in most other places. Still the fact remains that, although, of course, a good number of labourers do go, some bide upon the land, if not enough to supply its needs. The exodus is steady and increasing, but it is not furious.

A typical Somerset holding which I inspected was the

Aller Farm, near Williton, of 380 acres, rented by Mr. Hosegood, whose father or uncle—I forget which—held it before him. The rent value of this farm, which includes a large proportion of pasture, some of it laid down by the tenant, was, I think I am right in saying, about 22s. an acre, and the capital invested about £10 an acre, or a little more. It was worked on the four-course Norfolk shift, the layers being left for one year only, as in this kind of soil, which is somewhat sandy, the couch grass is apt to smother them if they stand longer. A fair average return from the land, which was very well done by, is four and a half quarters of wheat, seven and a half quarters of oats, and about five quarters of barley, per acre.

Much less wheat is now grown than formerly. Thus Mr. Hosegood used to have seventy acres under that cereal, but in 1900 he grew only twelve. In 1901 his acreage was thirty of wheat and eighty of barley. The cottages in his neighbourhood, he complained, were bad and small, while some were being pulled down and not replaced. He kept a good stock of cows, sheep, and other cattle, and, being a hard-working man of high intelligence, who farmed his land thoroughly, on the whole seemed to be doing well. His implements, I may add, were many of them of American make, which, he said, he had found to be superior to those that are made in England, as they combine lightness with great strength. This, however, is disputed by English manufacturers from whom I have received letters on the subject of the above remark. Whatever may be the rights of the case, upon which I can express no positive opinion, the fact remains, that I have found a great number of American implements employed in almost every county I visited in England.

On this farm kail was grown. Here the drills were set wide apart for that crop, with the result that it comes coarse, leaving the ground somewhat cumbered with large stalks which are troublesome in the subsequent ploughing. The reader may remember that in Wiltshire, as we saw upon Mr. Dibben's farm, the kail was cultivated very close, so that the stalks grew thin, whereby this evil was avoided. Upon part of a large field of forty acres, made by throwing down the fences of seven small enclosures, land was being prepared, I think for late barley, with a cultivator, to which three horses were harnessed abreast. For this crop six pecks of seed were sown to the acre, the drill being set eight inches apart. On some that was up I counted an average of forty plants to the yard. Superphosphate and bone manures are invariably used for the mangold crop. Swedes are sown about June 20, since they mildew if drilled earlier. The average allowance of artificial is 2 cwt. of superphosphate and 2 cwt. of dissolved bones per acre, either sown broadcast before the drill, or with the seed according to the fancy of the farmer. The water here was supplied by means of an hydraulic ram put in by Mr. Hosegood, who spoke of it with enthusiasm, saying that it saved him much anxiety and labour.

The country in that neighbourhood is wide, open, and rolling, with many elm trees. To the west lay Dunkerry Beacon and the Exmoor Spurs; to the east the Quantock Hills, still brown and bare of herbage ; to the north the Bristol Channel ; and to the south the Brendon Hills.

Mr. Hosegood was of opinion that in this humid climate it was the salvation of a farm to lay down grass, only, he added, it must be laid down well. Like everybody else, he complained of the state of the labour market, saying that Bristol drained away their best men, twelve or fifteen of whom had migrated thither not long before. Wages, he admitted, were perhaps at the bottom of it, though, for his part, he believed that a love of company and the desire for lighter work were equally responsible for the exodus, which he considered to be a national and ever-increasing evil.

Quite close to Mr. Hosegood's is the farm of Mr. Bowerman, the well-known breeder of pedigree Somerset Devons, which he exported to Germany and elsewhere. His stock of young bulls was very fine. When we visited the place some of these were being prepared to undergo the tuberculin test, an interesting and I believe effective, if somewhat intricate process. Those animals which are proved to be affected with tuberculosis by the guide of their registered temperatures are, I understand, butchered without delay. The cottages that I saw upon this farm were bad, and the buildings, to my fancy, indifferent.

Another holding which I went over at Stogumber, some miles away from Williton, is owned by its occupier, Mr. George Cornish. It was a prosperous-looking and well-managed place, with the usual large proportion of pasture. Mr. Cornish grazed a good many bullocks, which he sent to Guildford to be marketed. Personally he had sufficient labour, although skilled hands and thatchers were scarce. He said he did not believe that farmers were making more than a rent and a living, and that he did not intend to bring up his son to the trade. All the husbandry in this district struck me as of a high class.

Here I will give the opinions of some of the gentlemen with whom I had conversations at Williton and in its neighbourhood.

Mr. Andrew, the land agent, took a hopeful view of things. Thus he said that, although rents had fallen 25 per cent., they showed no tendency to drop any lower. The labour question, he thought also, was apparently not acute. The size of farms in this part of Somersetshire he put at an average of 250 acres in the lowlands, and from 500 to 600 acres in the hill country.

Mr. Tapp, a retired farmer, told me that tenants in Somersetshire could make no more than their rent and a living, which on holdings of any size would include the education of a moderate family. Thus, in a negative sense, they were prosperous, or at any rate not so badly off as in some other places. Almost without exception they were, he considered, industrious people, the tenant of 250 acres being his own stockman and shepherd. Doubtless a good deal of the capital invested in farming was borrowed, still there were plenty of men able and willing to increase their holdings when opportunity offered. Such people worked like slaves, paid their rents, and in some instances put by money. He thought that the outlook was doubtful, being afraid that as yet agriculture had not touched bottom. The fall in wool had made a great difference, especially to the holders of rough, feeding land. The average rent of farms, of which about two-thirds were arable, he put at from 20s. to 25s. the acre, but better land with more pasture fetched a higher price. The sale value was from twenty-two to twenty-four years, calculated on existing rents. The wages ran from 14s. to 15s. a week, with free cottages for horsemen and shepherds. There was an inconvenient scarcity of labour and an increasing exodus from the land, brought about by education, facility of transit, desire for a higher wage, and the good money that could be earned in the coal and iron trades. In many villages cottages were standing empty, and in some places being allowed to fall into ruins. He thought the old saying that if you have cottages you are sure to have men, no longer held in Somerset.

Mr. Nicholas Snow, J.P., who lives at Oare on Exmoor, and, I believe, is the owner of the site of the famous Doone Castle, about which he told me that a great deal of non-sense had been written and talked, said that some lands were going out of cultivation owing to lack of labour. The young men went away, but he thought that this exodus was not so marked as it had been ten years before; also that in time the towns would become congested. In his opinion the conversion of small farms into big ones had done a great injury to the country, as was recognised by landowners like Lord Fortescue, who were breaking them up again. Indeed there was a general tendency towards the re-establishment of these small holdings, although the difficulty was to pro-vide the necessary buildings. He saw no other solution of the labour question.

Mr. Fred Adams, who held a hill farm near Dunster, said that there the labour question was acute, and the more money they paid the less work they got done. The wages were from 11s. to 12s., with extras, and the general complaint among the men was that this was not enough. Many labourers would not stop upon the steep hill farms, but migrated to those that could be more easily worked.

Another gentleman said that he should be glad to get eight or ten more men whom he could employ for the following four months. Generally, this informant was very emphatic as to the farmer's evil case owing to the lack of labour.

I drove for a good many miles in the neighbourhood of Williton, studying the aspect of the country. The roads were steep and water-worn, the soil was of a red tinge, and the farming uniformly good. In the valleys all the land seemed rich, and on the high ground poor. Here and there a field was pointed out to us as 'hungry': such had a 'sharp sand' soil, but as a rule the pastures were lush-looking and evidently most productive. In this neighbourhood also I visited an ancient house, of which the condition can scarcely have changed since the middle ages. It stood in a hollow, surrounded by trees. Crossing an unmown lawn where peacocks wandered, we came to a porch ornamented with coats-of-arms, a half-obliterated inscription, and a date —1508. Within was a large flagged hall, hung round with age-darkened pictures, and strewn with the unmounted skins of deer, old cannon balls said to have been fired by Cromwell, and other untended relics, out of which opened a great kitchen with a wide, antique fireplace, and another chamber, also flagged, wherein stood a massive table of black oak. At the top of a flight of stairs of solid stone was a great room hung round with enormous faded tapestries representing scenes from the life of Alexander the Great, and, rising from the centre of the house, a square tower with a sloping four-sided roof that must have been built in or before the reign of Henry VII. The furnishings of the place were in keeping with its character : they looked as though nothing had been changed for generations. I do not think that I ever saw a house that impressed me more strongly. It spoke of the past, and the past alone ; nothing of our own age seemed to have found a footing there.

From Williton I travelled to Taunton, where I had a very instructive interview with Mr. Greenslade, the auctioneer of that town, and secretary to the Taunton Farmers' Club. He estimated the recent fall in rents at 25 per cent., with a corresponding reduction in the fee-simple value, and said that at present prices there was an active demand for farms. The vale lands around Taunton let at from 30s. to 40s. the acre, the proportion of pasture to arable being about half or a little more. He declared that the feeling between employer and employed was satisfactory, but that the cottages of the district were generally poor and without proper accommodation for a family. The wages averaged 12s. a week, with cottage, garden, and potato land. Of labour he said that they had plenty in the vale, but few young men were coming on, and for the most part these could boast but little skill.

On the poor, highland farms, however, the labour question was very acute, and the exodus from those districts rapid. Thus he mentioned that from the single parish of Coombe St. Nicholas, besides those who had drifted into other employment, no fewer than thirty-seven young fellows had gone to the war, mostly, I understood, as Yeomen. In this Blackdown Hill district, indeed, a few farms, Mr. Greenslade stated, were being left actually derelict for lack of labour wherewith to work them, while many were tumbling down bodily to such grass as they would bear.

He told me a pathetic story, not without its comic side, of a tenant who arrived a while ago at the house of his landlord, with the keys of his dwelling, and informed him, politely but firmly, that as his last labourer had just left the farm, agreement or no agreement, he was going too ! At Yeovil I heard of a somewhat similar case, where a gentleman who farmed 400 acres, was reported to be obliged to content himself with the services of a solitary man. I confess that the vision of this agriculturist instructing his faithful servitor each morning in his duties for the day, was one that caught my fancy. 'First you will plough the eight acres, then you will return and help me to milk the twenty cows, after which you will see to the lambing of the ewes,' and so forth.

While on this subject I cannot refrain from telling another story which I was assured is absolutely authentic. Not long before a labourer in the neighbourhood of Yeovil advertised for a situation in the local paper. On the next Saturday there appeared in the same weekly journal—the *Western Gazette*—an announcement from this man—a humorist, surely—thanking the seventy gentlemen who had so kindly applied for his services, and the following week yet another, thanking the sixty further gentlemen who also were so good as to wish to give him employment!

The local agricultural conditions, Mr. Greenslade thought, were depressed, but no worse than they had been seven years before. If anything, indeed, owing to the improved price of beef and mutton, they seemed a trifle better. Farmers, however, did no more than make a rent and live. The soil, for the most part, was loam, and in places so heavy that it needed some working; thus, south of Taunton, it was customary to plough with three horses. Some of the pasture was good enough to ripen bullocks with the help of cake. He said that there was not a bit of bad land within nine miles of Bridgewater. In North Somerset most of the cattle were Devons, and the sheep Devon long-wools, crossed with Hampshire Downs. There were still, however, a few Dorset-horns left, but the breed had become very unpopular. Of the Somerset-Devon cattle he spoke highly, saying that they do not eat so much as the cross-breds, and bear a spell of short commons better.

The only remedy which Mr. Greenslade could suggest for the troubles of the poor-land farmers and owners was an advance in the price of corn—in other words, Protection.

Beyond Taunton, upon the road to Yeovil, whither I travelled next, appear stretches of marshland, of which the dykes, which are lined with pollard willows, are kept very clean and trim. Some of these marshes are drained by the river Tone, into which the water is lifted by steam power. Then are passed Sedgemoor, the scene of Monmouth's battle, and Burrowbridge, with its church which never was completed, standing on 'The Mump,' and a monument among the marshes to some departed admiral, till on the left appear the Polden Hills, and on the right one of the Blackdown spurs. Next come more flats, across which the herons fly, and moors of clay soil overlying peat. At Langport these are left behind, and higher land begins. Then more moor-like marshes, some of them at that time inundated with water, and after them fields of lighter soil, where the water does not stand, and others of stiff clay. At Martock, on the Parrett, the moors have vanished. Here there is much pasture, but the soil seems to be stiff and heavy, and as yet in April the herbage showed no sign of spring.

At Yeovil I had the advantage of a conference with some of the leading farmers of the district, among them Colonel Harbin, Messrs. G. and H. Dampney, Roberts, Marsh, and Templeman. Also I inspected many farms. The space at my disposal will only allow me to summarise the resulting information. As a rule the neighbourhood is prosperous, the labour-bill being light, owing to the large proportion of grass lands. Thus on one farm that I inspected, out of 300 acres only twenty acres were arable, but three acres being given up to wheat. Here the labour came to less than 15s. the acre. Small farms were in eager demand, thus nice, mixed grass holdings of from 60 to 120 acres, if well placed and with good house and buildings, let readily at from 45s. to 60s. the acre. Mixed farms of from 120 to 160 acres fetched from 35s. to 45s. the acre, according to position and the quality of the land ; while large, mixed farms brought from 20s. to 35s. the acre.

The reason of the keen competition for grass farms is

DORSET HORN SHEEP                    *Page 239*

BIRD-SCARING!                    *Page 234*

that they suit little men who can do most of the work themselves with the aid of their families. Also they are largely taken by farmers who have given up or failed in more extensive holdings. Here, as everywhere else, the great outcry was over the labour question ; and the great fear that the ruin which has overtaken the corn farms will for this reason fall upon the dairy farms also, since cows must be milked on Sundays as well as week days.

At my conference I asked whether there was any complaint as to labour. Seven gentlemen, one after the other, answered me thus : (1) ' Yes, it is universal. . . . The movement is daily accelerated.' (2) ' I find them no good.' (3) ' It's only the duffers that stay.' (4) ' They go to Wales when the trade is good.' (5) ' They won't work on Sunday.' (6) ' There are a good many farmers giving up dairying owing to want of labour.' (7) ' My stepfather milked ninety cows, now he can only milk sixty,' and so forth. One gentleman added that the number of milch cows in the county had very much decreased.

Of cottages in this district I was told there were plenty, and that many stood empty. Some of these dwellings, such as those upon Lord Portman's Somerset estate, are excellent, as I can testify from inspection. Here, as elsewhere, however, people will not live in lonely cottages, or where children have to walk long distances to school. One gentleman, a large farmer, declared without hesitation that ' cider is the only thing that keeps the men on the land ; if it were not for cider we should not have a man.' Of this drink, by the way, he allowed each hand two hogsheads, or 108 gallons, annually ; while at times of extra stress another hogshead per head (or per throat), is consumed in the fields. Everywhere I heard that the amount of cider which the Somerset labourer can drink is gigantic, and I may add that it is by no means so feeble a beverage as is commonly supposed.

Among the holdings that I visited in the neighbourhood of Yeovil was the Great Lyde Farm of 300 acres, of which but twenty were arable, occupied by Mr. O. J. Rowles. As might be expected from this large extent of pasture, Mr. Rowles relied chiefly upon his cows, of which he kept from fifty to sixty. Five men and boys only were employed upon the place, the labour-bill coming to about £4 a week, a very light total. The carter received 11s. a week and a cottage, and good, steady day men 13s. a week. In Bristol they could earn from 18s. to £1, so it is not strange that many of them migrated thither, although probably there the money does not go so far as the smaller country wage.

In walking over the farm we came to a field with a northern aspect—'back sunded' is the local term, from the fact of its not facing to the sun—from which we had a beautiful view of the surrounding country, including the pinnacled and spired tower of Trent Church, and the river Yeo winding through the pastures, a silver line that marks off Somerset from Dorsetshire. The first piece of arable we saw was six and a half acres, very clean and well cultivated, under spring beans and white oats. Next came thirteen and a half acres of black oats and trifolium, the latter of which crops was to be succeeded by mangold in the following season. Of mangolds Mr. Rowles makes a speciality; indeed, in competition with all England for six years he took prizes given, I think, by Messrs. Proctor, of Bristol. His system was, first cabbages or some other green crop fed off with sheep; then thirty loads of farm manure ploughed in per acre; then 5 cwt. of superphosphate broadcast and harrowed in after the mangolds were drilled, with a result of fifty tons of splendid roots per acre. After the mangolds two white crops were taken in succession.

Of hay Mr. Rowles grew a hundred acres, producing in the season of 1900, 30 cwt. to the acre. In the case of this crop he saved labour by dragging up the grass with a hay collector and making the rick in the middle of the field, thus avoiding all loading and unloading of waggons. His milk fetched 5d. a gallon at the co-operative milk factory in or near Yeovil.

Another farm that I went over was that of Mr. G. Dampney, of Chilton Farm, near Ilchester, a holding of 500 acres, of which fifty acres, or 10 per cent., were arable. Here ten men were employed, the labour-bill coming to £1 an acre. The rent was 38s. the acre. Mr. Dampney, being a gentleman of great enterprise, ran his farm in conjunction with a butcher's shop in Yeovil, which was, I understood, doing very well, so well indeed that he could not keep pace with the demand. The expenses of the shop, at which butter, eggs, and poultry were also sold, were, however, considerable, as in addition to rent and rates, &c., some of the labour must be highly paid.

Only ten acres of wheat were grown upon this farm, of which the straw was used for thatching. The rest of the necessary straw Mr. Dampney bought. He kept more than 200 horned animals and about 1,000 sheep. The cultivation was high, the corn, cake, and artificial manure bills amounting to £1,100 a year. The average return of mangolds was from forty to fifty tons, and, as in the case of Mr. Rowles, here it is the fashion to follow them with two white crops. Mr. Dampney manured too high to grow barley satisfactorily, this being a cereal that when over-stimulated is apt to 'go down.' He considered oats, of which he grew about twenty acres, his best corn crop. Of trifolium he had ten or twelve acres, to be followed, first by kail and then by mangold. The trifolium with coarse grasses, &c., was manufactured into ensilage, his silo capacity being of no less than 500 tons. This ensilage, he said, would keep two years. In addition to other food his bullocks were fed twice a day with a ration of 12 lbs. of a mixture compounded of ground barley, oats and maize, chaff and pulped root, a small quantity of wheat meal being added. On this they did very well. He kept also ten or twelve sows of the Tamworth and Berkshire breeds. If I remember right this farm had the advantage of excellent water power conveyed to the buildings from a neighbouring stream by means of an underground channel.

On another day I visited the holding of Mr. Henry Dampney, The Manor Farm, Closworth, which is four and a half miles south of Yeovil and on the Dorchester road. On our way out I noted a very curious and lofty obelisk built of roughly-wrought stone and standing in a belt of Scotch firs. The local story about this monument is that with others it was erected to mark the boundaries of his property by some charitable landowner who desired to find employment for working men 'when labour only cost a penny a day.' At what period this philanthropist flourished I cannot tell, but from the general aspect of the obelisk I imagine that it is not older than the eighteenth century.

Mr. Henry Dampney farmed 640 acres under Lord Portman at a rent of 13s. the acre, which is some 2s. or 3s. lower than that which is generally paid in this district. Here the soil was of a very different character from what we saw on the farms that I have described, being for the most part clay (although in places sandy) with a subsoil of brick-earth and stone, which bakes and cracks badly in dry weather. Of the total acreage of the farm 200 were arable, 100 acres having been laid down to grass by Mr. Dampney and his father who was here before him. He kept no fewer than sixty cows, Somerset-Devons and cross-breds. The latter he declared to be 'the cow we like.' These animals will give an average of from twelve to fourteen pints of rich milk while in profit. Also they have the great advantage of fattening rapidly and well when they are no longer of use for the dairy. Thus a twelve-year-old cow, after being fed for a month on Bibby's Cake, would often fetch as much as £20 from the butcher. Indeed Mr. Dampney instanced a case in which one cow of fifteen years sold for £23 when fat.

On this farm there existed a curious custom, somewhat similar to that which I have described in Wiltshire, of leasing out the cows to a dairyman. I understood the arrangement, which must have proved satisfactory to all parties, as it had endured for twenty years, to be as follows : The cows, which

are calved down in spring, and not promiscuously throughout
the year, as when studying the agriculture of that country,
I found to be the custom in Holland, were let to the dairyman at an annual rent of £10 each, the resulting butter,
milk, and cheese being his property. Mr. Dampney fed the
animals, but Mr. Clarke, the dairyman, paid half the cake
bill. Also if for any reason it was not good enough, the
dairyman had the right to cast a cow within two or three
weeks of its being entered as one of his stock, but not later,
the subsequent risk being his. The calves also belonged to
him, and with the exception of the hay which was supplied,
were fed at his expense on beans and milk, but Mr. Dampney
bought them back from him on May 18 at an average price
of 75s. a piece.

Another arrangement seemed to be that, although each
party paid half the cake bill for the cows, in a dry summer
Mr. Dampney found it all. Each cow was reckoned to consume three acres of grass, supplemented by hay in the spring
of the year.

In addition to his cows Mr. Dampney kept a flock of
250 fine ewes of a race that his family had bred for a hundred
years. They were very good-looking creatures, with a close,
firm fleece. The practice seemed to be to drop the lambs in
March and to shear them in June. They are sold about the
end of August, and make from 38s. to 40s. Mr. Dampney's
custom was to feed the ewes with linseed cake for two
months before they lambed, as until he did this, for years
he lost about 10 per cent. of the lambs. Now he loses no
lambs, and in 1901 only nine ewes had died from chill contracted about a fortnight after lambing. Here a male of one
year is called a wether, and a female of one year a hog. A
teg is a lamb that has been shorn. The value of the tegs
was from 45s. to 48s.

On this farm 120 acres were mown for hay, but owing
to the variable quality of the soil the return is very
uneven. Thus some fields will yield a ton an acre, and
others but 5 cwt.; the average may perhaps be put at

15 cwt. It was the custom here to feed off the swedes as they stand. After the sheep have done with them the stump and root are jobbed out with an iron instrument and cleared away, as on this heavy land, if pulled before they are fed, they are apt to be trampled and spoilt. I made trial of this jobbing-out process, and found that to do it quickly and well requires a good deal of skill. When drilling artificial for roots, of which Mr. Dampney gave 4 cwt. of dissolved bones and superphosphate to the acre, it was his habit to mix the ash from burnt ant-hills with the manure in the proportion of half to half. He said that when thus prepared it went through the drill much better, and was otherwise more beneficial. The average produce of his corn land was four quarters of wheat and five quarters of oats, but the barley that this soil produces is of poor quality.

Adjoining the house stood the Church of All Saints, which I visited. It is Perpendicular in style, and in many ways very interesting. In the churchyard stands an ancient preaching cross and the tomb of the famous bellfounder Thomas Purdue, who died in 1711. On its east end is engraved the representation of a bell and this quaint epitaph :—

HERE LIES THE BELL FOUNDER HONEST & TRUE
TILL YE RESURRECTION MORN—PURDUE.

The population of the parish of Closworth is about a hundred ; since the last census it has lost twenty inhabitants.

From Closworth we drove to Haselbury to visit Mr. G. D. Templeman, of The Manor Farm. On our way we passed through four villages, in none of which was there to be found a public-house, or so I was informed. This, I may remark, is perhaps the greatest curiosity that I met with in my extensive wanderings throughout the length and breadth of England. When I questioned them about it, however, some local informants unkindly suggested that as the inhabitants got so much cider free, public-houses were superfluous. On this farm of 534 acres, rented at 22s. 6d. an acre, the soil is stone brash with a blue clay subsoil, and two-thirds of the area are under grass. In that district even adjoining fields vary very much in value ; thus I was shown some lying close at hand which were only worth 10s. the acre. On the east side of Haselbury, towards Hardington, where I believe the soil is clay over limestone rock, there is much poor land ; indeed, either Mr. Templeman or Mr. Slade, the land agent, whom I met at his house, told me that hundreds of acres of it were not worth a shilling an acre. One such farm had just been let to a tenant at a figure that could only suffice to cover the rates and taxes.

Although the labour question is pressing here, Mr. Templeman said that personally he had enough men. The wages for ordinary hands were 12s. a week nominal, with privileges and extras that brought them up to 16s. or even 18s. I remember that I talked to a shepherd on this farm who struck me as a man of a very good stamp. The total labour-bill ran out at about £1 an acre. The sheep were, I think, Dorset horns. I was informed that this breed will not pay unless they are lambed down in November, and turned into good mutton by about the following October, that is, within from ten to twelve months. Mr. Templeman kept seventy cows of the Shorthorn stamp, and one of the principal pro-ducts of his farm was Cheddar cheese, of which he made, I think, about fourteen tons annually. I visited his cheese rooms, which were very well arranged. Here the process of manufacture was explained to me whereby the sweet, whole milk is ultimately converted into great Cheddar cheeses that sell for some 60s. the hundredweight. Shorthorn cows may, he said, be divided into three classes, of which the best ought to yield about 4 cwt. of cheese during the season, the second best about 3 cwt., and the more ordinary animals about 2½ cwt. Cheese-making, Mr. Templeman told me, is not so remunerative as it used to be, and only pays if the best possible article is turned out.    Then it gives more profit than butter.

Once flax for making sailcloth was largely cultivated here, but I understood that this crop is no longer grown.

On our homeward way I noted between Crewkerne and the little village of Sutton Bingham—a district of clay and heavy sand with a lime-rock subsoil—that the land was extraordinarily poor, much of it being mossy and spotted with brakes of gorse. Indeed some farms seemed near to going out of cultivation. Near Sutton Bingham the woods reach down to the borders of the fields, which probably would be more valuable if they covered them altogether.

Having described some sample Somersetshire farms, I proceed to give the views of one or two sample Somersetshire men, as they were furnished to me by word of mouth, or in writing.

Mr. J. Quartly Carter, of Impens, North Petherton, in the Bridgewater division of the county, who occupied 320 acres of mixed land, said that since 1875 rents on large farms had fallen from 20 to 30 per cent., but the small holdings had not suffered so much. In some instances, indeed, where the land was particularly fertile and fit for market-garden purposes, it was quite as dear to rent as ever, although the proportion of such land was very small. The fee-simple value had shrunk in sympathy with the rents, but in the case of poor land to a larger extent, while the best land nearly held its own. Thus Mr. Carter had occasion a few months before my visit to purchase a six-acre field close to his house. It cost him over £100 an acre, but he did not think that the fact of its being so necessary to him, made any difference in the price he had to pay. The explanation of this was that he is surrounded by small owners who hunger for land. These men were mostly of the market-gardener class who had saved a little money, and perhaps borrowed more on mortgage. Such of them as occupy their own holdings 'do two days' work in the twenty-four hours, as they are working for themselves and not for employers.'

Indeed, Mr. Carter thought that if an average agricultural labourer, who had developed into a small owner, were to do no more for himself than he does for the farmer, ruin would soon overtake him.

In his neighbourhood no land was held under the Small Holdings Act, and he did not think that small-holders could be created to any considerable extent by Parliament. Their evolution must be left to the working of natural laws, nor, in his opinion, would they thrive except on the very best land. The ownership of larger farms was rarely changed, but these varied much in quality and value, say from £20 an acre for the poorest to £50 the acre for the best; perhaps £35 the acre would be a fair average price for mixed lands. In Mr. Carter's neighbourhood the principal landlords are Lord Portman, who lives on his estate in Dorsetshire, but whose eldest son resides on the Somerset-shire property; Mr. E. J. Stanley, M.P., and Sir Alexander Fuller-Acland-Hood, M.P. These gentlemen also reside upon their estates, and are typical English landlords who take a personal interest in their properties, and are readily accessible to the tenantry. Mr. Carter said that he had heard Mr. Stanley state publicly that the whole income derived from his Somersetshire estates is disbursed upon them. Of his own landlord also he spoke highly, adding that within a radius of ten miles there were many other gentlemen resident upon their properties.

In his district labour was very scarce. The average weekly wage was about 12s., with or without a cottage; two quarts of cider per diem, the Truck Amendment Act being, he said, a dead letter which was equally ignored by master and men; and 1s. a day extra in hay time and harvest, when over-time is worked. Cottage rentals are reckoned at about 1s. a week, but the tenant generally gives Sunday work in lieu of the rent. Now-a-days there was not much piecework, since the labourers did not care for it unless an exorbitant price was paid, as it involves more labour. Severe labour, Mr. Carter remarked, is the one thing that the modern farm-hand does not like. Since the introduction of self-binders piecework had gradually lessened, but this the men do not seem to regret. Still wages were rising, and, as he believed, within a few years would be higher by 2s. the week. Meanwhile day by day the labourers became more independent.

Cottages were scarce, but, owing to the advance of depopulation, were becoming more plentiful. At that time there were several to let in his village, a new thing in his experience. Nearly all these dwellings were old, and such as would not satisfy the sanitary authorities in the case of newly erected cottages. For the most part they consisted of two downstairs rooms—a living room and a wash-house—and two bedrooms. This could hardly be called decent accommodation for a mixed family; still it did not vary much; nor could such habitations be closed unless others were provided, which would never be done by private enterprise. Unless they married early and had a family, which handicapped them, the young men did not stay upon the land. From his neighbourhood they nearly all went to the Welsh coalfields, where during three or four days they earned good wages, and employed the remainder of the week in spending them. A boy who was perhaps taking 6s. a week at farm work would be enticed to the mines, where he receives 15s. a week, or more at a hazardous employment. Naturally he thinks it a grand thing to jump to a man's wage all at once, and on his first holiday returns home with glowing tales of the money that is to be had for the asking by those who are willing to follow his example. Is it wonderful, asked Mr. Carter, that nearly all of them go away, so that a boy to drive horses on the farm cannot be procured for love or money?

The initial cause of this exodus was, he thought, our system of education. Formerly if a boy went to school, at the age of nine or ten years he left it to earn five-pence or sixpence a day by scaring birds or doing odd jobs upon the farm. Now he must remain at his lessons until he was twelve or thirteen, by which time he had lost all taste for country pursuits, and was more fit to drive a pen than to follow the plough. By all means, said Mr. Carter, let a boy be taught to read and write and do the four elementary rules of arithmetic—knowledge that he could acquire by the time he was nine years of age; after which let him begin to earn his daily bread. Were they asked, this is what all boys of the labouring class would wish. Their parents would wish it also, and the plan would be approved by the common sense of the community, if this were not overruled by the dicta of educational enthusiasts and buried beneath departmental regulations. How, he asked, are the vast regions that we have recently conquered to be satisfactorily colonised? Not, he thought, by clerks and others of that ilk, but by the bone and sinew of the land, which can only be produced in perfection in the rural districts. Therefore, he said, if his parents approve, a boy should be permitted to leave school so soon as he can fairly master the three R's. Then he would take to the land naturally. In the eyes of a farm-boy scientific and technical teaching was a ridiculous fad. It was certain that a lad who migrated to the town must necessarily develope into a man of lower physique than one who stayed upon the land.

Farmers were always grumbling and generally with good cause, but he did not believe that in his district they had suffered so acutely as was the case in many others. Still there were not many who could put by for a future day, and a few disastrous seasons would empty farms and pull down the rents. The depression of the last twenty years had driven out most of the old tenantry. Landlords did not care to reduce the rents of the sitting men, but they had been compelled to relet to new ones at a much lower figure. In his neighbourhood there was no distress among landlords, whilst the labourer's position had doubtless improved, and would continue to do so.

He was not hopeful as to the future of agriculture, nor could he see any indication of its revival. The only thing that could possibly bring back prosperity to the land was Protection, and that we should never get. If we did it was the landowner who would ultimately profit by it; but leaving the incidence of benefit as between landlord and tenant out of the question, considered from the national aspect he was convinced that a duty on corn would be a blessing in disguise, as it would stimulate the growth of our own supplies of food, of which we could produce double as much as we did at present. Thus, formerly he himself grew sixty acres of wheat per annum, whereas now he only sowed twenty, and were it not that he needed the straw would grow even less.

Farming could not go on without labour, and if the labour was starved the farm was starved also. If the exodus of labourers could not be checked, a corresponding proportion of arable land must go out of cultivation. Double the wages and some men might be brought back, but no farm would stand that extra strain. If the labourer could be made to believe that a protective duty upon corn would go into his pocket in the shape of increased wages, instead of into those of the landlord or the tenant, there might be a possible solution of the difficulty. But no politician had the courage to propose anything of the sort, and it was heresy to breathe the word Protection. For his part he was gradually laying down his land to grass. During the season of 1901 he intended to put down another eighteen acres of good, deep, medium loam capable of producing a cereal crop of forty or fifty bushels to the acre every alternate year. It was a pity, ' yet one needs must go when the Devil drives.' ' Bad prices,' added Mr. Carter, ' to which the labour difficulty is now added, will break the back of agriculture.'

Colonel H. E. Harbin, of Newton Surmaville, Yeovil, said that in his district rents had fallen from 25 to 40 per cent., and with the exception of building land near towns, the selling value to a like amount. Of late, however, the letting value of farms that were principally grass and near railway stations, had improved. With the exception of

those that were mostly arable, farms let readily enough, and
the rents were fairly well paid. Labour was scarce and
getting scarcer, the wages being 14s. and 15s. a week, with
good cottage, garden, cider, and other perquisites. Save in
the case of a few old copyholds, the cottages were good in
his district, and generally contained two living rooms, three
bedrooms, and offices. The young men did not stay upon
the land, as the attractions of the towns, railway, police,
post office, army and navy, and foreign adventure were
taking the best of them away. Still he thought it was a
question of supply and demand which ultimately should
settle itself, although there would be great difficulty for some
time to come.

The condition of the tenant farmers was fairly good ; at
any rate in his district he had heard of no bankruptcies
amongst them, and financially the small landlords were
worse off, the demands upon them being so numerous. As
for the labourer, he was in better case than he had ever been
before. He could not say that he saw much sign of a revival
of agricultural prosperity at present, but he was hopeful that
things would come round. Worse times had been known,
and there never was any time of which no complaint was
made. The desertion of the land by the working-classes was a
very serious matter, but with more labour-saving appliances,
better wages, less luxury, plainer living, and greater economy
on the part of landlord and tenant, it was possible for
agriculture to struggle on in Somerset. The fact was, too,
much was expected from the land. Tithe, death-duties,
Imperial taxes, local rates, expenses of repairs, up-keep of
buildings, contributions to schools, the cost of valuers and
umpires, endless subscriptions, and the fierce pressure of
foreign competition, all piled on to it, were more than its
back could bear.

In conversation Colonel Harbin told me also that he did
not consider the labour question one that could be solved by
higher pay alone. Thus a tenant of his had offered very
good wages for a shepherd, but could find no one to fill the

place. He thought that in the future the small squires would be obliged to farm their own land, which would no longer pay three profits : that of the owner, the occupier, and the wage-earner. To show the extent of the depression in the corn-growing districts, he mentioned the case of a friend of his who used to draw £1,500 a year from land in the neighbouring county of Dorset. At the time of our interview it produced £300.

Mr. Wingfield Digby, M.P., with whom I had the pleasure of an interview, informed me also that the labour was a very great difficulty, chiefly owing to the influx into towns, the competition of Government works and of the Welsh mines.

Mr. J. D. Adams, M.D., a medical officer of health for the Yeovil Rural District, gave me an interesting view on the present position of the agricultural labourer in Somersetshire, which he thought would admit of much improvement. He said that it was difficult to understand how a man earning from 14s. to 16s. a week could support a wife and children in a decent fashion. In the neighbourhood of Yeovil, however, the takings of a family were in most cases largely increased by gloving work, an industry in which nearly all the women and girls were more or less engaged. It was the young lads and unmarried men who became dissatisfied with farm work and wages, and migrated to the towns, or from that immediate district to the collieries in Wales. Considered from the sanitary point of view, the labourers' cottages were by no means what they should be, but in his opinion this fact was not the cause of the unpopularity of farm labour.

His experience was that the education of the boys had the effect of rendering them gregarious, and of inducing in them a distaste for farm work and an inclination for the constant society of those of their own age and class. Thus the factories in that locality found no difficulty in obtaining boys, although the hours were as long and the pay no better than on the farms, because there they found society with its pleasures, and a half holiday on Saturdays. He believed also that the fact of all the farm labourers in a district being paid the same wage, whether they were able and industrious, or idle, was disastrous in its results. Take away hope and emulation from any class, and, whether they laboured with their hands or with their brains, both the workers and their work would certainly deteriorate. The circumstance of so much land that was formerly arable having of recent years been laid down to grass had of course enabled the farmer to dispense with some of his workmen. Still the demand for farm labourers was in excess of the supply; the work was there, but the young and active men would not accept it upon the terms offered to them.

Mr. Thomas Laurie, scientific apparatus maker, of Paternoster Row, London, has forwarded to me a very interesting correspondence between himself and the secretary of the Bath and West and Southern Counties Society, which illustrates in a striking manner the extraordinary neglect of agricultural education, not only in Somersetshire, but throughout England.

The Society, proposing to hold an exhibition 'for the purpose of illustrating, by means of specimens and diagrams, subjects connected with agriculture,' wrote to Mr. Thomas Laurie to suggest that he might like to take advantage of the opportunity to exhibit some of his collections and diagrams. Mr. Laurie has sent me a copy of his reply, which I reproduce, as it is impossible to state his case more clearly than does his letter :—

'December 5, 1901.

'We thank you for your favour of yesterday suggesting that we might with advantage to ourselves send a display of our models and cabinets for teaching agriculture. You will observe that the enclosed Catalogue from page 27 is wholly devoted to that subject. We have kept our lists well before all agricultural lecturers and teachers for many years, with no result whatever except numerous requests for the *loan* of our models from lecturers who were well paid for their work. Nothing whatever has resulted from our large outlay in this country. We then brought them before the notice of the Universities and Agricultural Colleges in the United States, and the response was immediate and satisfactory. We received many orders, and also letters of thanks for bringing the models and appliances before them. In this country there is no interest in the subject whatever; we mean that intelligent interest which searches for and seizes upon the best methods of instruction. If we sent a display of everything specified in our lists from pages 27 to 56 we would not sell 5s. worth of the goods.'

It is painful to an English agriculturist to read what Mr. Laurie has to say as to the difference of the reward of his enterprise in the United States, to that meted out to him by those who have authority in the matter in England. After all, however, it is only one more example of the neglect of agriculture and of everything that has to do with the land and its products in this country, where these excite no real interest and receive little practical support.

In conclusion, I repeat that the general body of evidence went to show that in Somersetshire the great majority of farmers—of course I speak of those on good land—are paying their rent and making a living, and no more. Said Mr. Marsh: ' A good many men have lost all and gone out. These were rented too dear, and the rent was reduced too late to save the sitting tenant.' The lesson of this county seems to be that now-a-days those farmers who wish to thrive should lay their land down to grass. Still, the keen competition for the best Somersetshire farms shows that there are many who continue to think the occupation one to be desired.

MR. TORY'S SHEEP

Page 202

# DORSETSHIRE

THE southern, sea-bordered shire of Dorset has an area of about 632,000 acres, and measures fifty-four miles from east to west by a breadth from north to south of from five to forty miles. Most of the county belongs to the chalk formation, the North Downs, which begin at Cranborne, stretching down to Beaminster, and the South Downs from Beaminster to Melcombe and Swanage. The best grazing lands lie in the valley of Blackmore and of the Frome and Piddle. There are many hills in the county and water is abundant. Agriculturally it is chiefly noted for its dairy products, Dorset butter being famous all over the world; but the soils vary greatly, and a large acreage is given up to the production of cereals.

From Yeovil to Dorchester, the capital of the county of Dorset, the country seems to rise gradually. It is pasture, pasture all the way, scarcely relieved by the sight of a single piece of arable. After passing Yetminster, however, the soil becomes more stony and of a light grey colour, which on the highest hills grows almost to white, denoting that we are once more on chalky land. Near Grimstone I observed that many of the cottages seemed to be in a bad state, some of them miserable—even squalid.

At Dorchester we were met by Mr. Tory, jun., who was to drive us sixteen miles to Turnworth, where his father—the well-known Dorsetshire tenant farmer—worked several thousand acres. Passing through the quaint old city of Dorchester, which, as I found in a county history, was a great barley market so long ago as 1730, we came to rich valley lands. These bottom lands still command up to

30s. an acre rent, in striking contrast to the hill farms, some of which bring in as little as 10s. an acre. It is from these pastures and those of the Blackmore Vale that we get the Dorset butter, although I was told in the county that much of what is sold as Dorset was really churned in Brittany. Excellent barley is also grown in this neighbourhood.

For nearly three hours, meeting very few people as we went, we drove over sodden roads through undulating, open country diversified by woods, the last hour of our journey taking us almost continually across land in the occupation of Mr. Tory. The first field of his that we saw, has for generations been known by the somewhat depressing title of ' Labour-in-Vain '—I cannot say why, as it did not look poorer than the others. Beyond it lies the village of Clenstone Winterborne. Here we stopped a few minutes to look at a beautiful and ancient house, full of carved oak and panelling, now in the occupation of Mr. J. Tory, and a great barn built, like the house, of Purbeck stone, with a marvellous roof of open and fluted oak-work that would be a glory to any church. The old monks were responsible for these things; no one else would have expended such material, skill, and labour on a barn—if, indeed, that was its original use. Next we passed a farm hired, I was informed, at 12s. 6d. an acre, the owner of which had recently been obliged to spend three years' rent upon the buildings. Seventy acres of this holding were grass and the other 220 good arable. Poor landowner! After he has paid the customary outgoings he will not grow rich upon that property.

Here I may mention that a landlord whom I met in this neighbourhood, who occupies some of his acres and lets the rest, told me that sometimes he made 1 per cent. on the land he farmed, but no more. He added that he received nothing from his property, and that landowners in Dorsetshire as a class were dependent on outside means, without which they would be ruined. In his opinion the industry, and everything connected with it, was hollow and artificial, and although the present race of farmers went on from force of habit, or because they must, their sons would not do so. As to labour, he said that of hedgers, ditchers, and dairymen there were none to be had, giving as an instance a neighbouring parish in which there used to be ten woodmen. Then only one was left.

Mr. Wood Homer, of Bardolf Manor, Dorchester, in an interesting letter said also that rents had dropped from one-third to one-half, and the fee-simple value of the land from 40 to 60 per cent. He thought the tenant farmers were barely holding their own ; that the landlords were poor, while the remaining labourers were in full work. He believed that in future there would be but two classes of farmers—small men who do their own labour, and what he termed ' prairie farmers,' holding at a very low rent and employing a little highly-paid labour. Such men, he thought, would produce much less than was grown under the old system, and allow hundreds of acres of land to go out of cultivation altogether. He was of opinion that the only thing that would keep the arable land in Dorsetshire under the plough, was a fair price for barley, by which he meant from 36s. to 42s. a quarter. He said that where the owner of the land was resident the population does not diminish very fast, but where the landlord lived away, it was about 33 per cent. less than it had been a quarter of a century before. The large farms were being broken up, but the small-holdings let fairly well. The wages were nominally 11s. a week, but to them must be added house and garden rent free, coal, faggots, potatoes, extras for overtime, piece work, hay and harvest, and beer or beer allowance. Thus the receipts of the best men averaged 18s. a week and per-quisites. Cottages were fairly plentiful, but many of them were not good. He thought the bottom had been reached in the matter of prices, but the higher wages which were being paid placed the large employers in a worse position by adding to their expenses.

At Turnworth we were most hospitably received by Mr. Tory. This gentleman belongs to the old school of yeoman farmers, of whom he is a perfect type. As I looked at him, surrounded by his stalwart sons and handsome daughters, I could not help wondering whether in another score of years rural England would have many such families to show. I trust that it may be so, for surely such as he and his are, or have been, the very backbone of the nation. Including his brother, who was also present, those of his family who were gathered round his table, farmed between them no fewer than 6,000 acres of Dorset land, and have so farmed for many years. Few can be better acquainted with the local conditions, and it is therefore with the more regret that I have to record their views of the agricultural outlook.

Mr. Tory, jun., the valuer, said he could see nothing ahead but ruin, and that the only hope of salvation lay in small holdings, whereas his uncle—note the contrast of opinion between the old man and the young—thought that the land must be divided into great farms and worked by capitalists. They all believed the outlook to be as bad as possible, and one of them, who had been abroad, added that Dorsetshire farming must fall to the level of that practised in the Colonies. It would be a case of 'peasant proprietors or ranches,' the small holder feeding himself and no more, and the big man breeding herds of half-wild cattle.

Of labour their tale was the same as that which I had heard in so many places, only, perhaps, worse. They said that it was a very great difficulty, and they could not guess what the future was to be; moreover, its quality was bad. They supposed that the farmers must do the work themselves, and that meant misery for everybody. Mr. J. Tory added that not one in fifty of the young fellows would stop upon the land, so the only thing to do was to lay it down to grass. Some people could find no hands to milk. In many cases the state of the cottages was very bad. How could a girl who had been in service be expected to live in a hovel when she married? Of course the result was that she and her husband went away. Without labour the land was worthless, and without proper cottages there could be no labour. But, in truth, I am weary of repeating that melancholy story.

Talking of the fall of prices, Mr. Tory, sen., mentioned that the difference in the value of the wheat from 200 acres of land between the best year and the worst in his long farming record, amounted to no less than £2,000. The fall of rentals during the same period he estimated at 50 per cent., and of selling values at from 50 to 75 per cent. Thus on one of his farms the rent had come down from £870 to £400, but he said that he would rather pay the old rent and sell his produce at the old prices, than the small rent and earn the present miserable return. I think he added that when he came into one of his holdings there were over sixty applicants, and that not long ago, when he thought of giving it up, the landlord could find no other tenant. As for their reasons for clinging to the land—well, they had always been farmers, and their capital was sunk in it. They would work the day through, and the future must look to itself.

Dorsetshire is a county of magnificent views. Thus, within a mile or two of our host's house at Turnworth, looking from the gorse-clad ridge of Okeford Hill, I saw great stretches of Wilts, Dorsetshire, and Somersetshire. Below lay the fertile Blackmore Vale, through which runs the river Stour, with the village of Fitzpaine half hidden among its apple orchards, and beyond it Shaftesbury and the wooded hill of Duncliff. This ridge divides the under-hill and the overhill men. Overhill, to the south, they raise corn and sheep; underhill, to the north, they are graziers and dairy-folk. In the vale the land fetches up to £3 an acre rent, and a hundred acres is a large holding; on the hill it is worth 10s. to 15s., and the farms may measure from 500 to 1,000 acres. Below the labour-bill may fall as low as 5s. an acre; above it comes to at least £1. On our way back from this walk I remember that I saw some cottages where people would not live because the position was lonesome.

The pride of Mr. Tory's farms are his beautiful barleys, grown from the same seed for many years—over thirty, I believe—which are plump, round in the berry, primrose-coloured, and very thin in the skin, and his 'smutty-faced' Dorset Down sheep, of the famous Watercombe blood, one of the best flocks in the county of Dorset. These sheep, of which I saw a great flock, are somewhat smaller than the Hampshire Downs, and produce a finer quality of mutton. Another point about them is that they can be profitably lambed up to a full mouth, also their under parts are extraordinarily well covered with wool. The average clip is 4½ lbs. of washed wool to a sheep, the rams producing as much as 9 lbs.

On the day that I inspected this flock we drove through many miles of country, yet on that long expedition met but four vehicles. Three of them were brewers' drays, and the fourth was a timber-drag! Indeed, I scarcely saw any travellers upon the road, but, by way of compensation, there were wild roebuck feeding outside the coverts. Noticing a number of unthrashed ricks, I remarked that this seemed to show that farmers who could leave their wheat so long without turning it into cash, must still be fairly prosperous. 'Oh! no,' answered Mr. Tory, jun., who was driving us, 'it only means they can't find men to do the thrashing.' Another curious sight was that of two women helping a shepherd to pull swedes. Here, by the way, they never 'hole' or 'pit' swedes, but feed them to the sheep from the ground.

Among other gentlemen whom I met I had the advantage of a conversation with the steward of a great estate in that neighbourhood. I quote a few of the very interesting figures which he gave me illustrative of the decay of agriculture in his district. The examples are taken from farms on the large property of which he has the management.

### Farm A.

In 1852 it let for £1 the acre.
In 1880 it let for 31s. 8d. the acre.
In 1901 it let for 12s. 6d. the acre.

### Farm B, of which one-third is pasture—549 acres.

In 1862 it let for £650.
In 1901 it let for £250, tithe free.

### Farm C.   Hill arable land—396 acres.

In 1852 it let for £300.
In 1862 it let for £450.
In 1901 it let for £240.

### Farm D.   Grass land—180 acres.

In 1852 it let for £235, plus £46 tithe, paid by tenant.
In 1878 it let for £352, plus £46 tithe, paid by tenant.
In 1901 it let for £262, minus tithe, paid by landlord.

He said that the labour was very short. This was his melancholy conclusion : 'Unless the owners combine they will lose the labour that remains, and the land will go out of cultivation.' I asked him how long he thought it would be before the crash came, suggesting the modest term of twelve years. 'Oh, less than that,' he answered confidently. He thought that the Government would be forced to face the question, and that farmers would have to give higher wages, adding, however, that the land could not afford to pay more.

That day we saw the famous views from Bulbarrow and Miltonhill. Very grand they were, notwithstanding the furious storms of sleet which swept over and obscured the landscape, though lonesome and desolate, for scarcely a house was to be seen for miles around. Also we visited

Milton Abbey and its ancient, lovely fane, rebuilt in the reign of Richard II. in the Decorated and Later English styles. This beautiful church is now little more than a chapel to the Abbey house, although I believe service is held here on Sunday afternoons during the summer. Formerly it was a place of worship for the Benedictine monks who founded it in the reign of King Athelstan. The present Abbey house was built by the first Earl of Dorchester, in the year 1771, upon the site of the old abbey. After inspecting the church we drove on to the village of Milton Abbas.

This settlement was moved bodily from the neighbourhood of the Abbey to its present situation something over a century ago by this same Earl of Dorchester, who thought that its proximity interfered with his comfort. As they were all built at the same time, its cottages are exactly similar, and placed facing each other on either side of a wide roadway that runs up a shallow valley. They are constructed of 'cob,' thatched, and very picturesque, the gardens lying behind them in long strips. Between each pair of cottages was planted a chestnut tree, most of which still flourish, although some of them have been broken by storms or mutilated by the hand of man.

From Milton Abbas we drove to Winterborne Stickland, where the soil is light, a chalky loam with a chalk subsoil. In this village the cottages have a dilapidated air. Here we saw sheep penned upon the rye, which was strong and well forward for the season. I noticed that, although labour is so scarce, the fences in this neighbourhood were for the most part neatly kept. The growth is partly cut through and laid all one way, so that the young shoots spring densely from the short stubs amongst and above the laid wood, binding it firmly together, making the hedge impervious, and preventing it from becoming hollow at the stems. Formerly donkeys were much used in this district for the purpose of chalking land, by means of panniers with bottoms that could be undone to let out the chalk. This chalk was dug from a depth of from six to eight inches below the soil and scattered about on its surface, where it acted as a fertiliser and as a preventive of 'finger and toe.' The odd thing is that, being present in such immense quantities beneath, it should still be necessary, in order to produce these beneficial effects, to dig it up and expose it to the air.

Another place that we visited was the seat of Lord Portman, a vast mansion situated at Bryanstone, near Blandford, where I had the pleasure of meeting Mr. James Forrester, the agent. Here, as might be expected, everything is managed without thought of cost. Never before have I seen such buildings or cottages : the very cows are provided with softer sorts of wood on which to kneel, and the electric-light machinery reminds the visitor of the engines of some great ship. Mr. Forrester said that the corn and sheep farms had depreciated 50 per cent. in value, but the grass land only 10 or 15 per cent. On that estate they had about 1,800 acres in hand. The tenants complained much of the labour, and their own case was little better. The young men went away continually. 'Please, sir, give me a character,' was the daily cry. The cottages upon the property were plentiful and good, and never had less than three bedrooms, two of them with fireplaces. The tenure of these cottages used to be quarterly, but of late, owing to the frequency of strikes amongst the labourers, they had been let subject to a weekly notice.

In addition to their model cottages, for which they pay very little—but 1s. 6d. a week—the labourers have pensions, clothing, and coal clubs, to which the subscriptions are doubled at the end of the year, liberal allowances in the case of sickness, allotments, and every other conceivable advantage. They are well paid also, up to 18s. a week, with fuel for carters. Yet they go, and, what is more, strike at hay-time or other inconvenient seasons, and are generally troublesome. 'They won't be kept,' said Mr. Forrester, but, male and female, depart, mostly to take service in shops. Few except the 'doodles' remain. Doodle, by the way, is the Dorsetshire equivalent for the Norfolk 'waster' and the Devonshire 'smike.' Yet if they will not stop on an estate like this, which, of course, is run absolutely without reference to expense—£10,000 a year, I understand, being spent in wages alone—where will they stop?

Everything has been tried. Thus, when some men asked for land, Mr. Forrester arranged for them to have a field of twenty-three acres, which was let at 24s. the acre, the landlord building a barn and providing a hand-power thrashing-machine. Fourteen men hired lots in this field, but in ten years there was only one of them left, the balance of the land having being rented by a miller. Again, cottages were sold to certain of the people upon special arrangements as to price. Mr. Forrester said that this was the worst thing that ever happened to them, and some of these cottages were now being condemned because their occupiers had reduced them to such a condition that they were no longer fit for folk to live in. Mr. Forrester seemed to think that the want of religious feeling that is so marked a symptom of the day, had much to do with the discontent of these people at the conditions of their life. Lack of principle was the root of it; also on that particular property there might have been some over-pampering.

Mr. Forrester took us to see the cattle on the home farm, North Devons and Guernseys. The Devons were splendid animals, especially the heifers and young bulls, the former of which were preparing for the show-yard. These Devons give but little milk, flesh production being their strong point, but what they do yield is extremely rich. I noticed that a Guernsey bull which we inspected, was nearly twice the size of those that we had seen in Guernsey itself, another example of how emigration to England changes the characteristics of that breed. The sheep were Hampshire Downs, but if I remember right, with a strain of blood from Mr. Tory's flock.

The area of wheat grown had much decreased of recent years—from 200 acres down to 40, indeed. I visited some of the cottages on the home farm, of which I think twenty had been built during the previous eight years. They were as commodious as they were picturesque, having three down- and three up-stair rooms. Before we parted, I asked Mr. Forrester if he could think of any remedies which would help to solve the labour difficulty, but, with the exception of machinery, he could suggest none. Little wonder that he added, 'Government will have to face the question.'

One of my correspondents, a large tradesman in Dorchester, described the situation very well, if somewhat forcibly. He said that thirty years ago they had a grand race of yeomen, or what might be called gentlemen-farmers, in the county. These were men who when wheat sold at from 70s. to 80s. a quarter, held their 600 or 1,000 acres of land, kept their hunters, and always had a good glass of port to give to a friend. Now they had nearly all disappeared, having gone under one by one. To-day there was a new type of farmer, who, as a rule, began life as a grocer, a village smith, or a shoemaker. This person lives on about 10s. a week and goes to a sale to buy an old wagon for 50s. He has not a good horse on his farm, and no one would give 2s. for the suit of clothes he wears. On an 800-acre holding he employs about four hands, and sometimes not so many, and is unprofitable to the landlord, the tradesman, and the labourer alike. But, after a fashion, he makes farming pay. My informant added that the wretched farm buildings that are common, were a great drawback to the dairy farmers, and that the railway rates supplied the last straw which broke their backs.

This picture may be drawn in strong colours, still there is truth in what the writer says.

Few people could be better qualified to speak of the rural conditions of Dorsetshire than the well-known authority on natural history, the Rev. Octavius Pickard-Cambridge. Mr. Cambridge, whose ancestors, I believe, have been connected with the county for a great number of generations, has since

1868 been rector of Bloxworth, Wareham, of which parish, I think I am right in saying, his father was the squarson. In kind response to my request for information on various points, Mr. Cambridge said that in Dorsetshire, as elsewhere, the scarcity of agricultural labourers was an undoubted fact, although he thought that there were still a fair number of them floating about the county; that actual scarcity was made to appear greater than it is by the fact that the labourers did not remain in the service of the same farmer, as many of them changed their situations every year. This was, he believed, owing partly to that universal feeling of restlessness which now-a-days seemed to pervade all kinds of labour, agricultural and domestic, but, on the labourer's part, even more to the lingering influence of the teaching of Joseph Arch.

Arch's great maxim was, 'Don't bind yourself at any rate for longer than a year,' that is, from Lady Day to Lady Day. The labourer, therefore, would make his bargain at the busy time, while the farmer retaliated by dispensing with his services at slack times, as in winter. As yet their employers could hardly be said to have tempted the labourers to remain by means of adequately increased wages, shorter hours, or other advantages. They preferred to run the risk of being left underhanded, trusting to a quick, fair-weather harvest, when the use of machinery enabled the work to be accomplished with half the number of labourers who were formerly employed, to the great relief of the wages bill. To one class, however, higher wages were now given—namely, to lads of eighteen or twenty and unmarried men, as distinguished from married men with wives and children, because the young fellows and bachelors, having no impedimenta, can tie all their worldly goods in a bundle on their backs and depart at a week's notice. Also the clergy and others, naturally interested in bettering the condition of lads and young men, assist the general exodus from the country by finding them situations as policemen, railway porters, gardeners, gamekeepers, domestic servants, &c., in all of which occupations they find not only better pay, but with it the attractions of higher companionship and more recreation. If the country-side and its labours offered a better wage and more of such advantages, with good, but not necessarily larger dwellings, he thought that the rush to the towns would be materially checked.

Here, perhaps, the question of small-holdings might come in. Every parish would, in his opinion, do well to have a number of these—not too small nor too large, say from ten to forty acres each—although their total acreage need not take up any great proportion of the available agricultural land. In his own parish the advantage of such holdings was very evident between 1840 and 1868, when Mr. Cambridge's late father used to provide them wherever possible, putting into them the most industrious and steadiest of the labourers. This was comparatively easy to do in Bloxworth, as in that village there was much waste and semi-waste land. Still, Mr. Cambridge believed that the bulk of the soil would never be cultivated in small-holdings to the advantage of the nation. The occupiers of such tenancies should, he thought, take them on short, renewable leases of, say, three years, the buildings being provided and kept up by the landlord. Any arrangement under which the tenant only held from year to year, or was responsible for the upkeep of the buildings, must, he thought, be doomed to failure.

The best prospect for the future success of agriculture lay, it seemed to him, in the cultivation of great areas by joint-stock companies. Even the largest farms now worked by individuals were not large enough to pay for the full separate employment of the most efficient machinery, steam-ploughs, traction-engines, and tramways. The present race of tenant-farmers would make good bailiffs, superintendents, &c., of such large areas, and if they invested their capital in the business would earn a better return for it and their work than they do to-day. Such company-managed farms would not, of course, check the depopulation of the country districts—in some ways they might even accentuate it—but the village population would be kept up by a more intelligent body of labourers, and by the occupiers of and the workers on the small-holdings, who would create a class of which we were now greatly in want.  Also many of the more advanced and skilled workmen might, and probably would, hold shares in these joint-stock farms.

With respect to the system of rural education now in force, Mr. Cambridge was strongly of opinion that the keeping of boys at school till they are thirteen, tends very much to decrease the number of agricultural hands.  No lad who did not begin farm work long before that age would embrace it unless he was obliged, and even if he began then he would escape from it as soon as he could, while if he stayed upon the land he never became so useful or efficient a labourer as those of the old times, when lads were always put to the business at eight or nine years old.  Under the system of farming to which Mr. Cambridge looked forward as one of the certainties of the future, it was probable that this delay in beginning farm work would not operate so prejudicially as it does to-day.  The whole *odour* of agriculture, as it were, would be essentially different, and the position of the farm-hand much changed for the better.  He could imagine that our representative squires, sportsmen, and others would contemplate with horror an agricultural era when the land should be worked by a few joint-stock companies ; but he said that all questions of rural advantages to the gentry, especially those of shooting and hunting, were gradually being solved by the more recent game Acts and barbed wire.  Shooting now-a-days meant, for the most part, the killing of tame pheasants, and hunting, the riding over country where barbed wire was indicated by flagstaffs, so that, in his opinion, the clearance of the stage for the next scene of the scientific culture of land in 20,000-acre farms would not be so abrupt as now appeared probable.

To deal with the smallest point first, if I may criticise, I would suggest that Mr. Cambridge's views are not altogether sound so far as they concern the matter of sport, to the purposes of which, indeed, the establishment of huge farms in the hands of companies would prove extremely favourable. Moreover, shooting does not mostly consist of 'shooting tame pheasants.' Rocketing pheasants are not by any means tame, and are very hard to hit, much more so than were the birds killed in the old fashion by our fathers, while driven partridges require more skill and judgment to bring to bag, than any winged game I know, unless it be snipe in a gale of wind. Nor, whatever else may be said against that sport, can it be construed into a reproach upon hunting even if the position of stretches of the cruelly dangerous barbed wire is indicated by means of flags.

Still this is a very little matter. For Mr. Cambridge's scheme of the co-operative farming of great areas of land there is doubtless much to be said, although, as he foresees, I fear that it would tend to increase, rather than to lessen, the depopulation of the country. Other objections are that farming by means of Boards of directors might not always prove satisfactory, unless, indeed, they were more fortunate in their managers than are many other commercial concerns. Secondly, would the required capital be forthcoming in sufficient sums, that is, about £200,000 for each 20,000-acre farm? Unless agriculture proves itself a much more paying business in the future than it has been in the immediate past, I think not. People who invest money in companies expect at any rate a better return than they can get in Consols. There is nothing to show that such a return will be forthcoming, as it is probable that the salaries of the managers, cost of offices, fees of directors, &c., would quite swallow up any extra moneys that might be earned through the use of the improved machinery that Mr. Cambridge advocates.

Individual farmers continue to farm for various reasons independent of that of the actual interest they earn, or hope to earn, upon their capital. Thus often they secure a good house rent free, and with it a certain social position; also they live a life that is more agreeable and suitable to them than any other. In the new joint-stock era these and other advantages would count for nothing. The question would be reduced purely to one of dividends which very often might not be forthcoming. That there is weight in these objections seems to be shown by the fact that in England we hear little of co-operative farms and nothing of any that have succeeded. I have, however, heard of some that failed. But with better prices things might be otherwise and, doubtless, like all other agricultural experiments, co-operative farming will have its turn.

Mr. Cambridge thought that sport and great farms would hardly prove compatible, but Mr. E. Barkworth, of South House, Piddletrenthide, Dorchester, of whose kind help I was unfortunately not able to avail myself when in the county, but who has favoured me with his views, believed that small-holdings would prove its absolute destruction. He said that his opinion of these holdings was that except in the neighbourhood of large towns they are a mistake. As soon as a man took a field or fields, he surrounded them with an entanglement of barbed wire and spent his spare time prowling round them with a gun, shooting anything that crossed it either running or flying. He thought that the increase of such holdings would quite put a stop to fox-hunting, and make England unfit to live in.

For my part I do not share Mr. Barkworth's apprehensions. England is a big place in which there is ample room for every kind of holding, large and small, and as regards the latter, in greater quantities than are likely to be needed. But although myself I like sport in its season, and from experience well know the nuisance of a little occupier or freeholder with his dog, his traps, and his gun, I must add that even if my informant be right, and the increase of small-holdings means the ruin of sport, that calamity—and for many reasons it would be nothing less—does not, to my mind, furnish a conclusive argument against the multiplication of such holdings. After all the prosperity of the land with the great national issues that are involved therein, is more important than the enjoyment of successful sport by the comparative few by whom it can be afforded. In short the welfare of farming, if there must be a choice, should, I think, be preferred to that of fox-hunting, and the preservation of people to that of partridges.

Mr. Barkworth said also that he did not think there was any scarcity of labour in his neighbourhood. He had, however, noticed amongst the younger men a growing disinclination to have anything to do with horses, cattle, or sheep, both on account of the Sunday work involved, and because the care of animals compelled shepherds and others to be out in every kind of weather, while the ordinary labourer would be in the barn making sacks, or perhaps doing nothing at all. The cottages in his village were very bad, but in many cases this was owing to their proprietors being only ' copyholders for lives ' under a Corporation, and therefore unwilling to spend a penny upon their houses. He could suggest no remedies for the present state of agriculture; all he knew was that in his case farming did not pay.

A very strange commentary on the views of Mr. Barkworth, which are those of hundreds of others throughout England, as regards the undesirability and general uselessness of small-holdings, is furnished by the experience of Sir Robert Edgcumbe with reference to the Rew Farm at Winterborne St. Martin, near to Dorchester, within a dozen miles indeed of Mr. Barkworth's own residence. On the history of this farm and his dealings with it, Sir Robert has most kindly drawn up for me the following clear and excellent report, which I earnestly commend to the attention of all who are interested in the matter of small-holdings, and in the question as to whether or no they can be multiplied in England with advantage to their owners and to the country.

### Rew Farm Small-Holdings.

#### *General Position.*

In 1888 I purchased Rew Manor Farm, in the parish of Martinstown (Winterborne St. Martin), about three miles from the county town of Dorchester, in order to convert it into small-holdings, as it seemed suitable for this purpose. Rew is a long narrow farm, nearly two miles in length, from its northern end, abutting on the high road (leading from Dorchester to Bridport) about three miles out of Dorchester, to its southern end, termi-nating near Hardy's Monument (the Sir Thomas Hardy in whose arms Nelson died). Near the southern end Rew Farm is crossed (about four miles from Dorchester) by the highway from Martins-town to Abbotsbury, and about the middle of the farm by the high road from Martinstown to Bridport.

#### *Roads.*

The farm being about two fields wide from east to west, though stretching nearly two miles from north to south, all that was needed to open it up was a road driven through it from north to south.

#### *Area.*

The size of the farm was 343 acres.

#### *Cost.*

The farm was sold by auction, and fell to me at £5,050. Tillages and tenant right added £490 to the price. I laid out £340 on the roadway; the materials—chalk, gravel, and flint—all came off the farm. £120 was laid out on wells, £140 on survey maps and law costs; the farm then stood me in £18 per acre.

#### *Soil.*

The soil is of the class of light Dorset soils—a thin black earth on the chalk for the most part, though some of it is richer, almost loamy. One-third of it might be classed as good, two-thirds as poor, though not worthless.

#### *Farmhouse and Meadow.*

The farmhouse, which was a comfortable little house, but too large for small-holders, was sold with two acres of land to a retired farmer. The water-meadow, about 25 acres, was very good land, worth 50s. an acre to let. It was not possible to break it up into portions, owing to the watering of it, so I tried to treat it as a 'common' meadow, but this was not acceptable, therefore I sold it as a whole to a neighbouring landlord. About 9 acres were taken for roads, leaving, after these deductions, some 307 acres for small-holdings.

### Terms of Sale.

The 307 acres were plotted out into 80 lots, varying in size from 1 to 9 acres, and lithographed plans of the whole farm so plotted were given to all applicants. The price of each plot I fixed beforehand, and when applicants stated what plots they desired to purchase, I gave them the price of those plots. The price included all costs of agreements and conveyance and tillages, so that it was in all cases an inclusive price.

The conditions were that one-tenth of the purchase-money should be paid on signing the agreement, and the other nine-tenths by equal half-yearly payments spread over nine years. Further, that at each half-yearly payment interest at the rate of $4\frac{1}{3}$ per cent. on the purchase-money outstanding was to be paid. The fact that there were no 'extras' gave general satisfaction. The agreement and conveyance is printed in the Report of the Royal Commission on Agriculture for Dorset (C. 7764). Apart from the farmhouse sold separately, there were four good cottages and a barton (that is a set of farm buildings without a dwelling-house). The price of each cottage was £50; these were purchased by four different buyers, and the barton by a fifth purchaser. Almost all elected to pay by instalments, though several preferred to pay up in five years instead of nine years. Many subsequently accelerated their payments, and six years from the start all had been paid off save about £500.

### Conditions of Success.

I advised each applicant who interviewed me, that he could not expect to live upon the produce of his land and meet his instalments at the same time. Twenty-seven purchasers in all took up the 307 acres, and of these three attempted the impossible—namely, to make a living upon their land and pay off the instalments at the same time. All three failed to do it. One had purchased a good cottage and 30 acres of land. Failing to keep up his instalments, he raised £300 on mortgage at 4 per cent. This enabled him to pay off his instalments and current debts, and live com-

T 2

fortably, thus getting his cottage and 30 acres subject to his payment of interest to the amount of £12 per annum. With this 'rent' he has done well. Another bought 18½ acres and built himself a house. He cleared off his instalments by a mortgage for £250 at 4 per cent. These two failures may be regarded as qualified successes. The third had only 5 acres, and put himself up a small house. He got into arrears and sold out to a railway ganger, who lets the holding to him, and he manages to live on it and pay his rent. Apart from these three, who attempted too much, the other twenty-four have made a thorough success of their holdings.

### Applicants and their Callings.

There was no trouble in advertising. The news spread rapidly, and I fixed three consecutive days to settle with applicants. If they could not get the exact lots they wanted, they readily took the next available. Of those who took up the land eight were agricultural labourers, three gardeners, two coachmen, two stone-masons, two watchmakers, one carpenter, one shopkeeper, one policeman, one blacksmith, one cooper, one carman, one postman, one porter, and one small general dealer.

One of the gardeners has erected a large amount of glass houses. He bought his glass and wood, and with a jobbing carpenter built the houses. The lime for the mortar was burnt out of chalk dug on the land.

### Prices of the Land.

The poorer part of the farm, some 200 acres, was sold at from £7 to £20 per acre. The delight of those who bought some five acres for £35 (£7 per acre) is not easily forgotten. Some of the better land, worth £2 per acre to rent, was sold at £35 per acre.

### Number of the Holdings.

The 27 holdings average about 11 acres each. These little farmers have helped each other in many ways. The blacksmith helps the others with their implements. One man ploughs for another. They arrange to get the threshing machine to follow on for their various crops, and the carman is a great help.

### Tithe and Land-Tax.

The farm was not subject to land-tax, and the tithe was light, about 1s. per acre. But I had some trouble with it. It would have cost £500 to redeem, and the Board of Agriculture seems to act on the principle that tithe should be redeemed and not apportioned. After much trouble I got a field apportionment, but the maximum apportionment is fixed by the Board at 5s., so that a purchaser of 5 acres with a tithe of 4s. 3d. must have his land joined with an adjacent owner, and both are liable for the continued tithe at the option of the tithe-owner.

### Poor Land suits Small Men.

I could have sold the poorer land (200 acres) four times over; it was the better-priced land that they hesitated about. I was advised in fixing my prices by most competent surveyors, and they and other land-agents all told me that I should sell the good land readily and be left with the poor land. I have found the same advice tendered to other landlords quite recently, and it has deterred them from selling out in small-holdings. I am confident that surveyors are entirely wrong in their advice, for they have no experience of the small purchaser who works his land himself. They only know the farmer who has a labour-bill to pay, and, as it costs the same to work poor land as it does good land, the profit varies and may mean loss. To the small man, who works for himself early and late, it only means a difference between a lesser or greater return for his labour, and not a difference between profit and loss. With my present experience I should have priced the good land lower and the poor land higher. It is the cheap land that they rush for, anything under £20 per acre. £20 per acre is 1d. per square yard, and when I told them a few glasses of beer would buy quite a nice little garden they caught at the idea.

### Boundaries.

As regards selling the land and getting payment, I had really no trouble at all. I had on several occasions later to settle disputes about boundaries—disputes which sometimes waxed hot, but the holders always fell in with my decision. The fact was in many cases I did not particularise the boundaries with great exactitude. When selling land at 1d. per square yard it does not seem important to settle boundaries to a foot, but later I found every inch possessed value in the eyes of the respective claimants.

### Population.

There were four cottages sold, and of the purchasers fourteen have erected dwellings. When I bought the farm the farmer dwelt upon it with three labourers and a boy—a population, all told, of 21. The population on the farm now is close upon 100, and this number is likely to be further increased, as more houses are to be built.

### Rateable Value.

The area of the parish of Winterborne St. Martin is 3,546 acres. Rew Farm is a fair sample of the pasture and arable land of which the parish consists. When I purchased Rew in 1888 the outgoing tenant was in financial difficulties and could not make it pay. He was rented on an old lease at £240, but the general opinion was that the farm could not be let for more than £200. Since that time the rateable value of the parish has steadily declined, while the rateable value of Rew Farm has as steadily risen. In 1888 the rateable value of the whole parish was £2,807, and now the rateable value is £2,073, a fall in fourteen years of 26 per cent. in value. In 1888 the rateable value of Rew was £215, and to-day it is rated at £346, a rise of 60 per cent.                   R. E.

*April* 19, 1902.

I can honestly say that I have rarely read a paper with greater pleasure than that which is printed above, especially as it entirely confirms my own views, formed after a great deal of consideration and some experience of the subject. In letters which I have received from him, written from his residence at Sandy (Beds), Sir Robert Edgcumbe points out, moreover, that the purchasers of the plots at Rew came from all over Dorset, only two of them being inhabitants of Winterborne St. Martin. He says also that he received so many inquiries from persons anxious to buy, as to when another farm would be dealt with in the same way, that he felt that if he could have found the time and money to proceed with the matter he would have been able to dispose of a further 1,000 acres. He adds:

Subject to small-holdings being situate within five miles of a good-sized town, I am satisfied that there is a large field for their creation. Why is this not largely done, seeing that small buyers are ready to give relatively a higher price than purchasers of a whole farm can afford? The first reason, I consider, is that it is necessary in dealing with land in this way that it should be free of mortgages. The mortgaged vendor must get his money down to clear his mortgage. Rew was mortgaged when I bought it. Every mortgaged vendor is precluded from selling in this way [*i.e.* from receiving the purchase-money in instalments.—*Author*], though he could get a better price for the land sold in small portions. It is the old story of one penny for a box of matches and a dozen for eightpence. Secondly, those who are free of mortgages, yet want to sell, hesitate to embark upon an experiment, especially when they are invariably wrongly advised that they 'will sell off their good land and be left with their bad land.' A little while ago —— was selling a large property near here which would have done exactly for small-holdings. His agent wrote to me that they had considered the matter, but were advised that there was some poor land, and that they would be left with it and the rest sold. The advice was utterly wrong, and prevented one who could have given a lift to small properties, from marketing a picture property for this sort of thing.

I sincerely hope that my readers will carefully consider the above statements, and that any of them who have the power so to do, may be moved by their perusal to follow the example of Sir Robert Edgcumbe. I would call special attention to what he says as to the effect of his experiment in raising the population of Rew Farm from 21 to 100 souls. How much it would mean if these results could be repeated even here and there throughout England! I believe that in Dorsetshire alone the number of farm-labourers decreased from 18,000 in 1871 to 12,500 in or about 1891. How many there are of them now, I do not know, but surely it is time, both here and in other counties, that some steps were taken to preserve upon the land those of this class who still remain. Sir Robert Edgcumbe, to his great honour, has succeeded in showing us one way in which this may be done. And, if he has succeeded, why should others fail?

Another exceedingly well-informed and experienced gentleman to whom I am indebted, is Captain John Acland, of Wollaston House, Dorchester. He said that a very typical agriculturist of Liberal views and a prominent member of the Dorsetshire County Council, stated to him as his opinion that the depopulation of the villages in the county was really caused by the agricultural depression. Farmers would not and could not employ so many labourers as they did in former days; also machine work enabled them to do with fewer hands. Personally, however, he could always get what labour he wanted. Evidently this gentleman's view of the problem was that the farmers have caused the labourers to leave the villages by their endeavours to cut down the labour-bill. To these opinions Captain Acland added his own, that the lads were not content to face the dulness of village life, and that what they read of more attractive professions, together with their opportunities of travelling to towns, unsettled them.

In Dorchester an annual hiring fair is held on February 14, that is, old Candlemas Day, when the streets are crowded with men seeking a change of situation and farmers who need fresh hands. This fair offered an easy means of satisfying restlessness of spirit, and owing to it many labourers moved regularly, every year or two, which, Captain Acland thought, by depriving them of the feeling for 'home,' must have a very bad effect upon their children's characters. He held that small-holdings may succeed in certain favoured districts or near a station, but could hardly pay in their great open country miles away from a town or railway. He heard, however, that the tendency was towards the decrease in the size of the very large farms. The profession of agriculture was not now-a-days sufficiently remunerative to tempt men to find the capital necessary to its pursuit. Still one department of farming remained fairly flourishing, that of dairy farms, since as yet we commanded the market for milk and fresh butter, which at present was much superior to the imported article. Also the demand was steady and increasing.

As bearing more or less on the question of the conditions of village life, Captain Acland said that he might state his own experiences in a profession very different from that of agriculture. During a period of five years he was responsible for all the Army recruits raised in London, and afterwards for those who enlisted in Dublin and Birmingham. In this capacity he had found that the country lad was always conspicuous for his superior size and healthiness, which proved that the village labourer is well able to supply his family with the necessaries of life. Hence he inferred that, notwithstanding his low wages, the farm-hand and his family are better off than the town man who earns nearly double the money. He remarked that, although the usual weekly wage was but from 12s. to 15s., the distressing air of poverty that is so commonly met with in towns, is but rarely seen in villages. Finally, in his opinion, the agricultural outlook in Dorsetshire was not nearly so bad as in some other counties.

Captain Acland has also forwarded me a letter from a tenant farmer who holds a large farm within a few miles of Dorchester. This gentleman said, writing in March 1902, that in the outlying districts of the county labour was certainly scarcer now than ever it had been before. The towns were more attractive to young men than the country, as there they could get amusement in the evening with shorter hours of work, and in the case of mechanics and persons employed in trade, a chance of promotion that was denied to the farm labourer. The agricultural outlook was worse now than it used to be owing to the scarcity of labour and the low prices commanded by produce. Undoubtedly dairy farms were the most profitable, but of late years the seasons had been too dry to produce a good grass crop, and therefore the cake bill was much higher than usual. Where the tenants had no capital he did not agree with small-holdings, which, as less labour was employed upon them, drove more young men into the towns. Within a few years he thought that the difference between their condition and that of the large farms would be very evident. He could recollect, however, that thirty years ago such farms in his neighbourhood were in a much better state as regards their fences and general management, than was the case to-day.

The last evidence that I shall quote deals exclusively with the past and present position of the agricultural labourer in Dorsetshire. It will, I am sure, command universal attention and respect, having been given me by my friend, Mr. Thomas Hardy, who, as all the world knows, has made lifelong observation of this and kindred matters connected with the land.

Mr. Hardy wrote to me in the spring of 1902 : ' As to my opinion on the past of the agricultural labourer in this county, I think, indeed know, that down to 1850 or 1855 his condition was in general one of great hardship. I say in general, for there have always been fancy farms, resembling St. Clair's estate in " Uncle Tom's Cabin," whereon they lived as smiling exceptions to those of their class all around them. I recall one such, the estate owner being his own farmer, and ultimately ruining himself by his hobby. To go to the other extreme ; as a child I knew by sight a sheep-keeping boy who, to my horror, shortly afterwards died of want, the contents of his stomach at the autopsy being raw turnip only. His father's wages were 6s. a week, with about £2 at harvest, a cottage rent free, and an allowance of thorn faggots from the hedges as fuel. Between these examples came the great bulk of farms, whereon wages ranged from 7s. to 9s. a week, and perquisites were better in proportion.

' Secondly, as to the present : things are of course widely different now. I am told that at the annual hiring-fair just past, the old positions were absolutely reversed, the farmers walking about and importuning the labourers to come and be hired instead of, as formerly, the labourers anxiously entreating the stolid farmers to take them on at any pittance. Their present life is almost without exception one of comfort, if the most ordinary thrift be observed. I could take you to the cottage of a shepherd, not many miles from here, that has brass rods and carpeting to the staircase, and from the open door of which you hear a piano strumming within. Of course, bicycles stand by the doorway, while at night a large paraffin lamp throws out a perfect blaze of light upon the passer-by. The son of another labourer I know takes dancing lessons at a quadrille class in the neighbouring town.

'But changes at which we must all rejoice have brought other changes which are not so attractive. The labourers have become more and more migratory, the younger families in especial, who enjoy nothing so much as fresh scenery and new acquaintance. The consequences are curious and unexpected. For one thing, village tradition—a vast amount of unwritten folk-lore, local chronicle, local topography and nomenclature—is absolutely sinking, has nearly sunk, into eternal oblivion. I cannot recall a single instance of a labourer who still lives on the farm on which he was born, and I can only recall a few who have been five years on their present farm. Thus, you see, there being no continuity of environment in their lives, there is no continuity of information, the names, stories, and relics of one place being speedily forgotten under the incoming facts of the next. For example, if you ask one of the workfolk (they used always to be called "workfolk" hereabout; "labourers" is an imported word) the names of surrounding hills, streams, the character and circumstances of people buried in particular graves, at what spots parish personages lie interred, questions on local fairies, ghosts, herbs, &c., they can give no answer; yet I can recall the time when the places of burial, even of the poor and tombless, were all remembered; the history of the squire's family for 150 years back was known; such and such ballads appertained to such and such localities; ghost ta es were attached to particular sites; and secret nooks wherein wild herbs grew for the cure of divers maladies were pointed out readily.

'On the subject of migration to the towns I think I have printed my opinions from time to time, so that I will only say a word or two about it here. In this consideration the case of the farm labourers merges itself in the case of rural cottagers generally, including that of jobbing labourers, artisans, and nondescripts of all sorts who go to make up the body

of English villagery. That these people have removed to
the towns of sheer choice during the last forty years it would
be absurd to say, except as to that percentage of young, adven-
turous, and ambitious spirits among them which is found
in all societies. The prime cause of the removal is, unques-
tionably, insecurity of tenure. If they do not escape this
in the towns, it is not fraught with such trying consequences
to them as in a village, where they may have to travel ten or
twenty miles to find another house and other work. Moreover, if in a town lodging an honest man's daughter should
have an illegitimate child, or his wife take to drinking, he
is not compelled to pack up his furniture and get his living
elsewhere, as is, or was lately, too often the case in the
country. (I am neither attacking nor defending this order
of things ; I merely relate it. The landlord sometimes had
reason on his side, sometimes not.)

' Why such migrations to cities did not largely take place
till within the last forty years or so is, I think, in respect
of farm labourers, that they had neither the means nor the
knowledge in old times that they have now. And they had
not the inclination, owing to the stability of villagers of the
other class, such as mechanics and small traders, who are
the backbone of village life. The tenure of these latter was
before that date a fairly secure one, even if they were not in
the possession of small freeholds. The custom of granting
leaseholds for three lives and other life-holding privileges
obtained largely in our villages, and though tenures by
lifehold may not be ideally good or fair, they did at least sub-
serve the purpose of keeping the native population at home.
Villages in which there is not now a single cottager other
than a weekly tenant, were formerly occupied almost entirely
on the lifehold principle, the term extending over seventy or
a hundred years ; and the young man who knows that he is
secure of his father's and grandfather's dwelling for his
own lifetime, thinks twice and three times before he embarks
on the uncertainties of a wandering career. Now, though,
as I have said, these cottagers were not often farm labourers,

their permanence reacted on the farm labourers, and made their lives with such associates richer in incident, better worth living, and more reluctantly abandoned.

'Thirdly, as to the future, and the ultimate results from such a state of things, it hardly becomes me to attempt to prophesy here. That remedies exist for them, and are easily applicable, you will readily gather from what I have stated above.'

Perhaps a further hint of what Mr. Hardy considers to be the remedies that he does not actually specify in his letter, may be gathered by the perusal of an article on the Dorsetshire labourer, from which he has given me leave to quote, published by him in 'Longman's Magazine' in 1883. In speaking of the peasant proprietors of Auvergne, and of the false conclusions that are drawn from the dirty and miserable condition of their dwellings, which lead the superficial observer into the error of supposing that slovenliness is necessarily accompanied by unhappiness, he says: 'But it must be remembered that melancholy among the rural poor arises primarily from a sense of the incertitude and precariousness of their position. Like Burns's field mouse, they are overawed and timorous lest those who could wrong them should be inclined to exercise their power. When we know that the Damocles' sword of the poor is the fear of being turned out of their houses by the farmer or squire, we may wonder how many scrupulously clean English labourers would not be glad with half-an-acre of the complaint that afflicts those unhappy freeholders of Auvergne.'

Again, in writing of the depopulation of the villages, which even in 1883 he described as 'in some quarters truly alarming,' and of the pulling down of the cottages of the lifeholders and other petty tenants who did not chance to be in the employ of the owners or farmers of estates as their leases fell in, he says: 'The occupants who form the back-bone of village life have to seek refuge in the boroughs. This process, which is designated by statisticians as "the tendency of the rural population towards the large towns " is really the tendency of water to flow uphill when forced. The poignant regret of those who are thus obliged to forsake the old nest can only be realised by people who have witnessed it, concealed as it often is under the mask of indifference.'

I have no express authority for the opinion beyond that of the views which I have quoted ; but I think that I am not wrong in concluding that Mr. Hardy believes the best way to retain labourers and their families on the land is to give them some opportunity of securing, as owners or occupiers, an interest in the land.

I have now adduced a considerable body of evidence collected from authorities who are well able to judge of the agricultural conditions of the county, of the general purport of which the reader must form his own opinion. My personal conclusion is that unless the outlook has much changed since the year 1901—which I do not imagine to be the case—it is impossible to take a favourable view of the present prospects of the land, or of any class connected with it, in Dorsetshire.

# HEREFORDSHIRE

HEREFORDSHIRE, which lies on the Welsh border, contains about 537,300 acres, and has an extreme length of thirty-eight miles and an extreme breadth of thirty-five miles. It is a hilly county with a moist climate and a large proportion of pasture and woodland. Also it is famous for its orchards and its hops. The soil varies, and in many places is under-laid by the Old Red sandstone. For the most part, especially in the east, it is a deep red, clayey loam, in appearance not unlike that of which we see so much in Devonshire. In the south this loam is sandy, and in the west the soil is very stiff and water-holding. Also there are patches of pure clay, marl, and gravel.

The eye of the traveller in Herefordshire in late April or early May, falls upon one of the most lovely sights that rural England can afford. The apple orchards are not out indeed, but on either side of him stretch the rich green pastures starred, or rather sheeted with wild daffodils that are, in places, spread upon the meadows like a veritable cloth of gold, while the woodlands are white with the frail anemone. I begin my comments upon this county with some remarks upon its rural industries and labour problems, after which I hope to deal with a selection of the evidence that I collected during my visit there.

Herefordshire has always been famous for its fruit, and of late the culture of strawberries has been added to its industries. For the actual profits of this crop I must rely upon the information given me by growers, and the figures which I am about to quote, should be read subject to this reservation. One gentleman, a large farmer, told me that

in 1900 from six and a half acres of strawberries he netted
£200 clear profit. Another plot of sixty acres was said to
have produced 150 tons, which sold at £25 a ton, the net
profit on this parcel amounting to £1,500. How often does
an ordinary cultivator of the soil clear £1,500 profit in
these days, even from a farm of, let us say, 1,000 acres?
The inference is suggestive, and in this connection I may
say that much of our English wheat land which is now
practically worthless, would be well suited to this crop.
My question leads to another. How many English farmers
can grow a strawberry, or, being ignorant, will take the
trouble to learn the craft?

Perhaps the prettiest and best cultivated fruit farm in
the neighbourhood of Ledbury is that of Mr. Riley, of
Putley Court, which, after an interval of some years, it was
now my good fortune to visit for the second time. In all
Mr. Riley has about forty acres of fruit, beautifully laid out
upon the slope of a hillside. Of these, twenty acres were
under plums which were planted in 1881, and had apples set
between them to take their place when, in another score of
years or so, they begin to fail.

Every fruit has its allotted period of profit. Thus pears
will stand to a great age; when in Herefordshire I drank perry
made from the produce of ancient trees that I saw, which are
known to have been set in the days of Queen Anne. Few
apples will endure a century; whereas the life of a cherry
is said to be that of a man—namely, threescore years
and ten. The plum's career is shorter, while not many
gooseberries or currants last for more than twenty years.
Between some of his trees—all of which, by the way, were
pictures of health and beauty—Mr. Riley had planted
strawberries, a 'moving-on crop' that must not be allowed
to stand upon the ground for more than two successive sets
of plants, or, say, a period of eight years. Among others,
gooseberries and black currants were the under-crop. Of
the latter he had three acres. There used to be more, but
some years ago he was obliged to grub up twelve acres

rendered worthless by the ravages of the winter moth. This pest spread to them from the apples, but has now practically been overcome by grease-banding the trees, and thus preventing the female moth from creeping up the trunk in winter. Pears Mr. Riley does not grow, as he considers them a most uncertain crop, except in selected positions on a warm, sandy loam.

The profit or loss on fruit-growing, even in the most favoured situations and under skilful management, depends necessarily upon the supply of labour. In addition to the men required to dig and hoe the ground, and to prune, graft, and bud the trees, extra hands must be employed to pick and pack. Many fruits ripen almost simultaneously, and spoil if they are not garnered upon the instant. To meet this need growers must hire a large number of additional hands. For the most part these are women and children, who come from the big cities and are lodged in huts or tents for the season, receiving an agreed sum for each bushel gathered. Hitherto, in the Midland Counties, the supply of these folk has been sufficient, since many of them look upon the fruit and hop picking as a summer holiday; but if for any cause it should fail, the growing of bush-fruit would have to be abandoned. Even on his area of forty acres, Mr. Riley employs as many as 150 pickers, with the result that his labour-bill never averages less than £15 an acre. His ordinary men receive about 14s. a week, with 3d. a day extra for spraying, but when on piece-work they can earn quite 3s. a day.

For centuries Herefordshire has been the chief home of the manufacture of cider and perry. Indeed, according to a work I am proud to possess, which the author quaintly calls 'a small piece of rusticity,' that of 'Vinetum Britannicum, or a Treatise of Cider,' by J. Worlidge, Gentleman, published in 1691, and dedicated to the famous Elias Ashmole, founder of the Ashmolean Museum at Oxford, it 'was a drink among the Antient Britons.' My experience of this beverage is that its name, like that

of Charity, covers a multitude of sins.  Details are superfluous, but while on this journey, before I knew as much
about its manufacture as I do to-day, I drank cider—
'family cider' is the correct appellation—the memory of
which, or of its effects, will never leave me so long as I may
live.  This dreadful draught, which tastes like steel filings
mixed with vinegar and mud, is, it appears, compounded of
more or less rotten apples heaped up in orchards for pigs
and fowls to feed on, whereof the juice, expressed into dirty
casks, may be at times diluted with water from a neighbouring
horse-pond.  Very different is the bright and health-giving
liquor now manufactured by the best makers, which is so
rapidly winning its way among the public as the most wholesome of summer beverages.  Much of this renewed popularity
is due doubtless to the energy and example of Mr. Radcliffe
Cooke, who was so kind as to show me over his cider works
and to explain its manufacture.

Cider is made from different sorts of apples—Kingston
Black and Fox-whelp are among the best of them, I understand—none of which, however, have any merit as an eating
fruit.  Perhaps in this connection it may be of interest if I
give here a list of the principal apples that, according to my
esteemed author, J. Worlidge, were cultivated in England in
the seventeenth century.  The Aromatick or Golden Russeting, which Mr. Worlidge says ' has no compeer . . . lives over
the winter,' and has ' a most delicate aromatick hautgust
and melting in the mouth ' ; the Orange Apple, the Golden
Pippin, the Russet Pearmain, and the Kirton Pippin, which
' yields very good cider.'  The Carlisle Pippin, the Bedford
Pippin and the Bridgewater Pippin ' are much commended
for excellent table fruits.'  The Golden Rennet, the Lincoln
Rennet, the Leather-coat, the Green Russeting, the Red Russeting, the John Apple or 'Deuxans,' ' so called from its dur-
ableness, continuing two years before it perisheth, are great
bearers and fit for our cider plantation.'  The Marigold Apple,
also called the Onion Apple or Kate Apple, or Joan's Pearmain
' to be propagated in your cider plantation ' ; the Harvey

Apple, the Queen Apple, the Paradise Apple, ' a curious fruit produced by grafting a Pearmain on a Quince'; the Devonshire Quarington, the Codling, the King Apple, the Famagusta (named, I suppose, after the city of Famagusta in Cyprus) ; the Giant Apple, the Cat's-head, the Fox-whelp— then as it is to-day ' esteemed amongst the choice cider fruits.' The Red Streak that ' above all cider fruit has obtained the preference '; the Non-such; the Angel's-bit; the Greening, another old English fruit of a green colour; the Pome-d'Appease, which ' the Madames of France carry in their pockets by reason they leave no unpleasant scent'; the Sodome Apple or Blody Pippin ; the Winter Belle and Bon ; the Winter Glory, and others too many to enumerate here. It will be seen that our ancestors did not lack for varieties of apples, and that some of their sorts have survived to this day.

To return : When the cider apples fall they should be collected, each sort by itself, and mellowed in heaps covered with straw to protect them from rain, frost, and animals, until they are dead ripe but not rotten. In this condition they are conveyed—I speak of the old and more simple method of manufacture—to the mill, which consists of a runner or round stone turned by horse-power in a trough, also of stone, which is known as the chase. This done, the pulp or ' must ' is placed in open vats, after which it is pressed through cloths and the juice pumped into other vats, where it ferments and is skimmed. Thence it is syphoned into casks of huge size, where the fermentation is completed. Ultimately, the cider is bottled or sold in the wood, as may be most convenient.

After he had shown us his cellars, in the cool recesses of which stood gigantic hogsheads, with the specific gravity of the liquors within recorded upon them, and we had inspected the bottling, Mr. Radcliffe Cooke escorted us to another factory, where cider is manufactured upon more modern principles. Thus, carbonic acid gas is forced into the liquor before bottling, in order to give it a champagne-like sparkle, and many other things are done to ensure rapidity and cleanliness in manufacture, and an even quality of product.

Cider and perry makers in Herefordshire complain a great deal of the adulterated drinks compounded or flavoured with chemicals, and treated with boracic acid, salicylic acid, formalin, &c., which are, they say, largely sold to the public as genuine juice of the apple and pear, thereby unfairly competing with their liquors and bringing them into disfavour. In short, like the manufacturers of much that we eat and drink, they protest against those forms of fraud, from which the consuming public suffers, that appear, in many instances, to be either beyond the reach of the law or beneath its notice. Of the virtues of cider and its parent fruit Mr. Radcliffe Cooke spoke in terms which I can only describe as enthusiastic. To those who desire to keep in perfect health he went so far as to recommend, indeed, that at midnight, or later, they should eat six medium (or three large) unpeeled apples, washing them down with a pint of cider. I presume, however, that this heroic recipe is intended only to be used by those who are so fortunate as to be born in Herefordshire. By weaker, alien folk it might be feared.

The third great agricultural industry in Herefordshire is that of breeding its famous cattle; in fact, it is scarcely too much to say that these animals are the mainstay of farming in the county. On almost every holding here and in Worcestershire may be seen a number of thick-set, fleshy, white-faced cows or oxen, every one of them Herefords of high or low degree. Indeed, in these counties no other breed can hold its own against them. The points of the Hereford are thriftiness, hardiness, and an extraordinary capacity for laying on flesh. It is said, perhaps with a touch of exaggeration, that the Hereford will grow fat on a pasture where a Shorthorn will starve, and it is certain that they flourish well upon ordinary grazing ground, whereas most other breeds require rich meadows to fat them. On the other hand, although attempts are being made, with more or less success, to raise a race of milking Herefords, they are 'very poor at the pail,' and as a rule can do no more than rear their own calves. It is its great qualities of rapid flesh production and early maturity that make the Hereford so popular a beast both in North and South America. There they are said to thrive well on pampas and prairie, where the ranchmen account them good 'wrostlers.' By this they mean that they will manage to get a living under the most adverse circumstances, even if they have to dig for it beneath the snow. When I visited the county, as I was informed by Mr. Britten, the honorary secretary of the Herefordshire Herd Book, there was a very large order out for heifers to be shipped to the States, which, when fulfilled, would put a good sum into the pockets of the breeders.

Of these cattle I inspected various herds, together with a pleasing variety of bulls, some of them of gigantic size and formidable aspect. It is, by the way, worthy of note, as a characteristic of agricultural nature, that every owner believes his own particular bull to be rather more peaceful than a lamb. Where so many are excellent to express an opinion seems almost invidious, but of the stock which I saw, those of Mr. Richard Green and Mr. Stephen Robinson, both of Lyonshall, and that of Lord Coventry at Croome Court, in Worcestershire, struck me as about the best. Mr. Green's cattle, which I shall describe at more length presently, have taken a great number of prizes during the past few years, and are consequently much in demand in America. To fit them for the show ring even the breeding heifers must be got up to an unsightly point of fatness; indeed, some of them that I inspected, were so huge that they could scarcely walk with any ease. As a result of this unnatural and, I venture to think, foolish habit, the calves dropped by such animals are, as a rule, puny.

In former days Lord Coventry's was, I believe, considered the premier herd of Herefords; indeed, it may still be so, but of late years he has not entered his animals for competition. Mr. Robinson is making an effort to improve the milking qualities of the breed, with a considerable measure of success; at least his bailiff informed me that when at their flush the cows gave an average of two gallons a day.

Having treated all too briefly of the special agricultural industries of the county, that of hop-growing excepted, I now pass on to its labour problems and general farming conditions.

One of the noblest mansions in Herefordshire—Hampton Court—is the seat of Mr. Arkwright. The castle, which is said to have been built by Henry IV., is situated about five miles from Leominster, in the midst of a lovely and fertile vale, through which flows the river Lugg. All around lies the estate of more than 10,000 acres, divided into 40 farms and 30 smaller holdings, with a total of 162 cottages. This fine domain has, of course, suffered through the bad times like others, although, perhaps, not so heavily as some, most of the land being of excellent quality. As in all properties of this class, Mr. Ashworth, the estate agent, pointed out to me how heavy is the burden of those repairs with which every landlord has made acquaintance. In this case they seem to amount to about seventeen per cent. of the rental, a heavy tax in such times as these.

More serious, to my mind, however, than the curtailment of income and the cost of upkeep, is the threatening aspect of the labour question in this part of Herefordshire. While staying at Hampton Court I was fortunate enough to see both Mr. Stephens, the sanitary inspector of the Leominster Rural District Council, and Mr. Noakes, the very well-informed schoolmaster of the parish of Hope. Among other information Mr. Stephens stated that labour was scarce, dear, and uncertain, and that the cottages in his district were good and ample. Indeed, he added that if things went on as at present they would soon be too ample for the population. On these matters, however, there is nobody who can be so well informed as the local school-master, since all the youth of the village that, in the ordinary course of events, should constitute the adult population of the future, pass through his hands. It is this fact which makes his evidence so important. Mr. Noakes told us that during the previous six years out of an average attendance of 100 lads, not more than a dozen remained in the parish, and that these were, for the most part, 'dullards.'

It seems that both boys and girls depart immediately on leaving school; indeed, six months before their course is finished, he said that it was the habit of the local lads to make inquiries in Leominster or other towns with a view to securing situations. This they do very frequently by under-bidding some other youth already in employment, who in his turn moves on to a larger town, where he does as he has been done by. Mr. Noakes informed me that he knew of absolutely no instance of a boy or girl returning from the cities to the country; indeed, many had told him, when on a visit to their friends, that nothing would induce them to leave what they call 'town sweets.' He added that in this parish of Hope, with its population of about 510, there were no fewer than thirty-seven houses which had in them no child of an age to attend school. For the most part they were occupied by old people whose children had left them for the cities, or, at any rate, departed from the land.

As regarded remedies, he seemed to think that agricultural education is none at all, since in his school four or five lessons on rural matters were given every week. His experience was that once the young people reached the town, an occasional half-holiday spent at their homes or in the fields quite satisfied any longing they might have to return to country life. Mr. Noakes was of opinion that higher wages and amusements might do something to anchor them to the villages, but that money alone would not hold them. Ownership, he thought, would prove more effective in this respect, that is, after they attained a certain age. Among the farmers the tale was very similar. Thus on the afternoon of the same day I visited two of them almost at hazard. The first was working his holding with the aid of three sons. He stated repeatedly that were it not for these young men he would 'jack it up at once,' adding that they—his sons—were dissatisfied with being obliged to stop upon the land, and that he thought perhaps they would do better to go away and leave him. He appeared to believe that the upshot of the labour trouble must be that the farms would be thrown back upon the hands of the landlords, 'whether they could work them or not.' Of the land he had no complaint to make, but said that he could save no money; that for thirty years, indeed, he had worked hard for his living, and no more. He added that in this matter of labour his neighbour was worse off than himself, since very often he had no men at all to help him to carry on his farm of 150 acres. How he managed he could not say, but luckily nearly all his land was grass.

The second farmer whom we visited was one of the most popular and respected men in this part of the county. He said he was not 'so bad off,' being 'pretty well known,' which was his modest way of defining his general reputation. Otherwise his story was much the same. I sum it up in his own words: 'The old uns be dying out, and the boys don't come on.' Although he had done well in the past, he stated that were it not for his son's help, he would give up farming, and that farmers in general had not 'made a bit lately.' Of course this lack of trained assistance entails very heavy and constant labour on the occupiers of the land, as is well exemplified by the following Arcadian tale. A farmer whose holding we saw was asked by the clergyman why he never came to church. 'Well, parson, if you wants to know,' he answered, 'it's because I'se too hellish busy to wash me.'

As I am dealing with this subject of the lack of labour, I will give the instance of a farm I visited quite by accident in one of the richest parts of Herefordshire. The land is good, as is shown by the fact that this holding of 180 acres used to let for £300 a year, and to produce, I was informed, excellent stock and heavy crops. As I approached it I noticed that the fences were wild and gappy, to such an extent, indeed, that sheep or cattle could travel from field to field without troubling the gates. Most of the land appeared to have tumbled down to grass of a very indifferent character, and to be full of rubbish, while some of it was sodden and waterlogged. The farmhouse itself seemed good and tidy, but the roof slates were falling from the buildings, the weather-boards were rotten, and the gates broken. In the unkempt rickyard stood two melancholy-looking stacks of hay, one with a little crinoline of thatch upon its ridge, the other totally unthatched, and therefore, as I presume, spoiled. Passing down a lane we came to a field, which I can best describe by saying that, not having been ploughed in the autumn after the crop, if any, was removed, it suggested to the mind a gigantic brickbat covered with a dense growth of twitch.

On the further side of this enclosure an active man, the occupier of the place, was engaged in ploughing with a pair of horses. He received us civilly enough, and an interesting conversation ensued. I asked him what he meant to plant upon the field. He replied turnips ; but as it was obvious that there could not be much chance of his raising a crop of this or any other root from the land in such a condition, I left the subject and passed on to that of labour. In reply to my queries on this point, he said that one small boy was his only assistant. I suggested that he might advertise for a man, as this staff seemed insufficient to work 180 acres. He replied that he had done so, but as to go on advertising 'made a man look foolish' he had given it up. In short, he could find no labour, with the result that the place had become the wilderness I have described. One man who was unable either to read or write had stayed with him fourteen years, and as no other was forthcoming, he did the best he could by himself. The remedy he suggested was primitive and thorough-going—viz. that an Act should be passed to abolish education ! Educated people, he said, would not labour on the land. Feeling unable to pursue the

argument on these lines, I bade him farewell, whereupon
he whipped up his horses and again began to guide the
plough through that ravenous growth of couch-grass, which
within a month must once more hide his furrow in its cloak
of unwholesome green. I may add that on inquiry in the
neighbourhood, I was informed that the reputations both of
this farmer and his wife were good in every way.

As I left the field a kind of hopelessness took hold of me.
My mind was filled with a vision of this lonely and unaided
man, striving from year to year against that devouring sea
of twitch, till at last he departed into some cottage or
through the portals of the workhouse. I wondered also
whether the condition of this holding, once so fertile, was or
was not typical of the destiny of much of our English land.
So far as it is possible to judge, unless the labour and other
conditions change for the better in some way which at
present it is difficult to foresee, within the next score of
years the wanderer in parts of rural England will find
many farms as desolate, a conclusion which seems absurd.
To the eye of the casual observer Herefordshire, for instance,
appears prosperous enough; nor must it be supposed that all
farmers lack the hands necessary to cultivate their fields,
since for this reason or for that some of them still have
plenty, and do well.

Yet as I write I have before me notes of interviews with,
or the written opinions of three of the most experienced land-
agents in the county, not to mention a mass of confirmatory
evidence. From these it appears that the average farm
rents have sunk from 10 to 40 per cent., and selling values in
proportion. 'Labour,' said one, 'is becoming scarcer and
scarcer. . . . The tenant farmer, even in the face of
reduced rents, complains bitterly, and seems to have lost heart.'
'Labour,' said another, 'is very scarce, days shorter, men
more independent, women and boy labour almost nil.'
'Labour,' declared Mr. Britten, whose opinion is perhaps
as valuable as that of anybody in the county, 'is very
short. The position is most acute. The land is going

back. The tenants complain, and say "Find the man and I will pay him." It is a most vital question.' And so on and on.

To give more of such extracts would be easy, but what is the use when their tenor is continually the same? The most hopeful view of the situation which I can find among all my mass of notes, is that of Mr. Russell, a leading auctioneer, who said, 'Without doubt I think there is a scarcity, but I think that I should always get enough myself. . . . There are not sufficient men in the county to properly cultivate the land, but there will be enough to last my time.'

As I set down the conclusions at which I have arrived in county after county, knowing the importance of the matter in hand, I am increasingly afraid that it may be thought of me that I exaggerate, with or without design. But indeed it is not thus. From the sum of the information which I gathered, I endeavour to express the truth, and that which I believe to be the truth I am obliged to write—did I not do so I should be false to the duty I have undertaken to fulfil. Thus it comes about that I find it impossible, considering the county as a whole, to prophesy smooth things of the future of agriculture in Herefordshire. Of course conditions may change—who can tell? But I have to deal with facts as I found them, and am therefore driven to say that the outlook seems black even in this beautiful and fertile land. Still there are bright spots on the horizon—I refer especially to the trade with America in cattle, and to the remunerative culture of fruit and hops. But to be successful, more perhaps than any other products, fruit and hops require an ample supply of reliable labour. Will it always be forth-coming? If not, what is there to look to except the increase of small-holdings that may tie the people to the land? Indeed, such was the opinion of many intelligent men with whom I spoke in Herefordshire, although others took a different view of the matter, alleging that the expense of their establishment would be prohibitive, and that the result, even if it could be attained, must prove unsatisfactory to the farmer.

Having dealt briefly with the general situation, I will set out some details of the evidence which I collected in the county. Mr. Somerville, a farm labourer whom I saw in Ledbury, told me that he had returned from the collieries, where he earned £2 a week, to the land, where he received 15s. a week, with an extra shilling in lieu of cider, a house, and a quarter of an acre of garden. His reason was that he liked agricultural work better than any other. 'You see, it's steady like, and you know what you've got,' while as for the colliery money, 'I threw it away there, travelling.' He said that there were enough men on the land in his district, and that the cottages seemed good as far as he knew, but added of the young fellows : 'I don't know any that are learning to plough or milk; they all go on somewhere.' He thought that 'it is well to be near a town, for then the little shopkeepers in the country don't get it all out of you.'

An auctioneer whom I met in Ledbury expressed himself very hopefully on the agricultural position in Herefordshire, saying that this county and Worcestershire were the garden of England. Although Kent also grew hops and fruit, it lacked their splendid grass lands, and speaking generally, Herefordshire was not in the same category with counties that only produced hay and corn. Even on the higher land sheep and barley were paying, and of bad soil there was none, except commonage and places like the shoulder of the Malvern Hills, which only brought in from 10s. to 15s. the acre. There was no serious depression in the county and no fall in rentals since 1875—evidence which, the reader will observe, is controverted by other witnesses. They rarely had a farm to let, and when they did there were twenty people after it. Thus a few days before, on a Saturday, he was instructed to let a farm, and on the day of our interview—a Tuesday— he had five applicants. He knew of land within three miles of Ledbury which was worth £200 an acre, and on Tuesdays his average sale of stock was to the value of £1,200. The farmers did well, making rent, interest, and putting money by, some of them enough to purchase their farms; in fact the man who had £10 an acre to invest in his business was bound to make money. The only doubtful point was labour, which was an increasing difficulty, and one of which he confessed that he did not quite see the end, especially where hay-making and hop-picking were concerned, as the people drew away into the towns. The farmers did not pay them enough, and the wages, which were 14s. a week and a cottage, ought to be more.

In view of what I heard from many other gentlemen of experience in the county, the above opinions may be thought somewhat optimistic. They were, however, to some extent confirmed by those of a farmer, whom I saw upon the same day, who worked about 400 acres, of which 124 were under hops. Of these I think he said that 100 acres were his own property, having been bought by him for £3,000, which, he added, was about the value of the buildings on them. It was this gentleman who told me that a net profit had been made of £1,500 off sixty acres of strawberries, of which crop he was planting thirty additional acres in 1901. He said that sixteen years before he started with £1,500, and since then had made ten times his capital. The hop and fruit business was very prosperous, and hop-lands in Herefordshire were the cheapest to buy or lease in the world. Although the factors were 'trying it on here' they had no trouble with them, as they sold to a merchant at Worcester, or in many cases straight to the brewer. Personally he had not found much difficulty about labour, but as a rule they only got the worst men, and the young ones were going. So long as the hops paid, however, they could keep the men. If he could not get a labourer, he would give more and more until he did. The wages were 14s., with a cottage and perquisites. The cost of producing strawberries he put at £5 the acre for the tillage, and at £3 the acre for the picking. The total expense of the production of hops he estimated at £45 a ton, adding that he did not know a man who had grown them properly who had not succeeded. He was of opinion that there ought to be a duty on foreign hops, but why a farmer who, according to his own showing, was so eminently successful should want any duty at all is more than I can say.

Another gentleman whom I saw at the same time did not speak in this hopeful strain. He farmed 350 acres of sheep and corn land, half pasture and half arable, at a rent of 24s. the acre, the soil being red clay and loam on marl. Fifteen years before the rent of this farm was 35s. the acre. He said that he had been in business for twenty years— fifteen with his father and five years on his own account —and had 'done no good.' Indeed, he had a 'hard job to make both ends meet,' and was laying down land to grass as fast as he could. The corn was worth nothing now; a load used to fetch £30; to-day it only brought £15. He had a mill out of which he made a little, and a good stock of Shorthorns in which he 'took pleasure.' They helped him, and he kept a dairy and manufactured butter. He did not complain of the rent as compared with his labour-bill, which came to £400 a year. That of the gentleman who grew hops on a little larger acreage, by the way, was £1,000 a year, this crop being so much more expensive to cultivate. Indeed, he stated that the labour was a matter of general complaint, as the exodus was rapid, and he thought that in consequence of it, a good deal of the land was 'bound to go out of cultivation.'

The Rev. H. J. Marshall, of Winforton, a parish on the northern bank of the Wye, that in 1891 had a population of 132, told me that there the exodus was very marked. Thus, out of the few cottages in this village, five were occupied by men over sixty, and one by a man over seventy. Two of the men had housekeepers and no children or relatives, two had wives and no children at home, and an old man, a pensioner, had one son.

Mr. W. E. Britten, to whose evidence I have already briefly alluded, a gentleman of great experience, who is agent for various large estates, said that the Herefordshire rents for the good lands now varied from 25*s*. to 32*s*. the acre. They used to run from 50*s*. the acre down to 25*s*. for isolated patches. Some of the higher grounds, however, which in old days let for 30*s*., now brought in from 15*s*. to £1. These were lands of which the general course of cultivation is turnips fed off by sheep, then three years lay, roots, oats, and down again to temporary lay. One method of sowing down was, after they had been fed off, to work fields of late roots very fine, and about May broadcast them with the grasses, in which were mixed three pounds of rape to the acre. In July, when the seed was up about four inches, the rape would be high. Then the sheep were turned in to eat it off and tread the land, and the result was a good layer. The 25*s*. an acre land would include a proportion of grass, fruit, hop, and tillage soil. Of such land the rent was low in comparison with its quality, because the labour necessary to the cultivation of hops was so scarce.

The best hop districts were round Leominster, Monkland, Dilwyn, from Hereford down to Ledbury, the Frome Valley, Withington, Ashperton, and Stoke Edith. The chief sheep and barley district was about Ross-on-Wye. The large, light farms ran from 500 acres in size upwards, and the hop and fruit farms from 150 up to 500 acres. Those hop-growers, who held 200 acres or more of land, were generally successful. The expense of cultivating this crop he put at from £20 to £25 the acre. The meadow lands in the hop districts were, with few exceptions, only good for grazing beasts for store and breeding purposes. The feeding lands, which would turn out fat stock, were in the north of the county, on the banks of the Arrow and Lugg, and between Leominster and Hereford; the very best being at Pembridge on the Arrow. The fruit business was still in its infancy, the old orchards having been allowed to go down. Now, however, owing to the growth of the cider trade, planting was on the increase.

The breeding of Herefordshire cattle was, Mr. Britten said, one of their great industries, and, in addition to the home markets, among which that of Hereford was excellent, they could always rely upon South America to buy their good animals. The points of the race were their great flesh production, hardiness, and capacity for doing well on poor and even new-laid pastures. They were not, however, milking cows, although they could rear their own calves. Most of the sheep were Shropshire Downs, which were often crossed with the Kerry Hill breed. The mutton of the Ryeland sheep was very like that of the Black Face, but these had white faces and were close-woolled. In the Ross neighbourhood they crossed the Shropshires with the Oxford Downs. On the whole farmers were fairly prosperous. Most of them were sportsmen, happy and contented by nature, and good workers. The labour was very short, and on this point complaints were universal. The wages he put at 13s. a week, with a cottage and cider, and for carters 15s. or 17s. a week. These, however, were most difficult to find, and objected to the extra hours. One result of the shortage was that the fences were not trimmed or mended, and the unscattered mole-heaps were spoiling the fields.

All the young men who were worth anything went away, only the dregs remaining on the land. The farmers who did best were those who had sons and kept them to help in the cultivation of their holdings. In fact, at 'each change you get nearer the smock-frock,' by which Mr. Britten meant nearer to a system of small-holdings. If things went on as at present he could see nothing before the country except the depopulation of the rural districts. He did not think that high wages would keep the best of the men. I asked him if he thought that a sense of ownership would have this result. He replied that undoubtedly it would, and so would more small-holdings, if they could be created, but the cost of the necessary buildings seemed to bar the way. As it was he knew of cases in which every one of the young men went to coal mines or brick manufactories, or to the Birmingham waterworks, and when once they had touched the 'big shilling' they would not come back. Those labourers who remained were nothing like what they used to be : they would not learn their business, as they knew that, without any special knowledge, they could always get £1 or 25s. a week in the towns, with a half-holiday on Saturdays. Indeed, now-a-days they took very little interest in their work, and were ' a lot of shirkers,' a state of affairs that the farmers attributed to our system of education. Mr. Britten added that the land used to fetch thirty years' purchase, but now it generally sold for about twenty-five years' purchase, estimated on the reduced rental.

At Lyonshall, a village about sixteen miles from Hereford and eleven from Leominster, where the soil is clay and gravel, we were the guests of my friend, Mr. Stephen Robinson at Lynhales, who, like Mr. Richard Green, of The Whittern, in the same parish, has a fine herd of Hereford cattle. Both of these gentlemen are practical farmers, and take a great interest in the cultivation of their land. While showing me his Hereford heifers, a level and good-looking lot, Mr. Robinson told us of a very curious murrain which killed out a number of his calves a few years before. These calves died one after the other when about two days old, and on examination it was found that the milk in their stomachs had turned to a kind of cheese which no physic seemed powerful enough to stir. This sickness was supposed to be due to some microbe that inhabited the calf-pens, which ultimately it was found necessary to destroy and rebuild, since when there has been no further trouble. Mr. Robinson informed me that a herd of which he knew in Worcestershire had been similarly affected. His steward, who went with us round the cattle, spoke with enthusiasm of the flesh-producing qualities of the Herefords, which, he said, could be got out fat at from fifteen to eighteen months. Also, as I have mentioned, both he and his master believe that their milking properties can be developed, and, indeed, they have met with some success in this direction. He told me that they had trouble about labour. Thus he had advertised for two months for a waggoner and only received one answer.

Shortly after he bought this property, thirty years or more ago, Mr. Robinson began planting woods of ash and larch, through which I walked. They have done wonderfully well, as also have the Wellingtonias planted at the same time, which for their age are the best I know. As the ash trees grow up thickly they are thinned out when they reach a diameter of about four inches, and sold as 'spittle wood,' which, I suppose, originally meant wood that is made into spits. At any rate, the supply of this wood furnishes a livelihood to certain men who manufacture it into the handles of miners' tools. Thus they are kept in the neighbourhood instead of migrating to the towns. The soil of this farm is a heavy loam, which takes grass readily and makes good permanent pasture in about five years. For instance, one piece of eighteen acres of a rather nasty white clay, which Mr. Robinson had laid down, is now throwing out capital herbage. From Lynhales, by the way, there is a fine view of the Black Mountains of Brecknockshire and of Robin Hood's Butts, conical hills upon their projecting spurs, that are seen far off across the well-wooded vale.

In returning from our walk over the land I met and conversed with a gentleman who farmed in the neighbourhood. He told me that he paid 24s. an acre rent, and used to employ eight hands, but now had only four. He said that if he had given up farming in 1896 he would have been worth £1,100 or £1,200 more than he was then. He had eight children, and would see that none of them took to farming. He thought the prospect very bad owing to the lack of labour. All the young men were leaving, and unless there was a change, the land would go out of cultivation. Generally this informant took a very black view of the agricultural prospects in that part of Herefordshire.

That evening I had an interview with Mr. Mainwaring, over some of whose land I had walked in the afternoon, and noted that it was exceedingly well farmed. He held 260 acres, of which eighty were tillage, under Mr. Robinson, who spoke very highly of him both as a man and a tenant. On this acreage he employed four men and a lad, but said that he ought to be able to manage with three, as he helped himself, and his wife, who struck me as being a very capable and energetic person, attended to the poultry and other matters. On the whole he had no cheerful tale to tell. Still he said that if a man persevered and attended to his business he ought to get on, but that it depended on the man. Such a person could pay his rent and live, but could make no interest on his money. He knew, however, that many would give up if they could afford to do so, and many more had borrowed money, and if they were sold up to-morrow would have nothing left.

Mr. Mainwaring's great complaint was of the labour. Thus for seven weeks he had advertised for a shepherd without an answer, and when at last he got one he was a man of fifty years of age who had fallen out with his employer. Still he was the youngest hand in his service. There were but few young men left, and 'as a rule they were wasters.' As things were he saw no solution; unless something happened, the business must come to an end. He thought that if a man had a bit of land he would be as good a servant as though he had none, as those men who wished for land generally took an interest in the land. But it must be pasture; he did not hold with a farm labourer taking tillage. The exodus was not altogether a question of wages, as the hands were well paid. In addition to their regular wage they had potato land and a free garden, £2 extra in harvest, with a shilling for each calf to the ploughman, half a crown a foal to the waggoners, &c.—counting everything, not much under £1 a week. Yet the serving-girl and the milking-man were no more; his wife could find no servant. His land was good for sheep, but not strong enough to fat cattle. He sold steers and cattle in store condition, and fed out the barren cows. His sheep were Radnorshire ewes crossed with Shropshire tups. He thought that Shire horse breeding was a paying business, but good land was needful to grow good bone. It was the land that made the bone. Unless conditions changed the only thing to do would be to lay down as much of the land to grass as possible and let the rest go.

In going over the estate of Mr. Richard Green, upon the following day, the first farmer whom I saw was Mr. R. Edwards, of Strangworth, in the neighbouring parish of Pembridge, who I think, held 200 acres, at a rent that used to be 30s., but is now £1 the acre. He said that the people were leaving the land fast; thus the population of Lyonshall had shrunk by 105 during the previous ten years. At that moment three young men were going away, and he thought that the girls were becoming even scarcer than the lads. If this continued, the end of it must be that the worst of the land would go out of cultivation. There was a tendency among the people to despise the business of working on the soil; but he thought that if the towns became congested, they might get some of the men back again.

The remedy that he had to propose—and on this point Mr. Edwards was very strong indeed—was a great increase in the number of small-holdings. Such small-holdings used to exist, but when agriculture was profitable they had been absorbed by the large farms. There ought, in his opinion, to be some scheme under which labourers could take land in lots varying in size from 5 to 100 acres. He knew of one place which had been thus split up. There were twelve applicants, and among these it was divided, with the result that the old rent was quite doubled. In Pembridge, also, sixteen applications were made to the parish Council for lots of land measuring from five to fifteen acres. Mr. Edwards, in his capacity of chairman to the Council, wrote to those who owned or occupied the land in the neighbourhood, but all he could secure was a grass field of nine acres, which was divided into three portions. After the expenses of fencing, &c., had been met, the Council was unable to let these at less than 45s. the acre. This rent, however, was paid, and the condition of the land was now much better than it had been seven years before. One of his own men occupied two acres of land, to which Mr. Edwards had added another three-quarters of an acre. This was rented with the cottage at £2 10s. the acre, and on it, amongst other things, the tenant kept three or four sheep. Besides taking care of his little holding, this man worked for him in a satisfactory fashion. Of course the small-holder looked to the farmer for occasional help, such as the loan of a horse now and again. Mr. Edwards had found that it paid him to give time and assistance to others, as when he was pressed they helped him in turn.

Most people will, I think, be of opinion that the above views upon these matters are wise and sound.

Mr. Williams, whose little place I saw, occupied thirty acres in Lyonshall, near to The Whittern, at a rent of 30s. the acre. Half of this holding was tillage, which he said he was laying down to grass. He told me that he began as a farm labourer, and by hard work had saved enough to enable him to take the thirty acres four years before, which he managed with the help of a boy who was a relative of his own. He kept eight or ten head of horned stock with twenty ewes, feeding out their lambs. He and a neighbour, another small-holder, worked their places more or less together, which they found cheaper than keeping two horses apiece. He said that he could pay his rent and make his way ; that he liked the life, and would advise his friends to follow his example. He knew plenty of men who would be glad to take suitable small-holdings if they could get the chance.

Immediately adjoining that of Mr. Williams I saw two other small-holdings, one of eighteen acres, where lived the neighbour with whom he co-operated, and another of twelve acres, with a good house, where the tenant kept three cows and sold milk and butter. I understood that all these men paid their rent, made a living, and were fairly con-tent. A neighbouring farm, I think of about 200 acres, was worked by three brothers from Carmarthenshire, with the assistance of one good servant and four horses. It seemed to be cultivated in excellent style, and I noted that the fences were particularly well kept. Doing the work of the place with their own hands, these brothers appeared to get on well.

Mr. Thomas Turner, the bailiff, in the absence of my friend, Mr. Richard Green, showed me his employer's splendid Herefordshire cattle. Among them was the bull Major-domo, by Diplomat, which was sold to America for £300; a heifer of two years old, that had taken nine first prizes; and four other heifers, which Mr. Turner thought were the best in England. They had only been shown once, I think in Ireland, when they took the first and second prizes. A beautiful cow also was Merry Maid, which had taken many medals. Mr. Turner had no opinion of the milking qualities of Herefords, which, he said, could only just manage to rear their own calves.

The rent of the land in the Lyonshall district he put at about 25s. the acre, more or less, according to the quality of the soil. The cottages in the neighbourhood, he said, were generally poor and bad, and the people were going away. Mr. Green's shepherd, also named Turner, a very intelligent man with whom I conversed, was of the same opinion. He said, 'They all clear out from here; they want lighter hours, more money, and social delights.'

Conducted by Mr. Robinson, I visited various farmers in Pembridge, a large parish on the Arrow, covering over 7,000 acres, that in old days was a market town. Here the soil is gravel and loam with a red sandstone subsoil, and there is much pasture. The first of these was Mr. Edward Farr, of Norke Court, a quaint old house with water in front of it, that I imagine had been part of an ancient moat. He led out for our inspection his champion Hereford bull, Britisher, which weighed over 23 cwt.; a tremendous animal, of formidable aspect. Mr. Farr said that, person-ally, he had enough labour, at wages which, with wood, coal, cider throughout the summer, cottage at 1s. a week, and 7s. 6d. a week extra at corn harvest, amounted to about

£1 a week. But then, he said, 'I work them light, treat them well, and ask them to drink often.'

At the Leen Farm I met Mr. A. P. Turner, the occupier, who holds under Mr. Evelyn, of Kinsham Court, Presteign, and Mr. Lawton Moore, of Brampton Bryan, on the river Teme, on the Shropshire border. Mr. Turner had a fine herd of Herefords, some of which I saw, and said that this breed had been the salvation of the county. He told me that the rents in the Arrow Valley ran up to £2, but the average was from 25s. to 30s. for land of which two-thirds would be pasture. He made the usual complaints about labour, saying that the young men went away, and that if it continued there might be a great difficulty. To stay on the land had become a reproach ; thus, if children were dull, the schoolmasters would twit them as ' only fit to follow the plough.'

Mr. Lawton Moore thought that the principal cause of the exodus was the merging of the small-holdings that used to exist, into the large farms. At Brampton Bryan he had sufficient labour, but then he was surrounded by small-holders, and the sons of these men came out to work upon the land with a view to saving money, and, in due course, becoming small-holders themselves. He knew many men who had been farm labourers and were now farmers ; for instance, one whose name he mentioned, who began as a labourer, at that moment occupied a holding of 500 acres. Mr. Turner said also that there was a man near by who began with thirty acres and then held 300, which his sons helped him to work. Mr. Moore believed that out of twenty acres of land and a sheep-run the small-holders in his neighbourhood made a living, which some of them supplemented by occasionally working for farmers. On the other hand many of the little proprietors or yeomen in Montgomeryshire had come to grief, owing generally to the mortgages that had been piled upon their lands. The wages in his district were 14s. a week with cottage, potato ground, and 50s. at harvest. Those men who worked on Sunday he allowed to keep a cow.    The rent was about 24s. or 25s. an acre.

Mr. John Price, of the Court House farm, whom I visited next, was the owner of some of the most famous Herefords in the county.    When I was there he was about to give up his farm, being, as he said, 'glad to slip out while I have a bit left,' and I think I have since seen that his herd was sold by auction at a high figure.    His sitting-room was hung round with portraits of prize Hereford cattle and adorned with trophies which he had won, amongst them the Elkington Challenge Cup, taken at the Birmingham Cattle Show in 1882, and the Elsmere Plate for the best animal in the same year.    He said that the position as regarded labour was very bad, and he could not see what the end would be.    All the lads went, and of late Herefordshire had suffered much. When the old men died he did not know how they would be replaced.

We next visited Mr. Henry Russell, farmer, auctioneer, and estate agent of Westonbury.    He farmed 333 acres, of which ten acres were wood, at a rent of 27s. an acre, and said that if it were put on the market the next day, it would fetch as much.    He considered his farm to be of medium quality, and out of it he made rent and interest on capital, but he did not live from the land.    He did not think that the farmers were really prosperous, unless they had some speciality which brought in money.    Herefordshire, however, had suffered as little as any other county, being supported by the variety of its agricultural products -- hops, fruit, Hereford cattle, and sheep, in addition to the ordinary cereal crops.    The fall in rents, he considered, was more than outweighed by the drop in the value of products, and the trouble was that farmers tried to go on where their fathers left off, which they could not do.    During the last fifteen or twenty years the lot of the labourer had improved more in proportion than that of any other class dependent on the land.    Some of his men received £1 a week, or its equivalent, and none of them got less than 13s. a week in cash.    Personally he had enough men, and if he became short he should clear out of farming, but many were going away. He doubted whether increased wages would keep them, and did not think that the brighter lads would stay in the country. He had sympathy with his labourers, but had no faith in rural sports and that kind of palliative, although now and again he gave them a day off.

Mr. Russell thought that a proportion of small-holdings would help, that is, where the woman worked the holding and the man worked for the farmer, but he had never seen a proper system of small-holdings tried. His experience was that relatively they did not produce as much as the large farms. In that neighbourhood there were plenty of very fair cottages with large gardens and potato grounds. Pigs also were kept, which ran on the farmer's land, and cider was given. He mentioned a man who had been a servant of his own, who had a little holding of eleven acres quite close by, and who had saved or made £2,000. But he was a very clever man, who bought well and sold well, and would get money anyhow. He was 'one of those who will have it.' A bad feature of the past had, in his opinion, been the joining of farms together to the exclusion of the little man. There was still a great demand for small farms. Thus for one of 400 acres there would be one or two applicants only, for 200 acres a good number, and for fifty acres there might be as many applications. Mr. Russell said that for shootings there was an enormous demand, even if they only covered 100 acres ; he thought this a very bad thing, for the shooting tenant had no real interest in the land.

Mr. R. Penhall, of Weston House, whose farm I also saw, is a gentleman-farmer, holding 260 acres. Like some of his neighbours, he made a business of breeding pedigree Hereford stock. I think that his account of the labour question was the most hopeful that I heard in this district. At any rate, he declared that, so far as he was concerned, he had no trouble in the matter.

The first letter which I shall quote from among those

of my correspondents in Herefordshire has a somewhat melancholy interest, as its writer, Mr. Thomas Duckham, one of the best-known agriculturists in England, died but the other day at the age of eighty-five. He began by making some complimentary allusions to my work on behalf of agriculture—that, coming from such a source, I value highly—and with the offer to give me every assistance in his power. But, he added, in words of which we can now appreciate the full meaning, 'Age is telling very seriously upon me; my memory sadly fails me, and now, far advanced in my eighty-fifth year, I cannot do as I have done.' He said that the Central and Associated Chambers of Agriculture were the emanations of his brain, and that he had fought hard against the cattle plague and other diseases. 'When in the House of Commons'—where Mr. Duckham served for many years as a Liberal member—'I pressed repeatedly for a Minister of Agriculture, and I think the fourth time I asked for the appointment, Mr. Gladstone promised a department. Also, when one of the trustees of the Smithfield Club, I carried a motion for the slaughter of all animals for food at the port of landing. When Mr. Long was appointed Minister of Agriculture I wrote pressing him for a Bill with that provision, and during its progress supported it in the Press.'

Truly Mr. Duckham's is a record of useful work. In his letter he spoke somewhat bitterly of the manner in which 'poor agriculture' had been sacrificed to the interests of wealthy manufacturers of margarine, and certainly it does seem hard that the law should still allow these traders to colour their merchandise in imitation of genuine butter, and thus give it an unfair advantage on the market.

A gentleman who has managed land in Herefordshire for over thirty years, said that on a sample property the farmers in 1875 paid £5,886 in rent and tithe, and in 1900 £4,032 in rent; the cottagers and small-holders up to about twelve acres paying about the same now as they did then. The average farm rents in his district in 1900 were about 20s. the acre, tithe free, and the fall in the selling value of land was probably about 40 per cent. There were not so many resident landlords as there used to be in his district. The farms let readily, but generally at lower rents, or with arrangements for the erection of additional hay barns or other buildings, upon the cost of which no interest was paid. Labour was very scarce; indeed, of that of women and boys there was almost none, while the men were more independent and worked a shorter day. Carters, cowmen, and shepherds received from 13s. to 16s. the week, with extras in the shape of house, garden, potato land, cider, and harvest money, worth in all 3s. a week. General labourers were paid 2s. 6d. a day. Cottages were plentiful and in good condition, most of them having three bedrooms, gardens of a quarter of an acre, good piggeries, and generally several profitable fruit trees. In many cases also the cottagers had small orchards varying in size from one up to twelve acres. These holdings let readily, and the rents were punctually paid.

The young men left the land and went to railway service, into the police and the army, to towns as trade porters, to the iron and coal works of South Wales and Monmouthshire, and into gentlemen's gardens and stables. He did not attribute this exodus to education, but because they earned more money with less Sunday work, light amusements, and greater liberty. They did not, however, appear to save money, or to rise to better positions than do those who remain upon the land, and he often heard of cases where their parents had to help them in sickness, or when trade was slack, or during a strike. On the other hand, as a guardian, he well knew the difficulty of forcing these young men who had emigrated, to contribute to the support of their poor old relatives when, growing too weak to do regular work, these became chargeable to the Union.

The tenant farmer, with his wife and children, had to work like slaves, and generally harder on Sundays than on other days, but he did not find that they grew poorer than they used to be. The landlord was certainly worse off than in the past. He had to live more economically, and in some cases to let his own house, or to go away altogether. This was an unfortunate state of affairs, as in such instances the farmer frequently suffered by his landlord's absence and the lack of the help which he was accustomed to receive from him. The labourer was certainly better off than he was twenty years ago, and often by his industry had gradually become the occupier of a few acres of grass or orchard land. In saying this he had in his mind about ten men whom he knew who, during the past twenty-five years, had worked their way up from the position of labourers to that of farmers of from five to forty acres.

My informant was sorry to say that he could not see any sign of a revival in the condition of agriculture, nor was he hopeful as to the future. He thought that farming would go on, but, owing to the scarcity of labour, the land will be indifferently cultivated, and that more of it will be allowed to go down—not to be properly laid down with good seeds—to grass; also that rents would fall still lower. His notion of a remedy was to increase the number of small-holdings furnished with cheap buildings and suitable for dairy, poultry, garden, and fruit-farming. This, however, would take capital, and the great difficulty was to know whence the money should come. Where the roads, water supply, and sanitary arrangements were satisfactory he would have no difficulty in finding plenty of good tenants for comfortable cottages with buildings sufficient to the working of from five to fifty acres. The population in his neighbourhood had sunk exactly 20 per cent. since 1881.

The following information, which was kindly furnished to me by Mr. J. P. Brown, F.S.I., of the well-known Herefordshire firm of Apperley & Brown, has many points of interest, especially as regards the small-holdings in Mr. Brown's parish of Whitchurch. Mr. Brown says that rents in his district had fallen from 10 to 30 per cent., and ran from 15s. to 30s. the acre according to position, the price of land having come down from thirty years' purchase of the rental value to twenty-five years'. Many of the mansions and residences were now let to strangers. There was a fair demand for farms, but those of small area, where little labour was required, let the best. The labourers were continually becoming scarcer. Their wages ran from 12s. to 17s. a week, in addition to harvest money, gratis cottages, and cider. Cottages were fairly plentiful, and generally contained from four to six rooms, but their quality varied. On some estates they were very good, on others inferior.

The young men were migrating more and more to the towns, in search of better pay, more excitement and amusement. Without doubt education had much to do with this exodus, but he was afraid it was too late to improve the system. Notwithstanding the reduced rents, the tenant farmers complained bitterly and seemed to have lost heart. The landlords in many instances were overburdened with charges and felt the pinch of the reduced rents; but the labourers had never done better and were never more independent, or, as a whole, more dissatisfied. He saw no signs of improvement, but, although not sanguine on the point, was hopeful that the nation might wake up to the fact that the interests of agriculture and the land were of national import. He believed that the effect of the desertion of the land by its inhabitants would be most serious and must prove a danger to the country. The question had been too long ignored, and in his opinion the Press was responsible for much of the apathy and callousness in this matter both of the people and the Government.

At my request Mr. Brown furnished me with the following particulars as to the small occupations in the parish of Whitchurch, near Ross-on-Wye, where he resides, or resided. He said that Doward Hill, in this parish, adjoins the river Wye near to Symonds Yat in the royal Forest of Dean, and was originally common-land. Years ago portions of the hill which was then common were enclosed and cultivated by labourers, who built small cottages, which in many instances were still occupied by their descendants. There were in 1901 more than 100 of these small proprietors living on their own holdings, which varied in size from half an acre to five acres of land, and often had been held from father to son for over eighty years. When not engaged in agricultural work these men found ample occupation in the Government woods; also in summer the younger ones were employed as boatmen and guides to tourists, who visited the Wye Valley in increasing numbers.

The principal characteristic of these small-holders was their attachment to their own property, thus, although many of the original cottages had been pulled down, they were not only being replaced but improved upon. Whilst in many parishes in Herefordshire the population had shrunk, in this Whitchurch district it had held its own, and although here, as elsewhere, agricultural labour was hard to come by, it was a satisfaction to find men who were willing to remain where they were bred and born, and anxious to increase and improve their little properties. It should be noted that much of the land there was orcharding, and that the gardens were early and productive.

Mr. Edwin W. Beaven, of Highfield House, Holmer, near Hereford, farmer and fruit grower, was so good as to furnish me with some information which, he stated, had also been considered and verified by his neighbour, the well-known auctioneer and land agent, Mr. Walter Pye, of Coldwells, in the same parish. He said that rents had fallen considerably in Herefordshire, though not to the same extent as in some other counties. Temporary abatements had been general on many estates, and a lowering of perhaps 25 per cent. on most of the poorer class of farms had been found necessary. On the other hand, some of the best holdings maintained their rent value, as the demand for really good farms had not diminished, which, even if large, were some of them rented as high as £3 the acre. The average rent of agricultural land, however, was from 15s. to 30s. the acre, small holdings being always in demand, and fetching more in proportion. The sale value had in some instances fallen quite 50 per cent., but generally from

25 to 30 per cent. In that district there were not many resident landlords. Good farms let readily enough, and even inferior holdings found tenants without much difficulty, and, provided that the price was adjusted to suit the times, the rents were fairly paid. Labour was of an inferior quality and becoming scarcer. The wages varied from 13*s.* to 18*s.* a week for ordinary farm hands, with £1 or 30*s.* extra at harvest, and on most farms an allowance of cider.

Although, owing to the shrinkage of the population of the agricultural districts, it might naturally be supposed that there were many unoccupied dwellings of the kind in the country, in his district good cottages were greatly in demand. Very few young men were content to stay on the land, and for the most part these were of an inferior type. Even boys willing to work on the farm were now scarcely to be met with; as soon as they left school they were off to the towns, attracted thither chiefly by the prospect of higher wages. In his opinion the system of education in our country schools was undoubtedly at fault. It was not practical enough, nor was the slightest interest shown in teaching those branches of learning which might tend to make a rural life more attractive. To judge from appearances, tenant farmers in general were fairly well-to-do, but often the landlords had not sufficient capital to keep the farmsteads in thorough repair and erect new buildings adapted to modern requirements. As to the labourer, he was much better off than formerly, and, when not in the habit of attending a 'public,' which too often lay close to his door, he ought to be in a fairly comfortable position.

The two or three seasons prior to 1901 had been favourable to farming generally, more so than several before them, hence there was a slight improvement in agricultural interests. The labour question might of course assume a still more serious aspect in the immediate future. Otherwise he saw no reason why farmers in his part of Herefordshire should not hold their own, and at the least gain a living when the seasons favoured them. Large grain-growing farms could not, it was true, pay their way except under exceptional circumstances, or unless special attention was given to some other and more profitable branch of agriculture, but on smaller farms near a town a certain degree of prosperity might be attained. A good crop of wheat, for instance, leaves some profit where the straw is sold at an advantage, and money might be earned in many extra ways with the team. The farmer must find out to what crops his land is particularly adapted, and if need be, strike out on fresh lines in some new branch of culture that will bring in a clear profit. Then, even in these times of competition, he may at least manage to win a livelihood out of the land.

There was not the least doubt but that this desertion of the land by the labouring classes, if not checked in some way, would prove in the end calamitous to the country at large. Any other Government but our own, Mr. Beaven thought, would take steps towards preventing so ruinous an exodus. Our land laws, he considered, were sadly at fault. Legal expenses and formalities connected with the purchase of small properties needed to be lessened and ameliorated. They were a great hindrance to the true progress of land culture. Also the occupier should be granted more liberty of action and an ampler security in his holding.

In the course of an interesting communication, a Herefordshire solicitor gave me but a poor account of the agricultural position in that county. He said that notwithstanding the assistance which the rearing of stock, poultry, and fruit-farming gave them, owing to the intensity of foreign competition, farmers found that they could hardly make the land pay. It was impossible to avoid coming to the conclusion that the agricultural interest was gradually growing poorer, and that the value of land had sunk at least 50 per cent. during the past thirty years. The gradual depopulation of the villages also was bringing the people into the small towns, where there was not sufficient employment for them all. Lawyers had grown very careful about advancing money upon mortgage of land, since such extreme caution

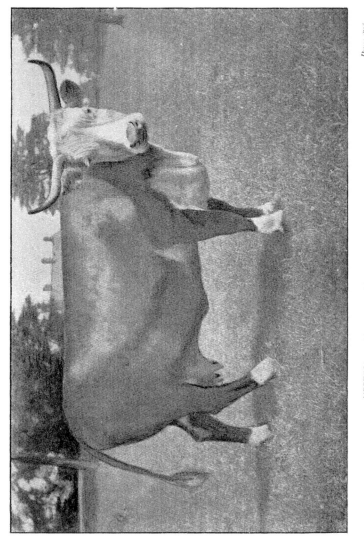

HEREFORD COW, THE PROPERTY OF MR. STEPHEN ROBINSON

had to be exercised that the investment was rarely worth the anxiety. He knew several villages in this and the adjoining counties where cottages stood unoccupied; the farmers were growing poorer; while the small country shopkeepers who used to thrive, were sinking one by one into the Bankruptcy Court. If some remedy could not be found, England, he thought, must drop behind in the race of nations.

Mr. John Arkwright, M.P., whom I had the pleasure of meeting when staying at his father's house, has been so kind as to write me a letter in which he suggests that I should bear in mind the great value of well-organised games as a means of keeping some of our village lads in the country. Also that I should ask myself whether it is not true that many a young fellow goes to the town because, when he leaves school, he finds himself utterly unable to face the hard work to which he is put upon the land, and whether a proper system of physical training would in any way over-come this difficulty. By a proper system of physical training he meant an orderly, intelligent curriculum designed in the first instance by experts and doctors, and carried out by teachers who understood at least the elements of anatomy. I had the advantage of talking over the matter with Mr. Arkwright, but I cannot say that I was converted to this view of the case. My belief is that the English lad who leaves the village school is not only as strong to-day as were his forefathers, but even stronger, since he has been brought up on better food and under healthier conditions than they enjoyed. I fear that it is not inability that prevents him from working on the land, but a rooted objection to that work, which he thinks, and is right in thinking, he will to a great extent avoid by migrating to the town.

I wish that I could add some more cheerful opinions on the present condition and prospects of agriculture in Hereford-shire. This, however, I am unable to do, since, although I have searched them carefully, in all my pile of notes and correspondence, with the exception of the few which are given in the text, I can find none. I am therefore driven to the conclusion that the sample views which are printed in the preceding pages accurately represent the conditions of the land and those dependent on it in Herefordshire as these were in the year 1901.

## WORCESTERSHIRE

THE midland county of Worcester has an area of about 480,500 acres and an extreme length from north to south of thirty-four miles by a breadth of thirty miles. It is hilly, with many well-watered and fertile valleys, and its scenery is among the most beautiful of any in England. Red marl and deep loam are perhaps the most common soils, but in the neighbourhood of Evesham a stiff blue clay is met with. In this county there is an enormous preponderance of permanent pasture, and it is also famous for its fruit and hops.

I purpose to begin my remarks upon Worcestershire by giving some account of the lovely Bewdley district. After this I shall treat of the hop and fruit growing, then of the Catshill small-holdings, the famous Vale of Evesham, and various farms that I inspected, as in the case of other counties, reserving some general evidence and individual views to be dealt with last of all.

Close to the borders of Shropshire stands the ancient and beautiful town of Bewdley, on the Severn, where, on May 19, 1499, Prince Arthur, the eldest son of Henry VII., was married in the chapel of Ticknell to the Princess Katherine of Arragon. The princess, by the way, did not appear upon the occasion, but was represented by her proctor, Roderic Gundesalvi de Puebla, which must have made the ceremony somewhat disappointing to witness.

In response to most kind invitations from the Bewdley and District Horticultural Society, thither I journeyed, prepared to inspect small-holdings, but not altogether for a reception by the mayor and many other gentlemen, or the

speeches of a public luncheon. Still to be entertained by
hosts so genial as the leading citizens of Bewdley was one
of the most pleasant experiences of my journey, and after
the feast and the speeches came the small-holdings, which
we visited in company with some of the chief agriculturists
of the district.

Before proceeding to describe them I print here a statement, which has been kindly prepared for me, showing
the number and sizes of the holdings on a total of 10,300
acres of land in the Bewdley district.

### Number of Holdings.

| | | | | | | | |
|---|---|---|---|---|---|---|---|
| Under 1 acre, including gardens of more than ¼ acre | | | | . | . | . | 233 |
| Between | 1 | acre and | 2 | acres | . | . | 46 |
| ,, | 2 | ,, | 3 | ,, | . | . | 37 |
| ,, | 3 | ,, | 5 | ,, | . | . | 44 |
| ,, | 5 | ,, | 10 | ,, | . | . | 54 |
| ,, | 10 | ,, | 15 | ,, | . | . | 29 |
| ,, | 15 | ,, | 20 | ,, | . | . | 13 |
| ,, | 20 | ,, | 30 | ,, | . | . | 24 |
| ,, | 30 | ,, | 50 | ,, | . | . | 22 |
| ,, | 50 | ,, | 60 | ,, | . | . | 10 |
| ,, | 60 | ,, | 80 | ,, | . | . | 6 |
| ,, | 80 | ,, | 100 | ,, | . | . | 15 |
| ,, | 100 | ,, | 150 | ,, | . | . | 16 |
| ,, | 150 | ,, | 200 | ,, | . | . | 7 |
| Over 200 acres | | . | . | . | . | . | 7 |

It will be observed that out of this total of 560 holdings,
no fewer than 233 are under one acre in extent, whereas
456 are of a size smaller than twenty acres, figures which
show how eagerly little tenancies of land are sought for in
this neighbourhood. The farming on these holdings may be
described as of a general character, although, for the most
part, it includes a fruit orchard, probably of cherry trees.
Here is a list of some of the industries which are practised

by individual small-holders as an adjunct to the working of their land :—Basket-making ; duck, fowl, and turkey raising ; cherry and other fruit growing ; egg producing ; breeding of high-class bulldogs ; hay, straw, pig, and general dealing. After seeing a considerable number of them, the general impression left upon my mind by these small-holders is that they are a singularly hard working and independent body of men, who, if they do no more, at least succeed in earning a good living by their toil.

The road from Bewdley leading to the parish of Rock, runs for a considerable distance through orchards of cherry trees, which clothe the steep, bordering banks. It is impossible to imagine anything more lovely than were these orchards at the time of my visit. Each tree was a cloud of dazzling white, and every bough, so thick did the blossoms hang about it, a veritable sceptre of frosted snow. The local growers seemed to anticipate another season like that of 1886, when cherries were in such plenty that for some days the Bewdley streets were blocked with the carts and barrows. It is said, indeed, that on this occasion 4,000 ' pots,' each containing 63 lbs. of fruit, were on offer at once, with the result that in a single day the price fell from 14s. to 5s. per pot, a quite unremunerative figure. Indeed, in 1901 growers feared a too plentiful crop, and some of them grumbled to me at the abundant promise of their orchards. I wonder whether it was realised.

The rent received for small-holdings in this district is very different from that which the larger farms command. Thus, as we went, we saw upon our right a tenancy of forty acres, which let at 50s. the acre. On the left lay one of 250 acres of similar land that brought in but £1 the acre. Another small-holding of twenty-four acres of poor land was rented at £40, whereas a large neighbouring farm of between 300 and 400 acres realised but 12s. or 13s. the acre. We were told also that in this same parish two large farms were without tenants, although their soil is much better than that of the twenty-four acre holding spoken of above.

Another small tenant said she had to pay no less than £4 an acre for three acres of very indifferent land. Although it must be remembered that little holdings are necessarily more expensive than large ones, since the landlord must be remunerated for the cost and upkeep of the extra set of buildings, I admit that the difference in the price asked seems to me excessive.

The explanation, of course, is, that we are all of us glad to get the full market value of our property. Thus there are few men philanthropic enough, when the eager, would-be tenants press offers of £3 an acre upon them, to bid them take their pen and write down 30s. So it comes about that small-holdings, for which there is much competition, are but too frequently over-rented. As a remedy, I suggest that such tenancies should, as far as possible, be under the management of county Councils or other public bodies, which could buy the land in large blocks and sell or let it out in small ones, without being exposed to the temptation of seeking to take advantage of the demand in order to secure an extravagant profit. This is done, at any rate to some extent, by the Bewdley and District Horticultural Society that rents a parcel of land *en bloc* and hires it out in allotments, which we saw, as indeed parish Councils can do if they wish. These allotments are taken eagerly by the townsfolk, of whom many may be seen working upon them every evening. Indeed, when I was there already more land was required.

By way of illustrating the conditions that prevail on the Bewdley small-holdings, I will now very briefly describe some of those which we visited. The first, of one and a half acres, all under mixed fruit trees, was cultivated by an engineer with damaged eyesight, to whose wife it belonged. He grumbled a good deal, and said that he would sooner have a steady job; I presume he meant at the wages usually received by engineers. Still, I gathered that with the help of a little light work done occasionally for others, he managed to make a living, which, under the circumstances, and taking into consideration the smallness of his holding, was a not unsatisfactory result.

No. 2 had eight acres, two in one plot and six in another. I think he owned it all, having succeeded to some and bought the rest. He said that he made a good living out of his eight acres, but to do this was obliged to work very hard. The cultivation of this land taking up all his time, he could do nothing else. Most of the plot that we saw was planted with fruit trees of different sorts, including an orchard of cherries, which had not yet come into bearing. Also he grew 'quick,' that is, young whitethorn, which he sold at £1 a thousand when they were five years from the seed, to be used in setting hedges. I asked him whether he thought it best to hire or to own, to which he answered tersely that an owner could not be turned out and a hirer would not plant. This remark suggested to my mind that there is much in what is alleged by many students of the subject, who declare that to make small-holdings really successful, fixity of tenure is necessary.

Here we noticed the good effects of tillage upon the growth of fruit trees. Part of this orchard of cherries was planted in garden ground which is dug and manured every year, and part on a little grass field. Although they were set in the same season and in the same soil, those trees which grew upon the grass were not more than half the size of those which grew in the garden. Afterwards, when visiting Evesham, that home of fertility and agricultural wealth of which I shall treat presently, I noticed the same thing on a larger scale. Those who wish to secure a sure and quick return from fruit should till the soil about its roots.

No. 3 was a bricklayer. He had three acres of land, and earned 5s. a day at his trade. Needless to say he was reported to be doing very well. No. 4 held twenty-four acres of indifferent 'brashy,' that is, stony land, at a rent of £40, which he considered too dear. On this point he said : 'We've got to pay for these little bits, and many more would be after it if I left. It would be better if it were my own.' The land was all pasture and fruit, out of which the tenant paid his rent and made a living by dint of hard work. He kept five cows and some fowls, selling the butter and eggs in Kidderminster and feeding the skim milk to pigs. As for hands to help, he said: 'We has 'em when we can get 'em,' but in practice he and his wife did all the work themselves. This man used to farm 109 acres, which he occupied for twenty-four years.

No. 5 also held twenty-four acres, of which twenty-one were owned, and three hired at the rent of £12 a year. In this case the husband was very ill and could do but little, but his wife received help from sons, who also worked elsewhere. They had horses, cows, eight or ten sheep, two pigs, and poultry. On the whole, notwithstanding the sickness of the father, they seemed to be doing well. No. 6 rented two acres of fruit, and kept pigs: he and another man worked at making strong baskets for coaling ships, which we saw in process of manufacture. They are constructed of thin broad bands of oak, which are split after boiling, and when finished fetch 12s. a dozen or a little more. I noticed the energy with which these men laboured; indeed, it struck me as almost ferocious. Even while speaking, they did not cease one moment from their task, at which, as it was easy to see, they were working for their own benefit, not for that of an employer.

No. 7 was a blacksmith, who cultivated about twenty acres of land—as I believe, his own property. He had fruit and stock, and made butter, the pigs being fed with the skim. Our interview with him was brief, as he seemed exceedingly busy drilling his mangolds, but we were informed that he was a hard-working and successful man. In his orchard we were shown a large cherry tree, which he said was worth £10 a year to him. Its fruit was of a sort that had no value to sell, but the birds were so fond of it that while a cherry hung upon that tree, they did not attempt to rob the rest. No. 8 rented between thirty and forty acres at about £2 an acre, half of it pasture and half arable; also he had two acres of fruit trees, and dealt in stock. He said that some of his land was very poor, but he added cheerfully, 'not so bad, after all, if it is well looked after.' This farmer impressed me as being a most intelligent man.

The conclusion to which I have come about the Bewdley small-holdings, whereof those described above may be taken as a fair sample, is, that notwithstanding the high rent, and in some cases the distance from a railway or market, none of their occupiers failed to make a living. Doubtless they are helped by the sale of fruit, of which all of them grow more or less; but, on the other hand, much of the soil is of indifferent quality, and in the main they rely upon the common products of the farm. Here, as elsewhere, the prevalence of the system seems to produce a class of sturdy and independent men, and to check the migration of the people from the land that bred them. It should be noticed that both Mr. Money-Kyrle and Mr. G. F. Eyre, clergymen respectively of the parishes of Bewdley and Far Forest, are deeply interested in the success of this movement, which they lose no opportunity of forwarding by every means in their power. These two gentlemen are, it is true, men of exceptional ability and force, but such qualities are not scarce among the clergy of the Church of England. I suggest that wherever the local circumstances are favourable, their example is one that should be followed.

Before I leave the subject of the Bewdley Small-Holdings I may state that in February 1902 I was very pleased to receive the following letter from Mr. E. P. Leacock, honorary secretary to the Bewdley Horticultural Society and secretary to the Bewdley Agricultural Supply Association, Limited, who says:—

I enclose you a report as to the fruit-drying experiments. I feel sure that it will give you very great pleasure to know that your visit has been of so much use to this district. We have already formed two co-operative societies, one here and one at Far

Forest. We also have several in course of formation. In addition to this we are working out a scheme for a society to assist in increasing the number of small-holdings. Co-operation seems to me to be the way to get people back to the land by giving them an interest in its products.

The newspaper cutting enclosed begins :—

When the Bewdley District Horticultural Society in May last invited Mr. Haggard to visit that section of the county, they did not contemplate that their action would lead to the commencement of an agricultural co-operative movement in Worcestershire. Such, however, has been the case. Mr. Rider Haggard's article called the attention of the Agricultural Organisation Society to the district, and their energetic vice-president, Mr. W. L. Charleton, put himself in communication with the Rev. G. F. Eyre, vicar of Far Forest. The idea of the introduction of co-operation amongst the small-holders in his parish, commended itself to Mr. Eyre, and he at once set to work to organise a society. The Rector of Bewdley also took up the idea, and, aided by a number of those interested in agriculture and horticulture, entered upon the work of getting the co-operative association registered.

In the result, experiments were made that proved the possibility of utilising the new 'Jones' system of hop-drying as a means of desiccating fruit and vegetables. This has now been done with complete success, thereby opening up a new agricultural industry. Mr. W. L. Charleton, in publicly thanking Messrs. Jones for allowing the tests to be made, said that the demand for dried vegetables was increasing all over the country. Both the Admiralty and the War Office had stated that they would be pleased to purchase English dried vegetables, but they bought £140,000 worth every year from Germany because they did not know where else to find them. He was satisfied that the system they had tried would be successful if undertaken on a commercial basis, and might be worked co-operatively by small associations of fruit farmers.

Mr. Brooke-Hunt, who represented the Board of Agriculture upon the occasion of the trial, said ' that there was not the slightest doubt that if means of drying vegetables could be invented, those grown by allotment holders and others might be treated with very profitable results. The process they had seen had great possibilities before it, and was particularly adapted to the purposes of agricultural co-operation, as it was doubtful if a machine would ever be designed that was sufficiently cheap to be owned by individual growers.' He suggested the establishment of co-operative drying-plants for the use of villagers and allotment holders, and promised to report upon the process to the Board of Agriculture.

Thus the matter stood in February 1902, but I believe I am right in saying that those concerned consider the success of the system to be assured. In this event the results of the experiment must be held to be very satisfactory, and may prove of a far-reaching character. Dried fruit and vegetables are articles in great demand, and there seems no reason why England should not supply her own instead of procuring them from Germany.

In March 1902 I received a second letter from Mr. E. P. Leacock, which I print as it stands, believing that it may be of interest to my readers. It says:—

Referring to your kind letter, in which you were so good as to express the pleasure which you felt in the results which had followed your visit to Bewdley last spring, and asking me to let you know of any further developments which took place, I now send you a newspaper report of a meeting which was held here on the 17th inst. You will note that we are largely depending on the A.O.S. for advice and support. Mr. Charleton was down, and, as usual, was of the greatest help; indeed, without the Society I do not think it would have been possible for us to have profited by your kind advice, and to have started the two associations at Far Forest and at Bewdley.

Following in their train we are now arranging for another society in the Forest, which is to run a small dairy farm, with a sterilising plant for milk, cream, and fruit, and also a poultry-breeding branch in connection with it. This we have placed under the management of a young lady, who has been trained at the 'Lady Warwick Hostel,' Reading, and we propose to use it principally for the instruction of the small-holders and of other persons who wish to study improved methods of dairying, treating milk, fruit-drying, poultry-keeping, &c., all of which will be done there. I trust that some day you may be again in the neighbourhood, and be able to look over these different societies, and see how far they fulfil your ideas as being of some use in effecting the solution of the problem which you have taken so very active a part in bringing under public notice.

Whilst in the Bewdley district I was kindly taken by Mr. Edward Smith, of The Heath, Wribbenhall, to whose opinions on education I may have occasion to refer later, to visit the farm of Mr. T. B. Potter, of Blackstone House, near Bewdley. Mr. Potter farmed 255 acres of rather light soil on gravel resting on Red sandstone, of which about half was tillage and the rest pasture. He said that he was ceasing to grow wheat, whereof the average return there was about three quarters to the acre, as he found it too expensive at the price for which the grain sold. He manured his land heavily, dressing it with 300 tons of well-rotted farmyard muck a year in addition to other stimulants. His cattle were Herefords, and he remarked that he found the heifers fatted quicker than the steers. They were fed scientifically, all food being weighed out to the beasts. One of his principal crops was eating-peas, for the Kidderminster and other markets. These peas, of which he had seventeen acres in 1901, were sown after wheat, for which the land had been well manured. When the green peas were fit to pull they were sold as they stood to merchants or middlemen, who picked them. As it is the custom for the purchaser to go over the crop but once, many immature pods are left which are subsequently mown by the farmer with the haulm and make a valuable and nutritious hay fodder. Generally after the peas are off, the land is sown with a catch crop of turnips, which in due course is fed to sheep.

Mr. Potter said that farming in the district was not in a flourishing condition, and that the soil, being light and sandy, was apt to scald. The average rents for light land were from 15s. to 23s. the acre, and for better quality land up to 30s. the acre. Such farms, however, would not include any waste or 'shin,' that is, poor, high-lying soil, of which the worst would not pay to work at all. There, however, it was the practice to take the good soil and a proportion of 'shin' together. The average size of farms in the district was from 100 to 200 acres, and he thought that those of their owners who depended upon the land were badly off. Farmers were scarcely living and the good old class was melting away, the general tendency being towards a contraction in the size of the holdings.

The state of the labour market was a very great drawback to the farmers, but personally he was not short of men, among whom one had been with him thirty, another seventeen, and another sixteen years. Still they were dissatisfied, as they saw the navvies earning higher wages at laying pipes or on the railways, and he was obliged to reason with them. Waggoners received 18s. a week, with cottage, garden, pigsty, and manure. He thought that every farmer should try to offer his men some inducement to stay on the land, as they must have an interest in life beyond that of their daily work. Another difficulty was that on some farms there were no cottages, so that the men employed there had to walk out from the towns where they lived, perhaps a distance of two miles.

In the course of this conversation Mr. Edward Smith, who was present, and who has a large business in one of the neighbouring cities, remarked that in their establishment they could get the pick of the country lads to do work that was more or less mechanical, at a wage of from 13s. to 15s. the week, rising ultimately to 30s. or £2 the week. Although he deplored the fact, under these circumstances he did not believe that they would return to live upon the land. Mr. Potter thought, however, that in this district things would ultimately right themselves in some way at present unforeseen.

There can be little doubt that the industry which is most prosperous in Worcestershire to-day, and especially in the Valley of the Teme and its tributaries, is that of hop growing. Indeed, the same may be said of Herefordshire, where I had the pleasure of meeting a gentleman who is reported to have realised a considerable fortune, and to have purchased an estate out of the profits earned by him in this industry. Why the gains should be so large in these counties when growers of the same crop find it very difficult to make both ends meet in Kent, is at first sight not easy to determine. There are, however, reasons which go far towards explaining the difference. To begin with, good hop lands can be hired at from £1 to 30s. in Worcestershire, whereas in Kent they would command about £3 the acre. But in hop growing it must be remembered that the sum payable as rent is comparatively of small account. Further, the system of cultivation is much cheaper; the difference amounting to at least £10 the acre in favour of the West Midland counties, which is accounted for, at any rate to some extent, by the substitution of horse for manual labour in the tillage of the planted land, and the greater abundance of casual hands in the summer months, drawn largely from the cities of the Black Country. Lastly, while the best Kent lands are said to be somewhat stale, those in the West, especially such of them as lie on the Old Red sandstone, are still fresh and perhaps better suited to the needs of the hop plant than any others in England. Another point in favour of the Hereford or Worcester grower is that in the great majority of instances he deals direct with the merchant and the brewer, thus keeping the factor's commission in his own pocket.

These general statements are confirmed in a very striking manner by an elaborate series of figures, which I believe to be quite accurate, that have been kindly furnished to me by one of the leading experts on hop culture in Western England. According to these tables between the years 1878 and 1900 the hop acreage of the kingdom has sunk from 71,789 acres to 51,308 acres. In Kent the loss is 32 per cent., in Sussex 56 per cent., in Hants 30 per cent., in Surrey 43 per cent., and elsewhere 34 per cent. Hereford and Worcester alone show increases, the first of 22 per cent., and the second of no less than 60 per cent., which seems to suggest that in these counties only is hop growing found to be a really profitable pursuit. That it ought to be remunerative everywhere is proved by the fact that while the beer brewed in the United Kingdom increased from twenty-seven million and odd barrels in 1881, to thirty-six million and odd barrels in 1900, the imports of foreign hops decreased from an average of 214,250 cwt. between 1877 and 1886 to an average of 196,754 cwt. between 1897 and 1900.

In the course of my stay in these Western Midlands I had the great advantage of inspecting the accounts, carefully kept over a number of years, of a very large grower of hops. On this estate, which is managed with much care and intelligence, the rent, tithes, and rates were put at £6 10s. per acre, while the cultivation, horse labour, and manure stood at £26 16s. per acre. Now comes the amazing part of the statement. The average profits of the previous ten or twelve years, after deducting every charge and providing for every expense, amounted to something over £30 an acre net. Until I had seen these incontestable figures, I confess I would not have believed that anything which the land could grow in England, was capable of producing so splendid a return. Indeed, he who ventured to tell farmers in the Eastern Counties that it was possible to net £9,000 a year clear profit over a long average of seasons from the produce of 300 acres, or £3,000 a year from the produce of 100 acres, would probably find his information received with incredulity, secret or expressed. The facts, however, are as I have stated them, nor in this instance does there seem to be any possibility of error or miscalculation. I believe also, although for this I have but a general authority, that similar profits are earned by sundry other growers, some of whom, indeed, are known to have accumulated fortunes.

I should add that on the farm of which I have spoken, the average crop over a period of eight years preceding my visit was 16 cwt. 2 qrs. 5 lbs. of hops per acre, and the average cost of production £3 8*s*. 9*d*. per cwt. Still it must be clearly understood that even in Hereford and Worcester, hops, like fruit, to be profitable require the best of everything and the most skilful management. Moreover, he will do most with them who farms his own land and has an ample kiln accommodation constructed on scientific principles. This not many tenant farmers possess, since, even if they can afford to do so, few landlords are prepared to put capital into the building of a number of expensive kilns for which the next tenant of the farm may declare that he has no use.

Of the agricultural fortunes of the various counties I visited, after I left them, I have of course no personal knowledge. It would seem, however, that the season of 1901 was not favourable to the English hop growers, although perhaps more so than 1902 has unfortunately proved to be. Thus in the 'Pall Mall Gazette' of September 26, 1901, was published a paragraph stating that a representative of that paper had interviewed a large hop grower, who pronounced it to be ' one of the worst years for hop cultivators ever known, hops which in 1900 fetched from £4 to £6 10*s*. the cwt. being only saleable at from £2 2*s*. to £3 the cwt.' According to this authority the National Association of English Hop Growers had issued a circular inviting their members to refuse to sell until remunerative offers were made, but the factors declared that they could see no prospect of a change for the better. Many of the farmers, moreover, could not wait ' because they have obtained advances from factors in order to pay their pickers, and must sell their produce as soon as possible. Altogether,' the report goes on, ' the outlook is considered most disheartening, and following a bad season will cause many either to relinquish their holdings or decrease their hop acreage next year.'

I imagine that this summary refers rather to Kent than to Hereford and Worcester, although in those counties I have

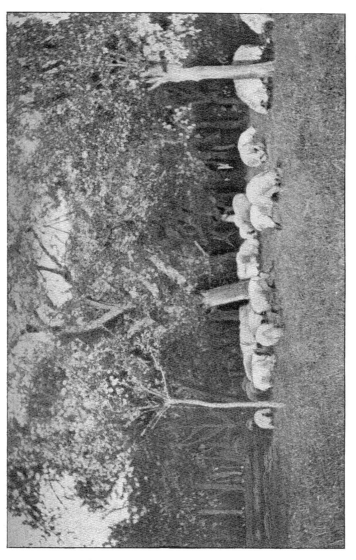

AN EVESHAM ORCHARD

read that there were last autumn grave differences of opinion
between growers and buyers as to the value of the produce
offered. The worst feature, perhaps, of the cultivation of
hops is the uncertainty of the price which the crop will ultimately command. It would be interesting to know whether
my informant realised his average profit of £30 an acre in
the season of 1901.

In the course of these agricultural wanderings I visited
various fine fruit farms, but none of them, I think, impressed itself quite so deeply on my mind as that of Mr.
Montagu Taylor, who owns and cultivates an estate at
Shelsley Walsh, in the Valley of the Teme. To begin with,
the situation of the place is one of the loveliest imaginable
—a tongue of land running up into the hill-side and looking
across the fertile meadows of the vale to Woodbury Hill and
the slopes of the opposing ridge. The house also, which, as
I understood, was for generations the home of the ancient
family of Walsh, is old, charming, and on one face, half-
timbered with black oak, while almost in the garden stands
the little Church of St. Andrew, the only one in England, I
believe, which, like St. Peter's in Rome, is built of Traver-
tine limestone. In this church the rood beam is exquisitely
carved, a very rare feature, I am told.

In all, Mr. Taylor, whom his neighbours described as ' one
of the best farmers in England,' cultivated about 500 acres, of
which fifty were under hops, twenty-five under plums, apples,
and bush-fruit, and forty under grass-fruit—that is, trees
grown upon pasture land. Quite near to the house, situated
on a sunny slope such as all fruit loves, stood fifteen acres of
the best cherry trees that I ever saw. The lower part of this
orchard is old and showed signs of decay, the trees having
been set some seventy years ago by Mr. Smith, a former
tenant of Shelsley Walsh, whose family farmed this place
for over two centuries. The larger portion, however, was
planted by Mr. Taylor himself twenty-five years ago, and is
therefore approaching its prime. He attributed its remarkable healthiness and vigour to the fact that the fruit-bearing

buds were set upon wild cherry stocks collected from the
woods, where the birds sow them, and to the suitability of
the soil and aspect.  Also, although heifers are now allowed
to graze upon the grass beneath the trees, the orchard has
been always carefully protected from damage by horses and
horned stock.  These cherries gave promise of a heavy crop
of fruit when I saw them, and, as I understood, bring in an
average return of about £30 the acre.

Passing through the garden, in which stands the largest
known specimen of the Weeping Pine that is to be found in
Europe, which was brought by some members of the Walsh
family from the Himalayas and planted here about two
hundred and fifty years ago, we came to the cultivated fruit
land, of which I can only say that I know no better.  The
apples—Lord Suffield, Devonshire Quarrenden, Worcester
Permain, Gladstone, Lord Derby, Grosvenor, and others—
are half-standards of various ages, but nearly all in bearing.
The system of pruning practised here was particularly
worthy of note, the central growths of the trees being cut
away to allow the outer boughs, which take the shape of a
tulip, to receive a maximum of sun and air.  This principle
is followed also in the case of bush-fruit and nuts, so that
each individual apple, plum, or berry comes to full size and
perfection.  How different is the case in most counties!
In Norfolk, for instance—and I may add in Devonshire—
the ordinary farm orchard is stocked as a rule with faggot-
headed trees pruned only by the wind.  Even the dead wood
is left uncut; yet it is common to hear farmers complain of
the quality of their fruit, and that it will not pay to grow.
The curse of the agricultural mind is that it will take no
account of little things, an attitude which, as I suppose, is
the heritage of high prices and of generations of corn-
growing.

On Mr. Taylor's farm, between the long lines of trees in
each square of plums and apples, stood the bush-fruits —
gooseberries, currants black and red, and raspberries—so
arranged that it remained easy to shallow-dig and hoe the

land. All of them looked most thriving, and gave promise of a great crop. The hoeing was done by piecework at an average price of 10s. an acre; the total cost of manure and labour for the fruit section of the farm, amounting, I understood, to £15 the acre per annum.

Of labour Mr. Taylor, who draws his pickers from the Black Country, said that he had as much as he wanted, perhaps because his farm is situated ten miles from a railway station. Another great grower, however, some of whose plantations I saw, told a different story. He said that he was obliged to a large extent to depend upon tramps and roadsters, who 'come out like flies in the hot weather,' and that were it not for this low class of men, he could not get through with his work. In this part of Worcestershire, speaking generally, if the cottages are first class and the wages good, there still remains a sufficiency of men who are willing to work upon the land.

I asked Mr. Taylor what such plantations as his would let for, supposing them to be thrown upon the market. To my astonishment he answered he did not think that an incoming tenant would bid more than £2 an acre, and that within ten years the place would be a worthless wilderness. I quote this opinion because it seems to me to touch the weak point of fruit farming in a district where the industry is not general, and where few cultivators have the knowledge, energy, and patience necessary to its pursuit. In such cases it may well happen that if a man dies who has spent his life in rearing up beautiful orchards which bring him a return of £20 or £30 an acre, no one will be found willing to pay a reasonable price for the inheritance of his skill and labour, with the result that all may soon be wasted. The good fruit farmer is in his way something of an artist, and, as we know, artistic gifts are always more or less personal to their possessor. In a district like that of Evesham, on the other hand, where many understand the business and are eager to take a profitable holding, such difficulties are not likely to arise.

While driving at a distance of about five miles from Mr. Taylor's farm, I caught sight of a pear tree so gigantic that I climbed the fence to measure its bole with a foot-rule which I carried. At a height of three feet from the ground I made the circumference to be no less than seventeen feet. I imagine that this must be the largest pear tree in England ; at least, I never heard of one so big. The lower boughs having been lopped because they overshadowed the road, its appearance is that of a great poplar, and its height, I was informed, makes the gathering of the fruit impossible. Unfortunately the photograph which we took of this tree was lost in the post, with others of objects and places of interest in the same district, so it cannot be reproduced in this book.

In 1892 Parliament passed a Small-Holdings Act, often, I believe, referred to as the Jesse Collings Act, which aimed at the creation of a number of small, cultivating owners and the wider distribution of land among the people. Under the provisions of this measure county Councils may acquire land which they can either let or resell in lots of not less than one acre and not more than fifty acres, to persons who desire to cultivate them. The purchaser of such a holding must pay down one-fifth of the cost in cash, and the balance in half-yearly instalments extending over a period of not more than fifty years. The Council has power, moreover, to leave one-fourth of the purchase money uncollected and secured as a perpetual rent-charge upon the holding. It may also advance money to the extent of four-fifths of the purchase price to sitting tenants who desire to acquire the holdings which they have rented from a landlord. It is provided further that every holding thus purchased must be cultivated by the holder, who has no power to sub-let.

This Act, so full of possibilities, is generally regarded as an utter failure, since few people even know of its existence, and, so far as I am aware, but a single county Council, that of Worcestershire—perhaps one of the best and most pro-

gressive in England—has taken advantage of its provisions
to any extent worthy of notice. This body, chiefly, I am
informed, upon the representations of Mr. Bigwood and
Mr. Frank Smith, the honorary secretary of the Rural
Labourers' League, purchased in or about the year 1895, at
a cost of £4,900, a farm of 140 acres, situated at Catshill,
in the county of Worcester, and about eleven miles from
Birmingham, which was divided up into thirty-two small-
holdings, ranging in size from two and a half to eight acres.

At Catshill there had for many years existed a colony
of people called 'Nailers.' These men, until the advent
of machinery destroyed their trade, used to earn a living
by the manufacture of nails in little sheds, many of which
can still be seen attached to their cottages. On the failure
of their business they were reduced to great poverty, and
forced to exist as best they could. Thus it came about
that when the plots of land were offered the Nailers took up
every one of them very eagerly, with the result that to-day,
instead of forging iron, they are growing strawberries for the
Birmingham market. Now for the issue of the enterprise
when I studied it in 1901, that is, after six years of trial.
It is with real pleasure that I am able to say that at this
date every instalment which was due had been paid up. In
other words, the small-holders—most of whom began with
little or nothing—have amply justified the confidence reposed
in them by the Council, and so far, at any rate, have proved
the experiment to be a triumphant success. With the
generosity and foresight that distinguish it, the Worcester
County Council, by a liberal interpretation of that section
of the Small-Holdings Act which refers to the erection of
buildings, has consented to advance 75 per cent. of the
cost of construction of dwelling-houses upon the several
plots. As a consequence of this policy, when I saw them
there were built upon lots Nos. 4, 6, 7, 21, 25, and
32 excellent houses of an average value of about £300,
while £118 had been advanced to the holder of Lot 1 to
enable him to commence a similar dwelling.

This man, Mr. Watt, was one of the first whom we interviewed. We found him working on his holding of soil that was somewhat light and stony, but fairly suited to the purposes of market gardening. These six and a quarter acres were, when necessary, ploughed by a farmer at a charge of 12s. the acre, but all other work on them was done by the owner without assistance. The land was planted with rye grass, potatoes, and strawberries. I asked Mr. Watt if he was satisfied with his present position. He replied that in past days he had been glad to earn 12s. a week, walking eight miles a day to get it, whereas now, by paying a rent of £2 an acre for his land, he was making a better living than he did as a labourer, and at the same time acquiring the freehold. He said he believed that if a thousand acres were to be offered on similar terms they would all oe taken up in that district, as the demand for land was large and active. His only complaints were that there is a good deal of competition in the strawberry trade, and of his distance from the Birmingham market, to reach which he was obliged to take his produce eleven miles in his father's cart. His method of avoiding the charges of the middleman was to stand on the market and sell his goods in person. Mr. Watt expected shortly to begin to build a house upon his land.

Considerations of space only allow me to allude to one more of these holdings. I take that of Mr. Banner (No. 21), who occupied three acres two roods, purchased at £132 14s. 10d., repayable as to the balance by equal half-yearly instalments of interest and capital combined of £2 13s. 5d., over a term of forty years, plus a tithe of 15s. 4d., £26 10s. 11d. having been paid down by the owner on completion of the contract. In addition, Mr. Banner had received an advance of £225 towards the cost of the dwelling and outbuildings which he has built upon his land. With this and other houses of the same stamp I have but one fault to find, that the wells are sunk far too close to the back door and to the sink drain. Unless great precautions are taken sickness will certainly result from this oversight. Otherwise these dwellings are excellent, commodious, and even ornamental.

Mr. Banner, who with his family had suffered severe illness from occupying his house before it was dry, joined his brother, another small holder, in cultivating their land, for which purpose each of them kept a horse. His crops were of the usual market-garden character, and he disposed of them by hawking, bringing back from Birmingham as a return load manure to fertilise his holding.

Such are the Catshill small holdings. To conclude that similar freeholds purchased with moneys advanced by county Councils would succeed in every district may be too optimistic, since it must be remembered that here was an energetic population reduced by circumstances to poverty and eager to discover some new way of earning a livelihood. Also the market of Birmingham lies at a reasonable distance. Further, I was told on good authority—although the view is not my own—that an ordinary county would not produce a sufficient number of men able and willing to make a success of such holdings, even if they were helped to acquire the freehold. I can only hope that this contention is not correct. The good results of this system and of the numerous allotments which have been provided in that district by the North Bromsgrove Rural District Council are easy of demonstration. Thus the reputation of the ' Nailers ' as a class, which used not to be of the best, has distinctly risen, and Mr. Frank Smith informed me that since this new departure in the matter of the provision of land, no able-bodied man has gone on to the rates.

Another place in Worcestershire where I spent several days as the guest of Mr. John Idiens, a member of the well-known fruit firm, and himself a large grower of fruit, is the beautiful and fertile valley of Evesham.

From quite early times Evesham has been a home of gardening. When Arthur Young passed that way in 1770 he found that between three and four hundred acres of land in its neighbourhood were cultivated as gardens. Now the area must cover thousands of acres—how many I do not know—and their number is still growing. All this increase has taken place since about 1853, and may for the most part be attributed to the invention and development of railways, which make it possible for produce to be placed upon the market in London and other great towns. The usual results of high culture on small-holdings are not wanting in this instance—general prosperity and an increase of population. Thus the census returns for 1901 of the Evesham Union show that the population has grown from 13,891 in 1841 to 17,629 in 1901, the increase over the return of 1891 being 1,560, and this in the face of the fact that a good many of the purely rural parishes show a decrease. The general prosperity cannot be doubted—it is borne witness to by the numbers of comfortable homesteads and the hundreds of plots of highly tended gardens.

Here, as elsewhere, the seeker after information hears, it is true, many grumbles at the competition and the low price of produce. It seems probable that this last evil might be met, or at any rate ameliorated by a better system of co-operation which would enable growers to lay their stuff into shops of their own, and thus save some of the profits of the middleman, or in other ways to regulate distribution. When I was at Evesham spring cabbages were selling at 9d. a 'pot' of two and a half dozen, whereas householders know well that the town greengrocer charges them 1½d. or 2d. for a single cabbage, which represents, at the lower figure, a difference of about 400 per cent. between the sum received by the producer and the sum received by the ultimate retailer. That this thing is not as it should be is obvious.

Another misfortune from which the district suffers is the present prevalence of asparagus blight, probably because the land is growing sick of asparagus, which used to be a great mainstay. Still personally I am convinced, and have the highest authority for saying, that, on the whole, the fruit and vegetable cultivators of Evesham and its neighbourhood are doing well. Indeed, as in the case of Guernsey and Jersey, with which it may be compared, it is by no means uncommon to meet men there who, beginning with nothing, have realised considerable fortunes out of the produce of the soil.

The crop of 1900, to take an example, was an exceedingly good one, and quite 50 per cent. of the total amount of fruit sold to jam makers, is said to have been bought by the Government to be consumed by our soldiers in South Africa. More trees and bushes are being planted every year, and it is indeed a pleasure to see land that some five seasons since was not worth 10s. an acre for agricultural purposes, now returning I know not how much from currants and other small fruit, and increasing annually in capital value as the plums and apples get their growth.

Wickhamford Manor, where we were the guests of Mr. John Idiens, of the firm of John Idiens & Sons, is one of those beautiful old houses for which Worcestershire and the neighbouring counties are famous, half-timbered in black oak, and standing upon the edge of a moat of clear water, in which on sunny days it is reflected as in a glass. The place is historical also, for in the little church which almost joins the house was buried, in the year 1697, a certain Penelope Washington, who married one of the Sandys family. On the gravestone of this Penelope, if I remember right, are cut her arms, which contain stripes and three five-pointed stars, from which arms, I was informed, is supposed to originate the world-famous banner of the United States of America, whose great general, Washington, is said to have descended from this family. In that church also are very beautiful monuments to two of the Sandys family—father and son—who died within a few days of each other in the Elizabethan period, and their wives.

Mr. Idiens gave me a great deal of interesting information, of which I quote a few items. He said that the rent of agricultural land had fallen heavily in that district, in some instances as much as 60 per cent., and mentioned a stiff clay farm which used to bring in £700 a year, and at that date was let for under £200. The ordinary agricultural

wage was 15s. a week and a cottage, but on the fruit farms
the men earned 16s. in winter and 18s. in the summer, the
average number employed being one hand to three acres of
ground. The local fruit output was enormous ; thus one
buyer took seven hundred tons of strawberries, and another
great firm dealt with three thousand tons of English fruit
during 1900, though I did not understand that all of this
came from the Evesham district.

Mr. Idiens spoke with enthusiasm of the Pershore plum,
of which this neighbourhood was the original home. The
parent tree was found growing in a wood at Pershore about
fifty or sixty years ago, and from it have sprung all the countless thousands in cultivation. Although it is a wild plum,
yellow and egg-shaped, both its quality and colour are good,
and there is no plum so suitable for jam making and bottling.
It can be picked in good hard condition for bottling, or partly
yellow for preserving, and it is so great a cropper that often
the fruit hangs on the trees ' like rigs of onions.' This plum
is now widely disseminated about England. Thus I myself
have found it planted in Essex ; but the Evesham growers
declare that it will not really thrive outside their district.
They have an interesting saying about it, that ' the good old
Pershore will buy the horse and cart while the fancy sorts are
paying for the harness.'

Average crops seem to be two tons to the acre of plums
and raspberries, and five to eight tons to the acre of gooseberries. Mr. Idiens said that the land in the fruit orchards
is never without a crop. Thus in the winter it can be planted
with winter cabbage. Then come radishes, lettuce, and peas,
with cucumbers and marrows between. Of course, to produce so much the soil must be heavily manured and with
strange substances. Thus leather dust from London—that
from the chamois-leather factories for preference—is a
favourite fertiliser for cabbage, while horse-parings are good
for all kinds of fruit trees, as are also Peruvian guano, nitrate
of soda, and shoddy from the cloth mills. He did not consider that the Evesham fruit output was overdone at present.

Mrs. Idiens gave me a receipt for preserving fruit in bottles which, to judge from the results as I tasted them, is well worthy of the notice of my readers. The fruit to be treated should be placed in wide-mouthed bottles that are filled up with water, corked, and wired so as to make them air-tight. The bottles must then be set in a copper or other vessel in cold water in such fashion that the necks stand above its level. The water must then be raised to a temperature of 160 degrees, after which it should be allowed to cool, with the bottles still standing in it. Treated thus the fruit will keep for any length of time and preserve its flavour so well that when cooked it can scarcely be distinguished from that which has been fresh gathered. Mr. Idiens—and there can be few greater authorities—considered that the three best apples grown in that part of England are Cox's Orange Pippin and Worcester Pearmain for eating purposes, and Warner's King for cooking. Wellington also, he said, is an excellent keeping cooker.

Before I describe various fruit farms which I visited in this district I will set down some general information that I gathered from sundry authorities in and about Evesham. Among other gentlemen I saw Mr. F. P. Webb, the well-known land agent in that town, with whom I had a long and interesting conversation. He told me that the great failure in the Evesham asparagus crop, owing to the blight of 1899, combined with the poor prices realised for all garden produce in 1900, had proved a heavy blow to the further development of the local fruit industry, and that unless lower rents were accepted by owners he expected that considerable difficulty would be experienced in letting out fresh lands for at least two years to come. Mr. Webb kindly furnished me with detailed schedules of certain farms which had been cut up into lots and leased to fruit growers during the previous twelve years. These are too long to print in full, but I give the summaries.

Farm No. 1, of 217 acres, of which 162 acres had been let in 1901 in lots for fruit and vegetable growing, the remainder being still devoted to ordinary agricultural purposes. In 1884 this farm was rented at £300. From that day forward various fields were taken from it, as shown in the schedule, a corresponding reduction in the rent of the farm being made as these lands were subtracted from its acreage. The rent in 1901 for all the land, agricultural and fruit-bearing, was £463 9s. 6d. The cost of making good roads to the various fruit and vegetable lots, with necessary gates, inclusive of alterations to farmhouse and buildings to make them suitable to the requirements of the present tenant, was at least £2,000. In addition four new cottages had been erected for various tenants at a cost of £800, which at present rentals paid about 3 per cent. net. Also the smallholders, owing to the bad prices of 1900, had all received an allowance of 10 per cent. on their rentals. It will be seen, therefore, that the gross increase of rent of £163 9s. 6d., in fact, only meant a very small actual gain to the owner of the land.

Farm No. 2, of 78 acres, was let for £180 in 1890, and having been cut up into lots brought in £249 in 1901. Being close to a station and very early land, this farm is exceptionally suitable to gardening purposes. The cost of road-making, alteration of buildings, &c., had been a little over £800.

Farm No. 3, of unusually good land close to a village, used to be let as a farm at £200. The best rent it had ever realised for gardening purposes was £245 ; but in 1901, owing to a number of the lots being unoccupied, it only brought in £199. In his note upon it Mr. Webb said: 'You will notice the number of void lots. This is entirely owing to the failure of the asparagus crop from blight.' He feared that much more of this land would be given up at the following Michaelmas, as there was great difficulty in collecting the rents of the lots that were left. The whole was subject to an allowance of 10 per cent., owing to failure of crops, &c.

If the above can be taken as fair samples, as I doubt

not is the case, it may be argued that, whatever profit fruit farming has brought to the small-holder and the district, it has at present added but little to the income of the land-owners. If an increase in population is any test, however, the benefit of the system to the neighbourhood cannot be questioned, since the parishes in the Evesham Union, where market gardening is practised, have most of them added to their numbers. Thus Hinton-on-the-Green numbered 175 in 1891, and in 1901 209; Bradley, 574 in 1891, in 1901 775; Great and Little Hampton, 742 in 1891, 977 in 1901; All Saints, Evesham, 1,917 in 1891, 2,642 in 1901; St. Lawrence, 2,547 in 1891, 2,711 in 1901; St. Peter's, Bengeworth, 1,372 in 1891, 1,748 in 1901.

Mr. Jones, the well-known Evesham fruit expert, whom I saw, is, I believe I am right in saying, a gentleman who during the last forty-five years has worked his way up from small beginnings. Indeed, he told me that he began work at a wage of 4d. a day. He said that the district was undoubtedly prosperous, but 'ever such a little bit of a depression made the growers complain.' They were apt to think that a fortune was to be made at once, but, as in every other business, this took time. He thought that, owing to the opening up of the country by the railways, the demand for their produce was increasing, and that cultivators had a better chance of doing well than ever was the case before. The charges of the middleman were very oppressive to the small grower, and sometimes made it almost impossible for him to live. Personally he paid nothing for commission, as all his goods were sent direct to shops in towns. In his day, Mr. Jones said, he had sold stuff in pennyworths and in £1,000 lots, and had got rid of it all, with a great deal more belonging to others as well, without the help of middlemen.

The present depression would doubtless cause a check, but this, he thought, would right itself in another year or so. The market for apples and pears was splendid, and it was only lately that they had come to appreciate the value of their soil, both as regards aspect and protection from the east. Also the average price of fruit during the last ten years was higher than it had ever been before. Mr. Jones added that he introduced tomato-growing for market purposes into Evesham in 1887, and had grown them ever since with but one failure. I was informed in the neighbourhood that there is no one there whose opinion is so valuable in all matters connected with fruit culture, or who understood better how to lay out an orchard so as to secure the best possible results from the local conditions of soil and exposure. The apples which he recommended as the very best to grow were Cox's Orange Pippin, Worcester Pearmain, Devonshire Quarrenden, Lord Grosvenor, Warner's King, Bramley's Seedling, Eclingville Seedling, and Stirling Castle.

Another gentleman, who, I suppose, knows as much about the fruit trade as anyone in the Evesham district, also obliged me with his views, of which the following is a summary. He said that fruit, &c., is sent from the Vale of Evesham to all parts of the United Kingdom, the district being well supplied with railway communications. Both the Midland and Great Western lines run special produce trains from May till the end of September. In the year 1900 about 20,000 tons of fruit and vegetables were sent away from the two Evesham stations, in addition to large quantities collected at all the small railway stations within a radius of ten miles of Evesham. Upon this point my informant said that the special cheap rates granted for the carriage of fruit and vegetables under the new Great Western scale had proved of great benefit, and that if this mileage scale was adopted by all railways it would be an enormous boon to English fruit growers. Already the special cheap rates had enabled the Evesham producer to despatch to the large towns, in competition with the foreigner, great quantities of fruit which he believed otherwise would have been unsaleable, especially in seasons of glut. He considered that this matter was most important to the industry, and that the Great Western Railway Company, by setting the example of introducing such a scale, had really helped fruit growers. He trusted that other companies would follow suit before long, and thought that it only needed combination on the part of those interested in the various districts to induce them to do so.

When the markets and shops were supplied the surplus Evesham fruits were, he said, sold direct to the jam makers in every part of the United Kingdom, a good supply of Pershore plums being sent yearly even to the preserving houses in the Kentish towns, which, to those unacquainted with the mysteries of the trade, sounds rather like despatching coals to Newcastle. Three years previously, a single factory had made 700 tons of black-currant jam, and in the clock tower of this establishment alone could be stored no fewer than 200,000 pots. Also there were other large factories, such as that of Messrs. Liptons, capable of dealing with as much as 4,000 tons of fruit each during a single season. In the year 1900 large importations of Dutch strawberries and raspberries, of which it is estimated that 3,000 tons were annually shipped to London alone, were kept out of this country because of the unsatisfactory condition of the cargoes received in the year 1899. Owing to the cancelling of these foreign orders in 1900 the demand for English strawberries far exceeded the supply, with the result that the price of this fruit advanced to £28 per ton.

This authority said that there was no reason whatever to prevent England from supplying all the soft fruit required by the jam makers. By way of example of his statement he quoted the case of Mr. William Porter, of Stoke Edith, near Hereford, who a few years ago was manager to Mr. Riley, of Putley Court, whose farm, it will be remembered, has already been described in this book. Mr. Porter rented ordinary farmland between Ledbury and Hereford for strawberry growing only, and in 1901 had nearly 200 acres of fine strawberries in a splendid state of cultivation. His crops in 1899 and 1900 were excellent, and, indeed, could not be beaten in England. Almost all his produce was

purchased by a single firm. It might be asked, how did
he manage for labour? The answer was simple. If 500
hands were required for picking, he sent his labour agents
into the thickly populated districts, where the demand was
readily met. When the hands arrived he erected bell-shaped
tents in the fields, each of which accommodated six or seven
persons, and was provided with a portable wooden floor and
out-places for boiling water and cooking.

The strawberries were all 'plugged,' that is, cleaned from
the stalks, on the farm, packed into small tubs with a capacity
of about forty pounds, and sent straight by train to the factory,
where they arrived perfectly fresh. In Evesham Vale itself, he
said, there were four local factories, of which that of Messrs.
Beach & Sons, of Toddington, was the largest, that between
them dealt with about 3,000 tons of fruit each season. Most
of the fruits sent to the factories were made into jam at once,
but any surplus, after partial boiling, was laid down into
three-gallon jars or freshly emptied wine casks and hermetically sealed, to be used as required. When treated thus
the fruit would, if necessary, keep fresh for two years. Large
quantities of small sour apples were also purchased by the
jam makers for the manufacture of jelly and of cheap jams,
which were in great demand among the working classes.

The Dutch Government, recognising the importance of
keeping their people on the land and the danger of losing
the English markets owing to the increased acreage of fruit
grown in this country, had, he said, decided some four years
before to give a bounty of about £2 a ton on all fruit kept in
their own country and manufactured into jam, or put down,
partly boiled, into hermetically sealed casks. More fruit also
was being dealt with in France for manufacturing purposes,
that is, by drying or crystallising.

This gentleman added that it was common to read letters
and suggestions from individuals asking why English fruit
growers did not wake up and go in for fruit drying. His
answer was that the great bulk of dried fruit sent into this
country was grown in the South of France, Bosnia, and the

WICKHAMFORD MANOR

*Page 345*

Australian colonies, places where they have the advantage of hot sun, which enables them to dry out the fruit on wooden trays in the open. Some eight or nine years ago machinery of this kind was tried on Lord Sudeley's fruit farm at Toddington under the superintendence of Messrs. Beach & Sons. It was then found that the English fruit, and especially the plum, retained 15 to 20 per cent. more moisture than fruit grown in the foreign countries which have been named; also that the utmost quantity that could be dried in twenty-four hours in one machine was 10 cwt., and that it took 7 lb. of good apples to produce 1 lb. of dried fruit. Further, he might point out that so long as we have our present fruit factories and a growing population who will consume fruit in an ever-increasing degree it would not pay to risk capital in such a very doubtful enterprise.

By way of comment upon this piece of evidence I ask the reader to turn back and consider what has been written about the new fruit-drying experiments at Bewdley. At the date of my interviews with him my informant of course did not know of this new invention, which may very possibly answer some of his objections in a satisfactory way. With regard to others of them I may remark that what will not pay in certain conditions in some districts, may pay in different conditions in other districts. Thus an enterprise which large growers in Evesham would not think profitable may possibly produce good returns to the little holders at Bewdley. In truth the market is large enough to consume every kind of product connected with fruit if only means can be found of manufacturing it at a profit, and of as good quality as that which is turned out abroad.

This gentleman said, moreover, he had seen it alleged that in some years hundreds of tons of apples were wasted, but, for his part, he did not believe that the statement would bear investigation. In this country there was always a good demand for the best sorts of large apples, while the sour small ones were saleable to jam makers, and all that were sweet and inferior could be crushed into cider, for which the market was increasing. But shortly before he had been in conversation with a small holder of land in Somersetshire who had ten acres of grass and two acres of orcharding, all cider fruit. This man from an average crop could make fifty hogsheads of cider, of sixty gallons to the hogshead, off the two acres. Now, if the selling price of cider were put at 6d. the gallon, and the cost of manufacture at 4s. per hogshead, he would be glad to know what better return a man could get from this common fruit, which certainly would not pay him so well if dried. Again, assuming all to be of a cooking class, only large, sound, good apples were suitable for drying, and, as he had said, such fruit was already in demand in the present market.

Speaking of the future of fruit growing in England, he was of opinion that there were at present sufficient gooseberries and plums planted to meet the requirements of the country for some years to come, but that there was still room for more black currants, raspberries, and strawberries. Indeed, the demand for this last fruit was continually on the increase, and it must be remembered that the plants only lasted five years. To succeed, the strawberry grower must reset on fresh ground after that period, which necessitated the taking up of a large acreage every year.

He believed that the market for good apples and pears in this country was unlimited. For apples alone we were paying to America and other countries £1,500,000 per annum, while thousand of acres of land in England, now almost derelict, could be utilised for orchards planted out on the Tasmanian principle. A help to such orchards would be the light implements invented by the Americans, which greatly facilitated their working and saved an enormous amount of manual labour. In Tasmania there were orchards that covered 200 acres of ground, and in America some of them were four times as large. The English climate was quite as suitable for apple growing as that of Tasmania or America, and taking into consideration

our measureless market, there was no reason why the cultivation should not be on a similar scale. It should be
remembered that pyramid apple trees, if well grown and
grafted on a Paradise stock, would commence to bear good
fruit in the second season after planting. He was glad to
say that in the Evesham district progress was being made
in the cultivation of this fruit, and there was no doubt that
the acreage under it would increase year by year. In this
matter he was speaking from practical experience, as one
who had tested the capabilities of the soil. Indeed, as an
experiment, he had planted apples on fifteen acres of land
which would not pay under corn, and was now arranging to
plant another thirty acres during the following autumn.

Since I visited the Evesham district, another gentleman,
who said that he had thirty years' experience in the fruit
market business, has written to me alleging that 'for years
past the jam houses have practically dictated their own
terms to English fruit growers.' This correspondent also
complained bitterly of the deceptive labelling of jams as
'made of best selected fruit,' whereas many of them are the
product of foreign fruit, which frequently arrived in bad
condition as deck cargo, and is soaked with rain or sea
water. He stated that on one day in 1901 he had seen no
less than ten tons of such fruit condemned and dumped into
a barge for removal. Much of it, however, escaped this
fate, and the sum of his argument was that jams manufactured from foreign fruit should be specified as such.

The first small-holder I visited at Evesham owned a
pretty and charming little house, different indeed from the
ordinary labourer's cottage, which I understood he had
built in the year 1889 out of profits made in the cultivation
of asparagus. Of this vegetable he said, however, that 'it
was no use now ; there is rust in it ; the land is sick. You
must start elsewhere ; it will never do in Evesham.' He
informed us that he bought his land at £80 the acre, but ' if
I wished to sell now I should want a lot of money.'

A good typical fruit-holding was that of Mr. Masters,

which I saw. Here the soil was a stony 'brash,' with a
stiff blue clay subsoil, upon which, curiously enough, the
almost universal Pershore plum did not flourish very well.
Fine plum trees, however, there were in abundance, planted
about twelve feet apart, with two lines of gooseberies, which
seemed to me rather crowded, between each row of them.
Under the trees were broad beans, lettuces, parsley, potatoes,
cabbages, and radishes, but of this last crop Mr. Masters
said the land was 'going sick.' The artificial manures that
he used, which had to be applied every year, were soot, fish
guano, and leather dust for cabbage, at the rate of about a
ton an acre. The lettuces were sown and planted out in
the orchard, and stood under the trees all the winter until
the spring, when they are cut and sold 'in pots' of from
three to four dozen. A pot of plums, by the way, seems to
contain 72 lb., of cherries 63 or 64 lb., of gooseberries 64 lb.,
and of radishes fourteen dozen bunches. The vegetables
that are grown in such gardens under the shade of closely
planted fruit trees must be early, and, for the most part, off
the ground before the leaf is full out upon the trees, otherwise they do not pay.

Mr. Masters still grew asparagus, but said that the local
stock was worn out and that new seed ought to be obtained.
In this respect Americans were most particular, always
selecting the seed from the best and strongest canes, and he
thought that perhaps their troubles in Evesham arose from
a lack of similar care. I think that the sort he grew was
called Palmetto, a giant, but not very prolific variety, imported from America. The practice seemed to be to sow
the seed in beds, and at one year old to plant out the roots
in single rows upon land that had been well sooted, but
not otherwise prepared. These rows were set 2 ft. 6 in.
apart, and would be ridged up the following year. Till this
was done the space between them was being utilised for the
growing of peas. Here we saw some asparagus that had
stood for twenty years and was unblighted, whereas other
beds which had been planted only five years were blighted

and would have to be dug up. I noted that in this orchard all the trees were grease-banded as a protection against the winter moth. This grease banding used to be done by smearing the material direct on to the tree, which, to judge from its rough and unhealthy appearance, appeared to injure the bark. Now that practice has been given up in most orchards, and the grease is spread on paper, which is fastened round the tree with string, at a height of about two feet above the ground.

Mr. Masters seemed to think highly of the Victoria plum, which he said was strong and a good bearer. Certainly the fruit on the trees of that variety in his orchard had set wonderfully well.

A fruit farm that struck me as particularly interesting was that held by Messrs. Idiens, and owned, I think—but of this I am not sure—by the Duke of Orleans, who has a fine place on the outskirts of Evesham. The soil of this farm, which covers thirty acres, strikes the observer as of an exceedingly unpromising nature, being of the stiffest and poorest clay, lying rather high—land that would scarcely be worth 7s. 6d. an acre for the growth of ordinary farm crops, at which rent, I believe, it was originally let. It is this circumstance which makes the results obtained by Messrs. Idiens during their first four or five years of tenancy—I do not think they had held it longer—so very remarkable.

Land, I should explain, which the tenant proposes to plant with permanent fruit trees is taken under the provisions of the Market Gardeners' Compensation Act of 1895, which, to the woe and grief of many such cultivators, has been held by the House of Lords not to be retrospective. The principal provision of this Act is to the effect that in the case of tenancies commencing after January 1896, where there is an agreement in writing that the ground is to be let or treated as a market garden, on the expiration of the said tenancy the tenant has a right to claim from the landlord compensation for the value of the trees planted by him as they stand, and for certain other improvements. This clause is of very great importance. Thus the rent of this holding of Messrs. Idiens is about £40 a year, but it is probable that if their tenancy should terminate, say twenty years hence, the value of the trees upon the thirty acres will amount to a large sum, perhaps thousands of pounds, which sum they would be entitled to recover from the landlord, or to receive by private agreement as tenant right from the incoming occupier. To take an example, I was told of a case where a man hired land some ten years before at 30s. an acre, and after he had held it for seven or eight years sold his tenant-right to another man for £80 an acre, that is, for a good deal more than the fee-simple value of the land.

After deep cultivation, I think with a steam plough, which cost about £10 an acre, such portions of this farm as were, when I saw it, already under fruit had been planted with plums, currant, and gooseberry bushes, (200 plums, and 1,000 currants or gooseberries, costing in all about £20 to the acre). The plums were set fifteen feet from row to row, and twelve feet from tree to tree. Two rows of black currants were planted between each row of plums, and one row of currants along the line of the plums in the spaces left between the trees, which, as these grow big, can, if necessary, be cut out. The black currant used was Lea's Prolific, which is supposed to have the power of resisting the fatal disease known as 'big bud,' and the plums, which are best planted with an eastern aspect and when one year old from the graft, were Early Orleans, Prolific, Czar, Monarque, King of the Damsons, Pershore, and Victoria, the last being one of the most excellent and vigorous known. Although the trees were quite young, their growth and condition were splendid; indeed I would not have believed that it was possible on such poor, cracking, cakey clay soil for slow growing trees like damsons to attain such dimensions in four years, or to bear such crops of fruit as I saw forming upon them. It must be remembered, however, that the cooler the bottom the better is the soil suited to the needs of the plum.

I noted in walking through the orchard that the variety known as Prolific makes a great deal of wood, whereas that called Czar did not make much wood but was loaded with fruit. The gooseberries used were Wynan's Industry and Keepsake. The custom is to prune them up well for the first two or three years, and to cut out the centres so as to let the light and sun into the heart of the bush. Most people who grow this fruit will be aware how rarely the gardener thinks it worth while to adopt such an obvious and commonsense method. But my experience of this class is that most of them have much to learn from business men who, not being paid a weekly wage, have their wits sharpened by the necessity of making a living from their gardens.

I saw also another holding of sixty acres, of which twenty-six were orchard and the rest grass, in the occupation of one of the Brothers Idiens, some of the orcharding being on grass land where sheep and fowls were allowed to run, to the great advantage of the ground. This farm had a charming house on it, recently built by the Duke of Orleans, on the cost of which the tenant paid interest at the rate of 5 per cent. Opposite to it was a holding of ten acres planted in the usual fashion. Its occupier was a gardener who used to earn but 15s. a week, and I mention the instance to show how men may rise by thrift and industry in the happy Vale of Evesham. Indeed, while driving back to the town I noticed on its outskirts a number of commodious and well-constructed villas which, I was told, had all been built by successful market-gardeners.

Another farm of a different class that I went over here was in the occupation of Mr. Savory, of Aldington Manor, quite close to Wickhamford, who had held it for many years—I think about twenty-five. This farm comprised 350 acres, of which thirty were under fruit, thirty under hops, eighty let in allotments at about 75s. the acre and averaging from one to three acres in size, the balance being half arable, half pasture. The soil was a splendid wheat land upon which the hops that were originally introduced by Mr. Savory twenty-five years before, throve to perfection. When we saw his plantation all hands were busily engaged in cutting out superfluous shoots and training the vines up the string, which, by the way, cost £24 a ton, and is used at the rate of a hundredweight per acre. Mr. Savory had a beautiful herd of pedigree Jerseys, about forty head in all, of which sixteen or seventeen were in milk. Each cow was expected to earn about £20 gross per annum. They were kept for ten or twelve years and then sold for £8 or £10, either fat or with their last calf. The butter from these cows was of a splendid quality, golden in colour and sweet to the taste. It was disposed of readily at 1s. 6d. per pound, carriage free.

Mr. Savory kindly took us to see some of the allotment holders. The first of these was Mr. Grant, whose land was beautifully cultivated, the peas being planted with six feet between the rows, having vegetable marrows set in the intervening space at distances of six feet from plant to plant. These marrows were protected from the cold spring wind by means of very simple and ingenious glass cones that are placed over them, and when the sun is hot either removed or tilted up a little, so that each plant has its own greenhouse, which helps it to early maturity. These excellent little shelters only cost £1 1s. a dozen, and ought, I think, to be more generally used. Mr. Grant said that in the past asparagus had been the making of the small man, but owing to blight the crop had deteriorated. He complained that now-a-days there was little gain in market-gardening. They used to make money, but the area under cultivation had increased so much that the competition killed the profit. The railway rates also were oppressive and the charges of the middlemen stiff—or so he declared.

Another holding that I saw of very similar character, rented at £4 the acre, was in a splendid state of cultivation, but report said that its owner did not make it pay. Mr. Mustoe, who in addition to other occupations, I think, kept a public-house near to Mr. Savory's farm, was a gentleman of very wide experience, and gave me some useful information. He said that market-gardening was doing better that season, and so was the asparagus crop, of which the best qualities were fetching a good price, although the average figure for 120 sticks was only 1s. 2d. Still, none of it was up to the old mark, and seven years before the crop had been twice as prolific. For instance, Badsey was built on asparagus, but that could not be done now. He thought that if market-gardening was much extended it would mean failure, and that owners were making a great mistake in cutting up more farms for this purpose; indeed, he was afraid that a good many men would throw up their holdings at the following Michaelmas. 'We have got to work hard for a little,' he said; 'in summer it means from three o'clock in the morning till eight at night.

He complained that the carriage to London was so much heavier than to other places, and that the Covent Garden charges of 6d. a bushel upon all fruit were higher than elsewhere. Also the proceeds varied so much. Thus not long before cabbage on the London market fell 1s. a pot in a single day, and beans from 3s. 6d. to 1s. 3d. also in one day. The farmers round about, he said, were very short of labour, especially on the hills, and the men were most independent. At Cirencester, recently, he had found the tenants borrowing hands from each other in order to get their ricks thrashed. 'It's a very bad thing to see all the people going into the towns,' he added. I remarked that a good many folk about Evesham seemed to be prosperous. He answered, 'Oh! yes; some of them are doing pretty well; it is the small men who do badly.'

It must be admitted that such evidence, of which I heard a good deal, is not altogether encouraging. Still I think that it ought to be discounted, since whenever prices happen to rule low the small-holder is apt to take a despondent view of the situation. On the whole, I believe that Evesham is prosperous, and likely to advance in prosperity, and incline to agree with Mr. Jones, whose views I have quoted, that, notwithstanding temporary checks, the fruit growers there have to-day a better chance of flourishing than ever they had before. Also I am sure that their industry is capable of almost indefinite expansion.

In the course of a debate on Mr. Lambert's Land Tenure Bill, which took place in the House of Commons during the month of May 1901, it was stated that the total annual import of fruit and vegetables into this country is of the value of £11,500,000. Some of this, of course, is paid for products which we cannot grow, such as oranges and bananas, and for apples which come in from Canada and Australasia at those seasons of the year when our own crop is not yet on the market. But why should not the rest, to the value, at a hazard, of five or six millions, be raised in this country, where there are tens of thousands of acres of land admirably suited to its production that now bring in little or nothing under corn and indifferent grass? To do this three things are wanted—enterprise, new ideas, and a moderate supply of capital. We send our sons to fruit farms in Florida and hot Australian valleys. Should we not do better to take up a patch of clay land with a suitable aspect, and grow apples, plums and black currants to satisfy the insatiable demand of the British millions? After visiting Evesham and studying its cultural methods, for my own part I have little doubt upon the point.

One of the most interesting estates that I visited in Worcestershire was that of the Earl of Coventry, at Croome Court, where, amongst other things, I saw his noted herd of Hereford cattle. Upon this property many improvements have been made within recent years. Thus, between 1869 and 1884, about 3,000 acres were drained, at a cost of £16,551, or, say, £5 10s. an acre. During the past thirty-two years also thirty-eight new cottages have been built, each of them containing three bedrooms, while additions and improvements have been made to many of the older cottages, and other dwellings have been purchased on various parts of the estate. The cottage rents here are low, varying from 1s. to 1s. 6d. a week, inclusive of a large garden. Of late years the allotments have been largely increased. When I visited Croome Court in 1901 they numbered 321, ranging from a quarter of an acre to one acre in size. Also there were forty-four small-holdings of from one to six acres, the majority of them in the neighbourhood of Pershore, which, for the most part, were occupied by working market-gardeners.

Labour, that is of men who could build or thatch a rick, cut or lay hedges, shear sheep, &c., Lord Coventry informed me, had always been scarce in that part, but within the last few years it had grown still scarcer, as the young able-bodied men were leaving for the towns, whither they were attracted by the higher wages and the seductions of city life. As the older hands died out, or became past work, it grew increasingly difficult to find young ones to take their places. There was a system of sick pay and old-age pensions in force for the benefit of those who are in the employ of Lord Coventry, under which labourers who were ill received half-pay after they had been laid up for a fortnight, and if permanently unfitted for work, at the expiration of twelve months were placed upon the pension list. Able-bodied men were paid 14s. a week during the winter months, and extra wages in the summer during hay and corn harvest. Also, whenever possible, opportunities were given to them to earn higher wages by piecework. Carters and stockmen received from 16s. to 17s. a week. At Christmas every cottager and his family were given presents of beef at the rate of 2 lb. and a 2 lb. loaf per head, a custom that has been in force upon this estate for upwards of a century. Also liberal contributions were made towards the coal clubs in the various parishes. During the previous thirty-two years a considerable sum had been spent in adapting the farm homesteads on this estate to modern requirements, and when I was there tanks, of which I saw one, were being constructed for the treatment of sheep suffering from scab and foot-rot. These, it was expected, would prove a great boon to tenants and others in the district.

A shire stallion was kept for the use of the tenants at a nominal fee. In 1900 the noted prize winner College Don was hired by Lord Coventry at a high fee, and in 1901 another prize winner, Curfew, had been hired by him at a still higher fee for the benefit of the tenants.

At an interview which I had with Lord Coventry and his agent, Mr. Hill, at Croome Court, before we set out to inspect the property, they told me that the average depreciation on arable land since the depression set in was about 30 per cent., and on pasture land about 10 per cent. The farming was mixed, with a proportion of fruit and market-gardening, and the demand for farms better than it had been a few years before, small holdings being in great request. Indeed, Mr. Hill said that these small holdings were fairly prosperous, and he thought that if there were many more of them they would be taken up at once. On most of such holdings there was some fruit, but landlords were not encouraged to plant orchards by the fact that many tenants did not take proper care of the trees. Lord Coventry remarked that one of the difficulties of the labour question was that people declined to inhabit the remoter cottages, whereas forty years ago they liked these solitary spots. Another was that farm work was looked down on, and it was common to hear it said of such and such a man that 'he is too good for a clodhopper.' The exodus had been going on progressively for the last ten or fifteen years, but Lord Coventry remarked that although he saw little light on the matter, he liked to hope that when the war was over many men would come back.

In a letter which he wrote to me, Lord Coventry summed up his views upon these subjects with much force and clearness. He said, 'The rural exodus I attribute to the low price of wheat, which has thrown so much good corn-growing land out of cultivation. The labourers, in consequence, were not employed regularly, especially in the winter season, so they migrated to the towns. The inadequate food supply of our country, if it is not dealt with shortly, will be our ruin, and it seems to me almost incredible that the nation has so little regard for its interest, and that it is impossible to move our statesmen to deal with the question. We ought to have a year's supply of breadstuffs in the country; without this the money expended upon national defence is wasted. I feel so strongly on this subject that I hope you will forgive me for thus expressing myself.' In another letter he added, 'I think the Chancellor of the Exchequer might have re-imposed a shilling duty upon wheat without hurting any-one. Until we in England are placed on even terms with the foreigner, agriculture will never flourish again.'

I must point out that these are the views of an agricul-turist and very large landowner of long and wide experience in the questions on which he speaks; they are therefore entitled to the earnest consideration of all thinking men

Mr. Hill said that nobody could foresee what would happen, but he did not despair. Four of their parishes had not decreased in population, although the pick of the men and women went away.

Lord Coventry's herds of Hereford cattle, many of which wandered on the lush meadows round the house, were on the whole the finest I have seen, or am likely to see. About ninety breeding cows were kept which brought up their calves in the fields. Here it is the practice not to sell the best of the heifers, but of the steers about a hundred are fatted off at three years of age. The bulls were magni-ficent animals, especially 'Champion,' a splendid beast in store condition; 'Mercury,' a three-year-old; and a youngster of one year that I think was named 'Vatican.' These creatures, which were descended from ancestors that have never been beaten in the prize ring, as might be expected, fetch a great deal of money when sold.

The orchards here were also very fine, the best of them being planted on cultivated ground. Plums were chiefly grown, of the Pershore, Victoria, and Pons — seedling varieties, while the favourite apples are Warner's King, Lord Suffield,

Peasgood Nonsuch, King of the Pippins, Cox's Orange
Pippin, Worcester Permain, and Eclingville Seedling.   The
produce of one plum orchard of two and a half acres, sold,
according to my notes, for £90, £100, and £66 respectively
in three successive years.   Apples do not seem to be so
remunerative; thus I have it that the crop of one orchard
of five and a half acres produced £70, and of eleven acres
£150.   Fifteen pounds an acre seems to be an average
return.   In the hop plantations it was explained to us that
in selecting the sprouts of the fruit-bearing vines, it was
better to save the later small green shoots, not the hollow,
quick-growing ones, which appear first.   These hops were
protected by excellent wind screens of belts of spruce fir
well pruned in.

One of the agricultural industries of Worcestershire, to
which I have already alluded briefly in describing Mr.
Potter's farming, is the growing of green peas for market
purposes in large fields.   This, I believe, Lord Coventry was
one of the first, if not the first, to undertake at Stoke
Severn.   These peas, of which we saw some, bring in from
£12 to £18 the acre, according to crop and season, and cost
about £5 the acre to cultivate.   They were sown in rows
set from ten to twelve inches apart.   The rotation seemed to
be first barley, then, after dressing with manure, peas, and
after the peas are off, a catch crop of turnips.

Another interesting sight on this Stoke Severn farm was
one of the new sheep tanks of which I have spoken.   This
foot-rot tank was so contrived that the sheep walk along
a cemented channel to which they are confined by sheets
of galvanised iron placed edgewise on either side, dabbling
their feet as they go in the special antiseptic and curative
mixture with which the channel is filled to a depth of
three or four inches.   The dipping tank is of course much
deeper, and after they have floundered about in it, the
sheep crawl one by one up a steep incline on the further
side, so that the liquid flows from their fleeces back into
the tank and is saved for further use.

At Pirton we saw one of the most beautiful half-timbered houses that I visited in Worcestershire, which, in addition to its plentiful black oak, was remarkable for its gables and fine stack of twisted chimneys. Before Croome Court was built this place, Pirton Court, was the home of Lord Coventry's family. Fortunately, standing as it does at some distance from the present house, it was not pulled down as was so often the case when owners of estates a hundred years or so ago found themselves in a position to build a more modern and splendid residence. Other interesting objects at Croome Court itself were a fine growing oak planted by the late Queen Victoria when she was five years old, and a gigantic elm measuring thirty feet round the base. Lord Coventry also kindly drove us to see another beautiful timbered house in the neighbourhood, which was, I think, in the occupation of one of his sons. Of the two, however, I preferred Pirton Court, which seemed to me to have undergone less renovation.

In driving from Malvern to Croome Court, a distance, if I remember right, of about ten or twelve miles through fertile, open country, I noted many fine meadows on the banks of the Severn, and further on a number of thriving orchards of from eight to ten years' growth. Also about five miles from Malvern we passed a solitary house which, our driver informed us, was called the Rats' Paradise. According to him an owner of this place, who died not so long ago, used to grow a large acreage of corn which year by year was stacked and left for the rats to feed on—a strange mania truly. In one or two places in England, however, I have seen stacks of rotting corn, now valueless, left thus because the owner had vowed not to thrash them until wheat rose again to a certain figure.

At Worcester I had an interview with Mr. Beauchamp, the secretary to the local Society of Agriculture, who was not in favour of either allotments or small-holdings. He thought that a good cottage with a fair-sized garden was enough for a labouring man to look after, as if he had half an acre in addition he must either neglect it or his master's work. In his opinion few of the small-holders could make a living, as the railway rates killed the profit on fruit. Indeed, he had known 'pots' of 72 lb. of plums, which cost fourpence or fivepence to pick, to be sold for ninepence a pot, and it was not uncommon for one place to be starving for plums, while another was burdened with an unsaleable plethora. At Pershore, in a good season, trees were, he said, sometimes left unplucked. Labour and packing were also great difficulties, as hands were scarce and fruit suffered very much in transit. For these reasons growers often preferred to sell their crop as it stood. In his opinion the labour trouble was that of which the Worcester farmer had most to complain, as both girls and boys were leaving for the towns, where very often they learnt no good. Over-education was one of the causes, as the fact remained that the best worker was the man who could neither read nor write.

At the house of our kind host, Admiral Britten, of Kenswick, near Worcester. I met, among other agricultural authorities of the county, Sir Harry Vernon, of Hanbury Hall, Droitwich ; Mr. James Best, of Holt Castle ; Mr. V. Wheeler, of Newnham Court; Mr. Montagu Taylor, of Shelsley ; and Mr. Dudley Clarke, the well-known land agent and rural architect, author of a valuable handbook entitled ' Modern Farm Buildings ' (Batsford). As I conversed with them all together I cannot attempt to do more than give a short summary of their collective views. They seemed to think that tenants were better off in Worcestershire than they had been, and that the rents were fair. These, they said, had fallen from 40 to 50 per cent. of late years, the best land then fetching from 25s. to 30s. the acre. As regarded the fee-simple value, one gentleman instanced to me an estate of between 300 and 400 acres, which in 1867 sold for £26,200, that he had bought of recent years, after an additional £1,000 had been spent upon the buildings, for £13,000. Most of them spoke badly of the position as regards labour. Thus one said : ' It is in a very bad way. I

FOUR-YEAR-OLD DAMSON TREE, GROWN ON COLD CLAY
*Page 358*

TRAINING HOP-BINE (EAST KENT SYSTEM) ON MR. SAVORY'S FARM
*Page 360*

think when the cottages are good you will get labour, but the small farmer does not pay enough.' Another added that neither good wages nor good cottages would keep men on the land, as the lads went at eighteen years of age, and that, speaking generally, the village population had gone down.

One gentleman said that the farmers of grass and corn were, at best, making a living and no more, but that those of hops and fruit were by comparison well off. These crops, however, required suitable land, capital, men who understood their business, and industry, the industry being the main point. Given these requisites, there was more to be made out of one acre of hops and fruit than from forty acres of wheat land. Most of them seemed to be in favour of small-holdings, under certain limitations, and if held by suitable men ; while one or two urged that more timber should be planted, and that a great deal of the stiff four-horse land should be put down to grass. They, or some of them, thought also that Government should advance money at reasonable rates to enable owners to build more cottages.

On a subsequent day I visited Mr. Wheeler's estate of Newnham Court in the Teme Valley, where he owns a large property and farms about 400 acres. Mr. Wheeler thought that the county Councils should have power to take the construction of light railways in hand, and I agree with him that this is a view for which there is much to be said. We want more local government in England : it is folly to leave everything to a congested and indifferent Parliament. He said also that there was great risk in planting fruit trees on farms that are not in hand, as the result too often is that the tenant takes no care of them ; 'if they live they live ; if they die they die.' At Mr. Wheeler's house we were shown the quarters occupied by the hop pickers in the season, a large building divided off by match-boarding, where as many as 200 people sleep, the men below and the women in a loft above. It was dry and comfortable, but must at times become a little crowded. On the left of this house were some banks that tradition says once were vineyards. The land here is too rich for sheep, and if kept longer than September the lambs are apt to scour and die. Mr. Wheeler said that in 1900 he lost four in one week from this cause. Here we saw old orchards, under the trees of which the land was farmed in the ordinary fashion; thus some of it was planted with beans and wheat. The rent of this beautiful Teme-side soil, by the way, Mr. Wheeler put at 35s. the acre, or, taking it all round, at 30s. He had a considerable number of Herefords, which he bought in at £14 and sold out at about £20 at Christmas or earlier.

The life of a hop plant, he told me, averaged from twenty to thirty years, but one of his fields was a hundred years old. He considered that hop growing was an 'awful speculation,' and said that he had sold them at 30s. the hundredweight and up to £11 the hundredweight. They cost from 22s. to 25s. the hundredweight for picking and drying, the price of the picking being approximately 1s. for the five bushels.

Leaving Mr. Wheeler I went on to one of the most interesting hop and fruit farms in Worcestershire, that of Mr. Wallace, of Eardiston, Tenbury. Mr. Wallace's estate covered, I understood, about 900 acres, of which 150 were under hops and no less than 250 or more under fruit, only sixty acres being in ordinary tillage. The cultivation on this property was wonderful, nor was any trouble or expense allowed to stand in the way of its success. Thus I saw a whole field of well-grown apple trees in the process of being regrafted. Originally they were Peasgood Nonsuch, but as for some reason this sort was not considered to be satisfactory, their tops had been removed in order to make room for scions of some more favoured variety. In short here beautiful land—I should say some of the best in England—was being worked by its owner with ample capital and great intelligence. As a result Mr. Wallace's farming is a triumphant success.

The wages paid were 15s. a week in winter and 17s. a week in summer, but the system of piece work which was in force raised them considerably above this total. Mr. Wallace

said that the young men were going, but he was not afraid.
'We have plenty of cottages, therefore we have labour.'
He thought the question of small ownerships was one of
great difficulty. The soil should, he thought, be farmed by
the man who owns it, and he agreed that people could only
be brought back to the land by giving them a living interest
in that land. How this was to be done he could not say, but
he did not approve of our system of primogeniture, under
which it is customary for the entire estate to pass to one
member of a family.

I went over some of Admiral Britten's farms under the
guidance of the bailiff, Mr. Thomas Webb. Mr. Webb said
that all the young men of any value were going away, and
that the farmers were very short of labour. They had but
few regular men in their employ and were glad to pick up a
tramp, or any casual hand to help them. He thought that
the question of wages had a great deal to do with the
exodus, and that if men were to be kept, the farmers must
pay them as much as they could earn in the towns. When
I asked him how they were to do this under present conditions, he replied that he supposed that landlords must
reduce the rents until tenants were in a position to give the
'big money.' As the said rents are by no means high, such
a prospect can scarcely be called cheerful for owners of
property. Mr. Webb also thought that the land must either
go down to grass or that Protection must be introduced to
improve present prices. Certainly the first receipt is being
largely followed; thus, a farm that Admiral Britten has in
hand used to be all arable. When I was there three-
quarters of it were grass and twenty more acres were to be
laid down. The land here is stiff and requires three horses
to work it in winter. Farms of this character in that neighbourhood do not command a very high price on the market;
thus we were told of, and I think saw two, of which the
first of ninety acres was bought at £15 the acre, and the
second of 240 acres, subject to a tithe of 3s. the acre, for
£11 10s. the acre.

Black currants are grown at Admiral Britten's farm, where I saw several acres of them. The bushes were set eight feet apart with thirty feet between the rows, and the custom appeared to be to hand-dig for a width of two feet on each side of them and to plough the intervening space. If the land proved workable these spaces were to be utilised for the growth of kail and cabbage during the following summer; but when we saw it, it was hard as iron and in lumps as big as a man's head, so that nothing could be done.

I was fortunate in finding Admiral Britten's sheep being clipped with a shearing machine, which I had never before seen at work. It is a simple implement to which a wheel turned by a lad supplies the power, the shearer holding the sheep and guiding the knife, which in principle is similar to that used to clip horses. One knife will clip about thirty sheep before it requires resharpening, the only requisite being that first the animals must be thoroughly washed. I timed the clipping of several sheep which were finished in an average of ten and a half to eleven minutes, and very well finished too, the cuts being rare and of a quite trivial nature. Now I think I am right in saying that it takes a good hand twenty minutes to do a sheep with the old-fashioned shears, and that for the day through two an hour is a fair average. It is therefore difficult to understand why this implement, which only costs £7 10s., is not more largely employed by farmers. Most of them, however, seem to have a prejudice against it, and some have told me that they consider it cuts too close; a quality that I should hardly have counted as a fault.

On this same day I went over a very fine 500-acre farm of which 120 acres were under hops and 120 under fruit, thirty acres being devoted to strawberries. One of the first orchards that we visited here was two and a half acres of plums, the ground beneath the plums being planted with tens of thousands of pheasant-eyed narcissi, just then in full bloom—truly a beauteous sight. The owner said, how-

THE EARL OF COVENTRY     *Page 362*

YOUNG HEREFORD BULL     *Page 362*

ever, that they did not pay to grow ; indeed, I think that they were not even being picked for sale. All this land was very highly manured with carpet shreddings that contain 15 per cent. of ammonia and other substances, in addition to the 1,200 tons of farm manure which it absorbs annually. For scale a wash was used on this farm which has been found effective, especially if the trees are first scraped. It is made of a pound of caustic soda and a pound of caustic potash mixed in ten gallons of water. Also the trees were grease-papered in the manner I have already described, as a protection against winter moth.

The favourite apples seemed to be Eclingville seedling, which here does best on high ground, Warner's King, Gladstone—which, by the way, does not flourish with me in Norfolk—Golden Pippin, and Golden Cluster. The vigorous and prolific Bramley seedling is found to bear best when it has attained a good age. This is also my experience in my own small orchard, as I have good trees of the species planted ten or eleven years ago off which up to the present I have scarcely gathered a single apple. This season (1902), however, they seem to be knotting for bloom. Our host favoured the planting of pyramids, and said that the Paradise stock was excellent for dwarfs on heavy land. Such bushes cost 1s. 6d. apiece in a nursery at two years from the bud, and even at this price were hard to get. Here the practice seemed to be to purchase the dwarf Paradise stock in France at, I think, 34s. the 1,000. They are then planted out for one year and in the following June cut down and budded in July at the bottom bud, above which the stock is left standing to a height of three inches to form a support for the young sprout.

Paxton was considered the best strawberry. The plants, which received eighteen tons of stable manure to the acre every alternate season, are allowed to stand four years and may then be replanted for another four years, but not more, on the same ground. They should be set out in August. All apples do not prove successful here ; thus we saw Warner's

Kings that had suffered from canker and were therefore cut down and grafted with Lord Grosvenors, which means a delay of five years before fruit is plucked. Again, a lot of Eclingville seedlings, not having fruited after nine years, were being regrafted, and Peasgood Nonsuch, which fruit, so magnificent in size and colour, I have heard called by the opprobrious name of 'Flat Catchers' in Worcestershire, had been converted into late Elizabeths, Warner's Kings, and Gladstones.

The process of grafting, as it was explained to me and as I saw it being practised on this farm, is as follows. Shoots of the sort desired to be worked are taken from the parent trees in winter before the sap rises and plunged into the ground. The trees that are to be converted into a different kind of apple are headed down in May, the severed ends being nicely pared. The grafts are then cut slanting-wise and four of them are set in slips made in the bark of each bough. After this the bark is bound round with bands of raffia to hold the grafts in place until they have time to unite with the wood, and then smeared over with the grafting wax which on most farms has now taken the place of clay, to keep the air and weather from the wound. The process sounds simple, but only skilful hands can execute it satisfactorily.

Black currants were also grown upon this farm, the 'Big Bud' being kept under by hand picking, and gooseberries of the sort known as Lancashire Lad. The labour upon the place cost, I understood, no less than £4,000 a year, which shows that the fruit and hop growers must do well to meet so heavy an expenditure and leave themselves in profit.

Altogether this was a most interesting and, I should imagine, prosperous farm, but the reader must be careful not to judge from such isolated instances of the agricultural conditions of that part of the county as a whole. Indeed, these splendid fruit holdings, of which I have now described several, are the exception rather than the rule. They may suggest riches, but around them is much poverty. Thus many of the arable lands are by no means in good condition, and great stretches of them have gone down to somewhat indifferent grass; nor do all the Worcestershire farmers make so much even as a good living.

Mr. Walter Wiggin, of the Fore Hill, in Alvechurch parish, within a few miles of Birmingham, a house which commands a magnificent view, who was our host in that district, farmed about 250 acres of land, which is owned by himself or by his father, Sir Henry Wiggin, Bart. The estimated letting value of this land was 30s. the acre, and although only twenty-five acres of it were arable, all the remainder being under grass, the labour-bill came to 24s. the acre. The character of the soil is rather cold, and I noticed that few of the trees there grow to any size. Also it is heavy, requiring three horses yoked abreast to work it, and of a ruddy colour. The fences were old and hollow, and the pastures, which were a good deal injured by rabbits, produced good sweet grass, but not in very heavy crops. Labour in this district was scarce and dear, although at haysel Irishmen are plentiful at the wage of a guinea a week with beer. The local wages were 19s. a week for a head man with a cottage, and 17s. to 18s. a week for the other hands.

The cows, of which there were a considerable number, were a very good-looking lot of dairy Shorthorns, although some of them seemed more adapted to butchering than to milk-pail purposes. The milk was sent by cart to Birmingham, where it fetched eightpence or tenpence a gallon in winter, but necessitated the keeping of two ponies for its conveyance. Out of the total area of the farm nearly 100 acres were laid up for hay. The cows had been turned out to grass a week before I saw them on May 11, and from that day forward would be left abroad all night. Their average value was said to be about £15, though some were worth much more, and they were estimated to produce 500 gallons of milk or over. The hay with which they were fed was steamed, and the bailiff, Mr. Youle, told me that he thought it twice as good for them when treated thus. The cowsheds were excellent, being very clean and sweet. In addition to the cattle there was a small flock of sheep and some horses.

Another holding that I visited was that of Mr. Morris, of the Big Fore Hill Farm, who was, I think, a tenant of Mr. Wiggin. He held sixty acres, all grass land, at a rent of 25s. the acre, which he worked with the assistance of his father and a boy. Mr. Morris said that labour was very scarce and commanded 18s. a week. His chief industry was the making of butter, which he disposed of to private customers. The hay on this farm was noted for being particularly good, that which I saw in stack being very green and fresh with an excellent 'nose.' At the time of my visit it was fetching £4 10s. a ton.

Whilst stopping with Mr. Wiggin I met and conversed with various gentlemen who were well acquainted, either through ownership of estates or otherwise, with the local conditions in Worcestershire and the neighbouring counties. Amongst these were Sir Henry Wiggin, Bart., Sir William Jaffray, Bart., and Dr. Gaunt, a medical man of experience who has a large practice in Alvechurch and its district. Sir Henry Wiggin seemed to take a fairly cheerful view of the situation and said, amongst other things, that he thought the price of milk would rise, as the producers in the midland grass counties were combining to keep it up. Hay dealers also seemed to make a living and get on, and some of them were now taking farms. He added that it was a great thing to have a good market like Birmingham close at hand, but that the holders of small farms could only live by the help of extraneous work or enterprise, such as carting or dealing. Sir William Jaffray said capital was scarce among small farmers, who often let the farmhouse and lived in a cottage. Thus out of eighty applicants for one of his farms he found that only two were responsible men who were really in a position to take the place. His experience was that the landlords had to look after the fences on a holding periodically, as it was a practice of most of the tenants to neglect them. Labour was scarce, and often the available supply in a district was taken up by some rich man who was building a house and laying out grounds. He paid his men 18s. a week, with a free cottage.

Dr. Gaunt said that Alvechurch was scarcely a typical agricultural neighbourhood, and that labour there was getting short, the men grumbling very much at Sunday work. On the bigger farms they paid higher wages and thus got the milking done. Some men would stop 'for 18s. or 19s. a week,' which, when the difference in rent and necessaries was taken into consideration, was as high a wage as they could earn in cities. Still the lads were not content to stay, and when employed in delivering milk in the town took that opportunity to ask for jobs on the railway or elsewhere. The old-fashioned agricultural labourers were almost extinct; practically there were no skilled men left in the neighbourhood. If a farmer were not very careful how he spoke to one of his servants, he would lose him. He knew of a man who had left the farm where he had been employed for ten years because he was asked to sow soot—a task, by the way, that is part of the daily round of a gardener—which he refused to do unless he was paid 1s. a day extra. He thought that the arable land would go out of cultivation or down to grass, and that wages must rise still higher with the result that outlying villages would be to a large extent deserted. There was no pauperism in that part of the county; he did not give a relief order once a month. Down Wootton way the big farms were certainly going back, and generally it would be found that scarcely a farmer was living well. Still, the days when they took things easily had gone by; they all worked, and worked hard.

As regards the effect upon the race of the exodus from the country, Dr. Gaunt said that it must mean its deterioration. It was true that the conditions of life in cities were improving, but it was most injurious for human beings to be herded together. At Edgbaston even plants would not thrive; how then could women and children be expected to do so? The time when the town dwellers might be observed to flag was during the hot summer months. It was well known that the nervous system and the physical system reacted on each other, and as a fact three children were reared in the villages to two in Birmingham. The extension of the big cities simply meant the continual engulphment and devitalising of a new area of country. Still the people went to the towns, as they must have their amusements; indeed the tendency of the day seemed to be for the rich folk to come out to the land and the poor ones to migrate to the cities.

On this point I may add that when driving on the Birmingham road in this neighbourhood on a Sunday we met various conveyances filled with shouting excursionists taking their Sabbath recreation in the country—and its inns. One drag I remember especially, as it seemed to be crowded with people all more or less the worse for liquor. Such are the pleasures, or certain of them, that our country youth seem so eager to garner in the towns. On this drive I noticed also that some of the land was very poor and that, as the ridge and furrow showed, a great deal of it had fallen down to indifferent grass.

An interesting little bit of evidence was given to me by the butler at Fore Hill House, Andrews by name, a very worthy man, with whom, as it chances, I was acquainted when he was in service in Norfolk. He told me that although he had offered 4s. a day he had found it impossible to get his garden dug, not because there were no men, but simply for the reason that they would not work. He added that in this neighbourhood it seemed to be the same story with every class of labour.

Thomas Barnett, a labourer in the employ of Mr. Wiggin, told me that he had been on the land for fifty-six years. He said that he did not know why the people went, for if some of them did not get enough wages others did. ' None of them won't farm unless they can help it. Farming folks must work and the young men like pleasure and won't stop to do Sunday labour. They might save money in the towns if they had the sense.' Mr. Barnett told me that as a boy of eight years old he received 3*d.* a day, as a plough-lad 6*d.* a day, as a labourer before the Russian war 1*s.* a day, and as a married man 8*s.* a week. From this meagre pay there were, however, no deductions; the rent of cottages was from 10*d.* to 1*s.*; his father paid 10*d.*, and the men, who were well treated, could live as comfortably then as they can now. Thus there was plenty of wood about and they were given 5 cwt. of coal in the year. Also mutton was 4*d.* a pound, and the farmer helped the man, as he could do, since 'he got a lot and had better chances then-a-days than now.' For instance, corn was 57*s.* for a bag of three bushels. He remembered that one winter a quartern loaf cost 10*d.*, and that then they were pinched and used to eat a mixture of wheat and barley. Still they never went hungry. In those times if a man misbehaved he must leave his master and his parish, since no farmer in the same place would employ him. Arch, he said, had upset things a great deal, but in some ways made it better for the labouring man.

I conclude my remarks upon Worcestershire by quoting some expressions of opinion collected from various gentle-men who are authorities upon the points with which they deal. One, a very large and enterprising farmer, wrote that he thought he might have left me under a wrong impression as to what he had said with reference to arable and grass land not being payable. What he intended to convey was that personally he did not care about farm-ing that class of land. Corn growing was played out in England, and the cereals he grew were more for con-venience than for profit. Where good live stock was produced and dairying and milk selling carried on, pasture land would pay; but unless fancy prices were made of stock, or the market for milk was good, the profits could not be large. The class of farming that paid him the best by far was the production of crops which were not readily obtained from abroad, such as hops, nearly all kinds of fruit, early peas, potatoes, &c., but this required large capital and of course could only be practised with success in certain districts. He believed that he would be in pocket if he had only very few acres of arable and grass, even if he were obliged to buy hay and straw, but in this matter he was speaking only from his own point of view.

He thought that a very large proportion of land was put to an unsuitable use. Thus where the soil was stiff and cold it should go down to turf, as even if it went down badly it would gradually increase in value. A 'ranch' thus formed would carry stock in summer, and with the help of hay some animals could be wintered mostly out of doors ; hardly any labour would be required, while the expenses would be cut down to the lowest possible point. Of course, however, this would not be high-class farming. Then there was a very large acreage, which was now cultivated at a loss, which would pay if planted with larch or other trees adapted to the district. I might think, he said, that all this would not tend to bring back men to the land, still it had a bearing on the question. Thus in this class of farming an employer could afford to pay a higher wage, and with good cottages, good gardens, and good money, men would still be found. He quite agreed with me that small-holdings on a limited scale were desirable, but the great want of the country was good houses and gardens, and if the Government would advance needy landlords money at an easy rate of interest, the repayment to be spread over a long period—say sixty years—it would be a great boon.

Certainly the average cottage was not what it ought to be, and lack of cottages must mean lack of labour, while if labour was not forthcoming even the present reduced rentals could not be maintained.

Another gentleman with whom I had the pleasure of conferring, the owner of a large estate, wrote that he thought that the following particulars of some small-

A TEME VALLEY ORCHARD  *Page 369*

SHEEP-SHEARING BY MACHINERY  *Page 372*

holdings in Worcestershire might be of service in my inquiry. These are situated round a common off which at some time or other they probably were 'cribbed,' and the houses erected by the 'cribbers.' In 1884 he put these parcels up to auction in twenty-one lots, with the result that all but six lots have now been purchased, most of them by the former occupiers. If his figures were correct the price for which the fifteen lots, totalling 11a. 3r. 6p., sold averaged about £150 per acre, the total price being £1,828. It should be stated that these small-holdings lie within three miles of a town and on good roads. The houses were inferior and in many cases much out of repair, but most of the gardens were well stocked with apple, pear, and plum trees. He thought that £100 would be a liberal allowance to make for the value of each of these houses, of which there were seven, leaving the sale value of the land at about £100 per acre. This, he remarked, was not a bad price as times went, and proved that where circumstances were favourable there was a demand for small-holdings in Worcestershire.

Among the most interesting communications that I received in Worcestershire were some from Mr. Silas Weaver, of Bricklands, Castle Morton, where he is, or was, chairman of the parish Council. Mr. Weaver, who is a strong believer in small-holdings, said that the results of his observation were that many labouring men accustomed to farm work would stay in the rural districts if there were more small-holdings available. Such men would be willing to work for farmers in the busy seasons at a fair wage, and thus make up the returns from the holdings to an amount sufficient to enable them to live decently. Owing to the poverty caused by agricultural depression farmers, except in the busy seasons, were not able to find regular work for their hands, and consequently, where such holdings and allotments are not provided, the young men drifted to the towns where wages are higher. Farmers complained of scarcity of labour, but 12s. a week, a cottage held at will, and the necessity of working long hours were conditions that were coming to an end.

The parish Council at Castle Morton took on lease a poor farm of 120 acres in foul state and relet it in four- and six-acre lots of mixed pasture and arable which the tenants fenced. This land, Mr. Weaver stated, was now greatly improved, and the rental, which varied from 12s. to 30s. the acre according to situation and quality, was promptly paid.

The Council had other lands in the neighbourhood, their total area being about 260 acres, and there was a demand for more. Further, they had established a co-operative loan society, started as an experiment with about £40 capital, the operations of which they desired to extend, as it had answered well. The result of this energy was that their population had increased from 720 in 1891 to 795 in 1901. He had studied the question for years, and was firmly convinced that the bitter hostility shown by landowners and large farmers against the subdivision of land either into small freeholds or in small-holdings, and the political power they had so long commanded, were alone responsible for the present state of affairs, and that unless public opinion was aroused and made to understand the vast importance of reform in these matters things would become even worse. He had long held the opinion that overcrowding in towns with the squalid misery, drunkenness, &c., of thickly populated centres was largely caused by our bad land laws.

In that parish there were three farms of a total acreage of 1,100 acres held by as many tenants at a rent of about 16s. an acre. He was sure that if these tenants were each of them allowed to retain 150 acres and the rest of the land was divided up into, say, forty- and sixty-acre holdings, many small tenants would be forthcoming who would take them at 25s. the acre. A suitable house and buildings could be erected for £500 on each holding, for which outlay the increased rental would recoup the owner. On such a holding the tenant and his family would do most of the work, and if they were multiplied the rateable value of the rural districts would rise, more stock and corn would be produced per acre, and outdoor relief would decrease to the general welfare of the country. Parish Councils, he thought, should have larger powers to deal with such matters, and also control over common lands, which would enable them to preserve such lands for the benefit of those who lived in their proximity.

Mr. Weaver added that in his opinion the irksome and vexatious building restrictions now enforced by nearly all the rural and district Councils were a further and very potent cause of the exodus from the country of thrifty working men. To erect a cottage and out-offices with the drains, &c., in accordance with the building by-laws of the Upton-on-Severn district Council, would entail an outlay of £250 minus the cost of the land that when small lots were for sale—which was seldom—would be £70 or £80 the acre. For instance, a person had lately erected such a cottage at a total cost, inclusive of the land, whereof there were only a few yards, of £300. The rent asked was £15, or the not exorbitant rate of 5 per cent. on the outlay. To working men, however, this had proved prohibitive, and the tenement remained unlet. The result was that small capitalists could not build, as they were unable to get a return on the heavy outlay from the only people who would take such houses. He did not find any desire amongst labouring men to occupy new and elaborate dwellings; what they wanted was a small tenement with a few acres of land out of which something could be earned. As building under such conditions was not possible, he feared that when the comfortable old-fashioned cottages could no longer be inhabited in his and other districts, more thrifty men, against their own inclinations, would drift away to the urban centres and the cities.

Mr. Weaver's very earnest and interesting views, with which in so far as they deal with the questions of small-holdings and building restrictions I am in sympathy, seem to require some comment. He speaks of the uncertain tenure of cottages as a hardship to the labouring man. As

I have treated of this matter at length in a previous chapter
of this work, that which dealt with Wiltshire, I think,
on this point, I refer the reader to what I have already
written. Mr. Weaver says that the tenants fenced the lands
that were let to them by his parish Council. In many
places they will not do this, and the fact that they were
ready to undertake such a labour and expense shows that
small holdings in Worcestershire must be more profitable
than is the case in some other counties. Thus I remember
that when I was chairman of the parish Council of the
village of Ditchingham in Norfolk, it was proposed that a
large field of grass land should be taken by the Council and
let out to various tenants who were said to desire pasturage.
The scheme, however, broke down over this very question of
fencing, since all concerned were unanimous in declaring
that the applicants would never go to such an expense,
which, for its part, the Council did not feel justified in laying
upon the parish.

Again, even if it is admitted that landowners and large
farmers have, for various reasons, shown hostility to the subdivision of land, is it a fact that this, together with the
political power which Mr. Weaver supposes them to have
commanded—before the extension of the franchise, I presume—'is alone responsible' for the present unfortunate
state of things in rural districts? Is not the terrible depression that has fallen upon the agricultural interests at large
really responsible? Again, what does he mean when he
talks of 'our bad land laws,' which he believes to have
largely caused, not only the overcrowding in the towns, but
also their squalid misery and drunkenness? How are they
so bad? If Mr. Weaver, or anyone else who can pay for it,
wishes to buy or hire a piece of land, he has as much right
to do so as, let us say, the Duke of Westminster, though
he may justly complain perhaps of the cumbersome and
expensive system of transfer which the lawyers have contrived to preserve in England. Primogeniture, it should be
remembered, is not a law except in the case of intestacy, but

a custom. No one whose estate is unentailed—and entail is
a matter of mutual agreement—is obliged to leave all his
land to a single person. Still it must be admitted that the
habit has resulted, and still results in many cases, in the
passing on of large blocks of land undiminished from one
holder to another, a system that has advantages and disadvantages too many and intricate to allow of my discussing
them here. Doubtless its abolition would in course of time
bring about division of the land, but this would be of little
use unless the land so divided would suffice to support its
owners. In many parts of England, even on considerable
holdings, this would not be the case. We must face the sad
fact that in such districts the land is nothing but a luxury—
in my opinion one of the most evil and ominous conditions
that can befall a nation. This being so, at any rate in such
instances it may as well be handed on in large blocks from
rich owner to rich owner, or if these cease to be rich, sold to
other wealthy men who spend money on it as a toy and a
means of obtaining sport, as be cut up into lots upon which
a number of poor owners would starve.

Were the bulk of it really of value, as it is, let us say, in
France, or in other countries where Protection is practised, the
question might perhaps be argued otherwise. Provided that
the individual estates do not become too small, thousands or
tens of thousands of landowners, each living on his own property and winning from it an honest and sufficient livelihood,
must in their sum furnish a population that would enable any
country to speak with her enemies in the gate, knowing at
least that she had food in her granaries and countless sons well
able to defend her in her need. But to dream of such a state
of affairs in England is somewhat Utopian. Of our own act
we have chosen that the bulk of our population should be
driven into cities, there to live by trade or on the wages of
traders, instead of remaining upon the land, there to live
upon the bountiful produce which, if farmed as it might be, it
was never more capable, as I believe, of producing to twice the
amount that it does to-day. In short, we have elected to put

our trust in money rather than in men, with results that the future will reveal.

Mr. Weaver thinks that the powers of parish Councils should be increased to the extent, it would appear, of enabling them to portion out the land of a parish in such lots and to such tenants as it might select, and of regulating the tenure of commons, which, subject to certain public rights, are frequently private property. On these points I regret to say I cannot at all agree with him. A parish Council is generally a body of limited ideas, education, and violent prejudices, shaped for the most part by local and private considerations. To increase its powers in the directions indicated would, in my humble judgment, be exceedingly dangerous to the comfort and welfare of the community. If, however, Mr. Weaver had said that greater authority and more scope should be given to the county Councils, which consist for the most part, of persons of education and standing, elected from an area sufficiently wide to insure their impartiality in most local matters that come before them, I should have been inclined to agree with him. There is no doubt that under suitable limitations, the principles of what is called Local Government might be much extended in England with advantage to the community at large.

To come to the last point raised by Mr. Weaver, that of the building regulations enforced by the district Councils, I agree with him that these are not infrequently very onerous. Many complaints have been made to me on the same matter in various counties, and I think that in the enforcement of these by-laws the zeal of local officials ought always to be tempered by discretion. Thus, upon a windy coast it is not always necessary to insist that the height of rooms should be the same as is thought desirable in a crowded town ; nor to take another instance, is there any advantage in forbidding the use of a wooden building or annexe where such building stands at a distance of hundreds of yards from any other habitation. At the same time elementary sanitary precautions cannot be too rigidly enforced.

Mr. Frederic Impey, of Longbridge Place, Northfield, near Birmingham, the Chairman of the Committee of the Allotments and Small Holdings Association, and the author of the well-known pamphlet 'Three Acres and a Cow,' which although it was largely used for political purposes, was in fact written to advocate social improvements that might retain the labouring population upon the soil, held views that were to some extent similar to those of Mr. Weaver. At least he said that he believed 'simplification of our land laws to be the greatest need in promoting agricultural prosperity.' He added that 'the housing question would also gain by this, as were it possible to get the land cheaply numbers of people would be content to build cottages for their own use, or a neighbour's, for a much smaller rent than a man who wants as good a return as possible and perhaps has to pay interest on borrowed money.'

Again I must remark that I do not see how the land laws can be simplified to any material extent, that is, if the rights of owners are to be respected. Nor do I understand how it could be made possible to acquire land otherwise than at its market value. Surely also, however cheaply the property was bought, the purchaser, being human, would wish to get 'as good a return as possible' from the houses which he built upon it, although of course—but of this I am not sure, public Bodies, who spend the ratepayers' and not their own money, might prove free from this temptation. Still I am entirely at one with Mr. Impey as to the desirability of promoting small-holdings by every legitimate means.

Mr. Edward Smith, whom I visited at the Heath, Wribbenhall, Bewdley, a gentleman who has done and is doing much for that district, said that in his opinion it was necessary to make the scholar in the elementary school acquainted with the principles of practical agriculture. He thought that if children were grounded in the knowledge of what the soil can do, when they discovered the joylessness of life in crowded cities, they would turn back from them. At present, however, they were only taught to look forward to the city as a field where many of the sons of the soil had found their fortunes.

Mr. E. Vincent Wheeler, of Newnham Court, Tenbury, where I visited him, the owner of an estate of some 4,000 acres, of which he farmed about 400, mostly in fruit and hops, wrote that to his mind the most serious question in the future of agriculture was that of labour. In his district, he added, 'there is no lack of work, but there are no men to do it.'

Mr. J. W. Willis Bund, the Chairman of the Small Holdings Committee of the Worcestershire County Council, very kindly forwarded to me the report of that committee, made about the time of my visit. From it I extract the following paragraph, which seems to me true and important:—

The depopulation in the last ten years is very great. For the reasons we have mentioned, we think it will continue. We are of opinion that it is part of the general movement going on all over the country of the rural labourers to urban and semi-urban districts, which is caused by the better wages and better accommodation they obtain there, and we do not see how it can be averted in this or other cases unless something can be done in each particular case to attract the labourers to such place ; and it is a matter requiring very careful consideration, and one on which we express no opinion, whether it is the duty of a public body to find that attraction at the cost of the rates.

With these sample opinions I close my observations upon Worcestershire and its small-holdings, trusting that the reader may find as much interest in the perusal of them as I did in their collection.

THE HYDE FARM

# GLOUCESTERSHIRE

FEW things seem more difficult to ascertain than the exact area of a county. Thus in Messrs. Bacon's 'Atlas' that of Gloucestershire, inclusive of Bristol south of the Avon, is given as 783,699 acres; in the 'Encyclopædia Britannica,' 9th edition, as 805,102 acres; in Kelly's 'Directory of Gloucestershire,' edition of 1897, as 802,875 acres; in 'Whitaker's Almanack' for 1902, wherein the size is estimated on the Poor Law areas, as 712,243; and in Longman's 'Gazetteer of the World,' 1895, as 795,734 acres. I must therefore leave the reader to form his own conclusion as to the exact number of acres that actually lie within the boundaries of the shire.

This county is divided into three great divisions of hill, vale, and forest, the hill consisting of the Cotswold, the vale extending from the Cotswold to the east bank of the Severn, and the forest a peninsula lying between the rivers Wye and Severn. The hill country is poor land, for the most part devoted to the grazing of sheep and the production of oats and barley; while the rich soil of the vale, where the climate is mild and moist, is largely under permanent pasture, and produces cattle, corn, and roots. Also there is much dairying in the county, and the double Gloucester cheeses of the Vale of Berkeley and elsewhere are known throughout the world.

In Gloucestershire my host was Mr. Alfred Apperley, of Rodborough Court, Stroud. Mr. Apperley has two farms, one small, of the model order, at Rodborough, and another not far from Chalford, some miles away. The latter holding, which is called the Hyde Farm, lies high and covers 450 acres. It was bought a few years ago by Mr. Apperley at £8 10s. the acre, which makes the purchase price £3,825. Twenty-five years before, as he informed me, the same farm was valued at £15,000. These figures are indeed an eloquent commentary upon the fall in the price of this class of land in the county. From Rodborough to Hyde Farm the road runs upwards, across a Down plateau of common-land, divided off from the surrounding farms by walls of limestone. The Hyde Farm, which lies on the limestone formation and is beautifully situated, commands a fine view of the Stroud Valley, and of the swelling sides and shoulders of the Cotswolds with their woods of larch and fir. To the north lies the village of Chalford, the larch groves running up to and among its dwellings, whilst at a distance down the valley can be seen the straggling town of Stroud. Near to the village and sloping upwards from the vale, is a glade of meadow land, flanked, when I saw it, by larch woods of vivid green and backed with the purple of new tilled fields, the whole furnishing a prospect such as is only to be seen in certain parts of England where for centuries the hand of man has been at work upon the face of nature.

Mr. Apperley has brought to farming the intelligence and ability which have made him successful as a manufacturer ; indeed, his case is another example of what I have noted in various instances, that men who have been trained in business often make the best farmers, perhaps because their minds are more open to the influence of new ideas. He employed ample labour, the bill on the farm, of which 380 acres were arable and the rest pasture and wood, amounting to £687 a year, or about 30s. the acre. The results appeared to be that after working the holding for a few seasons—how many I forget—he was paying himself 4 per cent. on the purchase price of the land and 5 per cent. on the capital invested, which was, I think, £10 the acre. One of the troubles of the place had been a lack of water, which Mr. Apperley overcame in a fashion that should be more often followed than it is in such situations. Over the well at the homestead, at a comparatively small expense, he erected a powerful windmill which raises 900 gallons an hour to a tank at a height of 130 feet, measuring from the bottom of the well, whence, after satisfying the local demand, the water delivers itself to some other buildings 900 yards away that are situated on the highest point of the farm. In addition to pumping, this wind-motor drives a crushing and cake mill, a grinding mill, and a circular saw. The saving that this machine effects upon the farm in the matter of water-carting alone was estimated to amount to from £60 to £100 a year.

The same enterprise was noticeable in every department. Thus the pig-house, in which Mr. Apperley kept fifty breeding sows, for the most part Berkshires, was one of the best thought-out and arranged buildings that I have seen, being fitted with tramways, shifting feed-screens, and other labour-saving and health-promoting devices. He sold out his pigs a hundred at a time, porkers at an average weight of fourscore at 10s. the score in the season, and bacon pigs at a weight from eight to nine score at about 9s. 6d. the score. Their staple food was barley meal with sharps and a little milk. On the value of their manure as a dressing for this brashy land it is not necessary to dwell.

But Mr. Apperley did not rely upon farmyard muck alone. Thus he bought sulphate of ammonia containing 25 per cent. of nitrogen at £10 the ton, and soot containing $4\frac{1}{2}$ per cent. of nitrogen at 30s. the ton ; also superphosphate containing from 30 to 32 per cent. of phosphates, bone dust at £4 the ton, refuse from the wool mills which is rich in nitrogen, and refuse salt from a bacon factory at a cost of 5s. the ton, which, when applied in the proportion of from 1–2 cwt. the acre, has manurial value and keeps the soil moist. The result was that he grew forty bushels of wheat to the acre, although he said that this was a crop that did not pay, and I saw great hales of mangolds estimated to contain 240 tons, which had been grown 'on the flat' upon seven and a half acres of land. These mangolds were manured with fifteen loads of farmyard muck, 2 cwt. of kainit, 1 cwt. of salt, 1 cwt. of sulphate of ammonia, and 3 cwt. of superphosphates to each acre of land. Liquid manure Mr. Apperley considered an over-rated stimulant, and one which it did not pay to carry far. Further, there was a small silo made of an old beer vat that would contain from seven to eight hundred bushels of grains for feeding purposes. These, however, Mr. Apperley only bought when there was a glut of them and they went cheap.

The gates on this farm were of oak, all carefully adjusted to the struts and having the top piece bowed. They were hung on stone posts, and cost 15s. each. There were no live fences, all walls being carefully built to a height of 4 ft. 6 in. of stone, which was extracted from Mr. Apperley's own quarry at a cost of 8d. the cubic yard. At one place a house was in course of construction to contain an engine and thrashing-machine. Here, again, Mr. Apperley saved expense by using sleepers of unusual length, obtained from the old broad-gauge line of the Great Western, as supporting posts. These sleepers cost him 15s. the ton of eighty foot run.

In walking over the Hyde farm I saw some fields which were being brought down to grass, not a very easy task on that soil. One, a pasture which had been sown four years, had in two successive seasons received a dressing of 3 cwt. to the acre of basic slag. It was thriving and had thrown up a nice plant of clover. Another two years' layer after barley looked lush and strong, and a field of winter oats was of a good colour but backward. It was, however, infested with wild garlic—a great pest here, which was then being hoed out.

At a fine set of outlying stone buildings which Mr. Apperley had recently repaired, were more pigs in sties made by Crumps of Gloucester. These cost £11 apiece, and were very convenient, being constructed with wooden floors and ventilated at the back. Here were Berkshire, Tamworth, and white Yorkshire boars, and with them some Gloucester pigs, a spotted, flop-eared, and long-bodied breed. Also there were young stock, Jersey and Shorthorn mixed, that seemed to be doing very well. Passing on over some late barley, grown after swedes fed off by sheep, which it was proposed to dress with a little sulphate of ammonia, we came to the ewes penned upon kohl-rabi, that will stand the winter here, and is not refused by them even when ' bolting' into flower. In addition they were receiving cut chaff, while the lambs were given a bite upon the clover and a few peas or beans. It was intended to sow this land with barley, but I thought it doubtful whether that crop would succeed so late, as on May 18 the field was still being fed, and suggested that kail might do better. Of Hampshire Down ewes there were 220, also 100 tegs, and during the summer 250 lambs. Mr. Apperley thought that having brought the farm into heart he would be able to keep fifty more sheep in following years. Of barley his area was fifty acres ; here the land is ploughed twice for this crop.

The wages paid were 15s. a week, and 13s. for lads, with 3d. an hour overtime for anything above fifty-four hours a week, and 3d. an hour extra during harvest, with cider or beer at 6d. the gallon. The horsemen were also given cottages and potato land.

Altogether this was a very interesting farm, especially as, although the capital employed was ample, no money had been wasted upon the land or buildings. Indeed, here the most was made of everything, the cost of all improvements being carefully considered, and materials or manure, &c., purchased with great judgment and economy. In short, the holding was run upon business principles, with the view of making it yield a fair return, which is more than can be said of many farms worked by gentlemen chiefly as an interesting and health-giving recreation.

At Rodborough, in the suburbs of Stroud, Mr. Apperley has a little grass farm of forty acres, on which he kept thirty head of choice Jersey cattle. Here his cows yielded 150 lbs. of butter a week, which sold for 1s. 2d. a pound, the milk fetching 1s. a gallon. Also there were eighty pigs. Three men were employed, and with the exception of some of the hay, most of the food for the animals was bought. Still—and it is another proof of his good management—this little place paid its owner rent, interest on capital, and a small profit of about £20 per annum.

Jersey bulls are always supposed to be vicious, and here I saw one that lived up to the character. This animal had a spite against the man who tended it. One day, neglecting the warnings he had received to be careful, he went too near the beast in its stall. Instantly it was at him, and, catching him on its sharp horns, tossed him into the air. Luckily the man fell across a rafter, to which, while the bull ramped below, he clung until he was rescued.

When I was staying with Mr. Apperley we discussed the possibility of making up English wool, which hitherto has been chiefly used for blankets and coarse cloths, into first-class goods for men's wear. This he has since succeeded in doing at his Stroud mills; indeed the specimens of cloths woven from the fleeces of Hampshire Down sheep which he has sent to me are, so far as I can judge, as good in appearance and to the touch as any that can be made. Mr. Apperley points out that the English farmers find it increasingly difficult to sell, at anything like profitable prices, even the limited amount of wool that they at present produce, and that they cannot be expected to grow more till they are certain of a better market. To provide such a market was his principal reason for undertaking the manufacture of special cloths made exclusively of this home-grown wool. As an expert in such materials, he states that this new cloth leaves nothing to be desired either in construction or manufacture, and that in the fixity of its dyes and the permanency of its colours, it is equal, if not superior, to any at present on the market; also that everything that science can do, has been done to produce a thoroughly sanitary fabric.

Of this cloth he writes to me : ' It is already taken up by some high-class London tailors whom I have seen, and they are very pleased indeed with the goods. We have our own special arrangements for softening the wool, so giving it a finer handle. These goods come out about the same in price as to cost, as those produced from a similar colonial or foreign wool, but we are going to make a speciality of English wool. I have bought several lots already of my neighbours, and now I have a lot of applications.'

I sincerely trust that Mr. Apperley will be well supported in this intelligent effort of his to develope a new home industry.

On a subsequent day we drove with Mr. Apperley to a village about five miles beyond Gloucester, which was I think called Rudford, to see Mr. H. W. Bruton, of the well-known Gloucester firm of auctioneers and valuers, Messrs. Bruton, Knowles & Co. The drive was long—over twenty miles, if I remember right—but for the most part through very beautiful scenery. From Stroud the road ascends steadily, running between swelling hills of which the sides are dotted with villages of grey stone, till beyond Pitchcombe it climbs the western slopes of the Cotswolds. The land in the broad vale which is spread out beneath, most of it pasture, was said to be worth from £80 to £100 an acre and to let for £2 the acre.

After Painswick Edge is passed the road debouches on to the high lands overlooking the valley in which lie Cheltenham and Gloucester. Here the country gradually opens out into a vast plain of fertile fields of small size, most of them pasture bordered by hedges in which grow many elms. On the day when I saw it the prospect, that faded gradually into a misty distance, was one of singular charm and beauty. The road also, bordered as it was with magnificent chestnut trees white with thousands of spikes of stately bloom, furnished a spectacle not easy to forget, while the grey old Tudor houses that appeared from time to time told the traveller that for many generations men have loved to dwell in a spot so favoured. At length all these beauties pass away and a thickening fringe of unattractive villas heralds the town of Gloucester.

Here, under the kind conduct of Mr. Herbert Brewer, the organist, we visited the cathedral, one of the most splendid fanes that I saw in all my travels. He told me an excellent story, which I trust I may be forgiven for repeating, about a verger, past or present, who in showing the glories of the place to a party of visitors, explained that the nave was Norman and the chancel Perpendicular, adding that of course 'the Perpendicular was built first.' One of his audience ventured to suggest that Norman architecture preceded Perpendicular. 'Ah!' answered the undefeated verger, 'that may be so in other places, but Gloucester folk always had ways of their own.'

There is another pleasing tale of a clergyman who took the members of a mothers' club round this cathedral, showing them amongst other things the famous lavatory of the monks. Afterwards one old lady stopped behind to thank him, and explained that in this lavatory naturally she had been more interested than the rest of the company, as for many years 'her aunts had always washed for them Monks.' For a while her pastor was puzzled until he remembered that the family name of the late bishop had been Monk!

Next to the cathedral and an old house near by, where it is said that Parliament once sat, and that Domesday Book was 'signed'—by whom I wonder—in a chamber now occupied by a maidservant, I thought the most noticeable thing in Gloucester was the number of pretty young women to be seen in the streets. I observed that most of these had dark eyes, an inheritance, I presume, of the Celtic blood of which there must be a large admixture in this population.

With Mr. Bruton I had a long and instructive interview at his place at Rudford, where he interests himself in working a small farm. He said that during the last two years there had been less trouble in letting land, and that most of the farmers were making rent and a living. A few years before many of them went under, but now there was a better class of tenant forthcoming, and the low rents with

*Page 490*

VIEW OF STROUD FROM THE COTSWOLD HILLS

the rather improved prospects were inducing some of them to bring up their sons to the land. In that district rents on typical vale estates had fallen about 30 per cent., and the fee-simple value a little more in proportion, say 40 per cent., for land of which, speaking generally, one-third would be arable and two-thirds pasture. Perhaps this was because the Agricultural Holdings Acts had to some extent scared buyers, who feared that heavy claims might be made upon them for unexhausted improvements. On the brashy Cotswold Hill lands, where barley and oats are grown, the depression was acute. Thus one estate there of 288 acres, which, however, had neither water nor buildings, was offered to him at the miserable price of £4 10s. the acre, but ultimately sold, I was told, for £6 10s. the acre.

The average letting value of a typical Cotswold estate was, he said, about 10s. an acre. Mr. Bruton mentioned one of 700 acres in excellent order with 200 acres of pasture, good buildings, cottages, &c., but subject to a tithe of 4s. the acre, which let for this sum. It used to fetch from 15s. to £1 an acre, and had a selling value of £30 the acre, so that putting the present sale value at twenty-five years' purchase, the drop would be nearly 60 per cent. The average price of Cotswold land he estimated at £10 the acre in 1901. On the other hand a pasture farm with cottages and buildings situated five miles from Gloucester, had sold not long before for £60 the acre, but a mixed Vale farm situated at Upleadon, four miles from a railway station, which thirty years before was bought for £50 the acre, sold lately for £25 the acre.

Labour, Mr. Bruton told me, was a difficulty in the county, especially on the hill lands, and the young men were leaving for the towns. Sunday work and milking caused a great deal of dissatisfaction, and another reason for the scarcity was that the farmers did not employ their men all the year through, but took their chance of getting them in the busy seasons. Thatchers were especially scarce, and the

art of skilled fence trimming and laying was almost extinct.
Personally, Mr. Bruton said he gave his men their bank
holidays, or other days in exchange for them, and he thought
that farmers would be wise to do the same.   In that district
the cottages were generally good, but speaking of Gloucestershire as a whole he could not say so much.

In the Vale the old landed families 'hung on,' and there
were still a good many resident landlords, of whom a fair
proportion owned moderate-sized or small properties.   On
the Hills, however, they had vanished.   There was a great
demand for small-holdings of from 50 to 100 acres, especially
in the fruit districts along the Severn, where the land grew
wonderful crops of plums and apples.

On the whole Mr. Bruton considered that the agricultural
outlook was brighter than it had been ; indeed, he said to
me : 'If I had money I should put it into land.'   He
pointed out that the area of English land is limited and
that our population was increasing ; also that commercial
prosperity might not always be so great as it is, and
that if it passed away the towns would not be able to afford
to pay such high wages, which would mean that the
labourers, or some of them, would stop in the country.
Still corn, mutton, and wool were hard hit, and at sevenpence a pound the last of these gave no profit   On the Hills
many Shorthorns were bred which were fatted in the Vales,
but there was a tendency to cross them with polled Angus
and Galloways.   He considered that the Gloucestershire
farmers, taken as a body, were of a good class, being for the
most part progressive and intelligent men.   He inclined to
believe in the advisability of multiplying small-holdings, and
thought that the man who worked a little farm with the
help of his family did well.

Subsequently Mr. Bruton forwarded to me some
particulars of the prices fetched not long before by certain
Cotswold farms, which were very kindly furnished by a well-
known Cheltenham auctioneer.   These, omitting names, I
print below, as they are instructive and authentic.

——, *Gloucestershire.*

Lot 1.  Freehold farm, cottages, and land, called —— Farm, in extent 367a. 2r. 38p., let to Mr. —— at £240 per annum.

Sold to ——, Esq., for £7,000.

Lot 2.  Two freehold farms, with cottages and buildings and land, called The —— and The —— Farm, let to Mr. —— at £270 per annum, in extent 980a. 1r. 19p.

Sold to —— for £5,850.

Lot 3.  Freehold farm, with cottages and land, called —— Farm, ——, in extent 219a. 0r. 21p., let to Mr. —— at £110 per annum.

Sold to ——, Esq., for £2,250.

——, *near Northleach, Gloucestershire.*

Freehold farm, six cottages and gardens, and 378a. 1r. 27p. of land.  Farm held by trustees of the estate, and known as —— Farm.

Sold to —— for £3,000.

——, *near Cheltenham, Gloucestershire.*

Freehold pasture farm, known as —— Farm, with house and buildings and 32a. 3r. 18p. of land, held by trustees of the estate.

Sold to Mr. —— for £1,400.

—— *Farm,* ——, *near Gloucester.*

Freehold farm, with house, cottages, and buildings, and 193a. 2r. 12p. of arable and pasture land, held by owner.

Sold to Mr. —— for £3,030.

In his letter he said :

As you will see, the prices range from £6 to £20 the acre.  It must be borne in mind, however, that the sales were principally by trustees, who, no doubt, were anxious to wind up their estates, and were reconciled to this low price.  Large estates on the Cotswolds that have been offered recently—as, for instance, the —— estate—did not find purchasers in the auction room.  I fear that you will have to report that a large area of the Cotswold land is letting now from 5*s*. to 10*s*. the acre. But, as I remarked to you when we met at Rudford, the Hill farmer has had to contend with a startling reduction in the price of corn and wool. He has also to transform his stock, substituting close-woolled sheep for the Cotswold.

Mr. Bruton was also good enough to send me through Mr. J. A. Peter, Lord Fitzhardinge's agent, the documents connected with the Berkeley Farmers' Association, Limited, of which Lord Fitzhardinge is the chairman, a most useful institution whereof the main object is 'to carry on the business of a co-operative society in all its branches.' I believe that this society has done a great deal of good in the neighbourhood of Berkeley, and I am glad to say that, as the balance sheet, published in 1901, which I give below, demonstrates, it is in a sound financial position. Indeed the Association was able to pay 5 per cent. dividend on its capital, a bonus of 8*d*. in the pound on members' purchases, a bonus of 5 per cent. each on net profits to manager and secretary, and to carry forward a small balance to reserve account. The success of this corporation shows once more the value of co-operative effort amongst English farmers. It might be well if more of them would recognise this and act thereon.

### THE BERKELEY FARMERS' ASSOCIATION, LTD.

*Balance Sheet, March* 31, 1901.

| LIABILITIES. | £ s. d. | ASSETS. | £ s. d. | £ s. d. |
|---|---|---|---|---|
| Nominal Capital, 1,000 Shares of £5 each £5,000 | | Plant, Horses, &c. .. 299 17 4 Less 10 per cent. Depreciation .. 29 19 9 | | 269 17 7 |
| Subscribed, 529 Shares, £4 10 0 paid.. .. .. .. .. | 2,380 10 0 | Sundry Debtors .. | | 1,927 15 2 |
| Sundry Creditors .. | 185 19 2 | Stock-in-Trade .. | | 827 15 7 |
| Reserve Account .. £303 12 10 Premiums on 17 Shares .. £11 5 0 | 314 17 10 | Cash at Bankers .. | | 390 14 8 |
| Profit and Loss Account Balance at Credit thereof .. | 534 16 0 | | | |
| | £3,416 3 0 | | | £3,416 3 0 |

While at Stroud I visited Mr. James Harper, who is well known as a lecturer on matters connected with agriculture. He was so kind as to show me a large machine for the artificial drying of all sorts of fruits and vegetables. This apparatus, which cost £65, will desiccate 2,500 lbs. weight of apples in the twenty-four hours with an expenditure of 3 cwt. of coal. The results, of which I saw and tasted samples, were certainly excellent. Mr. Harper stated that £4,000,000 worth of dried produce is imported annually into Great Britain, most of which could be manufactured in the country. The matter is one whereon I can express no opinion, but, as I have pointed out in treating of the Bewdley district, the sun of foreign lands which we lack, is a very serious competitor with machines that have to be worked by means of coal, which costs money. At Bewdley also, it will be remembered, after trial those concerned rejected this system of machine drying, adopting in its place a newly devised method modified from that used in hop-oasts.

However these things may be, the apparatus which Mr. Harper showed us was certainly most ingenious, and at the least, can no doubt be usefully applied in many cases where the quantities to be dealt with are not very large. In his house we saw also many admirable labour-saving contrivances, most of them, I imagine, of American origin, for paring, coring, and slicing potatoes, apples, pears, and almost every other kind of fruit and vegetable. It seems a pity that these clever inventions are not more largely used in private kitchens.

Dr. Martin, whom I saw when staying with Mr. Apperley, a medical officer who has to deal with an area of fifty square miles containing 33,000 people, said that the general health of the district was good, although the whole of the water supply was liable to pollution. The cottages were fair with good gardens, and there were very few cases of overcrowding; still he had been obliged to condemn some of them. Their average rent was 2s. a week, but some were let as low as 1s. a week. The character of the district allowed of a man working on the land while his wife and children were employed as mill hands or otherwise in the towns, a state of affairs that added to the general prosperity. His experience was, however, that as soon as the boys were old enough they took service in the mills.

I conclude my remarks upon this county with one or two brief expressions of opinion sent to me by persons of local experience. Thus Mr. T. Valentine Pettifer, Veterinary Inspector to the Board of Agriculture and Wilts and Gloucester County Councils, &c., wrote to me that if the migration of the rural population was not checked, he hardly knew what would become of agriculture. In the county of Gloucester the exodus for the most part was, he said, to the locomotive works of the Great Western Railway at Swindon. Also many labourers were drawn away to railways which were in course of construction. After a stay on such works they were spoiled and no longer took kindly to ordinary labour on the land. So short was the supply of men that farmers were even selling cows for lack of milkers to attend to them.

A lady who has for many years been a poor-law guardian in the county and a farmer of her own land, said that in no single season had she made her rent, much less a profit. Having other sources of income she and her husband were able to continue in their home, but during the past thirty years they had seen many of their neighbours ruined, and noticed that in numbers of instances the agricultural industry was only kept afloat by means of wealth that had been made in towns. This view was confirmed by that of Mr. H. J. Elwes, F.L.S., etc., of Colesborne, Cheltenham, a distinguished gentleman who for long past had farmed his own land in Gloucestershire, Hants, and Essex, and, as he employed no agent, had a very practical acquaintance with the business. Mr. Elwes said that the constant influx of large sums of money made in trade and spent upon the land and on so-called improvements, which rarely produce any pecuniary return, is the only circumstance that saves great parts of England from becoming waste. A very striking feature in his district was the number of instances in which areas of agricultural land were being laid down for rough grazing or made use of as sporting farms. Mr. Elwes was of opinion that tithe was the land's greatest and most pressing burden.

On the whole, however, I am of opinion that when compared with many other counties, the agricultural condition of Gloucestershire is not altogether unprosperous. Nor do the farmers there seem to have lost hope of better days to come.

## WARWICKSHIRE

THE midland county of Warwick has an area of about 577,000 acres. It is very picturesque, with a good soil and much pasture land, of which the extent is increasing.

At Webheath, on the borders of Warwickshire, near to the town of Redditch, I visited Mr. S. C. Thornton Jagger, who since 1893 has been agent to the Bentley Estate, that, I believe, covers 9,000 acres and lies partly in Worcestershire and partly in Warwickshire. Mr. Jagger said that it took farmers all their time to pay their rent and make a living, but that the industry was advancing slightly. Agriculturists were more prosperous than they had been, the rents were paid, and the 10 per cent. allowance had been discontinued. He thought that the Warwickshire farmers were, on the whole, superior to those of Worcestershire, and more careful to keep pace with the times. Most of the land, from two-thirds to five-eighths of the whole, was pasture, and the average rents ran from 18s. to £1 an acre. For labour they were not so badly off as they had been. A few years ago everybody flocked to Redditch, then local commercial depression set in, if I remember right, owing to a set-back in the bicycle trade, and some of them returned, having learnt a lesson. Still a number of the young men continued to go. Certain of the high-class farmers were, he thought, very prosperous. Thus he instanced one who had realised £1,250 off twenty-seven acres of spring cabbage, for which the best markets were the collieries of South Wales, and sold £1,700 worth of peas in a single year. Of course, however, cultivation of this character is rather market gardening on a large scale, than farming as the word is generally understood.

A curious example of the inability of the English farmer to meet local requirements, was furnished by the fact that Danish butter was served on Mr. Jagger's own table, as he said that he was unable to buy butter or cream fit to eat in the neighbourhood.

Mr. Jagger was a strong believer in small-holdings and in the planting of trees of which the fruit is suitable for manufacture into cider and perry, but he thought that the little farmer ought not to have less than fifty acres of land. He gave me an instance of a man in the neighbourhood who out of his wages and the produce of half an acre had saved enough to take such a fifty-acre farm. Skilled agricultural labour, by the way, in this district commanded from 18s. to £1 a week, with a cottage. Mr. Jagger also believed in co-operative creameries, but said that, owing to the obstinacy and suspicions of farmers, it was difficult to persuade them to support such establishments.

He showed me a most interesting map of the parish of Feckenham, in Worcestershire, where, I believe, some of the property that he manages is situated. This map was ordered to be made by Queen Elizabeth at the time of the 'dis-forestation' in 1591; but the copy that I saw was executed by hand in 1744 for a Mr. Blagrave by John Dobarte the younger, of Worcester. In Elizabeth's time, and before it, Feckenham was an important place, where the monarchs of England seem to have had wine cellars, fishponds, and a hunting lodge. Its total area was then 7,285 acres, but to-day, as I read in my notes, it measures only 6,654, the balance having gone I know not where, probably into some other parish. According to the map this total was at that date divided as follows: 2,898 acres, held by sixty-three different owners: Common Fields, 1,517 acres; the Lord's Wastes, 675 acres; the Lord's Demean Lands and his Tenants, 1,458 acres; Assart Land and reclaimed Woodlands, that is, copyhold lands reclaimed from bog and forest waste, 732 acres. The missing five acres were, I suppose, accounted for by roads and sites of buildings. Now comes the interesting point. This extent of land, of which nearly three thousand acres in Elizabeth's time was held by no fewer than sixty-three different owners, has to-day passed almost entirely into the hands of six people, who hold 6,000 out of the 6,654 acres which constitute the present area of the parish. Could a better example be found of the transference of the land of England from the hands of the people into those of a class?

Under the guidance of Mr. Jagger I visited various small-holders in the parish of Webheath. The first was Mr. James, a fish-hook maker with a large family, who had an allotment of a quarter of an acre, which he rented for 18s. a year. On this piece of ground, where we found him working, he grew roses and 'all manner of things.' He was a great exhibitor at local shows, and said that he took seventy-five or eighty prizes a year and had a thousand 'cards' at home. He told me that his allotment did not really pay him, as he could not make the best of the pro-duce when he sold a few trees or blooms, but his family consumed vegetables off it to the value of £6 a year. If only he could market his stuff satisfactorily, he thought that two acres of land would keep him. In this respect some system of collection would be helpful. The hospital and friendly societies in the neighbourhood gave honorary prizes in the shape of cards, the vegetables exhibited being sold for the benefit of charities. In return for their help towards the success of these shows, the exhibitors, when sick, received tickets of admission to the hospitals, and other benefits from the societies. Mr. James informed me that the rent of a cottage was from £4 to £5, including a garden or allotment worth 10s. a year.

Mr. Bartland, whom I saw next, hired thirty acres at a rent of £48 a year, of which four were tillage, two being under wheat and two under beans. He kept two sows, which were grazing on the meadow, two cows, and two young things. From the cows, in addition to the milk necessary to the calves, he made seven and a half pounds of butter a week, which he sold at 1*s*. 3*d*. a pound. Also he had bought in two heifers for £15 10*s*. the pair, and after keeping one of them for a while sold it out for £15. From his pigs he had realised over £60 in twelve months, and, having a nice house, added to his profits by taking in the curate as a lodger. One of his occupations was the growing of summer chrysanthemums, of which he showed me two plots about the size of asparagus beds that had brought him in £9 in a year. These flowers fetched an average price of 8*d*. per dozen bunches of twenty blooms per bunch, and he said that ' many and many a time his missus had made £1 a day out of them.' His system, if I remember right, was to plunge the old roots in a frame, then separate off the suckers and plant them out. The blooms, he said, have to be picked when dry and kept in a shed until they are sent to market, otherwise they would fade. Mr. Bartland thought that no flowers paid better than these chrysanthemums, and that anyone who had money to lay out might make a very good thing of them. Of labour he declared, ' You can't get nobody. You can't get a man to help ; there is no labour.'

Mr. Thomas Neasom, the land agent and auctioneer in Redditch, gave a very hopeful account of the agricultural position in Gloucester and Warwick. He said that the average rental of farms in the immediate neighbourhood, which would include about 80 per cent. of pasture, was 25*s*. the acre. Taking the county of Warwick through it was more, accommodation land fetching as much as £4 the acre. Rents had perhaps fallen 25 to 30 per cent. since 1879, the terrible year of fluke-rot among the sheep, and the fee-simple value 33 per cent., but in his opinion they were rising a little. Indeed, he had never known a greater demand for land, especially on large estates, as the big landowners did not disturb the sitting tenants. Also there seemed to be a considerable amount of money available for agriculture, and the tenants who came forward were solid men. On Lord

Windsor's estate in 1885 there were several void farms, but now such a thing was not known.

Skilled labour was very scarce indeed and indifferent labour scarce. He did not, however, think that things would get worse, for the reason that 90 per cent. of the agricultural labourers, at a wage of 15s. a week, with a good house and garden, were better off than the artisan. Generally the exodus was owing to the low price of corn, but he considered that the bicycle trade was the local cause; also in some cases the cottages were short. Thus Mr. Neasom mentioned an isolated farm of 250 acres that had none at all, and another estate where there was only one to the hundred acres. On the other hand his father, who farmed a thousand acres, had plenty of cottages, which kept the men together, and as these were within one mile of Redditch, the wives and children could work in the town. The average size of farms in that district he put at 300 acres, but some of them ran down to 40 or even to 20 acres. The capital employed was nearer £5 than £10 the acre, and they would let to a man who had that amount. The cost of labour averaged from 30s. to 33s. an acre on mixed farms, of which two-thirds were grass. Locally, he informed me, corn was measured by the bag, which contained three bushels or 196 lbs. A bushel of wheat should weigh 63 lbs., a quarter of oats 320 lbs., and a quarter of foreign barley 400 lbs. In conclusion Mr. Neasom said that a great deal of land was sold through his firm, and that he thought it the finest security in England.

From Alvechurch to Henley-in-Arden, near Stratford, whither I went to visit Mr. R. E. Cooper, agent to Sir W. Jaffray and other landowners, a gentleman of great experience in all matters connected with the land, is a distance of about ten miles. The scenery on the road was extremely pretty, but I noticed that a very large proportion of the land through which we passed, as the high ridge and furrow showed, had fallen and not been laid down to grass. The pasture struck me generally as fair but not good; indeed, in the vicinity of Umberslade Park it was exceedingly poor and used for the grazing of Scotch sheep.

Mr. Cooper said that he held seven agencies and had been all his life connected with Warwick land; indeed, his family began to be estate and land agents in the county in 1772, three generations ago. He thought that the position was decidedly more promising than it had been, and that the farms were better looked after. Small-holdings also were in more demand. The rents scarcely averaged £1 the acre. Thus, in the Wellesbourne district, where they used to be 50s., they were then 25s. The average drop in the rentals since 1875 was at least 50 per cent., and of the fee-simple value also about 50 per cent. The present price of land was, say, twenty-five years' purchase on the reduced rentals. It used to be thirty years' purchase on the old rents. Most of the strong land which required four horses to work it, had gone down to grass. Now there were very few farms of which half the area was arable, and it would be hard to find anyone to take such a place. Fifty per cent. of arable ' settled a tenant '; he would not come on. In some cases Mr. Cooper had advised his clients to allow the arable to go to waste and let the grass. Farmers, however, liked a little arable on which to grow straw, say twenty or thirty acres out of 200.

The value of bean and wheat lands was sometimes as low as £10 the acre on the blue lias. Indeed, much of this strong land was nothing but a rabbit run, and between Stratford and Kineton many hundreds of acres were out of cultivation. In Warwickshire, however, the soils were very mixed, and it was not unusual to find two or three classes of them in a single field. On the heaviest basic slag was very useful, as it put ' a face ' on the land and brought up the white clover.

Mr. Cooper told me that he never let on lease, as now-a-days that meant a case of ' no lease for the landlord, but a lease for the tenant,' nor did he think that many farms were held thus in Warwickshire. As regarded the character of the farming, he stated that holdings near a station were used for milk production and the best lands for grazing, rearing, and feeding out. Some of these were very good, but meadows were only to be found here and there, as along the banks of the Avon. Of sheep there were a fair amount, mostly of the Shropshire breed, and the cattle were principally Shorthorns; but he thought that the Herefords were creeping in. These suited the blue lias, which had a purging effect upon horned stock. The first cross between Herefords and Shorthorns was a very useful breed. A few years before the farmers were being sold up right and left, but now they seemed to do better on the reduced rents. If a man did two-thirds of the work himself, he could make his rent and a living, but he lived hard and did not save, and in some cases was eating into his capital. There was a good demand for farms, but the class of man who came forward was not always satisfactory. Indeed, changing tenants was a risky matter, as there were a great number of ‘travelling farmers’ about, who sprang up like mushrooms and went as quick. In this matter of selecting tenants it was necessary to be very particular.

Mr. Cooper added that there were a considerable number of large landlords in Warwickshire, such as Lord Willoughby de Broke, Lord Warwick, Lord Leigh of Stoneleigh Abbey, and others, all of whom owned about 10,000 acres. He did not think that much of the county was in the hands of small landowners of, say, from 500 to 1,000 acres. Those landlords who depended upon the proceeds of their estates were undoubtedly pinched. Labourers, whose ordinary wage was 15s. a week, were very scarce. Thus he had advertised for three months before he could get a waggoner; yet the villages seemed to contain many people without visible means of subsistence. If the men were spoken to they did not say that they were going—they went. It was common for the men to stay away a day or two without leave; thus one of his own people had gone to the Stratford races and only reappeared on the Wednesday of the following week.

The tendency had been to pull down cottages in order to save the rates payable upon them, but now that rates were thrown upon large districts, the owners of the cottages wanted them back again. The landlords were not building to any extent, but Mr. Cooper thought that they would be obliged to do so, as they were very short of labourers' dwellings, and the only hope of keeping people in the country lay in the erection of suitable houses for them to inhabit. He was of opinion, however, that the cottages ought to be under the control of the farmers and not let to the labourers direct. Generally the labour-bill amounted to more than the rent, say to 1l. an acre. They had no Irishmen although these came to districts ten miles away. He considered that the labour question was the most serious that agriculture had to face.

I asked Mr. Cooper whether he thought that small-holdings would help in this matter. He replied Yes ; he believed in either small-holdings or big holdings, that is :

(1) In little farms on which the tenant did all the work with the help of his family ; or

(2) Large farms with highly paid labour where every modern appliance and machine were used.

Mr. Cooper said that the expenses of repairs varied. Where everything was on a large scale and there were few buildings, these cost less than on small farms with many buildings, the cost of which ate up the rent. Perhaps 15 per cent. of the returns would be a fair average. This question of the cost of buildings was, in his opinion, a great stumbling-block in the way of the establishment of small-holdings.

Warwickshire he described as undulating and well-wooded, especially with elm, which was called the Warwick weed. The best hill country was in the neighbourhood of Stoneleigh, but here they were not planting much, and of fruit there was practically none. In many places pasture was hard to make, the red marl in particular taking grass with difficulty. Much of the land would not bear sheep well, and on the clay it was too wet for them. In the Wellesbourne district the barley was of a dark colour. In some parts of the county the breeding of Shire horses was an important industry, of which Mr. P. A. Muntz, of Dunsmore, who sold largely to America, was one of the pioneers and leaders. The average size of farms in the county was from 200 to 300 acres, and the capital required, but not always employed, £10 the acre.

In walking over Mr. Cooper's farm I saw an extremely ingenious form of hay shed invented by himself. The stack was built beneath an iron roof supported by uprights and cross-beams, and so contrived that by means of a windlass the roof could be lifted up and down as the hay was stacked or removed. The prime cost of this hay barn was about £20.

Mr. Cooper, since the date of our interview, has kindly forwarded to me some figures showing the rents of various farms in Warwickshire, exclusive of woods and plantations, as they were in 1877 and 1901 respectively. These I quote.

In the parish of Boddington a farm of 202 acres. Rent 1877, £380 ; 1901, £200.

In the parish of Warmington, a good district six miles from Banbury, farm of 173 acres. Rent in 1877, £320 ; 1901, £200. This farm is strong land and has only about twenty acres of arable, although just on the top of the hill, towards Banbury, the soil is chiefly light arable, growing turnips and barley.

An estate between Redditch and Studley of 984 acres. Rent in 1877, £1,402 ; 1901, £850.

An estate lying on the borders of Warwick and Worcester of 1,139 acres. Rent in 1877, £1,562 ; in 1901, £931.

An estate in the parishes of Kineton, Gaydon, &c. ; of 2,199 acres. Rent in 1877, £2,376 ; in 1901, £1,654.

Estimated rental (gross) of the parish of Wootton Wawen and of 8,012 acres (ordnance map) in 1873, £17,057. In 1894, after which some alterations were made in the area, £13,933.

Mr. Gibbs, of Cutler's Farm, Wootton Wawen, a very fine old gentleman who is said to have ridden and made more horses than any man in Warwickshire, told me that he took his farm over half a century ago. It was inferior land, and of the 270 acres eighty were arable, the total being divided into fifteen enclosures, of which eight were arable, four of them being three-cornered in shape. The land was very hilly and 'given to rabbits,' and a public road ran through many of the fields.

Mr. Gibbs said that when first he began to farm he did well and made money at £2 an acre rent, but now at £1 an acre he lost it as fast as he used to make it, and was obliged to spend £100 a year out of his private income to keep going. He thought that farmers in Warwickshire were 'doing very middling' and that two-thirds of the applicants for holdings were men without capital, adding emphatically, 'No one can farm without money.' In 1845 the labour cost 8s. a week, and even down to 5s. for an Irishman, 'and he stopped with me till he died.' Labour now was very short. The men wanted encouragement, better wages and 'more interest in the land—that is the only way to bring them back to the land.' Also there were not enough cottages; he had not one upon his farm. Mr. Gibbs was of opinion that the land was going down hill very fast, and that its price had been reduced by half 'since his time.' Personally he bred horses and rode them for other people, including the Rothschilds. This and farming generally he considered to be 'a nice occupation if a man is independent.'

Some two months later, about the end of July, when staying in Oxfordshire, I had the opportunity of visiting Mr. Henry A. Warriner at Weston Park, Shipston-on-Stour, Warwickshire. Mr. Warriner is agent to Lord Camperdown, who owns a large extent of land in Warwickshire, and has some of it in hand, which I inspected. Mr. Warriner said that the condition of the farming interest was not so bad as it had been in 1895 and 1896. The farmers made a living, and the best of them just managed to cling on, though some went out and developed into 'commercial travellers in artificial manures.' He thought that the 150-acre men with families did best, but generally speaking the larger farmers were

better business men than these were ; what they did now-a-
days they did well, and for the most part kept their heads
above water. When there was a holding to let there were
many applicants, but some of these would be men who had
nothing at all. Yet they would go over 400-acre farms as
though they had really the intention of taking them. Also
there was a class of tenant who would rather hire a good
house with a bad farm than a good farm with a moderate
house.

The average fall in rents since the prosperous time, Mr.
Warriner put at 33 per cent., but they had some farms that
had fallen 50 per cent. Thus he instanced two, one of
which used to let for 70s. and now brought in 30s., and a
second which had fallen from 60s., also to 30s. The land
was chiefly under grass, as most of the arable had been laid
down. Much of it was a sour clay on which basic slag was
the best manure ; but the strong point of the soil was its
capacity for growing cattle. Thus they had some that
would fat out an ox and some on which the aid of cake was
necessary.

The position as regarded labour was not so bad as it had
been in 1890, but the young fellows were going away, and
they were obliged to rely upon men between forty and fifty
years of age. Those of, say, twenty-four would not try to
thatch or drain ; they were just day men, and ' bad at that.'
Still he did not believe that in this respect things were so
hopeless as some people thought. He could remember that
in 1872 the case was much the same, and that his father
had to borrow hands. The towns would not always want
the services of country folk. Already some were coming
back. Thus the last four men whom he had taken on came
respectively one from Willesden, one from Stratford, where
he worked a steam-tram ; and two from Birmingham, where
they were timbermen. The reason of their return was
that they were tired of the towns. I suggested that, partly
as a result of education, the general impulse seemed to be
towards the cities. He replied that this was so, but not

always. Thus in that neighbourhood the population of Long Compton and Cherrington were down, but Whichford held its own. In this connection he remarked that most of the children born about there seemed to be girls. Speaking broadly, he did not think that the outlook in this matter was hopeful, but neither did he think that the position was likely to grow worse. It must be remembered, however, that he was talking of grass country.

Of cattle Mr. Warriner said that if you both bred and grazed them the business paid, but if you had to buy them in at £14, keep them for a season, and sell them out at, say, £16 or £18, they left no profit. On the arable land the mutton trade held its own fairly, but there was always ' cold storage ' to be faced. The Argentine Republic, where they seemed able to produce anything at a very small cost, was the great rock ahead of the industry.

The average cost of repairs and upkeep on the estate Mr. Warriner put at 17 per cent. of the rental, although their own timber was used and all material possible worked up at home, including the bricks, if I remember right. Thus they made their own gates with oak heads, heels, top-bars, and larch ledges. These gates, he said, they could sell at a profit for 12s. apiece, and Spanish chestnut, cut on the estate, was, they found, as good for gate-making purposes as oak.

In walking over this farm I saw the best field of swedes out of the hundreds that I had inspected in my travels. I can only describe it as magnificent. The oats also were a heavy crop, but had been beaten down in places by the rain. Of Shorthorn dairy cows there was a fine herd, their produce being made into butter which was marketed at Birmingham. Another herd of beasts from two to four years of age were fatting on very good pasture with the help of 6 lbs. of cake a head. Some of these were ripe for market.

On this 400-acre farm at Long Compton—there was another of 500 acres of clay land in hand at Stretton-on-the-

Foss, which I did not visit—147 Oxford Down ewes were kept. They were of high quality, as the photograph (facing page 412) of one of the tups shows, and of their produce sixty shearling rams were sold out annually at an average price of £7. Here all young sheep are called 'tegs' until sheared; shearling but unlambed ewes are 'theaves'; and a sheared sheep is a 'hog,' locally pronounced 'shearog.'

On this farm the four-course system was followed: wheat, beans or root, barley, seeds. Here I saw a meadow on the limestone formation, which was making a really good bottom under somewhat adverse circumstances. Ten years before it had been sown down with sainfoin, and in time became infested with 'squitch,' or couch-grass (*Triticum repens*) which, if left undisturbed, sooner or later will kill out the growths of sainfoin or lucerne. This particular field of squitch and sainfoin was heavily grazed with sheep, I presume cake-fed, with the result that the couch-grass had almost entirely vanished, leaving in its place amongst other grasses a fine plant of white clover. Here, again, is a proof that if only they are fed, manured by animals, and kept from becoming a thicket, most lands will in time lay themselves down to satisfactory pasture formed of grasses natural to the neighbourhood.

Near to this pasture was a fine field of wheat—by the way, it is the custom here to horse-hoe the corn. Mr. Warriner estimated the crop at no less than six quarters to the acre, but I judged it at five. He then told me that he did not wonder at my conclusion, as it was a peculiarity of that land that it always cast an extra quarter to the acre above the return the eye would estimate. A feature of this farm was its excellent machines. Thus there was a hay-turner, I think by Jarmain, of Great Haseley, Oxon, with the work of which Mr. Warriner said he was delighted, and an excellent horse-hoe that, by changing the feet, will serve for roots or corn, by Garrett & Sons, of Leiston, Suffolk. In a shed also stood a splendid thrashing-machine and engine which, I think, was manufactured by Messrs.

Clayton & Shuttleworth, of Lincoln, for one of the exhibitions. It cost, I believe, £319 for the thrasher and £190 for the 8 h.p. engine, and then after ten years' wear, inclusive of hiring out, seemed to be as good as new. It must be remembered, however, that much better care was taken of it than falls to the lot of most such implements.

Since I had the pleasure of meeting him Mr. Warriner has kindly sent to me the comparative rents of five typical farms on the Earl of Camperdown's estate, four of them situated in Warwickshire and one in Gloucestershire, for the years 1847, 1875, and 1901. This table I give below, marking the farms by initials. I should say that their average is just over 200 acres, a very usual size in Warwickshire. On Lord Camperdown's property are some of about 400 acres, but the rents are proportionately the same as those quoted. All these five farms, which lie at a considerable distance from each other, have good houses and buildings, more grass than arable, and are well watered.

| Farm | Rents per Acre | | |
|------|------|------|------|
|  | 1847 | 1875 | 1901 |
|  | s. d. | s. | s. d. |
| A. . . . | 32 4 | 39 | 20 7 |
| B. . . . | 37 0 | 40 | 19 0 |
| C. . . . | 40 0 | 44 | 24 0 |
| D. . . . | 30 0 | 31 | 20 0 |
| E. . . . | 38 0 | 44 | 22 0 |

Mr. Golding, of Whichford, Warwickshire, whom I saw on the same day that I visited Mr. Warriner, farmed 270 acres, of which 140 were arable. He said that the land was very good and the country very pretty, but owing to its hilliness it 'played the devil with men and horses.' Thus it took three horses to cart manure, and, owing to the strain upon them, the animals often went wrong. The soil was marl on oolite, or a variety of limestone. He informed me that the rent of his own farm had dropped quite 25 per cent., but the fall on most holdings in the neighbourhood was greater. His buildings were excellent, as were, he said, all those that belonged to Lord Camperdown, which was the reason why he could let his farms so well. He thought that if farmers earned their livings and paid their rents they were fortunate, and did not believe that any in that district were adding to their capital. Taking farms was a speculation, but the man who went in always imagined that he would do better than the man who was going out. He cultivated on a five-course shift: (1) Turnips or vetches, (2) barley, (3) oats, (4) seeds or beans, (5) wheat. His lambs he kept and sold out in the following January if fit, if not later, and it was his practice to buy young things to tread in the straw and eat rough hay for the first year, to be sold out as stores to fat for the following Christmas.

Labour, he said, was rather short, and the best hands went away. The young men were not there, and the old ones would die out, which made the outlook difficult. Of course it must be remembered that on stiff, heavy land the work in winter was very hard, and therefore unpopular. The girls also went away; still the population in that village showed an increase of three or four, but in the neighbourhood generally it had gone down. The average wages were 11s. for daymen and 13s. for horse and stockmen, with a cottage free. At harvest and haytime they received 3s. a day, with an allowance of malt and hops, and I think some other advantages. Now there were sufficient cottages, and Lord Camperdown kept his in very good condition. There were some small-holdings in the neighbourhood. Mr. Golding mentioned two, one a farm of 150 acres which a man worked successfully with the aid of his sons, and another of 50 acres, also managed by a tenant and his son. He seemed to think that to be successful on such occupations the holder must have the help of a family. All the young fellows, however, did not wish to take to farming; thus his own lad of nineteen had left the land to become an electrical engineer. There was no station nearer to the farm than four miles, which was a drawback to it, but they had good markets at Chipping Norton and Banbury.

In driving through this neighbourhood I noticed that most of the cottages were stone-built and slate-roofed, and that a good many of them, now converted into dwellings for labourers, had once been farmhouses. Here, too, I saw some of the S lands of which the origin and object have excited so much speculation among those who study such matters. As I hope, however, to treat of these more fully when I come to deal with Northamptonshire, I do not enter into the subject here.

A gentleman whom I had the pleasure of meeting in the county, the son of a large farmer who for many years had been mixed up with agricultural matters and agriculturists, and who is himself a landowner and a farmer, wrote me an interesting letter of which I quote the substance. He said that some twenty-five years before he bought an estate of good red marl which if properly farmed would produce from thirty-six to forty-eight bushels of wheat to the acre, and as many of beans. In 1876 he sold his wheat at 6s. a bushel, and in 1877 at 7s. the bushel. He gave up farming this land in 1893, when he sold his wheat for 3s. the bushel, the difference between the first year at 6s. and the last at 3s. estimated on a return of thirty-six bushels, being £5 8s. per acre, or, say, five annual rents of the land upon which the wheat was grown, a decrease in crop value of 50 per cent. Also he kept a flock of pedigree Shropshire sheep. In 1876 he sold their wool for about eighteenpence a pound, in 1893 for ninepence a pound. This was another decrease of 50 per cent., the difference between the two prices equalling the total amount paid away for labour in connection with the flock. In consequence of the heavy fall in the value of wheat he came to the conclusion that it was impossible to work his land as a wheat- and bean-producing farm, and determined to lay the whole of it down to permanent pasture, with the exception of a few acres. This he did, and in 1894 let the bulk of the estate for a very fair rent as a grass farm.

When he was farming the land as arable his wages bill was about £3 a week per hundred acres. When he let it for grazing and dairy purposes the wages bill certainly did not amount to £1 a week per hundred acres. What, then, he asked, became of the men who lost their employment through the change ? Without doubt they had to leave the neighbourhood, many of them going into the towns to compete with their artisans and labourers. Also the locality was robbed of a considerable annual expenditure. Moreover, what he had done in this and in other cases, had been done by great numbers of people in the Midland Counties. It appeared to him quite clear that this change was bad for the owner, for the occupier, for England generally, and, worst of all, for the labourer. It had almost destroyed the country markets for our manufactures, and it had seriously reduced the number and the profit of the small tradespeople, such as blacksmiths, wheelwrights, saddlers, and others who were dependent upon landowners and tenants for their living.

He considered that it was to the interest of the whole community that something should be done which would induce the occupiers of suitable English land to grow wheat as they used to do, and thus repeople the rural districts, increase our food supplies, and again bring prosperity to English agriculture. As things were, year by year the country became more dependent upon the foreigner for its food—a fact of which the consequences might be disastrous in time of war. He was a Free Trader, but as regarded this question of encouraging the growth of wheat he would be disposed to support the imposition of a moderate protective duty.

The only other possible course, so far as he could see, was to give to the grower of wheat a bonus either on the acreage or on the produce of his crop. This would be difficult but not impossible to arrange, and if the bonus were allotted to the man who actually grew the wheat, it appeared to him that it could not be fairly said that it was putting money into the landowner's pocket. But even if it did to some extent advantage the owner as well as the cultivator, he thought that the country would benefit as a whole by the large increase in the production of wheat, by the large increase in the number of labourers employed upon the land, and by the resulting large increase in the purchasing power of the rural districts, to say nothing of the fact that the kingdom would be made more independent of its supplies of imported food.

Unless they chance to be members of the Cobden Club, I think that most people will be of opinion that there is much sound sense in the views expressed by my informant, but this is a matter in which sense is of small avail.

In turning over my Warwickshire correspondence I find a letter from a clergyman in the county, whereof I summarise the contents, as it is a sample of many which future investigators of agricultural matters may expect to receive—that is, if I may judge from my own experience. The writer begins by invoking blessings on my labours, for which I thank him. He goes on to ask a number of questions, large, intricate, and difficult, as to the farming and management of his glebe, also for a list of literature that would be helpful to him. Finally he ends by saying, 'Your book, "A Farmer's Year," is, I hear, highly appreciated. May I venture to ask whether you will favour me with a copy, which I should like to read and also lend to some of my neighbours?' To play the rôle of an amateur land and general agent and adviser (no fees!) I am well accustomed—indeed it occupies a considerable portion of my time; but I confess that by my correspondent's kind offer not only to accept and read my work, but to lend it to his neighbours, I was deeply touched. Thus it is that authors grow so rich—as they are sometimes reported to be in the gossip paragraphs of the press.

To return to the county of Warwick. The general opinion that I formed was that landowners are considerably crippled; that most of the farmers are just making a living, and perhaps on the superior grass lands a little more; and that such of the labourers as remain are better housed, better fed, and better paid than they have ever been in the past. In considering this county it should be remembered that the markets for produce are large, constant, and remunerative.

## SHROPSHIRE

THE inland county of Shropshire, which lies upon the
border of Wales, and, especially upon the west, is of the
same hilly nature, appears to contain, although upon this
point sundry authorities vary to the extent of about
15,000 acres, 859,516 acres.  So far as I was able to
gather from various sources of information, the northern
division of the county is chiefly devoted to dairying,
grazing, and horse-breeding.  Here about one-third of the
land is pasture and two-thirds are arable.  In the south-
western division the chief agricultural industries are the
breeding and grazing of sheep and Hereford cattle and the
breeding of horses.  On the hill land in this division there
are many sheep-walks.  These lands are divided into about
seven-eighths pasture to one-eighth arable, but in the
lower-lying districts the proportions of arable and pasture
are almost equal.  In the south-eastern and central divisions stock are very largely fed ; also turnips and barley are
grown, and there exists a considerable sheep and horse
breeding industry.  Here the areas of pasture and arable
balance each other, or did some few years since, but probably a good deal of land has gone down to grass during
the last few seasons.  In the northern division the average
size of the farms is from 150 to 200 acres, about 500 acres
being the maximum area and 100 acres the minimum.  In
the south-western division they average from 200 to 250
acres, 1,000 acres being perhaps the largest and 120 acres
the smallest.  In the central and south-eastern divisions
there are sheep-walks which vary from 400 to 1,000 acres,

the other farms running from 500 acres down to eighty acres, about 200 acres being the average size.

The best farms are in very good demand, but not so those of inferior quality. The husbandry on the whole is fair, but owing to a want of capital to enable farmers to employ sufficient labour, not so good as it was in the past. Speaking generally, dairy farmers and graziers appear to be the most prosperous.

On the whole I suppose that the county may be called pastoral, and therefore more or less flourishing. The first agricultural authority with whom I spoke in Shropshire was a gentleman of very wide experience, Mr. R. H. Newill, of Lydbury North, agent to the Earl of Powis, who owns 21,000 acres in the county. He estimated the ordinary rentals in the district where he lives at about £1 an acre for good land, two-thirds of which would be pasture. In North Shropshire they seemed to run from 30s. to £2, and at Market Drayton from 33s. to 35s., while farms in the neighbourhood of Shrewsbury fetched about 28s. the acre. The average drop in rentals was somewhere about 20 per cent., and in selling values about 40 per cent., reckoning from 1875. For the most part, he said, the holdings are small, few of them exceeding 300 acres, but on the barley lands they vary from 300 to 500 acres. The smaller occupations were much in demand; but larger farms, which require a great deal of capital, let less readily. Shropshire farmers were, he considered, a hard-working set of men, and did well, making rent, interest, and a living. As usual, the worst feature in the outlook was, he declared, the question of labour. There was no doubt that the population was decreasing. The young folk migrated, leaving the aged in the villages, while the children lessened in number. Thus in the parish of Lydbury North fourteen years before the average school attendance was sixty. In 1901 it had fallen to twenty-six!

Mr. Newill kindly furnished me with a table of the comparative census returns of the Clun Union, in which

Lydbury is situated, for the decades of 1871, 1881, 1891, and 1901. Out of these nineteen parishes only five seem to have increased in population during that period, in one case owing to the advent of a rich family into the neighbourhood, whereas, unless my addition is at fault, the total number of inhabitants has been reduced by nearly two thousand souls. In some villages this shrinkage is very marked ; thus Norbury now returns 159 inhabitants, as against 421 in 1871 ; and Ratlinghope 197, as against 295. Still, Mr. Newill was hopeful of the future. He thought—upon what exact grounds I do not know—that although those who have gone will not come back, ' perhaps they will cease to go.' He said that taking the district through, they were pretty well off for cottages, although some were very bad indeed. The wages for an ordinary labourer seemed to be about 13s. a week, or, if he did Sunday work, up to 15s. In addition a cottage was supplied, together with the keep of a pig and some food and drink in harvest, with the privilege of free haulage of coal and wood. These extras, he estimated, brought the real value of the wage up to £1 a week. His conclusion was that its sheep, dairying, Hereford cattle, and barley growing still brought prosperity to Shropshire, on which, however, the shadow of the labour trouble lay deep.

While we were talking to Mr. Newill, although the weather was bitterly cold, a violent thunderstorm broke over the house. As I watched it through the window I saw a thunderbolt fall within twenty paces of me. It was shaped like a ball of fire, and seemed to vanish into the soil of the garden without doing any damage to the house or to the surrounding trees. Although I have heard of these globular bolts, I never before saw one, even in Africa, that land of thunderstorms.

Mr. Newill, among much other information, gave us an interesting example of what may be done by the judicious planting of larch. Waste heather land set in 1859 with about 4,000 trees per acre, at a cost of 30s. per 1,000, when cleared recently realised a profit of £40 an acre—that is, £1 an acre rent for land which was otherwise almost valueless. The thinnings, I may add, were estimated to cover the cost of setting and fencing.

On the day and morrow of our arrival at Lydham Manor our host, Mr. Arthur H. Sykes, took us to interview some farmers on the estate. These men had no notice of our coming. Indeed, we only called where the farms lay convenient to our path upon such of the tenants as happened to be at home, my object being to collect evidence from the ordinary run of agriculturists who might be taken as fairly representative of their class.

The first farmer whom we saw held 146 acres, of which fifty were arable. He grew ten acres of wheat 'for straw and bread corn,' and kept sixty-two ewes and twenty-eight head of cattle, of which ten were cows in milk. It will scarcely be believed, but at the time we saw this man he was carrying on his farm with no other assistance than that of his wife, who had eight young children. Until shortly before he had employed two men, both of whom, I think, lodged in his house, after the Shropshire custom. When the time for the spring hiring-fair came round, however, they left him, and up to that date he had not been able to find anyone to take their place. To one young fellow of twenty he offered £5 more than he had ever yet paid a man—viz. £20, with food and lodging (after all, only as much as a housemaid earns). The astute youth took his 'hiring-shilling' and then departed to someone else who offered him £4 more. According to this farmer such conduct is common. The hiring-shilling may bind the master, but unless he actually sets his foot upon the premises it does not bind the man, who, sure of a place in any event, enters on a quest for the highest obtainable wages. So keen is the competition, indeed, that he seldom fails in obtaining an advance on the amount for which he has contracted to give his services. As under the circumstances time was evidently of value to our host, who, with other business, had ten cows waiting to be milked, we did not trouble him for long. Often I wonder, however, whether he, his wife, and the eight infants are still the sole cultivators of those 146 acres of land.

Another farmer whom we saw, Mr. Gough, of the Glebe Farm, was a man of gigantic energy and considerable intelligence, who, I understood, had raised himself to his present position by dint of sheer hard work. Mr. Gough farmed 209 acres, of which between seventy and eighty were under the plough. Again I fear that the tale may seem incredible, but the fact remains that when we saw him he was running this farm with no other help than that of a lad of about nineteen and a little boy. His own words were, when speaking of Shropshire farming, ' The money in it is fairish, but the labour is awful. . . . Unless something is done the country is done. I don't complain of rents.' I asked him what he thought the end would be. He answered, ' I can tell you the end. We shan't have any labour soon—that will be the end. There won't be no man to cultivate the land—it will be for the crows to fly over.'

He said also that the labourers turned from the farmers and went to the gentry and well-to-do people; which was doubtless true, as I have often observed, that this was so. The work in a private garden, for instance, is very different from that on a farm; indeed, even where farms are concerned the labourer will almost invariably prefer to take service on those which are in the hands of a gentleman. Again and again I have found that if you ask the squire who has his own farm in hand about the labour supply, he will answer that there are some complaints, but that he has enough. To get at the facts of the matter the inquirer must take a walk and call on half a dozen farmers within a radius of three or four miles, when in nine cases out of ten he will hear a very different story.

One reason for this is that men like Mr. Gough are apt to expect their servants to work as hard as they do, forget-

ting that the master is toiling for himself and the hireling
for a hireling's wage. Now, Mr. Gough, according to his
own confession, laboured from five in the morning to nine or
ten at night. He said that the working farmer is the only
one that can make ends meet, but at the same time rather
illogically expressed a strong disbelief in small-holdings,
largely, I gathered, on account of the cost of the necessary
buildings. I pointed out to him that, according to all
accounts, he had himself risen to his present position. 'Yes,'
he answered; 'but where will you find men who have
"collared" (*i.e.*, worked) as I have?' The remedy he suggested for the present state of affairs was the common one
of Protection; and of our educational system he had no good
word to say.

Mr. David Lewis, of the Star Farm, in a neighbouring
parish, which was half arable and half pasture, said that
labour was a very grave difficulty. The wages of the men
came to about £26 a year, with food and lodging. He
declared that farming meant very hard work, with small
results, and that his son should not be a farmer. This land
grew good malting samples of barley.

Mr. Matthews, of Colebatch Farm, held 200 acres, of
which two-thirds were pasture, working this area with the
help of his brother and two men. He said that labour was
'terrible short,' and that 'you can't speak to a man but he
is off.' As regards the prospects, he did not 'know what it
was coming to.' On the bottom farms there was little to be
made, but the hill farms, where store-stock and sheep were
kept and little labour required, gave a good return. He
declared that they made a living, but a hard one.

Mr. Blakemore, of Minsterley, where he combined the
farming of 100 acres of land with a building and contracting
business, said that there was very little labour to be had, and
that if a young man was wanted, 'you must give him very
big money.' Thirteen years before a waggoner, who did as
much as two of the present men, used to cost 12s. a week.
Now his wage was £1, with house and garden extra,

and the land really could not afford to pay such wages. He declared that half the farmers were not working 'on their own bottom,' by which I think he meant that they were using borrowed money, but that if a man had a family who would work for him farming in Shropshire still paid well. They supplied the labour which otherwise was unobtainable, and he added, 'You can't farm without labour.'

In his opinion the landlords will suffer still further from the present state of affairs, as everything came back on them in the end. He mentioned the case of an owner of great estates who, when his tenants wanted a reduction some dozen years before, took a number of farms in hand. The result was a heavy loss. He changed his agent and tried again, and after dropping a great deal of money let the land for what it would fetch. Of small-holdings he said that they should not be larger than thirty or forty acres. To such holdings a man could attend himself, or he could supervise a farm of, say, 300 acres and find full employment. Tenancies such as his own of 100 acres he thought a mistake, as they were too much, and yet not enough. The 100-acre man could not put in the necessary personal labour and attend markets, &c., in addition.

Another farmer, Mr. Jones, whom we visited held 262 acres, of which 100 were tillage. He said that he was badly off for labour. He had two men, but wanted more. He complained much of the tremendous wages demanded at harvest. He did not know what to think of the future, but suggested that strikes in the towns and the big industrial works might bring the men back to the land. Thus fifty hands had recently been discharged from a neighbouring quarry, but those who had worked in quarries were not much use in farming.

Mr. Jones kept Welsh and Kerry sheep and Hereford cattle, which he fed out, buying cake and corn. He used a good deal of basic slag, and said that he found it act very well and quickly upon new-laid pasture.

Mr. Christie, a working man with whom I spoke, said

that the young fellows were all going off. Six had just left his village. He had four sons, of whom only one remained upon the land. The rest had gone into various occupations, and one of them was earning £38 a year as a butler. The reason that they went was low wages ; they asked for more money, and if it was not given, cleared off elsewhere. He thought that if people could get a little place of their own they would stop upon the land.

Mr. F. R. Armytage, the author of the valuable report made to the Shropshire County Council some years ago upon the state of agricultural education in the county, and a permanent official under the Council, wrote to me that in Shropshire they were well provided with means for imparting agricultural information both to boys and girls. He doubted, however, whether farmers' sons and daughters would avail themselves of the opportunities thus offered. Speaking generally, he was of opinion that Shropshire had suffered less from agricultural depression than any county in England, but that the labour question was becoming very serious.

Mr. R. S. Clease, the deputy clerk to the Shropshire County Council, also sent me a very interesting communication with reference to the steps that have been taken at the instance of the Shropshire authorities with a view of establishing a combined area of eight or nine counties for the purpose of dealing on uniform lines with sheep-scab. Certain conferences which were held had, he said, resulted in the formation of an area comprising the counties of Denbigh, Flint, Hereford, Montgomery, Radnor, Shropshire, Worcester, and Warwick. This, he thought, had done much good, although the joint committee of the combined counties were obliged to rely entirely upon public opinion to carry their resolutions into effect, as no Authority, except as a condition of allowing them to move from one county to another, could at present compel the enforcement of a rule that all sheep that had been infected or in contact with infection, should be dipped twice between May 1 and November 1.

He said in conclusion: 'We have not succeeded in stamping out the disease yet, but we believe that there would have been very many more cases had the joint committee not been in existence, and we have information on all hands that leads us to believe that the work of the committee is having a very good educational effect on the farmers in all the combined counties. When the combined area was first formed there were many complaints, and much discontent with the action of the individual authorities was shown; but so relieved are the farmers and dealers at having to comply with uniform regulations within the area, and so convinced are they that these regulations, though drastic, are beneficial, that they show their appreciation by assisting the police and inspectors in every way, and by intimating their desire (without compulsion) of dipping their sheep.'

These views were confirmed by Mr. W. E. Garnett-Botfield, of The Hut, Bishop's Castle, whom I had the pleasure of meeting in the county, and who has since written to me saying: 'The scab was rampant on our hill land, and is slowly but surely being stamped out. If we could do without Scotch sheep it would in a very few years be practically non-existent.'

A very interesting institution in Shropshire, but one of the results of which I can say nothing, as it was only opened in April 1901, shortly before the date of my visit to the county, is the Harper-Adams Agricultural College at Edgmond, Newport, founded under the will of the late Thomas Harper-Adams for the purpose of teaching practical and theoretical agriculture. This is, I believe, the only agricultural college that owns its own farm, a mixed pasture and arable holding of 180 acres. The college has accommodation for sixty resident students, who are admitted under the scheme of foundation at the low charge of £35 per annum, and the object of the course is to give a sound agricultural education, combined with the practical training which is required by those who intend to farm either at home or in the colonies, or who are qualifying as estate agents. I much regret that I was not able to avail myself of the kind invitation of the principal, Mr. P. Hedworth Foulkes, to visit this college.

One of the most able and interesting gentlemen with whom I conversed in Shropshire was Mr. H. B. M. Buchanan, of Hales, Market Drayton, where he owns an estate of 2,000 acres. Mr. Buchanan, who is the author of an excellent agricultural Reader for use in village schools, was a strong believer in small-holdings, and said that he had never any trouble in collecting the rents of this class of tenants. Amongst other examples he mentioned the case of a labourer who gave him notice, saying that he must go to where he could have a small-holding. Mr. Buchanan offered to let him five or six acres of land at 30s. the acre, and to put up the necessary buildings, on the condition that he paid 5 per cent. on the outlay, and asked if he would be satisfied with this arrangement. He replied Yes, and the result was, Mr. Buchanan added, that 'I saved that man to the property.' He said also that a tenant of his had two cottages, one with some land attached to it and the other without land. That with the land was always full, that without it always empty. To a tenant of his who opposed his action in increasing small-holdings, he had pointed out that it was to his own interest that they should be multiplied, otherwise it was quite possible that all his labourers might leave him in a body, which would mean his ruin, adding that it was better to keep them near him on the farm, even if they did not give him all their time, than run such a risk. I gathered that this farmer saw the force of the argument.

Mr. Buchanan said that his tenants were paying him 4 per cent. on the money actually laid out on the estate by himself and his predecessors, and were therefore paying nothing at all for the land they farmed. Now estates and farming—like everything else—must be conducted on business principles, and if the industry could not afford to pay Consols rate of interest on the capital advanced for the purchase and upkeep of the land, it was based upon unsound economic principles, and therefore sooner or later must come to utter ruin.

As regarded remedies, Mr. Buchanan was subsequently good enough to forward me a document, in which the gist of the opinions he expressed to me is summed up. As the views contained therein appear to me to be both practical and wise, I quote a portion of it almost in his own words. He wrote:—

Now do not suppose that the remedies I have to suggest are going to populate the country and place agriculture on a sound and prosperous footing. At the best they can do but little, but I believe they can do 'a little,' and, what is most important, they can do that little within the near future, and need not wait for the far future, with all its attendant suffering, before they can be put into operation. I do not think that it is a question of wage that is causing the young and more intellectual life to leave the country-sides for the town centres. In my opinion, the great force that is operating is dulness, and that the cottager has little or no prospect of improving his position. As regards dulness, I quite believe that more could easily be done, and this at once, to relieve the dulness of the villages. But at the very best village life can never, in this respect, as far as we can see at present, be on a level with town life.

But I believe men would put up with the necessary dulness of village life if they saw a chance, after some years of hard work and frugality, of investing their savings in stocking small convenient pastoral holdings, the man, as usual, working for the tenant farmer, while his wife and children looked after and did their best for the small place.

From my own inquiries and from what has passed under my own experience I believe that a man under such conditions is better off than he would be were he to take a larger place, that would entail the whole work of himself and his family, which was not supplemented by any outside earnings. I have christened these small pastoral 'farm-cottage-holdings,' in contradistinction to small-holdings.

There is another and great point that these 'farm-cottage-holdings' would do for the country and agriculture. A child or two who were most inclined for country life, after the school years were passed, might be induced to remain at home and assist to develop these holdings to their utmost capacity. The movement,

MR. COOPER'S LIFTING STACK-ROOF

*Page 412*

LORD CAMPERDOWN'S OXFORD-DOWN RAM

*Page 416*

therefore, would rear up amongst us a certain number of men and women who had some knowledge of the work necessitated by agriculture.

It is absurd to suppose that an inexperienced man, no matter how strong his muscles may be, is competent to do the work demanded of him on a farm. To call agricultural labour unskilled is the basest and most foolish libel that has ever been passed on a fine body of English working-men. If competent agricultural labour is not skilled, then for Heaven's sake show me what is! I am prepared, at any moment, to stand up before any body of town workmen and to show them that their labour is unskilled by comparison. But, remember, I refer to competent, experienced, willing work, and not to slovenly, inexperienced, and driven work.

Also as these farm-cottage-holdings multiplied, there would arise amongst us more movement, more life, more inquiry for papers, books, and amusements; and so they would help somewhat to relieve that very dulness which is accountable for much of the migration townwards. Still, moreover, these farm-cottage-holdings would produce larger quantities of those lesser agricultural products which ought to be raised in this country, and which, to our lasting disgrace, have been supplied to our town markets from over the seas.

I am aware that it is a mighty difficult and heroic task for a cottager who has a fairly large family to save sufficient to enable him to start in such a place with a fair prospect of success. Could not, then, some scheme be devised, by agricultural credit-banks or by Government loans, to advance to men of known character and experience (who had saved a bit for themselves) the balance necessary for a start, at low rates of interest, and with easy rates of repayment, and to landlords who possess the spirit, but not the cash, facilities to erect the necessary buildings at a cheaper rate than we can erect them at the present time? I wonder what a million or so of the nation's money lent out in this way would do? I would venture to predict that the capital and interest would be repaid, and the nation would be the stronger and richer for her loan to agriculture.

Could a landlord do a nobler work than to facilitate in all ways in his power the creation of these small 'farm-cottage-holdings,' and could he experience a deeper and more enduring pleasure than to go the round of his estate and watch the increasing prosperity and consequent contentment of his 'farm-cottage-holders'? As to the tenant farmer, what a sense of security he would experience, and how much more prosperous would be his farming if he were sure of permanent, willing, and intellectual labour. To help others to help themselves is surely Christianity put into practice, and is the wisest method of being useful in one's time and place.

I saw other agriculturists in Shropshire, some of whom were farmers and some who were not, but of these I need only say that with variations their tale was much the same as those which I have already told. Of the rent and general conditions of the industry they made little or no complaint; their cry was of the labour, continually of the lack of labour. The question is to what extent their stories of this trouble ought to be discounted. The reader must bear in mind that small husbandmen, especially in a grass country, will employ no more hands than are absolutely necessary; further, that unless they are driven to it they will not keep on men in slack times, preferring to take their chance of obtaining help when it is actually wanted, and thus save money in their pockets. The object is laudable, but their efforts to attain it in these days of scarcity do not tend to the solution of a very difficult problem.

I will conclude my sum of evidence by quoting a few figures connected with a large, and I believe typical, Shropshire estate the books of which I was kindly allowed to inspect. This property, which is a little under 7,000 acres in extent, used to bring in a rental of nearly 23s. an acre in the good times. In 1901 it brought in a gross rental of about 18s. an acre, from which must be deducted the repairs, that come to between 18 and 20 per cent. of the annual receipts; the tithe, that averages 2s. 6d. the acre; and the other usual charges. It is an instructive fact that on this property almost the entire loss is due to the reduced letting value of the farms *over* fifty acres, those *under* fifty acres having practically held their own as a source of income.

This estate may be divided into three classes—bottom

lands, which fetch about 24s. an acre; hillside farms, estimated at 12s. an acre; and hilltop sheep-runs, worth 5s. an acre. In addition the woods bring in a little money, and there are some very small holdings. A gentleman who was very largely interested in this property told me that the tenants farmed well as regards manure and keeping a good head of stock, but such matters as fencing, levelling mole-hills, and cutting out thistles were not attended to owing to the shortage of labour. He was a strong believer in the building of cottages, and disapproved of the smaller holdings being merged into the larger farms.

The general body of the testimony which I was able to collect went to show that the cottage accommodation in the county is 'middling,' and that more of it would be helpful in keeping the men on the land. A considerable number of gentlemen of all classes with whom I spoke declared themselves in favour of more small-holdings, for which there is doubtless a demand. On the whole, I am of opinion that farming in Shropshire is still a profitable industry, much more profitable, indeed, than in many other counties. But here, as elsewhere, the labour question is becoming very acute.

## ESSEX

In travelling from Warwickshire to Essex, which was the next county that I visited, I passed through Berkshire and noted there much poor and badly farmed land. Also there seemed to be great areas that had not been laid, but had tumbled down to grass of very inferior quality, always a sure sign of agricultural depression, recent and acute.

The metropolitan shire of Essex covers about 987,000 acres, coming tenth in size among the English counties, and has a length from north-east to south-west of sixty-three miles. The best soil, a friable loam well suited to cereals and beans, runs along the coast, forming a belt of eight or ten miles in depth ; indeed most of the good lands in Essex lie low, the richest pasture being found along the rivers and the marshlands, by the borders of the friths and creeks. Also there are numbers of islets of a marshy character, such as Havingore, Horsea, Mersea, Wallasea, Foulness, Potton &c. The highlands are situated in the interior of the county, the highest of all being on the London clay, as in the neighbourhoods of Waltham Abbey, Tiptree Heath, and Brentwood.

Certainly he who investigates the agricultural state of England must be prepared for surprises. Had I been asked before I went there in what part of the country I expected to find the labour conditions worst I should have answered in Essex, because of the prevailing depression and its nearness to London. The fact, as I found it, was that they were better than in any county I had visited so far, though how to explain the circumstance I know not. By this statement I mean that a certain proportion of the young men were stopping on the land; that in all districts labour could be had at a price; and that farmers as a whole did not seem to look forward with fear and trembling, as in many places, to a day when they might be left with no hands but their own to help them.

I do not mean, however, that there were no complaints upon this subject. Indeed, if I were to select individual opinions from the hundred and fifty pages of notes which we took in Essex, I could easily make it appear that the labour question was as pressing in this county as anywhere in England. But that was not the general view, although many were despondent on the point, and all agreed that the best men went. Indeed, taking it throughout, I heard more complaints of the highness of the wage and of the quality of the labour than of its scarceness. Strangely enough also the nearer we came to London, the more plentiful did we find labourers; a phenomenon that well may puzzle men and angels, unless indeed the explanation is that the dwellers in those parts know too much of the great city and its grinding poverty and competition to wish to spend their lives there. Or perhaps they have tried and failed to find fortune in the streets—who can say?

The agricultural position outside of the labour problems, I take roughly to be this. Excepting those who own suburban property valuable for building and accommodation lands, or some of the richest meadows by the rivers, the landlords of the million acres, more or less, which Essex contains are at the best receiving but an infinitesimal return from their estates. If, taking the county through, the average rent be put as high even as 15s., how much remains for the owner after tithe, land tax, repairs, and other outgoings have been deducted? Perhaps 5s. an acre, most of which will be absorbed every few years by the necessity for some new building. Of course, I am speaking now of totally unencumbered estates on which all the land is let to reliable tenants who pay their rents. What happens in the case of those that are burdened with mortgages, jointures, or other charges, or where the tenants default, leaving the soil foul and worked out, 'if I know I prefer not to say'? Speaking generally, however, it may be assumed that the landowner in Essex who has to depend solely on the produce of his acres is, in the vast majority of instances, a ruined man, who, to live at all, must let the home which he cannot sell, with its sporting rights, the only valuable assets that remain to him.

The tenant, on the whole, is in a better case. His rent has dropped enormously, often indeed to whatever sum he chooses to offer. Labour, it is true, is dear, but he meets this difficulty by employing fewer hands and not farming so much 'in detail' as he used to do. Being so near to London there are still crops which pay him, if he takes the trouble to grow them, such as green peas for market, or midsummer vetches for town horses, or mangold, swede, and radish seed raised to the order of the great seedsmen, and so forth.

Thus it comes about that they can make a living; indeed, I have not found one who fails to do so, to pay his rent, such as it is, to keep a horse and trap, and even in many cases, to treat himself to an occasional day with the hounds or gun. Of course, the farmer grumbles as he grumbled when wheat was 50s. a quarter, if with more reason; and there is no doubt that for the most part he lives close and puts nothing by. Still he does live, and in no disagreeable fashion; moreover, a fact which he is very apt to forget, he has a rent-free house over his head which in a town would cost him £50 a year; he occupies a position of authority and complete independence, and has many other incidental advantages such as are denied to the poor landlord with an empty pocket and a position to keep up.

But if the tenant does better than the owner in Essex, without a doubt the labourer does best of all. A good man, if he elects to remain on the land, can earn 18s. to £1 a week, and in some instances more. There is not the slightest need for him to suffer oppression or even just rebuke, since he can always find a market for his services elsewhere. Food is cheap and abundant, education is thrust upon him for nothing, and his children are well clothed and skilfully tended when they are sick at small cost to himself. The lot may not be ideal, with its lack of prospect and its monotony; moreover in Essex the cottages are for the most part bad, although, so far as I could ascertain, this fact does not seem to trouble the majority of their tenants. But compare it with that which fell to the fortune of our labourer's father or grandfather. Why, as I hope to show later on, it is Paradise to a pig-sty!

The Vale of Dedham, which lies below Langham Hall, the home of Mr. Nocton, the first of our kind hosts in Essex, is one of the most beautiful spots in Eastern England. Here it was indeed that Constable produced some of his finest pictures, the spot whence he painted his famous 'Vale of Dedham' being either a knoll now occupied by a sanatorium for wounded officers within the grounds, or the top of the church tower, which stands close to the Hall. Very charming did this Vale of Dedham look as I saw it from my window on the day of my arrival in the rich glow of a June evening.

Before me stretched flat, lush meadows through which wound the Stour, its waters rose-hued beneath the rose-hued sky. Beyond these lay a gentle slope of rising lands, some covered with the varying greens of wheat and barley, some bare, purple fallow, whereon in this season of drought no roots as yet appeared. Far away on the crest of the rise was a dense bank of slumbrous woodland, and just below me, in the immediate foreground, a brake of broom yellow with flower, marked by four trees—a clump of three twisted firs and a single ancient oak.

Mr. Nocton is a gentleman who has acquired his estate of 6,000 acres within recent years, who brings, moreover, intelligence, capital, and business capacity to bear upon the land and has sympathy with those of all classes who look to it for their livelihood. A summary of his views will therefore be instructive, especially as he himself farms about 800 acres. Since during the previous twelve years he had invested so largely in land, by way of a test question, I asked him whether he would put money into it which belonged to a ward.

He answered 'No,' but that, although the return on the investment was poor, the land afforded him sport and pleasure; also he thought that prospects were better and selling values improving. Of the labour he had no good word to say. Old men only were left, he declared; the young ones went away, and the quality was bad. He thought that farmers did not do well unless they combined dealing with husbandry. Mr. Nocton was also of opinion that the future of England depends very largely upon the manner in which the problem of the exodus from the rural districts is faced. He said that he had satisfied himself by personal observation that this question is the most vital of the day. The remedies he suggested were a tax upon imported flour, that would employ our mills—of which I have seen so many standing derelict in different parts of England, and bring an immense amount of 'offal' into the country—since imposed, although to a very trifling total—and the multiplication of small-holdings. Upon this point he was very strong indeed, although he was not prepared to say by what exact machinery they could be brought into being. He added that if he were able he would promote such holdings by every means in his power, and that he thought the subject one which earnestly demanded the attention of our Government, who should provide State aid and widen the powers of the county Councils. Further, he could see no valid reason why the transfer of land should not be greatly cheapened, and, indeed, made as easy as that of stocks and shares—a conclusion with which most people will agree, except, perhaps, those who are interested in maintaining the present system. As regards the outlook he said that he was 'living in hope.'

Another most valuable witness was Mr. J. Fenn, of Ardleigh, the well-known land agent and farmer, whose experience covers a period of no fewer than five-and-forty years.

He estimated the drop in rents at from 50 to 60 per cent., but said that the selling price was a little better than it had been a year or two before. The landlords, he declared, were cruelly hit, especially by the tithe, which in some places stood as high as 5s. or 6s. an acre. Farmers made a hard living, although a chance man saved some money, generally through dealing. As a class they were badly off for capital, and often secured farms which landlords were forced to let, because they had no money to work them, by bargaining that they should pay no valuation, or that they should have the land rent free for a year or two. Some also made a practice of 'land-skinning,' giving up the farm when it was worked out.

As regarded labour, he said that the wage was high and the quality bad, but that numerically they were better off for men than they had been. Mr. Fenn could see no hope for the future, and thought that the landed interests in Essex were marching towards ruin; that 'the land is going back, the crops are getting lighter, the capital is growing less.' Buildings, he said, were deteriorating, and the farms impoverished by the keeping of cows and ewes, that drag the land, instead of fat sheep and bullocks by which it is improved. In view of the drought and bad crops of the season of 1901, he characterised the outlook as 'awful.' In this connection it must be remembered that Mr. Fenn was speaking of the Ardleigh district, where the land is for the most part light, and had therefore felt the lack of rain more than some others.

Perhaps I may add here an expression of my own opinion. I drove through many miles of country in the neighbourhood of Dedham Vale. In June 1901 hays were not half a crop, corns were yellow, the ear showed on oats, some of which could not have been more than 9 in. in height, while the fly was ravaging great breadths of the young mangolds. In short it was difficult to see in that year to what the landlord could look for a rent and the farmer for his living upon the light lands of Northern Essex.

Wages, Mr. Fenn said, were 14s. or 15s. for daymen and
16s. for horsemen, with a house ; indeed, he knew a shepherd
at Langley who took £1 a week and a house. The upkeep
expenses of estates he put at from 10 to 12½ per cent. of the
gross rentals, but owing to the general impoverishment many
buildings were being let down. The money spent in connection with shooting, he thought, helped the county considerably. All the tenancies were yearly, and the system of
farming generally followed was (1) fallow or roots, (2) barley,
(3) seeds, that is, layers which were mown, (4) wheat, and
sometimes (5) oats. The cottages were fair and moderately
plentiful, but the water supply was bad. At a rental of
1s. 6d. a week they brought in no interest. Mr. Fenn informed me that he had an open mind on the subject of small-
holdings, but on the whole did not believe in them. Still
he knew some cases where they had been successful, but
more in which they were failures.

Upon the point of the abnormal drought that prevailed
in that season Messrs. Simpson, who for many years had
practised as farriers or veterinary surgeons throughout the
district, told me that they could scarcely remember such a
summer. They instanced a pond in the neighbourhood in
which the water was habitually 17 ft. in depth. That spring
there was not a pailful left. Among much other information
they said that the farming is no longer what it was in their
early days. Where five men were employed, there are now
only three, capital is scanty, and tenants take farms larger
than they can manage. The best young men were going or
gone from the land, but the wasters remained. They were
of opinion that ' it does not matter to the Government or the
towns whether we grow a sack of wheat or not.' The
farmers, they said, paid their rent, which ran from 30s. down
to 7s. 6d. per acre, according to the quality of the land, but
saved little or nothing. The present outlook they considered
very alarming, owing to the drought, and the labour question
' more serious than the prices,' yet they stated that the
prospects of North Essex farmers and farming were better

than they had been a few years ago. I am, I confess, not able to point out in what exact particulars the improvement lay.

Mr. Wilson, who was agent to Mr. Nocton, told me that the local wages were 14s. or 15s. a week, with £6 15s. for the harvest month and an allowance of malt and hops. Horsemen received a house in addition. Good horsemen were, however, very difficult to find. The cottages, he said, were on the whole bad : they brought in from 2s. down to 1s. a week, according to state and situation. There was a bare supply of labour of an inferior sort, but the question was not so much one of quantity as of quality, as it was almost impossible to find good, steady, skilled workmen, and many of the young men were going away. The rent of land varied from 5s. to 15s. an acre ; perhaps the average was about 12s. It had risen a little since 1891, and of late there had been a fair demand for farms, but those who applied for them generally lacked capital. As a rule the rents were paid ; thus out of his thirty or more tenants Mr. Nocton had hardly any in arrear. The great causes of failure among farmers were, he thought, want of capital, enterprise, and requisite knowledge. Also many of them were to a large extent in the hands of the dealers, who brought store cattle into the county, where very little stock was bred, from Shrewsbury and the Midlands. These they sold to the farmers, who when they could not pay for them in cash were debited with the amount, as may be imagined under such circumstances, to quite the full value of the beasts. When these stores have been fatted by the farmer, in practice they were obliged to resell them to the dealer from whom they had been bought, again at his own valuation, which it is not uncharitable to suppose would frequently be somewhat lower than that of a purchaser in the open market. Thus at the end of the transaction it would be found that the profit remaining to the farmer was exceedingly small.

The capital required in that district was £10 an acre, but as money was so short among agriculturists, the smaller farms let more readily than the large ones. Both Mr.

Wilson and Mr. Nocton put the selling value of most of the
land at from £15 to £20 an acre. Some of it, however,
such as light gravel farms, would not fetch more than £8
or £10 the acre, while on the other hand certain picked
lands in the Dedham Vale might be worth £50 an acre.
He described the district as a sheep and barley country with
but little cold clay. The proportion of grass to arable was
small, as the soil, with the exception of old stubbed woodlands, did not lay down well. In short it was for the most
part light, though not so light as that over the Suffolk
border. Mr. Wilson thought that cart-horses paid them
better than anything, the practice being to buy them in at
two years old and sell them out at five, the prices ranging
from £60 to £80. He said also that houses let very well to
tenants from London and elsewhere, as the neighbourhood
was very healthy and remarkable for its scenery. As I have
stated, Mr. Nocton was a great believer in small-holdings,
but his agent, Mr. Wilson, on the contrary, put more faith
in large farms, that is, if sufficient capital could be commanded.

Driving with Mr. Nocton over his land, I was first introduced to a labourer, Mr. Biles, who was at work on a field of
mangolds that sloped down to the Vale, and notwithstanding
the drought showed a good plant. He said that the young
men went away, leaving a few of the ' old uns ' behind. The
cottages he described as a ' fair average lot for such places,
but some of them a bit tumbled-down.' He told me he had
seen land at double the value it was then, although that was
' a nice spot ' and it was a funny season when they didn't get
a crop.

Mr. Borham, who lived at a farm of Mr. Nocton's of 500
acres, of which 130 were grass, called, I think, Broom House,
where stood a beautiful old mill surrounded with still water
edged by poplars, told me that the farmers in that district just
lived, and no more, which I gathered was his own case. For
labour they were not well off, though better than some others.
He complained that the best men went, while the ' duffers '

remained. Personally he believed in paying a good man a good wage, as opposed to the system, common in the Eastern Counties, of equal remuneration independent of merit; but his habit of giving more money for more value resulted, he said, in some friction. Mr. Borham kept 150 Suffolk ewes and 150 half-breeds, the produce of Lincoln tups, but said that he liked the Black-face best. His experience was that sheep and hay paid most on a farm, but that there was not any profit in bullocks.

Adjoining this place was a large common meadow of about fifty acres belonging, I believe, to Mr. Nocton, over which, however, the tenants of the neighbouring farms held certain rights in proportion to the size of their holdings. This field, of exceedingly rich pasture, lay low, and was mown once, after which it was fed, two head of cattle being allowed to the acre, but no bulls, shod horses, or sheep. Although the drought was so sharp that I was shown a dry pond that had not lacked water for twelve years, it looked beautifully lush and green, and the same may be said of several neighbouring pastures farmed by Mr. Nocton, where we were told sheep did wonderfully well after the hay was off. On these and other lands we saw large herds of young cattle belonging to Mr. Nocton, mostly of the Shorthorn stamp, which seemed in excellent case. Of these the rest of the heifers were to be kept for breeding and the remainder with the steers sold out as stores or fatted. The foreman told me that they were beginning to feel the drought. Of labourers, he said, they had 'plenty such as they are.' Here, by the way, in haysel and harvest the men stop to refresh themselves at eleven and four o'clock. These meals, or drinks, they call respectively 'elevens' and 'beavers.' These 'beavers,' derived, I suppose, from *boire*, to drink, are, I think, in Norfolk called 'fours,' whence perhaps the polite four-o'clock tea.

In the afternoon we drove through Langham village to Ardleigh, some five miles away, passing over some gravelly stretches of tableland which Mr. Nocton was planting with

Scotch fir and larch. Here the fields were small and the
fences ragged, with many hedgerow trees. On the brash
land some cherries were growing, which looked as well and
as full of fruit as those I saw in Worcestershire. In this
season of 1901 all the crops on that thirsty soil were much
shrunk; indeed during the entire drive of miles I did not
see a single field of which the produce looked as though
it would pay the cost of rent and labour. The grass was
short and thin; a field of peas that I noted, in which the
charlock was being hand-drawn, was going off; and the
beans and oats were very stunted. Among these and the
wheat also the gay red poppies were topping the dwarf
grain now coming into ear. Towards Ardleigh the country
became flatter and the land of a stronger character, although
as yet there was no sign of the stiff Essex clays with which
we were to make acquaintance later on. Here there were
considerable woods of birch, oak, and chestnut, and I noticed
that most of the cottages and farm buildings were roofed with
thatch.

Mr. T. Smith, a tenant of Mr. Nocton's at Ardleigh, was
a man able to speak with experience, as he had held his
farm for no less than fifty-one years, his father and grandfather having occupied another farm on the same property
before him. Outside his gate stood a fine spreading oak
timber. When Mr. Smith first passed that gate it was, he
told me, of such a size that it looked as though he could
pull it down. It must be a strange experience for a man to
have lived in one spot long enough to see a sapling develop
into a noticeable tree. Mr. Smith farmed 214 acres, for
which land he used to pay £400 a year, and £84 a year
tithe. In 1901 his rent was £135 a year, the landlord
paying the tithe. 'But,' he said, 'I was better off when I
paid the £400 than I am to-day.' Although two of his men
had been with him, one for forty-five and one for thirty-six
years, Mr. Smith spoke strongly on the labour question.
'What the land produces the labourer gets,' he said; 'they
don't do nothing, they don't do nothing!' How could

farmers get on, he asked, when each man took the value of a sack of wheat, that is, 14s. 6d. per week? The young men, he declared, were going away, and as regards the power of a bit of land to keep them, he remarked that they did not do their work as it was. I replied that then they would be working for themselves, to which he answered that if he was not able to get a living out of the land how could they?

The season of 1901, coming on the top of the bad year 1900, was, he said, the worst he had ever known. Practically in that part of Essex no rain had fallen for five years. The hay was very poor; the turnips had come up thick, but the fly had 'cleared the lot,' and the mangold was going too, he thought, down the birds' throats. He added that if Mr. Nocton would let him out, he should give up the following Michaelmas, as 'he was tired of it' and ought to have left off farming twenty years before.

Mr. Smith had a very nice lot of calves, which, as is customary in this district, were bought in Buckinghamshire when six days old at the high average price of 65s. each. He said that if they lived to the following Christmas twelve-month—that is, the December of 1902—they ought to make £30 apiece. The homestead buildings were very good on this farm, but noticing two long cracks in a gable I asked the reason, and was informed that they were due to the earthquake which, the reader may remember, visited Essex some years ago.

Driving in the neighbourhood of Ardleigh I found that here the land seemed deeper and cooler, with the result that the crops looked more promising. All of them, however, with the exception of the wheat, which, owing to its deep-rooting nature, drought affects but little, were coming into ear before their season. Beans were short and peas looked very languid, so much so, indeed, that it was doubtful whether rain, if it came, would not be too late to save them. In fact, the prospects of this part of Essex seemed ominous. There was only half a crop, but the rent, the cost of store stock and feeding stuffs, and, above all, of labour, remained the same. It is a melancholy thing to toil the year through at the grudging earth and after all to win no increase.

An interesting small-holder whom I visited in this neighbourhood was Mr. Chapman. He held forty-five acres, and I can never remember seeing land in better heart or more excellently cultivated. Although the season was so dry, he had an excellent crop of roots, which, owing, he alleged, to his system of frequent rollings in dry weather, the fly had not damaged. His peas, too, were good, and almost ready for picking, and a feature of the place was that, after searching it carefully with my eye, I could distinguish but one single weed. I gathered that Mr. Chapman was a very hard worker, and that, notwithstanding the disastrous conditions of recent seasons, his labours had been rewarded with a measure of success.

That there is a demand for little holdings in this district is, I think, suggested by the fact that I was shown two acres of land on which stood a shanty—I can scarcely call it a cottage. This plot had recently been sold to a small man for £160. The reader must remember that the top value of the best land in North Essex, not absolutely suitable for building purposes, is said to be about £50 the acre. Therefore, as the shed on the plot in question could have been worth but little, the purchaser of this piece, which, so far as I recollect, offered no special advantages, was willing to pay nearly 50 per cent. more than the highest value of larger parcels. The fact is, of course, that these little lots in which men are often ready to invest their savings seldom come upon the market.

Mr. Dunnett, of Stour House, Dedham, a large landowner, who, I think, had no less than 1,500 acres under small culture and seeds, the latter being grown for one of the large seed firms, told me that labour was short, that the quality was bad, and that they were working the land with the help of the old men. He said that in Dedham twenty years before he had put a hundred men to work in a single field, but now

IN DEDHAM VALE, NORTH ESSEX

*Page 439*

HOMESTEAD, DENGIE FLATS

*Page 469*

he did not believe that he could find a hundred agricultural labourers in the parish. On 1,500 acres he had not got twelve young men between the ages of eighteen and twenty-five, and on all his farms there was only one boy. The lads of fifteen or sixteen departed to London, where they found employment in the big shops, and all the girls went also. He mentioned the case of a greengrocer in the neighbourhood who bought twelve acres of standing peas and was obliged to import Frenchmen to pick them.

The average rent of land, the best grass excepted, Mr. Dunnett put at from 10s. to 15s. the acre. He informed me that in Essex the dealer was the 'top man,' who answered to the hop-factor in Kent, and the shopman or fruit-broker in Worcestershire. These dealers were men with knowledge, knack, and powers of work, who had often begun as drovers. He named one who, in fifteen years, was said to have risen from that position to be the owner of a fortune of £30,000. About every third farmer in the county dealt, in practice getting his living out of the other two. Not infrequently his 'commission' on a single beast, nominally sold to graziers in the manner that I have already described, would amount to as much as £4, that is, £2 above real value on going in thin, and £2 below real value on coming out fat into the hands of the same dealer. Mr. Dunnett told me that he kept a registered flock of Black-face Suffolk sheep and found that they paid. Also he believed in growing eating-peas for market, which fetched about £12 an acre, the farmer retaining the haulms and immature pods, as in Worcestershire, as the cost of their cultivation should not be more than about £5 the acre.

Dr. C. E. D. Maile, of Dedham House, a medical officer for the Lexden and Winstree Union, informed me that the cottages in the district were overcrowded and very bad. Still the general health was good and there were no epidemics. He did not think that he had treated a dozen cases of typhoid during the past seventeen years. He saw no signs of the exodus from the country districts coming to a stop,

and believed that the end of it would be that much of the
land must go out of cultivation.

Mr. G. F. Hempson, of Good Hall, Ardleigh, where he
farmed 400 acres, took a somewhat more cheerful view of the
labour question. He said that his best hands were the old
men, as the boys would not learn the work, but that his staff
then was better than it had been during the two or three
previous years. He put the average wage of the day labourer
at 17s. a week, and said that five years before he had employed five more men than he did when we met, although
he was still paying away as much for labour. The result
was that he found himself obliged to farm less in detail. He
considered that bad housing was one reason of the exodus.
Personally he had nine cottages, each with a garden, and
none of them were ever empty. Among his hands were men
who, having tried other trades, admitted that they were better
off on the land at the present rate of wages than they had
been in the towns.

Mr. Hempson sold a great deal of produce in London to
private customers, putting it up in the special railway boxes
which the Great Eastern will carry from many of their
stations, up to a weight of 20 lb. for fourpence. Here I may
state, both from my own experience and from that of others,
that this innovation on the part of the Great Eastern Railway, although it is not far-reaching and comprehensive
enough, has proved a boon to farmers who chance to live
upon their system, and, I should imagine, not unprofitable
to themselves. One of the chief evils from which English
agriculture has to suffer is the greed and obstinacy of railways, which in the pride of their monopoly, extort from the
British producer rates of carriage that often render his
industry unremunerative. Nor do they stop here; since
almost invariably, preferential terms are granted to the
foreigner, whose stuff arrives in bulk, and can if its
shippers choose, be disembarked at other ports and given to
rival lines to carry. Of course patriotism, or a care for
home interests other than their own, is not to be expected

from railway companies, or, indeed, where money is concerned, if we may believe a fifth of what we hear, from the great majority of trading bodies, who are not influenced by the traditions and finer feelings which sometimes have weight with the individual.

The marvel is, however, that British Governments should allow such a state of affairs to continue without even attempting to remedy it either by legislation, or by the better and perhaps more feasible way of competition. There is only one inference : that the interests of agriculture do not really count with them ; that its welfare to them is a matter of little import. On this day whereon I write there appears a report in the daily papers of a speech made by Mr. Hanbury at the annual meeting of the Agricultural Organisation Society. Had this address been delivered by any other Minister doubtless it would have been recorded at length ; but as the speaker was only President of the Board of Agriculture, representing the largest British industry, his remarks are compressed into a few lines. From this truncated report I gather Mr. Hanbury said that British farmers 'had not only to fight against a combination of foreign nations, but sometimes to fight against English companies and great English firms. . . . He admitted that the railway rates pressed very heavily on the small farmers.' In its comments upon these remarks the 'Morning Post' writes : 'The net effect is that the British farmer is left to compete single-handed, not merely against a combination of foreign rivals, who have been quick to learn that union is strength, but against the Government itself. . . . There is red tape enough at White-hall to strangle enthusiasm, and a stupid tradition that is not to be set aside by mere phrases, however valiant they be.'

True enough, but how melancholy to read ! How can Britain expect to continue to prosper when what is after all her most vital interest, since on its well-being depends the production, not only of food, but of the majority of those robust inhabitants without whom a nation must dwindle and fall—receives at the hands of our rulers neglect that

amounts almost to oppression ?   In what other country would
railways be allowed to give preferential rates to foreign produce ?   But to interfere with this privilege—I admit a very
difficult matter—would offend the monied interests by which
the policy of this land is in the main directed, and lose
votes ; therefore it is not interfered with, and to compete
with it would be costly and troublesome, therefore it is not
competed with.

To return.   Mr. Hempson said that flowers were so
plentiful and cheap in London that there was no profit in
supplying them, but that good chickens 'dressed but not
pulled' would always sell.   He kept a hundred bullocks,
but with beef at sixpence a pound had lost money on them ;
nor was Black-faced wool very remunerative at the same
price.   Mr. Hempson told me also that notwithstanding the
extra labour involved in the breaking up &c., in his opinion
three-year layers paid better than laying down the land to
permanent pasture, which often did not succeed, and at best
was very slow to establish itself.

At Great Bromley, a village about three miles south-
east of Ardleigh, I visited Mr. Charles Wenden, of Blagg's,
Thack's, and Hilliard's Farms, who with other land held
300 acres under Mr. Nocton.   He told me that the farmers
'wriggled along' ; they existed, although on the figures it
looked as though there were no profits.   The reason why
farms did not change hands more frequently was, he said,
that their occupiers clung to their homes, where often they
had lived all their lives, and perhaps their fathers had been
before them.   Not long before a really good agriculturist
had gone under in that neighbourhood—one who owned his
land and farmed it well, having the best of everything upon
the place.   But he was driven to raise money and now his
relatives were obliged to keep him.   Mr. Wenden said that
the younger farmers adapted themselves better to modern
conditions ; the old men could not shake off old habits and
suffered accordingly.   To be master of the situation the
holder of land ought to be able to command £10 an acre

'PUGGLING' STRAWBERRIES, TIPTREE FRUIT FARM

Page 461

capital, but he believed that there were many who 'schemed through' on £5 an acre. The fall in rents had been a help to tenants, but their present trouble was the labour. Still they had sufficient men at that time, and indeed he did not think there would be much difficulty as to supply, since certain of the brickyards had shut down and released a good many hands. The young men were not leaving Great Bromley so much as was the case in many places, but there were now few large families in the parish, and he felt sure that the population had sunk, as the school attendance was lower and some of the cottages were empty.

The wages, Mr. Wenden said, ran from 14s. to 16s. a week with harvest money, which meant another 1s. 6d. a week, beer at thrashing, &c. On his holding the labour-bill came to about 34s. an acre. He informed me that the year of 1900 was the worst that they had had, and that the prospects for 1901 were equally bad.

Out of the 600 acres which I understood Mr. Wenden farmed, only thirty were grass; a strange contrast truly to the holdings I have recently described when dealing with Warwickshire and other midland counties. His sheep were the Suffolk Black-face, and of course he had bullocks, but said that there was 'little hanging to them.' Here I saw a field of October-sown barley, rather a rarity in the Eastern Counties, or at any rate in Norfolk. It looked very well, indeed much better than the spring-sown, which it precedes by a week or so at harvest time.

Mr. H. E. Wenden, brother of the last gentleman and Secretary to the Tendring Hundred Farmers' Association, informed me that he thought the agricultural depression was not so bad as it had been, and that the farmers were economising more than they used to do. In agriculture, he said, as in other professions, talent told as did capital, a borrower of capital having no chance. The farming, he thought, was generally well done in that district. The average size of the holdings he put at from 500 to 600 acres and the average rent at about 15s. the acre. By way of showing that there was no cash to spare among the agricultural community, Mr. H. E. Wenden mentioned the fact that he collected the voluntary rates for Church and School and found it very difficult to get in the money. He said that the builders spoiled the labour market by offering higher wages, and that pig-keeping, which used to be a source of profit to the labourer, had been much checked by the prevalence of swine-fever. He told me that there were several small-holdings in the immediate neighbourhood of about thirty to fifty acres. One man did very well and paid 35s. an acre rent; others not so well. Thus, of two whose lands adjoined, one was flourishing and his neighbour very much the reverse. In this connection the reader will remember that the average rent for large holdings was put at 15s. the acre. In his opinion foremen, as a rule, made bad farmers, chiefly for the reason that they had no capital.

Mr. Wenden added that now-a-days it was impossible for the farmer to put any dependence on corn : he must 'scheme,' and grow such produce as might be in demand at the time. He thought that local agricultural clubs and shows did good, and that in this neighbourhood farmers would be willing to co-operate for their mutual benefit. I only trust that he may be right in his views, but my experience, gathered in many parts of England, is that large farmers absolutely refuse to combine. As I think I have already said, small-holdings seem to be essential to successful co-operation.

In driving through this Ardleigh district I observed that the churches were very numerous, and many of them of considerable size and architectural beauty. This seems to suggest that at the date of their erection, in or about the fifteenth and sixteenth centuries, the district must have been occupied by a large and thriving population.

Driving from Dedham to Lawford, near Manningtree, on the subsequent day, we passed through a somewhat dull succession of fields under wheat, oats, and barley, grown on good, mixed, light land, varied here and there by an occasional fallow on which the green lines of seedling roots were peeping through. In the village of Lawford many of the cottages are wooden, weather-boarded structures, small, but with good roofs. Here we visited Mr. William H. Richardson, a large farmer in the parish, who lived in a charming old house called Dale Hall. He said that the average rent in the neighbourhood was 15s. per acre, but it was 'not a question of the rent.' Farmers in general were not prosperous, and things had been going back with them during the last two years. They were making a living, and no more. Of labour they had just about enough, although they were not well off, as the able-bodied men departed to work in the factories. He thought that they had seen the worst of that difficulty; but so far as I could gather, the improvement was due to local causes, some brickworks having been shut down in the neighbourhood. Mr. Richardson added that the labour on his farm cost quite 40s. the acre, and even then such details as fence-trimming &c. had to be left to take care of themselves. Cottages, he said, were scarce, and more of them with good gardens were wanted. For such dwellings there was a demand, but he thought that landowners had not the money to build them. Chiefly owing to this labour question and its increased cost, he could not take a very bright view of the local agricultural outlook. The only hope lay in better prices.

Nearly all his land was arable, which would not lay down successfully, but he had a quantity of spring-tide marshland. After the salt water was off the rains washed this land and made it good, but he could not mow these marshes or feed them with sheep or young things; they had to be grazed with bullocks. In spite of the drought in 1901, Mr. Richardson had a very good plant of roots. His system was to plough and drill as soon as possible, and roll a good deal, so as not to give the land time to dry. He grew his roots on ridges, not on the flat. His farming course was as follows: (1) Fallow or root crop, for here were no long fallows; (2) barley or oats; (3) seeds; (4) wheat, which always followed seeds; (5) oats or barley. The land was manured twice in the five years, viz. for the roots and wheat. He kept Black-face sheep, and his custom was to buy in lambs in June or July, begin to fat them in the first week of October, and sell out at Christmas. When I was at his farm in June his peas were just fit for plucking. Mr. Richardson said that he was obliged to have a man guarding them night and day to prevent their being stolen.

He informed me that small-holdings were not in demand in that neighbourhood, although a man there who held a few acres and kept a beer-house did well out of fruit; but one of the risks of fruit growing would be the lack of suitable labour to gather the crop. He did not know whether small-holdings would help to keep people on the land, but this, he said, was not the case twenty years before, as in the old days the little men went first. I may add that Mr. Richardson's fields, which were of good, light land, seemed in excellent heart and without exception as well farmed as any that we saw in the whole district. Notwithstanding the drought which had proved fatal in many cases, his crops looked full of promise. My visit to him was the last that I made in North Essex.

Whilst waiting at the station at Ardleigh, I saw a whole train laden with wooden cases that looked like large, rough coffins. These were *en route* for Harwich to be shipped to Holland, whence they would return in a day or two full of foreign meat, for the most part veal and pork. The sight of these trains carrying their daily burden—I presume at preferential rates—cannot be very encouraging to the local Essex farmer.

A very typical Central Essex farm of the better sort was that of our host in that district, the Hon. C. H. Strutt, the well-known and able member of Parliament for the Maldon Division. Mr. Strutt held some 320 acres, whereof a fair proportion was grass, at Blunt's Hall, the property of his brother, Lord Rayleigh, and kept a herd of cows, the milk of which he sent to London. In addition to the ordinary Eastern Counties crops, such as wheat, barley, and clover-leys, he grew eating-peas for market, and, as is not unusual in these parts, various sorts of seeds. Thus in 1901 he had a field of radish seed, which was drilled in April and cultivated in the same fashion as mangolds—by cutting out, singling, hand and horse hoeing. Twenty bushels per acre, which should realise from £16 to £20, is a good return from this crop. The greatest enemies to the successful growth of radish seed are the small birds, especially those of the linnet tribe, which, notwithstanding any amount of scaring, will sometimes consume as much as half the yield. Another piece was planted with swedes for seed. These swedes are sown in August in beds and dibbled out about November. Twenty-four bushels of the seed, worth from 13s. to 16s. a bushel, is a good crop per acre. This seed is collected just before corn harvest, and its foe is canker at the root, which causes the affected plants to fall over. Some growers say that this crop will do as well if it is drilled and cut out in the usual fashion, which saves the labour of dibbling-in the plants from the seed-bed. Part of Mr. Strutt's field had been treated thus, but certainly this drilled portion did not look so well as the rest. It may be, however, that the difference was caused by that section of the land being higher and more droughty than the lower stretch, which overlies a damp bottom—at least so he seemed to think. At any rate the experiment was by no means conclusive.

A third field was given up to eating-peas of an early, dwarf variety, which grows without support. Of these peas, whereof many truck-loads are sent away daily during the season from Witham Station, a hundred bags, or 300 bushels, are considered a good crop per acre, but the earliest varieties seldom produce more than fifty bags. Their value varies very much : it may begin at 15s. a bag, or even more, and afterwards fall so low that the price realised will scarcely suffice to pay brokerage and railway charges.

Like most of the surrounding land, Mr. Strutt's farm was suffering severely from drought at the time of my inspection ; indeed, he stated that he never remembered to have seen it look worse, not even in the black year of 1893. This, how-

ever, was not his fault, but that of the season, and of the
lack of rainfall, which for some years past had afflicted Essex
so severely that, as I noticed in many places, the trees were
dying in great numbers. Night after night and week after
week the clouds gathered— 'Essex shows' is the local name
for them—only to belie their promise and carry the moisture
with which they were charged to some more favoured spot.
'It never do rain in Essex now,' said one despairing farmer
to me, 'and I begin to think it never will.' So far as the
cultivation and management of Mr. Strutt's land were concerned, I do not see how they could be improved upon, and I
am glad to be able to add that the financial results had on the
whole, proved as good as could be expected in these times.

Not far from Blunt's Hall I saw an old labourer named
John Lapwood, whose life experience, which I verified by
inquiry, is worth preserving. For half a century or more
he worked on the Post Hall and Oliver Farms in Witham,
and now, by the help of some kind friends, was spending his
last days in a little cottage, where he lived with his old wife.
We found him—an aged and withered but still an apple-
cheeked individual—seated upon a bank, 'enjoying of the
sweet air, although it be a bit draughty.' He told me that
in his young days wages for horsemen used to be down to
9s. a week, and for daymen to 8s., when the weather allowed
them to be earned. During the Crimean War bread cost
him a shilling a loaf, and other food a proportionate price.
He stated that for months at a time he had existed upon
nothing but a diet of bread and onions, washed down, when
he was lucky, with a little small-beer. These onions he ate
until they took the skin off the roof of his mouth, blistering
it to whiteness, after which he was obliged to soak them in
salt to draw the 'virtue' out of them. They had no tea,
but his wife imitated the appearance of that beverage by soak-
ing a burnt crust of bread in boiling water. On this diet he
became so feeble that the reek of the muck which it was his
duty to turn, made him sick and faint; and often, he said,
he would walk home at night from the patch of ground

where he grew the onions and some other vegetables, with swimming head and uncertain feet. I asked if his children, of whom there were eight, lived on onions also. He answered no; they had generally a little cheese and butter in the house, but he could not put it into his own stomach when they were hungry and cried for food. 'Things is better now,' he added.

Well, things are better now; indeed, it is scarcely too much to say that in many cases to-day, the labourer has more than his share of the rather plumless agricultural cake. But with such a record behind him, knowing what his fathers suffered, is it wonderful that he should strive to drive home the nail of opportunity, and sometimes to take advantage of the farmers who in the past too often were so merciless?

Let us try to understand his case and be just. Think, for instance, of this poor man Lapwood, whose condition was but that of ten thousand others, day by day forcing his hated food into a blistered mouth, starving that his children might be full. Think of him with his 9s. a week, and ten souls to feed, house, and clothe, while bread stood at a shilling a loaf. Remember, too, that from this lot there was no escape; that labour was in overflowing supply; and that to lift his voice against an employer, however tyrannous, meant instant dismissal and the hell of the poor-house—it was little better in those days—or the roadside ditch to lie in. Is it strange that, remembering these things, he—or rather his sons—should wax fat and kick, that they should be haunted also by the fear that the evil might return upon them, and bear in their hearts resentment, cloaked but very real, against those classes at whose hands they received that evil of which no subsequent kindness can obliterate the memory? With the agricultural labourer, as I believe, this resentment against past suffering, at any rate as yet, is deeper than gratitude for present benefits. Indeed, gratitude is scarcely his strong point. Thus, to take the example of the family of this very man, I was informed that those children for whom he starved, did not do all they might to make his last days easy.

Our drive from Blunt's Hall to the Tiptree Fruit Farm, where the Britannia Fruit Preserving Company carries on its industry, was full of interest. Thus, in the neighbourhood of Witham, and upon the land which used to be Tiptree Heath, are hundreds of garden plots devoted to the cultivation of various seeds, among them those of Shirley poppies, mangold, parsley, swede, nasturtium, and pansy. This class of cultivation, it is said, has turned the people of Tiptree and its neighbourhood, which used to be known as 'the Land of Heath and Thief,' into a law-abiding and prosperous community. First they squatted on the land and erected huts for shelter, and now, behold! the outcasts of a generation or two ago, touched by the wizard's wand of ownership, have become the thriving yeomen of to-day.

On our road we passed a seat called Braxted. The house was invisible from the road, but what struck me were the miles of massive brick wall, seven feet high or more, with which the park is enclosed. What must it have cost, I wonder? The dates upon the wall show that it was built in or about the year 1827, when corn was so high, and labour so cheap, and Essex landowners could afford to spend thousands of pounds to ensure a completer privacy. They could scarcely do it now, poor folk—that is, if they look to the land for a living. Since I saw it I have received a letter from Mr. Henry Siggers, who tells me that this wall was built by his father and grandfather for the late Peter Du Cane, Esq. He adds that he had heard his father say that it was four miles in length.

The Tiptree Fruit Farm, which we reached shortly after passing the holding once occupied by the late Mr. Mechi, of agricultural fame, owes its existence to the energy of the managing director, Mr. Wilkin. Including the farms at Kelveden and Dagenham the company now owns some 430 acres, of which about 300 are under fruit. We walked over the Tiptree Farm, that is planted with strawberries, currants, gooseberries, raspberries, and ordinary farm crops sown to rest the land. On the whole the fruit did not look

THE HONBLE. E. G. STRUTT'S DAIRY COWS

*Page 463*

well when I saw it, chiefly owing to the great drought following that of 1900, which had caused a maggot-like grub to attack the roots of the strawberries, and more especially those of the older plants. The raspberries also had died back very much; indeed, I do not consider that this soil is suitable to raspberries, and big-bud was playing havoc with the black currants. On the other hand, the small scarlet strawberry, supposed to be the best for jam-making purposes, does very well indeed.

It is pleasant to be able to record that, as the published balance-sheets show, Mr. Wilkin's skill and energy have been rewarded with complete success. In 1901 the company supplied jam to 9,700 customers, and if the preserve-loving public could see, as we did, the freshness of the fruit, the purity of the added sugar, and the care and cleanliness of the manufacture carried out by the aid of the most improved machinery, I am sure that this number would be considerably increased. Incidentally also this industry is of the greatest benefit to the neighbourhood, as will be easily understood when I state that even during the month of May 1901 the average amount paid away in wages was £145 per week, and that women can earn from 5s. to 8s. a day strawberry-picking, and about 1s. 4d. a day at strawing beneath the plants—'puggling' is, I believe, the local term—an occupation in which we found gangs of them engaged.

Another result has been to encourage the establishment of small-holders, about eighty of whom owned or rented plots of land in the immediate vicinity. Some of these men have done exceedingly well; indeed, Mr. Wilkin instanced one to me who had risen from the position of a ploughman, and then possessed a capital of several hundreds of pounds; and another, once a labourer, who had bought a holding. Also they were a great help to the fruit farm, upon which they were always willing to work during the busiest time. Mr. Wilkin is strongly in favour of small holdings, and informed us that had it not been for them the folk would have gone, as they are going, from the surrounding parishes.

The farmers, he said, complained that the fruit works drew the labourers from the land, but he answered that they brought people into the neighbourhood and prevented others from leaving it altogether. He thought that deserving men should be assisted to a small-holding, and instructed in its skilful cultivation. Indeed, he went further. ' I believe,' said Mr. Wilkin, ' that the remedy for the rural exodus is that the labourer should be enabled to acquire a piece of land,' a sentiment with which some of us will be inclined to agree.

I asked Mr. Wilkin if he thought that this fruit growing could be indefinitely extended; he replied that there was still room, but if largely taken up there might be times when there would be a glut and consequent failures. There was, however, place for many more growers, so long as they did not establish themselves in districts where the industry already existed on a large scale. Thus in that neighbourhood there was only sufficient labour to deal with the fruit grown by his company. Still if he were to build twenty or thirty more cottages, they would let readily enough to a good class of man, but he did not care to sink so much capital.

I believe the Hon. Edward Strutt, who manages the large Essex estates of his brother, Lord Rayleigh, to be one of the most skilful farmers in England. Certainly in the course of my somewhat extended experience I have met no one who impressed me as being quite so thoroughly master of his business, or, I may add, so successful in combating the difficulties of the times and prices. Of course there are reasons for this success. To begin with, he farms an enormous extent of land, in all some 10,000 acres, most of which is in excellent heart; there are, I believe, 3,000 acres in the neighbourhood of Witham alone. Further, there is no lack of capital; also London, which lies within thirty miles, furnishes a ready market for all sorts of produce, and especially for that of the cows, of which about 700 are kept.

Its true inner cause in my opinion, however, is to be found in the agricultural talent—if I may use the term—of

Mr. Strutt himself, with which he combines a business ability that is really remarkable.     Never before had I seen such books as those that he keeps.     One of them, which he had playfully christened the 'Bailiff Tormentor'—a tillage book—actually treats each field as if it were a separate farm. By this I mean that every expense, including proportion of rent, tithe, taxes, labour, manure, &c., is charged against that field and deducted from the value of what it produces, so that the farmer can tell at a glance whether the crop has or has not been profitable, and the exact extent of the gain or loss.     So beautifully is all this done that when the expenses and receipts on the various fields are added up, the results tally with the general profit and loss account of the farm concerned, thus showing that there can be no mistake in detail and apportionment.     I doubt if there is another farmer in England who keeps such books as these, and still more whether one in a thousand would be capable of keeping them.     Upon their value it is unnecessary to dwell, especially as they include distinct volumes devoted respectively to cows, cattle, sheep, pigs, poultry, and a summary book of milk sold and food bought.

It is the practice on these farms to measure the milk of each cow once a week, so that all unprofitable animals can be weeded out ; also the milk is frequently analysed.     This system of analysis has revealed to Mr. Strutt a curious fact, for which he is unable to account ; viz. that the evening milk is considerably richer in fatty matter than that yielded by the same cow in the morning.     The reader will observe that the interesting figures given to me by Mr. Mathews of Potter's Bar in Middlesex, which will be found in my chapter on Hertfordshire, entirely bear out Mr. Strutt's experience in this matter of morning and evening milk. I do not know whether agricultural chemists can give a satisfactory explanation of the circumstance.

Strangely enough, in face of the prevailing view to the contrary, Mr. Strutt's experience was that, even at the prevailing prices, in Essex wheat pays better than any other crop, more indeed than cows, and much more than bullocks, which make little or no return. It is true that it does not do what it did in the old days when wheat was expected to pay for itself and the rest of the rotation, whereas now it only pays for itself. Thus in 1894, exclusive of proportion of interest on capital and personal management expenses, wheat gave a net profit of £1 15s. 9d. per acre, in 1895 a profit of £1 1s. 10d., in 1896 a profit of £3 19s. 3d., in 1897 a profit of £4 5s. 6d., in 1898 a profit of £3 17s. 1d., and in 1899 a profit of £3 3s. Mr. Strutt pointed out, however, that the habits of millers deduct somewhat from the small return attainable on wheat. Thus when it is under eighteen stone the miller likes to weigh it in, but if the sample should chance to be over eighteen stone he refuses to buy in by weight, but takes it by measure only. Thus whoever loses he is advantaged. On the same period the return per acre from the barley crop was a trifle less. Here is a table of the profits from all sources earned over a period of fourteen years, upon what Mr. Strutt considered his best farm, which covers, I understand, about 1,000 acres :—

| Year | | | | | £ | Year | | | | | £ |
|------|---|---|---|---|-----|------|---|---|---|---|-----|
| 1887 | . | . | . | . | 957 | 1894 | . | . | . | . | 1,574 |
| 1888 | . | . | . | . | 855 | 1895 | . | . | . | . | 1,832 |
| 1889 | . | . | . | . | 1,604 | 1896 | . | . | . | . | 1,716 |
| 1890 | . | . | . | . | 2,005 | 1897 | . | . | . | . | 2,618 |
| 1891 | . | . | . | . | 1,883 | 1898 | . | . | . | . | 2,858 |
| 1892 | . | . | . | . | 409 | 1899 | . | . | . | . | 2,543 |
| 1893 | . | . | . | . | 219 | 1900 | . | . | . | (about) | 1,000 |

By way of contrast, I now give the figures over practically the same period, for what he considered his worst farm, 300 acres of mixed land, with a proportion of gravelly soil and grass :—

| Year | | | | | | £ | Year | | | | | | £ |
|------|---|---|---|---|------|-----|------|---|---|---|---|------|-----|
| 1887 | . | . | . | . | loss | 231 | 1894 | . | . | . | . | profit | 52 |
| 1888 | . | . | . | . | profit | 72 | 1895 | . | . | . | . | loss | 6 |
| 1889 | . | . | . | . | ,, | 367 | 1896 | . | . | . | . | ,, | 128 |
| 1890 | . | . | . | . | ,, | 363 | 1897 | . | . | . | . | profit | 410 |
| 1891 | . | . | . | . | ,, | 262 | 1898 | . | . | . | . | loss | 61 |
| 1892 | . | . | . | . | loss | 337 | 1899 | . | . | . | . | ,, | 21 |
| 1893 | . | . | . | . | ,, | 747 | | | | | | | |

In addition to the farms Mr. E. Strutt has two milk-shops in London. Although he was hopeful for the future, these shops had given him much trouble, expense, and anxiety of a sort familiar to those who attempt a retail trade in a great city, where competition is severe and many interests have to be 'conciliated.'

Allowing for all deductions, except interest on capital and cost of personal management, the net profits of his home farming for the year 1898 amounted, I understood, to £2 per acre. In these times this result must be looked upon as very satisfactory, although it should be remembered that the season of 1898 was one of the best in his record. If my experience in the county is any guide, I do not suppose, with perhaps a single exception, that there is another farmer of arable land in Essex who can show so good a balance-sheet, although no doubt some of them are still doing fairly well. I should add that Mr. Strutt estimated the cost of his labour, with which he seemed to have no difficulty, at the high figure of 50s. the acre.

In a letter which I have since received from him he expresses the following views upon labourers and small-holders in Essex, which, coming from so great an authority, are, I think, important. He says : 'I fear that there is no doubt that it is difficult to hold the labourer to the land, unless we offer him some opportunities of rising, and this can only be done by providing small-holdings. These I believe can be made to answer if proper men take them, though it is unfortunately the fact that many who have them do not prosper. Still I am sure if a man and his family really work and are careful, they ought to make a tolerable living out of a small holding by giving their attention to the smaller details of farm work. It is, as you say, either the very big or the very little farmer who succeeds. The man with from 300 to 400 acres has been driven out.'

I do not think that during all my agricultural wanderings I have made any more deeply interesting journey than that upon which we were most kindly conducted by Mr. Edward

Strutt through what are called the 'black' districts of Essex. Between Billericay and Althorne we saw hundreds, or rather thousands, of acres of strong corn lands which have tumbled down to grass. I can only describe the appearance of this land as wretched : it did not look as though it would support one beast upon ten acres of it, although, oddly enough, here and there we saw also a well-farmed and productive-looking holding. Much of this soil, which is only suitable to the growth of corn, beans, and lucerne, is in the hands of Scotsmen, who take it at a small price. Its selling value seems to be about £6 an acre, and some was pointed out to me, belonging to a public institution, which is said to bring in a rent of only 2s. 6d. the acre. Not far from Burnham-on-Crouch we saw a tract of country that through the breach of the sea wall during the great gale of 1897 was flooded with salt water to the extent of several thousands of acres. Indeed, some of it is still so flooded by every tide, since in the present depressed state of agriculture nobody seems able or willing to find the money to make sound the defences. The aspect of this land is most curious—as though it had been swept by fire. There stand the fences black and dead, and from them rise the stark, gaunt trees. The soil also is ' black like pitch when wet and like cinders when dry,' as one farmer described it to me ; indeed, the place appears a home of death and desolation. Even if the money were forthcoming to restore it to fertility, to do so would be the work of many years.

At Southminster we attended the market. Here, among many others, I had conversations with Mr. Clear, the auctioneer, and Mr. Horner, a large owner of London property, who farmed 650 acres in that neighbourhood in the best possible fashion. Mr. Clear estimated the rents on the good land in this district at 15s., and on the bad land at from 12s. 6d. downwards, adding that fifty years ago Maldon was the finest wheat-growing country in all England. He said that at the present time there were not a thousand acres of land utterly derelict in the Dengie Hundred, which is a striking commentary on the information I had received, that

in this particular hundred, many square miles lay entirely
waste. It only shows once more how the majority of
agriculturists lack knowledge of all districts and conditions
except their own. The local selling values he estimated at
from £20 down to £5 or £6 per acre for poor land that is
subject to sea-wall rates. Of the labour he said that it was
better than it had been; and of tenants that they could be
had at a figure, although capital was short. The future
prospects of the district depended entirely, he declared, upon
the price of wheat, which, he added, could not at present be
grown at a profit.

Mr. Horner, to whose ability and excellence as a farmer
everyone bore witness, including Mr. Strutt, said that in four
years' working of a holding, which during that time had
increased from 300 to 650 acres, allowing fully for rent and
interest on capital, he had lost £3,000, or, if he deducted
£1,000 for unexhausted manurial values, £2,000. He said
that he had bought the land cheap, and had every facility
for working it, such as an ample supply of manure and
proximity to a station and market, but that the speculation
had been disastrous, and he thought that his property must
decrease in value. Farming had disappointed him, and,
done well or ill, he did not see how it was to be made to pay
in Essex. They must scrape along as best they could, and,
for his part he was obliged to stick to his land, as he could
not sell it for what it cost him. Of labour he said that those
farmers who cared to pay men could get them, the wage of a
good hand amounting to about £1 a week.

Mr. Gale, of Bradwell, told me that he was very unfortunate, inasmuch as he had invested in land some twenty
years before, when even the heavy soils used to fetch over £40
the acre. Indeed, he had given more than £60 an acre for
property of which the selling price in 1901 would not be
more than £20 an acre. That land in this part of Essex
goes for much smaller sums is proved by the following
extract which I cut out of the Property Market Report of
the 'Daily News' for July 16, 1901:—'Mr. G. E. Hilliard

H H 2

(Messrs. G. B. Hilliard & Son) sold a freehold estate known as Gusted Hall and New England Farm, Rochford, Essex, comprising a farmhouse, two cottages, two lots of farm premises, and 221a. 3r. 13p. of arable pasture and woodland for £2,600; also Tilebarn Farm and Tillett Marsh Farm, Wallasea Island, Essex—in all, about 453 acres freehold—for £1,620.'

That is to say, the first property fetched a little under £12 the acre, and the second about £3 10s. an acre, in both cases exclusive of the value of buildings, cottages, &c. Imagine English land selling for £3 10s. the acre, although, of course, this particular property may have been subject to flooding or other troubles. Still, Mr. Gale had some confidence in the future, since he told me that were he a young man he would invest in land at present prices. He added that labourers for permanent staff were scarce, especially on outlying farms, and that a good man could earn £1 a week. Of cottages he thought there were enough—at any rate he had some standing empty, as the parish of Bradwell, which two decades before had a population of over a thousand, now returned between seven and eight hundred only. The last year, he said, had been a bad one, barley being the worst of the crops; also there was a loss on cattle in that and previous seasons.

Mr. Dow, a carrier, whose opinions, I was informed, were of an advanced order, was a strong believer in the merits of small-holdings. He told me that labourers in that locality did not earn more than 13s. a week. The Southminster station master, who was standing near, said by way of comment on this information that a little while before he had tried to hire a second porter with regular work and all the advantages and prospects of railway employment, at 16s. a week, and was unable to find a man. Upon this Mr. Dow's instructive comment was, ' Oh! they don't want to be tied.'

That afternoon, conducted by Mr. Strutt and his bailiff, we drove from flat field to flat field separated by dykes, over many miles of country between the Crouch and Blackwater

DENGIE FLATS, LOOKING SEAWARDS

Rivers, reaching the sea, or rather the mud foreshore, at or about that point which is known as the Dengie Flats. Much of this land, recovered from the ocean in past days, is farmed by Mr. Strutt, a portion of whose holding was unfortunately flooded in the great gale of 1897. Although only one tide invaded it, to that hour it was possible to see its exact limits. The poisonous effect upon the soil is really extraordinary; indeed, it is scarcely too much to say that from that day to this it has produced little of any value; nor is it expected that it will do so until a series of wet seasons have washed away the salt. The cost of labour on these farms, including thrashing expenses &c., was, I think, 30s. the acre.

The view looking over the Dengie Flats and St. Peter's Sands from the summit of the earthen bank which keeps out the sea, was very desolate and strange. Behind us lay a vast, drear expanse of land won from the ocean in days bygone, bordered on the one side by the Blackwater and on the other by the Crouch Rivers, and saved, none too well, from the mastery of the waves by the sloping earthen bank on which we stood. In front, thousands of acres of grey mud where grew dull, unwholesome-looking grasses. Far, far away on this waste expanse two tiny, moving specks, men engaged in seeking for samphire or some other treasure of the ooze-mud. Then the thin, white lip of the sea and beyond its sapphire edge in the half-distance, the gaunt skeleton of a long-wrecked ship. To the north, on the horizon a line of trees; to the west, over the great plain, where stood one or two lonely farms, another line of trees. On the distant deep some sails, and in the middle marsh, a barge gliding up a hidden creek as though she moved across the solid land. Then, spread like a golden garment over the vast expanses of earth and ocean, the flood of sunshine, and in our ears the rush of the north-west gale and the thrilling song of larks hanging high above the yellow, salt-soaked fields. Such seemed the Dengie Marsh as I saw it in June 1901. But what must it be like when buried beneath the snows of winter, or when the howling easterly winds of spring sweep across its spaces, and the combers of the North Sea sometimes reach and batter their frail embankment. Then indeed I should not care to be the tenant of one of those solitary steads.

Another district which we saw was that of Maldon, formerly, as Mr. Clear remarked, 'the finest wheat-growing country in England.' Here are thousands of acres which can only be described as derelict. In 1901, at any rate, few of the fields seemed to produce a crop of grass high enough to hide a lark; but such as it might be, that was their produce for the year. No wonder that we were told that of much of this land the tithe was higher than the rental. Yet once it grew not less than forty bushels of wheat to the acre, and with proper treatment doubtless could do so again.

The manufacture of small-arms at the Enfield Government factory alone excepted, I suppose that the chief industry of the Waltham Cross district of Essex is the cultivation of fruit under glass. Mr. Hamilton, of Gwendoline House, Waltham Cross, like so many other successful men in all walks of life a Scotsman by birth, is one of the largest of these growers, his houses covering, indeed, no less an area than twenty acres of land, which he held under our host in this district, Colonel Beale Colvin, C.B., of Monkhams. Mr. Hamilton, who had been twenty-six years in the business, told me that up to the previous two years, when it had been checked by over-production, reduced prices, and the increased cost of glass and building, the Essex fruit and tomato trade was increasing steadily. Although it might still be called prosperous, undoubtedly the value of its produce had sunk much of late.

Thus black Hambro' grapes, which used to realise 5s. a pound twenty years before, brought in only 1s., although the Canon Hall and Gros Colman varieties still commanded a higher figure. Tomatoes in twelve-pound baskets were sold from 6s. to 7s. a basket, and cucumbers at about 8s. a flat, containing from two to three dozen—prices that the housekeeper will compare with interest with those which she pays to the greengrocer. Certainly they leave no exorbitant profit to the producer. Of late also the competition has become very severe, since, in addition to that of Guernsey and other recognised growing centres, Danes, and indeed aliens of all descriptions, have started business on their own account in the neighbourhood. Their custom is to arrive as workmen, and thus learn the trade, after which they turn the knowledge they have acquired to a more profitable account. Mr. Hamilton said that they are for the most part steady and well-educated men. The ordinary hands employed in his houses received about 24s. a week and, in the case of foremen from 30s. to 40s., while women could earn 4d. an hour at grape thinning, which during the season brings them in 18s. to £1 a week. At this price they were plentiful, but owing to the competition of the Government factories, where very high wages are paid, male labour was growing scarce.

All Mr. Hamilton's produce was sent to London by road, and there sold by auction, whence came all the stable manure, which he found more valuable than any artificial fertiliser. His houses, whereof he had I know not how many, were a wonderful sight, the larger ones measuring 225 ft. in length by 30 ft. in width. Formerly these houses could, I understand, be erected at a cost of about £1 a foot run, including brickwork, glass, and piping; but now the price of building has risen by 25 per cent., and, owing to the frequent strikes in Belgium, that of glass by nearly 100 per cent. In 1901 the show of grapes, even of the shy-setting and expensive Canon Hall Muscat variety, was splendid; indeed, the houses had the appearance of great green arches from which the bunches hung by hundreds and by thousands.

Standing on steps, busily engaged in thinning these bunches with the help of scissors and bamboo forks, were bevies of girls, looking arcadian and picturesque in the quaint white caps they wear to shield them from the sun.

In other houses grew peaches, in others tomatoes by the thousand, planted in pots so constructed that the roots can travel through them into the ground beneath; and in yet others cucumbers, which were beginning to go over and to be replaced by later sowings of tomatoes. The soil of this nursery, I should add, is particularly well suited to glass culture, being loam with a gravel bottom the existence of which obviates any necessity for deep drainage.

On leaving Mr. Hamilton I visited the beautiful old abbey of Waltham, which I had never before seen. Being curious on the point I asked the good lady who showed us over if she could tell me whereabouts in the building King Harold was buried. She replied, 'I don't rightly know, but them there *archilogicals* tells me that they could find him in three hours, as they've got all his measurements!' 'Archilogicals' struck me as a useful and descriptive word.

On one day of our stay our host, Colonel Colvin, kindly took us for a sixty-mile jaunt in a motor-car from Waltham Abbey, through the Roothings and Easters of Western Essex and home again by Epping Forest. The Roothings —they number nine—were in existence before the time of Edward the Confessor; indeed the Romans occupied them, as their remains testify. They are, I suppose, so named after the river Roding, which runs through them, although for aught I know to the contrary the river may be named after them. How the Easters, or Estres, came by their appellation I have no idea. This tract, which lies high, is remarkable for its flatness, or rather for a series of tablelands separated from each other by shallow valleys, and for the heavy nature of its soil, which is admirably suited to the growth of wheat. Other characteristics are its lack of timber, its dearth of houses, and its complete sequestration from the world. Although it lies within thirty miles of London I do not think I have visited any place in England that impressed me as so utterly rural, so untouched by the push and bustle of our age. It is easy to imagine that these Roothings look to-day very much as they must have done in the time of Elizabeth, except that since then their population may have dwindled. At any rate, it is not increasing now, as one of our companions, who had known them for the best part of a generation, stated that during this period he could scarcely remember the building of a new house within their bounds. For the rest, the hand of agricultural depression has fallen upon them very heavily : rents have come down by a half or more, and farms which used to be worth £40 or £50 an acre may now be bought at from £7 to £12.

Upon this expedition our guide was Mr. Bailey, for many years the well-known and esteemed huntsman of the Essex Hounds, who is acquainted with every inch of the country, but now for the first time explored it on a motor-car. His 'Whoa, mare, whoa!' when we nearly came to grief down the bank of a stream was an amusing instance of the force of habit. Also he brought with him a hank of rope which he thought might be useful in emergencies. Before our journey was over an emergency arose!

Under Mr. Bailey's guidance we hissed and hustled down country lanes, and even dragged ourselves laboriously through straw yards and across field tracks, stopping from time to time at this homestead or at that. I will describe some of these and their occupants as specimens of Roothing farming and farmers.

Mr. Nicholas Lukies, a Cornishman—of whom there are many in Essex and Hertfordshire—lived at Cammas Hall, White Roothing, one of the most beautiful old moated granges that I ever saw, especially at that season of the year, when the water-lilies and the roses were in bloom. In the remoter parts of Essex there are, I believe, many such houses, which no one knows or visits. Mr. Lukies held 400 acres, and looked to wheat and barley as his mainstays. Also he fatted about forty bullocks, feeding his own straw to them with cake and maize. He farmed well, spending £150 a year on artificial manure, and from 35s. to 38s. on labour per acre, with which, like most of the Roothing farmers, he

seemed to have little trouble, more especially since he purchased two cottages for the use of his men. His practice
was to clean-fallow thirty acres every year, in addition to the
half-fallows of mangolds and beans. Of roots he had twelve
acres, of beans twenty-two, of lucerne three acres, and of
sainfoin no less than thirty-six acres. Sheep he bought in
during summer and sold out in autumn, as in winter they
will not flourish on this heavy land. Farms were, he said,
being taken readily at rents of from 12s. to 15s. the acre, which
sum, when the tithe of 4s. to 5s. an acre is deducted, means,
it must be remembered, that the landlord receives about
enough to pay outgoings and the costs of upkeep and no
more. As to the farmer's profits, Mr. Lukies said, ' We
make a living.'

Mr. John Wilson, of New Hall, High Roothing, or
rather his wife and brother, whose family have worked this
farm of 260 acres for several generations, could scarcely
admit as much. His house, by the way, which, although it
is called New Hall, dates from about 1480, was even more
interesting than Cammas Hall, and, I should judge, must at
some time have been a monastery. Indeed the fact that this
parish was presented by one Leofwin in the reign of Edward
the Confessor to a monastery in the Isle of Ely gives some
weight to this theory. Perhaps the Ely, monks had a branch
establishment at the building now known as New Hall.
Mrs. Wilson said that 1900 and 1901 were the worst years
they had ever known. She seemed to think that in these
times at present prices only ' land-skinners ' could make
a profit out of farming in the Roothings, and added that
labour was scarce, and although there were enough boys
about in the village, they were of little use.

Near to New Hall also we saw a farm of 500 acres, in
good order, which we were informed was to let at about
7s. 6d. an acre.

In the White Roothing, where the cottages are wood-clad,
I saw Mr. Edmund Grove, of Kingstons, who told me that
they could do no good grass-growing in that district ; indeed

he knew some fields that had been laid down for fifty years and were still bad. Three crops might be taken from new-laid land, then it began to go off. It was a grain and not a grass country, but sainfoin, clover, and tares did well. The selling value of land, he said, varied from £10 down to £5 the acre. A great deal had been sold at £10, and the price generally had improved a little, say to an average of £8. The farm he occupied fetched £5 the acre six or seven years before. The rents also had fallen a full half, but recently had risen a shilling or two the acre. Mr. Grove declared that labour was the great drawback and that many young men went away. There used to be a surplus population; now there were barely enough to meet the needs of the land. The wage was 15s. a week. The cottages were so abundant that many had been allowed to go to ruin, as there was nobody to live in them.

Mr. Alfred Oliver, of Marks Hall, in the same parish, whose farm I walked over, held 266 acres at a rent of £150. Twenty-five years before this land was let for £280 and the tithe. There were but ten acres of grass on the farm and about eight acres of root, of which six were mangolds. Mr. Oliver said that sainfoin did well and was the best crop they had. I saw one field of it here, although I do not think that this was in his occupation, which, having been down for over twenty years, had become so foul and weak that it was scarcely worth cutting. Crops sown after sainfoin, however, and indeed all broken-up grasses, are apt to suffer from wire-worm. Mr. Oliver's wheat was very good, a five-quarter crop, but in the previous year he had not harvested an average of three quarters. He told me that they sold every-thing, including straw, and manured with superphosphates and nitrate of soda. The farmers, he said, just made a living, and the Cornishmen seemed to do well, but the Essex people had no money left. The capital required was from £6 to £7 the acre. Of labour he made no complaint, saying that he had six as good men as anyone could want. Some of them went to London, but they came back. They were 'near enough to see the folly of it.' Cottages, he added, were plentiful, but poor.

This farm, which had a white clay subsoil, was steam mole-drained about twenty years before, and the drains were still working well, better, Mr. Oliver said, than pipes do on such soil. The wages were from 13*s.* to 15*s.* the week, in addition to harvest, which was sometimes worth £10.

In the neighbourhood of High Easter I saw an attempt at fruit farming—apparently the only one in the district—in the shape of a field, or fields, of black currants. These seemed to be in a very bad state and the land about them had not been cleaned. Near by was a wheat field smothered with charlock and, oddly enough, next to it one of the best crops of winter oats that I had met with anywhere. In this parish or in that of Good Easter, with which it may be identical, was a very fine farm, I believe, of 2,000 acres, that of Mr. Matthews, whom unfortunately we found from home. Here the fields were large, steam-cultivated and clean, and I was told that in autumn his corn stacks are a sight to behold. Doubtless with capital, intelligence, and energy corn-growing can still be made to pay in this part of Essex. That indeed, it will be remembered, was the experience of Mr. Edward Strutt. Not far away was another holding which contrasted strangely with that of Mr. Matthews. Here many of the fields were a mass of weeds and indeed practically untilled, while the hedge clippings of the previous year lay in rotting heaps where they had been placed. It was a melancholy spectacle of mismanagement and neglect, arising in all probability, though of the facts I know nothing, from the utter poverty of the tenant.

An interesting small farm that I visited in this district was that of Mr. Isaac Mead, of Waples Mill, Margaret Roding, who held about a hundred acres under University College, and combined farming with the management of a mill. Unfortunately Mr. Mead was away, but his wife showed us the grass lands and the chickens, ducks, and bees, of which they make a speciality. Mrs. Mead said that she

A MOATED GRANGE, THE ROOTHINGS          *Page 473*

A ROOTHINGS COTTAGE          *Page 474*

had no lack of labour, as she had three sons, who would not leave her. Mr. Mead, in letters I have received from him, told me that he was the son of a labourer, and had been at work since he was nine years of age; also that he had invented a patent poultry-food for which he claimed admirable results. I presume, therefore, that he has worked his way up by his own exertions; at which I am not in the least surprised, since I saw enough of his holding and family to assure me that he and his are very able and enterprising people who well deserve success.

In travelling on to Stanford Rivers, where I was to visit Mr. John Freeman, I noticed what is characteristic of all this part of Essex, that the cottages seemed to be uniformly poor, ill-kept, and small. Yet the people, or a fair proportion of them, remain upon the land. In the neighbourhood of Ongar, Fyfield, and Stanford Rivers the soil seemed good, and I noticed various fine stretches of grazing land. Obviously also the farmers were in a big way of business and fatted out much stock.

Mr. John Freeman, jun., held 370 acres under Sir Charles C. Smith, Bart., a landlord of whom he spoke with enthusiasm, of which 120 acres were arable and all the rest pasture. This, it will be observed, is a proportion very different from that which prevails in the Roothings. He kept a herd of Shorthorn cattle, which he bought in at St. Ives, Aylesbury, and other markets, and sent the milk to London by train, a distance of eighteen miles, the carriage coming to three halfpence a gallon. The price received by the Essex farmer at that time was a penny a pint, that by the London retailer twopence a pint, an advance of one hundred per cent. No wonder that the competition among the city vendors of milk is so keen that, as I was informed, touts are sent out by them into the country to canvas for the custom of families that are known to be moving to town. Cows that went wrong or proved bad milkers were fatted out with the bullocks, of which many are produced in this neighbourhood; thus, Mr. Freeman's father, who also farmed in the parish, grazed no fewer than two hundred of them a year. In short the mainstays of the local agriculture were milk and cattle-grazing, in addition to which the ordinary cereal and leguminous crops were grown upon this farm, where in 1901 the wheat and beans were good and the oats and barley bad.

The average rents which Mr. Freeman said were £2 an acre twenty years before had fallen to £1 the acre, but, he added, as so many have remarked to me throughout England, the success or failure of farming was not a question of rent, and that as a matter of fact they did better when they were paying on this account double what they do to-day. Farmers, he thought, were just holding their own and no more, and farms were in fair demand, but many of them about there were held by sitting tenants who had been in for years. For labour they were badly off, and, as I have always observed to be the case when coming to districts where there are, from districts where there are not railways, the young men were going away much faster than they did from the Roothings. So indeed were the young women, maid-servants being very difficult to find, a complaint that is universal throughout England. Skilled labour was especially scarce and men could not be hired to fye out the ditches. Sunday labour also was a great trouble. Thus, as Mr. Freeman was unable to find a reliable man to help him, his son, he said, was obliged to celebrate the Sabbath by milking ten or twelve cows. He had but two boys on the place, one of whom received 7s. 6d. and the other 13s. a week.

Mr. Harry Sworder, of Tawney Hall, Stapleford Tawney, where the soil is mixed with a heavy clay subsoil, whose large farm I visited, complained much of labour troubles. He said that he could not get sufficient; that he had ten men and could do with ten more for a time, if he were able to find them. As it was, there was only one hand at work on a ten-acre field of mangold. Four or five of his people had been on the place for an average of thirty years. The young ones were leaving the land, and they had to rely upon old folk. When they went, he asked, what shall we do ? He had a cottage standing empty, but it was bad. The wages were 16s. or 17s. a week, with a house, hay and harvest money, and the rent in that district averaged £1 an acre. He considered that £10 an acre or more was necessary as capital, and that the larger men with the most money had stood the strain best.

Except along the river the land was not very good, but neither was it the worst ; there was some which he would not have free of rent. It was patchy—'squally' was the term he used, I think—indeed in places there would be six or seven different soils in the same field. Mr. Sworder milked forty cows, but when I saw them he had thirty, and said that it was difficult to find milkers. He showed us an excellent Anglo-American sweep-rake which cost £12, and remarked that if it had not been for these rakes he did not know what he would have done during hay time. Labour, he declared, was scarcer and dearer, prices were low, and the prospect was not good. He could not say that he was hopeful as to the future.

The first farmer whom Colonel Colvin took me to see on his own and other estates in the neighbourhood of Waltham Abbey was Mr. Bott, of the Dallance Farm, who, I think—but of this I am not sure—was a tenant of Sir Hereward Wake, Bart., a gentleman whom I afterwards visited in North-amptonshire. Mr. Bott, who farmed 275 acres, of which two thirds were pasture, and had occupied his holding for fifty years, said that the prospect at the date when I saw him was the worst that he could remember, except that of 1893, and that the expense of everything was so heavy that but little profit was left. Thus a hay-cart cost £8 more than it did forty-five years ago. Like the great majority of his neighbours he was a hay farmer, only feeding about fifty acres, and sold all the hay that he produced, sending it by road to Whitchapel market. Here, as I understood, it was sold by agents at a fixed commission of 6s. a ton. Hay at that time was fetching £4 a ton, and a load of thirty-six trusses weighed 18 cwts.

Their normal crop he estimated at a little over a ton an acre, but owing to the drought in 1901 they had not more than half this weight. The year of 1900 was almost as bad; indeed he stated they could have got up the crop on the same day that it was cut. Of clover he said that they could get a plant, but it went off in the spring of the year; a fact for which he was not able to account.

Labour cost him £300 a year or a little more than £1 an acre, and there was general complaint of its short-ness and quality. They paid 18s. a week, or with haysel and harvest about £1 a week, for a decent man, and then he must be smoothly used. In short, he said that a farmer had become a kind of manager only; he had no control over his hands. He had no cottage on his farm; indeed the neighbourhood generally was very bare of cottages that rented without difficulty at 5s. or 6s. a week, which alone is sufficient to account for the high wage. Of those that had been built lately none had less than three bedrooms. Rents he thought had been reduced about twenty-five per cent.; at any rate that was so in his case. Generally he kept a hundred half-bred Scotch sheep, but he did not consider that this district with its clay soil and blue subsoil was a good sheep country. There were, he added, one or two milk-walks in the neighbourhood, but dairying gave a lot of trouble as it was so difficult to get the work done.

Next we visited the Aimes Green Farm which belongs to Colonel Colvin and was let at £1 the acre. Here the proportion of pasture was the same as on the holding of Mr. Bott, and the tenant also sold hay. While walking over this farm Colonel Colvin told me that he thought £5 an acre was sufficient capital for grass land. He said also that there were plenty of applicants for farms at a fair rent; indeed, he was letting one of eighty acres at an advance of 10s. the acre. He confirmed what I had heard about the labour, saying that it was hard to get, and that young men were scarce.

Our way back to Monkhams led us through very pretty

scenery, lying as it did on the outskirts of Epping Forest. Or I might say that it was impressive rather than pretty, owing, perhaps, to the massive foliage of the tall elms which against the leaden sky of that afternoon looked almost black. So marked was this effect that a quaint and red-tiled cottage with its bright, hedge-lined garden placed in a woodland glade, seemed to light up the somewhat solemn landscape in a fashion that was quite curious. In the midst of the gloom of trees and the dark green of grasses it caught and filled the eye, a single homely touch that relieved the rich yet melancholy prospect.

On another day Colonel Colvin took me to see a tenant of his, Mr. Brett, of Stubbings Hall Farm, who was one of the few small-holders of the neighbourhood. On our way we stopped to look at Colonel Colvin's Red-polls, of which, as a firm believer in the breed, I am glad to say he kept a small herd of the Henham strain. The bull, I remember, was one of the most lively of the scores of these animals that I have inspected in all parts of England. I have now had experience of a number of Red-poll bulls, and must, with regret, admit that their temper is uncertain. Thus of those which I have kept during the past dozen years, two, both young animals, have had to be destroyed upon the premises. The last of these, which was little more than a calf, got down my steward, Hood, not long ago, and had he not managed to cling on to its nose-ring until assistance came, it would, I believe, have killed him; after which the brute turned so savage that it was practically unapproachable. I am convinced, by the way, that no man ought to ring the bulls of which he has charge, or even to be present on that occasion. These brutes have a very long memory, and, in most cases, never forget or forgive a person who has caused them pain. A horse, however savage, can be mastered, and once mastered bears no malice, or at least is cowed; but with bulls the case is different. Punishment has no effect upon them.

I think that the lady we saw at Stubbings Hall was the daughter of Mr. Brett, an old man. She told me that her family had been there for three generations, her grandfather having come to the place when he was a little boy. They farmed sixty acres at £2 an acre rent, all or almost all of it grass land. She said that by the help of a little dairy work, poultry, and the fatting of heifers, of which they kept six, with cake and hay, they managed to make a living, but that the last ten or twelve years had been 'rather bad.' She complained much of the heavy commission they were obliged to pay to the hay-sellers at the London markets. This seemed to amount to 6s. a load, plus what was called ' the spending shilling,' which was charged against the farmer, plus 1s. 6d. fee to their own man who carted the hay. In addition, the cost of drawing was 4s., so that in all 12s. 6d. had to be deducted from the price of each load sold ; a heavy tax indeed.

It is from instances like these that we learn how great would be the advantage of co-operation among small farmers. Were such a system in force surely it would be possible for them to arrange some method of collection and disposal of produce, which would avoid the necessity of paying 8s. 6d. out-of-pocket expenses in the marketing of each load of hay. In this charming old farmhouse I noticed a set of Chippendale chairs of great beauty which without doubt must have been the property of the first of the family who occupied it, and everything else about the place had the same old-fashioned Georgian air.

On the estate of Mr. Ralph Bury at Nazeing, in this neighbourhood, I saw a number of very interesting plots of grass which had been experimented on, I think, by the county Council in order to determine what artificial manure, or manures, would give the best return in hay. The field was an old and good pasture which had been fairly farmed in the past, and the soil ten inches of loam lying over thirty feet of boulder clay. On Plot 0, unmanured, the grass was light; Plot 1, manured with 1 cwt. of nitrate of soda to the acre, still light, but of a darker colour and thicker bottom. Plot 2, ¼ cwt. of sulphate of ammonia ; results similar to those on unmanured land. Plot 3, 1 cwt. sulphate of potash, grass thinner than on unmanured land; Plot 4, 2 cwts. of super-phosphates. Here the clover was better, but general improvement scarcely appreciable. Plot 5, 2 cwts. of basic slag. Rather thicker at bottom than most, with a fair amount of clover. Plot 6, unmanured, thin by contrast with the last; Plot 7, 2 cwts. of superphosphates and 1 cwt. of nitrate of soda. Showed a fair bottom. Plot 8, 2 cwts. of superphosphates, 1 cwt. nitrate of soda and 1 cwt. sulphate of potash. More grass but scarcely in proportion to the outlay. Plot 9, farmyard manure. Showed an improvement on the unmanured land, but was not so good as the artificially manured plots. A strip at the edge of this field was under the shade of trees, and here I noticed that the grasses were thicker, if somewhat coarser, than on any of the treated plots. Perhaps the dry season was partly responsible for these not very satisfactory results, or cold may have affected them. Thus on the night previous to my visit, that of June 15, there was a sharp white frost.

Mr. Bury showed us another field that had received four dressings of basic slag in as many successive years. It was the best piece of grass on the farm, and looked as though it would cut $1\frac{1}{2}$ ton per acre. In the first year it was treated with 5 cwts. of slag; in the second with 4 cwts.; in the third with $3\frac{1}{2}$ cwts.; and in the fourth with $3\frac{1}{2}$ cwts. A field of beans also had been given 6 cwts. of basic slag to the acre a week before the beans were drilled in the previous autumn. The results were very satisfactory, as the haulms showed a dark green leaf and were podded to the ground. Mr. Bury said that personally he had sufficient labour.

I noticed that in the neighbourhood of this estate the forest trees looked very bad and sickly, and in some cases were actually dying owing to the effects of the continually recurring droughts.

Mr. J. Pegrum, of Bury Farm, Nazeing, where I visited him, held 600 acres, of which 200 were arable. He said that things could not look worse than they did in 1901. To earn a living a farmer had to work like a labourer, and he thought that as a class they were 'wasting rather than strengthening'; also that few of their sons would be willing to continue the business. It was difficult to hire skilled labour, or to find a lad who would learn ploughing. Out of all his hands, who numbered nearly forty, not one young fellow would 'walk the clods.' Indeed some whom he had told to plough refused and went away. It was, he said, much the same with milkers; you might advertise, but you would not get them, though he himself had one or two weakly men not fitted for other work, who did the milking. He arranged that they had a Sunday off in every three.

It will be observed that on this point Mr. Pegrum's evidence is of the usual, I might say of the universal, character. Why, I wonder, is there this general objection to milking, which is not altogether to be explained by the fact that it involves a certain amount of Sunday labour? I have a theory of my own which I will state for what it is worth. In the past to milk was the work of the women. But now Englishwomen will rarely work at all, either at this or at any other class of agricultural labour, that is, unless they happen to be the wives or daughters of small-holders, or can procure light and highly remunerative jobs, such as picking or 'puggling' strawberries or grape-thinning. In all my experience throughout England I cannot remember seeing or hearing of a single farmer whose cows were milked by female labour. Yet the tradition lingers in the minds of men that this milking is essentially a woman's job, and it is for this reason, I suggest, that they instinctively dislike the task.

Mr. Pegrum said also that the district was badly off for cottages, so that his elderly men had to live in what there were and take in the bachelors to board, not always a satisfactory arrangement. As regarded the cow-keeping business, he thought that much of the land would have to be used for other purposes owing to the labour trouble. A discussion followed as to whether cows, of which he kept forty, did or did not 'drag' the land, as many authorities allege to be the case, owing to the fact that their tether is not as stimulating and helpful to the soil as that of other cattle. Mr. Pegrum seemed to think that this deficiency could be remedied by careful feeding with cake; in short, he always kept the danger in view and took steps by which it might be obviated.

As a person who has kept cows for a good many years and at the same time been engaged in building up young pastures, my own opinion is that he who has milch kine should also keep sheep that he fats with cake, which in this important matter make up for the deficiencies of the cows. But of course this is only a view based upon my own experience. Mr. Pegrum said that in 1900 potatoes were very good, but it was a difficult crop to market through the London salesmen. Hay on the contrary was easily marketed, but he also made complaints of the salesmen's charges similar to those which I have quoted in the cases of Mr. Bott and Mr. Brett. Indeed, the grumbling on this matter was so universal in the district that it would be difficult to suppose it without foundation.

Milk was sold at tenpence a gallon in winter and sevenpence halfpenny a gallon in summer, but out of this amount farmers were obliged to pay carriage. Mr. Pegrum informed me in conclusion that he estimated the drop in rentals of grass lands in his neighbourhood at about 30 per cent.

In driving to visit Mr. Palmer, a gentleman renowned for his great skill as a judge of Hereford and other cattle at the larger agricultural shows, we passed over Nazeing Common, well known for its golf links. This common, which extends over a large stretch of ground, is covered with tens of thousands of ant-heaps that greatly damage, if they do not ruin, the pasture, while the surrounding land is practically free of these pests. Here we saw an instance of the evil of unenclosed land over which a number of persons have certain more or less limited rights. What is everybody's business is nobody's business, therefore the emmet-heaps remained unlevelled. The individual owner of a piece of property, knowing that he is working for his own benefit only, takes a different view of the matter, and is rid of them.

Mr. Palmer said—and I entirely agree with him—that the over-fatting of cattle for show purposes is ' all wrong,' although as a matter of fact the exhibitor who does not follow the common custom in this respect has but little chance of taking a prize. As regards oxen, of course the object is to show what can be done with the beasts, but, as he pointed out, in the case of heifers the practice is against nature and quite unfits them for breeding purposes. Mr. Palmer had some beautiful Herefords, young things of thirteen months that weighed 10 cwts., and a bullock of two and a half years preparing for the Christmas shows which was a positive monster. His farming was excellent, and of barley especially he grew very heavy crops per acre. It was not his custom to use artificial manure, as he preferred to rely upon large dressings of farmyard muck. Of labour he had sufficient, but said that the men must be gently handled.

Mr. Palmer was a believer in the theory advanced by Dr. Watney—who, I think, has a noted herd of Jerseys near Reading—that hay which is cut directly the grasses flower, that is, earlier than is usual, has much superior feeding properties to any other. This seems reasonable, but of course the crops secured in such circumstances must be lighter. He thought also that factories ought to be moved out of London in order to meet the matter of the deterioration of the health of the city populations. This also is reasonable. But unfortunately those concerned do not at present seem inclined to shift from the towns to the country, at least to any considerable extent. Amongst other drawbacks, to do so would of course involve a large expenditure of capital.

Among the farms which I visited in the neighbourhood of Waltham was one which had been held by the same family for nearly a hundred years. The rent was about £2 the acre, for half of this land is good grass situated in a convenient neighbourhood, which was practically the same as that paid by the holder's grandfather or great-grandfather a century ago, when of course money had a much higher value. Selling prices seem, however, to have decreased since then ; at any rate, the tenant informed me that he had lately sold some accommodation land, which was purchased by his forbears two generations since at £60 an acre. On the occasion of the resale it realised only £50 an acre, as I understood, for building purposes. This gentleman told us that he depended upon the sale of hay—at least that was his chief crop. Also he cultivated spring tares, which are bunched in August and sold as green-meat for London horses. Another catch crop was white turnips, sown very thick. These are purchased as a table vegetable by London buyers who harvest them at a price of from £5 to £7 an acre. Here spring beans were drilled in rows three feet apart, which admit of their being readily cleaned, so that in practice they serve the purpose of a fallow. Owing to the drought they looked very bad, and are being attacked by a black fly known locally as the ' collier.'

This farmer assured us that do what he would he could make no more than his rent and a fair living. I asked him of his labour, and was rewarded by a strange discovery. He was employing twenty hands at an average weekly wage of from 18s. to £1, some of whom we saw at work. As he was without cottage accommodation on the farm, I inquired where these men lodged. He answered, ' In one of the buildings.' I asked to see the place, and was shown a brick shed, measuring twelve or fourteen feet square, which might have served as a waggon house, and was, I think I am right in saying, windowless. In this place, upon sacks that were laid round the walls, slept the twenty men upon the floor. No washing apparatus was visible and no fireplace.

About a hundred yards away, on the slope of a hill, stands a hollow elm, at the foot of which were the ashes of a fire and an iron rod used to support the cooking pot. Round about lay some boughs, which served as benches.

This was at once the kitchen and the parlour of the twenty
men, who winter and summer did their cooking and spent
their Sundays and leisure hours with no other shelter than
that old tree afforded—or so I was informed. Any who
are interested in the matter of rural accommodation may
study the details of this delectable resort in the accompanying photograph, which was taken by ourselves. These
labourers, by the way, were all casuals, and presumably
unmarried; but their employer said that some of them had
been with him for as long as three years.

Let the reader realise the position. It meant that the
men, twenty, or perhaps less of them in winter, within
thirty miles of London, existed, and I presume still exist, at
all seasons of the year in a fashion that the lowest Kaffirs
would refuse. Their sleeping place, a crowded shed, their
bedding, sacks, their shelter by day, a tree, their food such
as unskilled hands can cook in an iron pot, their female
society none, their recreation the beer-house, where, as their
master told me, they spend the most of their good wages;
their refuge in sickness the public infirmary, to which when
I was at the place one of them had just been taken. Had
I not seen it with my own eyes I would not have believed
that such a state of affairs was possible. And yet who is to
be blamed? Not the farmer, as he had at most but one
cottage on his holding. The landlord? Very probably he
could not afford to build, and knew nothing of the matter.
The men? Work was plentiful; they might go elsewhere if
they liked, but so far as I was able to discover were satisfied
with their lot. The problem is too hard for me. Of one
thing only am I certain: it is not right that in a highly
civilised country human beings should pass their lives under
conditions that must be as comfortless and insanitary as they
are degrading.

I now propose to quote as briefly as I can a few of the
written opinions which I have received from various correspondents in Essex. Mr. C. Clarke, who, I believe, until
lately farmed at Maldon in Essex, said that in that district

rents had fallen to the extent of 50 per cent. on the better lands, and 75 per cent. on the poorer. In 1901 they ran from 10*s.* to 20*s.* per acre for the former, which used to let at from 40*s.* to 50*s.* per acre, and from nothing to 5*s.* the acre for the latter. In 1875 the poor heavy lands adapted to wheat growing were worth £30 an acre and downwards, which same lands in 1901 were worth £5 an acre. The better-class lands adapted to wheat and any other crop used to be worth £40 an acre and upwards, but in 1901 were worth from £10 to £15 an acre. There were no resident landlords in the district; farms did not let readily, rents were not regularly paid, and often were not paid at all. The labour was just sufficient but very inferior, the men being principally old.

Very few young people were coming on, and women refused to do general work as in the past, and often would not take even hay or harvest work. The average wage was 18*s.* a week, including harvest and extras. Cottages, he said, were scarce and in many cases in a deplorable condition, having only a living room with a back kitchen and two bedrooms. Where the landlords had been rich or wise enough to build decent houses, with two good downstair rooms, three bedchambers, and wash-house, the tenant farmer could command a much better class of labour. Nearly all the young men migrated to the towns, where they found more money, more amusement and more leisure. Education was not the cause of their departure, as men might be found working in the towns who were quite as ignorant as those upon the land.

The general condition of the tenant farmer was, he considered, very bad indeed, and although he put on a smiling face, at times his decent suit of clothes covered an aching heart. The landlords were much reduced, few depended entirely on their rents, having taken to commerce of one sort or another. Labourers, if prudent, were never better off. Mr. Clarke saw no signs of a revival of agricultural interests, and was not hopeful as to the future. He thought that the result of the present state of affairs would be that thousands of acres of land must go out of cultivation, following the thousands which had already gone, and that the country at large would have to depend upon foreign supplies of food. The cause of it all could be found in Hazell's Annual for 1901, which showed that whereas in 1873 the average price of wheat was 58s. 8d. per quarter, in 1899 it was 25s. 8d. The remedies that he had to suggest were (1): 'Find another Disraeli,' (2) put a moderate duty upon all imported wheat, barley, &c., with rebates in favour of our colonies, a double duty on meal and flour, and 20s. an acre bonus on every acre of home-grown wheat. These measures, in his opinion, would not greatly increase the price of bread, and in any event the extra cost would cause the entire community to contribute to the revenue.

Mr. Thomas Burleigh, of Great Chesterford, Essex, has sent me a very instructive summary of the costs that he found he would have to incur to enfranchise a single acre of agricultural land which he bought for £32. In all they amounted to £19 17s. 6d., which appeared to him so high a charge that he 'abandoned the proposal; and feeling sure that for so small a matter I should gain nothing by applying to the Board of Agriculture, I remain a serf.' He is of opinion that although the old class of tenant farmers cannot be brought back to the Essex land, a new and valuable body of small owners would be bred up if the labourers could buy holdings at a reasonable rate. The tenant farmer of thirty years ago, he said, was too big for his clothes. He did no more work than the large landowners, while his sons despised trade and spoke of a shopkeeper with the greatest contempt. Small farms were swallowed up; any rent was paid and no little man could get a holding. Thus the land had to support (1) the landlord, (2) the man who had lent him money, (3) the swell land agent, (4) the large farmer, (5) the large farmer's bailiff, (6) the labourer. The prices went down and with them 'for the most part down went the large farmer,' whose position was very often false from the beginning. He says that the tenant-farmer squire working with borrowed capital is not wanted, but that from a national point of view the owning farmer, however small, is much to be desired ; and after dwelling eloquently on the sorrows and sufferings which the agricultural classes have been called upon to bear, ends : ' It is very pitiful, but there have been grave faults, not only with the tenant, but sometimes in the landlord, and now both have their master in the labourer.'

A gentleman who does not wish his name to be mentioned has been so good as to write me several letters on the state of affairs in the Great Saling district of the county, where he is a landowner. Certainly his experience is great, since he says that he is eighty-nine years of age and has given up farming after harvesting sixty-nine crops on his own land, and has been for fifty years a poor-law guardian and twenty five years chairman of the Board. Also his family has lived in the same place since 1720. He feared that in the districts I had visited I might gather far too favourable an impression of Essex agriculture, unless it was qualified by actual obser- vation in the northern parts of the county. Also that some of the gentlemen from whom I had sought information, were not fully aware of the present difficulties arising from the loss of population and the lack of railways in the neighbour- hood of Braintree and elsewhere. Thus the population of Finchingfield, which thirty years ago was 2,600, in 1901 had fallen by over a thousand ; and Great Bardfield, which numbered 1,120 in 1858, had fallen to 750 in 1901. Further, a great quantity of land had been sold in that year at from £5 to £10 the acre, a friend of his having bought 125 acres within one and a half miles of a station for £600. No land, however, was out of cultivation, although it was very largely held off hand by people engaged in commercial pursuits. He thinks that all this part of the country is suffering much from the burden of tithe, which is heavier in Essex than in almost any other county, and has gone a long way towards ruining many landowners. Altogether his instructive communications are depressing to read ; but as their substance does but repeat much that I have recorded already, nothing can be gained by quoting them at length.

Mr. S. H. Sweetman, of Westcliff-on-Sea, is of opinion that what has appeared from my pen on the agriculture of the county has 'smacked too much of the Royal Agricultural Society method.' He says that 'the labourer and the land' —subjects about which I thought that I had written at some length—'are the rock-bottom factors, and if both of these are wrong, the superstructure is bound to be wrong also.' I admit the proposition; indeed I thought that I had advanced the same argument. He says that Essex is in the last stage of apathetic poverty, and is being cut up into areas by speculating land companies. He continues:

Yet, taking the country through, it is a fat land, and ought to do well, being so near London, the finest market in the world. What do we find in this town of Southend? If I want British butter I cannot get it, but I can Danish. My eggs are French, my cheese American, and my hams Canadian. The villages are dirty, and the people mostly on the poverty line. Nobody seems to care and there is no direction. Abroad the Government would help; we expand abroad and our rural population, the backbone of any country, is decreasing. If you visit this county, you will find a few well-to-do and they are satisfied. The poor don't care, and no opportunity appears to invite them to attain a higher level. Even the churches seem to be decaying, a sure sign of national poverty. Here and there are small settlements of freeholders, amateurs in cultivation, whose possessions show what can be done by people who have a real live interest in their own. Essex lies ready for an experiment on the lines of the Irish land system, as follows: (1) Land is cheap. (2) Let the Government purchase large tracts and build connecting light railways. (3) Lease to people who will take up so much as they can work themselves, assuring the workers the fruits of their own labours. (4) Establish co-operative agricultural councils to ensure a common trading basis and a common interest, and to enable the folk to hire or purchase for communal use the best of agricultural machinery, and so on. The Government who will start on these lines will do more for England than by hoisting flags abroad or imposing taxes at home.

With much of Mr. Sweetman's letter I agree, but his

remedies, or some of them, will only become practicable when British Governments develop that ' real live interest ' in English agriculture, which at present they seem to lack. Also I fear that however desirable these remedies may be, their carrying out would involve a certain amount of ' imposing taxes at home ' which would be energetically resented by the city populations, who would be called upon to help to pay them.

The Rev. Mr. Lach-Szyrma writes suggesting various ' palliatives for the present distress.' These include Protection, more light railways, the taxation of factories in towns until they remove themselves into the country, more allotments and peasant proprietors, rural education for rural schools, and more amusements for country folk, ' England,' he says, being ' hardly merry England for the farm labourer.' Excellent prescriptions most of them, but where is the chemist to make them up, and where are the nurses to administer them to sick and suffering rural England ?

I will only quote one more piece of evidence, that of Mr. Harold Rankin, of Broomhills, Rochford, who wrote that he was farming about a thousand acres, most of it very good land indeed, but he could not make the best of it ' because of the difficulty of getting labour, although our men are paid very high wages.'

At Hadleigh, thirty-six miles from London, the Salvation Army has a very interesting colony, which I much regret I was unable to visit. The object of this colony is to give employment, with food and lodging in return for his labour, to any able-bodied man who is willing to work, irrespective of the nationality or creed of the applicant. All sorts of agriculture, stock and poultry rearing, brick-making, &c., are there carried on with considerable success. There are 1,280 acres of farm land, 300 acres under fruit and market-gardening, and seventy acres given up to industrial undertakings. The first cost of the freehold land, together with that of planting orchards, was £40,390, but in addition I gather that £60,000 or £70,000 have been invested in buildings, brickworks, machinery, wharves, barges, stock, &c.

With reference to this colony and matters generally connected with my task, I had a most interesting interview with the head of the Salvation Army, General Booth, in my humble opinion one of the few great men of our time, using the word 'great' in its real, rather than in its common, complimentary sense. As his book 'In Darkest England' shows, no living man has larger experience of problems connected with the poor, and with the evils resulting from the crowding of country people into the towns, than has the Rev. Mr. Booth. For this reason I reproduce here the notes taken in shorthand at our interview, in so far as they refer to the matters under consideration in this work. To my mind they are full of interest and state in clear if every-day language, the views of a very remarkable man, formed in the course of a long lifetime devoted to good works.

*Notes of Mr. Rider Haggard's interview with General Booth. November 7, 1901.*

*Mr. Rider Haggard* : The object of my inquiries, General, has been largely to discover how things actually stand with reference to the migration of the people from the villages to the towns ; also if there is any special remedy for that migration, bearing in mind, as I do, the agricultural side of the question, which means, of course, under present circumstances, that labour is getting very short in many places ; also the national side of that question. I believe that it is a very ill thing for everybody to crowd into the cities. That has been the object of my inquiry. To be brief, I have visited, I think, twenty-six counties and several districts in each of them, and the upshot of my investigations is, that I find that this migration is undoubtedly going on—more in some places than in others—everywhere to a great degree. The country is being depleted and the towns have filled. Now, you have a vast experience in many ways and directions, and I have been anxious to see you, so as to get your views on the general question, and especially as to whether anything, and if so what, can be done to remedy this state of affairs, which I think you will admit to be a very great and a national evil.

*The General* : I am quite of your opinion. I agree with you as to the extent of the evil and its deplorable character. It must be, more or less, sooner or later, destructive of a great deal that is most desirable in a nation. But the question is how to prevent it. If you were to ask me, I should say that the only way of preventing the people from leaving the villages and coming to the towns, was to make things agreeable and profitable to them at home ; so that the boys could grow up and feel there was some sort of a future for them in their own neighbourhoods. As it is, they read the newspapers ; they come up to the towns by excursion trains ; they see the glitter and the glare ; they have relatives who have been to and fro to America, or who come to London, and they get letters from them. When people write letters they generally set forth the bright side of things, and in this way desires are created. The boys see the toil of their father and mother and they see the smallness of the supplies, the poorness of their food, the struggle there is to make things meet, and nothing before them at the end but the probability of pauperism. The young fellows say, ' No, I would sooner go and struggle and die in the towns in the attempt to get something better, than stop here in this misery.' Well, if you are going to keep them in the villages it seems to me that you must make life pleasanter for them. To do that you must give them a probability of getting something they can fall back upon. My notion is that they should be given something of their own, so that they can dig their own garden and mind their own pig, and look after their own chickens, and have something that really *is* their own. Proprietorship has a great charm, even if it is only in a small matter, and I think that there is a mass of these young fellows who, if they saw a chance of having something of their own, would prefer it to the chance of working for somebody else in the cities, even though they did get some other advantages. It must be borne in mind—although I don't know whether it is so or not—that these lads are probably born with some instinctive love of the land, love of its fruits and love of the animals, and if they could only see their way to stop there comfortably, the idea would be very attractive to them.

*Mr. Rider Haggard* : I think our system of education tends very much to eradicate that love.

*The General* : Yes, and the newspapers and periodicals and the glory of war. You have all these to contend with, and the railways and telegraphs and the penny postage which are put down as such great advantages. All these things are against your keeping a man on the land, especially if he can't get enough to eat. The question is, how is it going to be done?

*Mr. Rider Haggard* : Even when he does leave, he doesn't always get sufficient to eat, although in some cases he may do so.

*The General* : He goes to school and wants to rise above all that, and says ' Can't I do something better? '

*Mr. Rider Haggard* : There is another thing. You know there is a great desire on the part of the young to escape supervision. They want to get away from the parson and from public opinion. They don't want everybody to know what they are doing ; and in great cities they can do this. I think that is one of the difficulties.

*The General* : You should write a book in three volumes on the sorrows and disadvantages of the city for the benefit of these hobbledehoys, and put over against them the attraction of having a place of their own : there is no other way, Mr. Haggard. I have studied this question.

*Mr. Rider Haggard* : I know you have, and our opinions are perfectly identical upon that point.

*The General* : And that is the way—I was going to say God's way—but I suppose I must not bring in religion.

*Mr. Rider Haggard* : Probably our opinions are the same upon that point also.

*The General* : Put a man down on five hundred acres of land and he will perhaps have to slave and toil, and probably get into the Bankruptcy Court, but put a man on ten acres and help him on to his feet and you will make him a happy man.

*Mr. Rider Haggard* : To show that our opinions agree : just before leaving the Athenæum Club this morning I had a few minutes to spare and I was writing a letter to 'The Times' on these matters. Here is a sentence from it : ' I have only found one thing that will keep them, or the best of them—property in or on the land. Where small-holdings are fashionable my experience is that the population increases or at any rate does not dwindle. A man will do for himself what he will not do for another, and after all there are worse things than hard work in the open air.' I read that to show how completely our views are at one.

*The General* : Yes. I don't think there is any more important question for this country, so far as human affairs are concerned, than how we can get the land cultivated by its own

THE PARLOUR AND KITCHEN OF TWENTY ESSEX LABOURERS

children—those who belong to it, were born on it and brought up to it.

*Mr. Rider Haggard* : I agree, but have you any scheme ?

*The General* : I can make a scheme easy enough.

*Mr. Rider Haggard* : Let me hear it.

*The General* : It is all in a nutshell. You must give a man a certain amount of land ; you must give him a cottage to live in——

*Mr. Rider Haggard* : Give?

*The General* : I use the word in the sense of supplying. People who know us say, ' The Salvation Army give nowt for nowt.' When people come to us they all expect to have to work, or pay, or do something.

*Mr. Rider Haggard* : A good job too.

*The General* : My principles are well known : That which a man gets for nothing he underestimates ; make him work for what he gets. You supply five to ten acres of land ; you put him in a cottage ; you let him have a cow and some chickens ; you supply him with some seed and set him going, and if he has the fever or any trouble you must come in and help him along. You cannot do that without so much money per family. You must have carts to collect his chickens and milk, and give him the advantages of co-operation. If you will do that on my principles and the plan I follow, you can get four per cent. for your money and keep the people on the land.

*Mr. Rider Haggard* : You have a settlement ?

*The General* : No, we have not a settlement after that fashion ; we have a colony.

*Mr. Rider Haggard* : That is what I mean.

*The General* : We are bad to judge there because we take in the wastrels and scalliwags, people who get down through drink or misfortunes, through the prison or in some way or other. We raise them and float them back by hundreds into society, and they were lost to society. Nobody knows where they come from or anything about them. But then that is not the principle that I should like to see tried, which I should like to try, but I never had the money to do it. I have to beg my money from door to door, so to speak, as well as to raise the poor wretches.

*Mr. Rider Haggard* : You have a scheme, but you cannot carry it out because you have not the money. What is your scheme ?

*The General* : This would be my scheme. I would buy

estates—a dozen or so. I made a great mistake in buying my land—I don't like to say I make mistakes—because we bought hard clay land, and I have got out of the rain belt somehow—we have had seven years' drought.

*Mr. Rider Haggard* : Where is it ?

*The General* : Four miles outside Southend.

*Mr. Rider Haggard* : It is near a good market.

*The General* : That does not matter much. We are making bricks and we shall soon be making a million of them a week. I could sell some of it for £500 an acre ; it cost £20.

*Mr. Rider Haggard* : What do you grumble at, then ?

*The General* : It is not money I want to make, but men. I shall make a town there, lay out roads, build shops and little villas, and bring the people there. With the money I will buy land elsewhere.

*Mr. Rider Haggard* : Your scheme is to buy estates ?

*The General* : Buy the estates, and build cottages in the cheapest possible way. I was going in for this scheme, and got a nice lot of land, but they wouldn't let me put an iron cottage up.

*Mr. Rider Haggard* : You mean the District Councils ?

*The General* : No—the Government. By an Act of Parliament you cannot build a cottage of iron except you put a brick wall inside or outside. Well, my notion was to take the people from the town, but it is a better plan to keep them on the land.

*Mr. Rider Haggard* : You want to get this riff-raff, and take them back to the land. I want to keep them on the land ; that is what I am labouring so hard for, but I doubt how many will stop.

*The General* : You have the kind of man you require and the employment he has been born to, and grown up in. He has looked after the horse, gone into the fields and attended to things generally. I tell you if you give him five or ten acres——

*Mr. Rider Haggard* : He must have a market.

*The General* : You must make a market—carts will make a market.

*Mr. Rider Haggard* : You must have co-operation.

*The General* : We have five hundred fellows on our Farm and we have a co-operative store. We sell everything the people need on the ground.

*Mr. Rider Haggard* : You bought your land at £18 an acre ?

*The General* : And I have had to give £200 for some. It has largely increased in value ; hundreds of little villas have been built in the neighbourhood.

*Mr. Rider Haggard*: Who occupy them?

*The General*: Londoners.

*Mr. Rider Haggard*: What class of people? Is it because of this settlement that the accretion has happened, or is the case exceptional?

*The General*: Our settlement drew attention to that beautiful country, though they said we were going to ruin it.

*Mr. Rider Haggard*: But the land you have got and have cultivated has increased in value.

*The General*: Of course it has.

*Mr. Rider Haggard*: Very well. Your idea is now to buy large estates if you can get them?

*The General*: Buy large estates. You need not get them particularly near a railway; put up your little cottages and put your farmer's men into them. In the first go off, find some fellows that know what they are doing—decent fellows with families—help them until they are on their feet; collect their eggs, chickens, corn, and sell them back again the stuff they want.

*Mr. Rider Haggard*: What will these men get—a wage or a land interest?

*The General*: They get all the profit they make.

*Mr. Rider Haggard*: You charge them with interest.

*The General*: Yes, and a small return on the capital.

*Mr. Rider Haggard*: A sinking fund?

*The General*: Yes; money can be borrowed at 3 per cent., the Government says. We find a difficulty now—we are always borrowing. Supposing, for instance, that setting up a fellow would cost for a cottage——

*Mr. Rider Haggard*: £300 a pair.

*The General*: I don't think you can do it for £300.

*Mr. Rider Haggard*: I think you might, as you make your bricks.

*The General*: We should charge the bricks at market price. Well say £150, and £100 to put the man in—£250 at 5 per cent. That is £12 10s., or 5s. a week; say 3 per cent. for interest and 2 per cent. sinking fund.

*Mr. Rider Haggard*: Why don't you sell your valuable land and go into Suffolk? I know plenty there that is offered at £10 or £12 an acre.

*The General*: We are going to do better with ours—make roads and so on. Before I do any more—I am 72 years of age— I will have the money offered me if I will go and do it. I have done my share of begging to try and save the poor. Look at the city work. Three years ago I spent about £125,000 a year in helping the scalliwags and the poor homeless. Out of that I don't suppose I troubled the public for more than £8,000 ; the remainder was earned by the poor fellows themselves. If I had not to pay something like £10,000 for rates and taxes—they make me pay poor rates while I am doing all this ——

*Mr. Rider Haggard* : Of course they do ; they can hardly make an exception in your favour. I am going to suggest to you what I believe would be of great help in any such scheme as you are speaking of, and that is that you should establish a Bank on the principle of the Agricultural Credit Banks that are so prosperous abroad.

*The General* : We understand that Banking ; we are doing it in India, to the astonishment of everybody.

*Mr. Rider Haggard* : I maintain you would find that system of enormous assistance.

*The General* : We have a Bank on the premises. We also do insurance business ; we collect a penny a week per head.

*Mr. Rider Haggard* : You must also have co-operation.

*The General* : This plan ought to be tried by a syndicate, or the nation, or in some large way or other, not for the submerged but for the decent carter—the decent labourer who has got a wife and four or five strapping children. Let them show you what they will do ; they will grow some corn, rear chickens and so on.

*Mr. Rider Haggard* : That is why I want to see Banks established, so that such men will be able to borrow a little capital to do it with. Now you said when we began talking that there was great vice in London owing to poverty.

*The General* : Yes, vicious habits are created in the cities ; misery makes vice, and vice makes misery, and many of the people who come from the fields crowd into one room in the most shameless fashion—men and women together—and little children grow up in the midst of degrading influences, when they might be in the country.

*Mr. Rider Haggard* : In short, do you not think, General, that one of the great solutions of our modern poverty problems would be to keep people on the land, and to get many of those who have come from it back to the land ?

*The General* : Yes, and I believe that if I wrote in my ' War Cry ' I would have any number of applications from men and women of good character who would say, 'Let us go back to the village life ; I am sick of this.'

*Mr. Rider Haggard* : A certain number would, but a lot of them get so bitten with street life.

*The General* : I am talking about my own people. But all that is preliminary : get your decent people, and when you have your fire up to full blaze you can put any amount of rubbish on it. If you get a proper thing going it will bear putting more people in, and getting more land.

*Mr. Rider Haggard* : You are approaching it from a different side to what I have been approaching it. I have always thought it hopeless even to expect that any private organisation would rise up able to tackle this matter. Therefore I have had to confine myself to existing circumstances. Still we could do something if we would, and among the chief helps I have been able to see are these Banks and the extension of the Rural Housings Acts to enable landowners or corporate Bodies to borrow at a cheaper rate, repayable in sixty years, so that they can put up houses and buildings. I have always rather doubted the possibility of an artificial creation of small-holdings—don't you ?

*The General* : Yes.

*Mr. Rider Haggard* : I think you might do it—nobody else could.

*The General* : I have got this advantage, without which I think I should not have done what I have done. That is, the creating of a benevolent, loving spirit in the hearts of men and women that carries them on to do the work, not for their pay but for the good they are doing. If you are going to set the farmer on to do it for his servants, he will do as little as he can, and get as much out of them as he can, and the servant will get as much out of the master as *he* can.

*Mr. Rider Haggard* : The whole thing is very unsatisfactory as it is. They tell us that it is impossible—small-holdings. It seems to me they forget that England, at the beginning, and that is when we grew great, was a country of small-holdings, and it was always more or less in small-holdings until the last century.

*The General*· If you go to Illinois or California, they grow eight bushels an acre ; that is on a big holding. In England they raise twenty-seven bushels, in Scotland thirty-five, perhaps forty, in China eighty, and if you go to the spade-husbandman, you get seventy.

*Mr. Rider Haggard* : I would like to see a lot more spade-husbandry. I have seen derelict farms in Essex where every bit of the land would produce splendid vegetables and strawberries to any extent. We pay away hundreds of thousands for these things.

*The General*: Some years ago I was coming up from Clacton through Essex. As I came along I saw a garden full of cabbages, raspberry bushes and all manner of vegetables, while all around the land was lying comparatively idle. I said, ' What is the difference between the garden and field work ? '—labour very largely.

*Mr. Rider Haggard*: And manure.

*The General*: Very largely labour. I said to myself, ' I am going to the city, where people are dying for work, and here the land is dying for labour.'

*Mr. Rider Haggard*: Is there any real lack of work in London now ?

*The General*: To a certain extent things have been very much better lately. There were hundreds of people out of work.

*Mr. Rider Haggard*: Can any able-bodied man, who will put his back into it, lack work ?

*The General*: Take an ordinary dock labourer with 18s. a week. He has to pay 4s. 6d. for his room, and he has got a wife and several children. He loses a day here and a day there.

*Mr. Rider Haggard*: And yet he will come up from the country, where he is getting the same 18s. a week and paying only 1s. a week rent.

*The General*: The poor wretch don't know any better and all you highly learned men don't teach him any better. Look, too, how the masters treat their men. I have been amongst the farmers and I have heard them talk to their horses and pat them on the neck and speak to them like a gentleman, and talk to Tom, Dick, or Harry, as if he were a beast.

*Mr. Rider Haggard*: How about the employers at the docks ?

*The General*: They have to talk a deal more carefully than that or else men would strike.

*Mr. Rider Haggard*: I mean, as a matter of fact, that a man has probably come from getting 18s. a week in the country, and that he does not better himself by coming to London.

*The General*: He thinks he is going to do it, and then he can't get back.

*Mr. Rider Haggard*: Why can't he get back ?

*The General*: Perhaps he has no work to go to ; perhaps his wife won't go ; perhaps Dick and Sally won't go. They say, 'You can go but we sha'n't; we will go to America.'

*Mr. Rider Haggard*: I would rather work for 18*s.* a week in the country than at the docks.

*The General*: You have imagination ; they haven't.

*Mr. Rider Haggard*: The country is cleaner, healthier, and cheaper. It seems to me we are both perfectly agreed that this migration is the great evil of the day.

*The General* : You must show them how they can stop at home with some sort of prospect.

*Mr. Rider Haggard*: Heaven knows I would like to. I keep hammering at it hard enough. I don't see how it is to be done. It is perfect nonsense for the newspapers to turn to individuals to set such great schemes going.

(The General here gave details of the amount raised and expended on the Social Scheme, the annual sum he asked for and the amount contributed.)

*Mr. Rider Haggard* : I take it for the land experiment you mention you would want at least a quarter of a million ?

*The General*: I think you should put somebody into it who knows what he is doing. What is the use of setting the unskilled labourer down to work of this sort? We do it, but it is not a paying concern.

*Mr. Rider Haggard*: You would want a quarter of a million ?

*The General*: That would make the experiment, and by its example ultimately make England such a place as no other country is ; also it would pay.

*Mr. Rider Haggard*: I think so, provided you don't have too much waste on it.

*The General*: That is my point. I would only put good men on—men of character.

*Mr. Rider Haggard*: It is no use to put fellows there to look after cattle who don't know how to look after themselves.

*The General*: No. Managing a horse is a science ; managing a cow is a science.

*Mr. Rider Haggard*: I can only hope you will be able to do it. I am very glad you agree with me about the great seriousness of the position. I look at it as the question of the future ; to a very large extent the destiny of the country is involved in this question of the migration from the land to the cities.

(The General here spoke of the cultivation of the land in France, Denmark and Sweden—every corner being cultivated.)

*Mr. Rider Haggard* : And that—what is done in Denmark—is what you think ought to be done here ?

*The General* : You see here great stretches of beautiful land, and these only want working to grow five or six times the amount of food we are getting, instead of our going abroad for it.

*Mr. Rider Haggard* : One must bear in mind also the matter of our food supplies ; in case we went to war we should be in a very tight place.

*The General* : That is what I believe and am saying.

The upshot of the above interview is that General Booth's views and my own seem to be identical in all essentials. Evidently he is convinced of the greatness of the evils resulting from the desertion by the rural population of the villages for the towns, and earnestly desires that the movement should be checked in the interest of the country at large and its inhabitants.

In 1795 Mr. Charles Vancouver drew up 'for the consideration of the Board of Agriculture and Internal Improvement' a work called 'General View of the Agriculture in the County of Essex,' which I have been so fortunate as to obtain. I can only hope that a hundred and seven years hence these present volumes will not prove so difficult to read. Yet Mr. Vancouver was most laborious, and his statistical tables of information, though hard to understand, are masterpieces of intricate ingenuity. Also the student can derive much instruction from his pages, dull as they may be, and it is with a melancholy interest that he reads the familiar names of villages and reflects that of those who tilled their fields in 1795 not one in a thousand is even remembered to-day. An entry in the church register is their sole memorial, and one that nobody ever sees ; but if farmers go, farming is immortal, and here we find the same questions, troubles, hopes, and fears, if in a different degree, that agitate the Essex of to-day.

Oddly enough, the rentals of 1795 appear to have been practically identical with those that prevailed in the year of my visit (1901)— about £1 an acre for the best pasture, 14s. or 15s. for the sound arables, and less for the poor, waste, or unenclosed lands. Mr. Vancouver issued a set of queries proposed by the Board of Agriculture 'to be answered by intelligent farmers.' Four answers only seem to have been sent in, three of them signed by clergy and the fourth by, I presume, an intelligent farmer, who does not sign his name.

These replies are, in my opinion, the most valuable part of the book, and give the best and most concise information therein contained. From them I learn (Answer 1) that 'a *good* labourer gains at least 8s. a week the year round, beer included, more if working, as much is frequently done, when convenient on both sides, by the piece.' (Answer 2.) The price of labour is '1s. per day and beer; fourteenpence without; labour per grate' (*i.e.* by piece-work) 'varies; land-ditching,' that is, under-draining, 'a penny half-penny and twopence per rod; hedging and ditching one spit dry, threepence per rod.' (Answer 3.) 'The price of labour is 1s. 6d. per day of twelve hours, from six in the morning to six at eve; for in winter as long as it is light; but the chief of the work is done by the piece.' (Answer 4.) The cost of 'the best men-servants for farmers from £7 to £8 or £9 a year' (of course this means with food and lodging), 'maid-servants from £3 to £4 for ditto; servants to gentlemen considerably higher. Farmers' labourers, fourteenpence a day; by the piece they earn from 4s. or 6s. to 9s. or 10s. per week, according as the job turns out, or in proportion to the strength or dexterity of the labourer. The daily wages have been nominally raised within these few years about twopence in the shilling; but the annual earnings, comprehending all descriptions, young and old, strong and infirm, are perhaps not greatly advanced.'

These answers throw many other lights upon the condition of the county at the time. Thus the Rev. John Howlett, then vicar of Great Dunmow, which in those days had a population of 1,663, as against a population of 2,781 in 1891, states that 'the average annual mortality is one in

about 42⅜, an indication of at least tolerable healthiness.'
This gives a death-rate of a little over twenty per thousand,
which I presume would be thought satisfactory now-a-days.
We grumble at the rapid increase in our rates. But in
Great Dunmow the average for the preceding period of four
years of the poors-rates was in 1719, £260 6s. 8d.; in 1781
it was £951 19s. 8d.; in 1790, £698 11s. 4d.! Mr. Howlett
says: 'You see that during the last twelve years the three
averages of four years each have decreased more than £100
a year. This has been owing, I believe, to these two causes:
first, a determination in the parish officers to spare their
money to the utmost, and secondly, by admitting as few as
possible into the workhouse, where experience has taught
them that the maintenance of the poor is much more expensive in than out of it. . . . The price of provisions has
all the time been greatly advancing; the natural conclusion
seems to be that the necessities of the poor have not been so
well provided for. This, however, is not to be admitted in
its full apparent extent; for it is to be observed that in the
year 1782 a putrid fever took place, and carried off three times
the average number; and chiefly prevailing amongst the poor,
it at once raised the rates from about £800 to upwards of
£1,200.'

I confess that I cannot at all follow this argument of
the reverend gentleman's. I should have thought that the
putrid fever did show that the necessities of the poor had
not been so well provided for, unless indeed he means that
they continued to be provided for, the putrid fever notwithstanding.

Mr. Howlett also discourses on tithe. He says: 'I know
not anything that renders tithes more objectionable than
this disproportionate advance of the value compared with
that of the lands which produce them' (do we not make
much the same remark to-day?), 'and nothing but the for-
bearance and moderation of the clergy can make them
tolerable. As to a general commutation I know not any
better than that already referred to as made in the Agricul-

tural Return for Stafford.  The farmers are the only persons
who generally complain on this head ; but if they are wise,
they will never wish for their abolition ; for what they
now contingently get from the moderation of the clergy, the
landlords would immediately put in their own pockets,
and the farmers, burdened with increased rents, rates, and
taxes, would feel how indiscreet were their former complaints.'

The 'intelligent farmer,' who does not sign his name,
takes quite a different view of tithe.  He says : ' There is here
(as in other counties more or less) one grand obstacle to all
improvement ; for, great as is the industry and judgment
of our farmers in the cultivation of their land, still they
receive so severe a check to their spirit of improvement
when they see the tithe-owner taking from them a tenth
of all their produce, that it frequently puts an end to all
enterprise and experiment.'

How like is this voice from the past to that of the
authority, who also withholds his name, who wrote to me
from the Saling district that the tithe, which is heavier in
Essex than in almost any other county, had gone a long
way towards ruining many of the landowners by whom it is
now paid.  Times are changed, but the bitter tithe controversy remains the same.

At the date when Mr. Vancouver's book was written the
process of hollow-draining, or under-ditching, or land-ditching
was a recent introduction into Essex, pipe-draining being of
course unknown until a later day.  Says our author : ' There is
no improvement to which the heavy land husbandry in this
county owes so much as to the fortunate introduction, and
continuance of the practice, of hollow-draining.'  These
drains were dug three or four yards apart after first being
drawn with the plough.  They were then filled in, with straw,
which in twelve or eighteen months rotted away, leaving a
pipe of the nature of that which is formed by the modern
steam mole-plough.  Some farmers, however, used wood
and straw, or green broom ; also the loppings from elm
pollards were ' much esteemed.'  Drains thus made with

wood must have been exactly similar to those which are common with us on heavy land to-day.

Here, regretting that space will not allow me to quote from him more largely, I must bid farewell to Mr. Vancouver. Greatly do I wonder what changes another hundred and seven years have in store for the agriculture of Essex and of England, and greatly do I hope that when, my determined days fulfilled and my labours finished, I too have become an inhabitant of that immense Silence which has swallowed him, his generation, and all its works, my eyes and ears may still be open so that I may see and know these—and many other things.

Of the actual conditions of the rural interests in Essex as I found them, the reader must judge from the foregoing pages, which, I believe—although of course they are but a summary—give a sufficient and accurate view of the facts. For my part I cannot speak of them very hopefully. Essex is in the main, and I think must continue to be, a corn-growing country. It would seem, therefore, that until the price of that staple is increased, prosperity can scarcely return to those who own and cultivate her soil.

# HERTFORDSHIRE AND MIDDLESEX

The inland south-eastern county of Hertfordshire, which I visited after Essex, is one of the smallest in England, having an area of about 406,100 acres only and an extreme length from north-east to south-west of thirty-nine miles, with an extreme breadth of twenty-six miles.

Although so near to London it is almost purely agricultural in character. In addition to the ordinary cereal crops, potatoes, hay, vegetables, and fruit are grown in quantity for the markets of the metropolis, whither go also the bulk of its cattle, sheep, pigs, and poultry. On account of its situation it is a favourite place of residence for those whose occupations take them frequently to town; also here there are many landowners whose families have been established in the county for generations. It is well watered by numerous streams, for the most part tributaries of the Thames; but one of the great complaints of the residents is of the way in which the subsoil is being drained of its water by the great London companies, who pump it out of deep wells and from every other available source. For this damage, which threatens to injure the county materially, there seems to be no remedy at law. It appears that if a man buys half an acre of land, he has a right to sink in it wells of any depth he pleases, even if by doing so he renders all those of his neighbours useless, and impairs the value and utility of a large surrounding area.

After the examination of various districts in Hertfordshire, were I asked what struck me most in that county I think that I should answer, the submergence of the Hertfordshire farmer. 'But where are the home people?' I inquired after visiting a long succession of Scotch and Cornish agriculturists. 'You must look for them in the backwoods,' was the reply. By 'backwoods' I may explain was meant those districts which are a long way from the railway line or station, and therefore least desirable for the purposes of agriculture as it is practised in this county. In Herts, and in Essex also for that matter, this occupation of the best of the country by outlander farmers is a subject which not unnaturally excites a good deal of feeling. Therefore I touch on it with diffidence, and solely for the reason that to attempt to treat of the agriculture of the county without doing so would be misleading and even absurd. Of course some of the old local men still remain, some prosper even, but on the whole victory is to the Scotch and Cornish. Theirs are the best and the best worked farms, although in this respect there are Cornishmen *and* Cornishmen; theirs without a doubt is the largest share of prosperity.

In Hertfordshire, I think, almost for the first time in the course of all my journeying, except in the case of those who practise some special industry, when I have put to farmers the question of how their business did, I have in various instances received the reply: 'Well, sir, I have no reason to complain'—which, coming from the lips of an agriculturist, means a very great deal. As I do not wish to be invidious I will not attempt to write of the fundamental causes of the success of the strangers, even if I could be sure of them. Indeed, it is not necessary to travel further than their system of farming. The newcomers have thrown over the old shibboleths. The Scotchman introduced potato growing, which he has brought to a fine art, and practises in conjunction with dairying, the cows consuming all the unmarketable tubers, that are pulped and fed to them like roots. Also he imports from London vast quantities of manure purchased from the collecting merchants, with which he doses his potato lands, giving them as much as thirty loads to the acre or even more. Further he makes use of all the newest and best labour-saving machinery, and pays the highest wages for the pick of the men.

The Cornishman practises a system of three-year layers, which at the end of that time are ploughed up and put under other crops in rotation. In this way he saves labour, although in most instances, to a greater or less degree, he imitates the potato growing and dairying of his Scotch neighbour. It must be remembered that to be successful this style of farming is dependent upon proximity to the railway, without which it is impossible to import the necessary manure. In Hertfordshire prosperity is, in the main, confined to the neighbourhood of a railway line. Where means of communication are lacking, as a Scotch gentleman said to me, there is 'agricultural death.' It must not be imagined, however, because the energy, ability, and capital of a certain number of Scotch, Cornish, and local farmers, conveniently situated on the best lands, have enabled them to do well that the industry as a whole is prosperous in Hertfordshire. This I believe to be by no means the case; indeed, I think that the bulk of the farmers are slowly losing capital, and that the bulk of the remoter land is slowly going back, notwithstanding the proximity to London, and the fact that the labour question on the whole is perhaps not so pressing here as in many other counties.

Unfortunately when these remarks were publishe in my articles on the county, in one paper at least the above qualifying paragraph was omitted, owing, I suppose, to pressure on the journal's space. In consequence it would seem that I gave offence to many Hertfordshire farmers by my 'stories of the units who prosper when thousands fail.' Says the 'Mark Lane Express' in a leading article, 'There are some few farmers of the Mark Tapley genera, no doubt, and we are inclined to think Mr. Rider Haggard must have stumbled on such in Herts to have received the reply he states that he had from several when he inquired how the fates were dealing with them: "Well, sir, I have no reason to complain." We prefer to come to that conclusion rather than declare, as so many agriculturists did at the Herts Agricultural Show luncheon on Thursday last, that Mr. Rider Haggard by ill-conducting or misdirection got into a camp of idiots. The subject cropped up at that luncheon owing to Mr. Lloyd, the chairman, quoting this statement from Mr. Haggard's article, and thereupon congratulating Herts agriculturists that things were not so bad in their county as elsewhere. This false view was, however, very soon set aside by a practical farmer declaring that Herts crops, in his opinion, never had a worse appearance, and that the majority of farmers in that county, as well as most others, would be likely this year to suffer grievous loss.'

What I really wrote may be read on the preceding page —I repeat it : ' It must not be imagined, however, that . . . the industry as a whole is prosperous in Hertfordshire. This I believe to be by no means the case,' &c. Indeed, here as elsewhere, as I think the reader of this chapter will admit, I have striven, to the best of my ability, to give an impartial summary of the state of the various agriculturists and agricultural affairs in Herts judged from the samples that I saw. This includes the opinion that some of those farmers, mostly, I admit, Cornish and Scotchmen, are—or in the year 1901 were—prospering. Owing perhaps to their being strangers in the land, rather than to their success, this statement seems to have given offence, but it is impossible for a writer to set down what he believes to be the truth upon so great and varied a subject as I have undertaken to investigate, without from time to time offending certain persons or classes, however much he may wish to avoid so doing. He cannot please everybody and—he may be wrong in his conclusions. Also he may be right.

At the least I can plead innocence of any intention to offend by attributing to Hertfordshire farmers at large a prosperity to which I am the first to admit they have not attained.

Here is a summary of the opinions given to me by word of mouth and in writing by one of the most experienced land

MR. PROUT'S WHEAT, BLOUNT'S FARM

*Page 528*

agents in Hertfordshire, who, however, does not wish that his name should be mentioned. He said that certain farmers did well, but that many were in a bad way, while some threatened to give up their cows because of the labour difficulty. He remembered that between 1879 and 1882 a great many farmers went bankrupt, but now they were never forced through the court, since such a proceeding would give the landlord a bad name, and prevent him from getting other tenants.

The average rents he put at 13s. an acre, at which sum the tenant made a hard living, while after payment of land-tax, tithe, and repairs the owner received practically nothing. By this he meant that if a property was unencumbered and had not been let down, he could live in his house (of course upon means derived from outside sources) and keep his shooting if he could afford the additional outlay, doing ordinary estate repairs, but not reckoning the cost of new buildings. If, however, the farms were in a bad state or in any way encumbered, he must be absolutely out of pocket to a greater or less amount. He instanced a property upon which a moderate jointure was charged by will in 1876. In 1901, including the letting price of the house and shooting, a valuable asset in Hertfordshire, it did not produce enough to pay the annual sum due under the jointure. Still, farms let a little more readily than they had done a few years before, whereas land could be sold now at an average of £15 an acre, which at that time would only fetch £10. This is to say that, within thirty miles of London, the soil realises a price which would not be thought exorbitant for agricultural purposes in many of our colonies. In small-holdings he did not believe, owing to the cost of buildings and repairs.

He admitted that labour was still more plentiful here than in many other places, but considered the outlook somewhat hopeless because the rising generation 'refuses to take to the plough.' 'When the old men die and only the wasters are left what is to happen?' he asked. Like Shakespeare's soothsayer he adjured the owner of property to 'beware

the Ides of March!' since he thought that the blow of the
disastrous season of 1901 would fall upon them then. It
used to be a pleasure to look after the land, he declared, but
now it was 'a fight—a fight.' Finally he summed up his
views in a forcible phrase. 'The land is going to the devil!'
he said. Further, he expressed the opinion—which I find
to be very general, especially among tenants—that the
burden of all this disaster will be piled increasingly upon the
landlord's back, who, he thought, would in most cases do
well to sell his property for what it would fetch and invest
the proceeds in the funds.

I know that in the view of many people this is just as it
should be. Thus, to take rather an amusing instance of
this attitude of mind, as I wrote the above passage there
was put into my hand an article that appeared to be sent to
me from the offices of the 'Midland Mail,' which was, I
presume, published in that paper. As regards myself it
was not complimentary. The 'Midland Mail,' it seems,
always thought that I was not 'just the man' it would have
chosen for my present task. It always knew that I should
'start out with a stock of the old worn-out opinions and
bring nothing new in the way of thought to bear on the
subject.' It regretted to observe that I was justifying this
unfavourable estimate of my capacity. For this reason. It
appears that in an article published while I was on my tour
of investigation I said—I have said it several times: 'The
average farm rents have sunk from 10 per cent. to 40 per
cent. and settling' (I wrote selling) 'values in proportion.'

At first sight there might seem little in this allegation
of fact calculated to give offence; still, said the 'Midland
Mail,' 'What a barren and absurd statement that is!' Why
barren and absurd? Well, barren and absurd enough,
perhaps, to those who do not like the truth, unless it can
be made to fit in with or advance their aims and theories,
who think, moreover, that 'we had too much nonsense
about rents before Mr. Rider Haggard began.' Began what
—to exist or to write about agriculture? Then follows a

diatribe against landlords, ending with this bold declaration : 'If there is to be rural desolation, as Mr. Rider Haggard anticipates, landlords as a class will be responsible for it.'

Now I would occupy no space in commenting on the somewhat crude opinions of this not altogether unbiassed journal, were it not for the value of the instance. The scribe of the 'Midland Mail' is but one of many. From time to time I receive communications from social reformers of various degree, a number of whom seem to imagine that our present problems, or that branch of them under consideration, can be solved by some form of theft, veiled or open, of which the land-owning class is to be the victim.

Of course I do not know that the 'Midland Mail' holds any such opinions ; probably it does not; but the only meaning that I can extract from its remarks is that it thinks the landlord a very wicked person, who is responsible for all the trouble that has been, is, and is to be. Perhaps it may be owing to my incapacity to bring anything 'new in the way of thought to bear on the subject'; at any rate I cannot share this view. Indeed, I think it false. Moreover, I believe all schemes of reform which are built upon spoliation to be doomed *ab ovo*. The conscience of this nation will never permit of them, nor, in the long run, would the eternal law of right, which, whatever pessimists may say, permeates and directs the universe, allow them to succeed. If in the past landlords—I speak of agricultural landlords—have done wrong, at least it is true that they have paid its price. I hold no brief for them or for any other class. Still I ask, Did they do wrong as a body in taking a high rent—the market price, in short—while agriculture was prosperous for lands which, except in the case of some inherited estates, for the most part they bought at a high figure ? If anybody did wrong was it not rather the farmers in returning too small a share of their large profits to those labourers who made it possible for profits to be earned ?

However these things may be --and to discuss them would lead me too far afield--of this I am convinced, that to abuse the landlords, and still more to attempt to rob or tax them out of existence, will serve no useful purpose. On the contrary, it serves an evil purpose: it consolidates all holders of property in a resistance to reforms which they come to believe to be but a cloak of robbery, and discourages those who try to effect any salutary and moderate change. My thought, new or old, tends another way. I believe that a solution, if there is any, will be found in the indefinite multiplication of that much-vilified land-holding class. We need many more owners of the soil, and if that soil will no longer support landlord and tenant, then the landlord must become his own tenant or the tenant his own landlord—but not by predatory action or seizure on the part of the State or of individuals.

When the above remarks were published I gathered from a second printed slip forwarded to me from the office of the paper that the 'Midland Mail' replied to them, and was even more uncomplimentary to myself than before. They were 'a farrago of nonsense. . . . In this one quotation Mr. Rider Haggard has proved his incapacity for dealing with facts . . . as an investigator he is just nonsensical when not mischievous. We do not know any man who proposes to solve the land question by "theft veiled or open," and probably Mr. Rider Haggard does not; only that little insinuation might serve to arouse prejudice. We repeat that we had too much nonsense talked and written about "the fall in rents" before Mr. Rider Haggard began to add to it,' and so forth.

I may remark that I did not 'add' to this particular 'nonsense'; I merely chronicled, and chronicle, facts. I regret that I have not space here, and perhaps shall not be able to find it in these volumes, to enter at length into all the wild theories that have been and are continually promulgated with reference to the ownership of land. But by way of comment upon the above extract from the arguments of the 'Midland Mail' I will quote a few passages from a book called 'Birthright in Land,' published in 1891 by Messrs. Kegan Paul, Trench, Trübner & Co., and containing a reprint of Professor Ogilvie's well-known 'Essay on the

Right of Property in Land,' written about 1781, with a preface and other matter by Mr. D. C. MacDonald. In his preface Mr. MacDonald says amongst many other things:

'While labourers are content to remain deprived of their natural rights, they must pay whatever ransom the brigands who have seized these rights choose to demand. . . . The monster that would deprive a babe of its mother's milk, or would monopolise the breasts of several mothers, to the exclusion of several children, is not more deserving of being destroyed than the monster who seizes absolute possession of more than his share of the common mother of mankind' (that is, of the land) 'to the exclusion of his fellow creatures. Now as these monsters are comparatively few, and were always a very small minority of the human race, the question naturally arises, Why the vast majority submit —why, in short, they do not destroy such monsters without a moment's consideration?'

The answer seems to be because of the influence of the clergy, who somehow bring it about that woman 'as a parent is condemned to the position of a slave. In this position she brings forth her children. She generally does so by license from the clergy. But notwithstanding this "divine license" her children are treated as bastards. They are denied the right to draw one breath in their native land unless the parents beg permission of the landlord. They have to pay for the right to live on *his* land.'

I never knew before that landlords were air-lords as well.

I continue. Of this unhappy condition of the female sex it seems 'the usual result is universal ignorance, slavery, and suffering of mankind. It is here we may read the real fall of man—the loss of his birthright—his miserable and slavish position—an outcast

> Who begs a brother of the earth
> To give him leave to toil——

who like a dog has to submit to the oppressor's rod, in the shape of insolent robbery or insulting expatriation at the

instance  of  a  Duke  of  Argyll,  a  Lord  Clanricarde,  or  a  Mr.
A. J. Balfour.'

To those who know anything about Mr. A. J. Balfour—
but  I  forbear.   Then  we  have  some  poetry  written  by  I
know not whom.   Here are a few sample verses :

> Asses, swine, have litter spread,
> And with fitting food are fed ;
> All things have a home but one ;
> But thou, O Englishman, hast none !
>
> .        .        .        .        .        .
>
> 'Tis to hunger for such diet
> As the rich man in his riot
> Casts to the fat dogs that lie
> Surfeiting beneath his eye.
>
> Men of England, wherefore plough
> For the lords that lay ye low ?
> Wherefore weave with toil and care
> The rich robes your tyrants wear ?
>
> .        .        .        .        .        .
>
> Sow seed, but let no tyrant reap ;
> Find wealth, let no impostor heap ;
> Weave robes, let not the idle wear ;
> Forge arms in your defence to bear.
>
> .        .        .        .        .        .
>
> Rise like lions after slumber
> In unvanquishable number !
> Shake your chains to earth like dew
> Which in sleep has fallen on you :
> Ye are many, they are few !

I  return  to  prose.    ' England !  as  the  sanctuary  of  landlordism,  thy  cup  is  filling  fast ;  and  whether  the  next
revolution will be bloodless or otherwise who can tell ? '

After  this  it  is  not  strange  to  learn  that  for  the  same
landlordism ' there  is  only  one  cure :  Cut  it  down ;  why
cumbereth it the ground ? '

The  reader  may  consider  such  writing  somewhat
exaggerated.   However this may be, it is without doubt
seriously  meant,  and,  moreover,  presented  to  the  world
through the medium of publishers of repute, as an introduc-

tion to a reprint of the work of a well-known thinker of the eighteenth century. Certainly also those who are interested in the subject can find more of the same tenor from other pens. I commend it, with the lessons it inculcates, to the attention of the ' Midland Mail.'

In what way, I would ask, does the author quoted from propose ' to solve the land question ' ?

I may add that Captain J. W. Petavel, R.E., who appears to be a student of the subject, states of such opinions in a magazine article published in the present year :

It is natural that some people who have studied the land question should demur to paying up all land values, and that they should contemplate a partial confiscation by the public of a wealth which should never have been possessed by private individuals ; especially is this natural as, in addition to the injustices of private landownership in any industrial country, landownership in England is, strictly speaking, illegal, and all possession of land is based originally upon fraud. In the words of Professor F. W. Newman, ' The history of the gradual, stealthy, but truly nefarious revolution in which land *lords* by their own legislative power and by their influence over lawyers, changed themselves into land *owners*, needs to be popularised.'

To return, with many apologies for a digression, in its way perhaps instructive and not uninteresting. One of the first farms I inspected in Hertfordshire was the Warren, in the neighbourhood of Braughing, of over 500 acres, held by Mr. Lanyon, a Cornishman, who had lived in the county for six years. This is a very typical holding, comprising both heavy and light soil of average quality, which was exceedingly well done by and in good heart. Mr. Lanyon did not, I think, grow potatoes, and was too far from the station to import London manure with profit. He relied upon the farmer's old standbys, corn, sheep, cattle, and a herd of about forty cows, of which the milk was sent daily by road to a factory at Ware, some eight miles away. Being an agriculturist of great energy and intelligence he was, I am glad to say, doing fairly well at the low prevailing rent—at least that was my conclusion. Some of his corn had suffered badly from wire-worm ; but taking the crops through, it was wonderful how well they had stood that season of drought, especially the mangolds, which were really a fine plant.

Of the labour he complained a good deal, saying that he had enough, but that the quality was bad, and the young men would not stop upon the land. The local rate of wages was 13s., and 15s. for carters, to which must be added harvest and haysel money. By the way, Mr. Lanyon overcame the milking difficulty in an ingenious fashion new to my experience. Under a contract which he made with a man, in consideration of a wage of 50s. a week, with a house and a quart of milk thrown in daily, this person and his family engaged to milk and tend the cows in a husbandlike fashion, and to drive the produce once a day to the factory at Ware. It seems to me that this system might be extended with advantage to all concerned.

Mr. Lanyon's bullocks, of which one or two truckloads had arrived on the morning when I saw them, were imported by him from Cornwall to be fatted out on the Warren Farm. They were Devons, which he said he preferred to any other breed, as they cut up so well and would make fourpence a stone more than Herefords. This particular consignment he expected to finish off in about two months on cake and grass. His barley was badly injured by wire-worm. I think, though of this I am not sure, that it was sown after mustard, which had been ploughed in with the object of destroying this pest, as it is said to do. If so, the result was a failure. Indeed, Mr. Lanyon said that the only plan which he believed to be effective against it was to drill nitrates and phosphates mingled with soot and ashes—the latter to make the mixture run—along with the seed corn. His spring oats also were suffering from Hessian fly. The maggot of this fly is white and feeds upon the stem and leaves, causing the plant to shoot again, and thus make an uneven sample at harvest. The chrysalis, of which we found some, is of a red-brown hue, and lies just above the root until it is developed into a fresh maggot about August, the insect being of the double-brooded order. Mr. Lanyon has found nitrate of soda a good preventive against this plague. Of his 535 acres three quarters were arable. He said that this land did not lay down well, and that he would rather have the corn than the grass. If the straw was sold and replaced by cake-feeding he thought that wheat would pay at 30s. a quarter on an average of not less than four quarters to the acre.

He used steam cultivators a good deal, which are suitable to these large Hertfordshire fields, at a cost of from 7s. to 9s. the acre. A field of wheat, he said, looked better after the steam tackle than after the plough ; also it broke up the land more effectively and let in the sun and air. Weeds he abhorred, as every good farmer should, telling me that he had paid as much as £1 the acre to pull the docks out of clover. He said that whatever it cost ' I will have them ; I can't farm with docks.' For charlock he had ' sprayed ' with good results ; the mixture killed out the weed which had since given him but little trouble.

Of Hampshire Down sheep he kept a considerable number, and had already sold out his lambs at from 40s. to 53s., and fatted off several lots. He said that they helped the land since they ' go dung carting on Sunday as well as week-days.'

His sheep we found penned on trefoil which was to be sown immediately with rape and mustard, then folded again and go down to wheat. As each fold was cleared the plough followed, so that no time was lost, indeed promptness was a feature of Mr. Lanyon's farming ; nothing was put off till to-morrow that could be done to-day. Thus in his mangolds the horse-hoes were at work, and after them came the men with the hand-hoes to deal with the weeds left upon the lines of the drill. The labour on his farm of 500 acres cost him £700 a year.

Mr. A. Percival, who has been agent to Mr. H. Shepherd Cross, M.P., I think since 1884, very kindly showed me over the 900 acres which are kept in hand at Hamels Park, upon June 18, a date that I remember, as on that night in

1901 there was a sharp frost in Hertfordshire. Mr. Percival said that the agricultural prospect in that part of the county was better than it had been three or four years before, although the season of 1900 was bad and that of 1901 promised no improvement. Thus average land with some grass, which in 1897 used to fetch 12s. or 13s. the acre, now commanded 15s. or 16s. on that estate and in the neighbourhood. Of course, however, Mr. Cross was a good landlord, and taking the average the buildings were also good. They had 900 acres in hand, on which the labour-bill amounted to between £1,000 and £1,200 a year, not because these farms could not be let, but because it suited their convenience for shooting and other reasons. Up to 1900 the tenants were doing well, but in that year some of them had been hit. He thought, however, that they were holding their own. Still their capital had undoubtedly wasted, and not all of them could afford to buy sheep. Scarcely one of the old farmers of 1884 was now left in the neighbourhood. In districts there was some very poor farming, as certain of the husbandmen employed but little labour and did their land badly.

The average size of the farms ran from 250 to 300 acres, with but a small proportion of pasture. Thus one of 286 acres had 31 acres of grass, and one of 173 acres only 15 acres of grass. The average capital employed was from £6 to £8 the acre. Personally he never left valuations unpaid by incoming tenants, and there were no arrears on the estate. On the labour question Mr. Percival said that in outlying places he considered the prospect very serious—bad enough indeed to threaten the entire industry. Everywhere the men were unpleasant to work with : they dared not speak to them at critical times of the year, and they had no skilled young fellows. Boys also were very difficult to get ; in fact only the worst of the younger men were left. The sole remedy he knew for this state of affairs was the building of more cottages. Of these they had put up sixteen during the last ten years. Speaking generally, the cottages in the county were very bad. The wages were 15s. a week for carters, or

13*s.* and a free cottage, with threepence an hour overtime.   In 1890 his books showed that they paid shepherds 19*s.* 2*d.* a week, cowmen 17*s.* 6*d.*, waggoners 16*s.* 5*d.*, labourers 16*s.*, and aged labourers 14*s.* 3*d.*   Since then there had been an all-round rise of 2*s.* a week.   Landlords, Mr. Percival thought, must be badly hit.   The tithe on the Hertfordshire land varied from 2*s.* 6*d.* to 4*s.* the acre ; then there were land tax, erection of buildings and cottages, repairs, management expenses and sundries, all to come out of a rent of, say, 15*s.* the acre, so that if the owner had 5*s.* the acre left it was the most he could count on.

The run of the soil, he said, was rather heavy, but it was not the custom to take two white straw crops in succession unless it had been manured between them.   The local system was—(1) Barley ;   (2) clover and rye grass sown with the barley, which was mown the first year and fed with sheep after mowing, mowed the second year, broken up with steam tackle and sown with autumn crop of (3) wheat or winter oats.   These were followed (4) by spring oats or roots, which in turn would be succeeded by barley.   Also there were several large milk farmers in the neighbourhood and a good many sheep were kept ; they themselves had 200 ewes.   Milk fetched 1*s.* 8*d.* per barn gallon of seventeen pints from Michaelmas to Lady Day, and 1*s.* 3*d.* from Lady Day to Michaelmas.   The carriage to London came to three-halfpence per barn gallon, or about as much as was charged from Staffordshire, which was more than 100 miles further away !   Of laying land to grass he said that it did not pay, as fences had been so generally let down and there was no water.   Indeed, most of the water seemed to be drained out of the county, and the lack of it was a great difficulty.   Also the rainfall had been small of late ; thus in that season the grass seeds sown with barley were dying of drought, if not already dead.   Of barley they had reduced their acreage, as they could not get a malting sample, but on wheat they made a profit.

The hours of labour were—for horsemen from 6 A.M., and

ordinary men 6.30 A.M. till 5.15 P.M., with half an hour off for breakfast and an hour for dinner. Mr. Percival said emphatically that the present-day agricultural labourers were a miserable set, who for the most part took no pains or pride in their work. It was the custom in the neighbourhood to sell much of the hay and straw, but the good farmers replaced them with manure brought from London. Practically there were no small-holders, to whom the country was not suited, as grass and water were so scarce.

One of the first fields we saw in walking over the land was a good old grass meadow, which would fat out cattle with the help of 6 lbs. of cake a head per day. Then came a pasture which had been down for twelve years and was now chiefly made up of daisies and coarse grass. Still it was pasture, and, as Mr. Percival remarked, would not cost any more to cultivate. Here water was led to drinking troughs for the cattle by means of pipes. Near by we saw some land for which £34 an acre was asked in 1884. It was bought in 1900 for £15 the acre, which Mr. Percival thought its full value. He said that plenty of land was sold for £10 or £11 the acre, which was more than it was worth in such places as the Great and Little Mundens, not far away, where the soil was poor and heavy, with no cottages, no labour, and no station. The winter oats that we saw next were a good crop. Mr. Percival said that he preferred them to spring oats and was planting them more and more.

Next we visited some plots of clover hay upon which experiments were being made with various manures, I think, under the direction of the Cambridge University Department of Agriculture. So far as I could judge none of the stimulants had produced any great results, as not one of the plots looked as though it would yield more than three quarters of a load of hay to the acre. Perhaps, however, as in the case of Mr. Bury's farm in Essex, this comparative failure was to some extent due to the dryness of the season. Other experiments were being carried on with the object of investigating the results of various manurial dressings of both dung and artificials upon mangolds and upon the succeeding wheat.

Of these Mr. Percival has since kindly forwarded me the tabulated report, which unfortunately is too long to quote in full. The manures that seemed to give the best results, however, were fifteen tons of dung with 3 cwt. of mixed artificials per acre for mangolds in 1899, followed by 3 cwt. of mixed artificials for wheat in 1900, which returned twenty-one tons of roots in 1899, and 37·4 bushels of wheat in 1900 —not an excessive yield, considering the heaviness of the dressing. The report says : ' Summing up the above results, and bearing in mind that there must be a considerable residue of the dung still in the soil for succeeding crops, it would appear that the most profitable manurial treatment of these crops on this soil, is a fair dressing of about fifteen tons of dung per acre for the mangolds, supplemented by a top dressing of nitrate of soda, and for the wheat a small dressing of superphosphate and kainit in the autumn, and a top dressing of 1 cwt. of nitrate of soda in the spring.'

Next we came to a crop of red wheat which looked well after clover. Clover, by the way, is not here grown upon the same land more than once in eight years. A field of lucerne followed which was originally sown with barley and had been down for five years. It was to be ploughed up in the following autumn. The soil on which it grew and much more about it was a brick earth with a subsoil of heavy clay, apt to bake badly if it is meddled with in a wet time. Other fields we visited were thirty-five acres of spring oats, a thin and patchy crop but fair in places. Another of spring oats which had received ten or twelve loads of farm-yard manure after wheat and were well got in on good soil, now towards the end of June, owing to drought, stood from twelve to eighteen inches in height only, and were thin, yellow, and stunted. In the same way some crops of clover and lucerne which were being cut, looked fit to stack from lack of moisture, while the fly had sawed off the first of the swedes. Also we saw forty-three acres of grass which were laid down in 1887. A fair head of cattle on them looked well, and although the herbage was scarce and rather coarse, there were feed and a moderate bottom. Still for such a crop fourteen years seems long to wait. Clearly grass does not lay down well in this district.

Another farm I visited at Braughing was that of Mr. Weir, a Scotch gentleman, who was reported to be one of the best farmers in the neighbourhood. In addition to what he farmed elsewhere, here he held 307 acres of fairly good but somewhat scattered land quite near to the station, at a rent that had been reduced from £1 to 17s. the acre. Mr. Weir, who seemed satisfied with his lot and prospects, had been ten years in occupation of this holding, and said that he was glad that he came south and would not farm again in Scotland. Formerly he was at Little Munden, which he called The World's End, but left because the owners of his farm would not lower his rent. He offered 23s. an acre for it, which was refused. Now it was let for 15s. ! He thought that landlords did wrong ten years ago to send away the sitting tenants rather than give them a reduction. Farmers now-a-days had 'to pay up and look pleasant,' but he thought that they were 'doing.' When speaking of farmers, however, he meant Scotchmen and Cornishmen round about there, the latter of whom, he remarked, liked to have a *fat* farm to start on.

Of Mr. Weir's 307 acres at Braughing 70 were permanent pasture, 40 sainfoin, 4 lucerne which did pretty well, and 100 wheat. Of this last crop he said that by getting a return of four and a half quarters to the acre and selling the straw it could still be grown at a profit. Of potatoes he had thirty acres on a chalk subsoil, from which last year he had realised £30 the acre ; but in some seasons —wet ones, I suppose—they had been so bad that nobody would take them away. To his mangolds he gave 5 cwt. of superphosphate and 1½ cwt. of sulphate of ammonia to the acre, with the result that he lifted forty tons to the acre of root. These artificials were, I think, in addition to

London manure, of which he bought a great deal at a cost of 1s. 4d. or 1s. 6d. a ton plus 2s. 5d. railway carriage. In Glasgow, he said, such manure cost 8s. or even 10s. the ton.

Mr. Weir had a herd of cows, some of which he bred from a Shorthorn bull, and sent milk to London twice a day. These were kept in an admirable building where everything was arranged for convenience and to save labour, and all the drains were disinfected with carbolic. Up to the time that I saw them towards the end of June, his cows had only been out of their shed to drink, as Mr. Weir seemed to think that they did better under cover. He fed them upon a mixture of potatoes, pulped mangold, brewer's grains from London, wheat, oats, and ground maize. Also he used a meal compounded of maize, beans, and light oats, which were all ground upon the premises. The beans, and of course the maize, he purchased. The water supply upon this farm was excellent—a great consideration in Hertfordshire—being delivered from a spring by gravitation. Also there was a ram that pumped up as much as might be required.

Of labour he said that they were paying 5s. a week more than they used to do, but being near the village got sufficient hands. Cottages, of which he rented three good ones, were scarce and bad. There was a good deal of trouble about labour which was the worst feature in the local farming outlook. He thought that the result of our system of education was to send the people from the country to the towns.

One of the most deeply interesting agricultural experiments ever carried out over a series of years in England, is that which has been in progress since 1861—more than a generation—upon Blount's Farm, near Sawbridgeworth, in Hertfordshire. On our way thither we passed a beautiful house known as Hadham Palace that once belonged to the Bishops of London. It is situated in a deep hollow backed by trees, so that the traveller looks down on it from the road that skirts the tableland. The effect of this three-gabled, ancient dwelling, with its tiled roofs, dormer windows, and walls covered by an abundance of creeping plants, was singularly charming. Close to it stands the church, with its quaint, leaden spire and a wall-encircled graveyard dotted with white tombstones. Between the church and house is a verdant lawn, while in front of it lie the gardens, and, falling sheer from the roadside to a flat tableland lined out with elms, the steep slope of a hill.

When Mr. Prout, the father of the present proprietor, became possessed of Blount's Farm of 450 acres, it was in such a low condition that it was said of it 'that it would starve a donkey.' Also, it was undrained, made up of small enclosures, and cumbered with many fences. Now all this has been changed. Indeed, I never saw a better arranged or, I may add, in its own fashion a better cultivated holding. The fields were large, averaging perhaps thirty or forty acres, and pierced with convenient roads; the fences were low and well trimmed, and the drainage, that is done with the steam mole, a system of which I hope to speak in due course, was perfect. The peculiarity of Mr. Prout's farm is this. He keeps no cattle and no sheep, he grows nothing but cereals, clover, beans, and some mangolds for the horses, and year by year he sells everything off the soil that it produces. Further, he has no scruple about growing wheat or other cereals for many years in succession upon the same field, a thing hitherto supposed to be impossible to do in England at a profit. Nor does he replace the grain and straw sold off the farm by stable manure imported from elsewhere. Yet he makes his farming pay.

The experienced reader will naturally ask how this can be done. Here is the explanation. Four years after Mr. Prout, senior, who had farmed in Canada for ten years, took the holding in hand in a desperate state, the happy thought occurred to him to consult the late Dr. Augustus Voelcker, perhaps the greatest agricultural chemist of his day. In 1865 he submitted to him samples of the soil of Blount's Farm. Dr. Voelcker analysed these carefully, and in his report pointed out what elements should be added from time to time, to

LORD SALISBURY'S COTTAGES, NEAR HATFIELD  *Page 534*

A HERTFORDSHIRE FARMHOUSE  *Page 549*

ensure the permanent fertility of the land while producing successive crops of cereals. Accordingly the chemicals were added in the proportions which he advised, and, with the exception of deep and thorough tillage and draining, every other recognised rule of farming was set at defiance. In 1877, after twelve years of constant corn-growing and the annual sale of every stalk of straw, the land was again analysed, and found to be richer in all necessary constituents than it was in 1865. Nor, although as many as eight corn crops had been taken consecutively, did the yield lessen by a single bushel.

From 1865 to the present date the same extraordinary system has been carried on with precisely identical results, nor does there seem to be any valid reason why it should ever stop. In short, the fertility of the land is quite unimpaired. Up to the year 1879 it was the custom of Mr. Prout, senior, to sell his crops as they stood in the field, leaving the purchaser to harvest them; but since that time, as buyers no longer cared to speculate in corn at the prevailing low prices, he and his son have done the harvesting themselves, selling the grain in the ordinary manner, and the straw by auction. Indeed, when we visited the farm such a sale had recently been held, for we saw the tickets still fixed upon the stacks. Here it will be convenient to state that I inspected Mr. Prout's accounts, which are, however, not for publication. I will only add on this point, therefore, that he was, and in practice always had been, in the proud position of farming at a profit.

Now for a few figures. The average production of wheat per acre, I think for the year 1895, given in bushels, was: India 10, Argentina 11, United States 13, France 17, Great Britain 28, Russia 8, Australasia 6, of the whole world 12 bushels. The average production in the same year for the county of Herts was: Wheat 26 and a fraction bushels, barley 29 and a fraction, oats 35 and a fraction, and for the county of Lincolnshire, perhaps the most fertile in England, wheat 32 and a fraction, barley 35 and a fraction, oats 51 and a fraction bushels. On Blount's Farm in 1895 the returns were as follows: Wheat 36 bushels, barley 40 bushels, oats 40 bushels, and beans 32 bushels. These figures speak for themselves. It may be thought, however, that they refer to an exceptional year. That this is not so is shown by the fact that the average production of wheat on Blount's Farm, taken over a period of seventeen years, has been four and a half quarters, or thirty-six bushels per acre, and of barley five quarters, or forty bushels per acre.

The analysis of the clay lands of Blount's Farm showed its cultivators that it contained all the elements necessary to the growth of cereals, a sufficiency of phosphates and ammonia alone excepted. Their object, therefore, has been to supply these elements in just sufficient quantities to satisfy the needs of the growing crop, but no more. By this I mean that after the removal of the crop, land dressed thus scientifically should—and, as a matter of fact, on Blount's Farm does—show absolutely no loss of those constituent parts which are necessary to fertility, the main minerals, such as lime, potash, and soda, being, of course, as in most clays, present in this soil in quantities so large that it would take centuries of cultivation to exhaust them. To supply what is lacking if the crop to be grown is wheat, Mr. Prout doses the land by means of a manure distributor with 4 cwt. of mineral superphosphates per acre, which in this case would be applied in the month of January, or about three months after sowing, and $1\frac{1}{2}$ cwt. of nitrate of soda per acre applied about the middle of April. It must be remembered, however, that these chemicals are absolutely necessary to each other; thus it would be practically useless to apply the superphosphates without following them up with the nitrate, or the nitrate unless it had been preceded by the superphosphates. Of this fact we saw by good fortune a very striking example on the occasion of our visit.

In one of the wheat fields the man employed upon the task had by accident missed a strip when giving the nitrate dressing, although this strip, in common with the rest of the field, had received its full allowance of mineral superphosphates. There before our eyes was the result. On either side the corn grew stout and green, whereas along the line of this defrauded strip it was yellow, backward, and short in straw. Probably there was a difference of five bushels to the acre between the yield of this portion and that of the rest of the piece.

The other points about Mr. Prout's system are that he steeps all his seed-wheat for an hour or two upon the day before it is drilled, in a solution of blue-stone, a precaution which he finds quite effective against the disease known as 'smut'; and that he invariably makes use of the steam plough, thereby saving time and money, and insuring thorough cultivation of the land. Almost before the crops are off the field the steamer is at work in them, with the result that it is no unusual thing for him to begin drilling his wheat about September 20, and to finish it before the end of October— that is, at the season which nature appointed, when, too, in our climate it is always possible to get upon the land. With wire-worm, which the use of artificials is vulgarly supposed to produce, he has not been troubled for years, rolling and the application of nitrate having been quite sufficient to keep it down.

We visited every field on Blount's Farm, and as a sample I will transcribe the notes taken concerning two or three of them. I should add that, speaking generally, although they varied somewhat according to the condition and tilth of the land when they were got in, the appearance of the crops, including the beans and clover, was extraordinarily good. Even in that season of drought some of the wheats stood quite five feet high, showing the rich colour which denotes a perfect health.

No. 1 Field. Twenty-two acres of land under barley sown on April 19, and dressed at a total cost of £1 5s. immediately before seeding, with 3 cwt. of mineral superphosphates, and 1 cwt. of guano applied at the same time per acre, followed on May 14 by 1 cwt. of nitrate per acre.

The crop looked splendid in colour, and was thick and level in height.

No. 2. 'Brookfield,' thirty-one acres. Oats after barley. Steam ploughed. Sown on October 5 with three pecks to the acre of black winter oats. Received on January 25 a dressing of 4 cwt. of superphosphates, and on April 19 1¼ cwt. nitrate per acre.

No. 3 'Beadles Top,' twenty-seven acres. Wheat after oats. Steam ploughed. Sown on October 30 with eight pecks per acre of white-chaff Browick wheat, dressed on January 23 with 4 cwt. mineral superphosphates per acre, and on April 9 with 1¼ cwt. of nitrate per acre. Upon May 3 10 lbs. of clover seed per acre was cross-drilled among the wheat to form a layer for the ensuing year.

Although the subject is somewhat technical, I have described Mr. Prout's farm in detail because of the great agricultural importance of the system which he follows, farmyard manure, produced by his twelve horses, being used nnly in the growth of beans and mangold. Of course this system is only applicable in its entirety to farms so situated that there is a ready market for the sale of straw. But given this condition, and that of a heavy clay land not deficient in lime, there is no doubt that it has proved itself a triumphant success. Yet even among his neighbours no one follows his example, although this could be done at a profit in all the district of the Roothings, the only requisites being careful analysis of the soil, good cultivation, and some intelligence in the application of artificial manures. Indeed, I was actually informed in other parts of the county that Mr. Prout had abandoned the experiment as a failure.

Whether or not it is a failure the reader may judge; personally I was able to discover but one drawback against it, that after a long period of growth by the aid of chemicals the corn is apt to come rather light for its bulk. Why, then, is this practice not more widely followed, seeing that even where the straw must be used upon the premises the corn lands could be profitably treated with artificials, leaving the farmyard manure to be applied to the roots, beans, and pastures, to the great enrichment of the holding?

I suppose that the answer must be looked for in the conservatism, not to say the obstinacy, of farmers at large. Still, gentlemen working their own land might follow on the path pointed out by Mr. Prout, only then they would have to reckon with their bailiffs, who, as a class, do not love any new thing, and by accident or design often cause that to fail which they have not themselves discovered or approved. I should add that Mr. Prout has also a small light-land farm which we saw, where the same system is followed to a limited extent. Light land, however, does not lend itself so readily to treatment with chemical manures. Mr. Prout said that the greatest difficulty in the way of the land was that of labour, but he thought that this would right itself in some fashion. Perhaps the men would come back from the towns. Thus he had one who after four years' absence, returned looking very cadaverous, because he had fallen sick in the city. If they did not, it would be necessary to get them from elsewhere.

At Sawbridgeworth I went over the nurseries of Messrs. Rivers, who in past years have introduced so many new sorts of fruit trees to the British public. To the lover of horticulture their houses, gardens, and orchard grounds were full of interest. The Duchess of Oldenburg apple was, I noticed, setting extremely well in the bad season of 1901, while Early Rivers seemed to be the best and most promising plum. Mr. Rivers told me that the young men were going away a good deal from the neighbourhood and that labour was generally scarce.

Whilst driving on that day I passed a considerable orchard that must have cost a good deal of money to plant, which furnished a strange contrast to those of Messrs. Rivers. Indeed, as an example of how fruit should not be treated it could scarcely be surpassed. Here the standards and bush trees appeared on land that was just cut for hay. Evidently they were choked by the tall grass by which they had been surrounded, for aught I know, for several years, that, sucking the moisture from their roots, had left the young trees starved, dying, or dead. Doubtless if we had questioned the owner, or more probably the farmer to whom the orchard had been let, he would have told us that 'fruit did not pay to grow.'

In the Hatfield district of Hertfordshire our host was Mr. Wilson Fox, who, I suppose, knows as much about British agriculture at large as any man in the country. Under his kind guidance and that of Lord Lytton I went over a considerable number of farms in this part of Herts and at Knebworth, some miles away, a selection of which I shall now describe.

Perhaps I cannot begin better than by giving a brief summary of the views of Mr. McCowan, agent of Lord Salisbury, with whom I had the pleasure of an interesting conversation. Lord Salisbury, by the way—I do not take this from Mr. McCowan, but from what I learnt from farmers and others—has the local reputation of being one of the best and kindest of landlords, so kind indeed that a tenant upon his estate, unless he does something outrageous, is there for life. 'A man would have to be very bad indeed before Lord Salisbury would turn him out,' said the agent of a neighbouring property to me, confirming the statement by instances of various generous acts which he had done to help those who were struggling against circumstances. As regards his relations with the labouring class the story was the same : 'Lord Salisbury will always build cottages, but there are others who are not so forward,' said this informant.

Mr. McCowan thought that the farmers in the immediate neighbourhood of Hatfield, that is, near to the stations, were prosperous. Indeed, he said that some of the larger Scotch tenants were doing well and putting money by, chiefly out of potatoes and the milk trade, which on all hands was admitted to be an expanding industry. As to those who lived further off, however, he had another tale to tell, although he said there was no difference in the quality of the land they farmed. They were, he declared, 'in a bad way,' and added that those who succeeded were few in comparison with those who did not succeed. The rents, he said, varied from 30s. per acre for the best and most conveniently situated farms, down to nothing, quoting land at Much Hadham which was let for the amount of the tithe, and holdings three miles from a station that brought in from 10s. to 7s. 6d. the acre. For the choice lands there was considerable competition, but the majority of the good men were on the railway, so the other farms went back. As regarded selling values these also varied very much. Thus, in the neighbourhoods of Baldock and Hitchin land might be purchased for £10 the acre. He instanced a farm of about 230 acres which was bought in not long ago at £2,300. That same farm was acquired in 1864 for £7,000, the difference representing a fall of 67 per cent.

The small tenant farmers were, he considered, badly off for capital, but for the better class who were well provided in this and other respects he thought that the outlook was hopeful. Here, however, Mr. McCowan was careful to point out that, whatever might be the case with the hirer, at any rate in this district, it was by no means hopeful for the owner of land, which now-a-days would only support two classes instead of three, viz. the labourer and the tenant. ' The tenant,' he said, ' is the man who lives'; the landlord without other resources had gone under. Indeed, even those who had such resources were, in his opinion, extremely hard hit as a class. His views upon this matter, in short, so exactly confirmed those of another Hertfordshire land agent whose opinions I have already quoted that I need not enlarge upon them further. It comes to this : few landlords in Hertfordshire net any appreciable return from their estates ; they are, as one of them said, ' mere receivers.' How can it be otherwise when, as is the case at Hatfield, they are, in some instances, obliged to disburse as much as 25 per cent. of the gross rental for the costs of upkeep ?

Of labour Mr. McCowan said that a great many of the young men were leaving the land, and that most farmers were much hampered for hands and forced to work themselves from dawn to dark. At the same time he expressed the view, or hope, that people would return from the towns when they came to understand that the wages there are little better than they could earn in the country. In the year 1901, however, I am bound to add that in Hertfordshire they were not doing this in any numbers. Personally, in all the county I was only able to hear of a few cases, one of them being that of the young man in the employ of Mr. Prout, who returned because his health broke down in London, looking, as his master remarked, very different from what he did when he went away. Mr. McCowan said that his experience was that to keep the people at all they must have society, a necessity which is being met on the Hatfield estate by building the new cottages in groups of twelve.

These cottages, some of which I inspected on a subsequent day, are constructed upon a novel, and I think excellent plan, by workmen employed upon the estate, at the very moderate cost, when the present high price of building is considered, of £156 per house. Each row is divided into three blocks of four dwellings, with a road frontage, from which they are separated by a gravel path and the necessary outbuildings, the gardens lying in long strips behind them. The cottages, which were designed by Mr. W. Marshall, the architect to the Hatfield Estate, who has kindly furnished me with the accompanying plan, are of one storey only, measure about 21 feet deep by 29 feet long—at least so I paced them—and contain a living room, scullery, and three bedrooms. (The plan shows four, but the fourth belongs to the adjoining house.) The floors are boarded, with the exception of the scullery and pantry, which are cemented, and the walls, as I observed, hollow, constructed with a proper damp course and roofed in with an excellent patent tile—Major's double Roman roofing.

I asked two of their occupants how they liked them, and they both replied that they were warm, dry, and very comfortable. It seems to me that the plan is one which might be copied with advantage on other estates. The rent, I should add, was from 2s. 6d. to 3s. a week, which here was willingly paid for the accommodation. Speaking of this district generally, Mr. McCowan said that cottages were scarce, and I may say, from my own observation, that a good many of them were bad. Indeed, one large farmer went so far as to declare that half of them wanted burning, being in such a condition that you could kick down their ancient studwork or wood-cladding 'with a pair of shooting boots.' These delectable dwellings, however, were not on the Hatfield estate. The wages on this property were high, but

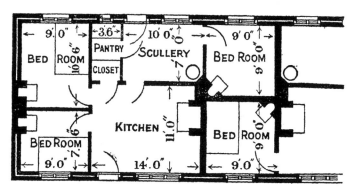

PLAN OF LABOURERS' COTTAGES ON LORD SALISBURY'S ESTATE.

the average price of the neighbourhood for horse and cowmen seemed to be about 18s. and a cottage, including extra moneys.

While speaking of this labour question, I may mention a curious and suggestive circumstance which was narrated to me by a large and successful Scotch farmer in this neighbourhood. Being in want of a cowman, and unable to find one, the idea occurred to him of advertising in 'Lloyd's Newspaper,' a journal which circulates largely among the labouring classes in London. To his surprise he received thirty replies from applicants, one of whom, a Cambridge man resident in London, he engaged. The reason given by many of these people of their wish to leave town was that the house rent there was higher than they could pay. Whether or not there are many such folk who would be glad of an opportunity of returning to country life if it could be brought to their notice, is, of course, more than I can say; but perhaps those employers who desire to make the experiment, would do well to try the effect of an advertisement in 'Lloyd's Newspaper.'

The first farm I went over in the neighbourhood of Hatfield was that of Mr. Sinclair, of Essendon, one of a Scotch family of which there are various representatives in this district. Mr. Sinclair farmed about 400 acres under Lord Salisbury, of which 250 acres were arable and 110 acres permanent pasture. He had been ten years on the farm, whereof the rent was 26s. the acre, the rates coming to another 2s. 6d. the acre. His land was light, and he complained bitterly of the drought, which he said had lasted seven years. During the previous two months it had only rained on three days, April 15 and May 8 and 9. In such seasons he declared that it was impossible to make money, and what the Middlesex hay farmers would do he did not know. Of labour he said he had plenty, as men could be got 'if you were willing to pay them.' The wages ran from 16s. to £1; one of his men took a guinea a week, besides beer and haysel. The milkers received 16s. and the first ploughman £1 and a cottage. There was a good deal of casual labour in the neighbourhood; thus when we arrived at Mr. Sinclair's farm two men who looked like tramps were there asking for employment. The cost of labour he put at £1 1s. an acre per annum.

I walked all over Mr. Sinclair's farm, which in its way was an object lesson, showing as it did how, when thoroughly well cultivated and in excellent heart, even light land can bear the effects of drought, aggravated though it was here through the pumping of water by the London companies. Of course, however, it had suffered. Thus one field that had received thirty tons to the acre of London manure, of which

Mr. Sinclair carted a great quantity in the winter, showed a
splendid plant of seeds that in an ordinary season would
have given not much less than three tons to the acre.   In
1901 I doubt whether more than a ton and a quarter were
secured.   The mangold, however, had come up without a
single miss and looked large and fresh.   Everywhere I found
the drought-resisting mangold increasing in popularity after
so many rainless years, while the breadth of swedes seemed
to grow less and less.

Of potatoes Mr. Sinclair had forty acres of the Up-to-
Date variety, which seemed to be doing well.   I do not
think that the potato minds any moderate amount of
drought ; wet is its great enemy.   He kept fifty cows and
sent the milk to London, but no sheep.   These cows had an
admixture of Dutch blood, which is popular in Hertfordshire
and some other milk-producing counties.   Personally, having
visited the cheese and dairy farms in Holland and studied
the cow of that country at home, I may say that I believe
in the breed.   They are enormous producers of milk of a
quality that is unsurpassed for cheese-making purposes, and
though rather thin not unsatisfactory in other respects.   If
I had a milk farm in England I should keep Dutch cattle,
especially if there were marsh lands on which to graze them,
with just sufficient Guernseys or Red Polls to raise the milk
to the standard of richness required by the towns.   Here
the cows were fed on mangolds and grains, with bean meal
and decorticated cake.   Speaking generally, Mr. Sinclair
followed the four-course system, but, he said, ' it's a job to
make it pay.'

Another fine farm that I visited was that of a Scotch gentleman who did not wish that his name should be mentioned.
His opinion was that those farmers who attended to business
did well, while others who neglected it failed.   Still he
admitted that there was general complaint among agriculturists.   Wages, he said, had advanced 3s. during the last
seven years, and were now 18s. a week all the year round and
a cottage.   The young men were going off, but he hoped

that in this respect things would take a turn. Rents varied from 17s. to 30s. an acre, but some of the 30s. land was in fact, he declared, cheaper than the 17s.

The average size of farms ran from 300 to 400 acres, and there were, he said, none to let in that neighbourhood ; all had been taken up. His arable soil was medium and his grass lands were heavy. Of cows, mostly Shorthorns, he had sixty, which were fed twice a day on mangold, cake, and grain, and kept in all the winter. Also he had a few Dutch cows, one of which, he said, gave twenty-eight quarts of milk when in flush ; indeed he considered half-bred Dutch to be the best dairy breed. Of potatoes there were forty acres, to manure which he bought 600 or 700 tons of London muck, in addition to basic slag for cabbages grown on the heavy land. This gentleman said that he did not see how corn farmers could make the business pay, but those who went in for stock did fairly well. Milk meant ready money coming in, but gave a lot of trouble ; also the competition of the Derby men, who had better grass, was very severe.

Of the local labourers he declared that two Scotchmen were worth any three of them. He did not, however, seem to think it strange that farmers should come to Hertfordshire from north of the Tweed, seeing that land in the neighbourhood of Glasgow rented for as much as £4 10s. the acre. Truly the Scotch are a wonderful people ! How in these days can they afford £4 10s. an acre rent and still make their farming pay ? On this farm is a brook that in 1901 was vanishing away, owing, the tenant thought, to the presence of water-pumping stations in the neighbourhood.

Mr. David M'Kinlay, on whom I called, who for thirty-five years had been agent to Mrs. Culling Hanbury, of Bedwell Park, said that the condition of local agriculture was not very prosperous. The Scotchmen, however, of whom there were a great many in Herts, seemed to do well. One of the reasons of this perhaps, was, that no Scotchman would 'farm without a muck-cart,' and he knew nothing which returned a kindness sooner than the land, except of course in

seasons of absolute drench or drought.   Rents varied a good
deal, farms in the neighbourhood which he instanced commanding 24s. and 27s. the acre, while others on a great estate
close by which used to fetch up to 30s., now brought in only
10s. or 15s.   The poor heavy lands of the Buntingford
district also, the worst in Hertfordshire, where the labour
was troublesome and the crops were poor, only commanded
about 10s. the acre.   Selling values also varied very much ;
thus, accommodation lands close by had fetched £60 the
acre, while good heavy land a few miles farther away, which
would have fetched £50 or more some years ago, sold for £18
the acre.   In some cases also old residents had been bought
out at a high price by rich men from London.

 With labour he had found no difficulty up to 1901, but
it was upon him at last.   Further he thought that things
were bound to get worse as the education got better, and
that if they did, farming must be given up.   As it was boys
or girls could not be had unless they came out of school
' with the dunce's certificate.'   The market gardeners also
ate into the supply of labour, as they could give from 24s. to
30s. a week against the farmer's 16s.   There was no difficulty in getting in the rents, such as they were, but the
farming generally was not so good as it had been.   He did
not advocate small-holdings in Hertfordshire, though he
thought that Scotchmen might succeed in such tenancies,
as their women were not afraid of work.   In the south they
would not work.

 Most of the dairy business of the district had been
started within the previous twenty years, and he did not
think that it was being overdone, as London could consume every drop of milk produced.   Indeed he mentioned
one farmer who had made a contract at an advance of £50
over that of the previous year, and said that some of these
men, after they had done with her, got as much for a fat
cow as they gave for a down-calver.   For farms there
was as much competition, at a rent, as there had ever been,
but Mr. M'Kinlay said that there were now no leases, only

yearly agreements. Neither were there any restrictions, as tenants might farm as they pleased.

At Knebworth Lord Lytton kindly took me to see some of his tenants. The first of these, a gentleman who did not wish that his name should appear, farmed 780 acres in the best possible style at a rent, I think, of about 23s. the acre, which was rather more than the average of the neighbourhood, that may perhaps be put at from 15s. to £1. The rates, which were paid by the tenant, were somewhat high in this neighbourhood; thus in the adjoining parish of Datchworth they were said to amount to 5s. 3d. in the pound, while the labour of this highly cultivated farm came, I understood, to no less than £2 the acre. This tenant said that some of the farmers were making a living and some were 'going backwards.' His practice was to sell all he could, such as milk, potatoes, and straw, and buy as little as possible. Of London manure, however, he bought a great deal, no less than from 4,000 to 5,000 tons being put upon the farm annually, in addition to that which was made at home by 150 cattle and twenty horses. Indeed he said that if it were not for this London muck, he would not have the land at a gift. He did not depend upon any one product, or cling to a fixed rotation.

One seventh of his land was permanent pasture, on which the hay in 1901 was little better than half a crop. Also he grew lucerne and fifty acres of sainfoin, which food, although so valuable, had, he said, the effect of making the milk smell. This gentleman told me a curious story of a case he had known at Stevenage, where the milk on a certain farm suddenly became offensive to the taste and smell. Every attempt was made to discover the cause, but without result. Food, water, and buildings were changed, but although on analysis the milk showed no contamination or poisonous quality, it still continued to stink and taste offensive. The end of the story was that the unfortunate farmer found himself obliged to abandon dairying. My informant told me that once his milk became tainted in the same way, but he was able to trace the infection to a single cow, which was got rid of, and the evil did not spread. To what this strange phenomenon was due I have not the slightest idea, unless it might be to some herb that grew upon the land. Perhaps a reader of this book may be able to furnish an explanation; if so, I shall be grateful.

On this farm no fewer than 100 cows were kept, mostly of the Shorthorn stamp, with a large admixture of Dutch blood. These fine creatures would yield up to 6 gallons of milk in a day, and one or two of them as much as 500 lbs. in a week, reckoning 10 lbs. to the gallon, that is, about 29 quarts a day. If, however, a cow would return a barn gallon of 17 pints a day throughout the year, the result was considered satisfactory. No sheep were kept on this farm; indeed I saw few in that part of Hertfordshire.

Here as elsewhere the tenant complained much of the drought; indeed he said, 'The seasons are killing us; this is the seventh year that the rainfall is not up to average. We have suffered more from drought than anything else.' His labour was mostly 'tramp labour,' on which he declared they depended in that district. These men are professional tramps, who go about the country salting herrings, picking hops, planting potatoes, doing jobs at gasworks &c., according to the season, and wandering from Union to Union when they have nothing to do. When they have money they eat, drink, and are merry, and when they have none 'they pull up their belts a hole.' He observed, however, that the same faces turned up from year to year. All the best of the young men went away to London, but he knew one who had come back. Were it not for the tramps they would 'be left.' Also there were a certain number of Irish labourers who worked at turnip-hoeing, potato-planting, and hay harvest. The cowmen were engaged for twelve months, and he gave them a bonus of £2 at the end of the year.

The wages for regular men, including extra money at harvest &c., came to 16s. a week and a house. Of Scotch

labourers, he said, 'they are very particular about hours and
very fidgety,' but they did more work and took more interest
in their tasks than the English. He added that he thought
the northern climate had something to do with this. Hertfordshire he had found very hot and enervating about
August. Our friend had also visited and, I think, farmed in
America, where he said that much of the land is 'the picture
of misery and as poor as Lazarus.' As for labour there was
rarely more than one man to a hundred acres, but 'they do
work; you have to go there to know what work is.'

This I can well believe from what I myself have witnessed
in the States. Never shall I forget one scene—a flat stretch
of land stubbed from the forest and fringed with fir trees, of
whose roots its untidy fence was made, and painfully toiling
up and down it beneath a wet and windy sky, at the tail of
a plough to which were harnessed a cow and a mule, a worn
and weary-looking woman. Evidently she represented that
farmer's available stock of labour. It is a great mistake
to suppose that all American farmers are well-to-do. I remember talking to a clergyman there who had some vast
agricultural district in his charge—I forget in which State—
who told me that his flock were poor to the verge of penury.
At any rate our Hertfordshire friend seemed to think the
agricultural chances were better here than in America, since
he said that with capital and intelligence money could still
be made in England.

After visiting his herds of cows, I was shown the pure-
bred Dutch bull, the first of these animals I have seen in
England. He was a tremendous beast, black and white
like all the breed, with an ugly head. This bull was
bought in London. For imported Dutch cows up to £30
a piece had been given on this farm. The barley here was
of a good colour, but short owing to the drought, and in
a pasture that had been five years laid down, I noticed that
the fine grasses were burnt out from the same cause. Part
of this field had been dressed with gas lime and road
scrapings, and part with moss-litter manure from London

A DAIRY COW, KNEBWORTH ESTATE

stables, of which the return was much superior to that from the lime dressing.   Cottages in this district were, I was told, scarce and in some cases bad.   Those which Lord Lytton has built cost from £380 to £500 the pair, and were let at from 2s. to 3s. the week—from an investment point of view not a very remunerative rent.   Three which I saw—good dwellings with parlour, kitchen, and three bedrooms—cost £560 for the set.

Mr. George Muirhead, of Deardsend, whose farm I visited, had a splendid two-year-old Shire horse bred by himself, an animal that looked fit to win in any company.   Here also was an excellent shed, sixty feet by twenty, which Lord Lytton, or his agent, told me had only cost £175 to build. I rather pride myself upon a quite useless faculty of being able to estimate the cost of buildings with some success, but here it failed me altogether, as I did not imagine that this one could have been erected for less than £250.

Mr. Milne, who was agent to Lord Lytton, put the average rents in that neighbourhood at from 15s. to £1 an acre ; some, however, were as low as 10s., while the best grass lands would fetch more than £1.   The upkeep expenses and the repairs, that on this estate had been extensive, he estimated at 20 per cent. of the rentals, which is rather higher than is common.   He said that the farms we had seen were worked by Scotchmen, and therefore highly cultivated, but there were others in not so good a case. More than half the Knebworth property was farmed by Scotchmen, who used a great deal of London manure, which cost from 3s. to 4s. the ton delivered at the local station.   Mr. Milne showed us a farm of 540 acres, rather highly rented, but in whose occupation I forget, where the soil was gravel and clay on chalk, and the chief industries were potato-growing and cow-keeping, which in Hertfordshire indeed nearly always go together.

One field of potatoes that we saw had been manured in part with peat-moss muck and in part with straw dung. Those drills which had received the peat-moss were much finer and of a better colour than those which had received the straw, the fact being that moss is more absorbent than straw. One of the troubles with potatoes is that a drought early in the year ripens off the tubers. These, if rain should then fall, start into a second growth, and become only suitable for food for cows, to which they are given raw and pulped. Here the potatoes were being earthed up with special implements. As they go down every second row the horses are harnessed abreast, but after this they are put tandem fashion to avoid injury to the crop. We also saw another farm of an inferior character. This was let for less than 10s. the acre. Mr. Milne informed us that the insurance premiums, tithe, income tax, and other expenses more than swallowed up every halfpenny it returned to its owner.

Mr. Williams, whom we visited next (by way of a change a Welshman, hailing from Montgomeryshire), had been six years on his farm of 230 acres, of which 130 were arable, twenty being under potatoes. He farmed well, buying some 500 or 600 tons of London manure annually and paying away about £2 an acre in labour. Of the quality of this labour he complained a good deal, saying that few of the young men stopped on the land unless they were deficient in intellect, and that they had to rely on tramps in the potato season. Mr. Williams declared that they had suffered from five or six bad seasons running, and that the hay was much wasted. If they had cut it three weeks earlier, twice the crop might have been secured. His mangolds, however, were pretty good, and his wheat, which had kept a capital colour, looked like giving a crop. Still he announced his intention of abandoning the cultivation of wheat, growing more roots and potatoes, and keeping an extra head of cows. He made his contracts for the sale of milk in March, to remain in force for twelve months. In 1901 the price he realised per barn gallon, I think, was fifteen pence for the summer months and twenty pence for the winter months.

A very interesting farmer whom I saw on a subsequent day was Mr. Charles Honour, of Moffat's Farm, North

Mimms. Mr. Honour told me that he had worked his own way, and that what he possessed he had made, for he did not start with a penny. Since the Russian war he had been climbing up, till he took his present farm of 350 acres, of which only twenty-two were pasture. He had a family of sons, all of them teetotalers like himself, of whom one was a baker. Three of them stayed at home and helped him, and he said of these three that they got through as much work as five hired men—the old story of men labouring for their own house—and that he paid them according to what they did. Labour, he told me, was very expensive and inferior, and the young men, many of whom were 'neither use nor ornament to themselves or anyone else,' kept going away. Rents in that district he put at from 15s. to 25s. the acre, according to the quality of the land.

Farmers he thought were not doing 'so very well.' The business required great perseverance and practical men to make it succeed. There was very little margin for profit. He had managed to get along, but if he were asked, he could scarcely say how, perhaps because they all worked together, daughters as well as sons, but many only 'scratched along' and were not able to do their land as it ought to be done. He kept pigs and cows, retailing the pork and milk himself, which, he said, paid better than sending them to London ; also he did a great deal of carting, and were it not for the money earned thus would, he declared, be sometimes hard pressed. Mr. Honour said that there were no small-holdings in that neighbourhood ; indeed, if he could do so he should like to find a little farm of from fifty to 100 acres in which to put one of his sons. 'When starting lads,' he added, 'let them have a pinch to begin with,' in my opinion a wise saying.

In driving to visit Mr. John Lloyd, J.P., of Astwick Manor, in the company of Mr. C. W. Gaussen, manager, I think, of the large property of his brother, the owner of the Brookman estate, who gave me much useful information, I noticed that a number of the oaks and other trees in the neighbourhood were becoming 'stag-headed' and dying, owing, I presume, to the drainage of the subsoil. One tree that I measured, an oak upon Captain Gaussen's property, is worthy of record. I made its girth to be 18 feet 6 inches at a height of five feet from the ground; but if I remember right, like so many others, it was beginning to die at the top. Mr. Gaussen said that his experience was that oaks should be grown straight away from the acorn and not transplanted, as they never forgave an injury to their tap-root.

Here cottages with three bedrooms let exceedingly well. We saw some which had cost about £200 apiece, and were bringing in a rent of £13 a year, or nearly 7 per cent., a very different return from that which is given by such property in most counties. These were not, I imagine, however, hired by agricultural labourers. Another block of four which had cost £800 were let to a farmer at an annual rent of £8 each. Others that we saw were worn out. From one of these an ancient couple, both of them over eighty, were with difficulty removed, on the understanding that when it was rebuilt they should be allowed to go back. It seemed that, having occupied the place for more than half a century, they were quite willing to put up with its deficiencies, although it was almost tumbling about their ears.

Mr. Lloyd farmed about 600 acres of his own property at Astwick Manor. This was quite the best land that I saw in Hertfordshire, being deep, rich loam lying on a bed of chalk many feet below; also it was in splendid order, everything about it, down to the trimming of the fences, being a pleasure to look at. Mr. Lloyd said that the English farmers were being thrust off all the best Hertfordshire land by the Scotchmen, who understood their business. These were doing well, in proof of which Mr. Lloyd mentioned one of them who came from the North to St. Albans years ago with little or no capital and had put out three sons on to 300- or 400-acre farms. As regarded labour he said that the work was being carried on by worn-out odds and ends of men. When they were done for he thought that they would be replaced by others who had been used up in the

NEW HAY-SWEEP ON A HERTFORDSHIRE FARM

Page 551

cities. All the best of the people went away, and he did not know what they were going to do for ploughmen. The wages with extras came to over £1 a week, and he gave a cottage and garden in, with as much more land as a man wanted. He had eight cottages which were used for farm servants only.

On his land, of which I think Mr. Lloyd said the rental value would be 25s. the acre or over, he employed rather more than £10 an acre capital. Also he bought manure, to the extent of no less than 2,000 tons per annum, at a cost of 5s. per ton, which was collected in London by the manure dealers and forwarded to his station. At that time of the year—June—when the demand was less, it could be had at half the price. Mr. Lloyd kept stock and horses, but no sheep, which as manure is so readily obtainable are much less needed in this part of Hertfordshire than in most places. Of cows he had only twenty, but said that the farm, of which a quarter was pasture, would carry eighty, and that to work it to its full profit this number ought to be kept. From these cows, which were half-blood Shorthorns, he bred with an Angus bull, keeping all his black stock and fatting them out in due season. Once he was troubled with tuberculosis, but rid himself of it by selling the herd. Mr. Lloyd was of opinion that hay and potatoes were the most profitable crop to grow, and that the secret of success in Hertfordshire agriculture was to have a farm which lay near a railway station.

One of the best cultivated and managed holdings which I went over in Hertfordshire, was that of Mr. Sinclair, who farmed 730 acres in Hatfield, abutting upon the property of Mr. Lloyd. Mr. Sinclair's father was among the first Scotchmen who immigrated into Hertfordshire. He began to work this farm some thirty-eight years ago, and the system of cultivation pursued on it to-day is still the same as he inaugurated. No cows are kept, and, as there is a railway siding but a quarter of a mile away, everything is sold off the farm and replaced by large importations of London manure.

Here is Mr. Sinclair's usual shift. Potatoes, for which the land receives a dressing of thirty tons of muck to the acre. These are grown once in five years on the light soil, and once in six on that which is heavier, the same seed being used for two years only, after which fresh is procured. Then wheat, then clover, and rye-grass layers for two years, then wheat on the heavy and oats on the light land with manure. Then potatoes again as a fallow. He had fifty or sixty acres of grass upon which he fatted bullocks, giving them cake, and in winter rough potatoes, but grew no mangolds or swedes.

He said that he was pretty well off for labour, some of his men having been on the farm for thirty years. He employed no tramps, all his being permanent hands. For the potato gathering he hired women and boys, and said that he got on pretty well with the women, who still came out to work, but not so freely as they used to do, at a wage of 1s. 6d. a day. Also he had a good supply of cottages, seven in all, of which four were new. 'If I had not the cottages,' said Mr. Sinclair, 'I don't know what I should do for labour.' The item of wages, by the way, figured in his books at no less than 50s. an acre per annum. Of potatoes, which he called a speculative crop, he generally grew about 100 acres, all of which he often sold to one man, who took them as he wanted them. A very good crop was twelve tons the acre, and the normal return about seven tons, which sold at an average price of from £3 to £4, delivered on rail. The sorts which he used chiefly were 'Up-to-Date' and 'British Queen.'

On one of Mr. Sinclair's fields we had a curious object lesson in the effect of seed on crop. This field was planted with the same potato, 'Up-to-Date,' I think, but part of the seed tubers came from Yorkshire and the rest from Scotland. The results were curious, the haulm of the Scotch section being dark, strong, and vigorous, while by comparison that on the Yorkshire part was light, small, and backward, though perhaps this crop would have looked well enough by itself. It would seem that the best of everything comes from Scotland, even of potato seed.

Some of Mr. Sinclair's land was gravelly, but most of it was the same good loam that we had seen at Mr. Lloyd's. His oats were suffering a little from smut, which he said they often found in the winter-sown, but never in the spring-sown oats. In one field the hay was being dragged up to the elevator that delivered it on to the stack, by an excellent gatherer or sweep, to which two horses were harnessed. It was made by Cottis & Sons, of Epping, and cost £12, the elevator, that was driven by horse power, costing £40. These machines save nothing in the number of hands or horses employed, but they can do in a day nearly twice as much work as could be accomplished with waggons alone. Therefore the economy in time, which means money, was very great.

It was curious to my companion, Mr. Cochrane, and myself to look at this gatherer sweeping the hay before it, since once many years ago, when we were farming together in South Africa, we invented and made with our own hands a rude implement of wood drawn by two oxen upon a similar principle. But we had no elevator, and were forced to be content with making our hay into stacks that resembled great cocks, and were, I remember, roofed with tarpaulins. Mr. Sinclair's wheat looked wonderfully good, the straw even in that drought standing five feet high. It was quite the longest we had seen. He told us that those who really farmed in Hertfordshire were making it pay; at any rate up to that time he had lost nothing at the business.

About five miles from Hatfield is Potter's Bar, in Middlesex, where I visited Mr. Mathews, the well-known expert in Jersey cattle, which he judges at the great shows.

Middlesex is a grass county with very little plough land, and farmers there rely chiefly upon their hay, all of which they sell in London. As a consequence they do not employ much labour, a fortunate circumstance for them, seeing that here the commodity was dear. For six days' work men took 18s., or with Sunday £1, carters and shepherds earning more. The farmers, who for the most part hold from 200 to 300 acres, at a rent of from 25s. to 30s., were said just to pay their way and no more, although those of them who deal may do better.

Generally speaking, the cottages were poor. Mr. Mathews farmed 200 acres under the Duchy of Lancaster, for which he paid £1 an acre rent. The land was very heavy, and somewhat rough, being much infested with thistles and marguerites, the result probably of its having tumbled down to grass in past years. Still, its produce must have very good feeding qualities, since his flock of pedigree Southdown ewes, even in that dry season and without the help of cake, looked extraordinarily fat and well, although the lambs were still on them; while his Jersey cattle, of which he kept about fifty head, were, and I suppose still are, famous throughout England. Mr. Mathews had twenty cows in milk, as beautiful a herd as I have ever seen, even in the Channel Islands, and his weekly output of butter at the time of our visit averaged 120 lbs. Indeed, each cow was estimated to produce 300 lbs. of butter a year, for which he found a ready sale winter and summer at 1s. 6d. the lb.

I suppose no other breed could show so good a record, but it must always be remembered that Channel Islands cattle are milk and butter machines and no more.

Mr. Mathews has kindly furnished me with the following useful and interesting table compiled by him from tests made at one of the great shows, the proportionate butter-producing qualities of the milk of various breeds of cattle. The difference between the morning and evening milk in the cases where it is given is well worthy of notice. Mr. Mathews suggests that this to a great extent is caused by forcing the cows for milk, as these cows were all competing for weight of milk, overlooking the fact that they could be disqualified, as many of them were, for quality. Of course I cannot set up an opinion against so great an authority, but it seems to me that this reason or argument would also apply to the evening milk.

No. of lbs. of milk required to make 1 lb. of butter.

|            | Morning Milk lbs. | Evening Milk lbs. |
|------------|-------------------|-------------------|
| Shorthorns | 33·38             | 25·14             |
| Jersey     | 18·91             | 13·89             |
| Guernsey   | 27·05             | 14·04             |
| Kerry      | 25·71             | 20·28             |
| Redpoll    | about 30 lbs.     | not stated        |
| Ayrshire   | about 25 lbs.     | not stated        |

Is not the true cause perhaps that the animals—at any rate under artificial conditions—feed much more in the daytime than at night, with proportionate results upon their milk product?

It was a melancholy sight that met the eye of the traveller between Baldock and Ashwell in the drought-stricken season of 1901. He saw stretched about him huge, flat fields, some of them sown with barley half hidden in the yellow blooms of charlock, their scanty, stunted corn ravaged by wireworm, and some with wheat for the most part of a faded, sickly hue. Here and there, it is true, the land seemed better farmed or more productive; but whatever the cause, the crops on most of it looked as if they would scarcely pay for the reaping. After Ashwell appeared many acres of pasture which had been laid or tumbled down, very bare in places, and producing at the best a scanty growth of grass, varied now and again by a cornfield, stained blood-red with poppies, that sure sign of thin, unfruitful land. In these parts the soil is grey, light, and stony, and the landscape wide and open. Occasionally, however, its poverty-stricken aspect was relieved by some good pieces of winter oats and wheat, which seemed to have withstood the drought better than other cereals.

Between Royston and Cokenach, the residence of our host, Mr. Crossman, the view is very striking, and in great contrast to that of those parts of Hertfordshire which we had visited. The road wanders up and down over a vast chalky plain that embraces many thousand acres of absolutely open land, ruled here and there by white lines of highway, and blotted here and there with dark clumps of wood. In parts it was green with crops, in parts grey and brown with fallows or stained yellow by the growth of flowering charlock, while in this place or in that, like gigantic ant-heaps on the veld of Africa, appeared the rich brown roofs of stacks.

It is a lonely region even for rural England, since in all its area I could see but two houses, and this sense of solitude was, if anything, accentuated by the hard-hued dome of the sky, the rushing of the north-west wind, and the eternal ripple of the ripening corn. A mile or two further on, and the change is complete. Suddenly the road dips into woodlands, pasture, and the hedge-bound fields that are common in the Eastern Counties.

Mr. Crossman, who owns a considerable acreage in this neighbourhood, only acquired his property of recent years, since when, however, he has spared neither labour nor money in its improvement. Foul fields have been fallowed and drained, cottages have been built, pastures laid down or mended, ponds dug, roads constructed of burnt earth (since stone is unattainable), fences erected, hedges trimmed and laid, and plantations improved or reset. This is a gigantic task, only to be faced by those who have ample command of capital; but as in this case everything has been done with knowledge and economy, unless things become worse even than they are at present, I do not doubt that in time he will meet with his reward.

All this is very much as it should be; indeed it is delightful to see the wilderness in process of being made to blossom like the rose—at some future date—yet the sense of contrast is almost painful. I mean that in contemplating such improvements it is impossible to avoid the reflection that they are not—and I fear never can be—applied to more than a small proportion of those lands in England which stand in sad need of similar care to-day. Rich men, it is true, still buy suitable residential properties with good sporting advantages, and reclaim them, but after all their number is limited, and so indeed is the number of properties that they would care to own.  There remain and always must remain millions of acres which can never hope to fall under the beneficent influence of their wealth.  Moreover, even among those who care for sport, and are prepared to pay heavily to enjoy it, how many are there who, like Mr. Crossman, take a real and living interest in rural and agricultural problems and conditions, and enter upon their possessions prepared to spend thousands of pounds, which possibly may never be remunerative, in the betterment of the land and its inhabitants?  I greatly fear that, although in places they may be mitigated, the troubles which, in some counties at any rate, threaten the very existence of agricultural England will never be dispersed through the occasional purchase of estates by moneyed men.  Also it should be remembered that, speaking generally, the further such properties lie from London or the other great cities, and the less their sporting advantages, the fewer there will be who desire to own them.  Of course I except the case of Scotland.

Of the labour conditions in this district I have to report that they were better than in many others, especially in the neighbourhood of the parishes of Barkway, Barley, Langley, and the surrounding villages which lie at a distance of from five to six miles from a railway station.  By this I do not mean that there were no complaints, for here, too, complaints were many ; also it was generally admitted that the majority of the young men were leaving, while, as one large farmer, Mr. Edward Pigg, of Chipping, said, ' Not one in fifty comes back from the towns.'  Other complaints were that they do not marry freely, and that when they are married their families are small, which is a tale that I have heard in many other counties.  It was said further that on bank holidays young men who have settled in London return to their homes ' with a blustering tale,' and entice away those who remain.

The facts, however, as I understood them, were that there was still a good supply of old, middle-aged, and some younger men to be had by such employers as would pay for them, especially in those districts where lands have practically gone out of cultivation, or where the farmers are so impoverished that they have been obliged to cut down their number of hands. It is a curious fact also, as I was informed by Mr. Basham, an old resident and farmer, that villages such as Langley, in which he lived, where there is a large green belonging to the inhabitants, retain their population much better than others. In short, on most farms there was a sufficiency of labour; but as one man said to Mr. Pigg, ' What be you a-going to do when we old uns is done ?  You won't get no turnups set out then ! '

Another thing that I noticed here was that allotments have small attraction for the labouring man.   Mr. Crossman said that his had been given up, and that ten acres at Newsells had also been given up.   Moreover, I saw, myself, as I drove through the country, two parcels of allotments of which quite one half had gone out of cultivation.

On one day of our stay with him Mr. Crossman drove us to visit a great block of about 2,000 acres of derelict land, some of which belongs to his own and some to other properties.   I believe that this unfortunate strip of country, or most of it, used to be within the borders of Hertfordshire, but owing to a rectification of frontier is now claimed by Essex.   On our way we passed the interesting church of Little Chishall.   It is said to have been built by the Saxons, but, although in fair order, is now practically deserted, as, with the exception of the inhabitants of a single farmhouse, there seemed to be little or no population in the place.   Once there was a village here, but, as I was informed, the cottages had been pulled down to save the rates upon them.   I visited this church, of which the first recorded rector was one Alanus.   A more desolate place I have seldom seen.   In the flooring of the porch and along the bases of the stone seats, worn by centuries of use and carved with the names of boys who flourished perhaps in the time of Elizabeth, grew thistles and elders.   Within the place was empty, save for

MOLE-DRAINING DERELICT LAND                    *Page 559*

MOLE-DRAINING PLOUGH                    *Page 559*

one dead starling that lay upon the floor. The ancient
naked walls leaned this way and that, the pews were gone,
a few deal benches and two chairs serving the purpose of
such congregation as on rare occasions is gathered here, and
in the vestry stood a decaying chest containing the Bibles
and Prayer-books thumbed by successive generations of
rectors. The antiquity of the building is extreme, especially of the chancel with its round Saxon window. For
ages folk have worshipped here, but now as a consequence of
the decay that has fallen upon this part of rural England
this fane consecrated from of old, and crowded with dead
and memories, is fast becoming but a home for bats and owls.

Nor far from the church is a farm called Shaftenhoe End,
where stands an ancient house with a projecting gable within
which runs a stair. Across this gable is placed a moulded
oaken beam, supported by grotesque, carved figures of men
playing on flute-like instruments and wearing plumed head-
dresses, exceedingly like those which I have seen upon Aztec
buildings in Mexico. Indeed these figures, to judge from
their appearance, might easily have been removed from some
temple at Palenque. Carved on this beam was the following
quaint inscription which I copied :—

W. L.      1624.

So God May Still Me Blesse
I Care The Lesse;
Let Envy Say Her Worst
And After Burst.

What was the genesis of that screed, one wonders ?
Probably some neighbours' quarrel whereof here is the only
monument.

Further on we passed a farm of 300 acres, which used
to be let for £300 a year. Now the tenant paid no rent at
all. After stopping to look at a pond which Mr. Crossman
had dug at a cost of £100, burning the excavated clay for
use upon the roadways, we came to the deserted territory
which lies between and around some woods. Truly I never
saw anything more desolate than was this land. The gates

were gone, the fences were wild and high, the ditches choked. Thorns and young trees, nibbled down by rabbits, sprang amid an unwholesome growth of twitch, black grass, plantain, water grass, wild carrots, dandelion, and other evil-odoured, flowering plants of which I do not know the names.

Nothing nutritious seemed to flourish in that iron-crusted, water-logged soil where, I believe, even in summer no beasts are turned to graze because they could not live there for a single week. Yet—and this is the melancholy part of the story— Mr. Basham, who had farmed in this neighbourhood from his youth, informed us that up to 1879 all of it grew good crops of corn. Indeed, he said that a certain field we saw, within his own memory once produced no less than £18 an acre for clover seed that was grown upon it, which shows what the land could do under proper cultivation. Britain, as everyone knows, lives for the most part on imported corn, and, as its feverish anxiety and continually recurring terrors about the condition of the Navy show, is well aware of what may happen to it in the event of a serious and prolonged war with a European Power. Yet it is quite content to allow land that could grow from thirty to forty bushels of corn per acre, to become utterly barren and useless for any purposes except those of the sportsman. Well, I suppose that the people love to have it thus, so there is nothing more to be said.

Mr. Crossman thought of trying to reclaim some of these fields, but this at present prices, it seemed almost impossible to do at a profit, or indeed without a heavy loss. They lie six miles from a station, and the negotiations for a light railway had fallen through owing to the exorbitant terms demanded of the local landowners, who, it seems, were required to furnish the land and half the capital, without interest or security, which was more than they could afford to do. In London, within thirty-six miles, Mr. Crossman's firm pays a contractor £400 a year to remove the manure of 160 horses. Yet owing to the lack of reasonable railway facilities the cost of delivering that manure upon these fields would be prohibitive. One of them, however, he was then engaged in steam-draining, although local opinion was much against his incurring an expenditure which it held would be thrown away. 'If you don't want to lose money,' I heard one authority say to Mr. Crossman, when speaking of this land, 'use it for shooting—leave it alone. There's rough cover, that is all it is worth.' I suggested that it might be planted, but the answer was that it would be difficult to prevent the rabbits from destroying the young trees.

This draining is done with two steam engines which stand on opposite sides of the field and by means of a double steel rope that winds and unwinds itself on drums, drag backwards and forwards an iron framework whereon sits a man. Beneath this frame projects a knife-shaped movable bar at the foot of which is a solid, sharp-pointed ingot of steel, about two feet in length, with a diameter of three inches. At the commencement of each drain a hole is dug to a depth of about eighteen or twenty inches, into which the mole or ingot is dropped. Then the engine on the far side of the field begins to work, the cable tightens, and the mole starts on its underground journey. Its course terminated, it is lifted from the soil by special machinery where the drain joins the pipe main, leaving behind it a neat hole bored through the stiff clay subsoil, which for the next score of years or so will carry off the water that collects above.

These drains are drawn twelve feet apart, the engines moving forward that distance after each journey, at a cost of 15s. the acre, the employer finding coal and carting water. Under good conditions as much as twelve acres can be dealt with in a day, the mole travelling at any depth that may be required down to thirty inches. On really heavy soils without gravel or other faults that will fill in the bore, and in large fields, this system of steam mole-draining is the most economical and effective that has yet been invented. That it is not more commonly employed seems strange.

Mr. Basham told us that once he held the Lawn Farm in this neighbourhood at the rent of a guinea an acre. Up to

1879 he made a profit of £300 a year plus his rent. Then
he lost £1,000 at one swoop, after which he continued to lose
money, although the rent was dropped to 10s. an acre,
until at length he abandoned the enterprise. Many farmers
in this neighbourhood seemed to have met with a somewhat
similar experience. At least Mr. Basham declared that they
made no money in the heavy land districts. I asked what was
the end of them. He replied grimly, ' The Agricultural Benevolent Society ! ' This statement was to a limited extent borne
out by a gentleman who serves upon the Board or Committee
that has to do with the hearing of income-tax appeals in
the neighbourhood. He informed me that a great number of
the farmers had proved to the satisfaction of the authorities
that they were making nothing, adding that there was an
average of three appeals where there used to be but one. In
short, so he said, the majority of them paid no income tax
at all. Still it must not be imagined that all agriculturists
in the Royston district were unprosperous, since many of
them who held the best lands near the railways, and some
who did not, flourished in various degrees. Especially was
this the case if they happened to be natives of Scotland or of
Cornwall.

The country in the neighbourhood of Cokenach is singularly beautiful. Thus from the rise in Shaftenhoe, to the
west is seen a hamlet embowered in trees and to the east
the villages of Great and Little Chishall. Beyond a down
then hazy with the heat, lies a wide landscape of chalk soil
like that of Wiltshire, and to the north the eighty acres of
Chishall Big Wood, a mass of solid green, while in the
shallow dip of the vale beneath stand some solitary trees
and a single, brown-thatched homestead. Unfortunately the
farming conditions are not always as attractive as the views,
since in this neighbourhood I saw a good deal of land in an
indifferent state, some of the corn having more charlock in
it than is generally thought desirable.

A tenant of Mr. Crossman's, whom I visited, whose rent
was, I think, 15s. the acre, complained as usual of the labour,

which he said was getting steadily worse. Extra hands, he declared, were not to be had unless they could be borrowed. The wages he paid were 15s. and a cottage for a horseman, and 12s. for daymen. He said also that the distance from a station was a great drawback and made it difficult to sell his hay. Generally this farmer struck me as a man struggling with adversity.

After leaving him we drove to some lands which Mr. Crossman had been laying down to grass. These were doing fairly well, but will, I imagine, cost one way or another nearly double their fee-simple value before they become sound, remunerative pasture. Here the fences were very high, some of them measuring ten feet, and there was much woodland. What land I saw under crop seemed to be largely devoted to wheat and beans. Indeed these have always been grown in this district. Thus the Rev. J. Frome Wilkinson, the Rector of Barley, told me that his researches into leases some of which dated as far back as 1300, showed that anciently the invariable shift was (1) wheat, (2) beans, (3) fallow. In those old days the light lands were used as sheep-down, while on the heavy soil wheat and beans were the only crops grown; and as in those times, owing to the lack of roads, it was impossible to cart manure on to the land, even if any manure was made, the triennial fallow was a necessity.

In driving through this neighbourhood I saw but one fruit farm, or rather what had been a fruit farm, for the condition of these nine acres of trees was lamentable. The apples and plums were very ancient, sixty or seventy years old, moss-grown, pest-infected, and generally in a wretched state. Near by were several acres of young trees, mostly plums, that might have been five or six years in the ground, and must have been planted at great expense. Now they were grass-choked, bent, wind-torn for lack of support, and in most cases dying. I do not know the history of the place, but I imagine that through death or some other cause it must have changed hands, and that the labours of the departed owner or tenant were being brought to nothing by his successors. Earlier in this book I have pointed out that this is one of the great dangers of fruit farming in places where the industry is not common, and here was a striking example of the truth of my remark.

After lunching with Mr. Bowen, of Ickleton Grange, which is, I think, in Cambridgeshire, and going over his farm where the Dexter and Kerry cattle, which looked respectively like small Shorthorns and Jerseys, were especially remarkable, we went on to visit Mr. Gray, a Scotch gentleman who was agent to Lord Hampden, and farmed 860 acres on his own account, of which eighty-one were grass. On our way there we saw some land in a very bad state, and I was told that the crop of oats on one field of thirty acres had been sold for £10, I think, in 1900. Also we saw s wood of four acres, composed entirely of laburnum trees, which was said to be a gorgeous sight in spring.

Mr. Gray's house, a very good one, was built by a Duke of Leeds for a shooting lodge, and a peculiarity of his large farm was that it had been divided into eight gigantic fields. There were 181 acres of barley, 180 acres of oats, 30 acres of mangold already singled, 50 acres of wheat, and 45 acres of potatoes with other crops. Also there were 70 cows and 350 Hampshire Down ewes. Mr. Gray paid, I understood, 15s. an acre rent, or £700 a year, for the farm that used to let for £1,000. In addition to this the partridge shooting, which I think remained in his hands, brought in £250 a year—not a bad return for 800 brace of birds, the average bag. But, as a gentleman said to me, one of the great 'agricultural' industries in those parts is the letting of shootings to rich sportsmen from London. Mr. Gray had held this place for three years, and already was getting it into excellent order. He farmed high, spending £400 a year on cake and I know not how much on manure, of which he had used 1,650 loads in 1900. He complained much of the drought, saying that what they needed there were rain and a railway, and that 1900 was the worst year that he remembered, owing chiefly to the late frosts. With the prospects of 1901 he was better pleased.

His course was potatoes, which received about seventeen loads per acre of manure and 1 cwt. of nitrate later, a crop of eight tons being reckoned good, then wheat, then clover, then another straw crop, then roots, for which the land was again manured. The land for mangold was dunged on the stubble and the manure turned in deep with a steam plough ; the oat land, which was heathy, had been ploughed thirteen inches deep without manure, and the resulting crop looked very satisfactory; but other oat land which had not been ploughed so deep was giving an inferior return. The cabbages had been dressed with salt and nitre to keep them going, and in spite of the drought the clover was growing well. The barley crop was above the general average for the season, and the wheat, of the square-headed variety, was really excellent. Mr. Gray's oats were of the Tartar King and Abundance kinds, both of them supplied, I think, by Messrs. Garton. His method of improving new-laid pastures was to lamb the ewes on them and sow additional seeds amongst their feet. It seems to me to have merit.

Of labour he said he had no reason to complain and that he did not see much difference between Scotch and English hands. It was generally a question of fair wages and good cottages. On that farm he had seventy-five people to keep and pay before he took anything for himself. He did not look down upon the young men or pay all his hands alike. His best man had a guinea a week, the others 15s., and there were twelve cottages, all free to their occupiers. Also they, or some of them, had free potatoes, with fourpence an hour overtime and a pint of beer when they had finished at night. One family in his employ took £120 per annum. Mr. Gray has kindly sent me his labour sheet for the year 1900, which I append, since it is of interest, showing as it does the cost of running a highly cultivated and well-managed farm in this part of Hertfordshire.

FARM 860 ACRES, 81 ACRES GRASS, MOSTLY NEW LAID DOWN.

*Chrishall Grange.　Wages for the year ending June 14, 1901.*

| 1900. | | | £ | s. | d. | £ | s. | d. |
|---|---|---|---|---|---|---|---|---|
| June 29. | Chrishall Grange Labour . | | 30 | 19 | 9 | | | |
| July 13. | ,, | ,, | . 33 | 13 | 2½ | | | |
| ,, 27. | ,, | ,, | . 33 | 17 | 3 | | | |
| August 11. | ,, | ,, | . 29 | 3 | 2 | | | |
| ,, 24. | ,, | ,, | . 27 | 9 | 3 | | | |
| Sept. 7. | ,, | ,, | . 79 | 3 | 1 | Harvest | | |
| ,, 21. | ,, | ,, | . 25 | 7 | 5 | | | |
| Oct. 5. | ,, | ,, | . 28 | 11 | 9 | | | |
| ,, 19. | ,, | ,, | . 29 | 4 | 0 | | | |
| Nov. 2. | ,, | ,, | . 32 | 10 | 6 | | | |
| ,, 16. | ,, | ,, | . 34 | 5 | 2 | | | |
| ,, 30. | ,, | ,, | . 32 | 18 | 8 | | | |
| Dec. 14. | ,, | ,, | . 30 | 7 | 11 | | | |
| ,, 28. | ,, | ,, | . 27 | 11 | 2 | | | |
| 1901. | | | | | | | | |
| Jan. 11. | ,, | ,, | . 27 | 7 | 7 | | | |
| ,, 26. | ,, | ,, | . 26 | 15 | 2 | | | |
| Feb. 8. | ,, | ,, | . 31 | 4 | 3 | | | |
| ,, 22. | ,, | ,, | . 30 | 11 | 0 | | | |
| March 8. | ,, | ,, | . 28 | 13 | 1 | | | |
| ,, 22. | ,, | ,, | . 30 | 13 | 5 | | | |
| April 5. | ,, | ,, | . 30 | 0 | 11 | | | |
| ,, 19. | ,, | ,, | . 31 | 11 | 11 | | | |
| May 3. | ,, | ,, | . 36 | 9 | 9 | | | |
| ,, 17. | ,, | ,, | . 34 | 16 | 5 | | | |
| ,, 31. | ,, | ,, | . 35 | 4 | 5 | | | |
| June 14. | ,, | ,, | . 31 | 3 | 8 | | | |
| | | | | | | 849 | 13 | 10 |
| | Christmas Boxes . . . . . | | | | | 8 | 0 | 0 |
| | Beer . . . . . . . | | | | | 30 | 0 | 0 |
| | | TOTAL . | | | | 887 | 13 | 10 |

His opinion of the local agricultural position was that the farmers were getting on 'middling,' but not making much money.

In driving from Mr. Gray's farm I saw four boys and two men engaged in spreading manure on a field. During the four or five minutes that we took in coming up to them I observed that none of these four lads did a single hand's-turn. They stood staring at the road and talking, nor did the men seem to remonstrate with them. On various occasions I have noticed the same thing in different parts of England, but the idlers were not always boys. A master cannot be everywhere, and thus it often happens that his time is wasted. The wheat about here looked very well on the heavier lands in the neighbourhood of Heydon and Great Chishall, both of them very pretty villages where the roses in the cottage gardens were a great feature.

Mr. Gardiner, who was Mr. Crossman's ganger, or bailiff, at Cokenach, a man of intelligence and experience, told me that he did not think that farmers were doing so very badly ; that is, the best did well, the others as best they might. Much of the land, however, had been left to go to ruin by poor tenants who farmed poorly. There was plenty of labour for those who paid for it ; and the men were skilled, though not so willing as they used to be. He did not suppose, however, that half as many hands were employed in the district as used to be the case two or three years before. He paid the men, of whom twenty-two in all were employed, according to what they were worth. For the most part they took piecework at which their earnings varied. Thus he could pick out six who were able to earn a shilling a day more than another six.

The drive from Cokenach through Barkway and Buckland to Chipping whither I went to visit Mr. Edward Pigg, chairman of the district Council, was very pretty. About Buckland, where I observed the Workmen's Club and the public-house placed side by side in the most friendly fashion, the chalk crops up and the country is well wooded, ash trees being numerous. The tall fences, many of them unkempt, bore elder bloom in masses white as snow, and were sweetly starred with unnumbered wilding roses. Such things did not mind the drought or the unseasonable north-east wind rushing beneath a hard sky lined with 'mares'-tails.' But this weather, combined with a hot sun, was proving fatal to the swedes, many of which, it was evident, must be redrilled. The winter oats and wheat, however, had not suffered, especially on the clay lands which reappeared at Chipping.

Mr. Pigg—who farmed 1,200 acres, of which 250 were pasture—said that owing to the badness of the season his produce sold for £1,280 less in 1900 than it had in 1899, and that the prospect was not much better for 1901. Many of the crops would not bear going into, especially the spring corn and roots, but if the wheat had a nice blooming time the cast would be good. Rents, which had fallen 50 per cent. since 1879, were now 15s. the acre or less, but Mr. Pigg said, 'I did better at 30s. than I do at 15s.' After paying the tithe of about 3s. 6d. an acre and the usual expenses of upkeep, and outgoings, the landlords, he added, received little or nothing, and the fee-simple values had fallen more heavily in proportion than the rents. On the other hand the rates were heavier than they had been. He did not think that many of the ordinary run of farmers had sufficient capital.

Nearly all the small farms had been, he said, merged into the large ones. Mr. Pigg instanced several cases of little men who had failed and said that 400 or 500 acres was the size of farm from which a man could get a living, that is, except in the case of families who took up little holdings and worked them themselves, the wife or daughters doing the dairying. Farming was not a very grand trade, but his sons, who were fond of horses, bullocks, and sheep, insisted on clinging to it; he had put the youngest in a brewery for a year, but he was back on the land. With reference to labour they paid high enough to get men, but the industry would bear no further increase of wage. Of the young men who went away in such numbers, he knew one who had come back and married, as he said that he could not afford to make a home for his wife in London; but this was a case of an old attachment. The young men did not marry as they used to, the towns having altered their ideas in this and many other respects.

Mr. Pigg bred a few good hunters and showed us two very promising young animals. Also he bred Shires, but the luck that year had been bad, as out of eleven foals five were dead. On this farm I saw a pasture of which the drains were still working, that had been mole-ploughed in 1863.

On our road to Westmill Bury, the farm of Mr. Russell, we passed through Throcking, a rather deserted-looking, heavy-land parish, to Buntingford, a straggling and somewhat melancholy little town on a hill, outside of which a fine church seemed to be falling to ruin. Before Mr. Russell, a Cornish gentleman, who began by farming 30 acres in Cornwall, and now hired 800 in Hertfordshire, this Westmill Bury farm was held for several generations by an old Hertfordshire family, the last of whom, I was told, fell a victim to the bad times. It is heavy land, clay over chalk, good for corn and excellent for sainfoin. Of the 800 acres 150 were old pasture. The exact rent I did not inquire, but in that neighbourhood it was said to average 15s. the acre. The cost of labour on the farm came out at a little over £1 an acre per annum, as against 25s. the acre paid by Mr. Pigg, who employed two engine-men. In these estimates, however, the expenses connected with the hire of the steam cultivator were not included.

Mr. Russell's great complaint was of labour, which he said was scarce and for the most part aged. Nearly all the young men went away, and on his great farm he had but one boy. At one time five of his milkers left him to go to London, when he really thought that he would have to give up his cows, but at the date of our meeting, his family were doing the most of this work and he got on better. The wages were 15s. a week with a cottage and extras for milkmen, and 13s. a week with extras for the other men, and he informed me that he should not be surprised if they went up another 3s. or 4s. Of cottages he said they could do with twenty more, and that if there were an ample supply of good houses, there would be less trouble about labour.

Mr. Russell kept sixty cows, which were receiving rations of meal, cake and chaff.  Also he gave them brewers' grains, salted and trampled down into pits, which when treated thus would, he said, keep for many weeks.  The cowsheds were very good and commodious, and the apparatus by means of which the milk was cooled down to sixty degrees with running water, was admirably arranged.  After cooling, the milk was put upon the train for London, if I remember right, at a siding on the farm.  Mr. Russell thought that this trade looked like going better, as a baby-food factory at Ware was taking a great deal of the local milk, and he contemplated selling his to it at an agreed price on rail.

The values at that time were from 1s. 3d. to 1s. 8d. per barn gallon according to the season of the year, which, after paying carriage, meant a penny a pint net to the producer; but he expected that it would be worth 1s. 9d. or 1s. 10d. in the following winter.  His cows were milking Shorthorns, which were bought in with calves at foot, or as down-calvers, and afterwards weeded out fat, the best of them being bred from again.  The calves were not weaned but sold out at once.  A milker was allotted to each twelve cows, and it was one man's duty to feed them and keep the sheds clean.  Owing to the drought he lost twenty acres of kohlrabi, which he had been obliged to resow.  His swedes were up and showing a plant, and there was also a fair plant of mangold ; indeed these looked as good as any I saw in the neighbourhood.  The cabbage were a trifle blue in colour owing to the lack of moisture, but still a nice, growing crop. When once it is started, cabbage can stand drought better than most things.

Owing to the high cost of feeding stuffs, the low price of produce, and the lack of rainfall, Mr. Russell thought the look-out bad.  Still I imagine that he is a man who will always overcome such difficulties as he is called upon to face.  He told me that several Cornishmen were looking for farms in the neighbourhood but could find none.  It must be remembered, however, that the immigrants into Hert-

fordshire from Scotland and Cornwall are not satisfied with
a common kind of holding. They want good land with up-
to-date buildings that lies near a railway station, but such
farms are for the most part already occupied by their com-
patriots.

In driving back to Cokenach I passed three farms lying
together, all of which I was told were occupied by Cornishmen. Also I saw three and a half acres of allotments, of
which quite half were derelict and growing every kind of
evil weed. This seemed the more strange as a village within
half a mile of them, near to the seat of Major Heaton Ellis,
contained a number of really good cottages.

Mr. Crossman, with whom I had various interesting conversations, told me that when he bought his property, which
was tithe and land-tax free, and covered some 2,600 acres,
of which he farmed about 1,100, it was thoroughly run out.
He had been farming all his life, as it was his hobby, and
during the last four or five years he had done what he could
to bring the land back into a sound condition, but nothing
rash or needless. Thus he had built cottages, laid down
pastures, made roads and drains, and manured the soil, but
he had not bought expensive artificials or incurred unnecessary costs. Still if he looked to his estate for an income, there was none ; indeed it was worth more for sporting
than for agricultural purposes. Nor did he consider land a
desirable investment, as a purchaser could scarcely expect
a return of more than one per cent., especially if he had to
bear the severe tax of bringing derelict acres back to fertility.
All his outlay was on permanent landlord's improvements,
which he thought would pay in due course, though to a
poor man such a property would be but a white elephant.
Everything came back on the landlord at last, and although
his receipts could not sink to lower than nothing, they
might reach that level.

In his opinion the rural exodus was a very serious thing
and part of the general social change. Thus men of all
classes in the country as well as in the towns no longer

married, or had the same number of children they used to do ; moreover, many of the mothers would not nurse their infants. People lived more for pleasure and less for duty. He thought, however, that the migration from the land to the city was more or less a question of wages. The farmer must either raise them or give up farming, and he believed that a man who looked after his business and the labour could afford to pay more than he did at present. If the wages were as high as the land could bear, and the labourers had good cottages and gardens, it would help to keep them. They were better off for labour in that district than they had been three years before, and if only the young men could be induced to marry, they would be anchored to the soil.

However, the general prospects of the land and all connected with it depended upon prices, and so far as the farmer was concerned, while there was any rent that could be remitted, he still had a chance. He did not believe in small-holdings in that county. Better facilities of communication would help agriculture, but in their district the Great Eastern demanded terms for the construction of a light railway, that it was impossible for the landowners to face. On the whole he did not think that the position of the land and those connected with it was worse than it had been ten years before.

Mr. Crossman is a thinking man with great business experience, whose views deserve respect even from those who may not agree with all of them. I therefore supplement the above summary by some written opinions with which he has been so kind as to furnish me, that touch upon many points of interest connected with the land and its social conditions.

I should say that the cause, or rather the commencement of the cause, of the exodus of the rural population was simply bad wages for uncertain work. The farmers round here now admit that labour is more plentiful than it was three years ago, which I think is greatly owing to their realising that they could no longer keep the able-bodied young men in the villages, unless they gave a fair equivalent for their work as compared with the town worker. The farmers, as a class, hardly realised the great change that was going on, owing to increased education, cheaper railway travelling, exchange of ideas between town and country on bank holiday visits, and kept saying ' Can't afford it at price of wheat,' ' Go if you like,' &c., till they found they had only the old or imbecile man left to work for them. The farmer now finds he can pay better wages, and that, in fact, it pays him to do so for better labour, and he is getting more men again.

To sum up. To keep the labourer in the country these are necessary :

1. A higher rate of *weekly wage*; as much piecework as possible, and stockkeepers and shepherds to have a small interest in stock reared or sold.

2. Good cottages with as large gardens as possible, well planted with fruit trees, so that in good fruit years there is some to sell.

3 Landlords and residents to support in every way soundly conducted sick clubs. There should be also cricket and football fields in every village.

4. As to small (freehold or leasehold) holdings, where there is a natural demand for them, some system of help through Government loans might be advantageous ; but to create them artificially would prove as great a failure as the allotments have in so many parishes, and at a considerably greater loss to the community. There is a keen competition for small grass farms in the Midlands, but in the Eastern Counties' corn lands, the men are not there to work them successfully.

*Outlook.*—I cannot see that the prospect of farming is any worse than it was, say, five years ago. Farms are readily letting at reduced rents as compared with twenty years ago, labour is improving, and the man who now takes a farm, lives on a lower scale and is not ashamed to work himself.

The landlord is impoverished, and death duties have settled him.

Since 1879, when one may say the prosperity of the British farmer departed, no one connected with the land has suffered more than the average owner of the country. Whether it be the squire, Church, or hospital, all have had to face reduced incomes and still been expected to meet all the general charges on the land of buildings, which they have not been able to do—necessary repairs, draining, &c., all lapsing from want of funds. Added to this the death duties, which have, in very many cases indeed, driven the squire from his home and transferred the income left to him to London or some other society resort, all helped to drag down the prosperity of the country village and to make a considerably less demand for labour ; helped also to drive the labourer away, no one wanting him.

*Light Railways.*—I consider that it would be an enormous help to many outlying parts of the country, if they could get railway communication, and that it would benefit landlord, tenant, and labourer if the Light Railway Act could be made more workable for districts isolated at present from the railways, either by Government guaranteeing a small percentage on the outlay made by the railway companies or by the landlords, or by the county Councils being deputed *to work* them. This I consider an important point.

*Tithes.*—As it is to the advantage of land to be free of incum·brances, I consider that landlords who are desirous of freeing their land of the burden of tithe should have the compulsory power of redeeming it at the last three years' value, twenty-five years' purchase instead of the commuted value.

I quite agree with you that if the labourer could be fixed on the land on a self-supporting basis, either as owner or occupier, it would go a long way to solve the question of depopulation ; but as there is no heroic way of doing this I fear it would be a work of ages, and that at present we must depend more upon the spending power of the landlords and tenant farmers to support the labourers and keep them contented. Agriculture, though the largest industry in the country, always has and always will come in for the least recognition from the Government, and in their present financial straits there will be no support to light railways &c. for years.

Everyone must admit that there is at present, quite apart from the question of wages, a general spirit of unrest among the younger of the rural population, a growing desire for change and excitement, a wish to see something beyond the confines of the village, and have some experience of the great world of which their friends give such glowing accounts. This feeling, with education, cheap press, and easy railway travelling, is likely to increase than otherwise, though fortunately many return after a time.

A. C.

July 1, 1901.

The Rev. J. Frome Wilkinson, M.A., F.S.A., F.S.S., the Rector of Barley, a gentleman who has given much consideration to agricultural problems, differed from Mr. Crossman on the matter of small-holdings. He said that the reason of the failure of many of these was that after the death of the landlord who began the experiment, his estate fell into the hands of agents, who detested the whole system and quickly brought it to an end.

What he proposed was that such holders should have fixity of tenure dependent upon proper cultivation of land, to be bought by and rented from Government Commissioners. I suggested that the same result might be arrived at more simply and with greater completeness by allowing, or assisting, men to purchase their own holdings. He replied that he had found no desire to purchase, which may be true of that part of the country, but certainly is not true everywhere. I then suggested that co-operation and much better and quicker transport arrangements might help. Mr. Wilkinson was of the same opinion, and we agreed that what was wanted was an Agricultural Post that would convey stuff by hundredweights as well as by pounds, a scheme that I have gone into more fully in my concluding chapter. Why should not Government organise such a post? I believe that it could be done by the help of a motor service, and that if done it would pay, besides proving of inestimable benefit to the rural districts by the cheap and certain carriage of their produce, and to the inhabitants of towns to whom that produce would be delivered. I can only trust that I may be successful in inducing the authorities to give this project the consideration of which it is, I think, most worthy.

Mr. Wilkinson considered that the exodus from the country was not only serious, but vital, and that involved in it, was nothing less than the fate of the manhood of the nation. The passing from a natural to an artificial life must. he said, weaken, and in the end kill, that manhood which, unless continually recruited, could not endure more than three generations of existence in cities. Mr. Wilkinson, who had studied agricultural education, declared that in order to make it effective, you must first educate the educator. At present the schoolmaster was uniformly of an urban mould. Men were wanted who understood the country and could give practical instruction in rural matters. Meanwhile, as he informed me, the exodus was increasing from almost every village in that district. It was the desertion of the villages that made the villages so dull. If their inhabitants stopped in the country and used the power which their numbers would give them, they might obtain some helpful legislation. In the time of Elizabeth an Act was passed providing that no house should be built unless four acres of land went with it. Something of the sort was wanted now.

An argument followed about allotments, Mr. Wilkinson saying that in his parish there were five applicants for every one that was vacant, and Mr. Crossman answering that he knew of twenty acres of them which had been abandoned. To this Mr. Wilkinson replied that it was because their tenants tried to use them for the cultivation of corn. Also he quoted the success of Lord Carrington's allotments in Lincolnshire as a shining example of what might be done. When these were started, he said, farmers were frightened, but now they found that the allotment-holders made the best and most intelligent labourers. Further, the result had been to check the exodus from that district.

Of course the fact of the matter is that the success or failure of allotments and small-holdings depends enormously upon the local conditions, and upon the character of the population. This truth is, I think, clearly demonstrated in the pages of the present work by many and varied examples.

After our conversation Mr. Wilkinson, who is, I forgot to say, a member of the Agricultural Education Committee, was so good as to write me some notes on this and kindred subjects. These I print below almost in his own words, as they seem to me to contain valuable suggestions.

1. *Education.*—What is needed is *real* differentiation of rural schools, the curriculum to include some such course as that

outlined by the Board of Education, for which the Agricultural Education Committee is mostly responsible. This committee has worked hard, and is so doing, to get an elementary education suitable to the needs and surroundings of rural children.

Suitable education is a first necessity to keep the young on the land and in the country. Upper standards should in the afternoons be taught the use of tools, taken to see horticultural and agricultural operations, cultivate school gardens, and observe natural phenomena and objects. Evening continuation schools should exist to carry them on and to give genuine technical instruction, open to *all*, of whatever age, who are over the day school age or free from attending day school. Special departments in training colleges, or an entirely new college for the training of teachers for rural schools, are greatly needed. Nothing much can be done without this reform. At present education as applied in country districts is a prime factor in causing and increasing the 'rural exodus.' It is held that there is no dignity about manual labour. An educated boy or lad must be careful not to dirty his boots. To work on the land is to take the lowest place, fit only for 'dullards'! The dignity of labour, the true natural life in the country as opposed to the artificial and non-natural conglomeration in the town—these things are not inculcated.

2. A revival of village industries would be of great assistance in keeping the people in the villages.

3. The lost rungs of the social ladder, leading from horse and plough boy to the occupier and possessor of land, should be replaced. They are :

(*a*) Garden allotments till all cottagers have sufficient land on which the cottage is built. No new cottage should be allowed to be built without a certain minimum of land round it, a quarter or third of which should be planted with fruit trees.

An allotment committee, rules, and co-operative management.

(*b*) Small-holdings (farm) graduated from over one acre to fifty acres, with co-operation in horse labour and cutting and harvesting of crops.

For (*a*) and (*b*) *an agricultural collecting service* which shall have communication with all available markets and dispatch collected goods in bulk. *Agricultural banks* are also necessary. They have been the saving of rural Italy, &c. The result of them is that the producer or collector is not *forced* to sell at the worst time and in the lowest market.

Small farm allotments (like many in my neighbourhood) of

twenty rods or more are of no use now-a-days, and so have been given up. Many people are obliged to leave the country because they have no houses to live in. When a young man wants to marry he cannot find a home.

The *girls* should be especially taught domestic economy and first principles of dairy and poultry farming. In grass country cow-runs of five to ten acres each should be provided. But cow-keeping need not be restricted to grass country. Arable lands produce the necessary keep, and in some ways the *fed* and stalled beasts are better for dairy purposes, their produce being more uniform.

Finally I [*i.e.* Mr. Wilkinson] quote Lord Salisbury on this matter.

'We are told that the first effort of the State in agricultural matters should be to increase the produce of the land. I firmly deny that. I quite admit that it is an important thing to increase the produce of the land, *but it is not the most important. It is not so important as maintaining in happiness and respectability a large class of our fellow subjects.*'—Speech at Hitchin, Dec. 7, 1882, by Lord Salisbury.

A very large and enterprising farmer in this neighbourhood told me he feared that the smaller men were not holding their own, and that farmers could not afford to pay the labourers enough to keep them on the land. Many of them were doing no good and many more had lost all their capital. There was at that time a little better demand for farms, but most of the applicants were not good tenants, and even at a rent of from 12s. to 15s., had not sufficient capital to work the places they hired. Labour was a great trouble; one farm he had given up because that question beat him altogether. If it were not for this difficulty he would farm on a much larger scale. He thought that wheat was still the best crop they grew, taking the return on the high basis of five quarters to the acre and remembering that the straw and offal must be considered. Also a little dealing was a good thing; the dealers were the men who made the money. He could remember the derelict lands in that neighbourhood paying well; the prices had killed them. His sons declared that they would be farmers, and if they could be brought to keep their eyes open there was still a living to be made in the business. But he would not recommend anyone who wanted to make money to go in for farming.

Another gentleman—or rather other gentlemen—said that the good old sort of labour was gone, and that now-a-days there were a great many farmers who did not know how to set a man to plough. All were going back, farmers and labourers together. Let anyone who doubted it, go out in the winter and see how the land was ploughed.

Said one, 'The men don't know how to do it, and mine won't do it when I show them. As for the young ones, they don't want to learn.'

Mr. Gardiner Wilson, of North Mimms, wrote me a letter containing some interesting views and information on matters connected with rural Hertfordshire. He began by stating—the letter was written while my articles were in the course of appearing—that he was sorry to say, 'I have so far studied your comments without deducting therefrom any idea which would lead to the restoration of the labourer to the land.'

I am a person well accustomed to criticism; few perhaps have had experience of more thereof, favourable and unfavourable, but there are two styles of comment which still irritate me mildly. One is that based upon views— especially agricultural views—I am supposed to have expressed or written, but in fact have neither expressed nor written, which I may call the imaginative style; and the other, that directed against matter not yet written, or only half written—the premature style. Now when my correspondent posted his letter only a portion of the articles to which he refers had appeared, whereof it seems that he had read 'some.' It does not appear to have struck him that I should reserve the expression of my deliberate opinions till the end, since few people care to give judgment till they have heard the evidence. There he might have found a summary of my views of what is immediately necessary to

bring back the labourer to the land, or at any rate to deter
him from leaving it for the towns. Indeed I thought that
I had indicated those views with some clearness from the
beginning, and that they amounted to this: To keep the
labourer on the land—if anything can do so—you must
either pay him as much as he can earn elsewhere, or give
him a reasonable chance of acquiring some individual interest
in that land.

The matter—so far as it concerns me personally—is,
however, a small one, and I only touch upon it because,
having received various letters containing similar cavils, I
take this opportunity of saying to their writers, that before
they set me down as void of light or suggestion, I trust that
they will be at the pains to study the pages of this work.
It is probable indeed that even in that case they will not be
satisfied, especially if they chance to belong to some extreme
school of thought. The man who could announce any
absolute specific against the great evil of the rural exodus,
might, perhaps with justice, be named a self-sufficient person,
or even a quack. All that the best of us can do, or at any
rate all that I can do, is to study this vast subject humbly
and with patience, and present my conclusions for the consideration of my fellow-countrymen, trusting that they will
weigh them in the balance of their own judgments, and if
they find them sound, try to induce those who have authority
to take moderate and reasonable action in the matter.

Mr. Wilson said also that I had seen the wrong people
in Hertfordshire; that 'it is not from the information such
men can give, that the all-important question to the nation
generally of building up the physique of our manhood who
will be capable of defending our rights and competing
successfully with the men of other countries in their class
is likely to be rectified.' I observe that in almost every
county, however catholic may have been the selection of the
persons to be interviewed, there are individuals who declare
that I have seen the 'wrong people.' I wonder whether,
considered from the point of view set out in the above

sentence, my correspondent holds the Rev. Mr. Frome Wilkinson, to take a single example, to be one of these wrong people.

Mr. Wilson was of opinion that it was altogether chimerical to hope that townsmen would ever return to farms in any considerable number. He said that what would happen and what was happening in my own immediate neighbourhood—I suppose he meant in Norfolk and Suffolk—is that 'decrepit, worn-out, and partly insane men' take the employment that no able-bodied persons can be found to fill. He added—and this is interesting—that in an agricultural area of between 2,000 and 3,000 acres round Colney Heath, during his twenty years' residence no fewer than sixteen farms had been absorbed into other farms, or the farmhouses converted into private residences. This concentration, he said, naturally produced a reduction in expenses—by which he meant wages—fewer men being required on the farms than used to be the case.

The following example had come under his personal notice. A farm of 200 acres absorbed a farm of sixty acres occupied for forty years by a man and his wife, who had brought up a large family of sons and daughters. After the small farm had been swallowed up, the only additional labour expense which the tenant of the large farm had to meet in order to deal with the added land, was that of one more horse and the employment of a man where he used to employ a boy.

Mr. Wilson continued that he could not see that it was 'possible for worn-out land like ours to satisfy by its produce so many claimants.' As a consequence nationalisation of the land seemed to be the remedy. How would that help, I wonder, seeing that there must still be the landlord—that is, the State—the farmer, and the labourer, all wanting their share of the profits? As, he continued, this appeared to be out of the question, other means must, however, be adopted, such as higher wages, better and properly drained cottages, the transference of industries from the large towns to the villages, and 'the exclusion of the brewer, except at the wish of the inhabitants.' Also, he added, landed proprietors must reside on their estates and take an interest in the welfare of their poorer neighbours as they did of old.

As a matter of fact, do they not reside on their estates whenever they can afford to do so, at any rate in England? Few men enjoy being obliged to let their homes. And are they less kindly to their poorer neighbours than they used to be of old? Another thing, why does Mr. Wilson speak of our 'worn-out land'? I deny that the land of England is worn out, though often enough, I admit, it is neglected. While we can grow a heavier crop of wheat per acre, with everything else in proportion, and produce better stock than any other country in the world, can our land justly be spoken of as worn out?

Mr. Wilson stated in conclusion that the old yeoman class of farmer is fast disappearing (which is true), having lost his capital, some of them probably through 'riotous living,' and some through depression of the markets, 'the middleman being also a terrible scourge to him. In his place you have the man without capital, with only a crude knowledge of agriculture ; a man of no intellect, no better than a labourer, who is satisfied with an income something more than the wage of a labourer.' Surely Mr. Wilson is rather hard upon the average Hertfordshire farmer.

A great authority resident in Hertfordshire, whose views I value as highly as those of any man in England, told me that in his opinion, if it is desired to keep the labourer on the soil, he must be provided with a decent house and a good garden. To be kept on the land, its sons must have found for them some counter-attractions to the high wages and greater excitement of life in a town. There were a number of rural districts with an insufficient supply of cottages, while even those that existed were often very bad. This was especially the case when the owners were small people. The large landlords in many places had done much to set an example in the way of building cottages, with which great estates were often well equipped. Also cottages should be grouped together as much as possible, as the wives of labourers did not like being isolated, or the necessity of walking long distances over muddy fields to shop and of sending their small children several miles to school. For these reasons labourers' dwellings ought, where possible, to be near to a village. In order to provide a suitable supply of cottages, landlords should be able to borrow money at a very low rate of interest to be employed in building them.

If the present law were properly enforced by Sanitary Authorities, existing cottages would, he thought, be much better than they are. Sufficient pressure was not put on the owner of bad dwellings to make him bring them into decent and healthful condition. What stronger weapon could be placed in the hands of Sanitary Authorities than the power they now possess of securing the closing of a cottage if not in a fit state of repair, or if unwholesome? Even the threat to close would in many cases have the desired effect. His points were that Sanitary Authorities should know the state of every cottage in their districts and all particulars about it, and that the owner should be required to furnish an annual return, giving certain particulars as to the existing accommodation, &c.; further, that the onus should be thrown on him of declaring that his cottages are in a habitable condition. After the first year it would be no great trouble for the Authorities to make a digest of the returns, and the yearly form required to be filled up by owners might be made very simple. He also considered that Sanitary inspectors should be a well-paid class of men, and that there should be periodical inspection by Government officials, who would be free from all local influences and prejudices.

Upon these suggestions I may remark that if the law affecting the condition of cottage property is to be more rigorously enforced, or perhaps amended, the Government should be prepared to advance money at a very moderate rate for the repair as well as for the building of cottages. Every additional expense is much felt in these hard times, and particularly so in the case of those whose properties are encumbered, or in that of small proprietors. I should be surprised if in many instances owners did not prefer to allow their utterly unremunerative cottage property to go to ruin rather than face the expense of bringing it up to a considerably higher standard, with the result that the number of cottages in the country, already far too few, would be still further decreased. Also, unless they were helped in the way I have suggested, the majority of small proprietors would be quite unable to find the funds necessary to costly repairs and renovations.

Of small-holdings my informant said that freeholds and leaseholds ought to be multiplied wherever possible ; but in these difficult days the question of expense was very serious, and most landowners had no money wherewith to erect new buildings. Therefore, admitting the desirability of the creation of such ownerships, the Government should advance money on the lowest possible terms for the purchase of the necessary lands. Public Authorities might also buy land for this purpose, provided that they did so on business-like principles, and did not make foolish experiments and put their cost upon the rates. He felt sure that in the neighbourhood of large agricultural villages a good deal of land, especially if pasture, could be let in small plots. Also it would be a great benefit to the farmers to have a class of men, such as existed in some districts, who held enough land to enable them to keep a couple of cows and a pony which they used for carting, and to grow a few vegetables, who at the same time would occasionally work for wages on the land.

There ought to be greater opportunities for capable and industrious men to better their position. In districts where only large farms existed, the labourer must remain a labourer. Of course, however, small farmers would only succeed in certain localities, where the soil was suitable and the markets were accessible. In his opinion, such men would never really prosper until there was some system of co-operation in the selling of produce, and the purchase of feeding stuffs, manures, &c., of which they could take advantage. They must be in a position to combine, to send away truckloads of produce to the proper markets at the proper time, instead of despatching very small quantities at expensive rates. At present, cases were not infrequent in which small-holders had been absolutely eaten up by the charges of the railways and the salesmen.

Lastly, farmers must recognise the necessity of paying labourers higher wages and giving regular employment, as the best of them did without grumbling, accepting the fact as one of the conditions of modern farming. Against this obligation it was useless to struggle; the employer who wanted good men must give a good wage, and it was but poor economy to pay a small wage for inferior or worthless hands.

Of these opinions I need only say that, with the slight modification I have suggested above, they are practically the same as those at which I have arrived after much study and investigation of the subjects wherewith they deal. As we are all glad to see our own views ably expressed, it only remains for me, therefore, to recommend them to the earnest attention of the reader.

Mrs. Ernest Hart, of Fair Lawn, Totteridge, wrote to me, pointing out the strange fact that where she lived, within the twelve-mile radius of the devouring millions of London, the whole country was under grass. The high rents and the enormous cost of carriage by road or rail made even dairying an unprofitable business, while the leases provided that the land should not be broken up. Labour, she said, was almost impossible to get, and cottages could not be hired. She compared the depopulation of the English country districts ' with the busy habitation of those upon the Continent,' and lamented the hopelessness of wringing a profit from purely agricultural land. Of course the reason of the difference is that abroad small proprietors, who have the advantage of Protection, are many, whereas here they are few and unprotected; neither are they assisted in England by Co-operation and Agricultural Banks. Mrs. Hart speaks of leases and high rents. Personally I found few of either in Hertfordshire, but in her immediate district the case may be different.

My general conclusions on this county have already been stated at the commencement of the chapter, and need not, therefore, be enlarged upon. I may say, or repeat, however, that while on the whole its agriculture does not seem to be prosperous, certain farmers with enterprise, capital, and ability, who hold the best land near the railway lines, produce potatoes and milk, and purchase London manure in large quantities, were undoubtedly doing well in 1901. Whether their number can be very largely increased is, however, open to question. The lack of good and reliable labour is, perhaps, the greatest difficulty that the agricultural community in Hertfordshire and Middlesex has to face. If not to the same extent as in some other counties, still the farm-servant is practically master of the situation. Also he knows it. A gentleman I met was given notice to by a cowman who, after being in his service for many years, had secured more remunerative employment elsewhere. The hour of parting came, and the man arrived to say good-bye. He was very regretful over this severance of old ties, and his last words to his quondam master—who had *not* secured another cowman—were: ' I'm real sorry for ye, but, I'll tell ye what, I'll keep my eye on ye.'

Could the position be more amusingly exemplified?

END OF THE FIRST VOLUME.

THE ABERDEEN UNIVERSITY PRESS LIMITED.

1116328R0

Printed in Great Britain by
Amazon.co.uk, Ltd.,
Marston Gate.